readings in

moral

philosophy

readings in moral philosophy

Jonathan Wolff

Blavatnik Professor of Public Policy
Blavatnik School of Government, Oxford University

W. W. NORTON & COMPANY
NEW YORK · LONDON

W. W. Norton & Company has been independent since its founding in 1923, when William Warder Norton and Mary D. Herter Norton first published lectures delivered at the People's Institute, the adult education division of New York City's Cooper Union. The firm soon expanded its program beyond the Institute, publishing books by celebrated academics from America and abroad. By midcentury, the two major pillars of Norton's publishing program—trade books and college texts—were firmly established. In the 1950s, the Norton family transferred control of the company to its employees, and today—with a staff of four hundred and a comparable number of trade, college, and professional titles published each year—W. W. Norton & Company stands as the largest and oldest publishing house owned wholly by its employees.

Editor: Ken Barton
Assistant Editor: Shannon Jilek
Project Editor: Diane Cipollone
Managing Editor, College: Marian Johnson
Managing Editor, College Digital Media: Kim Yi
Production Manager: Ashley Horna, Ben Reynolds
Media Editor: Erica Wnek
Media Assistant Editor: Ava Bramson
Media Project Editor: Cooper Wilhelm
Digital Production: Lizz Thabet, Mateus Teixeira
Marketing Manager, Philosophy: Michael Moss
Design Director: Lissi Sigillo
Permissions Manager: Megan Schindel
Permissions Associate: Bethany Salminen
Composition: Six Red Marbles Inc.
Manufacturing: Quad Graphics—Taunton

ISBN: 978-0-393-92360-5 (pbk.)

W. W. Norton & Company, Inc., 500 Fifth Avenue, New York, NY 10110
wwnorton.com
W. W. Norton & Company Ltd., 15 Carlisle Street, London W1D 3BS

1 2 3 4 5 6 7 8 9 0

To Tom, Kirra-Lee, Kayley, and
Jaxon John

contents

PART 2
Normative Ethics 84

PART 3
Applied Ethics 208

preface

This book is designed to accompany my textbook *An Introduction to Moral Philosophy*, also published by W. W. Norton. Although they are produced so that they can be used independently of each other, together they provide an extensive and substantial introduction to moral philosophy. Part 1 of this volume, Meta-Ethics, provides fuller versions of texts discussed in *An Introduction to Moral Philosophy*, but can provide only a sample of issues and texts rather than aiming to be comprehensive. Part 2, Normative Ethics, also provides support for *An Introduction*, with selections from philosophers discussed in depth there, including Bentham, Mill, Kant, Aristotle, and their critics, but also extends the range of sources by including philosophers such as Confucius and Sartre. Part 3, Applied Ethics, takes the extension further by including readings on a wide range of applied topics that are only touched on, or not covered at all, in *An Introduction*.

A particular effort has been made to include pieces written by women and people of color, and this has led to the inclusion of several readings from writers who are not generally regarded as philosophers, such as Nelson Mandela and the poet and radical thinker Audre Lorde. These writers have been selected because they raise important ethical questions, even if they do not discuss them in the standard terms of Western moral philosophy. The readings allow us to reflect on the nature of the central issues they raise, as well as the boundaries of what should be studied under the heading "moral philosophy." Some may question their inclusion; if so, I welcome the debate.

Readings in Moral Philosophy includes introductions to each part and section as well as study questions, which test reading comprehension, and compare and contrast questions, which test a student's ability to synthesize different philosophical viewpoints. The book is also supported by a full test bank and a coursepack of assignable quizzes and discussion prompts that loads into most learning management systems. Access these resources at digital.wwnorton.com/readmoral.

This book would not exist without the efforts, encouragement, and various methods of persuasion of a number of people, most notably Roby Harrington, Peter Simon, and especially Ken Barton and Michael Moss, all at W. W. Norton. I originally conceived the project on a much more modest level, simply to provide fuller versions of texts quoted or discussed in *An Introduction*. Ken and Michael persuaded me to think on a grander scale and conducted extensive research with instructors to identify what they most wanted to see in a book like this. Of course it is not possible to satisfy everyone completely, or indeed anyone, and hard choices had to be made. We hope we have made the right ones, but very much welcome further feedback for future editions.

It would be impossible to thank everyone who gave their opinion on the contents of this book, but a number of people gave substantial help and advice. I'd like to give my grateful thanks to Paul Abela, Acadia University; Caroline T. Arruda, University of Texas at El Paso; Andrew D. Chapman, University of Colorado, Boulder; Eric Gampel, California State University–Chico; Don Hatcher, Baker University; Carol Hay, University of Massachusetts, Lowell; Rodger Jackson, Stockton University; Julie Kirsch, D'Youville College; Michael McKeon, Barry University; Timothy J. Nulty, University of Massachusetts, Dartmouth; Andrew Pavelich, University of Houston; Arina Pismenny, Montclair State University; Aleksandar Pjevalica, University of Texas at El Paso; Weaver Santaniello, Penn State University; Daniel Star, Boston University; and Glenn Tiller, Texas A&M University Corpus Christi.

I would particularly like to thank Derek Bowman, Providence College; Rory Kraft, York College of Pennsylvania; and Joanna Smolenski, CUNY, for their work in preparing the test bank and coursepack.

readings in
moral
philosophy

meta-
ethics

T he collection starts with a selection from Thomas Nagel's introductory
book on philosophy *What Does It All Mean?* Nagel raises the fundamental question in moral philosophy of what it is we mean when we
say that some conduct is wrong, using examples of stealing a library
book and an umbrella in a rainstorm. It is not simply a matter of following rules, for not all behavior is covered by rules and some rules
are themselves wrong. Often a sense that something is wrong is related to
potential harm that could be caused to others, but suppose you just don't
care. Does that mean you no longer have a reason to avoid wrongdoing?

Nagel considers the response that God's punishment or love provides a
reason to avoid acting wrongly or, alternatively, that we should act well so
that others act well to us, but he points out a number of limitations to those
arguments. More promising is the idea that morality provides reasons that
apply to everyone, and therefore in considering the morality of an act such
as stealing another person's umbrella we should ask "How would you like it
if someone did that to you?" He answers that if we find that we would resent
it, then this response shows that there is a type of universal reason not to
steal the umbrella.

Nagel suggests that morality requires us to adopt a general point of view, taking everyone's interests into account and not just our own. Nevertheless, it would be very hard to live according to a morality in which I literally took everyone's interests as seriously as I take my own, for example by giving to charity all but the bare minimum of my money. Somehow a line has to be drawn to allow me to pursue my own interests rather than devote myself entirely to the interests of others.

A further question is whether right and wrong are the same for everyone. Moral customs have changed over the centuries, which may lead us to think that moral standards should be relative to the standards of our own society. This is the question of cultural relativism, to which we will return shortly. Nagel comments that he finds cultural relativism very hard to believe, as it would seem to cut off the possibility of being critical about our own society's moral standards.

Finally Nagel considers a challenge to morality that claims we always act selfishly and that any apparent morally good action is done purely to avoid guilt or to achieve the "warm glow" of self-satisfaction. But Nagel suggests that we would not feel guilty or experience a warm glow unless there were external moral standards to follow. Morality, he says, tries to appeal to impartial motivation, even though it may sometimes give way to selfish or personal motives.

Nagel raises numerous important issues and argues for particular positions. But he recognizes that he has not provided a definitive answer to any of the questions raised. Therefore his discussion is a perfect springboard for further reflection and an excellent introduction to moral philosophy.

We move next to David Hume, who, writing in the 18th century, aims to bring out a distinction between two ways of thinking about morality. One is that morality is based on "reason," the other that it is based on what he calls "passions," which we might now call "feelings" or perhaps "preferences" or "desires." Hume claims that morality is a practical matter, leading to action, but, he also claims, reason alone cannot lead to action. He argues that reason reveals relations between ideas and hence concerns thought and belief alone. In order to motivate human action, something more than thought and belief is needed: desire. I can believe that there is a refreshing drink in front of me, but this will not lead me to drink it unless I have a desire to drink. Insofar as morality is a practical sphere, requiring people to be motivated to act, then morality must be based not merely on reason but also on desire or passion.

Hume's discussion suggests only a limited way in which we can use ideas of reason in our thinking about action. If we desire something, then reason can help us calculate how to achieve it. And we can sometimes use our reason to discover that something we desire is possible or available (or not). But the ultimate ends of our action cannot be criticized for being reasonable or unreasonable, or rational or irrational. There are some things that "excite our passions," which is to say that we desire them, and some things that do not. On this view, no desire is irrational, unless it is a desire for something that will frustrate a more important desire. Similarly, Hume claims, we must come to understand that something is morally good through the fact that it accords with our passions, rather than because it is derived by our reason.

Hume next, in a very influential argument, points out that it has been very common for writers about moral questions to move from passages that describe some factual state of affairs to a judgment of right or wrong, without making clear how that transition is made. Hume wants us to appreciate that no statement about facts logically implies any moral judgment. On a literal reading of the text, Hume is simply pointing out that there is often a gap in the argument between "facts" and "values" and is criticizing other philosophers for leaving that gap unfilled. However, Hume is often read as suggesting that such a gap cannot be filled and that it is simply illegitimate to move from an "is"—a statement of fact—to an "ought"—a statement of values. And indeed this may well have been Hume's subtle intention, raising a very significant question of how the "is/ought gap" can be filled.

The next reading is a short extract from the anthropologist Ruth Benedict which provides examples of cultural difference with respect to moral attitudes. Benedict lists different practices regarding the taking of life, and suicide, to support the claim that there are no universal values and that values differ from culture to culture. As an anthropologist her project is to understand cultures, rather than to make a philosophical argument. However, the type of evidence that Benedict draws on is often used in arguments for the view that there are no universal moral standards, but that moral standards differ from culture to culture and there is no external standpoint from which one can be judged "right" and another "wrong." This is the view known as cultural relativism, mentioned above in relation to Nagel, and it is certainly encouraged, whether or not directly advocated, by Benedict's writing.

Mary Midgley's task is to consider the merits of the type of cultural relativism suggested by the writings of Benedict and others, which Midgley calls "moral isolationism." Such a view prevents us from criticizing other cultures, for each culture's value system is said to be relative to that particular culture and hence immune to external judgment. Midgley points out that moral isolationism blocks praise as well as blame and makes it impossible to learn from other cultures. Indeed, she argues that moral isolationism makes it problematic for us even to judge our own culture, for what standards could we use if not comparisons with other cultures?

Midgley asks us to reflect on what is claimed to be the ancient Samurai practice of "trying out one's new sword" on an innocent wayfarer, who would be sliced in half as a result. An external critic might well condemn such a practice as barbaric. Midgley points out that one way of replying to the critic is to explain the practice as arising within Japanese culture and even to suggest that the wayfarer may well consent. In addition to raising the question of whether such consent is likely, Midgley points out that even to enter into such a discussion is to reject moral isolationism. The true isolationist response would be that it is simply not for us to try to judge or attempt to understand. But those tempted to say anything substantive in criticism or justification are applying one set of values (their own) to try to justify other practices. Moral isolationism turns out to be a very difficult theory to live by, and, Midgley argues, very misguided, as any real culture has been formed by a good number of different traditions, many from "outside," which should not be possible on an isolationist view.

The challenge to conventional morality begun by cultural relativism or moral isolationism is continued in the extract of Friedrich Nietzsche's brilliant but rather elusive writings. He begins by applauding the role of strong people in human development and achievement. He moves on to a deeply paradoxical position: that refraining from injuring, exploiting, and being violent to others, which is normally thought to be morally required, will lead to the *denial* of morality. Life, Nietzsche says, is "will to power," by which he means the drive to impose one's own goals on others, even at their expense. Therefore, conventional morality, in curbing the will to power, is contrary to life.

Nietzsche then goes on to distinguish what he calls "master morality" and "slave morality." Master morality identifies the good with the aims of the nobility or aristocracy, which attempts to separate itself from the mass. The noble have contempt for the "cowardly" and inferior. They have the power even to determine their own values, and although they may help the weak, it is simply an exercise of their own power. "Good" is the exercise of the will of the nobility, and "bad" its frustration. Slave morality, by contrast, is the morality of "good" and "evil." Nietzsche regards slave morality as a type of agreement or conspiracy among the weak, to protect them from the "evil" that they fear: those very people who are the masters of master morality. Hence slave morality turns out to be a conspiracy of the weak to protect themselves from the strong. And it is clear that Nietzsche regards slave morality as a highly undesirable system, opposed to "life" and in urgent need of replacement by master morality.

From Nietzsche we move to A. J. Ayer's equally radical, though more calmly expressed, critique of ethics. Ayer's position flows from a more general philosophical position known as logical positivism, which is a theory of how statements can be meaningful. For the logical positivist, statements are meaningful only if they meet one of two conditions concerning how they can be tested, which Ayer calls the "criterion of verifiability." The first is if they can be tested by logic; the second if they can be tested by experience.

Two moral theories could meet the criterion of verifiability, according to Ayer. These are subjectivism and utilitarianism. Subjectivism is here defined as identifying the good with what is generally desired, and utilitarianism with what maximizes happiness. Ayer's objection to both takes the same form: It is not contradictory to say that something is good but not desired, or good but not maximizing of happiness. Hence the good cannot be defined as subjectivists or utilitarians do.

This failure leads to the startling conclusion that statements expressing moral beliefs appear to be classified as meaningless, for there is no conceivable test we can use to decide a moral dispute. Rather than take this path, Ayer provides a different way of understanding moral statements as expressing our attitudes. To say that something is good is rather like cheering for it, and to say it is bad is akin to booing it. Hence, on this view, moral judgments do not aim to be true, but rather, they express our emotions. Hence the position defended by Ayer is known as "emotivism." And it has the further feature that any apparent moral disagreement is just that: apparent. For it is perfectly possible, and no contradiction, for two people to take opposed attitudes to the same state of affairs.

In reply to the objection that his theory makes it impossible to argue about moral questions, Ayer replies that typically moral disagreements concern the background matters of fact that give rise to the moral judgment, such as whether someone really did take something from a shop without paying for it. When we agree on all the facts, Ayer suggests that further moral argument is not possible and that different moral judgments simply reflect different emotions or attitudes toward the case.

Like Ayer, J. L. Mackie wishes to argue against the view that moral standards are in some sense objective. Unlike Mackie, however, he does not rest his argument on a theory of meaning. Rather, he concedes that the meaning of an ethical judgment such as "stealing is wrong" is that it states that it is an objective fact that stealing is wrong. However, Mackie wishes to convince us that all such statements are false. For they presuppose that there are objective values in the world—in this case, the "wrongness" of stealing—but, he says, there are no such things as objective values. All moral judgments contain the same error of presupposing the existence of moral values. For this reason, Mackie's view has become known as "error theory."

Mackie presents two main arguments for his conclusion. The first is the argument from cultural relativity that we have seen in Ruth Benedict's writing. Mackie suggests that the great cultural diversity in moral values we observe in the world is a good reason for believing that there are no objective truths about morality. The second is known as the argument from "queerness" (using the term in its old-fashioned sense) that if there were objective values, they would be very odd or queer, unlike anything that exists in the world. This argument has two parts. The first is metaphysical, in that it concerns what, fundamentally, exists in the world. Objective values would be very strange objects. The second part is epistemological, concerning how we can know values. If values are subjective, then it is very easy to see how we could know them, for we would have made them for ourselves. But if they are objective, how do we have the type of engagement with them that would lead to knowledge? For all these reasons, Mackie concludes that objective values do not exist and hence our ordinary moral judgments are false.

Harry Frankfurt's journal article moves us to a different topic. He considers the thesis that people are morally responsible for their actions only if they could have acted otherwise. Frankfurt calls this thesis the "principle of alternate possibilities." It, or something very like it, is often taken for granted in ordinary understandings of morality, for if you had no alternative to doing something, how could you be blamed (or praised) for doing it? Consider, for example, someone who acts under hypnotic suggestion or under extreme coercion. But this principle has far-reaching consequences. For if it turns out that human beings do not have free will and that all our actions are determined by factors outside our control, then human beings have no alternative to acting as we do. Then it will also turn out that we have no moral responsibility and cannot be praised or blamed for anything.

Frankfurt sets out to cast doubt on the principle of alternate possibilities by imagining a case in which someone voluntarily performs an action which, had that person not chosen to perform the action, someone else would have forced the person to do. In one example, another person has taken control of my brain and could change my choices if need be. Whatever happens, I would have performed the action and hence had no alternative to doing so. But in this case, because I have voluntarily chosen to undertake the action, and no intervention was necessary, we have very little hesitation in saying that I am indeed morally responsible for the action. Frankfurt wishes to replace the principle of alternate possibilities with the principle that people are not morally responsible for what they have done if they did it *only because* they could not have done otherwise. Through this simple argument, Frankfurt provides a possible basis for what is known as a compatibilist position in the free will debate, in which determinism is compatible with moral responsibility.

Changing topics again, we move to Plato's *Euthyphro*, which contains one of the most important arguments in the history of moral philosophy, even though the dialogue form and the literary writing style may somewhat obscure its significance. The topic is whether God's command can be foundation of morality. The context of the extract is that Euthyphro has told Socrates that he is bringing a prosecution against his own father who has unjustly brought about the death of a slave. The discussion moves on to the nature of "piety," raising the question of whether some actions are pious because the gods command those actions, or whether the gods command them because these actions are pious for other reasons. The context in which Plato is writing is that of Greek polytheism, in which there are many gods, often in dispute with each other. Hence it may seem that Plato is concerned with a local theological question that has little general application. But in fact this argument has been taken as presenting exactly the same question for the relation between morality and God in a monotheistic religion. The question for us today is this: On a view that founds morality on religion, are actions good because God commands them, or does God command them because they are independently good? This is now known as the *Euthyphro* dilemma.

The dilemma is that if we take the latter alternative and say that God commands certain actions because they are independently good, then it seems we have denied that there is a religious basis to morality. Goodness would not, then, depend on God's command. So someone who wishes to find a religious foundation for morality seems compelled to take the first alternative and argue that actions are good because God commands them. But this, it seems, is problematic in a different way. If actions are good simply because God commands them, it seems that morality is unconstrained. Hence whatever God commands becomes morally correct, however repellent those commands appear to us to be. Can this consequence be accepted? If not, then it appears that it will be very difficult to find a religious basis for morality.

Our final reading in this section jumps forward 2,500 years to explore the links between recent theorizing in genetics and in moral philosophy. Given that human beings are a product of evolution, it is reasonable to suppose that elements of human behavior can be explained in evolutionary terms. Moral behavior would be no exception, and therefore it could be fruitful to explore how much moral behavior can be explained as a product of evolution, in that it could have evolved in order to facilitate human survival and reproduction. This is the area known as sociobiology.

Peter Singer understands altruism as behavior that helps others at some cost to oneself, and the puzzle is to explain how genes for this sort of self-sacrificing behavior could evolve and survive when it would seem to be against the interests of the being that developed them. Singer identifies three possible mechanisms that have been thought to be candidates for playing a role in the evolution of moral norms: kin altruism, reciprocal altruism, and group altruism. Kin altruism starts from the insight that my close relatives contain much of the same genetic material as I do, and so my own genes can survive through their survival. Hence there is any easy genetic explanation for why I might sacrifice my own interests to those of my close relatives, especially my children, if this sacrifice would better preserve my genes. Reciprocal altruism arises from the insight that although cooperation can be a cost, it is generally better to live under cooperative arrangements than ones in which we ignore or cheat each other. These two mechanisms seem plausible explanations of at least part of morality. The third mechanism, group altruism, is more controversial. It is the idea that cooperative groups will do better as a whole than noncooperative groups. However, cooperative groups are likely to be subject to free riders (those who reap the benefits without paying the costs), which could lead to destruction of the group. Consequently, Singer sees only a limited role for group altruism, perhaps as a way of helping reciprocal altruism get established, at which point group and reciprocal altruism reinforce each other, especially when combined with hostility to outside groups, to prevent new free riders from entering.

THOMAS NAGEL
Right and Wrong

Thomas Nagel (b. 1937) is an American philosopher, particularly noted for his contributions to moral philosophy, political philosophy, and philosophy of mind.

Suppose you work in a library, checking people's books as they leave, and a friend asks you to let him smuggle out a hard-to-find reference work that he wants to own.

You might hesitate to agree for various reasons. You might be afraid that he'll be caught and that both you and he will then get into trouble. You might want the book to stay in the library so that you can consult it yourself.

But you may also think that what he proposes is wrong—that he shouldn't do it and you shouldn't help him. If you think that, what does it mean, and what, if anything, makes it true?

To say it's wrong is not just to say it's against the rules. There can be bad rules which prohibit what isn't wrong—like a law against criticizing the government. A rule can also be bad because it requires something that *is* wrong—like a law that requires racial segregation in hotels and restaurants. The ideas of wrong and right are different from the ideas of what is and is not against the rules. Otherwise they couldn't be used in the evaluation of rules as well as of actions.

If you think it would be wrong to help your friend steal the book, then you will feel uncomfortable about doing it: in some way you won't want to do it, even if you are also reluctant to refuse help to a friend. Where does the desire not to do it come from; what is its motive, the reason behind it?

There are various ways in which something can be wrong, but in this case, if you had to explain it, you'd probably say that it would be unfair to other users of the library who may be just as interested in the book as your friend is, but who consult it in the reference room, where anyone who needs it can find it. You may also feel that to let him take it would betray your employers, who are paying you precisely to keep this sort of thing from happening.

These thoughts have to do with effects on others—not necessarily effects on their feelings, since they may never find out about it, but some kind of damage nevertheless. In general, the thought that something is wrong depends on its impact not just on the person who does it but on other people. They wouldn't like it, and they'd object if they found out.

But suppose you try to explain all this to your friend, and he says, "I know the head librarian wouldn't like it if he found out, and probably some of the other users of the library would be unhappy to find the book gone, but who cares? I want the book; why should I care about them?"

The argument that it would be wrong is supposed to give him a reason not to do it. But if someone just doesn't care about other people, what reason does he have to refrain from doing any of the things usually thought to be wrong, if he can get away with it: what reason does he have not to kill, steal, lie, or hurt others? If he can get what he wants by doing such things, why shouldn't he? And if there's no reason why he shouldn't, in what sense is it wrong?

Of course most people do care about others to some extent. But if someone doesn't care, most of us wouldn't conclude that he's exempt from morality. A person who kills someone just to steal his wallet, without caring about the victim, is not automatically excused. The fact that he doesn't care doesn't make it all right: He *should* care. But *why* should he care?

There have been many attempts to answer this question. One type of answer tries to identify something else that the person already cares about and then connect morality to it.

For example, some people believe that even if you can get away with awful crimes on this earth and are not punished by the law or your fellow men, such acts are forbidden by God, who will punish you after death (and reward you if you didn't do wrong when you were tempted to). So even when it seems to be in your interest to do such a thing, it really isn't. Some people have even believed that if there is no God to back up moral requirements with the threat of punishment and the promise of reward, morality is an illusion: "If God does not exist, everything is permitted."

This is a rather crude version of the religious foundation for morality. A more appealing version might be that the motive for obeying God's commands is not fear but love. He loves you, and you should love Him, and should wish to obey His commands in order not to offend Him.

But however we interpret the religious motivation, there are three objections to this type of answer. First, plenty of people who don't believe in God still make judgments of right and wrong, and think no one should kill another for his wallet even if he can be sure to get away with it. Second, if God exists, and forbids what's wrong, that still isn't what *makes* it wrong. Murder is wrong in itself, and that's *why* God forbids it (if He does). God couldn't make just any old thing wrong—like putting on your left sock before your right—simply by prohibiting it. If God would punish you for doing that it would be inadvisable to do it, but it wouldn't be wrong. Third, fear of punishment and hope of reward, and even love of God, seem not to be the right motives for morality. If you think it's wrong to kill, cheat, or steal, you should want to avoid doing such things because they are bad things to do to the victims, not just because you fear the consequences for yourself, or because you don't want to offend your Creator.

This third objection also applies to other explanations of the force of morality which appeal to the interests of the person who must act. For example, it may be said that you should treat others with consideration so that they'll do the same for you. This may be sound advice, but it is valid only so far as you think what you do will affect how others treat you. It's not a reason for doing the right thing if others won't find out about it, or against doing the wrong thing if you can get away with it (like being a hit and run driver).

There is no substitute for a direct concern for other people as the basis of morality. But morality is supposed to apply to everyone: and can we assume that everyone has such a concern for others? Obviously not: some people are very selfish, and even those who are not selfish may care only about the people they know, and not about everyone. So where will we find a reason that everyone has not to hurt other people, even those they don't know?

Well, there's one general argument against hurting other people which can be given to anybody who understands English (or any other language), and which seems to show that he has *some* reason to care about others, even if in the end his selfish motives are so strong that he persists in treating other people badly anyway. It's an argument that I'm sure you've heard, and it goes like this: "How would you like it if someone did that to you?"

It's not easy to explain how this argument is supposed to work. Suppose you're about to steal someone else's umbrella as you leave a restaurant in a rainstorm, and a bystander says, "How would you like it if someone did that to you?" Why is it supposed to make you hesitate, or feel guilty?

Obviously the direct answer to the question is supposed to be, "I wouldn't like it at all!" But what's the next step? Suppose you were to say, "I wouldn't like it if someone did that to me. But luckily no one is doing it to me. I'm doing it to someone else, and I don't mind that at all!"

This answer misses the point of the question. When you are asked how you would like it if someone did that to you, you are supposed to think about all the feelings you would have if someone stole your umbrella. And that includes more than just "not liking it"—as you wouldn't "like it" if you stubbed your toe on a rock. If someone stole your umbrella you'd *resent* it. You'd have feelings about the umbrella thief, not just about the loss of the umbrella. * * *

When our own interests are threatened by the inconsiderate behavior of others, most of us find it easy to appreciate that those others have a reason to be more considerate. When you are hurt, you probably feel that other people should care about it: you don't think it's no concern of theirs, and that they have no reason to avoid hurting you. That is the feeling that the "How would you like it?" argument is supposed to arouse.

Because if you admit that you would *resent* it if someone else did to you what you are now doing to him, you are admitting that you think he would have a reason not to do it to you. And if you admit that, you have to consider what that reason is. It couldn't be just that it's *you* that he's hurting, of all the people in the world. There's no special reason for him not to steal *your* umbrella, as opposed to anyone else's. There's nothing so special about you. Whatever the reason is, it's a reason he would have against hurting anyone else in the same way. And it's a reason anyone else would have too, in a similar situation, against hurting you or anyone else.

But if it's a reason anyone would have not to hurt anyone else in this way, then it's a reason you have not to hurt someone else in this way (since *anyone* means *everyone*). Therefore it's a reason not to steal the other person's umbrella now.

This is a matter of simple consistency. Once you admit that another person would have a reason not to harm you in similar circumstances, and once you admit that the reason he would have is very general and doesn't apply only to you, or to him, then to be consistent you have to admit that the same reason applies to you now. You shouldn't steal the umbrella, and you ought to feel guilty if you do.

Someone could escape from this argument if, when he was asked, "How would you like it if someone did that to you?" he answered, "I wouldn't resent it at all. I wouldn't *like* it if someone stole my umbrella in a rainstorm, but I wouldn't think there was any reason for him to consider my feelings about it." But how many people could honestly give that answer? I think most people, unless they're crazy, would think that their own interests and harms matter, not only to themselves, but in a way that gives other people a reason to care about them too. We all think that when we suffer it is not just bad *for us*, but *bad, period*.

The basis of morality is a belief that good and harm to particular people (or animals) is good or bad not just from their point of view, but from a more general point of view, which every thinking person can understand. That means that each person has a reason to consider not only his own interests but the interests of others in deciding what to do. And it isn't enough if he is considerate only of some others—his family and friends, those he specially cares about. Of course he will care more about certain people, and also about himself. But he has some reason to consider the effect of what he does on the good or harm of everyone. If he's like most of us, that is what he thinks others should do with regard to him, even if they aren't friends of his.

Even if this is right, it is only a bare outline of the source of morality. * * * There are many disagreements among those who accept morality in general, about what in particular is right and what is wrong.

For instance: should you care about every other person as much as you care about yourself? Should you in other words love your neighbor as yourself (even if he isn't your neighbor)? Should you ask yourself, every time you go to a movie, whether the cost of the ticket could provide more happiness if you gave it to someone else, or donated the money to famine relief?

Very few people are so unselfish. And if someone were that impartial between himself and others, he would probably also feel that he should be just as impartial *among* other people. That would rule out caring more about his friends and relatives than he does about strangers. He might have special feelings about certain people who are close to him, but complete impartiality would mean that he won't favor them—if for example he has to choose between helping a friend or a stranger to avoid suffering, or between taking his children to a movie and donating the money to famine relief.

This degree of impartiality seems too much to ask of most people: someone who had it would be a kind of terrifying saint. But it's an important question in moral thought, how much impartiality we should try for. You are a particular person, but you are also able to recognize that you're just one person among many others, and no more important than they are, when looked at from outside. How much should that point of view influence you? You do matter somewhat from outside—otherwise you wouldn't think other people had any reason to care about what they did to you. But you don't matter as much from the outside as you matter to yourself, from the inside—since from the outside you don't matter any more than anybody else.

Not only is it unclear how impartial we should be; it's unclear what would make an answer to this question the right one. Is there a single correct way for everyone to strike the balance between what he cares about personally and what matters impartially? Or will the answer vary from person to person depending on the strength of their different motives?

This brings us to another big issue: Are right and wrong the same for everyone? * * *

Many things that you probably think are wrong have been accepted as morally correct by large groups of people in the past: slavery, serfdom, human sacrifice, racial segregation, denial of religious and political freedom, hereditary caste systems. And probably some things you now think are right will be thought wrong by future societies. Is it reasonable to believe that there is some single truth about all this, even though we can't be sure what it is? Or is it more reasonable to believe that right and wrong are relative to a particular time and place and social background?

There is one way in which right and wrong are obviously relative to circumstances. It is usually right to return a knife you have borrowed to its owner if he asks for it back. But if he has gone crazy in the meantime, and wants the knife to murder someone with, then you shouldn't return it. This isn't the kind of relativity I am talking about, because it doesn't mean morality is relative at the basic level. It means only that the same basic moral principles will require different actions in different circumstances.

The deeper kind of relativity, which some people believe in, would mean that the most basic standards of right and wrong—like when it is and is not all right to kill, or what sacrifices you're required to make for others—depend entirely on what standards are generally accepted in the society in which you live.

This I find very hard to believe, mainly because it always seems possible to criticize the accepted standards of your own society and say that they are morally mistaken. But if you do that, you must be appealing to some more objective standard, an idea of what is *really* right and wrong, as opposed to what most people think. It is hard to say what this is, but it is an idea most of us understand, unless we are slavish followers of what the community says. * * *

I should answer one possible objection to the whole idea of morality. You've probably heard it said that the only reason anybody ever does anything is that it makes him feel good, or that not doing it will make him feel bad. If we are really motivated only by our own comfort, it is hopeless for morality to try to appeal to a concern for others. On this view, even apparently moral conduct in which one person seems to sacrifice his own interests for the sake of others is really motivated by his concern for himself: he wants to avoid the guilt he'll feel if he doesn't do the "right" thing, or to experience the warm glow of self-congratulation he'll get if he does. But those who don't have these feelings have no motive to be "moral."

Now it's true that when people do what they think they ought to do, they often feel good about it: similarly if they do what they think is wrong, they often feel bad. But that doesn't mean that these feelings are their motives for acting. In many cases the feelings result from motives which also produce the action. You wouldn't feel good about doing the right thing unless you thought there was some other reason to do it, besides the fact that it would make you feel good. And you wouldn't feel guilty about doing the wrong thing unless you thought that there was some other reason not to do it, besides the fact that it made you feel guilty: something which made it *right* to feel guilty. At least that's how things should be. It's true that some people feel irrational guilt about things they don't have any independent reason to think are wrong—but that's not the way morality is supposed to work.

In a sense, people do what they want to do. But their reasons and motives for wanting to do things vary enormously. I may "want" to give someone my wallet only because he has a gun pointed at my head and threatens to kill me if I don't. And I may want to jump into an icy river to save a drowning stranger not because it will make me feel good, but because I recognize that his life is important, just as mine is, and I recognize that I have a reason to save his life just as he would have a reason to save mine if our positions were reversed.

Moral argument tries to appeal to a capacity for impartial motivation which is supposed to be present in all of us. Unfortunately it may be deeply buried, and in some cases it may not be present at all. In any case it has to compete with powerful selfish motives, and other personal motives that may not be so selfish, in its bid for control of our behavior. The difficulty of justifying morality is not that there is only one human motive, but that there are so many.

STUDY QUESTIONS

1. How does Nagel think you should respond to your friend who wants you to help steal a library book?
2. How impartial should we be, according to Nagel?
3. How does Nagel respond to the suggestion that we act morally only in order to get the "warm glow" of acting well?

DAVID HUME
Moral Distinctions Not Derived From Reason

David Hume (1711–1776) was a Scottish philosopher who wrote enormously influential works on a very wide range of philosophical topics, although he was better known in his own day as a historian.

If morality had naturally no influence on human passions and actions, it were in vain to take such pains to inculcate it; and nothing would be more fruitless than that multitude of rules and precepts, with which all moralists abound. Philosophy is commonly divided into *speculative* and *practical*; and as morality is always comprehended under the latter division, it is supposed to influence our passions and actions, and to go beyond the calm and indolent judgments of the understanding. And this is confirmed by common experience, which informs us, that men are often governed by their duties, and are deterred from some actions by the opinion of injustice, and impelled to others by that of obligation.

Since morals, therefore, have an influence on the actions and affections, it follows, that they cannot be derived from reason; and that because reason alone, as we have already proved, can never have any such influence. Morals excite passions, and produce or prevent actions. Reason of itself is utterly impotent in this particular. The rules of morality, therefore, are not conclusions of our reason. * * *

Reason is the discovery of truth or falsehood. Truth or falsehood consists in an agreement or disagreement either to the *real* relations of ideas, or to *real* existence and matter of fact. Whatever, therefore, is not susceptible of this agreement or disagreement, is incapable of being true or false, and can never be an object of our reason. Now it is evident our passions, volitions, and actions, are not susceptible of any such agreement or disagreement; being original facts and realities, complete in themselves, and implying no reference to other passions, volitions, and actions. It is impossible, therefore, they can be pronounced either true or false, and be either contrary or conformable to reason.

This argument is of double advantage to our present purpose. For it proves *directly*, that actions do not derive their merit from a conformity to reason, nor their blame from a contrariety to it; and it proves the same truth more indirectly, by showing us, that as reason can never immediately prevent or produce any action by contradicting or approving of it, it cannot be the source of moral good and evil, which are found to have that influence. Actions may be laudable or blamable; but they cannot be reasonable or unreasonable: laudable or blamable, therefore, are not the same with reasonable or unreasonable. The merit and demerit of actions frequently contradict, and sometimes control our natural propensities. But reason has no such influence. Moral distinctions, therefore, are not the offspring of reason. Reason is wholly inactive, and can never be the source of so active a principle as conscience, or a sense of morals. * * *

It has been observed, that reason, in a strict and philosophical sense, can have an influence on our conduct only after two ways: either when it excites a passion by informing us of the existence of something which is a proper object of it; or when it discovers the connection of causes and effects, so as to afford us means of exerting any passion. These are the only kinds of judgment, which can accompany our actions, or can be said to produce them in any manner; and it must be allowed, that these judgments may often be false and erroneous. A person may be affected with passion, by supposing a pain or pleasure to lie in an object, which has no tendency to produce either of these sensations, or which produces the contrary to what is imagined. A person may also take false measures for the attaining his end, and may retard, by his foolish conduct, instead of forwarding the execution of any project. These false judgments may be thought to affect the passions and actions, which are connected with them, and may be said to render them unreasonable, in a figurative and improper way of speaking. But though this be acknowledged, it is easy to observe, that these errors are so far from being the source of all immorality, that they are commonly very innocent, and draw no manner of guilt upon the person who is so unfortunate as to fall into them. They extend not beyond a mistake of *fact*, which moralists have not generally supposed criminal, as being perfectly involuntary. I am more to be lamented than blamed, if I am mistaken with regard to the influence of objects in producing pain or pleasure, or if I know not the proper means of satisfying my desires. No one can ever regard such errors as a defect in my moral character.

Should it be pretended, that though a mistake of *fact* be not criminal, yet a mistake of *right* often is; and that this may be the source of immorality: I would answer, that it is impossible such a mistake can ever be the original source of immorality, since it supposes a real right and wrong; that is, a real distinction in morals, independent of these judgments. A mistake, therefore, of right may become a species of immorality; but it is only a secondary one, and is founded on some other, antecedent to it.

As to those judgments which are the *effects* of our actions, and which, when false, give occasion to pronounce the actions contrary to truth and reason; we may observe, that our actions never cause any judgment, either true or false, in ourselves, and that it is only on others they have such an influence. It is certain, that an action, on many occasions, may give rise to false conclusions in others; and that a person, who thro' a window sees any lewd behaviour of mine with my neighbour's wife, may be so simple as to imagine she is certainly my own. In this respect my action resembles somewhat a lie or falsehood; only with this difference, which is material, that I perform not the action with any intention of giving rise to a false judgment in another, but merely to satisfy my lust and passion. It causes, however, a mistake and false judgment by accident; and the falsehood of its effects may be ascribed, by some odd figurative way of speaking, to the action itself. But still I can see no pretext of reason for asserting, that the tendency to cause such an error is the first spring or original source of all immorality. * * *

But to make these general reflections more clear and convincing, we may illustrate them by some particular instances, wherein this character of moral good or evil is the most universally acknowledged. Of all crimes that human creatures are capable of committing, the most horrid and unnatural is ingratitude, especially when it is committed against parents, and appears in the more flagrant instances of wounds and death. This is acknowledged by all mankind, philosophers as well as the people: the question only arises among philosophers, whether the guilt or moral deformity of this action be discovered by demonstrative reasoning, or be felt by an internal sense, and by means of some sentiment, which the reflecting on such an action naturally occasions. This question will soon be decided against the former opinion, if we can show the same relations in other objects, without the notion of any guilt or iniquity attending them. Reason or science is nothing but the comparing of ideas, and the discovery of their relations; and if the same relations have different characters, it must evidently follow, that those characters are not discovered merely by reason. To put the affair, therefore, to this trial, let us choose any inanimate object, such as an oak or elm; and let us suppose, that by the dropping of its seed, it produces a sapling below it, which springing up by degrees, at last overtops and destroys the parent tree: I ask, if in this instance there be wanting any relation, which is discoverable in parricide or ingratitude? Is not the one tree the cause of the other's existence; and the latter the cause of the destruction of the former, in the same manner as when a child murders his parent? It is not sufficient to reply, that a choice or will is wanting. For in the case of parricide, a will does not give rise to any *different* relations, but is only the cause from which the action is derived; and consequently produces the *same* relations, that in the oak or elm arise from some other principles. It is a will or choice, that determines a man to kill his parent; and they are the laws of matter and motion, that determine a sapling to destroy the oak, from which it sprung. Here then the same relations have different causes; but still the relations are the same: and as their discovery is not in both cases attended with a notion of immorality, it follows, that that notion does not arise from such a discovery.

But to choose an instance, still more resembling; I would fain ask any one, why incest in the human species is criminal, and why the very same action, and the same relations in animals have not the smallest moral turpitude and deformity? If it be answered, that this action is innocent in animals, because they have not reason sufficient to discover its turpitude; but that man, being endowed with that faculty, which *ought* to restrain him to his duty, the same action instantly becomes criminal to him. Should this be said, I would reply, that this is evidently arguing in a circle. For, before reason can perceive this turpitude, the turpitude must exist; and consequently is independent of the decisions of our reason, and is their object more properly than their effect. According to this system, then, every animal, that has sense and appetite and will, that is, every animal must be susceptible of all the same virtues and vices, for which we ascribe praise and blame to human creatures. All the difference is, that our superior reason may serve to discover the vice or virtue, and by that means may augment the blame or praise: but still this discovery supposes a separate being in these moral distinctions, and a being, which depends only on the will and appetite, and which, both in thought and reality, may be distinguished from reason. Animals are susceptible of the same relations, with respect to each other, as the human species, and therefore would also be susceptible of the same morality, if the essence of morality consisted in these relations. Their want of a sufficient degree of reason may hinder them from perceiving the duties and obligations of morality, but can never hinder these duties from existing; since they must antecedently exist, in order to their being perceived. Reason must find them, and can never produce them. This argument deserves to be weighed, as being, in my opinion, entirely decisive.

Nor does this reasoning only prove, that morality consists not in any relations, that are the objects of science; but if examined, will prove with equal certainty, that it consists not in any *matter of fact*, which can be discovered by the understanding. This is the *second* part of our argument; and if it can be made evident, we may conclude, that morality is not an object of reason. But can there be any difficulty in proving, that vice and virtue are not matters of fact, whose existence we can infer by reason? Take any action allowed to be vicious: Wilful murder, for instance. Examine it in all lights, and see if you can find that matter of fact, or real existence, which you call *vice*. In whichever way you take it, you find only certain passions, motives, volitions and thoughts. There is no other matter of fact in the case. The vice entirely escapes you, as long as you consider the object. You never can find it, till you turn your reflection into your own breast, and find a sentiment of disapprobation, which arises in you, towards this action. Here is a matter of fact; but it is the object of feeling, not of reason. It lies in yourself, not in the object. So that when you pronounce any action or character to be vicious, you mean nothing, but that from the constitution of your nature you have a feeling or sentiment of blame from the contemplation of it. Vice and virtue, therefore, may be compared to sounds, colours, heat and cold, which, according to modern philosophy, are not qualities in objects, but perceptions in the mind: and this discovery in morals, like that other in physics, is to be regarded as a considerable advancement of the speculative sciences; though, like that too, it has little or no influence on practice. Nothing can be more real, or concern us more, than our own sentiments of pleasure and uneasiness; and if these be favourable to virtue, and unfavourable to vice, no more can be requisite to the regulation of our conduct and behaviour.

I cannot forbear adding to these reasonings an observation, which may, perhaps, be found of some importance. In every system of morality, which I have hitherto met with, I have always remarked, that the author proceeds for some time in the ordinary way of reasoning, and establishes the being of a God, or makes observations concerning human affairs; when of a sudden I am surprised to find, that instead of the usual copulations of propositions, *is*, and *is not*, I meet with no proposition that is not connected with an *ought*, or an *ought not*. This change is imperceptible; but is, however, of the last consequence. For as this *ought*, or *ought not*, expresses some new relation or affirmation, it is necessary that it should be observed and explained; and at the same time that a reason should be given, for what seems altogether inconceivable, how this new relation can be a deduction from others, which are entirely different from it. But as authors do not commonly use this precaution, I shall presume to recommend it to the readers; and am persuaded, that this small attention would subvert all the vulgar systems of morality, and let us see, that the distinction of vice and virtue is not founded merely on the relations of objects, nor is perceived by reason.

STUDY QUESTIONS

1. What are Hume's reasons for claiming that moral distinctions are not derived from reason?
2. What does Hume mean by "passions"? What role do they play in moral motivation?
3. What is wrong, according to Hume, with deriving an "ought" from an "is"?

RUTH BENEDICT
Patterns of Culture

Ruth Benedict (1887–1948) was a major American anthropologist. Her documentation of cultural difference has influenced the development of cultural relativism in moral philosophy.

The diversity of cultures can be endlessly documented. A field of human behaviour may be ignored in some societies until it barely exists; it may even be in some cases unimagined. Or it may almost monopolize the whole organized behaviour of the society, and the most alien situations be manipulated only in its terms. Traits having no intrinsic relation one with the other, and historically independent, merge and become inextricable, providing the occasion for behaviour that has no counterpart in regions that do not make these identifications. It is a corollary of this that standards, no matter in what aspect of behaviour, range in different cultures from the positive to the negative pole. We might suppose that in the matter of taking life all peoples would agree in condemnation. On the contrary, in a matter of homicide, it may be held that one is blameless if diplomatic relations have been severed between neighbouring countries, or that one kills by custom his first two children, or that a husband has right of life and death over his wife, or that it is the duty of the child to kill his parents before they are old. It may be that those are killed who steal a fowl, or who cut their upper teeth first, or who are born on a Wednesday. Among some peoples a person suffers torments at having caused an accidental death; among others it is a matter of no consequence. Suicide also may be a light matter, the recourse of anyone who has suffered some slight rebuff, an act that occurs constantly in a tribe. It may be the highest and noblest act a wise man can perform. The very tale of it, on the other hand, may be a matter for incredulous mirth, and the act itself impossible to conceive as a human possibility. Or it may be a crime punishable by law, or regarded as a sin against the gods.

The diversity of custom in the world is not, however, a matter which we can only helplessly chronicle. Self-torture here, head-hunting there, prenuptial chastity in one tribe and adolescent licence in another, are not a list of unrelated facts, each of them to be greeted with surprise wherever it is found or wherever it is absent. The tabus on killing oneself or another, similarly, though they relate to no absolute standard, are not therefore fortuitous. The significance of cultural behaviour is not exhausted when we have clearly understood that it is local and man-made and hugely variable. It tends also to be integrated. A culture, like an individual, is a more or less consistent pattern of thought and action. Within each culture there come into being characteristic purposes not necessarily shared by other types of society. In obedience to these purposes, each people further and further consolidates its experience, and in proportion to the urgency of these drives the heterogeneous items of behaviour take more and more congruous shape. Taken up by a well-integrated culture, the most ill-assorted acts become characteristic of its peculiar goals, often by the most unlikely metamorphoses. The form that these acts take we can understand only by understanding first the emotional and intellectual mainsprings of that society.

Such patterning of culture cannot be ignored as if it were an unimportant detail. The whole, as modern science is insisting in many fields, is not merely the sum of all its parts, but the result of a unique arrangement and interrelation of the parts that has brought about a new entity. Gunpowder is not merely the sum of sulphur and charcoal and saltpeter, and no amount of knowledge even of all three of its elements in all the forms they take in the natural world will demonstrate the nature of gunpowder. New potentialities have come into being in the resulting compound that were not present in its elements, and its mode of behaviour is indefinitely changed from that of any of its elements in other combinations.

Cultures, likewise, are more than the sum of their traits. We may know all about the distribution of a tribe's form of marriage, ritual dances, and puberty initiations, and yet understand nothing of the culture as a whole which has used these elements to its own purpose. This purpose selects from among the possible traits in the surrounding regions those which it can use, and discards those which it cannot. Other traits it recasts into conformity with its demands. The process of course need never be conscious during its whole course, but to overlook it in the study of the patternings of human behaviour is to renounce the possibility of intelligent interpretation.

This integration of cultures is not in the least mystical. It is the same process by which a style in art comes into being and persists. Gothic architecture, beginning in what was hardly more than a preference for altitude and light, became, by the operation of some canon of taste that developed within its technique, the unique and homogeneous art of the thirteenth century. It discarded elements that were incongruous, modified others to its purposes, and invented others that accorded with its taste. When we describe the process historically, we inevitably use animistic forms of expression as if there were choice and purpose in the growth of this great art-form. But this is due to the difficulty in our language-forms. There was no conscious choice, and no purpose. What was at first no more than a slight bias in local forms and techniques expressed itself more and more forcibly, integrated itself in more and more definite standards, and eventuated in Gothic art.

What has happened in the great art-styles happens also in cultures as a whole. All the miscellaneous behaviour directed toward getting a living, mating, warring, and worshipping the gods, is made over into consistent patterns in accordance with unconscious canons of choice that develop within the culture. Some cultures, like some periods of art, fail of such integration, and about many others we know too little to understand the motives that actuate them. But cultures at every level of complexity, even the simplest, have achieved it. Such cultures are more or less successful attainments of integrated behaviour, and the marvel is that there can be so many of these possible configurations.

Anthropological work has been overwhelmingly devoted to the analysis of culture traits, however, rather than to the study of cultures as articulated wholes. This has been due in great measure to the nature of earlier ethnological descriptions. The classical anthropologists did not write out of first-hand knowledge of primitive people. They were armchair students who had at their disposal the anecdotes of travellers and missionaries and the formal and schematic accounts of the early ethnologists. It was possible to trace from these details the distribution of the custom of knocking out teeth, or of divination by entrails, but it was not possible to see how these traits were embedded in different tribes in characteristic configurations that gave form and meaning to the procedures.

Studies of culture like *The Golden Bough* and the usual comparative ethnological volumes are analytical discussions of traits and ignore all the aspects of cultural integration. Mating or death practices are illustrated by bits of behaviour selected indiscriminately from the most different cultures, and the discussion builds up a kind of mechanical Frankenstein's monster with a right eye from Fiji, a left from Europe, one leg from Tierra del Fuego, and one from Tahiti, and all the fingers and toes from still different regions. Such a figure corresponds to no reality in the past or present, and the fundamental difficulty is the same as if, let us say, psychiatry ended with a catalogue of the symbols of which psychopathic individuals make use, and ignored the study of patterns of symptomatic behaviour—schizophrenia, hysteria, and manic-depressive disorders—into which they are built. The rôle of the trait in the behaviour of the psychotic, the degree to which it is dynamic in the total personality, and its relation to all other items of experience, differ completely. If we are interested in mental processes, we can satisfy ourselves only by relating the particular symbol to the total configuration of the individual.

There is as great an unreality in similar studies of culture. If we are interested in cultural processes, the only way in which we can know the significance of the selected detail of behaviour is against the background of the motives and emotions and values that are institutionalized in that culture. The first essential, so it seems today, is to study the living culture, to know its habits of thought and the functions of its institutions, and such knowledge cannot come out of post-mortem dissections and reconstructions. * * *

It is one of the philosophical justifications for the study of primitive peoples that the facts of simpler cultures may make clear social facts that are otherwise baffling and not open to demonstration. This is nowhere more true than in the matter of the fundamental and distinctive cultural configurations that pattern existence and condition the thoughts and emotions of the individuals who participate in those cultures. The whole problem of the formation of the individual's habit-patterns under the influence of traditional custom can best be understood at the present time through the study of simpler peoples. This does not mean that the facts and processes we can discover in this way are limited in their application to primitive civilizations. Cultural configurations are as compelling and as significant in the highest and most complex societies of which we have knowledge. But the material is too intricate and too close to our eyes for us to cope with it successfully.

The understanding we need of our own cultural processes can most economically be arrived at by a détour. When the historical relations of human beings and their immediate forbears in the animal kingdom were too involved to use in establishing the fact of biological evolution, Darwin made use instead of the structure of beetles, and the process, which in the complex physical organization of the human is confused, in the simpler material was transparent in its cogency. It is the same in the study of cultural mechanisms. We need all the enlightenment we can obtain from the study of thought and behaviour as it is organized in the less complicated groups.

STUDY QUESTIONS

1. What evidence does Benedict provide to support the claim that moral standards can differ from culture to culture?
2. How can such evidence be used in an argument for cultural relativism?
3. What does Benedict think can be gained through the study of relatively less developed societies?

MARY MIDGLEY
Trying Out One's New Sword

Mary Midgley (b. 1919) is an influential English moral philosopher who has written more than 15 books, the first of which was published when she had reached the age of 59.

All of us are, more or less, in trouble today about trying to understand cultures strange to us. We hear constantly of alien customs. We see changes in our lifetime which would have astonished our parents. I want to discuss here one very short way of dealing with this difficulty, a drastic way which many people now theoretically favour. It consists in simply denying that we can ever understand any culture except our own well enough to make judgements about it. Those who recommend this hold that the world is sharply divided into separate societies, sealed units, each with its own system of thought. They feel that the respect and tolerance due from one system to another forbids us ever to take up a critical position to any other culture. Moral judgement, they suggest, is a kind of coinage valid only in its country of origin.

I shall call this position "moral isolationism." I shall suggest that it is certainly not forced upon us, and indeed that it makes no sense at all.

People usually take it up because they think it is a respectful attitude to other cultures. In fact, however, it is not respectful. Nobody can respect what is entirely unintelligible to them. To respect someone, we have to know enough about him to make a *favourable* judgement, however general and tentative. And we do understand people in other cultures to this extent. Otherwise a great mass of our most valuable thinking would be paralysed.

To show this, I shall take a remote example, because we shall probably find it easier to think calmly about it than we should with a contemporary one, such as female circumcision in Africa or the Chinese Cultural Revolution. The principles involved will still be the same. My example is this. There is, it seems, a verb in classical Japanese which means "to try out one's new sword on a chance wayfarer." (The word is *tsujigiri*, literally "crossroads-cut.") A Samurai sword had to be tried out because, if it was to work properly, it had to slice through someone at a single blow, from the shoulder to the opposite flank. Otherwise, the warrior bungled his stroke. This could injure his honour, offend his ancestors, and even let down his emperor. So tests were needed, and wayfarers had to be expended. Any wayfarer would do provided, of course, that he was not another Samurai. Scientists will recognize a familiar problem about the rights of experimental subjects.

Now when we hear of a custom like this, we may well reflect that we simply do not understand it; and therefore are not qualified to criticize it at all, because we are not members of that culture. But we are not members of any other culture either, except our own. So we extend the principle to cover all extraneous cultures, and we seem therefore to be moral isolationists. But this is, as we shall see, an impossible position. Let us ask what it would involve.

We must ask first: Does the isolating barrier work both ways? Are people in other cultures equally unable to criticize us? This question struck me sharply when I read a remark in *The Guardian* by an anthropologist about a South American Indian who had been taken into a Brazilian town for an operation, which saved his life. When he came back to his village, he made several highly critical remarks about the white Brazilians' way of life. They may very well have been justified. But the interesting point was that the anthropologist called these remarks "a damning indictment of Western civilization." Now the Indian had been in that town about two weeks. Was he in a position to deliver a damning indictment? Would we ourselves be qualified to deliver such an indictment on the Samurai, provided we could spend two weeks in ancient Japan? What do we really think about this?

My own impression is that we believe that outsiders can, in principle, deliver perfectly good indictments—only, it usually takes more than two weeks to make them damning. Understanding has degrees. It is not a slapdash yes-or-no matter. Intelligent outsiders can progress in it, and in some ways will be at an advantage over the locals. But if this is so, it must clearly apply to ourselves as much as anybody else.

Our next question is this: Does the isolating barrier between cultures block praise as well as blame? If I want to say that the Samurai culture has many virtues, or to praise the South American Indians, am I prevented from doing *that* by my outside status? Now, we certainly do need to praise other societies in this way. But it is hardly possible that we could praise them effectively if we could not, in principle, criticize them. Our praise would be worthless if it rested on no definite grounds, if it did not flow from some understanding. Certainly we may need to praise things which we do not *fully* understand. We say "there's something very good here, but I can't quite make out what it is yet." This happens when we want to learn from strangers. And we can learn from strangers. But to do this we have to distinguish between those strangers who are worth learning from and those who are not. Can we then judge which is which?

This brings us to our third question: What is involved in judging? Now plainly there is no question here of sitting on a bench in a red robe and sentencing people. Judging simply means forming an opinion, and expressing it if it is called for. Is there anything wrong about this? Naturally, we ought to avoid forming—and expressing—*crude* opinions, like that of a simple-minded missionary, who might dismiss the whole Samurai culture as entirely bad, because non-Christian. But this is a different objection. The trouble with crude opinions is that they are crude, whoever forms them, not that they are formed by the wrong people.

Anthropologists, after all, are outsiders quite as much as missionaries. Moral isolationism forbids us to form *any* opinions on these matters. Its ground for doing so is that we don't understand them. But there is much that we don't understand in our own culture too. This brings us to our last question: If we can't judge other cultures, can we really judge our own? Our efforts to do so will be much damaged if we are really deprived of our opinions about other societies, because these provide the range of comparison, the spectrum of alternatives against which we set what we want to understand. We would have to stop using the mirror which anthropology so helpfully holds up to us.

In short, moral isolationism would lay down a general ban on moral reasoning. Essentially, this is the programme of immoralism, and it carries a distressing logical difficulty. Immoralists like Nietzsche are actually just a rather specialized sect of moralists. They can no more afford to put moralizing out of business than smugglers can afford to abolish customs regulations. The power of moral judgement is, in fact, not a luxury, not a perverse indulgence of the self-righteous. It is a necessity. When we judge something to be bad or good, better or worse than something else, we are taking it as an example to aim at or avoid. Without opinions of this sort, we would have no framework of comparison for our own policy, no chance of profiting by other people's insights or mistakes. In this vacuum, we could form no judgements on our own actions.

Now it would be odd if *Homo sapiens* had really got himself into a position as bad as this—a position where his main evolutionary asset, his brain, was so little use to him. None of us is going to accept this sceptical diagnosis. We cannot do so, because our involvement in moral isolationism does not flow from apathy, but from a rather acute concern about human hypocrisy and other forms of wickedness. But we polarize that concern around a few selected moral truths. We are rightly angry with those who despise, oppress or steamroll other cultures. We think that doing these things is actually *wrong*. But this is itself a moral judgement. We could not condemn oppression and insolence if we thought that all our condemnations were just a trivial local quirk of our own culture. We could still less do it if we tried to stop judging altogether.

Real moral scepticism, in fact, could lead only to inaction, to our losing all interest in moral questions, most of all in those which concern other societies. When we discuss these things, it becomes instantly clear how far we are from doing this.

Suppose, for instance, that I criticize the bisecting Samurai, that I say his behaviour is brutal. What will usually happen next is that someone will protest, will say that I have no right to make criticisms like that of another culture. But it is most unlikely that he will use this move to end the discussion of the subject. Instead, he will justify the Samurai. He will try to fill in the background, to make me understand the custom, by explaining the exalted ideals of discipline and devotion which produced it. He will probably talk of the lower value which the ancient Japanese placed on individual life generally. He may well suggest that this is a healthier attitude than our own obsession with security. He may add, too, that the wayfarers did not seriously mind being bisected, that in principle they accepted the whole arrangement.

Now an objector who talks like this is implying that it is possible to understand alien customs. That is just what he is trying to make me do. And he implies, too, that if I do succeed in understanding them, I shall do something better than giving up judging them. He expects me to change my present judgement to a truer one—namely, one that is favourable. And the standards I must use to do this cannot just be Samurai standards. They have to be ones current in my own culture. Ideals like discipline and devotion will not move anybody unless he himself accepts them. As it happens, neither discipline nor devotion is very popular in the West at present. Anyone who appeals to them may well have to do some more arguing to make *them* acceptable, before he can use them to explain the Samurai. But if he does succeed here, he will have persuaded us, not just that there was something to be said for them in ancient Japan, but that there would be here as well.

Isolating barriers simply cannot arise here. If we accept something as a serious moral truth about one culture, we can't refuse to apply it—in however different an outward form—to other cultures as well, wherever circumstance admit it. If we refuse to do this, we just are not taking the other culture seriously.

This becomes clear if we look at the last argument used by my objector— that of justification by consent of the victim. It is suggested that sudden bisection is quite in order, *provided* that it takes place between consenting adults. I cannot now discuss how conclusive this justification is. What I am pointing out is simply that it can only work if we believe that *consent* can make such a transaction respectable—and this is a thoroughly modern and Western idea. It would probably never occur to a Samurai: if it did, it would surprise him very much. It is *our* standard.

In applying it, too, we are likely to make another typically Western demand. We shall ask for good factual evidence that the wayfarers actually do have this rather surprising taste—that they are really willing to be bisected. In applying Western standards in this way, we are not being confused or irrelevant. We are asking the questions which arise *from where we stand*, questions which we can see the sense of. We do this because asking questions which you can't see the sense of is humbug. Certainly we can extend our questioning by imaginative effort. We can come to understand other societies better. By doing so, we may make their questions our own, or we may see that they are really forms of the questions which we are asking already. This is not impossible. It is just very hard work. The obstacles which often prevent it are simply those of ordinary ignorance, laziness and prejudice.

If there were really an isolating barrier, of course, our own culture could never have been formed. It is no sealed box, but a fertile jungle of different influences—Greek, Jewish, Roman, Norse, Celtic and so forth, into which further influences are still pouring—American, Indian, Japanese, Jamaican, you name it. The moral isolationist's picture of separate, unmixable cultures is quite unreal. People who talk about British history usually stress the value of this fertilizing mix, no doubt rightly. But this is not just an odd fact about Britain. Except for the very smallest and most remote, all cultures are formed out of many streams. All have the problem of digesting and assimilating things which, at the start, they do not understand. All have the choice of learning something from this challenge, or, alternatively, of refusing to learn, and fighting it mindlessly instead.

This universal predicament has been obscured by the fact that anthropologists used to concentrate largely on very small and remote cultures, which did not seem to have this problem. These tiny societies, which had often forgotten their own history, made neat, self-contained subjects for study.

No doubt it was valuable to emphasize their remoteness, their extreme strangeness, their independence of our cultural tradition. This emphasis was, I think, the root of moral isolationism. But, as the tribal studies themselves showed, even there the anthropologists were able to interpret what they saw and make judgements—often favourable—about the tribesmen. And the tribesmen, too, were quite equal to making judgements about the anthropologists—and about the tourists and Coca-Cola salesmen who followed them. Both sets of judgements, no doubt, were somewhat hasty, both have been refined in the light of further experience. A similar transaction between us and the Samurai might take even longer. But that is no reason at all for deeming it impossible. Morally as well as physically, there is only one world, and we all have to live in it.

STUDY QUESTIONS

1. What does Midgley mean by "moral isolationism"?
2. Why does Midgley suggest that moral isolationism leaves us in difficulty in forming judgments on our own culture?
3. What is Midgley's example of "trying out one's new sword" intended to show?

FRIEDRICH NIETZSCHE
Beyond Good and Evil

Friedrich Nietzsche (1844–1900) was a German philosopher who produced a number of brilliant and revolutionary works, though he suffered a breakdown and severe mental illness for the last decade of his life.

201

As long as the utility reigning in moral value judgments is solely the utility of the herd, as long as one considers only the preservation of the community, and immorality is sought exactly and exclusively in what seems dangerous to the survival of the community—there can be no morality of "neighbor love." Supposing that even then there was a constant little exercise of consideration, pity, fairness, mildness, reciprocity of assistance; supposing that even in that state of society all those drives are active that later receive the honorary designation of "virtues" and eventually almost coincide with the concept of "morality"—in that period they do not yet at all belong in the realm of moral valuations; they are still *extra-moral*. An act of pity, for example, was not considered either good or bad, moral or immoral, in the best period of the Romans; and even when it was praised, such praise was perfectly compatible with a kind of disgruntled disdain as soon as it was juxtaposed with an action that served the welfare of the whole, of the *res publica*.

In the last analysis, "love of the neighbor" is always something secondary, partly conventional and arbitrary-illusory in relation to *fear of the neighbor*. After the structure of society is fixed on the whole and seems secure against external dangers, it is this fear of the neighbor that again creates new perspectives of moral valuation. Certain strong and dangerous drives, like an enterprising spirit, foolhardiness, vengefulness, craftiness, rapacity, and the lust to rule, which had so far not merely been honored insofar as they were socially useful—under different names, to be sure, from those chosen here—but had to be trained and cultivated to make them great (because one constantly needed them in view of the dangers to the whole community, against the enemies of the community), are now experienced as doubly dangerous, since the channels to divert them are lacking, and, step upon step, they are branded as immoral and abandoned to slander.

Now the opposite drives and inclinations receive moral honors; step upon step, the herd instinct draws its conclusions. How much or how little is dangerous to the community, dangerous to equality, in an opinion, in a state or affect, in a will, in a talent—that now constitutes the moral perspective: here, too, fear is again the mother of morals.

The highest and strongest drives, when they break out passionately and drive the individual far above the average and the flats of the herd conscience, wreck the self-confidence of the community, its faith in itself, and it is as if its spine snapped. Hence just these drives are branded and slandered most. High and independent spirituality, the will to stand alone, even a powerful reason are experienced as dangers; everything that elevates an individual above the herd and intimidates the neighbor is henceforth called *evil;* and the fair, modest, submissive, conforming mentality, the *mediocrity* of desires attains moral designations and honors. Eventually, under very peaceful conditions, the opportunity and necessity for educating one's feelings to severity and hardness is lacking more and more; and every severity, even in justice, begins to disturb the conscience; any high and hard nobility and self-reliance is almost felt to be an insult and arouses mistrust; the "lamb," even more the "sheep," gains in respect.

There is a point in the history of society when it becomes so pathologically soft and tender that among other things it sides even with those who harm it, criminals, and does this quite seriously and honestly. Punishing somehow seems unfair to it, and it is certain that imagining "punishment" and "being supposed to punish" hurts it, arouses fear in it. "Is it not enough to render him *undangerous?* Why still punish? Punishing itself is terrible." With this question, herd morality, the morality of timidity, draws its ultimate consequence. Supposing that one could altogether abolish danger, the reason for fear, this morality would be abolished, too, *eo ipso:* it would no longer be needed, it would no longer *consider itself* necessary.

Whoever examines the conscience of the European today will have to pull the same imperative out of a thousand moral folds and hideouts—the imperative of herd timidity: "we want that some day there should be *nothing any more to be afraid of!*" Some day—throughout Europe, the will and way to this day is now called "progress." * * *

257

Every enhancement of the type "man" has so far been the work of an aristocratic society—and it will be so again and again—a society that believes in the long ladder of an order of rank and differences in value between man and man, and that needs slavery in some sense or other. Without that *pathos of distance* which grows out of the ingrained difference between strata—when the ruling caste constantly looks afar and looks down upon subjects and instruments and just as constantly practices obedience and command, keeping down and keeping at a distance—that other, more mysterious pathos could not have grown up either—the craving for an ever new widening of distances within the soul itself, the development of ever higher, rarer, more remote, further-stretching, more comprehensive states—in brief, simply the enhancement of the type "man," the continual "self-overcoming of man," to use a moral formula in a supra-moral sense.

To be sure, one should not yield to humanitarian illusions about the origins of an aristocratic society (and thus of the presupposition of this enhancement of the type "man"): truth is hard. Let us admit to ourselves, without trying to be considerate, how every higher culture on earth so far has *begun*. Human beings whose nature was still natural, barbarians in every terrible sense of the word, men of prey who were still in possession of unbroken strength of will and lust for power, hurled themselves upon weaker, more civilized, more peaceful races, perhaps traders or cattle raisers, or upon mellow old cultures whose last vitality was even then flaring up in splendid fireworks of spirit and corruption. In the beginning, the noble caste was always the barbarian caste: their predominance did not lie mainly in physical strength but in strength of the soul—they were more *whole* human beings (which also means, at every level, "more whole beasts").

258

Corruption as the expression of a threatening anarchy among the instincts and of the fact that the foundation of the affects, which is called "life," has been shaken: corruption is something totally different depending on the organism in which it appears. When, for example, an aristocracy, like that of France at the beginning of the Revolution, throws away its privileges with a sublime disgust and sacrifices itself to an extravagance of its own moral feelings, that is corruption; it was really only the last act of that centuries-old corruption which had led them to surrender, step by step, their governmental prerogatives, demoting themselves to a mere *function* of the monarchy (finally even to a mere ornament and showpiece). The essential characteristic of a good and healthy aristocracy, however, is that it experiences itself *not* as a function (whether of the monarchy or the commonwealth) but as their *meaning* and highest justification—that it therefore accepts with a good conscience the sacrifice of untold human beings who, *for its sake*, must be reduced and lowered to incomplete human beings, to slaves, to instruments. Their fundamental faith simply has to be that society must *not* exist for society's sake but only as the foundation and scaffolding on which a choice type of being is able to raise itself to its higher task and to a higher state of *being*—comparable to those sun-seeking vines of Java—they are called *Sipo Matador*—that so long and so often enclasp an oak tree with their tendrils until eventually, high above it but supported by it, they can unfold their crowns in the open light and display their happiness.

259

Refraining mutually from injury, violence, and exploitation and placing one's will on a par with that of someone else—this may become, in a certain rough sense, good manners among individuals if the appropriate conditions are present (namely, if these men are actually similar in strength and value standards and belong together in *one* body). But as soon as this principle is extended, and possibly even accepted as the *fundamental principle of society*, it immediately proves to be what it really is—a will to the *denial* of life, a principle of disintegration and decay.

Here we must beware of superficiality and get to the bottom of the matter, resisting all sentimental weakness: life itself is *essentially* appropriation, injury, overpowering of what is alien and weaker; suppression, hardness, imposition of one's own forms, incorporation and at least, at its mildest, exploitation—but why should one always use those words in which a slanderous intent has been imprinted for ages?

Even the body within which individuals treat each other as equals, as suggested before—and this happens in every healthy aristocracy—if it is a living and not a dying body, has to do to other bodies what the individuals within it refrain from doing to each other: it will have to be an incarnate will to power, it will strive to grow, spread, seize, become predominant—not from any morality or immorality but because it is *living* and because life simply *is* will to power. But there is no point on which the ordinary consciousness of Europeans resists instruction as on this: everywhere people are now raving, even under scientific disguises, about coming conditions of society in which "the exploitative aspect" will be removed—which sounds to me as if they promised to invent a way of life that would dispense with all organic functions. "Exploitation" does not belong to a corrupt or imperfect and primitive society: it belongs to the *essence* of what lives, as a basic organic function; it is a consequence of the will to power, which is after all the will of life.

If this should be an innovation as a theory—as a reality it is the *primordial fact* of all history: people ought to be honest with themselves at least that far.

260

Wandering through the many subtler and coarser moralities which have so far been prevalent on earth, or still are prevalent, I found that certain features recurred regularly together and were closely associated—until I finally discovered two basic types and one basic difference.

There are *master morality* and *slave morality*—I add immediately that in all the higher and more mixed cultures there also appear attempts at mediation between these two moralities, and yet more often the interpenetration and mutual misunderstanding of both, and at times they occur directly alongside each other—even in the same human being, within a *single* soul. The moral discrimination of values has originated either among a ruling group whose consciousness of its difference from the ruled group was accompanied by delight—or among the ruled, the slaves and dependents of every degree.

In the first case, when the ruling group determines what is "good," the exalted, proud states of the soul are experienced as conferring distinction and determining the order of rank. The noble human being separates from himself those in whom the opposite of such exalted, proud states finds expression: he despises them. It should be noted immediately that in this first type of morality the opposition of "good" and *"bad"* means approximately the same as "noble" and "contemptible." (The opposition of "good" and *"evil"* has a different origin.) One feels contempt for the cowardly, the anxious, the petty, those intent on narrow utility; also for the suspicious with their unfree glances, those who humble themselves, the doglike people who allow themselves to be maltreated, the begging flatterers, above all the liars: it is part of the fundamental faith of all aristocrats that the common people lie. "We truthful ones"—thus the nobility of ancient Greece referred to itself.

It is obvious that moral designations were everywhere first applied to *human beings* and only later, derivatively, to actions. Therefore it is a gross mistake when historians of morality start from such questions as: why was the compassionate act praised? The noble type of man experiences *itself* as determining values; it does not need approval; it judges, "what is harmful to me is harmful in itself"; it knows itself to be that which first accords honor to things; it is *value-creating*. Everything it knows as part of itself it honors: such a morality is self-glorification. In the foreground there is the feeling of fullness, of power that seeks to overflow, the happiness of high tension, the consciousness of wealth that would give and bestow: the noble human being, too, helps the unfortunate, but not, or almost not, from pity, but prompted more by an urge begotten by excess of power. The noble human being honors himself as one who is powerful, also as one who has power over himself, who knows how to speak and be silent, who delights in being severe and hard with himself and respects all severity and hardness. "A hard heart Wotan put into my breast," says an old Scandinavian saga: a fitting poetic expression, seeing that it comes from the soul of a proud Viking. Such a type of man is actually proud of the fact that he is *not* made for pity, and the hero of the saga therefore adds as a warning: "If the heart is not hard in youth it will never harden." Noble and courageous human beings who think that way are furthest removed from that morality which finds the distinction of morality precisely in pity, or in acting for others, or in *désintéressement;* faith in oneself, pride in oneself, a fundamental hostility and irony against "selflessness" belong just as definitely to noble morality as does a slight disdain and caution regarding compassionate feelings and a "warm heart."

It is the powerful who *understand* how to honor; this is their art, their realm of invention. The profound reverence for age and tradition—all law rests on this double reverence—the faith and prejudice in favor of ancestors and disfavor of those yet to come are typical of the morality of the powerful; and when the men of "modern ideas," conversely, believe almost instinctively in "progress" and "the future" and more and more lack respect for age, this in itself would sufficiently betray the ignoble origin of these "ideas."

A morality of the ruling group, however, is most alien and embarrassing to the present taste in the severity of its principle that one has duties only to one's peers; that against beings of a lower rank, against everything alien, one may behave as one pleases or "as the heart desires," and in any case "beyond good and evil"—here pity and like feelings may find their place. The capacity for, and the duty of, long gratitude and long revenge—both only among one's peers—refinement in repaying, the sophisticated concept of friendship, a certain necessity for having enemies (as it were, as drainage ditches for the affects of envy, quarrelsomeness, exuberance—at bottom, in order to be capable of being good *friends*): all these are typical characteristics of noble morality which, as suggested, is not the morality of "modern ideas" and therefore is hard to empathize with today, also hard to dig up and uncover.

It is different with the second type of morality, *slave morality.* Suppose the violated, oppressed, suffering, unfree, who are uncertain of themselves and weary, moralize: what will their moral valuations have in common? Probably, a pessimistic suspicion about the whole condition of man will find expression, perhaps a condemnation of man along with his condition. The slave's eye is not favorable to the virtues of the powerful: he is skeptical and suspicious, *subtly* suspicious, of all the "good" that is honored there—he would like to persuade himself that even their happiness is not genuine. Conversely, those qualities are brought out and flooded with light which serve to ease existence for those who suffer: here pity, the complaisant and obliging hand, the warm heart, patience, industry, humility, and friendliness are honored—for here these are the most useful qualities and almost the only means for enduring the pressure of existence. Slave morality is essentially a morality of utility.

Here is the place for the origin of that famous opposition of "good" and "evil": into evil one's feelings project power and dangerousness, a certain terribleness, subtlety, and strength that does not permit contempt to develop. According to slave morality, those who are "evil" thus inspire fear; according to master morality it is precisely those who are "good" that inspire, and wish to inspire, fear, while the "bad" are felt to be contemptible.

The opposition reaches its climax when, as a logical consequence of slave morality, a touch of disdain is associated also with the "good" of this morality—this may be slight and benevolent—because the good human being has to be *undangerous* in the slaves' way of thinking: he is good-natured, easy to deceive, a little stupid perhaps, *un bonhomme.* Wherever slave morality becomes preponderant, language tends to bring the words "good" and "stupid" closer together.

One last fundamental difference: the longing for *freedom,* the instinct for happiness and the subtleties of the feeling of freedom belong just as necessarily to slave morality and morals as artful and enthusiastic reverence and devotion are the regular symptom of an aristocratic way of thinking and evaluating.

This makes plain why love *as passion*—which is our European specialty—simply must be of noble origin: as is well known, its invention must be credited to the Provençal knight-poets, those magnificent and inventive human beings of the *"gai saber"*[1] to whom Europe owes so many things and almost owes itself.

---

1 "Gay science": in the early fourteenth century the term was used to designate the art of the troubadours.

STUDY QUESTIONS

1. What does Nietzsche mean by "will to power"?
2. What is the distinction between master morality and slave morality?
3. What are Nietzsche's objections to slave morality?

A. J. AYER
A Critique of Ethics

A. J. Ayer (1910–1989) was an English philosopher who was especially known as one of the first defenders of logical positivism writing in the English language. His writings on ethics concern the implications of logical positivism for ethical thought.

The criterion which we use to test the genuineness of apparent statements of fact is the criterion of verifiability. We say that a sentence is factually significant to any given person, if, and only if, he knows how to verify the proposition which it purports to express—that is, if he knows what observations would lead him, under certain conditions, to accept the proposition as being true, or reject it as being false. If, on the other hand, the putative proposition is of such a character that the assumption of its truth, or falsehood, is consistent with any assumption whatsoever concerning the nature of his future experience, then, as far as he is concerned, it is, if not a tautology, a mere pseudo-proposition. The sentence expressing it may be emotionally significant to him; but it is not literally significant. And with regard to questions the procedure is the same. We enquire in every case what observations would lead us to answer the question, one way or the other; and, if none can be discovered, we must conclude that the sentence under consideration does not, as far as we are concerned, express a genuine question, however strongly its grammatical appearance may suggest that it does. ∗ ∗ ∗

∗ ∗ ∗ It is our business to give an account of "judgements of value" which is both satisfactory in itself and consistent with our general empiricist principles. We shall set ourselves to show that in so far as statements of value are significant, they are ordinary "scientific" statements; and that in so far as they are not scientific, they are not in the literal sense significant, but are simply expressions of emotion which can be neither true nor false. ∗ ∗ ∗

The ordinary system of ethics, as elaborated in the works of ethical philosophers, is very far from being a homogeneous whole. Not only is it apt to contain pieces of metaphysics, and analyses of non-ethical concepts: its actual ethical contents are themselves of very different kinds. We may divide them, indeed, into four main classes. There are, first of all, propositions which express definitions of ethical terms, or judgements about the legitimacy or possibility of certain definitions. Secondly, there are propositions describing the phenomena of moral experience, and their causes. Thirdly, there are exhortations to moral virtue. And, lastly, there are actual ethical judgements. It is unfortunately the case that the distinction between these four classes, plain as it is, is commonly ignored by ethical philosophers; with the result that it is often very difficult to tell from their works what it is that they are seeking to discover or prove.

In fact, it is easy to see that only the first of our four classes, namely that which comprises the propositions relating to the definitions of ethical terms, can be said to constitute ethical philosophy. The propositions which describe the phenomena of moral experience, and their causes, must be assigned to the science of psychology, or sociology. The exhortations to moral virtue are not propositions at all, but ejaculations or commands which are designed to provoke the reader to action of a certain sort. Accordingly, they do not belong to any branch of philosophy or science. As for the expressions of ethical judgements, we have not yet determined how they should be classified. But inasmuch as they are certainly neither definitions nor comments upon definitions, nor quotations, we may say decisively that they do not belong to ethical philosophy. A strictly philosophical treatise on ethics should therefore make no ethical pronouncements. But it should, by giving an analysis of ethical terms, show what is the category to which all such pronouncements belong. And this is what we are now about to do. ＊ ＊ ＊

What we are interested in is the possibility of reducing the whole sphere of ethical terms to non-ethical terms. We are enquiring whether statements of ethical value can be translated into statements of empirical fact.

That they can be so translated is the contention of those ethical philosophers who are commonly called subjectivists, and of those who are known as utilitarians. For the utilitarian defines the rightness of actions, and the goodness of ends, in terms of the pleasure, or happiness, or satisfaction, to which they give rise; the subjectivist, in terms of the feelings of approval which a certain person, or group of people, has towards them. Each of these types of definition makes moral judgements into a sub-class of psychological or sociological judgements; and for this reason they are very attractive to us. For, if either was correct, it would follow that ethical assertions were not generically different from the factual assertions which are ordinarily contrasted with them; and the account which we have already given of empirical hypotheses would apply to them also.

Nevertheless we shall not adopt either a subjectivist or a utilitarian analysis of ethical terms. We reject the subjectivist view that to call an action right, or a thing good, is to say that it is generally approved of, because it is not self-contradictory to assert that some actions which are generally approved of are not right, or that some things which are generally approved of are not good. And we reject the alternative subjectivist view that a man who asserts that a certain action is right, or that a certain thing is good, is saying that he himself approves of it, on the ground that a man who confessed that he sometimes approved of what was bad or wrong would not be contradicting himself. And a similar argument is fatal to utilitarianism. We cannot agree that to call an action right is to say that of all the actions possible in the circumstances it would cause, or be likely to cause, the greatest happiness, or the greatest balance of pleasure over pain, or the greatest balance of satisfied over unsatisfied desire, because we find that it is not self-contradictory to say that it is sometimes wrong to perform the action which would actually or probably cause the greatest happiness, or the greatest balance of pleasure over pain, or of satisfied over unsatisfied desire. And since it is not self-contradictory to say that some pleasant things are not good, or that some bad things are desired, it cannot be the case that the sentence "x is good" is equivalent to "x is pleasant," or to "x is desired." And to every other variant of utilitarianism with which I am acquainted the same objection can be made And therefore we should, I think, conclude that the validity of ethical judgements is not determined by the felicific tendencies of actions, any more than by the nature of people's feelings; but that it must be regarded as "absolute" or "intrinsic," and not empirically calculable. ＊＊＊

In admitting that normative ethical concepts are irreducible to empirical concepts, we seem to be leaving the way clear for the "absolutist" view of ethics—that is, the view that statements of value are not controlled by observation, as ordinary empirical propositions are, but only by a mysterious "intellectual intuition." A feature of this theory, which is seldom recognized by its advocates, is that it makes statements of value unverifiable. For it is notorious that what seems intuitively certain to one person may seem doubtful, or even false, to another. So that unless it is possible to provide some criterion by which one may decide between conflicting intuitions, a mere appeal to intuition is worthless as a test of a proposition's validity. But in the case of moral judgements, no such criterion can be given. Some moralists claim to settle the matter by saying that they "know" that their own moral judgements are correct. But such an assertion is of purely psychological interest, and has not the slightest tendency to prove the validity of any moral judgement. For dissentient moralists may equally well "know" that their ethical views are correct. And, as far as subjective certainty goes, there will be nothing to choose between them. When such differences of opinion arise in connection with an ordinary empirical proposition, one may attempt to resolve them by referring to, or actually carrying out, some relevant empirical test. But with regard to ethical statements, there is, on the "absolutist" or "intuitionist" theory, no relevant empirical test. We are therefore justified in saying that on this theory ethical statements are held to be unverifiable. They are, of course, also held to be genuine synthetic propositions. ✳ ✳ ✳

We begin [our radical empiricist theory] by admitting that the fundamental ethical concepts are unanalysable, inasmuch as there is no criterion by which one can test the validity of the judgements in which they occur. So far we are in agreement with the absolutists. But, unlike the absolutists, we are able to give an explanation of this fact about ethical concepts. We say that the reason why they are unanalysable is that they are mere pseudo-concepts. The presence of an ethical symbol in a proposition adds nothing to its factual content. Thus if I say to someone, "You acted wrongly in stealing that money," I am not stating anything more than if I had simply said, "You stole that money." In adding that this action is wrong I am not making any further statement about it. I am simply evincing my moral disapproval of it. It is as if I had said, "You stole that money," in a peculiar tone of horror, or written it with the addition of some special exclamation marks. The tone, or the exclamation marks, adds nothing to the literal meaning of the sentence. It merely serves to show that the expression of it is attended by certain feelings in the speaker.

If now I generalise my previous statement and say, "Stealing money is wrong," I produce a sentence which has no factual meaning—that is, expresses no proposition which can be either true or false. It is as if I had written "Stealing money!!"—where the shape and thickness of the exclamation marks show, by a suitable convention, that a special sort of moral disapproval is the feeling which is being expressed. It is clear that there is nothing said here which can be true or false. Another man may disagree with me about the wrongness of stealing, in the sense that he may not have the same feelings about stealing as I have, and he may quarrel with me on account of my moral sentiments. But he cannot, strictly speaking, contradict me. For in saying that a certain type of action is right or wrong, I am not making any factual statement, not even a statement about my own state of mind. I am merely expressing certain moral sentiments. And the man who is ostensibly contradicting me is merely expressing his moral sentiments. So that there is plainly no sense in asking which of us is in the right. For neither of us is asserting a genuine proposition.

What we have just been saying about the symbol "wrong" applies to all normative ethical symbols. Sometimes they occur in sentences which record ordinary empirical facts besides expressing ethical feeling about those facts: sometimes they occur in sentences which simply express ethical feeling about a certain type of action, or situation, without making any statement of fact. But in every case in which one would commonly be said to be making an ethical judgement, the function of the relevant ethical word is purely "emotive." It is used to express feeling about certain objects, but not to make any assertion about them.

It is worth mentioning that ethical terms do not serve only to express feeling. They are calculated also to arouse feeling, and so to stimulate action. Indeed some of them are used in such a way as to give the sentences in which they occur the effect of commands. Thus the sentence "It is your duty to tell the truth" may be regarded both as the expression of a certain sort of ethical feeling about truthfulness and as the expression of the command "Tell the truth." The sentence "You ought to tell the truth" also involves the command "Tell the truth," but here the tone of the command is less emphatic. In the sentence "It is good to tell the truth" the command has become little more than a suggestion. And thus the "meaning" of the word "good," in its ethical usage, is differentiated from that of the word "duty" or the word "ought." In fact we may define the meaning of the various ethical words in terms both of the different feelings they are ordinarily taken to express, and also the different responses which they are calculated to provoke.

We can now see why it is impossible to find a criterion for determining the validity of ethical judgements. It is not because they have an "absolute" validity which is mysteriously independent of ordinary sense-experience, but because they have no objective validity whatsoever. If a sentence makes no statement at all, there is obviously no sense in asking whether what it says is true or false. And we have seen that sentences which simply express moral judgements do not say anything. They are pure expressions of feeling and as such do not come under the category of truth and falsehood. They are unverifiable for the same reason as a cry of pain or a word of command is unverifiable—because they do not express genuine propositions.

Thus, although our theory of ethics might fairly be said to be radically subjectivist, it differs in a very important respect from the orthodox subjectivist theory. For the orthodox subjectivist does not deny, as we do, that the sentences of a moralizer express genuine propositions. All he denies is that they express propositions of a unique non-empirical character. His own view is that they express propositions about the speaker's feelings. If this were so, ethical judgements clearly would be capable of being true or false. They would be true if the speaker had the relevant feelings, and false if he had not. And this is a matter which is, in principle, empirically verifiable. Furthermore they could be significantly contradicted. For if I say, "Tolerance is a virtue," and someone answers, "You don't approve of it," he would, on the ordinary subjectivist theory, be contradicting me. On our theory, he would not be contradicting me, because, in saying that tolerance was a virtue, I should not be making any statement about my own feelings or about anything else. I should simply be evincing my feelings, which is not at all the same thing as saying that I have them.

The distinction between the expression of feeling and the assertion of feeling is complicated by the fact that the assertion that one has a certain feeling often accompanies the expression of that feeling, and is then, indeed, a factor in the expression of that feeling. Thus I may simultaneously express boredom and say that I am bored, and in that case my utterance of the words, "I am bored," is one of the circumstances which make it true to say that I am expressing or evincing boredom. But I can express boredom without actually saying that I am bored. I can express it by my tone and gestures, while making a statement about something wholly unconnected with it, or by an ejaculation, or without uttering any words at all. So that even if the assertion that one has a certain feeling always involves the expression of that feeling, the expression of a feeling assuredly does not always involve the assertion that one has it. And this is the important point to grasp in considering the distinction between our theory and the ordinary subjectivist theory. For whereas the subjectivist holds that ethical statements actually assert the existence of certain feelings, we hold that ethical statements are expressions and excitants of feeling which do not necessarily involve any assertions.

We have already remarked that the main objection to the ordinary subjectivist theory is that the validity of ethical judgements is not determined by the nature of their author's feelings. And this is an objection which our theory escapes. For it does not imply that the existence of any feelings is a necessary and sufficient condition of the validity of an ethical judgement. It implies, on the contrary, that ethical judgements have no validity.

There is, however, a celebrated argument against subjectivist theories which our theory does not escape. It has been pointed out by Moore that if ethical statements were simply statements about the speaker's feelings, it would be impossible to argue about questions of value.[1] To take a typical example: if a man said that thrift was a virtue, and another replied that it was a vice, they would not, on this theory, be disputing with one another. One would be saying that he approved of thrift, and the other that *he* didn't; and there is no reason why both these statements should not be true. Now Moore held it to be obvious that we do dispute about questions of value, and accordingly concluded that the particular form of subjectivism which he was discussing was false.

It is plain that the conclusion that it is impossible to dispute about questions of value follows from our theory also. For as we hold that such sentences as "Thrift is a virtue" and "Thrift is a vice" do not express propositions at all, we clearly cannot hold that they express incompatible propositions. We must therefore admit that if Moore's argument really refutes the ordinary subjectivist theory, it also refutes ours. But, in fact, we deny that it does refute even the ordinary subjectivist theory. For we hold that one really never does dispute about questions of value.

This may seem, at first sight, to be a very paradoxical assertion. For we certainly do engage in disputes which are ordinarily regarded as disputes about questions of value. But, in all such cases, we find, if we consider the matter closely, that the dispute is not really about a question of value, but about a question of fact. When someone disagrees with us about the moral value of a certain action or type of action, we do admittedly resort to argument in order to win him over to our way of thinking. But we do not attempt to show by our arguments that he has the "wrong" ethical feeling towards a situation whose nature he has correctly apprehended. What we attempt to

---

1 cf. G. E. Moore, *Philosophical Studies*, "The Nature of Moral Philosophy."

show is that he is mistaken about the facts of the case. We argue that he has misconceived the agent's motive: or that he has misjudged the effects of the action, or its probable effects in view of the agent's knowledge; or that he has failed to take into account the special circumstances in which the agent was placed. Or else we employ more general arguments about the effects which actions of a certain type tend to produce, or the qualities which are usually manifested in their performance. We do this in the hope that we have only to get our opponent to agree with us about the nature of the empirical facts for him to adopt the same moral attitude towards them as we do. And as the people with whom we argue have generally received the same moral education as ourselves, and live in the same social order, our expectation is usually justified. But if our opponent happens to have undergone a different process of moral "conditioning" from ourselves, so that, even when he acknowledges all the facts, he still disagrees with us about the moral value of the actions under discussion, then we abandon the attempt to convince him by argument. We say that it is impossible to argue with him because he has a distorted or undeveloped moral sense; which signifies merely that he employs a different set of values from our own. We feel that our own system of values is superior, and therefore speak in such derogatory terms of his. But we cannot bring forward any arguments to show that our system is superior. For our judgement that it is so is itself a judgement of value, and accordingly outside the scope of argument. It is because argument fails us when we come to deal with pure questions of value, as distinct from questions of fact, that we finally resort to mere abuse.

In short, we find that argument is possible on moral questions only if some system of values is presupposed. If our opponent concurs with us in expressing moral disapproval of all actions of a given type *t*, then we may get him to condemn a particular action A, by bringing forward arguments to show that A is of type *t*. For the question whether A does or does not belong to that type is a plain question of fact. Given that a man has certain moral principles, we argue that he must, in order to be consistent, react morally to certain things in a certain way. What we do not and cannot argue about is the validity of these moral principles. We merely praise or condemn them in the light of our own feelings. * * *

Having upheld our theory against the only criticism which appeared to threaten it, we may now use it to define the nature of all ethical enquiries. We find that ethical philosophy consists simply in saying that ethical concepts are pseudo-concepts and therefore unanalysable. The further task of describing the different feelings that the different ethical terms are used to express, and the different reactions that they customarily provoke, is a task for the psychologist. There cannot be such a thing as ethical science, if by ethical science one means the elaboration of a "true" system of morals. For we have seen that, as ethical judgements are mere expressions of feeling, there can be no way of determining the validity of any ethical system, and, indeed, no sense in asking whether any such system is true. All that one may legitimately enquire in this connection is, What are the moral habits of a given person or group of people, and what causes them to have precisely those habits and feelings? And this enquiry falls wholly within the scope of the existing social sciences.

It appears, then, that ethics, as a branch of knowledge, is nothing more than a department of psychology and sociology.

STUDY QUESTIONS

1. What is the "criterion of verifiability"? What is its significance for moral philosophy?
2. Explain Ayer's emotivist theory of ethics.
3. How is argument about moral questions possible in Ayer's view?

J. L. MACKIE
Inventing Right and Wrong

J. L. Mackie (1917–1981) was an Australian philosopher who spent his working life in New Zealand, Australia, and the United Kingdom. Noted especially for his moral philosophy, he wrote on a wide range of philosophical topics.

MORAL SCEPTICISM

There are no objective values. This is a bald statement of the thesis of this chapter, but before arguing for it I shall try to clarify and restrict it in ways that may meet some objections and prevent some misunderstanding.

The statement of this thesis is liable to provoke one of three very different reactions. Some will think it not merely false but pernicious; they will see it as a threat to morality and to everything else that is worthwhile, and they will find the presenting of such a thesis in what purports to be a book on ethics paradoxical or even outrageous. Others will regard it as a trivial truth, almost too obvious to be worth mentioning, and certainly too plain to be worth much argument. Others again will say that it is meaningless or empty, that no real issue is raised by the question whether values are or are not part of the fabric of the world. But, precisely because there can be these three different reactions, much more needs to be said.

The claim that values are not objective, are not part of the fabric of the world, is meant to include not only moral goodness, which might be most naturally equated with moral value, but also other things that could be more loosely called moral values or disvalues—rightness and wrongness, duty, obligation, an action's being rotten and contemptible, and so on. It also includes non-moral values, notably aesthetic ones, beauty and various kinds of artistic merit. * * *

Since it is with moral values that I am primarily concerned, the view I am adopting may be called moral scepticism. But this name is likely to be misunderstood: "moral scepticism" might also be used as a name for either of two first order views, or perhaps for an incoherent mixture of the two. A moral sceptic might be the sort of person who says "All this talk of morality is tripe," who rejects morality and will take no notice of it. Such a person may be literally rejecting all moral judgements; he is more likely to be making moral judgements of his own, expressing a positive moral condemnation of all that conventionally passes for morality; or he may be confusing these two logically incompatible views, and saying that he rejects all morality, while he is in fact rejecting only a particular morality that is current in the society in which he has grown up. But I am not at present concerned with the merits or faults of such a position. These are first order moral views, positive or negative: the person who adopts either of them is taking a certain practical, normative, stand. By contrast, what I am discussing is a second order view, a view about the status of moral values and the nature of moral valuing, about where and how they fit into the world. These first and second order views are not merely distinct but completely independent: one could be a second order moral sceptic without being a first order one, or again the other way round. A man could hold strong moral views, and indeed ones whose content was thoroughly conventional, while believing that they were simply attitudes and policies with regard to conduct that he and other people held. Conversely, a man could reject all established morality while believing it to be an objective truth that it was evil or corrupt.

With another sort of misunderstanding moral scepticism would seem not so much pernicious as absurd. How could anyone deny that there is a difference between a kind action and a cruel one, or that a coward and a brave man behave differently in the face of danger? Of course, this is undeniable;

but it is not to the point. The kinds of behaviour to which moral values and disvalues are ascribed are indeed part of the furniture of the world, and so are the natural, descriptive, differences between them; but not, perhaps, their differences in value. It is a hard fact that cruel actions differ from kind ones, and hence that we can learn, as in fact we all do, to distinguish them fairly well in practice, and to use the words "cruel" and "kind" with fairly clear descriptive meanings; but is it an equally hard fact that actions which are cruel in such a descriptive sense are to be condemned? The present issue is with regard to the objectivity specifically of value, not with regard to the objectivity of those natural, factual, differences on the basis of which differing values are assigned.

SUBJECTIVISM

Another name often used, as an alternative to "moral scepticism," for the view I am discussing is "subjectivism." But this too has more than one meaning. * * * What is often called moral subjectivism is the doctrine that, for example, "This action is right" *means* "I approve of this action," or more generally that moral judgements are equivalent to reports of the speaker's own feelings or attitudes. But the view I am now discussing is to be distinguished in two vital respects from any such doctrine as this. First, what I have called moral scepticism is a negative doctrine, not a positive one: it says what there isn't, not what there is. It says that there do not exist entities or relations of a certain kind, objective values or requirements, which many people have believed to exist. Of course, the moral sceptic cannot leave it at that. If his position is to be at all plausible, he must give some account of how other people have fallen into what he regards as an error, and this account will have to include some positive suggestions about how values fail to be objective, about what has been mistaken for, or has led to false beliefs about, objective values. But this will be a development of his theory, not its core: its core is the negation. Secondly, what I have called moral scepticism is an ontological thesis, not a linguistic or conceptual one. It is not, like the other doctrine often called moral subjectivism, a view about the meanings of moral statements. * * *

The denial that there are objective values does not commit one to any particular view about what moral statements mean, and certainly not to the view that they are equivalent to subjective reports. No doubt if moral values are not objective they are in some very broad sense subjective, and for this reason I would accept "moral subjectivism" as an alternative name to "moral scepticism." But subjectivism in this broad sense must be distinguished from the specific doctrine about meaning referred to above. Neither name is altogether satisfactory: we simply have to guard against the (different) misinterpretations which each may suggest. * * *

THE CLAIM TO OBJECTIVITY

* * * The main tradition of European moral philosophy includes the * * * claim, that there are objective values of just the sort I have denied. * * *

But this objectivism about values is not only a feature of the philosophical tradition. It has also a firm basis in ordinary thought, and even in the meanings of moral terms. * * *

Someone in a state of moral perplexity, wondering whether it would be wrong for him to engage, say, in research related to bacteriological warfare, wants to arrive at some judgement about this concrete case, his doing this work at this time in these actual circumstances; his relevant characteristics will be part of the subject of the judgement, but no relation between him and the proposed action will be part of the predicate. The question is not, for example, whether he really wants to do this work, whether it will satisfy or dissatisfy him, whether he will in the long run have a pro-attitude towards it, or even whether this is an action of a sort that he can happily and sincerely recommend in all relevantly similar cases. Nor is he even wondering just whether to recommend such action in all relevantly similar cases. He wants to know whether this course of action would be wrong in itself. Something like this is the everyday objectivist concept of which talk about non-natural qualities is a philosopher's reconstruction.

The prevalence of this tendency to objectify values—and not only moral ones—is confirmed by a pattern of thinking that we find in existentialists and those influenced by them. The denial of objective values can carry with it an extreme emotional reaction, a feeling that nothing matters at all, that life has lost its purpose. Of course this does not follow; the lack of objective values is not a good reason for abandoning subjective concern or for ceasing to want anything. But the abandonment of a belief in objective values can cause, at least temporarily, a decay of subjective concern and sense of purpose. That it does so is evidence that the people in whom this reaction occurs have been tending to objectify their concerns and purposes, have been giving them a fictitious external authority. A claim to objectivity has been so strongly associated with their subjective concerns and purposes that the collapse of the former seems to undermine the latter as well. * * *

I conclude, then, that ordinary moral judgements include a claim to objectivity, an assumption that there are objective values in just the sense in which I am concerned to deny this. And I do not think it is going too far to say that this assumption has been incorporated in the basic, conventional, meanings of moral terms. Any analysis of the meanings of moral terms which omits this claim to objective, intrinsic, prescriptivity is to that extent incomplete; and this is true of any non-cognitive analysis, any naturalist one, and any combination of the two.

If second order ethics were confined, then, to linguistic and conceptual analysis, it ought to conclude that moral values at least are objective: that they are so is part of what our ordinary moral statements mean: the traditional moral concepts of the ordinary man as well as of the main line of western philosophers are concepts of objective value. But it is precisely for this reason that linguistic and conceptual analysis is not enough. The claim to objectivity, however ingrained in our language and thought, is not self-validating. It can and should be questioned. But the denial of objective values will have to be put forward not as the result of an analytic approach, but as an "error theory," a theory that although most people in making moral judgements implicitly claim, among other things, to be pointing to something objectively prescriptive, these claims are all false. It is this that makes the name "moral scepticism" appropriate.

But since this is an error theory, since it goes against assumptions ingrained in our thought and built into some of the ways in which language is used, since it conflicts with what is sometimes called common sense, it needs very solid support. It is not something we can accept lightly or casually and then quietly pass on. If we are to adopt this view, we must argue explicitly for it. Traditionally it has been supported by arguments of two main kinds, which I shall call the argument from relativity and the argument from queerness, but these can, as I shall show, be supplemented in several ways.

THE ARGUMENT FROM RELATIVITY

The argument from relativity has as its premiss the well-known variation in moral codes from one society to another and from one period to another, and also the differences in moral beliefs between different groups and classes within a complex community. Such variation is in itself merely a truth of descriptive morality, a fact of anthropology which entails neither first order nor second order ethical views. Yet it may indirectly support second order subjectivism: radical differences between first order moral judgements make it difficult to treat those judgements as apprehensions of objective truths. But it is not the mere occurrence of disagreements that tells against the objectivity of values. Disagreement on questions in history or biology or cosmology does not show that there are no objective issues in these fields for investigators to disagree about. But such scientific disagreement results from speculative inferences or explanatory hypotheses based on inadequate evidence, and it is hardly plausible to interpret moral disagreement in the same way. Disagreement about moral codes seems to reflect people's adherence to and participation in different ways of life. The causal connection seems to be mainly that way round: it is that people approve of monogamy because they participate in a monogamous way of life rather than that they participate in a monogamous way of life because they approve of monogamy. Of course, the standards may be an idealization of the way of life from which they arise: the monogamy in which people participate may be less complete, less rigid, than that of which it leads them to approve. This is not to say that moral judgements are purely conventional. Of course there have been and are moral heretics and moral reformers, people who have turned against the established rules and practices of their own communities for moral reasons, and often for moral reasons that we would endorse. But this can usually be understood as the extension, in ways which, though new and unconventional, seemed to them to be required for consistency, of rules to which they already adhered as arising out of an existing way of life. In short, the argument from relativity has some force simply because the actual variations in the moral codes are more readily explained by the hypothesis that they reflect ways of life than by the hypothesis that they express perceptions, most of them seriously inadequate and badly distorted, of objective values.

But there is a well-known counter to this argument from relativity, namely to say that the items for which objective validity is in the first place to be claimed are not specific moral rules or codes but very general basic principles which are recognized at least implicitly to some extent in all society—such principles as provide the foundations of what Sidgwick[1] has called different methods of ethics: the principle of universalizability, perhaps, or the rule that one ought to conform to the specific rules of any way of life in which one takes part, from which one profits, and on which one relies, or some utilitarian principle of doing what tends, or seems likely, to

---

1 *Editor's note*: Henry Sidgwick, *Methods of Ethics* (Hackett, 1981; original work published 1874).

promote the general happiness. It is easy to show that such general principles, married with differing concrete circumstances, different existing social patterns or different preferences, will beget different specific moral rules; and there is some plausibility in the claim that the specific rules thus generated will vary from community to community or from group to group in close agreement with the actual variations in accepted codes.

The argument from relativity can be only partly countered in this way. To take this line the moral objectivist has to say that it is only in these principles that the objective moral character attaches immediately to its descriptively specified ground or subject: other moral judgements are objectively valid or true, but only derivatively and contingently—if things had been otherwise, quite different sorts of actions would have been right. And despite the prominence in recent philosophical ethics of universalization, utilitarian principles, and the like, these are very far from constituting the whole of what is actually affirmed as basic in ordinary moral thought. Much of this is concerned rather with what Hare[2] calls "ideals" or, less kindly, "fanaticism." That is, people judge that some things are good or right, and others are bad or wrong, not because—or at any rate not only because—they exemplify some general principle for which widespread implicit acceptance could be claimed, but because something about those things arouses certain responses immediately in them, though they would arouse radically and irresolvably different responses in others. "Moral sense" or "intuition" is an initially more plausible description of what supplies many of our basic moral judgements than "reason." With regard to all these starting points of moral thinking the argument from relativity remains in full force.

THE ARGUMENT FROM QUEERNESS

Even more important, however, and certainly more generally applicable, is the argument from queerness. This has two parts, one metaphysical, the other epistemological. If there were objective values, then they would be entities or qualities or relations of a very strange sort, utterly different from anything else in the universe. Correspondingly, if we were aware of them, it would have to be by some special faculty of moral perception or intuition, utterly different from our ordinary ways of knowing everything else. These points were recognized by Moore when he spoke of non-natural qualities, and by the intuitionists in their talk about a "faculty of moral intuition."

---

2   R. M. Hare, *Freedom and Reason* (Oxford University Press, 1963).

Intuitionism has long been out of favour, and it is indeed easy to point out its implausibilities. What is not so often stressed, but is more important, is that the central thesis of intuitionism is one to which any objectivist view of values is in the end committed: intuitionism merely makes unpalatably plain what other forms of objectivism wrap up. Of course the suggestion that moral judgements are made or moral problems solved by just sitting down and having an ethical intuition is a travesty of actual moral thinking. But, however complex the real process, it will require (if it is to yield authoritatively prescriptive conclusions) some input of this distinctive sort, either premisses or forms of argument or both. When we ask the awkward question, how we can be aware of this authoritative prescriptivity, of the truth of these distinctively ethical premisses or of the cogency of this distinctively ethical pattern of reasoning, none of our ordinary accounts of sensory perception or introspection or the framing and confirming of explanatory hypotheses or inference or logical construction or conceptual analysis, or any combination of these, will provide a satisfactory answer; "a special sort of intuition" is a lame answer, but it is the one to which the clear-headed objectivist is compelled to resort.

Indeed, the best move for the moral objectivist is not to evade this issue, but to look for companions in guilt. For example, Richard Price argues that it is not moral knowledge alone that such an empiricism as those of Locke and Hume is unable to account for, but also our knowledge and even our ideas of essence, number, identity, diversity, solidity, inertia, substance, the necessary existence and infinite extension of time and space, necessity and possibility in general, power, and causation. If the understanding, which Price defines as the faculty within us that discerns truth, is also a source of new simple ideas of so many other sorts, may it not also be a power of immediately perceiving right and wrong, which yet are real characters of actions?

This is an important counter to the argument from queerness. The only adequate reply to it would be to show how, on empiricist foundations, we can construct an account of the ideas and beliefs and knowledge that we have of all these matters. I cannot even begin to do that here, though I have undertaken some parts of the task elsewhere. I can only state my belief that satisfactory accounts of most of these can be given in empirical terms. If some supposed metaphysical necessities or essences resist such treatment, then they too should be included, along with objective values, among the targets of the argument from queerness. ＊＊＊

Plato's Forms give a dramatic picture of what objective values would have to be. The Form of the Good is such that knowledge of it provides the knower with both a direction and an overriding motive; something's being good both tells the person who knows this to pursue it and makes him pursue it. An objective good would be sought by anyone who was acquainted with it, not because of any contingent fact that this person, or every person, is so constituted that he desires this end, but just because the end has to-be-pursuedness somehow built into it. Similarly, if there were objective principles of right and wrong, any wrong (possible) course of action would have not-to-be-doneness somehow built into it. * * *

Another way of bringing out this queerness is to ask, about anything that is supposed to have some objective moral quality, how this is linked with its natural features. What is the connection between the natural fact that an action is a piece of deliberate cruelty—say, causing pain just for fun—and the moral fact that it is wrong? It cannot be an entailment, a logical or semantic necessity. Yet it is not merely that the two features occur together. The wrongness must somehow be "consequential" or "supervenient"; it is wrong because it is a piece of deliberate cruelty. But just what *in the world* is signified by this "because"? And how do we know the relation that it signifies, if this is something more than such actions being socially condemned, and condemned by us too, perhaps through our having absorbed attitudes from our social environment? It is not even sufficient to postulate a faculty which "sees" the wrongness: something must be postulated which can see at once the natural features that constitute the cruelty, and the wrongness, and the mysterious consequential link between the two. Alternatively, the intuition required might be the perception that wrongness is a higher order property belonging to certain natural properties; but what is this belonging of properties to other properties, and how can we discern it? How much simpler and more comprehensible the situation would be if we could replace the moral quality with some sort of subjective response which could be causally related to the detection of the natural features on which the supposed quality is said to be consequential.

STUDY QUESTIONS

1. Why does Mackie call his approach to ethics "error theory"?
2. What is the argument from relativity, and what does Mackie hope to achieve with it?
3. What is the argument from queerness? (Explain both its metaphysical and epistemological aspects.)

HARRY G. FRANKFURT
Alternate Possibilities and Moral Responsibility

Harry Frankfurt (b. 1929) is an American philosopher, known for his work defending compatibilism, as well as political philosophy and a best-selling short book called On Bullshit *(2005).*

A dominant role in nearly all recent inquiries into the free-will problem has been played by a principle which I shall call "the principle of alternate possibilities." This principle states that a person is morally responsible for what he has done only if he could have done otherwise. Its exact meaning is a subject of controversy, particularly concerning whether someone who accepts it is thereby committed to believing that moral responsibility and determinism are incompatible. Practically no one, however, seems inclined to deny or even to question that the principle of alternate possibilities (construed in some way or other) is true. It has generally seemed so overwhelmingly plausible that some philosophers have even characterized it as an *a priori* truth. People whose accounts of free will or of moral responsibility are radically at odds evidently find in it a firm and convenient common ground upon which they can profitably take their opposing stands.

But the principle of alternate possibilities is false. A person may well be morally responsible for what he has done even though he could not have done otherwise. The principle's plausibility is an illusion, which can be made to vanish by bringing the relevant moral phenomena into sharper focus.

I

In seeking illustrations of the principle of alternate possibilities, it is most natural to think of situations in which the same circumstances both bring it about that a person does something and make it impossible for him to avoid doing it. These include, for example, situations in which a person is coerced into doing something, or in which he is impelled to act by a hypnotic suggestion, or in which some inner compulsion drives him to do what he does. In situations of these kinds there are circumstances that make it impossible for the person to do otherwise, and these very circumstances also serve to bring it about that he does whatever it is that he does.

However, there may be circumstances that constitute sufficient conditions for a certain action to be performed by someone and that therefore make it impossible for the person to do otherwise, but that do not actually impel the person to act or in any way produce his action. A person may do something in circumstances that leave him no alternative to doing it, without these circumstances actually moving him or leading him to do it—without them playing any role, indeed, in bringing it about that he does what he does.

An examination of situations characterized by circumstances of this sort casts doubt, I believe, on the relevance to questions of moral responsibility of the fact that a person who has done something could not have done otherwise. I propose to develop some examples of this kind in the context of a discussion of coercion and to suggest that our moral intuitions concerning these examples tend to disconfirm the principle of alternate possibilities. Then I will discuss the principle in more general terms, explain what I think is wrong with it, and describe briefly and without argument how it might appropriately be revised.

II

It is generally agreed that a person who has been coerced to do something did not do it freely and is not morally responsible for having done it. Now the doctrine that coercion and moral responsibility are mutually exclusive may appear to be no more than a somewhat particularized version of the principle of alternate possibilities. It is natural enough to say of a person who has been coerced to do something that he could not have done otherwise. And it may easily seem that being coerced deprives a person of freedom and of moral responsibility simply because it is a special case of being unable to do otherwise. The principle of alternate possibilities may in this way derive some credibility from its association with the very plausible proposition that moral responsibility is excluded by coercion.

It is not right, however, that it should do so. The fact that a person was coerced to act as he did may entail both that he could not have done otherwise and that he bears no moral responsibility for his action. But his lack of moral responsibility is not entailed by his having been unable to do otherwise. The doctrine that coercion excludes moral responsibility is not correctly understood, in other words, as a particularized version of the principle of alternate possibilities.

Let us suppose that someone is threatened convincingly with a penalty he finds unacceptable and that he then does what is required of him by the issuer of the threat. We can imagine details that would make it reasonable for us to think that the person was coerced to perform the action in question, that he could not have done otherwise, and that he bears no moral responsibility for having done what he did. But just what is it about situations of this kind that warrants the judgment that the threatened person is not morally responsible for his act?

This question may be approached by considering situations of the following kind. Jones decides for reasons of his own to do something, then someone threatens him with a very harsh penalty (so harsh that any reasonable person would submit to the threat) unless he does precisely that, and Jones does it. Will we hold Jones morally responsible for what he has done? I think this will depend on the roles we think were played, in leading him to act, by his original decision and by the threat.

One possibility is that Jones$_1$ is not a reasonable man: he is, rather, a man who does what he has once decided to do no matter what happens next and no matter what the cost. In that case, the threat actually exerted no effective force upon him. He acted without any regard to it, very much as if he were not aware that it had been made. If this is indeed the way it was, the situation did not involve coercion at all. The threat did not lead Jones$_1$ to do what he did. Nor was it in fact sufficient to have prevented him from doing otherwise: if his earlier decision had been to do something else, the threat would not have deterred him in the slightest. It seems evident that in these circumstances the fact that Jones$_1$ was threatened in no way reduces the moral responsibility he would otherwise bear for his act. This example, however, is not a counterexample either to the doctrine that coercion excuses or to the principle of alternate possibilities. For we have supposed that Jones$_1$ is a man upon whom the threat had no coercive effect and, hence, that it did not actually deprive him of alternatives to doing what he did.

Another possibility is that Jones$_2$ was stampeded by the threat. Given that threat, he would have performed that action regardless of what decision he had already made. The threat upset him so profoundly, moreover, that he completely forgot his own earlier decision and did what was demanded of him entirely because he was terrified of the penalty with which he was threatened. In this case, it is not relevant to his having performed the action that he had already decided on his own to perform it. When the chips were down he thought of nothing but the threat, and fear alone led him to act. The fact that at an earlier time Jones$_2$ had decided for his own reasons to act in just that way may be relevant to an evaluation of his character; he may bear full moral responsibility for having made *that* decision. But he can hardly be said to be morally responsible for his action. For he performed the action simply as a result of the coercion to which he was subjected. His earlier decision played no role in bringing it about that he did what he did, and it would therefore be gratuitous to assign it a role in the moral evaluation of his action.

Now consider a third possibility. Jones₃ was neither stampeded by the threat nor indifferent to it. The threat impressed him, as it would impress any reasonable man, and he would have submitted to it wholeheartedly if he had not already made a decision that coincided with the one demanded of him. In fact, however, he performed the action in question on the basis of the decision he had made before the threat was issued. When he acted, he was not actually motivated by the threat but solely by the considerations that had originally commended the action to him. It was not the threat that led him to act, though it would have done so if he had not already provided himself with a sufficient motive for performing the action in question.

No doubt it will be very difficult for anyone to know, in a case like this one, exactly what happened. Did Jones₃ perform the action because of the threat, or were his reasons for acting simply those which had already persuaded him to do so? Or did he act on the basis of two motives, each of which was sufficient for his action? It is not impossible, however, that the situation should be clearer than situations of this kind usually are. And suppose it is apparent to us that Jones₃ acted on the basis of his own decision and not because of the threat. Then I think we would be justified in regarding his moral responsibility for what he did as unaffected by the threat even though, since he would in any case have submitted to the threat, he could not have avoided doing what he did. It would be entirely reasonable for us to make the same judgment concerning his moral responsibility that we would have made if we had not known of the threat. For the threat did not in fact influence his performance of the action. He did what he did just as if the threat had not been made at all.

III

The case of Jones₃ may appear at first glance to combine coercion and moral responsibility, and thus to provide a counterexample to the doctrine that coercion excuses. It is not really so certain that it does so, however, because it is unclear whether the example constitutes a genuine instance of coercion. Can we say of Jones₃ that he was coerced to do something, when he had already decided on his own to do it and when he did it entirely on the basis of that decision? Or would it be more correct to say that Jones₃ was not coerced to do what he did, even though he himself recognized that there was an irresistible force at work in virtue of which he had to do it? My own linguistic intuitions lead me toward the second alternative, but they are somewhat equivocal. Perhaps we can say either of these things, or perhaps we must add a qualifying explanation to whichever of them we say.

This murkiness, however, does not interfere with our drawing an important moral from an examination of the example. Suppose we decide to say that Jones$_3$ was *not* coerced. Our basis for saying this will clearly be that it is incorrect to regard a man as being coerced to do something unless he does it *because of* the coercive force exerted against him. The fact that an irresistible threat is made will not, then, entail that the person who receives it is coerced to do what he does. It will also be necessary that the threat is what actually accounts for his doing it. On the other hand, suppose we decide to say that Jones$_3$ *was* coerced. Then we will be bound to admit that being coerced does not exclude being morally responsible. And we will also surely be led to the view that coercion affects the judgment of a person's moral responsibility only when the person acts as he does because he is coerced to do so—i.e., when the fact that he is coerced is what accounts for his action.

Whichever we decide to say, then, we will recognize that the doctrine that coercion excludes moral responsibility is not a particularized version of the principle of alternate possibilities. Situations in which a person who does something cannot do otherwise because he is subject to coercive power are either not instances of coercion at all, or they are situations in which the person may still be morally responsible for what he does if it is not because of the coercion that he does it. When we excuse a person who has been coerced, we do not excuse him because he was unable to do otherwise. Even though a person is subject to a coercive force that precludes his performing any action but one, he may nonetheless bear full moral responsibility for performing that action.

IV

To the extent that the principle of alternate possibilities derives its plausibility from association with the doctrine that coercion excludes moral responsibility, a clear understanding of the latter diminishes the appeal of the former. Indeed the case of Jones$_3$ may appear to do more than illuminate the relationship between the two doctrines. It may well seem to provide a decisive counterexample to the principle of alternate possibilities and thus to show that this principle is false. For the irresistibility of the threat to which Jones$_3$ is subjected might well be taken to mean that he cannot but perform the action he performs. And yet the threat, since Jones$_3$ performs the action without regard to it, does not reduce his moral responsibility for what he does.

The following objection will doubtless be raised against the suggestion that the case of Jones$_3$ is a counterexample to the principle of alternate possibilities. There is perhaps a sense in which Jones$_3$ cannot do otherwise than perform the action he performs, since he is a reasonable man and the threat he encounters is sufficient to move any reasonable man. But it is not this sense that is germane to the principle of alternate possibilities. His knowledge that he stands to suffer an intolerably harsh penalty does not mean that Jones$_3$, strictly speaking, *cannot* perform any action but the one he does perform. After all it is still open to him, and this is crucial, to defy the threat if he wishes to do so and to accept the penalty his action would bring down upon him. In the sense in which the principle of alternate possibilities employs the concept of "could have done otherwise," Jones$_3$'s inability to resist the threat does not mean that he cannot do otherwise than perform the action he performs. Hence the case of Jones$_3$ does not constitute an instance contrary to the principle.

I do not propose to consider in what sense the concept of "could have done otherwise" figures in the principle of alternate possibilities, nor will I attempt to measure the force of the objection I have just described. For I believe that whatever force this objection may be thought to have can be deflected by altering the example in the following way. Suppose someone—Black, let us say—wants Jones$_4$ to perform a certain action. Black is prepared to go to considerable lengths to get his way, but he prefers to avoid showing his hand unnecessarily. So he waits until Jones$_4$ is about to make up his mind what to do, and he does nothing unless it is clear to him (Black is an excellent judge of such things) that Jones$_4$ is going to decide to do something *other* than what he wants him to do. If it does become clear that Jones$_4$ is going to decide to do something else, Black takes effective steps to ensure that Jones$_4$ decides to do, and that he does do, what he wants him to do. Whatever Jones$_4$'s initial preferences and inclinations, then, Black will have his way.

What steps will Black take, if he believes he must take steps, in order to ensure that Jones$_4$ decides and acts as he wishes? Anyone with a theory concerning what "could have done otherwise" means may answer this question for himself by describing whatever measures he would regard as sufficient to guarantee that, in the relevant sense, Jones$_4$ cannot do otherwise. Let

Black pronounce a terrible threat, and in this way both force Jones$_4$ to perform the desired action and prevent him from performing a forbidden one. Let Black give Jones$_4$ a potion, or put him under hypnosis, and in some such way as these generate in Jones$_4$ an irresistible inner compulsion to perform the act Black wants performed and to avoid others. Or let Black manipulate the minute processes of Jones$_4$'s brain and nervous system in some more direct way, so that causal forces running in and out of his synapses and along the poor man's nerves determine that he chooses to act and that he does act in the one way and not in any other. Given any conditions under which it will be maintained that Jones$_4$ cannot do otherwise, in other words, let Black bring it about that those conditions prevail. The structure of the example is flexible enough, I think, to find a way around any charge of irrelevance by accommodating the doctrine on which the charge is based.

Now suppose that Black never has to show his hand because Jones$_4$, for reasons of his own, decides to perform and does perform the very action Black wants him to perform. In that case, it seems clear, Jones$_4$ will bear precisely the same moral responsibility for what he does as he would have borne if Black had not been ready to take steps to ensure that he do it. It would be quite unreasonable to excuse Jones$_4$ for his action, or to withhold the praise to which it would normally entitle him, on the basis of the fact that he could not have done otherwise. This fact played no role at all in leading him to act as he did. He would have acted the same even if it had not been a fact. Indeed, everything happened just as it would have happened without Black's presence in the situation and without his readiness to intrude into it.

In this example there are sufficient conditions for Jones$_4$'s performing the action in question. What action he performs is not up to him. Of course it is in a way up to him whether he acts on his own or as a result of Black's intervention. That depends upon what action he himself is inclined to perform. But whether he finally acts on his own or as a result of Black's intervention, he performs the same action. He has no alternative but to do what Black wants him to do. If he does it on his own, however, his moral responsibility for doing it is not affected by the fact that Black was lurking in the background with sinister intent, since this intent never comes into play.

V

The fact that a person could not have avoided doing something is a sufficient condition of his having done it. But, as some of my examples show, this fact may play no role whatever in the explanation of why he did it.

It may not figure at all among the circumstances that actually brought it about that he did what he did, so that his action is to be accounted for on another basis entirely. Even though the person was unable to do otherwise, that is to say, it may not be the case that he acted as he did *because* he could not have done otherwise. Now if someone had no alternative to performing a certain action but did not perform it because he was unable to do otherwise, then he would have performed exactly the same action even if he *could* have done otherwise. The circumstances that made it impossible for him to do otherwise could have been subtracted from the situation without affecting what happened or why it happened in any way. Whatever it was that actually led the person to do what he did, or that made him do it, would have led him to do it or made him do it even if it had been possible for him to do something else instead.

Thus it would have made no difference, so far as concerns his action or how he came to perform it, if the circumstances that made it impossible for him to avoid performing it had not prevailed. The fact that he could not have done otherwise clearly provides no basis for supposing that he *might* have done otherwise if he had been able to do so. When a fact is in this way irrelevant to the problem of accounting for a person's action it seems quite gratuitous to assign it any weight in the assessment of his moral responsibility. Why should the fact be considered in reaching a moral judgment concerning the person when it does not help in any way to understand either what made him act as he did or what, in other circumstances, he might have done?

This, then, is why the principle of alternate possibilities is mistaken. It asserts that a person bears no moral responsibility—that is, he is to be excused—for having performed an action if there were circumstances that made it impossible for him to avoid performing it. But there may be circumstances that make it impossible for a person to avoid performing some action without those circumstances in any way bringing it about that he performs that action. It would surely be no good for the person to refer to circumstances of this sort in an effort to absolve himself of moral responsibility for performing the action in question. For those circumstances, by hypothesis, actually had nothing to do with his having done what he did. He would have done precisely the same thing, and he would have been led or made in precisely the same way to do it, even if they had not prevailed.

We often do, to be sure, excuse people for what they have done when they tell us (and we believe them) that they could not have done otherwise. But this is because we assume that what they tell us serves to explain why they did what they did. We take it for granted that they are not being disingenuous, as a person would be who cited as an excuse the fact that he could not have avoided doing what he did but who knew full well that it was not at all because of this that he did it.

What I have said may suggest that the principle of alternate possibilities should be revised so as to assert that a person is not morally responsible for what he has done if he did it because he could not have done otherwise. It may be noted that this revision of the principle does not seriously affect the arguments of those who have relied on the original principle in their efforts to maintain that moral responsibility and determinism are incompatible. For if it was causally determined that a person perform a certain action, then it will be true that the person performed it because of those causal determinants. And if the fact that it was causally determined that a person perform a certain action means that the person could not have done otherwise, as philosophers who argue for the incompatibility thesis characteristically suppose, then the fact that it was causally determined that a person perform a certain action will mean that the person performed it because he could not have done otherwise. The revised principle of alternate possibilities will entail, on this assumption concerning the meaning of "could have done otherwise," that a person is not morally responsible for what he has done if it was causally determined that he do it. I do not believe, however, that this revision of the principle is acceptable.

Suppose a person tells us that he did what he did because he was unable to do otherwise; or suppose he makes the similar statement that he did what he did because he had to do it. We do often accept statements like these (if we believe them) as valid excuses, and such statements may well seem at first glance to invoke the revised principle of alternate possibilities. But I think that when we accept such statements as valid excuses it is because we assume that we are being told more than the statements strictly and literally convey. We understand the person who offers the excuse to mean that he did what he did *only because* he was unable to do otherwise, or *only because* he had to do it. And we understand him to mean, more particularly, that when he did what he did it was not because that was what he really wanted to do. The principle of alternate possibilities should thus be replaced, in my opinion, by the following principle: a person is not morally responsible for what he has done if he did it only because he could not have done otherwise. This principle does not appear to conflict with the view that moral responsibility is compatible with determinism.

The following may all be true: there were circumstances that made it impossible for a person to avoid doing something; these circumstances actually played a role in bringing it about that he did it, so that it is correct to say that he did it because he could not have done otherwise; the person really wanted to do what he did; he did it because it was what he really wanted to do, so that it is not correct to say that he did what he did only because he could not have done otherwise. Under these conditions, the person may well be morally responsible for what he has done. On the other hand, he will not be morally responsible for what he has done if he did it only because he could not have done otherwise, even if what he did was something he really wanted to do.

STUDY QUESTIONS

1. What is the principle of alternate possibilities, and what consequences does it have for the debate about free will and moral responsibility?
2. Explain Frankfurt's counterexample to the principle of alternate possibilities.
3. Does Frankfurt show that moral responsibility does not depend on free will?

PLATO
God and Morality

Plato (429?–347 BCE), an ancient Greek philosopher, stands as perhaps the most significant of the founders of the Western philosophical tradition. He was a pupil of Socrates and teacher of Aristotle. He wrote in dialogue form, generally featuring Socrates as the lead figure in the debate. It has been said that all subsequent philosophy is "footnotes to Plato."

EUTHYPHRO: ✳✳✳ What is dear to the gods is pious, what is not is impious.

SOCRATES: Splendid, Euthyphro! You have now answered in the way I wanted. Whether your answer is true I do not know yet, but you will obviously show me that what you say is true.

EUTHYPHRO: Certainly.

SOCRATES: Come then, let us examine what we mean. An action or a man dear to the gods is pious, but an action or a man hated by the gods is impious. They are not the same, but quite opposite, the pious and the impious. Is that not so?

EUTHYPHRO: It is indeed.

SOCRATES: And that seems to be a good statement?

EUTHYPHRO: I think so, Socrates.

SOCRATES: We have also stated that the gods are in a state of discord, that they are at odds with each other, Euthyphro, and that they are at enmity with each other. Has that, too, been said?

EUTHYPHRO: It has.

SOCRATES: What are the subjects of difference that cause hatred and anger? Let us look at it this way. If you and I were to differ about numbers as to which is the greater, would this difference make us enemies and angry with each other, or would we proceed to count and soon resolve our difference about this?

EUTHYPHRO: We would certainly do so.

SOCRATES: Again, if we differed about the larger and the smaller, we would turn to measurement and soon cease to differ.

EUTHYPHRO: That is so.

SOCRATES: And about the heavier and the lighter, we would resort to weighing and be reconciled.

EUTHYPHRO: Of course.

SOCRATES: What subject of difference would make us angry and hostile to each other if we were unable to come to a decision? Perhaps you do not have an answer ready, but examine as I tell you whether these subjects are the just and the unjust, the beautiful and the ugly, the good and the bad. Are these not the subjects of difference about which, when we are unable to come to a satisfactory decision, you and I and other men become hostile to each other whenever we do?

EUTHYPHRO: That is the difference, Socrates, about those subjects.

SOCRATES: What about the gods, Euthyphro? If indeed they have differences, will it not be about these same subjects?

EUTHYPHRO: It certainly must be so.

SOCRATES: Then according to your argument, my good Euthyphro, different gods consider different things to be just, beautiful, ugly, good, and bad, for they would not be at odds with one another unless they differed about these subjects, would they?

EUTHYPHRO: You are right.

SOCRATES: And they like what each of them considers beautiful, good, and just, and hate the opposites of these?

EUTHYPHRO: Certainly.

SOCRATES: But you say that the same things are considered just by some gods and unjust by others, and as they dispute about these things they are at odds and at war with each other. Is that not so?

EUTHYPHRO: It is.

SOCRATES: The same things then are loved by the gods and hated by the gods, and would be both god-loved and god-hated.

EUTHYPHRO: It seems likely.

SOCRATES: And the same things would be both pious and impious, according to this argument?

EUTHYPHRO: I'm afraid so.

SOCRATES: So you did not answer my question, you surprising man. I did not ask you what same thing is both pious and impious, and it appears that what is loved by the gods is also hated by them. So it is in no way surprising if your present action, namely punishing your father, may be pleasing to Zeus but displeasing to Cronus and Uranus, pleasing to Hephaestus but displeasing to Hera, and so with any other gods who differ from each other on this subject.

EUTHYPHRO: I think, Socrates, that on this subject no gods would differ from one another, that whoever has killed anyone unjustly should pay the penalty.

SOCRATES: Well now, Euthyphro, have you ever heard any man maintaining that one who has killed or done anything else unjustly should not pay the penalty?

EUTHYPHRO: They never cease to dispute on this subject, both elsewhere and in the courts, for when they have committed many wrongs they do and say anything to avoid the penalty.

SOCRATES: Do they agree they have done wrong, Euthyphro, and in spite of so agreeing do they nevertheless say they should not be punished?

EUTHYPHRO: No, they do not agree on that point.

SOCRATES: So they do not say or do just anything. For they do not venture to say this, or dispute that they must not pay the penalty if they have done wrong, but I think they deny doing wrong. Is that not so?

EUTHYPHRO: That is true.

SOCRATES: Then they do not dispute that the wrongdoer must be punished, but they may disagree as to who the wrongdoer is, what he did, and when.

EUTHYPHRO: You are right.

SOCRATES: Do not the gods have the same experience, if indeed they are at odds with each other about the just and the unjust, as your argument maintains? Some assert that they wrong one another, while others deny it, but no one among gods or men ventures to say that the wrongdoer must not be punished.

EUTHYPHRO: Yes, that is true, Socrates, as to the main point.

SOCRATES: And those who disagree, whether men or gods, dispute about each action, if indeed the gods disagree. Some say it is done justly, others unjustly. Is that not so?

EUTHYPHRO: Yes, indeed.

SOCRATES: Come now, my dear Euthyphro, tell me, too, that I may become wiser, what proof you have that all the gods consider that man to have been killed unjustly who became a murderer while in your service, was bound by the master of his victim, and died in his bonds before the one who bound him found out from the seers what was to be done with him, and that it is right for a son to denounce and to prosecute his father on behalf of such a man. Come, try to show me a clear sign that all the gods definitely believe this action to be right. If you can give me adequate proof of this, I shall never cease to extol your wisdom.

EUTHYPHRO: This is perhaps no light task, Socrates, though I could show you very clearly.

SOCRATES: I understand that you think me more dull-witted than the jury, as you will obviously show them that these actions were unjust and that all the gods hate such actions.

EUTHYPHRO: I will show it to them clearly, Socrates, if only they will listen to me.

SOCRATES: They will listen if they think you show them well. But this thought came to me as you were speaking, and I am examining it, saying to myself: "If Euthyphro shows me conclusively that all the gods consider such a death unjust, to what greater extent have I learned from him the nature of piety and impiety? This action would then, it seems, be hated by the gods, but the pious and the impious were not thereby now defined, for what is hated by the gods has also been shown to be loved by them." So I will not insist on this point; let us assume, if you wish, that all the gods consider this unjust and that they all hate it. However, is this the correction we are making in our discussion, that what all the gods hate is impious, and what they all love is pious, and that what some gods love and others hate is neither or both? Is that how you now wish us to define piety and impiety?

EUTHYPHRO: What prevents us from doing so, Socrates?

SOCRATES: For my part nothing, Euthyphro, but you look whether on your part this proposal will enable you to teach me most easily what you promised.

EUTHYPHRO: I would certainly say that the pious is what all the gods love, and the opposite, what all the gods hate, is the impious.

SOCRATES: Then let us again examine whether that is a sound statement, or do we let it pass, and if one of us, or someone else, merely says that something is so, do we accept that it is so? Or should we examine what the speaker means?

EUTHYPHRO: We must examine it, but I certainly think that this is now a fine statement.

SOCRATES: We shall soon know better whether it is. Consider this: Is the pious being loved by the gods because it is pious, or is it pious because it is being loved by the gods?

EUTHYPHRO: I don't know what you mean, Socrates.

SOCRATES: I shall try to explain more clearly: we speak of something carried and something carrying, of something led and something leading, of something seen and something seeing, and you understand that these things are all different from one another and how they differ?

EUTHYPHRO: I think I do.

SOCRATES: So there is also something loved and—a different thing—something loving.

EUTHYPHRO: Of course.

SOCRATES: Tell me then whether the thing carried is a carried thing because it is being carried, or for some other reason?

EUTHYPHRO: No, that is the reason.

SOCRATES: And the thing led is so because it is being led, and the thing seen because it is being seen?

EUTHYPHRO: Certainly.

SOCRATES: It is not being seen because it is a thing seen but on the contrary it is a thing seen because it is being seen; nor is it because it is something led that it is being led but because it is being led that it is something led; nor is something being carried because it is something carried, but it is something carried because it is being carried. Is what I want to say clear, Euthyphro? I want to say this, namely, that if anything is being changed or is being affected in any way, it is not being changed because it is something changed, but rather it is something changed because it is being changed; nor is it being affected because it is something affected, but it is something affected because it is being affected. Or do you not agree?

EUTHYPHRO: I do.

SOCRATES: Is something loved either something changed or something affected by something?

EUTHYPHRO: Certainly.

SOCRATES: So it is in the same case as the things just mentioned; it is not being loved by those who love it because it is something loved, but it is something loved because it is being loved by them?

EUTHYPHRO: Necessarily.

SOCRATES: What then do we say about the pious, Euthyphro? Surely that it is being loved by all the gods, according to what you say?

EUTHYPHRO: Yes.

SOCRATES: Is it being loved because it is pious, or for some other reason?

EUTHYPHRO: For no other reason.

SOCRATES: It is being loved then because it is pious, but it is not pious because it is being loved?

EUTHYPHRO: Apparently.

SOCRATES: And yet it is something loved and god-loved because it is being loved by the gods?

EUTHYPHRO: Of course.

SOCRATES: Then the god-loved is not the same as the pious, Euthyphro, nor the pious the same as the god-loved, as you say it is, but one differs from the other.

EUTHYPHRO: How so, Socrates?

SOCRATES: Because we agree that the pious is being loved for this reason, that it is pious, but it is not pious because it is being loved. Is that not so?

EUTHYPHRO: Yes.

SOCRATES: And that the god-loved, on the other hand, is so because it is being loved by the gods, by the very fact of being loved, but it is not being loved because it is god-loved.

EUTHYPHRO: True.

SOCRATES: But if the god-loved and the pious were the same, my dear Euthyphro, then if the pious was being loved because it was pious, the god-loved would also be being loved because it was god-loved; and if the god-loved was god-loved because it was being loved by the gods, then the pious would also be pious because it was being loved by the gods. But now you see that they are in opposite cases as being altogether different from each other: the one is such as to be loved because it is being loved, the other is being loved because it is such as to be loved. I'm afraid, Euthyphro, that when you were asked what piety is, you did not wish to make its nature clear to me, but you told me an affect or quality of it, that the pious has the quality of being loved by all the gods, but you have not yet told me what the pious is. Now, if you will, do not hide things from me but tell me again from the beginning what piety is, whether being loved by the gods or having some other quality—we shall not quarrel about that—but be keen to tell me what the pious and the impious are.

EUTHYPHRO: But Socrates, I have no way of telling you what I have in mind, for whatever proposition we put forward goes around and refuses to stay put where we establish it.

STUDY QUESTIONS

1. Why is it a challenge to religious morality if God commands certain actions because those actions are independently good?
2. Is it a problem for religious morality if it asserts that whatever God commands is good?
3. Does the *Euthyphro* dilemma show that there is no religious basis to morality?

PETER SINGER
Evolution and Morality

Peter Singer (b. 1946) is an Australian utilitarian philosopher, known for his uncompromising views on many issues of contemporary morality, such as animal liberation and the moral necessity to address global poverty.

THE ORIGINS OF ALTRUISM

We are not just rather like animals; we *are* animals.
—Mary Midgley, *Beast and Man*

A New Look at Ethics

Human beings are social animals. We were social before we were human. The French philosopher Jean-Jacques Rousseau once wrote that in the state of nature human beings had "no fixed home, no need of one another; they met perhaps twice in their lives, without knowing each other and without speaking." Rousseau was wrong. Fossil finds show that five million years ago our ancestor, the half-human, half-ape creature known to anthropologists as *Australopithecus africanus*, lived in groups, as our nearest living relatives—the gorillas and chimpanzees—still do. As *Australopithecus* evolved into the first truly human being, *Homo habilis*, and then into our own species, *Homo sapiens*, we remained social beings.

In rejecting Rousseau's fantasy of isolation as the original or natural condition of human existence, we must also reject his account of the origin of ethics, and that of the school of social contract theorists to which he belonged. The social contract theory of ethics held that our rules of right and wrong sprang from some distant Foundation Day on which previously independent rational human beings came together to hammer out a basis for setting up the first human society. Two hundred years ago this seemed a plausible alternative to the then orthodox idea that morality represented the decrees of a divine lawgiver. It attracted some of the sharpest and most skeptical thinkers in Western social philosophy. If, however, we now know that we have lived in groups longer than we have been rational human beings, we can also be sure that we restrained our behavior toward our fellows before we were rational human beings. Social life requires some degree of restraint. A social grouping cannot stay together if its members make frequent and unrestrained attacks on one another. Just when a pattern of restraint toward other members of the group becomes a social ethic is hard to say; but ethics probably began in these pre-human patterns of behavior rather than in the deliberate choices of fully fledged, rational human beings.

Eighteenth-century philosophers like Rousseau had little information to draw on about the social behavior of non-human animals; and they knew even less about the evolution of human beings. * * * Only in recent years have both the study of animal behavior in the wild and the study of human evolution advanced to the point at which we can claim with some confidence to know something about ourselves and our animal ancestors and relatives. * * * Sociobiology [is] "the systematic study of the biological basis of all social behavior" [and therefore] ethics falls within the scope of sociobiology. One might, of course, raise questions about the extent to which ethics has a biological basis; but if the origins of ethics lie in a past which we share with many non-human animals, evolutionary theory and observations of non-human social animals should have some bearing on the nature of ethics. So what does sociobiology offer us in place of the historical myth of the social contract?

Sociobiology bears on ethics indirectly, through what it says about the development of altruism, rather than by a direct study of ethics. Since it is difficult to decide when a chimpanzee or a gazelle is behaving ethically, this is a wise strategy. If we define altruistic behavior as behavior which benefits others at some cost to oneself, altruism in non-human animals is well documented. * * * Understanding the development of altruism in animals will improve our understanding of the development of ethics in human beings, for our present ethical systems have their roots in the altruistic behavior of our early human and pre-human ancestors.

Altruism intrigues sociobiologists. [Edward O.] Wilson calls it "the central theoretical problem of sociobiology." It is a problem because it has to be accounted for within the framework of Darwin's theory of evolution. If evolution is a struggle for survival, why hasn't it ruthlessly eliminated altruists, who seem to increase another's prospects of survival at the cost of their own?

ANIMAL ALTRUISM

Let us look at some examples of altruistic behavior in non-human animals. We can start with the warning calls given by blackbirds and thrushes when hawks fly overhead. These calls benefit other members of the flock, who can take evasive action; but giving a warning call presumably also gives away the location of the bird giving the call, thus exposing it to additional risk. ∗ ∗ ∗ If, as we would expect, birds who give warning calls are eaten at a higher rate than birds who act to save themselves without warning the rest of the flock, how does such altruism survive?

Another illustration comes from the behavior of Thomson's gazelles, a species of small antelope that is hunted by packs of African wild dogs. When a gazelle notices a dog pack, it bounds away in a curious, stiff-legged gait known as "stotting." Here is a description of this behavior and an indication of the puzzle it suggests:

> Undoubtedly a warning signal it [stotting] spread wavelike in advance of the pack. Apparently in response to the stotting, practically every gazelle in sight fled the immediate vicinity. Adaptive as the warning display may seem, it nonetheless appears to have its drawbacks; for even after being singled out by the pack, every gazelle began the run for its life by stotting, and appeared to lose precious ground in the process. ∗ ∗ ∗ It is therefore hard to see any advantage to the individual in stotting when chased, since individuals that made no display at all might be thought to have a better chance of surviving and reproducing.

Nor is altruism limited to warnings. Some animals threaten or attack predators to protect other members of their species. African wild dogs have been observed attacking a cheetah at considerable risk to their own lives in order to save a pup. Male baboons threaten predators, and cover the rear as the troop retreats. Parent birds frequently lead predators away from their nests with bizarre dances and displays which distract the predator's attention from the nest to the parent itself.

Food sharing is another form of altruism. Wolves and wild dogs bring meat back to members of the pack who were not in on the kill. Gibbons and chimpanzees without food gesture for, and usually receive, a portion of the food that another ape has. Chimpanzees also lead each other to trees with ripe fruit; indeed, their altruism extends beyond their own group, for when a whole group of chimpanzees is at a good tree, they make a loud booming noise which attracts other groups up to a kilometer away.

Several species help injured animals survive. Dolphins need to reach the surface of the water to breathe. If a dolphin is wounded so severely that it cannot swim to the surface by itself, other dolphins group themselves under it, pushing it upward to the air. If necessary they will keep doing this for several hours. The same kind of thing happens among elephants. A fallen elephant is likely to suffocate from its own weight, or it may overheat in the sun. Many elephant hunters have reported that when an elephant is felled, other members of the group try to raise it to its feet.

Finally, the restraint shown by many animals in combat with their fellows might also be a form of altruism. Fights between members of the same social group rarely end in death or even injury. When one wolf gets the better of another, the beaten wolf makes a submissive gesture, exposing the soft underside of its neck to the fangs of the victor. Instead of taking the opportunity to rip out the jugular vein of his foe, the victor trots off, content with the symbolic victory. From a purely selfish point of view, this seems foolish. How is it that wolves who fight to kill, never giving a beaten enemy a second chance, have not eliminated those who pass up opportunities to rid themselves of their rivals forever?

Evolution and Altruism

Many people think of evolution as a competition between different species; successful species survive and increase, unsuccessful ones become extinct. If evolution really worked mainly on the level of whole species, altruistic behavior between members of the same species would be easy to explain. The individual blackbird, taken by the hawk because of its warning call, dies to save the blackbird flock, thus increasing the survival prospects of the species as a whole. The wolf who accepts the submissive gesture of a defeated opponent exhibits an inhibition without which there would be no more wolves. And so on, for the other instances of altruism among animals.

The flaw in this simple explanation is that it is hard to see how, except under very special and rare conditions, the evolution of altruism could occur on so general a level as the survival or extinction of whole species. The real basis of selection is not the species, nor some smaller group, nor even the individual. It is the gene. Genes are responsible for the characteristics we inherit. If a gene leads individuals to have some feature which enhances their prospects of surviving and reproducing, that type of gene will itself survive into the next generation; if a gene reduces the prospects of leaving offspring for those individuals who carry it, that type of gene will itself die out with the death of the individual carrier.

For selection at the level of whole species to counteract this individual selection of genes, evolution would have to select species at something like the rate at which it selects genes. This means that old species would have to become extinct, and new species come into existence, nearly as often as individuals either succeed or fail in reproducing. But of course nature does not work like that; species evolve slowly, over many, many generations. Hence any genes that lead to altruism will normally lose out, in competition between members of the *same* species, to genes that lead to more selfish behavior, before the altruistic genes could spread through the species and so benefit the species as a whole in its competition with *other* species. And even if, under special circumstances, altruistic behavior did lead one species to survive where others without the genes for altruism became extinct, competition within the species would still work against the persistence of altruistic behavior in the surviving species, once the external competition was over.

✳ ✳ ✳ How could the genes for such self-sacrificing behavior get established? How is it that, as soon as the combination of genes necessary for giving warning calls appears, this type of combination is not rapidly wiped out along with the individual birds who, by giving the warning, reduce their own prospects of living long enough to leave descendants? It may be true that if this happened the species as a whole would be less likely to survive; but all this shows is that there is a real puzzle as to how the species does survive, since the species as a whole is powerless to prevent the elimination of altruism within it. ✳ ✳ ✳

Darwin himself was aware of this difficulty in the way of an evolutionary account of social and moral traits in humans. In *The Descent of Man* he wrote:

> But it may be asked, how within the limits of the same tribe did a large number of members first become endowed with these social and moral qualities, and how was the standard of excellence raised?
>
> It is extremely doubtful whether the offspring of the more sympathetic and benevolent parents, or of those who were the most faithful to their

comrades, would be reared in greater numbers than the children of selfish and treacherous parents belonging to the same tribe. He who was ready to sacrifice his life, as many a savage has been, rather than betray his comrades, would often leave no offspring to inherit his noble nature. The bravest men, who were always willing to come to the front in war, and who freely risked their lives for others, would on an average perish in larger numbers than other men. Therefore it hardly seems probable that the number of men gifted with such virtues, or the standard of their excellence, could be increased through natural selection, that is, by the survival of the fittest; for we are not here speaking of one tribe being victorious over another.

Darwin thought that part of the explanation was that as human reasoning powers increased, early humans would learn that if they helped their fellows, they would receive help in return; the remainder of his explanation was that virtuous behavior was fostered by the praise and blame of other members of the group. Sociobiologists do not invoke the institution of praise and blame for an explanation of altruism, since altruism occurs among non-human animals who do not praise or blame as we do. Sociobiologists have, however, developed Darwin's suggestion of the importance of the principle of reciprocity. They have suggested that two forms of altruism can be explained in terms of natural selection: kin altruism and reciprocal altruism. Some also allow a minor role for group altruism, but this is more controversial.

Kin Altruism

Evolution can, as we have seen, be regarded as a competition for survival among genes. "Gene" as I use the term does not refer to the physical bits of DNA—which cannot survive any longer than the individual wolf, blackbird, or human in which they are present—but to the type of DNA. In this sense, genes can survive indefinitely, for one bit of DNA in one generation can lead to the existence of similar bits of DNA in the next. The most obvious way in which this can be done is by reproduction. Each sperm I produce contains a random sample of half my genes; therefore each time I fertilize an egg which grows into a child, a set of half my genes takes on an independent existence, with a chance of surviving my death and in turn passing some of its genes on down through the generations. So, for example, by "the gene for brown eyes" I do not mean the particular bit of biological matter I carry which will cause my child to have brown eyes; I mean the type of biological matter which, passed on in reproduction, leads human beings to have brown eyes.

Thus strictly selfish behavior—behavior aimed at furthering my own survival without regard for anyone else—will not be favored by evolution. I am doomed in any case. The survival of my genes depends largely on my having children, and on my children having children, and so forth. Evolution will favor, other things being equal, behavior which improves the prospects of my children surviving and reproducing. Thus the first and most obvious way in which evolution can produce altruism is the concern of parents for their children. This is so widespread and natural a form of altruism that we do not usually think of it as altruism at all. Yet the sacrifices that humans as well as many non-human animals constantly make for their children represent a tremendous effort for the benefit of beings other than themselves. Thus they must count as altruism, as we have defined the term so far. * * *

But taking care of one's children is only one way of increasing the chances of one's genes surviving. When I reproduce, my children do not have all the genes I have. * * * Each child I produce contains half my genes; the other half of my children's genes comes, of course, from their mother. Each of my sisters and brothers will also, on average, have 50 percent of the same genes as I have, since, like me, they have half of my mother's and half of my father's genes. (This 50 percent is an average figure because, depending on how the genetic lottery fell out, they could have anything from all to none of their genes in common with me—but the huge number of genes involved makes either extreme fantastically unlikely.) Therefore in genetic terms my siblings are as closely related to me as my children; there is no special significance in the fact that the genes my children share with me replicate through my own body, whereas those I share with my sister did not. Assisting my brothers and sisters will enhance the prospects of my genes surviving, in much the same way as assisting my children will. (That care for siblings is not ordinarily as intense as care for offspring may be due to the fact that the difference in age makes parents able to care for their offspring when the offspring most need it, whereas siblings usually are too young to do so. In addition, in non-monogamous species full siblings are the exception, and half siblings—where the genetic relationship is only 25 percent—the rule.)

This is the basis of kin altruism: the genetically based tendency to help one's relatives. The relationship does not have to be as close as that of parents to their children or siblings to each other. The proportion of genes in common does fall off sharply as it becomes more distant—between aunts (or uncles) and their nieces (or nephews) it is 25 percent; between first cousins 12½ percent—but what is lacking in quality can be made up for by an increased quantity. Risking my life will not harm the prospects of my genes surviving if it eliminates a similar risk to the lives of two of my children, four of my nieces, or eight of my first cousins. Thus kin selection can explain why altruism should extend beyond the immediate family. In close-knit groups, where most members are related to other members, kin selection may explain altruistic behavior like giving the alarm when predators are near, which benefits the entire group.

Kin altruism does not imply that animals know how closely related they are to each other—that they can distinguish full sisters from half sisters, or cousins from unrelated animals. The theory says only that animals can be expected to act roughly as if they were aware of these relationships. In fact, since we are talking about complex living beings, there are many instances where animals do not behave in accordance with the nicely calculated fractions of genetic relationships. A female chimpanzee with many reproductive years ahead of her may sacrifice her life for a single child. African wild dogs have been observed risking their lives by attacking a cheetah that was threatening a pup that was at most a nephew to them. Evolved behavioral tendencies are not as predictable as the motions of the planets. Nevertheless, kin selection can explain some otherwise mysterious facts. For instance, why do adult zebras defend any calf in the herd attacked by a predator, whereas wildebeest do not? The reason could be that zebras live in family groups, so that adults and calves would generally all be related; wildebeest interbreed much more with other groups and adults would not be related to randomly selected calves. More startling still is the infanticide practiced by male langur monkeys. Female langurs live in groups, each under the control of a dominant male who prevents any other male from breeding with them. The other males, being unwilling bachelors, try to overthrow the dominant male and take his harem. If one should succeed, he will set about killing all the infants in his newly acquired group. This may not be good for the species as a whole, but the killer is not related to his victims; moreover, females nursing infants do not ovulate, so by removing the infants the male is able to have his own children earlier than would otherwise be possible. To these children he will be a better father. In the difference between his behavior toward infants genetically related to him and his behavior toward those that are not, the langur monkey demonstrates in a brutally clear form the kind of "altruism" that may evolve through kin selection. (Male lions have also been observed to kill infants on taking over a pride. Is there a human parallel in the wicked stepparents so common in fairy tales? Or in the mass rapes that for centuries have characterized military conquests?)

Reciprocal Altruism

Kin altruism exists because it promotes the survival of one's relatives; but not all altruistic acts help relatives. Monkeys spend a lot of their time grooming each other, removing parasites from those awkward places a monkey cannot itself reach. Monkeys grooming each other are not always related. Here reciprocal altruism offers an explanation: you scratch my back and I'll scratch yours.

Here's another example: I see a stranger drowning and I jump in to save her. Suppose that in so doing I run a 5 percent risk of drowning myself; suppose too that without my help the stranger would run a 50 percent risk of drowning, but that with my help she will be saved, except in the 5 percent of cases in which we both drown. At first glance, jumping in seems to be a purely altruistic act. I run a 5 percent risk of death in order to help a stranger. But suppose that one day I myself will need to be rescued, and the person I saved this time will then jump in and help me. Suppose that without help I would have a 50 percent chance of drowning, but with help my prospects improve to 95 percent. Then, taking the two acts together, it is in my interest to save the drowning stranger, for I thus exchange two separate small risks (the 5 percent risk I incur when I help the stranger and also when I am helped) for one large risk (the 50 percent risk I would have if I were not helped). Obviously two 5 percent risks are better than one 50 percent risk.

This is an artificial example, with the risks made precisely measurable in order to make the benefit clear. One might question the example on that ground; but there is a more important question that needs to be asked about the example: What is the link between rescuing a stranger and being rescued oneself? If one can arrange to get rescued without having to do any rescuing oneself, that seems the best strategy, from a self-interested standpoint. Why isn't that what happens? What ensures that this form of altruism is reciprocal?

On one level, the answer to this question could be that individuals can remember who has helped them and who has not, and they will not help anyone who has refused to help them. Cheats—those who take help but refuse to give it—never prosper, for their cheating is noticed and punished. If this is right we would expect reciprocal altruism only among creatures capable of recognizing other individuals, sorting them into those who help and those who do not. Reciprocity may not require human reasoning powers, but it would require intelligence. It would also be more likely in species with a relatively long life span, living in small, stable groups. For in this way, opportunities for repeated reciprocal acts would occur more frequently.

The evidence supports this conclusion. Reciprocal altruism is most common among, and perhaps limited to, birds and mammals; its clearest cases come from highly intelligent social animals like wolves, wild dogs, dolphins, baboons, chimpanzees, and human beings. In addition to grooming each other, members of these species often share food on a reciprocal basis and help each other when threatened by predators or other enemies.

On another level, there is still a problem: How did this reciprocal altruism get going? * * * If there was no deliberate contract of the "you scratch my back and I'll scratch yours" kind, the first animals to risk their lives for other, unrelated members of their species were risking their lives without much prospect of anything in return. If reciprocal altruism is widely practiced, it pays to take part—chances are, you'll benefit later. But if reciprocal altruism is rare, it might be better, from the self-interested point of view, not to put yourself out. In the drowning example just given, it would not pay to rescue another, running a 5 percent risk of drowning oneself, unless by doing so one significantly raises the chances that one will oneself be rescued when the need arises. So it is not quite true that cheats never prosper. Cheats prosper until there are enough who bear grudges against them to make sure they do not prosper. If we imagine a group consisting partly of those who accept help but give none—"cheats"—and partly of those who accept help and give help to all except those who have refused to help—call them "grudgers"—there is a critical number of how many grudgers there must be before it pays to be a grudger rather than a cheat. One grudger in a population of cheats will get cheated often and never be helped; but the more grudgers and fewer cheats there are, the more often the grudger will be repaid for her help and the more rarely she will be cheated. So while we can understand why reciprocal altruism should prosper after it gets established, it is less easy to see why the genes leading to this form of behavior did not get eliminated as soon as they appeared.

Group Altruism

It may be that to explain how reciprocal altruism can get established, we need to allow a limited role for a form of group selection. Imagine that a species is divided into several isolated groups—perhaps they are monkeys whose terrain is divided by rivers which, except in rare droughts, are too swift to cross. Now suppose that reciprocal altruism somehow appears from time to time in each of these groups. Let us say that one monkey grooms another monkey, searching for disease-carrying parasites; when it has finished it presents its own back to be groomed. If the genes that make this behavior probable are rare mutations, in most cases the altruistic monkey would find its kindness unrewarded; the groomed monkey would simply move away. Grooming strangers would therefore bring no advantage, and since it leads the monkey to spend its time helping strangers instead of looking after itself, in time this behavior would be eliminated. This elimination may not be good for the group as a whole, but as we have seen, within the group it is individual rather than group selection that dominates.

Now suppose that in one of these isolated groups it just happens that a lot of monkeys have genes leading them to initiate grooming exchanges. (In a small, closely related group, kin altruism might bring this about.) Then, as we have seen, those who reciprocate could be better off than those who do not. They will groom and be groomed, remaining healthy while other members of the group succumb to the parasites. Thus in this particular isolated group, possessing the genes for reciprocal grooming will be a distinct advantage. In time, all the group would have them.

There is one final step. The reciprocal grooming group now has an advantage, as a group, over other groups who do not have any way of ridding themselves of parasites. If the parasites get really bad, the other groups may become extinct, and one dry summer the pressure of population growth in the recipocal grooming group will push some of its members across the rivers into the territories formerly occupied by the other groups. In this way group selection could have a limited role—limited because the required conditions would not often occur—in the spread of reciprocal altruism.

* * * A group would have to keep itself distinct from other groups for group altruism to work—otherwise more egoistically inclined outsiders would work their way into the group, taking advantage of the altruism of members of the group without offering anything in return. They would

then outbreed the more altruistic members of the group and so begin to outnumber them, until the group would cease to be more altruistic than any other group of the same species. Although this would cost it its evolutionary advantage over other groups, there would be no mechanism for stopping this. If the group altruism had been essential to the group's survival, the group would simply die out.

This suggests that group altruism would work best when coupled with a degree of hostility to outsiders, which would protect the altruism within the group from penetration and subversion from outside. Hostility to outsiders is, in fact, a very common phenomenon in social animals. Although there is a popular myth that human beings are the only animals who kill members of their own species, other species can be as unpleasant toward foreigners as we are. Many social animals, from ants through chickens to rats, will attack and often kill outsiders placed in their midst. * * *

It may be objected that in a small, isolated group of the kind I have described, there will be so much interbreeding that all members of the group will be related to each other, and so what we have is not group selection at all, but rather kin selection in the special case in which all the group are kin to each other. This may be so; certainly kin and non-kin selection will be hard to distinguish in this situation. Nevertheless, when members of the group behave in certain ways toward all other members of the group—irrespective of whether they are full siblings or very distant cousins—and when this behavior gives the entire group a selective advantage over other groups, it is reasonable to describe what is going on as "group selection" even if it may ultimately be possible to explain what is going on in terms of kin selection.

Keeping outsiders away would not be enough to prevent erosion of high levels of self-sacrificing behavior for the benefit of the group. Evolutionary theory would lead us to expect a drift back toward selfishness within the group, since individuals who behaved selfishly would reap the benefits of the sacrifices of others without making any sacrifices themselves. Perhaps, though, a group could develop a way of dealing with a small number of free-riders who emerge within it. Human societies, at least, have institutions which serve this end; but here we are beginning to look beyond the development of altruism in non-human animals to its existence in our own species.

STUDY QUESTIONS
1. Explain the difference between kin, reciprocal, and group altruism.
2. Why is group altruism susceptible to free-riding and breakdown?
3. Can evolutionary arguments explain our moral duties to people to whom we are not closely related?

PART 2

normative
ethics

I n Part 2 we turn to normative ethics, where the issues move away from the meta-ethical problems of the nature of ethics to the more practical questions of what morality requires of us. Of course there will often be close connections between meta-ethics and normative ethics, but normative ethics has a much more direct tie to action.

We start with St. Thomas Aquinas on "natural law." Aquinas distinguishes between what he calls "the eternal law," which is God's plan for the world based on his divine wisdom; "the natural law," which is that part of the eternal law accessible to human reason; and "the human law," which concerns the way human beings order the world for themselves, albeit in accordance with reason and the natural law. As mentioned, our main topic here is the natural law. Aquinas explains his position both by contrasting natural law with eternal and human law, and by setting out and replying to objections to his account.

For Aquinas, all laws, ultimately, concern themselves with the happiness of the community, and, indeed, all laws presuppose a proper end or outcome, to which we have a natural inclination. In the case of the natural law, the end includes our desire to pursue our own good, in the sense of self-preservation. Aquinas claims that our natural inclinations also include the union of man and woman and the education of children and the desire to know the truth about God and to live in society with others. The natural law, then, is that set of laws, accessible through the use of our reason, to achieve these goals.

The natural law, says Aquinas, can be derived by natural reason. It is in that sense self-evident. Yet he admits that not everyone is equally capable of easily making the necessary derivations. Whether something is self-evident is ultimately a matter of logic, but Aquinas further argues that in many cases only the wise are capable of making the deductions in order to grasp the truth. Furthermore, although the natural law is the same for all people at the level of principle, when we look at particular cases the law can require what seem to be exceptions, such as not repaying a debt to someone who intends evil with the money. The highest-level principles of the natural law are said to be unchanging, but they can be added to by God's command or human invention.

We move next to a very different figure, Ayn Rand, a novelist and public intellectual who has had an enormous influence in American public thought, inspiring citizens, think tanks, and businesspeople. Her influence in academic philosophy is much more limited: She is often dismissed as having little to contribute, a crude advocate of a form of dogmatic selfish individualism. However, in this extract we see her sketching a view that, while clearly advocating a form of individualism and rejecting altruistic self-sacrifice, equally involves concern for others. Rand uses an expanded concept of benevolence, in which one contributes to the lives of others through love or affection, rather than by making sacrifices.

Rand displays impatience with traditional ethics, which often raises questions that are far from ordinary experience and depicts others as passive victims in need of help. Commonly, moral philosophy contrasts the self-sacrificing altruist to the almost psychopathic person who pays no attention to others. Neither alternative, argues Rand, does justice to our situation as human beings, in which benefiting particular others can often be an expression of our highest values. Rand uses the example of a man who can save his wife's life by spending a great deal of money or, alternatively, can save ten other women, letting his wife die. Rand claims that altruism would call for saving the strangers. Objectivism, which is the name she gives to her view, says that the morally good action depends on both self-interest and the hierarchy of your own values, which in this case is very likely to instruct you to save your wife, even if the strangers will die. The virtue in saving the life of the one you love Rand calls "integrity" rather than altruism.

Rand does admit that in emergencies we can have extensive duties to strangers. However, she criticizes advocates of altruism for treating ordinary life as if it is always an emergency.

Next we return to Plato. This extract is taken from Book II of Plato's *Republic*, one of the most important works in the Western philosophical tradition. It is written in dialogue form, with Plato's teacher Socrates as the central figure. We enter at a point where Thrasymachus, a character in the dialogue, has just departed, after energetically presenting the view that "justice is the interest of the stronger." This skeptical thesis presents justice as a type of cloak or screen by which the powerful attempt to legitimize their power. Socrates, refusing to accept this argument, wants to defend the thesis that justice is good for its own sake, as well as for the results it can bring. However, he has not satisfied the others who are also listening to the discussion. So the skeptical case is restated, in a more reasoned form, by Glaucon and Adeimantus, who, in real life, were Plato's brothers.

Glaucon begins with three arguments, not, he says, because he believes them, but because he thinks they state the common position and he wants to hear Socrates' reply. First, Glaucon presents the view that justice is a kind of compromise. Ideally, we would all wish to act according to our own selfish interests. Yet if we did this, each of us would be liable to harm caused by others in pursuit of their own interests. Hence morality is a kind of social contract, or compromise, as it is the best we can collectively achieve (this argument is very similar to the theory of reciprocal altruism, mentioned in Peter Singer's essay in Part 1). This position denies that justice is good in itself, of course.

Glaucon develops this line of argument by introducing "the ring of Gyges," a mythical ring that gave the person who wore it the power to become invisible. Glaucon argues that anyone who really did have this ring would use it unjustly in order to obtain advantages at the cost of others. This, he suggests, is further evidence that people act justly because of the consequences and not because of any intrinsic motivation for justice. And Glaucon's third challenge is to compare an unjust person who has a reputation for justice with a just person who is wrongly thought to be unjust and is punished for this supposed injustice. Glaucon suggests that everyone would consider the life of the unjust person preferable to that of the just.

Adeimantus adds that when parents educate their children to act justly, they say that justice is important because of the value of having the reputation for justice, rather than for its intrinsic good. And that reputation is valuable for the good fortune it is likely to bring. Adeimantus adds that the rich and powerful are admired and the poor and weak despised, independently of whether they are, in fact, just or not.

Glaucon and Adeimantus set these objections out in order for Socrates to reply. The rest of the long dialogue known as *The Republic* is Socrates' attempt to answer these very powerful arguments.

The theme of the social contract is continued in Thomas Hobbes's *Leviathan*, perhaps the most important work of political philosophy written in English. Hobbes sets out his bleak vision of what life would be like in a "state of nature," without government. Life, he says, would be "solitary, poore, nasty, brutish and short." In a state of nature, without laws and punishment to constrain people, everyone would live in fear of others, for no one is strong enough to be invulnerable to others. As a result, people would attack each other and their property, for three reasons: for gain, as a preemptive strike for safety, and for glory or reputation. It would be a war of all against all, at least in the sense that all people would need to be on their guard at all times.

Although our predicament in the state of nature leads us to war, Hobbes believes that the "law of nature" suggests "convenient articles of peace," by which human beings can live together in cooperation. The immediate difficulty is how to avoid war and achieve peace. The solution, for Hobbes, is for each person to lay down the right to attack others, in favor of the sovereign, the Leviathan, who can ensure peace. Of course, the laying down of the right especially of self-defense has to be conditional on all other people doing the same thing, to avoid extreme vulnerability. Under such circumstances, which Hobbes regards as a social contract, we would be able to reap the fruits of cooperation and civilization. Hobbes makes a point of arguing that the fact that the contract is entered into out of fear does not invalidate it. For Hobbes, the social contract is the basis of right and wrong: Injustice is defined in terms of not performing "covenants."

Hobbes's position bears comparison with the idea of "justice as a compromise" put forward by Glaucon in the previous extract from Plato's *Republic*. Glaucon presented it as a skeptical thesis for Plato to refute, but Hobbes takes a different perspective, regarding the social contract as the welcome truth about morality.

John Rawls's *A Theory of Justice* takes the idea of the social contract in a new direction. This book is often regarded as the most important contribution to political philosophy of the 20th century. Rawls introduces the related ideas of the "original position" and the "veil of ignorance" to provide a modern development of social contract theory. Part of the heart of the social contract theory of morality is the idea that our moral duties are what we would agree to in a contract made between all people. The difficulty is that, because people have different interests and values, it is not obvious that they would agree to very much beyond mutual noninterference, if even that.

Rawls's extension to the theory is to suppose that we should imagine a hypothetical contract made between free and equal people who want to advance their own interests but are placed behind what he calls a "veil of ignorance." Rawls's assumption of freedom and equality has radical consequences. It leads him to model the contract as being made between people who are ignorant about the sorts of facts about themselves that are likely to lead them to different views about justice. These facts include such things as your sex, race, or religion, your skills, your family background, your age, and even your ideas about justice or what you want out of life (your conception of the good). Such ignorance means that you need to be very cautious in what you would agree to, for you could otherwise agree to an outcome that would be highly problematic. For once the veil of ignorance is lifted, you would find yourself in whatever society you agreed to. If, for example, you had agreed to religious intolerance but then find that you are a member of a minority religion, your life would be very badly affected. Hence you are much more likely to seek agreement to tolerant, inclusive arrangements. In this way we can see Rawls's hypothetical contract, made under conditions of ignorance, as a very promising method to use when thinking about moral questions. In essence it asks you to consider what solution would be acceptable if you didn't know what role in the situation you were playing and therefore could find yourself suffering if a one-sided decision were made.

Rawls argues that particular principles would be chosen from behind the veil of ignorance (and we will return to this idea in a later reading). Those principles are to be tested by considering their consequences for the real world and whether those consequences match our "considered convictions," such as, for example, the idea that racial discrimination is unjust. Rawls imagines that we can adjust the conditions of the original position so that it yields principles that generate acceptable consequences. Going between principles and consequences in this way Rawls calls the process of "reflective equilibrium," suggesting that we can make adjustments to any of our beliefs so that they finally constitute a set that we can accept.

We move next to an extract from Jeremy Bentham, who was the first systematic defender of the moral theory known as utilitarianism. According to utilitarianism, the right action to do in any circumstance is that which will lead to the greatest balance of happiness over unhappiness, or pleasure over pain. Hence it is also known as the "greatest happiness principle." In this extract from his book *An Introduction to the Principles of Morals and Legislation*, Bentham sets out the basic concepts of the theory. He also compares it to alternative theories, which he calls "the principle of asceticism" (maximize the balance of pain over pleasure) and "the principle of sympathy and antipathy" (actions are right or wrong depending on how the theorist feels toward them). Bentham finds it easy to argue against both these alternatives, leaving utilitarianism as the only theory standing. Whether this is a good argument for utilitarianism is highly debatable, but the arguments help illustrate what Bentham was seeking in a moral theory. First, it must take human (and animal) pleasure and pain very seriously, and second it must provide an external standpoint that can be used to assess the morality of actions, rather than leaving it to individual judgment. The utilitarian moral theory does both of these things.

Bentham goes on to explain how pleasure and pain are to be measured, which is an issue of critical importance for a utilitarian. If we seek to maximize something, then it is obvious that it has to be quantified. Questions remain about whether Bentham has really said enough to make this possible, and in particular whether he has given enough attention to the question of how to measure the intensity of pleasures and pains.

John Stuart Mill, a philosophical "disciple" of Bentham, also sets out to defend utilitarianism. Mill follows much of Bentham's own definition and position. Part of Mill's purpose is to ward off what he regards as misunderstandings of the theory that treat the greatest happiness principle as a doctrine "worthy only of swine" because it focuses on pleasure and pleasure alone. Replying that human beings are capable of much more refined pleasures than pigs, Mill modifies the theory, adding that pleasures can be of different qualities. Mill suggests that there are higher and lower pleasures. The higher pleasures seem to be those that engage the intellect, such as the enjoyment of poetry. How the distinction between higher and lower pleasures is to be made, and the consequences for utilitarianism, are matters for debate. For example, once we admit that there are different types of pleasures, it is much harder to understand what it would mean to maximize the sum total of pleasure, for how are higher and lower pleasures to be measured against each other?

Mill adds a further development to the theory by attempting to provide a type of proof for utilitarianism. Mill argues that just as the only proof that something is visible is that people see it, the only proof that something is desirable is that people desire it. As people do desire happiness, it would then follow that happiness is desirable, which is part of the utilitarian position. (The other part is to argue that happiness is the only thing that is desirable as an ultimate end, for which Mill also argues.) Some have objected that this argument problematically assumes too close an analogy between the terms "visible" and "desirable." Visible means "capable of being seen," whereas desirable does not mean "capable of being desired" but rather "ought to be desired." It is, therefore, not clear that the proof does establish what Mill wants.

The next extract, from *Anarchy, State, and Utopia* by Robert Nozick, attempts to show readers that they do not believe one of the key elements of utilitarianism: that happiness is the only thing that is desirable. Nozick imagines that a machine has been invented that can provide people with any experience that they want. Accordingly, you will be able to experience whatever it is that makes you happy. When in the machine, you would not know that you were plugged in; instead, you would have experiences that match how you would feel in real life. Would you plug in? If you have any resistance to this idea (other than on the grounds that you do not believe it would work as described), then it seems you cannot believe that happiness is the sole good, for this machine could give you all the happiness you desire. For those reluctant to surrender to the machine, there must be something else that makes life valuable. Nozick suggests that the extra element is a type of authenticity: You want actually to achieve things and be someone, not simply have the experience of doing so. Therefore, Nozick concludes, utilitarianism in its classic formulation is unsatisfactory.

We turn next to a very different theory of morality. In this extract from *Groundwork of the Metaphysics of Morals*, Immanuel Kant sets out the heart of his moral philosophy in terms of the fundamental principle, which he calls "the categorical imperative": "Act only in accordance with that maxim through which you can at the same time will that it become a universal law." The maxim of an action is a type of general rule. For example, if I am tempted to lie to get out of a difficulty, my maxim, turned into a universal law, would be "Always tell a lie if it will get you out of a difficulty." Yet, Kant thinks, we could not have such a law, for if people were free to tell lies, conventions of truth-telling would come to an end and it would be impossible to tell a lie. The fact that it is impossible to universalize the maxim of your action shows, for Kant, that your action is immoral.

Kant has several different formulations of the categorical imperative. The formula just set out is known as the formula of universal law. Equally important is the formula of humanity, which states, "So act that you use humanity, whether in your own person or in the person of any other, always at the same time as an end, never merely as a means." Kant does not preclude using others as means to an end so long as you respect their own ends too. And notice that Kant suggests it is possible to treat yourself as a mere means too, a concept which has echoes in ordinary morality such as when we accuse people of lacking self-respect. A third formulation of the categorical imperative, very similar to the first, makes use of the idea of a "kingdom of ends." When we act in accordance with universal laws and treat all other people as ends, we can regard ourselves, through our actions, as sovereign, making law for the kingdom of ends.

In the next article, we see a feminist critique of the type of moral philosophy set out both by utilitarians and by Kant. Annette Baier draws on the important psychological work of Carol Gilligan. Gilligan distinguishes what she calls "the ethics of justice" from the "ethics of care." The ethics of justice is exemplified especially in Kantian moral philosophy but also in utilitarianism, by supposing that the highest form of moral reasoning consists in the use of abstract general principles that can be applied broadly to moral questions. The ethics of justice is very appealing in that, if correct, it provides a principled and rigorous way of settling moral questions. However, Gilligan argues that the ethics of justice is a distinctively male way of approaching moral questions and that her empirical research revealed another way, based on what she calls "the ethics of care," more typically used by women. The ethics of care refuses to attempt to reduce complex moral situations to abstract problems that can be resolved by the application of reason. Rather it pays attention to the complexities of each particular situation, giving special concern to the individuals affected and their relations to each other. It takes relationships and human interdependence as a given part of life, rather than acquired through voluntary agreement. The ethics of care opposes the detachment of the moral subject as depicted within the ethics of justice. It also sees emotion as essential to moral perception, rather than a clouding factor.

While it may be highly plausible that men and women are likely to approach ethical questions in these different ways, it is important to consider what is meant to follow from this assumption. As Baier points out, one problematic interpretation is that the research provides evidence that men and women have different natures. Pushed further, this assumption could be used to bolster an argument that men are better suited to professions such as the law and politics, in which impartial abstract reasoning is required, and women more suited to "caring" roles. But this would be a deeply retrograde step for feminist philosophers, reinscribing the sexist culture that feminism has tried so hard to undo over recent decades. Baier is determined not to take this supposed lesson from Gilligan's research, instead using it to point out a kind of one-sidedness in the ethics of justice, including Kantian moral philosophy, arguing instead that both justice and care must be part of a complete ethical account.

It is common now to suggest that there are three main traditions of moral philosophy. We have seen two of them, utilitarianism and Kantian ethics (also sometimes called deontology). The next selection, from Aristotle's *Nicomachean Ethics*, introduces the third, virtue ethics. A virtue is a disposition of character, such as bravery, which typically involves characteristic patterns of deliberation, emotion, and action. On this approach, morality is as much about becoming the right sort of person as it is about performing the right sort of actions. Virtue, says Aristotle, is an activity of the soul rather than the body.

The virtues, for Aristotle, are those character traits that will help us live well and achieve happiness over a complete life. For many people, Aristotle says, virtue and pleasure conflict, but those who have genuinely achieved virtue will take pleasure in acting well. Achieving virtue, Aristotle argues, is facilitated by the possession of external goods such as wealth, friendship, and good children. Moral virtue is not innate and has to be acquired or cultivated. It is largely a matter of practice. For example, we learn how to become just by performing just actions.

Aristotle suggests that, typically, virtue is a "mean" or intermediate between excess and deficiency. For example, the virtue of pride is intermediate between two vices: "empty vanity," which is the excess, and "undue humility," which is the deficiency. Although, as Aristotle admits, not all virtues fall into this pattern—an excess of justice, for example, might not be possible—it is a helpful way of thinking about many virtues. Aristotle runs through many examples, concluding that it is not always an easy task to be good.

The work of the ancient Chinese philosopher Confucius makes a very interesting comparison with the ancient Greek philosopher Aristotle, who lived 200 years later. In these two chapters from his great work *The Analects,*

Confucius sets out his approach to moral wisdom. Although the style of their writing is very different, Confucius, like Aristotle, is very focused on conditions under which people will be able cultivate the most desirable forms of virtues of character. Morality, for Confucius, is a form of wisdom as well as action. To this degree, the ideas of Aristotle and Confucius are similar. However, Confucius's doctrines differ from Aristotle's in a number of important ways.

One immediate contrast with Aristotle is Confucius's attitude to what Aristotle called "external goods." While Aristotle argues that virtue is facilitated by possession of wealth, Confucius confronts the issue that acting virtuously could lead to poverty and exile. In that case, Confucius suggests that principle should be put above wealth, very difficult though that will be. Here Confucius is closer to Plato than to Aristotle. Confucius's model of a virtuous person is someone who acts with humility and integrity. While these are, of course, virtues for Aristotle too, Aristotle also emphasizes much more outward facing virtues, such as generosity and being a good companion.

A further notable difference is that Confucius pays a great deal of attention to the value of ritual, which does not appear in Aristotle's account. For Confucius, loyalty and obedience are primary virtues. Confucius's writings contain much wisdom about what is most valuable in life, what we should aim for, and how we should conduct ourselves in relation to others, emphasizing the value of humanity. Even though he wrote so long ago and in a quite different world, we still have much to learn from him.

Like Aristotle and Confucius, contemporary philosopher Virginia Held is also interested in thinking about ethics from the perspective of character traits and their development. However, she adds to the analysis a distinctively feminist aspect. Like Annette Baier, she draws on the insights from the "ethics of care," which understands persons as interdependent and relational, embedded in family and social historical contexts. Held begins by setting out her understanding of a "moral subject," drawing on a narrative conception in which our identities are partly constituted by the stories we construct. By such means, we both respond to the context in which we live but also shape our own lives.

Held notes that some feminists have felt that an Aristotelian, virtue-based approach to ethics is a useful way of incorporating the ethics of care into a moral theory. However, Held makes a subtle distinction between what she calls the virtue of caring and being a caring person. Virtue ethics, she says, typically sees virtues as attaching to individuals, whereas the ethics of care is more interested in relations between persons. She notes that two people who display the virtue of caring may still fail to develop a caring relationship between the two of them, for example by being hostile or even intrusively caring on occasion. The right types of relations are more important than simply developing the right types of dispositions. Hence she regards the ethics of care as an alternative to virtue ethics rather than a component of it. Indeed, the virtue of care can go too far, in the direction of servility.

Held raises the question of whether autonomy is consistent with being a caring person, for having obligations to others could be thought to be in conflict with the type of freedom of choice associated with autonomy. Held argues that such a traditional conception of autonomy rests on a myth of natural independence and self-sufficiency. In its place she develops a concept of mutual autonomy that starts from the facts of our mutual interdependence and emphasizes the centrality of cooperation to the development of our capacities and aims.

In the final extract of Part 2, Jean-Paul Sartre provides an introduction to a different type of moral theory compared to those considered so far, existentialist ethics. He initially provides a response to criticisms and then develops the heart of the theory and its consequences.

The existentialist slogan is "Existence precedes essence." This is best understood by contrast with an object such as a knife, which has a purpose and is made to fulfill that purpose. For a knife, its purpose or function, and hence its essence, precedes its existence. On a theological worldview, we can say the same thing about human beings. If human beings are born to fulfill God's purposes, as we saw, for example, in the excerpt from Aquinas, then the essence of each human being is determined by God, even before any particular individual exists. Hence essence precedes existence. But Sartre's atheism asserts that there is no God, and hence there is no plan for us set out by God. This assumption leads Sartre to declare that our existence precedes our essence, meaning in effect that each one of us has to work out our life plan for ourselves—a view combining an exhilarating level of freedom with heavy responsibility. And this freedom and responsibility are the heart of the existentialist ethic. Human beings, says Sartre, are "condemned to be free," and this freedom is also a source of anguish.

To illustrate the depth of our individual freedom and responsibility, Sartre tells the story of a student who, during the Second World War, had to choose between staying with his mother or joining the French Resistance. Sartre argues that neither Christian nor Kantian morality can provide an answer to this dilemma, and in the end the student has no choice but to rely on his instincts. There is no way of delegating the decision to an external system of thought, whether religious or secular. The fact that there is nothing outside of ourselves to turn to is the reason why Sartre claims that existentialism is a form of humanism: There is nothing other than the human world to rely on.

ST. THOMAS AQUINAS
The Natural Law

St. Thomas Aquinas (1225–1274) was probably the most important theologian and philosopher in the Catholic tradition, notable especially for his Summa Theologica, *in which ethical and religious questions are treated together. He is also a major natural law theorist.*

THE TREATISE ON LAW

Qu. 90. The Essence of Law

* * *

2 Is Law Always Directed toward the Common Good? Every part is ordered to the whole as the imperfect is to the perfect. The individual is part of a perfect whole that is the community. Therefore law must concern itself in particular with the happiness of the community. * * *

Qu. 91. The Kinds of Law

1 Is There an Eternal Law? We have stated above that law is nothing else than a certain dictate of practical reason by a ruler who governs some perfect community. Assuming that the world is governed by divine providence as we argued in Part I, it is evident that the whole community of the universe is governed by the divine reason. Therefore the rational governance of everything on the part of God, as the ruler of the universe, has the quality of law. And since the divine reason's conception of things is not subject to time but is eternal, this kind of law must be called the eternal law.

2 Is There a Natural Law? Since everything that is subject to divine providence is regulated and measured by the eternal law, as we have shown above, it is evident that all things participate in the eternal law in a certain way because it is imprinted upon them through their respective inclinations to their proper actions and ends. Rational creatures are under divine providence in a more excellent way than the others since by providing for themselves and others they share in the action of providence themselves. They participate in eternal reason in that they have a natural inclination to their proper actions and ends. Such participation in the eternal law by rational creatures is called the natural law.

3 Is There Human Law? The speculative reason proceeds from naturally known indemonstrable principles to the conclusions of the various sciences which are not innate in us but are acquired by the effort of our reason. In the same way human reason must proceed from the precepts of the natural law as from certain common and indemonstrable principles to other more particular dispositions. Those particular dispositions arrived at by reason are called human laws.

4 Was There a Need for Divine Law? Besides the natural law and human law it was necessary to have the divine law to direct human life. This is for four reasons: First, law directs man to actions that are appropriately ordered to his final end. If man were destined to an end which did not exceed the natural capacity of mankind, there would be no need for his reason to direct him in any other way than through the natural law and the humanly enacted law that is derived from it. But because man is destined to the end of eternal bliss (*beatitudo*) which exceeds the capacity of the natural human faculties, as explained above, it was necessary for him to be directed to this end by a divinely revealed law, in addition to the natural and human law. Secondly, because of the uncertainly of human judgment, especially in contingent and particular matters, it happens that different decisions are made about different human acts, so that laws are often divergent and even contradictory. For man to know what he should do and not do without any doubt it was necessary for him to be directed in his actions by a law given by God, for it is certain that such a law cannot err. Thirdly, man can make laws about matters that are capable of being judged. But man cannot make a judgment about internal motivations that are hidden, but only about external actions that are public. To be perfectly virtuous, however, man must be upright in both kinds of action. Therefore since human law could not punish or direct interior actions sufficiently, it was necessary for there to be a divine law. Fourthly, as Augustine says, human law cannot punish or prohibit every evil action because in trying to eliminate evils it may also do away with many good things and the interest of the common good which is necessary for human society may be adversely affected. Therefore in order for no evil to go unforbidden and un-punished, it was necessary for there to be a divine law which forbids all sin.

• • •

By the natural law human nature participates in the eternal law in pro-portion to the capacity of human nature. But man needs to be directed to his supernatural end in a higher way. Hence there is an additional law given by God through which man shares more perfectly in the eternal law. ✳ ✳ ✳

• • •

A tyrannical law, since it is not in accordance with reason, is not a law in the strict sense, but rather a perversion of law. However it has something of the character of law to the extent that it intends that the citizens should be good. It only has the character of a law because it is a dictate of a superior over his subjects and is aimed at their obeying law—which is a good that is not absolute but only relative to a specific regime.

Qu. 93. The Eternal Law

1 Does the Eternal Law Exist in the Highest Reason of God? Just as in the mind of every artist there is a plan of what he will create by his art, so in the mind of every ruler there must already exist a plan as to what is to be done by those subject to his government. And just as the plan of the things to be produced by an art is called the art or exemplar of the things to be produced, so the plan of a ruler concerning the actions of his subjects has the quality of law, provided that the other conditions for a law that we have mentioned are met. God in his wisdom is the creator of all things and is related to them in the same way as an artist is related to his works of art, as we said in Part I. He governs all the actions and motions that are found in individual creatures, as we also explained in Part I. Therefore just as the plan of divine wisdom in accordance with which all things are created by it has the character of an art, or exemplar, or idea, so the plan of divine wisdom moving all things to their appropriate ends has the quality of law. Accordingly, the eternal law is nothing else than the rational plan of divine wisdom considered as directing all actions and movements.

3 Is All Law Derived from the Eternal Law? Human law has the quality of a law in so far as it is in accordance with right reason and in this respect it is evident that it is derived from the eternal law. If it deviates from the right reason it is said to be an unjust law, and thus does not have the character of a law but rather that of an act of violence. ✳ ✳ ✳

Qu. 94. The Natural Law

2 Does the Natural Law Contain One Precept or Many? The precepts of the natural law are related to the practical reason as the first principles of [logical] demonstration are related to the speculative reason. Both are principles that are self-evident. Something can be described as self-evident in two ways—either, in itself, or in relation to us. A proposition is said to be self-evident in itself if its predicate is contained in its subject—although it may happen that someone who does not know the subject will not know that the proposition is self-evident. Thus the proposition, "Man is a rational being" is by its nature self-evident since when we say "man" we are also saying "rational," but for someone who does not know what a man is, this is not a self-evident proposition. Thus Boethius says that certain axioms and propositions are generally known in themselves by everyone. The terms of these propositions are known to everyone—for example, that every whole is greater than its parts or that two things equal to the same thing are equal to each other. But some propositions are only known to the wise who understand the meaning of the terms used in the proposition. For example to someone who knows that an angel is not a body it is self-evident that it is not located in a particular place, but this is not evident to the unlearned for they can not grasp it.

A certain order is to be found in the things that are apprehended by men. The first thing that is apprehended is being, and a knowledge of this is implied in every act of apprehension. Therefore the undemonstrable first principle is that something cannot be affirmed and denied at the same time. This principle is based on the notion of being and non-being. All other principles are based on this, as Book IV of the *Metaphysics* says. Just as being is the first thing that is apprehended absolutely, so also good is the first thing that is apprehended by the practical reason which is directed towards action, since everything that acts does so for an end which possesses the quality of goodness. Therefore the first principle of the practical reason is based on the nature of the good, i.e., "Good is that which all things seek." Hence the first precept of law is that good is to be done and pursued, and evil is to be avoided. All the other precepts of the law of nature are based on this, so that all the things that are to be done or evils to be avoided belong to the precepts of the natural law which the practical reason naturally apprehends as human goods.

• • •

Since good has the nature of an end and evil its opposite, all the things to which man has a natural inclination are naturally apprehended by the reason as good and therefore as objects to be pursued, and their opposites as evils to be avoided. Therefore the order of the precepts of the natural law follows the order of our natural inclinations. There is in man, first, an inclination to the good that he shares by nature with all substances, since every substance seeks to preserve itself according to its own nature. Corresponding to this inclination the natural law contains those things that preserve human life and prevent its destruction. Secondly, there is in man an inclination to certain more specific ends in accordance with the nature that he shares with other animals. In accordance with this, the natural law is said to contain "what nature has taught all animals," such as the union of man and woman, the education of children, etc. Thirdly, there is in man a natural inclination to the good of the rational nature which is his alone. Thus man has a natural inclination to know the truth about God and to live in society. Thus the things that pertain to inclinations of this kind belong to the natural law, such as that man should avoid ignorance, that he should not offend others with whom he must associate, and other related actions. . . .

4. Is the Natural Law the Same for All Men? *Obj. 3.* We have said above that whatever man is inclined to by his nature belongs to the natural law. But different men are naturally inclined to different things—some to a desire for pleasure, others to a desire for honor and other men to other things. Therefore the Natural Law is not the same for all men.

I answer that, as we have just said, all the things to which man is inclined by nature belong to the natural law. One of the things that is proper to man is that he is inclined to act in accordance with reason. Reason proceeds from general principles to particulars, as is stated in Book I of the *Physics.*[1] However the speculative reason differs from the practical reason in the way that it does this. The speculative reason is concerned with necessary truths which cannot be other than they are, so that truth is found as surely in its particular conclusions as in its general principles. Practical reason, however, works with the contingent things related to human actions. Therefore although there is a certain necessity in its general principles, the further one goes down into specifics the more frequently one encounters exceptions.

. . . And so it is evident that as to the general principles of reason, whether speculative or practical, there is a single standard of truth and right for everyone which is known by everyone. However when it comes to the

---

1   Aristotle, *Physics*, I, I.

specific conclusions of the speculative reason, the truth is the same for everyone but it is not equally known by everyone. It is universally true, for instance, that the three angles of a triangle are equal to two right angles but not everyone knows this. When we come to the particular conclusions of the practical reason there is neither the same standard of truth and rightness for everyone nor are these conclusions equally known by everyone. It is right and true for everyone to act in accordance with reason. A particular conclusion that follows from this principle is that loans should be repaid. This is true in most cases, but it can happen in a particular case that it would be harmful and therefore irrational to repay a loan, for instance if someone wanted to use it to make war on his country. And exceptions become more likely the more we come down to particular cases, for instance, if the loan was to be repaid with a certain guarantee or in a certain way. The more particular conditions are involved, the more exceptions there can be as to whether it is right to repay or not to repay the loan.

Thus we must conclude that as far as its general first principles are concerned the natural law is the same for all, both as a standard of right action and as to the possibility that it can be known. However as to more particular cases which are conclusions, as it were, from its general principles it is the same for everyone in most cases, both as a standard of right action and as known (by all). However in particular instances there can be exceptions both with regard to their rightness because of certain obstacles (just as obstacles can produce exceptional cases among the things that grow and decay in nature) and to their being known. This can happen because the reason of some has been corrupted by passion or bad habits, or because of an evil disposition of nature, as Julius Caesar writes that at one time robbery was not considered wrong among the Germans even though it is expressly contrary to the law of nature. . . .

5 Can the Natural Law Be Changed? *Obj. 2.* The killing of the innocent, adultery, and theft are contrary to the natural law. But we find these things changed by God. God commanded Abraham to kill his innocent son; He commanded the Jews to steal the borrowed vessels of the Egyptians; and He commanded Hosea to take a "wife of fornication." Therefore the natural law can be changed.

Obj. 3. Isidore [of Seville] says that "the possession of all things in common and universal freedom are part of natural law." However we see that these things have been changed by human laws. Therefore it seems that natural law is changeable.

I answer that the natural law can be changed in two ways. First, something can be added to it. Nothing prevents the natural law from being changed in this way, since both the divine law and human laws have added to the natural law many provisions that are useful to human life. Secondly, the natural law can be understood to have changed by having something taken away from it, so that what was previously in accordance with the natural law ceases to be part of it. In this respect as far as its first principles are concerned, the natural law is altogether unchangeable. But as to the secondary precepts which we have said follow as immediate conclusions from the first principles the natural law does not change in the sense that what the natural law contains is always right in the majority of cases. However it can be changed in some particular aspect and in a few cases because some special reasons make its precepts impossible to observe. . . .

Reply to Obj. 2. Both the guilty and the innocent die natural deaths. Natural death is inflicted by the power of God as a result of original sin, according to I Kings [Samuel], "The Lord killeth and maketh alive." Therefore it is not unjust for God to command that death be inflicted on any man, whether guilty or innocent. In the same way adultery is intercourse with the wife of another man who has been given to him by the divine law that comes from God. Therefore for someone to have intercourse with another woman at the command of God is not adultery or fornication. The same thing is true of theft which is taking something that belongs to someone else. If someone takes something because of the command of God to whom everything belongs he is not taking something against the will of its owner which is what theft is. It is not only in human things that whatever God does is right. In the natural world as well whatever God does is in a certain sense natural.

Reply to Obj. 3. Something is said to be part of the natural law in two ways. First because there is a natural inclination to it, for example, that one should not harm other persons. Second, if nature does not produce the contrary. Thus we could say that man goes naked by natural law because human invention, not nature, has given him clothes. In this sense "the possession of all things in common and universal freedom" can be said to be part of natural law since neither separate possessions nor slavery resulted from nature, but they were produced by human reason for the benefit of human life. Thus in these cases the law of nature was not changed but added to.

STUDY QUESTIONS

1. Explain the relation between eternal law, natural law, and human law.
2. What, for Aquinas, is the basis of natural law?
3. How do human beings come to know the natural law, according to Aquinas?

AYN RAND
The Ethics of Emergencies

Ayn Rand (1905–1982) was a Russian/American novelist and philosopher. She continues to be highly influential in American public intellectual life as a defender of free market economics and, relatedly, a form of individualism.

The psychological results of altruism may be observed in the fact that a great many people approach the subject of ethics by asking such questions as: "Should one risk one's life to help a man who is: a) drowning, b) trapped in a fire, c) stepping in front of a speeding truck, d) hanging by his fingernails over an abyss?"

Consider the implications of that approach. If a man accepts the ethics of altruism, he suffers the following consequences (in proportion to the degree of his acceptance):

1. Lack of self-esteem—since his first concern in the realm of values is not how to live his life, but how to sacrifice it.
2. Lack of respect for others—since he regards mankind as a herd of doomed beggars crying for someone's help.
3. A nightmare view of existence—since he believes that men are trapped in a "malevolent universe" where disasters are the constant and primary concern of their lives.
4. And, in fact, a lethargic indifference to ethics, a hopelessly cynical amorality—since his questions involve situations which he is not likely ever to encounter, which bear no relation to the actual problems of his own life and thus leave him to live without any moral principles whatever.

By elevating the issue of helping others into the central and primary issue of ethics, altruism has destroyed the concept of any authentic benevolence or good will among men. It has indoctrinated men with the idea that to value another human being is an act of selflessness, thus implying that a man can have no personal interest in others—that *to value* another means *to sacrifice* oneself—that any love, respect or admiration a man may feel for others is not and cannot be a source of his own enjoyment, but is a threat to his existence, a sacrificial blank check signed over to his loved ones.

The men who accept that dichotomy but choose its other side, the ultimate products of altruism's dehumanizing influence, are those psychopaths who do not challenge altruism's basic premise, but proclaim their rebellion against self-sacrifice by announcing that they are totally indifferent to anything living and would not lift a finger to help a man or a dog left mangled by a hit-and-run driver (who is usually one of their own kind).

Most men do not accept or practice either side of altruism's viciously false dichotomy, but its result is a total intellectual chaos on the issue of proper human relationships and on such questions as the nature, purpose or extent of the help one may give to others. Today, a great many well-meaning, reasonable men do not know how to identify or conceptualize the moral principles that motivate their love, affection or good will, and can find no guidance in the field of ethics, which is dominated by the stale platitudes of altruism.

On the question of why man is not a sacrificial animal and why help to others is not his moral duty, I refer you to *Atlas Shrugged*. This present discussion is concerned with the principles by which one identifies and evaluates the instances involving a man's *nonsacrificial* help to others.

"Sacrifice" is the surrender of a greater value for the sake of a lesser one or of a nonvalue. Thus, altruism gauges a man's virtue by the degree to which he surrenders, renounces or betrays his values (since help to a stranger or an enemy is regarded as more virtuous, less "selfish," than help to those one loves). The rational principle of conduct is the exact opposite: always act in accordance with the hierarchy of your values, and never sacrifice a greater value to a lesser one.

This applies to all choices, including one's actions toward other men. It requires that one possess a defined hierarchy of *rational* values (values chosen and validated by a rational standard). Without such a hierarchy, neither rational conduct nor considered value judgments nor moral choices are possible.

Love and friendship are profoundly personal, selfish values: love is an expression and assertion of self-esteem, a response to one's own values in the person of another. One gains a profoundly personal, selfish joy from the mere existence of the person one loves. It is one's own personal, selfish happiness that one seeks, earns and derives from love.

A "selfless," "disinterested" love is a contradiction in terms: it means that one is indifferent to that which one values.

Concern for the welfare of those one loves is a rational part of one's self-ish interests. If a man who is passionately in love with his wife spends a fortune to cure her of a dangerous illness, it would be absurd to claim that he does it as a "sacrifice" for *her* sake, not his own, and that it makes no difference to *him*, personally and selfishly, whether she lives or dies.

Any action that a man undertakes for the benefit of those he loves is *not a sacrifice* if, in the hierarchy of his values, in the total context of the choices open to him, it achieves that which is of greatest *personal* (and rational) impor-tance to *him*. In the above example, his wife's survival is of greater value to the husband than anything else that his money could buy, it is of greatest importance to his own happiness and, therefore, his action is *not* a sacrifice.

But suppose he let her die in order to spend his money on saving the lives of ten other women, none of whom meant anything to him—as the ethics of altruism would require. *That* would be a sacrifice. Here the difference between Objectivism and altruism can be seen most clearly: if sacrifice is the moral principle of action, then that husband *should* sacrifice his wife for the sake of ten other women. What distinguishes the wife from the ten others? Nothing but her value to the husband who has to make the choice—nothing but the fact that *his* happiness requires her survival.

The Objectivist ethics would tell him: your highest moral purpose is the achievement of your own happiness, your money is yours, use it to save your wife, *that* is your moral right and your rational, moral choice.

Consider the soul of the altruistic moralist who would be prepared to tell that husband the opposite. (And then ask yourself whether altruism is motivated by benevolence.)

The proper method of judging when or whether one should help another person is by reference to one's own rational self-interest and one's own hier-archy of values: the time, money or effort one gives or the risk one takes should be proportionate to the value of the person in relation to one's own happiness.

To illustrate this on the altruists' favorite example: the issue of saving a drowning person. If the person to be saved is a stranger, it is morally proper to save him only when the danger to one's own life is minimal; when the danger is great, it would be immoral to attempt it: only a lack of self-esteem could permit one to value one's life no higher than that of any random stranger. (And, conversely, if one is drowning, one cannot expect a stranger to risk his life for one's sake, remembering that one's life cannot be as valuable to him as his own.)

If the person to be saved is not a stranger, then the risk one should be willing to take is greater in proportion to the greatness of that person's value to oneself. If it is the man or woman one loves, then one can be willing to give one's own life to save him or her—for the selfish reason that life without the loved person could be unbearable.

Conversely, if a man is able to swim and to save his drowning wife, but becomes panicky, gives in to an unjustified, irrational fear and lets her drown, then spends his life in loneliness and misery—one would not call him "selfish"; one would condemn him morally for his treason to himself and to his own values, that is: his failure to fight for the preservation of a value crucial to his own happiness. Remember that values are that which one acts to gain and/or keep, and that one's own happiness has to be achieved by one's own effort. Since one's own happiness is the moral purpose of one's life, the man who fails to achieve it because of his own default, because of his failure to fight for it, is morally guilty.

The virtue involved in helping those one loves is not "selflessness" or "sacrifice," but *integrity*. Integrity is loyalty to one's convictions and values; it is the policy of acting in accordance with one's values, of expressing, upholding and translating them into practical reality. If a man professes to love a woman, yet his actions are indifferent, inimical or damaging to her, it is his lack of integrity that makes him immoral.

The same principle applies to relationships among friends. If one's friend is in trouble, one should act to help him by whatever nonsacrificial means are appropriate. For instance, if one's friend is starving, it is not a sacrifice, but an act of integrity to give him money for food rather than buy some insignificant gadget for oneself, because his welfare is important in the scale of one's personal values. If the gadget means more than the friend's suffering, one had no business pretending to be his friend.

The practical implementation of friendship, affection and love consists of incorporating the welfare (the *rational* welfare) of the person involved into one's own hierarchy of values, then acting accordingly.

But this is a reward which men have to earn by means of their virtues and which one cannot grant to mere acquaintances or strangers.

What, then, should one properly grant to strangers? The generalized respect and good will which one should grant to a human being in the name of the potential value he represents—until and unless he forfeits it.

A rational man does not forget that *life* is the source of all values and, as such, a common bond among living beings (as against inanimate matter), that other men are potentially able to achieve the same virtues as his own and thus be of enormous value to him. This does not mean that he regards human lives as interchangeable with his own. He recognizes the fact that his own life is the *source*, not only of all his values, but of *his capacity to value*. Therefore, the value he grants to others is only a consequence, an extension, a secondary projection of the primary value which is himself.

"The respect and good will that men of self-esteem feel toward other human beings is profoundly egoistic; they feel, in effect: 'Other men are of value because they are of the same species as myself.' In revering living entities, they are revering their *own* life. This is the psychological base of any emotion of sympathy and any feeling of 'species solidarity.'"[1]

Since men are born *tabula rasa*, both cognitively and morally, a rational man regards strangers as innocent until proved guilty, and grants them that initial good will in the name of their human potential. After that, he judges them according to the moral character they have actualized. If he finds them guilty of major evils, his good will is replaced by contempt and moral condemnation. (If one values human life, one cannot value its destroyers.) If he finds them to be virtuous, he grants them personal, individual value and appreciation, in proportion to their virtues.

It is on the ground of that generalized good will and respect for the value of human life that one helps strangers in an emergency—*and only in an emergency*.

It is important to differentiate between the rules of conduct in an emergency situation and the rules of conduct in the normal conditions of human existence. This does not mean a double standard of morality: the standard and the basic principles remain the same, but their application to either case requires precise definitions.

An emergency is an unchosen, unexpected event, limited in time, that creates conditions under which human survival is impossible—such as a flood, an earthquake, a fire, a shipwreck. In an emergency situation, men's primary goal is to combat the disaster, escape the danger and restore normal conditions (to reach dry land, to put out the fire, etc.).

By "normal" conditions I mean *metaphysically* normal, normal in the nature of things, and appropriate to human existence. Men can live on land, but not in water or in a raging fire. Since men are not omnipotent, it is metaphysically possible for unforeseeable disasters to strike them, in which case their only

---

1   Nathaniel Branden, "Benevolence versus Altruism," *The Objectivist Newsletter*, July 1962.

task is to return to those conditions under which their lives can continue. By its nature, an emergency situation is temporary; if it were to last, men would perish.

It is only in emergency situations that one should volunteer to help strangers, if it is in one's power. For instance, a man who values human life and is caught in a shipwreck, should help to save his fellow passengers (though not at the expense of his own life). But this does not mean that after they all reach shore, he should devote his efforts to saving his fellow passengers from poverty, ignorance, neurosis or whatever other troubles they might have. Nor does it mean that he should spend his life sailing the seven seas in search of shipwreck victims to save.

Or to take an example that can occur in everyday life: suppose one hears that the man next door is ill and penniless. Illness and poverty are not metaphysical emergencies, they are part of the normal risks of existence; but since the man is temporarily helpless, one may bring him food and medicine, *if* one can afford it (as an act of good will, not of duty) or one may raise a fund among the neighbors to help him out. But this does not mean that one must support him from then on, nor that one must spend one's life looking for starving men to help.

In the normal conditions of existence, man has to choose his goals, project them in time, pursue them and achieve them by his own effort. He cannot do it if his goals are at the mercy of and must be sacrificed to any misfortune happening to others. He cannot live his life by the guidance of rules applicable only to conditions under which human survival is impossible.

The principle that one should help men in an emergency cannot be extended to regard all human suffering as an emergency and to turn the misfortune of some into a first mortgage on the lives of others.

Poverty, ignorance, illness and other problems of that kind are not metaphysical emergencies. By the *metaphysical* nature of man and of existence, man has to maintain his life by his own effort; the values he needs—such as wealth or knowledge—are not given to him automatically, as a gift of nature, but have to be discovered and achieved by his own thinking and work. One's sole obligation toward others, in this respect, is to maintain a social system that leaves men free to achieve, to gain and to keep their values.

Every code of ethics is based on and derived from a metaphysics, that is: from a theory about the fundamental nature of the universe in which man lives and acts. The altruist ethics is based on a "malevolent universe" metaphysics, on the theory that man, by his very nature, is helpless and doomed—that success, happiness, achievement are impossible to him—that emergencies, disasters, catastrophes are the norm of his life and that his primary goal is to combat them.

As the simplest empirical refutation of that metaphysics—as evidence of the fact that the material universe is not inimical to man and that catastrophes are the exception, not the rule of his existence—observe the fortunes made by insurance companies.

Observe also that the advocates of altruism are unable to base their ethics on any facts of men's normal existence and that they always offer "lifeboat" situations as examples from which to derive the rules of moral conduct. ("What should you do if you and another man are in a lifeboat that can carry only one?" etc.)

The fact is that men do not live in lifeboats—and that a lifeboat is not the place on which to base one's metaphysics.

The moral purpose of a man's life is the achievement of his own happiness. This does not mean that he is indifferent to all men, that human life is of no value to him and that he has no reason to help others in an emergency. But it *does* mean that he does not subordinate his life to the welfare of others, that he does not sacrifice himself to their needs, that the relief of their suffering is not his primary concern, that any help he gives is an *exception*, not a rule, an act of generosity, not of moral duty, that it is *marginal* and *incidental*—as disasters are marginal and incidental in the course of human existence—and that *values*, not disasters, are the goal, the first concern and the motive power of his life.

STUDY QUESTIONS

1. How does Rand define altruism? What does she think is wrong with it?
2. Does Rand's Objectivism suggest that we should always pursue our own self-interest?
3. Under what circumstances does Rand think that it is right to assist strangers?

PLATO
What Is the Value of Justice?

Plato (429?–347 BCE), the ancient Greek philosopher, stands as perhaps the most significant of the founders of the Western philosophical tradition. He was a pupil of Socrates and teacher of Aristotle. He wrote in dialogue form, generally featuring Socrates as the lead figure in the debate. It has been said that all subsequent philosophy is "footnotes to Plato."

* * * With his usual energy, Glaucon * * * went on to ask: Socrates, do you really want to convince us that justice is preferable to injustice, or will you be content if we only seem to be persuaded?

I would really like to persuade you.

Well, so far you haven't succeeded. Consider this question. Is there some kind of good we ought to strive for, not because we expect it to bring about profitable results but simply because we value the good for its own sake? Joy might be an example, or those sorts of harmless pleasures that leave nothing behind except the memory of enjoyment.

These are good pleasures to savor.

And can we agree that there is a second and different kind of good, valuable not only for its own sake but also for the desirable effects it produces? I think of sight, of knowledge, of health.

Of course.

How about a third kind of good? Gymnastic, medicine, the art of making money—all these yield benefits but are tiresome in the doing. Hence we think of them not as goods in themselves but value them only for their effects.

Yes, this is certainly another kind of good. But what is your point?

I want to know in which of these three categories or classes of goods you locate justice.

Justice belongs in the most valuable category. It is the good that the happy man loves both for its own sake and for the effects it produces.

But the multitude does not think so. Most people consider the practice of justice a burdensome affair. They think it a task to be avoided, if possible, and performed only if necessary to maintain one's reputation for propriety—and to collect whatever rewards such a reputation may be worth.

You are right. I know that is the common opinion. * * * But I am too stupid to be convinced of it Glaucon.

Well, then, Socrates, listen to what I have to say on the subject too. * * * As for me, neither the nature of justice or injustice is yet clear. I want to consider both of them quite apart from their effects or the rewards they might bring. What are they in themselves? What power do they exert within the confines of a man's soul?

To begin with, * * * I will speak first of all of the common view of the nature and origin of justice. Second, I shall argue that all who practice justice do so against their own will. This is so because they regard just behavior as something necessary but not as something good. Third, I shall stress that the rationale for such attitudes is rooted in the common view that the life of the unjust man is far better and happier than the life of the just man.

I do not believe these things myself, Socrates. But I admit that I become perplexed when I listen to the arguments of Thrasymachus and all those who believe as he does. My uncertainty is all the greater when I reflect that I have never yet heard an unambiguous proof that justice is always superior to injustice.

What I desire most, Socrates, is to hear someone praise justice for its own sake, and you are the one most likely to do so. Thus my purpose in praising the unjust life is to provoke a response from you that will effectively repudiate injustice and vindicate justice. * * *

Most men say that to be unjust is good but to suffer injustice is bad. To this opinion they add another: the measure of evil suffered by one who is wronged is generally greater than the good enjoyed by one who does wrong. Now, once they have learned what it is to wrong others—and also what it is to be wronged—men tend to arrive at this conclusion: justice is unattainable and injustice unavoidable.

Those so lacking in strength that they can neither inflict injustice nor defend themselves against it find it profitable to draw up a compact with one another. The purpose of the compact is to bind them all neither to suffer injustice nor to commit it. From there they proceed to promulgate further contracts and covenants. To all of these they attach the name of justice; indeed, they assert that the true origin and essence of justice is located in their own legislation.

Their lawmaking is clearly a compromise, Socrates. The compromise is between what they say is best of all—to do wrong without incurring punishment—and what is worst of all—to suffer wrong with no possibility of revenge. Hence they conceive of justice not as something good in itself but simply as a midway point between best and worst. Further, they assert that justice is praised only by those too weak to do injustice and that anyone who is a real man with power to do as he likes would never agree to refrain from doing injustice in order not to suffer it. He would be mad to make any such agreement.

As you very well know, Socrates, this is the orthodox account of the nature and origin of justice. Its corollary is that when people practice justice, they do so against their own wills. Only those are just who lack the power to be unjust. Let us test this proposition by altering the power distribution and assigning the just and the unjust equal power to do what they please. We shall then discover that the just man and the unjust man will follow precisely the same path. They will both do what all nature decrees to be good. They will pursue their own interests. Only if constrained by law will they be confined to the path of justice.

The test I propose makes the assumption that both the just and the unjust enjoy the peculiar liberty said to have been granted to Gyges, ancestor of Croesus the Lydian. Tradition has it that Gyges was a shepherd in the service of the king of Lydia. While he was feeding his flock one day, there was a great storm, after which an earthquake opened a chasm directly in front of the place where Gyges stood with his flock. Marveling at the sight, Gyges descended into the chasm. There he beheld many wonders, among them a hollow bronze horse fitted with doors. When he opened one of the doors and looked within, he saw the corpse of a huge man, nude except for a gold ring on his finger. Gyges removed the ring and made his way up and out of the chasm.

Now when the shepherds next met to prepare their customary monthly report to the king concerning their flocks, Gyges attended wearing the ring. While there, he chanced to turn the stone of the ring on his finger inward, toward the palm of his hand. Instantly he became invisible to all eyes. He was amazed to hear those who sat near him speak of him as if he were absent. Fumbling with the ring again, he turned the stone outward, away from the palm, and became visible once more. Now he began to experiment, turning the ring this way and that and always with the same results— turning it inward he became invisible, turning it outward he became visible again. Once he discovered the ring's power, he hastily managed to have himself appointed one of the messengers to the king's court. On arrival he seduced the queen and then, with her help, murdered the king. Thus it was that he became king of Lydia.

Supposing now there were two such rings, the just man wearing one and the unjust man the other. No man is so unyielding that he would remain obedient to justice and keep his hands off what does not belong to him if he could steal with impunity in the very midst of the public market itself. The same if he could enter into houses and lie with whom he chose, or if he could slay—or release from bondage—whom he would, behaving toward other men in these and all other things as if he were the equal of a god. The just man would act no differently from the unjust; both would pursue the same course.

One might argue that here is the great proof that no one is willingly just; men will be just only if constrained. This is because every man believes that justice is really not to his interest. If he has the power to do wrong, he will do wrong, for every man believes in his heart that injustice will profit him far more than justice.

These are the settled convictions of all those who choose to adopt them. They hold that anyone who acquires extraordinary power and then refuses to do wrong and plunder others is truly to be pitied (and a great fool as well). Publicly, however, they praise the fool's example, convinced that they must deny what they really think so that they will not encourage unjust acts against themselves. I think I have spoken sufficiently to this point.

Next, if we are to choose between the lives of justice and injustice, we must be precise in distinguishing the one from the other. Otherwise we cannot choose rightly. We can make the distinction only by treating the two as strictly separate. We must assume the just man to be entirely just and the unjust man entirely unjust. Each must possess all the qualities appropriate to his character and role as a just—or unjust—man.

First, the unjust man: his behavior must be like that of a clever craftsman. Like any good physician or pilot, he must practice his art with an intuitive sense for what is possible and what is impossible, holding fast to the first and shunning the latter. When he makes a mistake, he must be able to recover and correct himself. This means that the unjust man must pursue injustice in the proper way. If he is altogether unjust, he must possess an unerring capacity to escape detection; otherwise, if he fails and is caught, he shows himself to be a mere bungler. After all, the highest form of injustice is to appear just without being so.

Perfect injustice denotes the perfectly unjust man. Nothing belonging to injustice must be withheld from him. He must be allowed to enjoy the greatest reputation for justice all the while he is committing the greatest wrongs. If by mistake any of his misdeeds should become known, he must be endowed with ample powers of persuasion so that he can cover them up. Should he need to use force, let him do so with boldness and manly strength—and by mobilizing friends and money.

Having constructed a model of the unjust man, we must now do the same for the just man. He will be noble and pure—in Aeschylus's words, one who wants to be good rather than to seem good. Accordingly, he must be deprived of the seeming. Should he retain the appearance of being just, he would also enjoy an esteem that brings with it honors and gifts. In that case we could not know whether he serves justice for its own sake or because he covets the honors and gifts. He must therefore be stripped of everything but justice;

his situation must be the opposite of his unjust counterpart. Though the best of men, he must be thought the worst. Then let him be put to the test to see whether he will continue resolute in the service of justice, even though all the while he must suffer the opprobrium of an evil reputation. Let him so persevere—just in actuality but unjust in reputation—until death itself.

Here we have charted the full course for both the unjust and the just man and should be in a better position to judge which of the two is happier.

My compliments, Glaucon. You have given your characters high finish and form. One might think you were modeling a pair of sculptures intended to vie for first honors at the exhibition.

I have spoken of them to the best of my ability. And if I have also spoken truly, I think it should be an easy matter to anticipate and describe what life holds in store for each. If I now use language in my description that is sometimes rude—and even brutal—please remember, Socrates, that my words should be attributed not to me but to those who value injustice more than justice.

They will tell you that every man who is just, but whose reputation stamps him as unjust, will learn what it is to feel the lash, the rack, the chains, and the branding iron burning out his eyes. And after suffering all the other agonies he will be impaled on spikes, there finally to learn his lesson that it is better to seem just than to be so.

They will say that those words of Aeschylus apply far better to the unjust man. He who wills to be unjust but not to seem so is the real man of truth. He is the one who does not allow himself to be governed by opinion; instead he orders his affairs in accord with the way life really is:

He plows deep the furrows of his intellect
and brings home prudence as his harvest.

His reputation for justice will bring him high office. He can enter into marriage with whom he will and arrange the same for his children when their time comes. He will do business or not at his option. His contracts and partnerships will always be profitable for he does not hesitate to be unjust. When he becomes involved in law suits or other kinds of disputes, he bests all who stand against him. In gaining the decision in each contest he enters he also augments his wealth. Hence he is increasingly capable of benefiting friends and injuring enemies. He is able to make sacrifices and other gifts to the gods in such a way as will display his magnificence. Consequently, he pays court both to the men he favors and to the gods far more effectively than just men can; he may therefore reasonably expect that heaven will bestow its favors on him rather than on the just.

So do both men and gods favor the unjust man over the just. This is what the multitude believes.

I was about to respond to Glaucon when his brother, Adeimantus, intervened with a question. Surely, Socrates, you don't believe the statement of the case is now complete?

What else would you add?

The quintessential point. It has not yet even been mentioned. * * *

Do listen to this further point. Unless we go on to examine the reasoning and the language of the others—I mean those who extol justice and condemn injustice—Glaucon's case remains incomplete, at least in my view. You know well how fathers lecture their sons (and guardians their charges) about a man's obligation and also how they use words that compliment not justice but the good repute that comes with it. They calculate that a reputation for justice will gain a man public office and fortunate alliances and all the good things that Glaucon already said would accrue to the unjust man who wears the cloak of righteousness. Expanding still further on the value of reputation, they summon up the gods themselves to certify in abundant detail the heavenly blessings in store for the pious.

They bring the worthy Hesiod as well as Homer into their testimony. They cite Hesiod's lines where the gods make the very oaks belonging to the just man

> Bear acorns upon their topmost branches
> and honey from beeswarms far below on the midtrunk.
> His sheep are weighted down by their own soft fleece.

Hesiod adds on many similar blessings, and Homer concurs:

> To the good king who governs in fear of the high gods
> and upholds justice and the right the black earth
> yields reward: barley and wheat and trees
> laden and weighted with fair fruits.
> His flocks increase, and the teeming seas bring him fish.

Musaeus and his son sing of more tantalizing gifts from the gods to the righteous. With song and story they lead them down into the house of Hades. There they join the chosen ones, lying down on couches and feasting, crowned with garlands and drunk for all time. Indeed, in that place the fairest reward of virtue and the just life is an eternal drunk.

Other poets spin out the rewards from the gods to greater lengths. They will have it that the fair legacy of the just and faithful shall be handed down to the third and fourth generations. So much for this style in praise of justice. But the same poets sound a different note where the wicked are concerned. These they bury in the mud of Hades; some are also compelled to fetch water in a sieve. Still alive in death, the unjust are suffered to have infamy heaped upon them and to endure the very same collection of evils Glaucon said would befall those who, though deemed unjust, are truly just. That is all they have to say; such is the way they praise justice and condemn injustice.

But we must proceed still further, Socrates, and observe that both prose and poetry play with still other variations on our theme. All the world declares that justice and right living are honorable and fair but at the same time tedious and unpleasant. Vice and injustice, on the other hand, are easy to learn and offer a profusion of pleasures. Only law and conventional opinion condemn them. For the most part, the argument continues, injustice pays better than justice. All hail the rich and those with other kinds of power and hasten to do them indiscriminate honor in public and private. But the poor and the weak they despise, even though admitting that they are better men than the mighty.

The most bizarre of all these variations has to do with the relationship between the gods and virtue. The gods are said to visit sorrow and evil on many good men while bestowing happiness on many a scoundrel. Then come the priests with begging cups and itinerant soothsayers to the doors of the rich, talking up the powers they claim to have acquired from the gods and their skills at sacrifice and incantation. They declare that if a man—or any of his ancestors—should have committed a misdeed, it can be atoned for by entirely pleasurable festivals. Or else, if a man have an enemy, whether justly or not, he need pay only a small fee to cause his enemy to suffer injury—all because these seedy characters claim knowledge of charms and enchantments that will constrain the very gods to do their bidding.

Finally, the poets are brought forward again, this time as witnesses to the allure and ubiquity of vice. Hesiod is recalled once more:

Of evil there is plenty, easy for a man to find,
and smooth is the path to its door.
But the gods have decreed
that toil, sweat, and a steep and weary road
shall mark the quest for virtue.

On the other hand, Homer is called upon to testify that men are also able to lead these same gods astray:

> The will of gods can also be divorced from purpose.
> Having transgressed against them, erring men apologize
> with burning incense and libations.
> By prayers and sacrifice and vows of future temperance
> they would annul the heavenly wrath.

Next the sorcerers bring out a whole bushel of books by Musaeus and Orpheus, whom they call children of the moon and the Muses. These they use in their rituals, whose purpose is to persuade not only private individuals but whole societies that guilty deeds can be expiated and injustices forgiven. For the living, these objectives can be achieved by following a prescribed set of sacrifices interspersed with pleasant games. Nor do they neglect the dead. There are special rites for the defunct which they call functions, or mysteries. These promise us deliverance from the evils of the other world; if we disregard these liturgies, however, we shall suffer terrible things. ✳ ✳ ✳

What further argument could persuade us to prefer justice to the most base injustice? Let us choose the latter, but when in the public eye let us counterfeit the former. Then shall we prosper mightily with both men and gods, in life and death. ✳ ✳ ✳

I have always admired the brilliance of Glaucon and Adeimantus, but on this occasion their words gave me special pleasure. So I said to them: Sons of a noble father—Glaucon's friend put it well in the elegy he wrote to honor you both for your heroic deeds in the battle of Megara:

> Sons of Ariston, you honor the godlike
> heritage of a famous father.

There must indeed be some divine spark at work in your natures that you should be able to make such formidable arguments on behalf of injustice and yet resist being convinced by your own reasoning. And I believe that you are really not convinced. I infer this, however, from my knowledge of your characters: if I had to deal with your words alone, I would be suspicious of you.

STUDY QUESTIONS

1. What view is Socrates hoping to be able to defend?
2. What is the purpose of Glaucon's argument that justice is a compromise?
3. What is shown by the tale of the ring of Gyges?

THOMAS HOBBES
The State of Nature

Thomas Hobbes (1588–1679) is a very widely discussed English political philosopher, most famous for his book Leviathan, *in which he argued that in order to secure peace it is necessary, by means of a social contract, to submit to absolute government.*

CHAP. XIII.

Of the Naturall Condition *of Mankind, as concerning their Felicity, and Misery.*

Nature hath made men so equall, in the faculties of body, and mind; as that though there bee found one man sometimes manifestly stronger in body, or of quicker mind then another; yet when all is reckoned together, the difference between man, and man, is not so considerable, as that one man can thereupon claim to himselfe any benefit, to which another may not pretend, as well as he. For as to the strength of body, the weakest has strength enough to kill the strongest, either by secret machination, or by confederacy with others, that are in the same danger with himselfe.

And as to the faculties of the mind, (setting aside the arts grounded upon words, and especially that skill of proceeding upon generall, and infallible rules, called Science; which very few have, and but in few things; as being not a native faculty, born with us; nor attained, (as Prudence,) while we look after somewhat els,) I find yet a greater equality amongst men, than that of strength. For Prudence, is but Experience; which equall time, equally bestowes on all men, in those things they equally apply themselves unto. That which may perhaps make such equality incredible, is but a vain conceipt of ones owne wisdome, which almost all men think they have in a greater degree, than the Vulgar; that is, than all men but themselves, and a few others, whom by Fame, or for concurring with themselves, they approve. For such is the nature of men, that howsoever they may acknowledge many others to be more witty, or more eloquent, or more learned; Yet they will hardly believe there be many so wise as themselves: For they see their own wit at hand, and other mens at a distance. But this proveth rather that men are in that point equall, than unequall. For there is not ordinarily a greater signe of the equall distribution of any thing, than that every man is contented with his share.

From this equality of ability, ariseth equality of hope in the attaining of our Ends. And therefore if any two men desire the same thing, which neverthelesse they cannot both enjoy, they become enemies; and in the way to their End, (which is principally their owne conservation, and sometimes their delectation only,) endeavour to destroy, or subdue one an other. And from hence it comes to passe, that where an Invader hath no more to feare, than an other mans single power; if one plant, sow, build, or possesse a convenient Seat, others may probably be expected to come prepared with forces united, to dispossesse, and deprive him, not only of the fruit of his labour, but also of his life, or liberty. And the Invader again is in the like danger of another.

And from this diffidence of one another, there is no way for any man to secure himselfe, so reasonable, as Anticipation; that is, by force, or wiles, to master the persons of all men he can, so long, till he see no other power great enough to endanger him: And this is no more than his own conservation requireth, and is generally allowed. Also because there be some, that taking pleasure in contemplating their own power in the acts of conquest, which they pursue farther than their security requires; if others, that otherwise would be glad to be at ease within modest bounds, should not by invasion increase their power, they would not be able, long time, by standing only on their defence, to subsist. And by consequence, such augmentation of dominion over men, being necessary to a mans conservation, it ought to be allowed him.

Againe, men have no pleasure, (but on the contrary a great deale of griefe) in keeping company, where there is no power able to over-awe them all. For every man looketh that his companion should value him, at the same rate he sets upon himselfe: And upon all signes of contempt, or undervaluing, naturally endeavours, as far as he dares (which amongst them that have no common power to keep them in quiet, is far enough to make them destroy each other,) to extort a greater value from his contemners, by dommage; and from others, by the example.

So that in the nature of man, we find three principall causes of quarrell. First, Competition; Secondly, Diffidence; Thirdly, Glory.

The first, maketh men invade for Gain; the second, for Safety; and the third, for Reputation. The first use Violence, to make themselves Masters of other mens persons, wives, children, and cattell; the second, to defend them; the third, for trifles, as a word, a smile, a different opinion, and any other signe of undervalue, either direct in their Persons, or by reflexion in their Kindred, their Friends, their Nation, their Profession, or their Name.

Hereby it is manifest, that during the time men live without a common Power to keep them all in awe, they are in that condition which is called Warre; and such a warre, as is of every man, against every man. For WARRE, consisteth not in Battell onely, or the act of fighting; but in a tract of time, wherein the Will to contend by Battell is sufficiently known: and therefore the notion of *Time*, is to be considered in the nature of Warre; as it is in the nature of Weather. For as the nature of Foule weather, lyeth not in a showre or two of rain; but in an inclination thereto of many dayes together: So the nature of War, consisteth not in actuall fighting; but in the known disposition thereto, during all the time there is no assurance to the contrary. All other time is PEACE.

Whatsoever therefore is consequent to a time of Warre, where every man is Enemy to every man; the same is consequent to the time, wherein men live without other security, than what their own strength, and their own invention shall furnish them withall. In such condition, there is no place for Industry; because the fruit thereof is uncertain: and consequently no Culture of the Earth; no Navigation, nor use of the commodities that may be imported by Sea; no commodious Building; no Instruments of moving, and removing such things as require much force; no Knowledge of the face of the Earth; no account of Time; no Arts; no Letters; no Society; and which is worst of all, continuall feare, and danger of violent death; And the life of man, solitary, poore, nasty, brutish, and short.

It may seem strange to some man, that has not well weighed these things; that Nature should thus dissociate, and render men apt to invade, and destroy one another: and he may therefore, not trusting to this Inference, made from the Passions, desire perhaps to have the same confirmed by Experience. Let him therefore consider with himselfe, when taking a journey, he armes himselfe, and seeks to go well accompanied; when going to sleep, he locks his dores; when even in his house he locks his chests; and this when he knowes there bee Lawes, and publike Officers, armed, to revenge all injuries shall bee done him; what opinion he has of his fellow subjects, when he rides armed; of his fellow Citizens, when he locks his dores; and of his children, and servants, when he locks his chests. Does he not there as much accuse mankind by his actions, as I do by my words? But neither of us accuse mans nature in it. The Desires, and other Passions of man, are in themselves no Sin. No more are the Actions, that proceed from those Passions, till they know a Law that forbids them: which till Lawes be made they cannot know: nor can any Law be made, till they have agreed upon the Person that shall make it.

It may peradventure be thought, there was never such a time, nor condition of warre as this; and I believe it was never generally so, over all the world: but there are many places, where they live so now. For the savage people in many places of *America*, except the government of small Families, the concord whereof dependeth on naturall lust, have no government at all; and live at this day in that brutish manner, as I said before. Howsoever, it may be perceived what manner of life there would be, where there were no common Power to feare; by the manner of life, which men that have formerly lived under a peacefull government, use to degenerate into, in a civill Warre.

But though there had never been any time, wherein particular men were in a condition of warre one against another; yet in all times, Kings, and Persons of Soveraigne authority, because of their Independency, are in continuall jealousies, and in the state and posture of Gladiators; having their weapons pointing, and their eyes fixed on one another; that is, their Forts, Garrisons, and Guns upon the Frontiers of their Kingdomes; and continuall Spyes upon their neighbours; which is a posture of War. But because they uphold thereby, the Industry of their Subjects; there does not follow from it, that misery, which accompanies the Liberty of particular men.

To this warre of every man against every man, this also is consequent; that nothing can be Unjust. The notions of Right and Wrong, Justice and Injustice have there no place. Where there is no common Power, there is no Law: where no Law, no Injustice. Force, and Fraud, are in warre the two Cardinall vertues. Justice, and Injustice are none of the Faculties neither of the Body, nor Mind. If they were, they might be in a man that were alone in the world, as well as his Senses, and Passions. They are Qualities, that relate to men in Society, not in Solitude. It is consequent also to the same condition, that there be no Propriety, no Dominion, no *Mine* and *Thine* distinct; but onely that to be every mans, that he can get; and for so long, as he can keep it. And thus much for the ill condition, which man by meer Nature is actually placed in; though with a possibility to come out of it, consisting partly in the Passions, partly in his Reason.

The Passions that encline men to Peace, are Feare of Death; Desire of such things as are necessary to commodious living; and a Hope by their Industry to obtain them. And Reason suggesteth convenient Articles of Peace, upon which men may be drawn to agreement. These Articles, are they, which otherwise are called the Lawes of Nature: whereof I shall speak more particularly, in the two following Chapters.

CHAP. XIV.

Of the first and second NATURALL LAWES, *and of* CONTRACTS.

THE RIGHT OF NATURE, which Writers commonly call *Jus Naturale*, is the Liberty each man hath, to use his own power, as he will himselfe, for the preservation of his own Nature; that is to say, of his own Life; and consequently, of doing any thing, which in his own Judgement, and Reason, hee shall conceive to be the aptest means thereunto.

By LIBERTY, is understood, according to the proper signification of the word, the absence of externall Impediments: which Impediments, may oft take away part of a mans power to do what hee would; but cannot hinder him from using the power left him, according as his judgement, and reason shall dictate to him.

A LAW OF NATURE, (*Lex Naturalis*,) is a Precept, or generall Rule, found out by Reason, by which a man is forbidden to do, that, which is destructive of his life, or taketh away the means of preserving the same; and to omit, that, by which he thinketh it may be best preserved. For though they that speak of this subject, use to confound *Jus*, and *Lex*, *Right* and *Law*; yet they ought to be distinguished; because RIGHT, consisteth in liberty to do, or to forbeare; Whereas LAW, determineth, and bindeth to one of them: so that Law, and Right, differ as much, as Obligation, and Liberty; which in one and the same matter are inconsistent.

And because the condition of Man, (as hath been declared in the precedent Chapter) is a condition of Warre of every one against every one; in which case every one is governed by his own Reason; and there is nothing he can make use of, that may not be a help unto him, in preserving his life against his enemyes; It followeth, that in such a condition, every man has a Right to every thing; even to one anothers body. And therefore, as long as this naturall Right of every man to every thing endureth, there can be no security to any man, (how strong or wise soever he be,) of living out the time, which Nature ordinarily alloweth men to live. And consequently it is a precept, or generall rule of Reason, *That every man, ought to endeavour Peace, as farre as he has hope of obtaining it; and when he cannot obtain it, that he may seek, and use, all helps, and advantages of Warre.* The first branch of which Rule, containeth the first, and Fundamentall Law of Nature; which is, *to seek Peace, and follow it.* The Second, the summe of the Right of Nature; which is, *By all means we can, to defend our selves.*

From this Fundamentall Law of Nature, by which men are commanded to endeavour Peace, is derived this second Law; *That a man be willing, when*

others are so too, as farre-forth, as for Peace, and defence of himselfe he shall
think it necessary, to lay down this right to all things; and be contented with so
much liberty against other men, as he would allow other men against himselfe.
For as long as every man holdeth this Right, of doing any thing he liketh;
so long are all men in the condition of Warre. But if other men will not lay
down their Right, as well as he; then there is no Reason for any one, to devest
himselfe of his: For that were to expose himselfe to Prey, (which no man
is bound to) rather than to dispose himselfe to Peace. This is that Law of
the Gospell; *Whatsoever you require that others should do to you, that do ye to*
them. And that Law of all men, *Quod tibi fieri non vis, alteri ne feceris.* ✳ ✳ ✳

There be some Rights, which no man can be understood by any words,
or other signes, to have abandoned, or transferred. As first a man cannot
lay down the right of resisting them, that assault him by force, to take away
his life; because he cannot be understood to ayme thereby, at any Good to
himself. ✳ ✳ ✳

The mutuall transferring of Right, is that which men call CONTRACT. ✳ ✳ ✳

If a Covenant be made, wherein neither of the parties performe presently, but trust one another; in the condition of meer Nature, (which is a
condition of Warre of every man against every man,) upon any reasonable
suspition, it is Voyd: But if there be a common Power set over them both,
with right and force sufficient to compell performance; it is not Voyd. For
he that performeth first, has no assurance the other will performe after;
because the bonds of words are too weak to bridle mens ambition, avarice,
anger, and other Passions, without the feare of some coerceive Power; which
in the condition of meer Nature, where all men are equall, and judges of
the justnesse of their own fears, cannot possibly be supposed. And therfore
he which performeth first, does but betray himselfe to his enemy; contrary
to the Right (he can never abandon) of defending his life, and means of
living.

But in a civill estate, where there is a Power set up to constrain those that
would otherwise violate their faith, that feare is no more reasonable; and for
that cause, he which by the Covenant is to perform first, is obliged so to do. ✳ ✳ ✳

Covenants entred into by fear, in the condition of meer Nature, are obligatory. For example, if I Covenant to pay a ransome, or service for my life,
to an enemy; I am bound by it. For it is a Contract, wherein one receiveth
the benefit of life; the other is to receive mony, or service for it; and consequently, where no other Law (as in the condition, of meer Nature) forbiddeth
the performance, the Covenant is valid. ✳ ✳ ✳

CHAP. XV.

Of other Lawes of Nature.

From that law of Nature, by which we are obliged to transferre to another, such Rights, as being retained, hinder the peace of Mankind, there followeth a Third; which is this, *That men performe their Covenants made:* without which, Covenants are in vain, and but Empty words; and the Right of all men to all things remaining, wee are still in the condition of Warre.

And in this law of Nature, consisteth the Fountain and Originall of Justice. For where no Covenant hath preceded, there hath no Right been transferred, and every man has right to every thing; and consequently, no action can be Unjust. But when a Covenant is made, then to break it is *Unjust:* And the definition of INJUSTICE, is no other than *the not Performance of Covenant.* And whatsoever is not Unjust, is *Just.*

But because Covenants of mutuall trust, where there is a feare of not performance on either part, ∗ ∗ ∗ are invalid; though the Originall of Justice be the making of Covenants; yet Injustice actually there can be none, till the cause of such feare be taken away; which while men are in the naturall condition of Warre, cannot be done. Therefore before the names of Just, and Unjust can have place, there must be some coërcive Power, to compell men equally to the performance of their Covenants, by the terrour of some punishment, greater than the benefit they expect by the breach of their Covenant; and to make good that Propriety, which by mutuall Contract men acquire, in recompence of the universall Right they abandon: and such power there is none before the erection of a Common-wealth. And this is also to be gathered out of the ordinary definition of Justice in the Schooles: For they say, that *Justice is the constant Will of giving to every man his own.* And therefore where there is no *Own,* that is, no Propriety, there is no Injustice; and where there is no coërceive Power erected, that is, where there is no Common-wealth, there is no Propriety; all men having Right to all things: Therefore where there is no Common-wealth, there nothing is Unjust. So that the nature of Justice, consisteth in keeping of valid Covenants: but the Validity of Covenants begins not but with the Constitution of a Civill Power, sufficient to compell men to keep them: And then it is also that Propriety begins.

The Foole hath sayd in his heart, there is no such thing as Justice; and sometimes also with his tongue; seriously alleaging, that every mans conservation, and contentment, being committed to his own care, there could be no reason, why every man might not do what he thought conduced thereunto: and therefore also to make, or not make; keep, or not keep Covenants, was not against Reason, when it conduced to ones benefit. He does not therein deny, that there be Covenants; and that they are sometimes broken, sometimes kept; and that such breach of them may be called Injustice, and the observance of them Justice: but he questioneth, whether Injustice, taking away the feare of God, (for the same Foole hath said in his heart there is no God,) may not sometimes stand with that Reason, which dictateth to every man his own good; and particularly then, when it conduceth to such a benefit, as shall put a man in a condition, to neglect not onely the dispraise, and revilings, but also the power of other men. ∗ ∗ ∗ This specious reasoning is neverthelesse false.

For the question is not of promises mutuall, where there is no security of performance on either side; as when there is no Civill Power erected over the parties promising; for such promises are no Covenants: But either where one of the parties has performed already; or where there is a Power to make him performe; there is the question whether it be against reason, that is, against the benefit of the other to performe, or not. And I say it is not against reason. For the manifestation whereof, we are to consider; First, that when a man doth a thing, which not-withstanding any thing can be foreseen, and reckoned on, tendeth to his own destruction, howsoever some accident which he could not expect, arriving may turne it to his benefit; yet such events do not make it reasonably or wisely done. Secondly, that in a condition of Warre, wherein every man to every man, for want of a common Power to keep them all in awe, is an Enemy, there is no man can hope by his own strength, or wit, to defend himselfe from destruction, without the help of Confederates; where every one expects the same defence by the Confederation, that any one else does: and therefore he which declares he thinks it reason to deceive those that help him, can in reason expect no other means of safety, than what can be had from his own single Power. He therefore that breaketh his Covenant, and consequently declareth that he thinks he may with reason do so, cannot be received into any Society, that unite themselves for Peace and Defence, but by the errour of them that receive him; nor when he is received, be retayned in it, without seeing the danger of their errour; which errours a man cannot reasonably reckon upon as the means of his security: and therefore if he be left, or cast out of Society, he perisheth; and if he live in Society, it is by the errours of other men, which he could not foresee, nor reckon upon; and consequently against the reason of his preservation; and so, as all men that contribute not to his destruction, forbear him onely out of ignorance of what is good for themselves. ∗ ∗ ∗

And though this may seem too subtile a deduction of the Lawes Nature, to be taken notice of by all men; whereof the most part are too busie in getting food, and the rest too negligent to understand; yet to leave all men unexcusable, they have been contracted into one easie sum, intelligible, even to the meanest capacity; and that is, *Do not that to another, which thou wouldest not have done to thy selfe.* * * *

The Lawes of Nature oblige *in foro interno*; that is to say, they bind to a desire they should take place: but *in foro externo*; that is, to the putting them in act, not alwayes. For he that should be modest, and tractable, and performe all he promises, in such time, and place, where no man els should do so, should but make himselfe a prey to others, and procure his own certain ruine, contrary to the ground of all Lawes of Nature, which tend to Natures preservation. And again, he that having sufficient Security, that others shall observe the same Lawes towards him, observes them not himselfe, seeketh not Peace, but War; & consequently the destruction of his Nature by Violence. * * *

The Lawes of Nature are Immutable and Eternall; For Injustice, Ingratitude, Arrogance, Pride, Iniquity, Acception of persons, and the rest, can never be made lawfull. For it can never be that Warre shall preserve life, and Peace destroy it.

STUDY QUESTIONS

1. What, according to Hobbes, are the reasons why the state of nature would be a state of war?
2. What, for Hobbes, is the route out of the state of war?
3. What does Hobbes regard as the relation between the social contract and ideas of justice?

JOHN RAWLS
The Original Position

John Rawls (1921–2002) was an American philosopher, regarded as the most important political philosopher writing in English in the twentieth century. He is best known for his book A Theory of Justice *(1971).*

1. THE ROLE OF JUSTICE

Justice is the first virtue of social institutions, as truth is of systems of thought. A theory however elegant and economical must be rejected or revised if it is untrue; likewise laws and institutions no matter how efficient and well-arranged must be reformed or abolished if they are un-just. Each person possesses an inviolability founded on justice that even the welfare of society as a whole cannot override. For this reason justice denies that the loss of freedom for some is made right by a greater good shared by others. It does not allow that the sacrifices imposed on a few are outweighed by the larger sum of advantages enjoyed by many. Therefore in a just society the liberties of equal citizenship are taken as settled; the rights secured by justice are not subject to political bargaining or to the calculus of social interests. The only thing that permits us to acquiesce in an erroneous theory is the lack of a better one; analogously, an injustice is tolerable only when it is necessary to avoid an even greater injustice. Being first virtues of human activities, truth and justice are uncompro-mising.

These propositions seem to express our intuitive conviction of the pri-macy of justice. No doubt they are expressed too strongly. In any event I wish to inquire whether these contentions or others similar to them are sound, and if so how they can be accounted for. To this end it is necessary to work out a theory of justice in the light of which these assertions can be interpreted and assessed. I shall begin by considering the role of the prin-ciples of justice. Let us assume, to fix ideas, that a society is a more or less self-sufficient association of persons who in their relations to one another recognize certain rules of conduct as binding and who for the most part act in accordance with them. Suppose further that these rules specify a system of cooperation designed to advance the good of those taking part in it. Then, although a society is a cooperative venture for mutual advantage, it is typically marked by a conflict as well as by an identity of interests. There is an identity of interests since social cooperation makes possible a better life for all than any would have if each were to live solely by his own efforts. There is a conflict of interests since persons are not indifferent as to how the greater benefits produced by their collaboration are distributed, for in order to pursue their ends they each prefer a larger to a lesser share. A set of principles is required for choosing among the various social arrangements which determine this division of advantages and for underwriting an agreement on the proper distributive shares. These principles are the principles of social justice: they provide a way of assigning rights and duties in the basic institutions of society and they define the appropriate distribution of the benefits and burdens of social cooperation. * * *

3. THE MAIN IDEA OF THE THEORY OF JUSTICE

My aim is to present a conception of justice which generalizes and carries to a higher level of abstraction the familiar theory of the social contract as found, say, in Locke, Rousseau, and Kant. In order to do this we are not to think of the original contract as one to enter a particular society or to set up a particular form of government. Rather, the guiding idea is that the principles of justice for the basic structure of society are the object of the original agreement. They are the principles that free and rational persons concerned to further their own interests would accept in an initial position of equality as defining the fundamental terms of their association. These principles are to regulate all further agreements; they specify the kinds of social cooperation that can be entered into and the forms of government that can be established. This way of regarding the principles of justice I shall call justice as fairness.

Thus we are to imagine that those who engage in social cooperation choose together, in one joint act, the principles which are to assign basic rights and duties and to determine the division of social benefits. Men are to decide in advance how they are to regulate their claims against one another and what is to be the foundation charter of their society. Just as each person must decide by rational reflection what constitutes his good, that is, the system of ends which it is rational for him to pursue, so a group of persons must decide once and for all what is to count among them as just and unjust. The choice which rational men would make in this hypothetical situation of equal liberty, assuming for the present that this choice problem has a solution, determines the principles of justice.

In justice as fairness the original position of equality corresponds to the state of nature in the traditional theory of the social contract. This original position is not, of course, thought of as an actual historical state of affairs, much less as a primitive condition of culture. It is understood as a purely hypothetical situation characterized so as to lead to a certain conception of justice. Among the essential features of this situation is that no one knows his place in society, his class position or social status, nor does any one know his fortune in the distribution of natural assets and abilities, his intelligence, strength, and the like. I shall even assume that the parties do not know their conceptions of the good or their special psychological propensities. The principles of justice are chosen behind a veil of ignorance. This ensures that no one is advantaged or disadvantaged in the choice of principles by the outcome of natural chance or the contingency of social circumstances. Since all are similarly situated and no one is able to design principles to favor his particular condition, the principles of justice are the result of a fair agreement or bargain. For given the circumstances of the original position, the symmetry of everyone's relations to each other, this initial situation is fair between individuals as moral persons, that is, as rational beings with their own ends and capable, I shall assume, of a sense of justice. The original position is, one might say, the appropriate initial status quo, and thus the fundamental agreements reached in it are fair. This explains the propriety of the name "justice as fairness": it conveys the idea that the principles of justice are agreed to in an initial situation that is fair. * * *

* * * No society can, of course, be a scheme of cooperation which men enter voluntarily in a literal sense; each person finds himself placed at birth in some particular position in some particular society, and the nature of this position materially affects his life prospects. Yet a society satisfying the principles of justice as fairness comes as close as a society can to being a voluntary scheme, for it meets the principles which free and equal persons would assent to under circumstances that are fair. In this sense its members are autonomous and the obligations they recognize self-imposed. * * *

4. THE ORIGINAL POSITION AND JUSTIFICATION

* * * One conception of justice is more reasonable than another, or justifiable with respect to it, if rational persons in the initial situation would choose its principles over those of the other for the role of justice. Conceptions of justice are to be ranked by their acceptability to persons so circumstanced. Understood in this way the question of justification is settled by working out a problem of deliberation: we have to ascertain which principles it would be rational to adopt given the contractual situation. This connects the theory of justice with the theory of rational choice.

If this view of the problem of justification is to succeed, we must, of course, describe in some detail the nature of this choice problem. A problem of rational decision has a definite answer only if we know the beliefs and interests of the parties, their relations with respect to one another, the alternatives between which they are to choose, the procedure whereby they make up their minds, and so on. As the circumstances are presented in different ways, correspondingly different principles are accepted. The concept of the original position, as I shall refer to it, is that of the most philosophically favored interpretation of this initial choice situation for the purposes of a theory of justice.

But how are we to decide what is the most favored interpretation? I assume, for one thing, that there is a broad measure of agreement that principles of justice should be chosen under certain conditions. To justify a particular description of the initial situation one shows that it incorporates these commonly shared presumptions. One argues from widely accepted but weak premises to more specific conclusions. Each of the presumptions should by itself be natural and plausible; some of them may seem innocuous or even trivial. The aim of the contract approach is to establish that taken together they impose significant bounds on acceptable principles of justice. The ideal outcome would be that these conditions determine a unique set of principles; but I shall be satisfied if they suffice to rank the main traditional conceptions of social justice.

One should not be misled, then, by the somewhat unusual conditions which characterize the original position. The idea here is simply to make vivid to ourselves the restrictions that it seems reasonable to impose on arguments for principles of justice, and therefore on these principles themselves. Thus it seems reasonable and generally acceptable that no one should be advantaged or disadvantaged by natural fortune or social circumstances in the choice of principles. It also seems widely agreed that it should be impossible to tailor principles to the circumstances of one's own case. We should insure further that particular inclinations and aspirations, and persons' conceptions of their good do not affect the principles adopted. The aim is to rule out those principles that it would be rational to propose for acceptance, however little the chance of success, only if one knew certain things that are irrelevant from the standpoint of justice. For example, if a man knew that he was wealthy, he might find it rational to advance the principle that various taxes for welfare measures be counted unjust; if he knew that he was poor, he would most likely propose the contrary principle. To represent the desired restrictions one imagines a situation in which everyone is deprived of this sort of information. One excludes the knowledge of those contingencies which sets men at odds and allows them to be guided by their prejudices. In this manner the veil of ignorance is arrived at in a natural way. This concept should cause no difficulty if we keep in mind the constraints on arguments that it is meant to express. At any time we can enter the original position, so to speak, simply by following a certain procedure, namely, by arguing for principles of justice in accordance with these restrictions.

It seems reasonable to suppose that the parties in the original position are equal. That is, all have the same rights in the procedure for choosing principles; each can make proposals, submit reasons for their acceptance, and so on. Obviously the purpose of these conditions is to represent equality between human beings as moral persons, as creatures having a conception of their good and capable of a sense of justice. The basis of equality is taken to be similarity in these two respects. Systems of ends are not ranked in value; and each man is presumed to have the requisite ability to understand and to act upon whatever principles are adopted. Together with the veil of ignorance, these conditions define the principles of justice as those which rational persons concerned to advance their interests would consent to as equals when none are known to be advantaged or disadvantaged by social and natural contingencies.

There is, however, another side to justifying a particular description of the original position. This is to see if the principles which would be chosen match our considered convictions of justice or extend them in an acceptable way. We can note whether applying these principles would lead us to make the same judgments about the basic structure of society which we now make intuitively and in which we have the greatest confidence; or whether, in cases where our present judgments are in doubt and given with hesitation, these principles offer a resolution which we can affirm on reflection. There are questions which we feel sure must be answered in a certain way. For example, we are confident that religious intolerance and racial discrimination are unjust. We think that we have examined these things with care and have reached what we believe is an impartial judgement not likely to be distorted by an excessive attention to our own interests. These convictions are provisional fixed points which we presume any conception of justice must fit. But we have much less assurance as to what is the correct distribution of wealth and authority. Here we may be looking for a way to remove our doubts. We can check an interpretation of the initial situation, then, by the capacity of its principles to accommodate our firmest convictions and to provide guidance where guidance is needed.

In searching for the most favored description of this situation we work from both ends. We begin by describing it so that it represents generally shared and preferably weak conditions. We then see if these conditions are strong enough to yield a significant set of principles. If not, we look for further premises equally reasonable. But if so, and these principles match our considered convictions of justice, then so far well and good. But presumably there will be discrepancies. In this case we have a choice. We can either modify the account of the initial situation or we can revise our existing judgments, for even the judgments we take provisionally as fixed points are liable to revision. By going back and forth, sometimes altering the conditions of the contractual circumstances, at others withdrawing our judgments and conforming them to principle, I assume that eventually we shall find a description of the initial situation that both expresses reasonable conditions and yields principles which match our considered judgments duly pruned and adjusted. This state of affairs I refer to as reflective equilibrium. It is an equilibrium because at last our principles and judgments coincide; and it is reflective since we know to what principles our judgments conform and the premises of their derivation. At the moment everything is in order. But this equilibrium is not necessarily stable. It is liable to be upset by further examination of the conditions which should be imposed on the contractual situation and by particular cases which may lead us to revise our judgments. Yet for the time being we have done what we can to render coherent and to justify our convictions of social justice. We have reached a conception of the original position.

I shall not, of course, actually work through this process. Still, we may think of the interpretation of the original position that I shall present as the result of such a hypothetical course of reflection. It represents the attempt to accommodate within one scheme both reasonable philosophical conditions on principles as well as our considered judgements of justice. In arriving at the favored interpretation of the initial situation there is no point at which an appeal is made to self-evidence in the traditional sense either of general conceptions or particular convictions. I do not claim for the principles of justice proposed that they are necessary truths or derivable from such truths. A conception of justice cannot be deduced from self-evident premises or conditions on principles; instead, its justification is a matter of the mutual support of many considerations, of everything fitting together into one coherent view.

A final comment. We shall want to say that certain principles of justice are justified because they would be agreed to in an initial situation of equality. I have emphasized that this original position is purely hypothetical. It is natural to ask why, if this agreement is never actually entered into, we should take any interest in these principles, moral or otherwise. The answer is that the conditions embodied in the description of the original position are ones that we do in fact accept. Or if we do not, then perhaps we can be persuaded to do so by philosophical reflection. Each aspect of the contractual situation can be given supporting grounds. Thus what we shall do is to collect together into one conception a number of conditions on principles that we are ready upon due consideration to recognize as reasonable. These constraints express what we are prepared to regard as limits on fair terms of social cooperation. One way to look at the idea of the original position, therefore, is to see it as an expository device which sums up the meaning of these conditions and helps us to extract their consequences. On the other hand, this conception is also an intuitive notion that suggests its own elaboration, so that led on by it we are drawn to define more clearly the standpoint from which we can best interpret moral relationships. We need a conception that enables us to envision our objective from afar: the intuitive notion of the original position is to do this for us.

STUDY QUESTIONS

1. Explain the concept of the original position.
2. Why does Rawls modify standard social contract theory?
3. How can the methodology of the original position be used in relation to moral problems?

JEREMY BENTHAM
An Introduction to the Principles of Morals and Legislation

Jeremy Bentham (1748–1832) was an English philosopher and legal theorist who, in his copious writings, argued for substantial legal reform around the world, based on the "greatest happiness principle," otherwise known as utilitarianism.

CHAPTER I: OF THE PRINCIPLE OF UTILITY

I. Nature has placed mankind under the governance of two sovereign masters, *pain* and *pleasure*. It is for them alone to point out what we ought to do, as well as to determine what we shall do. On the one hand the standard of right and wrong, on the other the chain of causes and effects, are fastened to their throne. They govern us in all we do, in all we say, in all we think: every effort we can make to throw off our subjection, will serve but to demonstrate and confirm it. In words a man may pretend to abjure their empire: but in reality he will remain subject to it all the while. The *principle of utility* recognizes this subjection, and assumes it for the foundation of that system, the object of which is to rear the fabric of felicity by the hands of reason and of law. Systems which attempt to question it, deal in sounds instead of sense, in caprice instead of reason, in darkness instead of light.

But enough of metaphor and declamation: it is not by such means that moral science is to be improved.

II. The principle of utility is the foundation of the present work: it will be proper therefore at the outset to give an explicit and determinate account of what is meant by it. By the principle of utility is meant that principle which approves or disapproves of every action whatsoever according to the tendency it appears to have to augment or diminish the happiness of the party whose interest is in question: or, what is the same thing in other words to promote or to oppose that happiness. I say of every action whatsoever, and therefore not only of every action of a private individual, but of every measure of government.

III. By utility is meant that property in any object, whereby it tends to produce benefit, advantage, pleasure, good, or happiness, (all this in the present case comes to the same thing) or (what comes again to the same thing) to prevent the happening of mischief, pain, evil, or unhappiness to the party whose interest is considered: if that party be the community in general, then the happiness of the community: if a particular individual, then the happiness of that individual.

IV. The interest of the community is one of the most general expressions that can occur in the phraseology of morals: no wonder that the meaning of it is often lost. When it has a meaning, it is this. The community is a fictitious *body*, composed of the individual persons who are considered as constituting as it were its *members*. The interest of the community then is, what is it?—the sum of the interests of the several members who compose it.

V. It is in vain to talk of the interest of the community, without understanding what is the interest of the individual. A thing is said to promote the interest, or to be *for* the interest, of an individual, when it tends to add to the sum total of his pleasures: or, what comes to the same thing, to diminish the sum total of his pains.

VI. An action then may be said to be conformable to the principle of utility, or, for shortness sake, to utility, (meaning with respect to the community at large) when the tendency it has to augment the happiness of the community is greater than any it has to diminish it.

VII. A measure of government (which is but a particular kind of action, performed by a particular person or persons) may be said to be conformable to or dictated by the principle of utility, when in like manner the tendency which it has to augment the happiness of the community is greater than any which it has to diminish it.

VIII. When an action, or in particular a measure of government, is supposed by a man to be conformable to the principle of utility, it may be convenient, for the purposes of discourse, to imagine a kind of law or dictate, called a law or dictate of utility: and to speak of the action in question, as being conformable to such law or dictate.

IX. A man may be said to be a partizan of the principle of utility, when the approbation or disapprobation he annexes to any action, or to any measure, is determined by and proportioned to the tendency which he conceives it to have to augment or to diminish the happiness of the community: or in other words, to its conformity or unconformity to the laws or dictates of utility.

X. Of an action that is conformable to the principle of utility one may always say either that it is one that ought to be done, or at least that it is not one that ought not to be done. One may say also, that it is right it should be done; at least that it is not wrong it should be done: that it is a right action; at least that it is not a wrong action. When thus interpreted, the words *ought*, and *right* and *wrong* and others of that stamp, have a meaning: when otherwise, they have none.

XI. Has the rectitude of this principle been ever formally contested? It should seem that it had, by those who have not known what they have been meaning. Is it susceptible of any direct proof? it should seem not: for that which is used to prove every thing else, cannot itself be proved: a chain of proofs must have their commencement somewhere. To give such proof is as impossible as it is needless.

XII. Not that there is or ever has been that human creature breathing, however stupid or perverse, who has not on many, perhaps on most occasions of his life, deferred to it. By the natural constitution of the human frame, on most occasions of their lives men in general embrace this principle, without thinking of it: if not for the ordering of their own actions, yet for the trying of their own actions, as well as of those of other men. There have been, at the same time, not many, perhaps, even of the most intelligent, who have been disposed to embrace it purely and without reserve. There are even few who have not taken some occasion or other to quarrel with it, either on account of their not understanding always how to apply it, or on account of some prejudice or other which they were afraid to examine into, or could not bear to part with. For such is the stuff that man is made of: in principle and in practice, in a right track and in a wrong one, the rarest of all human qualities is consistency. ✳ ✳ ✳

CHAPTER II: OF PRINCIPLES ADVERSE TO THAT OF UTILITY

I. If the principle of utility be a right principle to be governed by, and that in all cases, it follows from what has been just observed, that whatever principle differs from it in any case must necessarily be a wrong one. To prove any other principle, therefore, to be a wrong one, there needs no more than just to show it to be what it is, a principle of which the dictates are in some point or other different from those of the principle of utility: to state it is to confute it.

II. A principle may be different from that of utility in two ways: 1. By being constantly opposed to it: this is the case with a principle which may be termed the principle of *asceticism*. 2. By being sometimes opposed to it, and sometimes not, as it may happen: this is the case with another, which may be termed the principle of *sympathy* and *antipathy*.

III. By the principle of asceticism I mean that principle, which, like the principle of utility, approves or disapproves of any action, according to the tendency which it appears to have to augment or diminish the happiness of the party whose interest is in question; but in an inverse manner: approving of actions in as far as they tend to diminish his happiness; disapproving of them in as far as they tend to augment it. ✳ ✳ ✳

V. There are two classes of men of very different complexions, by whom the principle of asceticism appears to have been embraced; the one a set of moralists, the other a set of religionists. Different accordingly have been the motives which appear to have recommended it to the notice of these different parties. Hope, that is the prospect of pleasure, seems to have animated the former: hope, the aliment of philosophic pride: the hope of honour and reputation at the hands of men. Fear, that is the prospect of pain, the latter: fear, the offspring of superstitious fancy: the fear of future punishment at the hands of a splenetic and revengeful Deity. I say in this case fear: for of the invisible future, fear is more powerful than hope. These circumstances characterize the two different parties among the partizans of the principle of asceticism; the parties and their motives different, the principle the same. ✳ ✳ ✳

VIII. The principle of asceticism, however, with whatever warmth it may have been embraced by its partizans as a rule of private conduct, seems not to have been carried to any considerable length, when applied to the business of government. In a few instances it has been carried a little way by the philosophical party: witness the Spartan regimen. Though then, perhaps, it maybe considered as having been a measure of security: and an application, though a precipitate and perverse application, of the principle of utility. * * * Whatever merit a man may have thought there would be in making himself miserable, no such notion seems ever to have occurred to any of them, that it may be a merit, much less a duty, to make others miserable: although it should seem, that if a certain quantity of misery were a thing so desirable, it would not matter much whether it were brought by each man upon himself, or by one man upon another. It is true, that from the same source from whence, among the religionists, the attachment to the principle of asceticism took its rise, flowed other doctrines and practices, from which misery in abundance was produced in one man by the instrumentality of another: witness the holy wars, and the persecutions for religion. But the passion for producing misery in these cases proceeded upon some special ground: the exercise of it was confined to persons of particular descriptions: they were tormented, not as men, but as heretics and infidels. To have inflicted the same miseries on their fellow-believers and fellow-sectaries, would have been as blameable in the eyes even of these religionists, as in those of a partizan of the principle of utility. For a man to give himself a certain number of stripes was indeed meritorious: but to give the same number of stripes to another man, not consenting, would have been a sin. We read of saints, who for the good of their souls, and the mortification of their bodies, have voluntarily yielded themselves a prey to vermin: but though many persons of this class have wielded the reins of empire, we read of none who have set themselves to work, and made laws on purpose, with a view of stocking the body politic with the breed of highwaymen, housebreakers, or incendiaries. If at any time they have suffered the nation to be preyed upon by swarms of idle pensioners, or useless placemen, it has rather been from negligence and imbecility, than from any settled plan for oppressing and plundering of the people. If at any time they have sapped the sources of national wealth, by cramping commerce, and driving the inhabitants into emigration, it has been with other views, and in pursuit of other ends. If they have declaimed against the pursuit of pleasure, and the use of wealth, they have commonly stopped at declamation. * * *

IX. The principle of asceticism seems originally to have been the reverie of certain hasty speculators, who having perceived, or fancied, that certain pleasures, when reaped in certain circumstances, have, at the long run, been attended with pains more than equivalent to them, took occasion to quarrel with every thing that offered itself under the name of pleasure. Having then got thus far, and having forgot the point which they set out from, they pushed on, and went so much further as to think it meritorious to fall in love with pain. Even this, we see, is at bottom but the principle of utility misapplied.

X. The principle of utility is capable of being consistently pursued; and it is but tautology to say, that the more consistently it is pursued, the better it must ever be for human-kind. The principle of asceticism never was, nor ever can be, consistently pursued by any living creature. Let but one tenth part of the inhabitants of this earth pursue it consistently, and in a day's time they will have turned it into a hell.

XI. Among principles adverse to that of utility, that which at this day seems to have most influence in matters of government, is what may be called the principle of sympathy and antipathy. By the principle of sympathy and antipathy, I mean that principle which approves or disapproves of certain actions, not on account of their tending to augment the happiness, nor yet on account of their tending to diminish the happiness of the party whose interest is in question, but merely because a man finds himself disposed to approve or disapprove of them: holding up that approbation or disapprobation as a sufficient reason for itself, and disclaiming the necessity of looking out for any extrinsic ground. Thus far in the general department of morals: and in the particular department of politics, measuring out the quantum (as well as determining the ground) of punishment, by the degree of the disapprobation.

XII. It is manifest, that this is rather a principle in name than in reality: it is not a positive principle of itself, so much as a term employed to signify the negation of all principle. What one expects to find in a principle is something that points out some external consideration, as a means of warranting and guiding the internal sentiments of approbation and disapprobation: this expectation is but ill fulfilled by a proposition, which does neither more nor less than hold up each of those sentiments as a ground and standard for itself.

XIII. In looking over the catalogue of human actions (says a partizan of this principle) in order to determine which of them are to be marked with the seal of disapprobation, you need but to take counsel of your own feelings: whatever you find in yourself a propensity to condemn, is wrong for that very reason. For the same reason it is also meet for punishment: in what proportion it is adverse to utility, or whether it be adverse to utility at all, is a matter that makes no difference. In that same *proportion* also is it meet for punishment: if you hate much, punish much: if you hate little, punish little: punish as you hate. If you hate not at all, punish not at all: the fine feelings of the soul are not to be overborne and tyrannized by the harsh and rugged dictates of political utility.

XIV. The various systems that have been formed concerning the standard of right may all be reduced to the principle of sympathy and antipathy. One account may serve for all of them. They consist all of them in so many contrivances for avoiding the obligation of appealing to any external standard, and for prevailing upon the reader to accept of the author's sentiment or opinion as a reason for itself. The phrases different, but the principle the same. * * *

XVI. The principle of sympathy and antipathy is most apt to err on the side of severity. It is for applying punishment in many cases which deserve none: in many cases which deserve some, it is for applying more than they deserve. There is no incident imaginable, be it ever so trivial, and so remote from mischief, from which this principle may not extract a ground of punishment. Any difference in taste: any difference in opinion: upon one subject as well as upon another. No disagreement so trifling which perseverance and altercation will not render serious. Each becomes in the other's eyes an enemy, and, if laws permit, a criminal. This is one of the circumstances by which the human race is distinguished (not much indeed to its advantage) from the brute creation.

XVII. It is not, however, by any means unexampled for this principle to err on the side of lenity. A near and perceptible mischief moves antipathy. A remote and imperceptible mischief, though not less real, has no effect. * * *

CHAPTER IV: VALUE OF A LOT OF PLEASURE OR PAIN, HOW TO BE MEASURED

I. Pleasures then, and the avoidance of pains, are the *ends* that the legislator has in view; it behoves him therefore to understand their *value*. Pleasures and pains are the *instruments* he has to work with: it behoves him therefore to understand their force, which is again, in other words, their value.

II. To a person considered *by himself,* the value of a pleasure or pain considered *by itself,* will be greater or less, according to the four following *circumstances:*

1. Its *intensity.* 2. Its *duration.* 3. Its *certainty* or *uncertainty.* 4. Its *propinquity* or *remoteness.*

III. These are the circumstances which are to be considered in estimating a pleasure or a pain considered each of them by itself. But when the value of any pleasure or pain is considered for the purpose of estimating the tendency of any *act* by which it is produced, there are two other circumstances to be taken into the account; these are,

5. Its *fecundity,* or the chance it has of being followed by sensations of the *same* kind: that is, pleasures, if it be a pleasure: pains, if it be a pain.

6. Its *purity,* or the chance it has of *not* being followed by sensations of the *opposite* kind: that is, pains, if it be a pleasure: pleasures, if it be a pain.

These two last, however, are in strictness scarcely to be deemed properties of the pleasure or the pain itself; they are not, therefore, in strictness to be taken into the account of the value of that pleasure or that pain. They are in strictness to be deemed properties only of the act, or other event, by which such pleasure or pain has been produced; and accordingly are only to be taken into the account of the tendency of such act or such event.

IV. To a *number* of persons, with reference to each of whom the value of a pleasure or a pain is considered, it will be greater or less, according to seven circumstances: to wit, the six preceding ones; viz.,

1. Its *intensity.* 2. Its *duration.* 3. Its *certainty* or *uncertainty.* 4. Its *propinquity* or *remoteness.* 5. Its *fecundity.* 6. Its *purity.* And one other; to wit: 7. Its *extent;* that is, the number of persons to whom it *extends;* or (in other words) who are affected by it.

V. To take an exact account then of the general tendency of any act, by which the interests of a community are affected, proceed as follows. Begin with any one person of those whose interests seem most immediately to be affected by it: and take an account,

1. Of the value of each distinguishable *pleasure* which appears to be produced by it in the *first* instance.

2. Of the value of each *pain* which appears to be produced by it in the *first* instance.

3. Of the value of each pleasure which appears to be produced by it *after* the first. This constitutes the *fecundity* of the first *pleasure* and the *impurity* of the first *pain.*

4. Of the value of each *pain* which appears to be produced by it after the first. This constitutes the *fecundity* of the first *pain,* and the *impurity* of the first pleasure.

5. Sum up all the values of all the *pleasures* on the one side, and those of all the pains on the other. The balance, if it be on the side of pleasure, will give the *good* tendency of the act upon the whole, with respect to the interests of that *individual* person; if on the side of pain, the *bad* tendency of it upon the whole.

6. Take an account of the *number* of persons whose interests appear to be concerned; and repeat the above process with respect to each. *Sum up* the numbers expressive of the degrees of *good* tendency, which the act has, with respect to each individual, in regard to whom the tendency of it is *good* upon the whole: do this again with respect to each individual, in regard to whom the tendency of it is *bad* upon the whole. Take the *balance* which if on the side of *pleasure,* will give the general *good tendency* of the act, with respect to the total number or community of individuals concerned; if on the side of pain, the general *evil tendency,* with respect to the same community.

VI. It is not to be expected that this process should be strictly pursued previously to every moral judgment, or to every legislative or judicial operation. It may, however, be always kept in view: and as near as the process actually pursued on these occasions approaches to it, so near will such process approach to the character of an exact one.

STUDY QUESTIONS

1. What are Bentham's arguments against the principle of asceticism?
2. What are Bentham's arguments against the principle of sympathy and antipathy?
3. How, according to Bentham, are pleasures and pains to be measured?

JOHN STUART MILL
Utilitarianism

John Stuart Mill (1806–1873) was born in England, of Scottish descent. Mill was initially a disciple of Bentham but branched out to develop his own distinctive and highly influential moral views. He wrote on a very wide range of moral, political, philosophical, and economic issues, including arguing for the emancipation of women.

The creed which accepts as the foundation of morals, Utility, or the Greatest Happiness Principle, holds that actions are right in proportion as they tend to promote happiness, wrong as they tend to produce the reverse of happiness. By happiness is intended pleasure, and the absence of pain; by unhappiness, pain, and the privation of pleasure. To give a clear view of the moral standard set up by the theory, much more requires to be said; in particular, what things it includes in the ideas of pain and pleasure; and to what extent this is left an open question. But these supplementary explanations do not affect the theory of life on which this theory of morality is grounded—namely, that pleasure, and freedom from pain, are the only things desirable as ends; and that all desirable things (which are as numerous in the utilitarian as in any other scheme) are desirable either for the pleasure inherent in themselves, or as means to the promotion of pleasure and the prevention of pain.

Now, such a theory of life excites in many minds, and among them in some of the most estimable in feeling and purpose, inveterate dislike. To suppose that life has (as they express it) no higher end than pleasure—no better and nobler object of desire and pursuit—they designate as utterly mean and grovelling; as a doctrine worthy only of swine, to whom the followers of Epicurus were, at a very early period, contemptuously likened; and modern holders of the doctrine are occasionally made the subject of equally polite comparisons by its German, French, and English assailants.

When thus attacked, the Epicureans have always answered, that it is not they, but their accusers, who represent human nature in a degrading light; since the accusation supposes human beings to be capable of no pleasures except those of which swine are capable. If this supposition were true, the charge could not be gainsaid, but would then be no longer an imputation; for if the sources of pleasure were precisely the same to human beings and to swine, the rule of life which is good enough for the one would be good enough for the other. The comparison of the Epicurean life to that of beasts is felt as degrading, precisely because a beast's pleasures do not satisfy a human being's conceptions of happiness. Human beings have faculties more elevated than the animal appetites, and when once made conscious of them, do not regard anything as happiness which does not include their gratification. ∗ ∗ ∗ There is no known Epicurean theory of life which does not assign to the pleasures of the intellect; of the feelings and imagination, and of the moral sentiments, a much higher value as pleasures than to those of mere sensation. It must be admitted, however, that utilitarian writers in general have placed the superiority of mental over bodily pleasures chiefly in the greater permanency, safety, uncostliness, &c, of the former—that is, in their circumstantial advantages rather than in their intrinsic nature. And on all these points utilitarians have fully proved their case; but they might have taken the other, and, as it may be called, higher ground, with entire consistency. It is quite compatible with the principle of utility to recognise the fact, that some *kinds* of pleasure are more desirable and more valuable than others. It would be absurd that while, in estimating all other things, quality is considered as well as quantity, the estimation of pleasures should be supposed to depend on quantity alone.

If I am asked, what I mean by difference of quality in pleasures, or what makes one pleasure more valuable than another, merely as a pleasure, except its being greater in amount, there is but one possible answer. Of two pleasures, if there be one to which all or almost all who have experience of both give a decided preference, irrespective of any feeling of moral obligation to prefer it, that is the more desirable pleasure. If one of the two is, by those who are competently acquainted with both, placed so far above the other that they prefer it, even though knowing it to be attended with a greater amount of discontent, and would not resign it for any quantity of the other pleasure which their nature is capable of, we are justified in ascribing to the preferred enjoyment a superiority in quality, so far outweighing quantity as to render it, in comparison, of small account.

Now it is an unquestionable fact that those who are equally acquainted with, and equally capable of appreciating and enjoying, both, do give a most marked preference to the manner of existence which employs their higher faculties. Few human creatures would consent to be changed into any of the lower animals, for a promise of the fullest allowance of a beast's pleasures; no intelligent human being would consent to be a fool, no instructed person would be an ignoramus, no person of feeling and conscience would be selfish and base, even though they should be persuaded that the fool, the dunce, or the rascal is better satisfied with his lot than they are with theirs. They would not resign what they possess more than he for the most complete satisfaction of all the desires which they have in common with him. If they ever fancy they would, it is only in cases of unhappiness so extreme, that to escape from it they would exchange their lot for almost any other, however undesirable in their own eyes. A being of higher faculties requires more to make him happy, is capable probably of more acute suffering, and certainly accessible to it at more points, than one of an inferior type; but in spite of these liabilities, he can never really wish to sink into what he feels to be a lower grade of existence. We may give what explanation we please of this unwillingness; we may attribute it to pride, a name which is given indiscriminately to some of the most and to some of the least estimable feelings of which mankind are capable: we may refer it to the love of liberty and personal independence, an appeal to which was with the Stoics one of the most effective means for the inculcation of it; to the love of power, or to the love of excitement, both of which do really enter into and contribute to it: but its most appropriate appellation is a sense of dignity, which all human beings possess in one form or other, and in some, though by no means in exact, proportion to their higher faculties, and which is so essential a part of the happiness of those in whom it is strong, that nothing which conflicts with it could be, otherwise than momentarily, an object of desire to them. Whoever supposes that this preference takes place at a sacrifice of happiness—that the superior being, in anything like equal circumstances, is not happier than the inferior—confounds the two very different ideas, of happiness, and content. It is indisputable that the being whose capacities of enjoyment are low, has the greatest chance of having them fully satisfied; and a highly endowed being will always feel that any happiness which he can look for, as the world is constituted, is imperfect. But he can learn to bear its imperfections, if they are at all bearable; and they will not make him envy the being who is indeed unconscious of the imperfections, but only because he feels not at all the good which those imperfections qualify. It is better to be a human being dissatisfied than a pig satisfied; better to be Socrates dissatisfied than a fool satisfied. And if the fool, or the pig, is of a different opinion, it is because they only know their own side of the question. The other party to the comparison knows both sides.

It may be objected, that many who are capable of the higher pleasures, occasionally, under the influence of temptation, postpone them to the lower. But this is quite compatible with a full appreciation of the intrinsic superiority of the higher. Men often, from infirmity of character, make their election for the nearer good, though they know it to be the less valuable; and this no less when the choice is between two bodily pleasures, than when it is between bodily and mental. They pursue sensual indulgences to the injury of health, though perfectly aware that health is the greater good. It may be further objected, that many who begin with youthful enthusiasm for everything noble, as they advance in years sink into indolence and selfishness. But I do not believe that those who undergo this very common change, voluntarily choose the lower description of pleasures in preference to the higher. I believe that before they devote themselves exclusively to the one, they have already become incapable of the other. Capacity for the nobler feelings is in most natures a very tender plant, easily killed, not only by hostile influences, but by mere want of sustenance; and in the majority of young persons it speedily dies away if the occupations to which their position in life has devoted them, and the society into which it has thrown them, are not favourable to keeping that higher capacity in exercise. Men lose their high aspirations as they lose their intellectual tastes, because they have not time or opportunity for indulging them; and they addict themselves to inferior pleasures, not because they deliberately prefer them, but because they are either the only ones to which they have access, or the only ones which they are any longer capable of enjoying. It may be questioned whether any one who has remained equally susceptible to both classes of pleasures, ever knowingly and calmly preferred the lower; though many, in all ages, have broken down in an ineffectual attempt to combine both.

From this verdict of the only competent judges, I apprehend there can be no appeal. On a question which is the best worth having of two pleasures, or which of two modes of existence is the most grateful to the feelings, apart from its moral attributes and from its consequences, the judgment of those who are qualified by knowledge of both, or, if they differ, that of the majority among them, must be admitted as final. And there needs be the less hesitation to accept this judgment respecting the quality of pleasures, since there is no other tribunal to be referred to even on the question of quantity. What means are there of determining which is the acutest of two pains, or the intensest of two pleasurable sensations, except the general suffrage of those who are familiar with both? Neither pains nor pleasures are homogeneous, and pain is always heterogeneous with pleasure. What is there to decide whether a particular pleasure is worth purchasing at the cost of a particular pain, except the feelings and judgment of the experienced? When, therefore, those feelings and judgment declare the pleasures derived from the higher faculties to be preferable *in kind*, apart from the question of intensity, to those of which the animal nature, disjoined from the higher faculties, is suspectible, they are entitled on this subject to the same regard. ***

According to the Greatest Happiness Principle, as above explained, the ultimate end, with reference to and for the sake of which all other things are desirable (whether we are considering our own good or that of other people), is an existence exempt as far as possible from pain, and as rich as possible in enjoyments, both in point of quantity and quality. *** This, being, according to the utilitarian opinion, the end of human action, is necessarily also the standard of morality; which may accordingly be defined, the rules and precepts for human conduct, by the observance of which an existence such as has been described might be, to the greatest extent possible, secured to all mankind; and not to them only, but, so far as the nature of things admits, to the whole sentient creation.

Against this doctrine, however, arises another class of objectors, who say that happiness, in any form, cannot be the rational purpose of human life and action; because, in the first place, it is unattainable: and they contemptuously ask, What right hast thou to be happy? a question which Mr. Carlyle clenches by the addition, What right, a short time ago, hadst thou even *to be?* Next, they say, that men can do *without* happiness; that all noble human beings have felt this, and could not have become noble but by learning the lesson of Entsagen, or renunciation; which lesson, thoroughly learnt and submitted to, they affirm to be the beginning and necessary condition of all virtue.

The first of these objections would go to the root of the matter were it well founded; for if no happiness is to be had at all by human beings, the attainment of it cannot be the end of morality, or of any rational conduct. Though, even in that case, something might still be said for the utilitarian theory; since utility includes not solely the pursuit of happiness, but the prevention or mitigation of unhappiness; and if the former aim be chimerical, there will be all the greater scope and more imperative need for the latter, so long at least as mankind think fit to live, and do not take refuge in the simultaneous act of suicide recommended under certain conditions by Novalis. When, however, it is thus positively asserted to be impossible that human life should be happy, the assertion, if not something like a verbal quibble, is at least an exaggeration. If by happiness be meant a continuity of highly pleasurable excitement, it is evident enough that this is impossible. A state of exalted pleasure lasts only moments, or in some cases, and with some intermissions, hours or days, and is the occasional brilliant flash of enjoyment, not its permanent and steady flame. Of this the philosophers who have taught that happiness is the end of life were as fully aware as those who taunt them. The happiness which they meant was not a life of rapture, but moments of such, in an existence made up of few and transitory pains, many and various pleasures, with a decided predominance of the active over the passive, and having as the foundation of the whole, not to expect more from life than it is capable of bestowing. A life thus composed, to those who have been fortunate enough to obtain it, has always appeared worthy of the name of happiness. And such an existence is even now the lot of many, during some considerable portion of their lives. The present wretched education, and wretched social arrangements, are the only real hindrance to its being attainable by almost all. * * *

I must again repeat, what the assailants of utilitarianism seldom have the justice to acknowledge, that the happiness which forms the utilitarian standard of what is right in conduct, is not the agent's own happiness, but that of all concerned. As between his own happiness and that of others, utilitarianism requires him to be as strictly impartial as a disinterested and benevolent spectator. In the golden rule of Jesus of Nazareth, we read the complete spirit of the ethics of utility. To do as you would be done by, and to love your neighbour as yourself, constitute the ideal perfection of utilitarian morality. * * *

Again, defenders of utility often find themselves called upon to reply to such objections as this—that there is not time, previous to action, for calculating and weighing the effects of any line of conduct on the general happiness. This is exactly as if any one were to say that it is impossible to guide our conduct by Christianity, because there is not time, on every occasion on which anything has to be done, to read through the Old and New Testaments. The answer to the objection is, that there has been ample time, namely, the whole past duration of the human species. During all that time, mankind have been learning by experience the tendencies of actions; on which experience all the prudence, as well as all the morality of life, is dependent. People talk as if the commencement of this course of experience had hitherto been put off, and as if, at the moment when some man feels tempted to meddle with the property or life of another, he had to begin considering for the first time whether murder and theft are injurious to human happiness. Even then I do not think that he would find the question very puzzling; but, at all events, the matter is now done to his hand. It is truly a whimsical supposition that, if mankind were agreed in considering utility to be the test of morality, they would remain without any agreement as to what is useful, and would take no measures for having their notions on the subject taught to the young, and enforced by law and opinion. There is no difficulty in proving any ethical standard whatever to work ill, if we suppose universal idiocy to be conjoined with it. * * *

The remainder of the stock arguments against utilitarianism mostly consist in laying to its charge the common infirmities of human nature, and the general difficulties which embarrass conscientious persons in shaping their course through life. We are told that a utilitarian will be apt to make his own particular case an exception to moral rules, and, when under temptation, will see an utility in the breach of a rule, greater than he will see in its observance. But is utility the only creed which is able to furnish us with excuses for evil doing, and means of cheating our own conscience? They are afforded in abundance by all doctrines which recognise as a fact in morals the existence of conflicting considerations; which all doctrines do, that have been believed by sane persons. It is not the fault of any creed, but of the complicated nature of human affairs, that rules of conduct cannot be so framed as to require no exceptions, and that hardly any kind of action can safely be laid down as either always obligatory or always condemnable. There is no ethical creed which does not temper the rigidity of its laws, by giving a certain latitude, under the moral responsibility of the agent, for accommodation to peculiarities of circumstances; and under every creed, at the opening thus made, self-deception and dishonest casuistry get in. ∗ ∗ ∗

CHAPTER IV

Of what sort of proof the principle of utility is susceptible

It has already been remarked, that questions of ultimate ends do not admit of proof, in the ordinary acceptation of the term. To be incapable of proof by reasoning is common to all first principles; to the first premises of our knowledge, as well as to those of our conduct. But the former, being matters of fact, may be the subject of a direct appeal to the faculties which judge of fact—namely, our senses, and our internal consciousness. Can an appeal be made to the same faculties on questions of practical ends? Or by what other faculty is cognisance taken of them?

Questions about ends are, in other words, questions what things are desirable. The utilitarian doctrine is, that happiness is desirable, and the only thing desirable, as an end; all other things being only desirable as means to that end. What ought to be required of this doctrine—what conditions is it requisite that the doctrine should fulfil—to make good its claim to be believed?

The only proof capable of being given that an object is visible, is that people actually see it. The only proof that a sound is audible, is that people hear it: and so of the other sources of our experience. In like manner, I apprehend, the sole evidence it is possible to produce that anything is desirable, is that people do actually desire it. If the end which the utilitarian doctrine proposes to itself were not, in theory and in practice, acknowledged to be an end, nothing could ever convince any person that it was so. No reason can be given why the general happiness is desirable, except that each person, so far as he believes it to be attainable, desires his own happiness.

This, however, being a fact, we have not only all the proof which the case admits of, but all which it is possible to require, that happiness is a good: that each person's happiness is a good to that person, and the general happiness, therefore, a good to the aggregate of all persons. Happiness has made out its title as *one* of the ends of conduct, and consequently one of the criteria of morality.

But it has not, by this alone, proved itself to be the sole criterion. To do that, it would seem, by the same rule, necessary to show, not only that people desire happiness, but that they never desire anything else. Now it is palpable that they do desire things which, in common language, are decidedly distinguished from happiness. They desire, for example, virtue, and the absence of vice, no less really than pleasure and the absence of pain. The desire of virtue is not as universal, but it is as authentic a fact, as the desire of happiness. And hence the opponents of the utilitarian standard deem that they have a right to infer that there are other ends of human action besides happiness, and that happiness is not the standard of approbation and disapprobation.

But does the utilitarian doctrine deny that people desire virtue, or maintain that virtue is not a thing to be desired? The very reverse. It maintains not only that virtue is to be desired, but that it is to be desired disinterestedly, for itself. Whatever may be the opinion of utilitarian moralists as to the original conditions by which virtue is made virtue; however they may believe (as they do) that actions and dispositions are only virtuous because they promote another end than virtue; yet this being granted, and it having been decided, from considerations of this description, what *is* virtuous, they not only place virtue at the very head of the things which are good as means to the ultimate end, but they also recognise as a psychological fact the possibility of its being, to the individual, a good in itself, without looking to any end beyond it; and hold, that the mind is not in a right state, not in a state conformable to Utility, not in the state most conducive to the general happiness, unless it does love virtue in this manner—as a thing desirable in itself, even although, in the individual instance, it should not produce those other desirable consequences which it tends to produce, and on account of which it is held to be virtue. This opinion is not, in the smallest degree, a departure from the Happiness principle. The ingredients of happiness are very various, and each of them is desirable in itself, and not merely when considered as swelling an aggregate. The principle of utility does not mean that any given pleasure, as music, for instance, or any given exemption from pain, as for example health, are to be looked upon as means to a collective something termed happiness, and to be desired on that account. They are desired and desirable in and for themselves; besides being means, they are a part of the end. Virtue, according to the utilitarian doctrine, is not naturally and originally part of the end, but it is capable of becoming so; and in those who love it disinterestedly it has become so, and is desired and cherished, not as a means to happiness, but as a part of their happiness. * * *

It results from the preceding considerations, that there is in reality nothing desired except happiness. Whatever is desired otherwise than as a means to some end beyond itself, and ultimately to happiness, is desired as itself a part of happiness, and is not desired for itself until it has become so. Those who desire virtue for its own sake, desire it either because the consciousness of it is a pleasure, or because the consciousness of being without it is a pain, or for both reasons united; as in truth the pleasure and pain seldom exist separately, but almost always together, the same person feeling pleasure in the degree of virtue attained, and pain in not having attained more. If one of these gave him no pleasure, and the other no pain, he would not love or desire virtue, or would desire it only for the other benefits which it might produce to himself or to persons whom he cared for.

We have now, then, an answer to the question, of what sort of proof the principle of utility is susceptible. If the opinion which I have now stated is psychologically true—if human nature is so constituted as to desire nothing which is not either a part of happiness or a means of happiness, we can have no other proof, and we require no other, that these are the only things desirable. If so, happiness is the sole end of human action, and the promotion of it the test by which to judge of all human conduct; from whence it necessarily follows that it must be the criterion of morality, since a part is included in the whole.

And now to decide whether this is really so; whether mankind do desire nothing for itself but that which is a pleasure to them, or of which the absence is a pain; we have evidently arrived at a question of fact and experience, dependent, like all similar questions, upon evidence. It can only be determined by practised self-consciousness and self-observation, assisted by observation of others. I believe that these sources of evidence, impartially consulted, will declare that desiring a thing and finding it pleasant, aversion to it and thinking of it as painful, are phenomena entirely inseparable, or rather two parts of the same phenomenon; in strictness of language, two different modes of naming the same psychological fact: that to think of an object as desirable (unless for the sake of its consequences), and to think of it as pleasant, are one and the same thing; and that to desire anything, except in proportion as the idea of it is pleasant, is a physical and metaphysical impossibility.

STUDY QUESTIONS

1. What are Mill's reasons for introducing the distinction between higher and lower pleasures, and how is that distinction to be made?
2. Assess Mill's "proof" that happiness is desirable.
3. How does Mill attempt to demonstrate that only happiness is desirable as an ultimate end?

ROBERT NOZICK
The Experience Machine

Robert Nozick (1938–2002) was an American political philosopher who wrote on a wide variety of topics; he was especially noted for his defense of the political philosophy of libertarianism.

There are ∗ ∗ ∗ substantial puzzles when we ask what matters other than how *people's* experiences feel "from the inside." Suppose there were an experience machine that would give you any experience you desired. Superduper neuropsychologists could stimulate your brain so that you would think and feel you were writing a great novel, or making a friend, or reading an interesting book. All the time you would be floating in a tank, with electrodes attached to your brain. Should you plug into this machine for life, preprogramming your life's experiences? If you are worried about missing out on desirable experiences, we can suppose that business enterprises have researched thoroughly the lives of many others. You can pick and choose from their large library or smorgasbord of such experiences, selecting your life's experiences for, say, the next two years. After two years have passed, you will have ten minutes or ten hours out of the tank, to select the experiences of your *next* two years. Of course, while in the tank you won't know that you're there; you'll think it's all actually happening. Others can also plug in to have the experiences they want, so there's no need to stay unplugged to serve them. (Ignore problems such as who will service the machines if everyone plugs in.) Would you plug in? *What else can matter to us, other than how our lives feel from the inside?* Nor should you refrain because of the few moments of distress between the moment you've decided and the moment you're plugged. What's a few moments of distress compared to a lifetime of bliss (if that's what you choose), and why feel any distress at all if your decision *is* the best one?

What does matter to us in addition to our experiences? First, we want to *do* certain things, and not just have the experience of doing them. In the case of certain experiences, it is only because first we want to do the actions that we want the experiences of doing them or thinking we've done them. (But *why* do we want to do the activities rather than merely to experience them?) A second reason for not plugging in is that we want to *be* a certain way, to be a certain sort of person. Someone floating in a tank is an indeterminate blob. There is no answer to the question of what a person is like who has long been in the tank. Is he courageous, kind, intelligent, witty, loving? It's not merely that it's difficult to tell; there's no way he is. Plugging into the machine is a kind of suicide. It will seem to some, trapped by a picture, that nothing about what we are like can matter except as it gets reflected in our experiences. But should it be surprising that what *we are* is important to us? Why should we be concerned only with how our time is filled, but not with what we are?

Thirdly, plugging into an experience machine limits us to a man-made reality, to a world no deeper or more important than that which people can construct. There is no *actual* contact with any deeper reality, though the experience of it can be simulated. Many persons desire to leave themselves open to such contact and to a plumbing of deeper significance. This clarifies the intensity of the conflict over psychoactive drugs, which some view as mere local experience machines, and others view as avenues to a deeper reality; what some view as equivalent to surrender to the experience machine, others view as following one of the reasons *not* to surrender!

We learn that something matters to us in addition to experience by imagining an experience machine and then realizing that we would not use it. We can continue to imagine a sequence of machines each designed to fill lacks suggested for the earlier machines. For example, since the experience machine doesn't meet our desire to *be* a certain way, imagine a transformation machine which transforms us into whatever sort of person we'd like to be (compatible with our staying us). Surely one would not use the transformation machine to become as one would wish, and there-upon plug into the experience machine! So something matters in addition to one's experiences *and* what one is like. Nor is the reason merely that one's experiences are unconnected with what one is like. For the experience machine might be limited to provide only experiences possible to the sort of person plugged in. Is it that we want to make a difference in the world? Consider then the result machine, which produces in the world any result you would produce and injects your vector input into any joint activity. We shall not pursue here the fascinating details of these or other machines. What is most disturbing about them is their living of our lives for us. Is it misguided to search for *particular* additional functions beyond the competence of machines to do for us? Perhaps what we desire is to live (an active verb) ourselves, in contact with reality. (And this, machines cannot do *for* us.)

STUDY QUESTIONS

1. What reasons could there be for not plugging into the experience machine for the rest of one's life?
2. What does the example of the experience machine show regarding utilitarianism?
3. Would you plug into the experience machine?

IMMANUEL KANT
The Categorical Imperative

Immanuel Kant (1724–1804) was an exceptionally significant and influential philosopher, who wrote on many topics. He was born and lived in Konigsberg, Germany. He is particularly noted for his fundamental but difficult writings on metaphysics, especially his Critique of Pure Reason, *but equally renowned for his rigorous, principled approach to moral philosophy.*

The present groundwork is ✳ ✳ ✳ nothing more than the search for and establishment of the *supreme principle of morality*, which constitutes by itself a business that in its purpose is complete and to be kept apart from every other moral investigation. ✳ ✳ ✳

It is impossible to think of anything at all in the world, or indeed even beyond it, that could be considered good without limitation except a good will. Understanding, wit, judgment and the like, whatever such *talents* of mind may be called, or courage, resolution, and perseverance in one's plans, as qualities of *temperament*, are undoubtedly good and desirable for many purposes, but they can also be extremely evil and harmful if the will which is to make use of these gifts of nature, and whose distinctive constitution is therefore called *character,* is not good. It is the same with *gifts of fortune.* Power, riches, honor, even health and that complete well-being and satisfaction with one's condition called *happiness,* produce boldness and thereby often arrogance as well unless a good will is present which corrects the influence of these on the mind. ✳ ✳ ✳

✳ ✳ ✳ Moderation in affects and passions, self-control, and calm reflection are not only good for all sorts of purposes but even seem to constitute a part of the *inner* worth of a person; but they lack much that would be required to declare them good without limitation (however unconditionally they were praised by the ancients); for, without the basic principles of a good will they can become extremely evil, and the coolness of a scoundrel makes him not only far more dangerous but also immediately more abominable in our eyes than we would have taken him to be without it.

A good will is not good because of what it effects or accomplishes, because of its fitness to attain some proposed end, but only because of its volition, that is, it is good in itself and, regarded for itself, is to be valued incomparably higher than all that could merely be brought about by it in favor of some inclination and indeed, if you will, of the sum of all inclinations. Even if, by a special disfavor of fortune or by the niggardly provision of a stepmotherly nature, this will should wholly lack the capacity to carry out its purpose—if with its greatest efforts it should yet achieve nothing and only the good will were left (not, of course, as a mere wish but as the summoning of all means insofar as they are in our control)—then, like a jewel, it would still shine by itself, as something that has its full worth in itself. ✳ ✳ ✳

To be beneficent where one can is a duty, and besides there are many souls so sympathetically attuned that, without any other motive of vanity or self-interest they find an inner satisfaction in spreading joy around them and can take delight in the satisfaction of others so far as it is their own work. But I assert that in such a case an action of this kind, however it may conform with duty and however amiable it may be, has nevertheless no true moral worth but is on the same footing with other inclinations, for example, the inclination to honor, which, if it fortunately lights upon what is in fact in the common interest and in conformity with duty and hence honorable, deserves praise and encouragement but not esteem; for the maxim lacks moral content, namely that of doing such actions not from inclination but *from duty.* ✳ ✳ ✳

Thus the moral worth of an action does not lie in the effect expected from it and so too does not lie in any principle of action that needs to borrow its motive from this expected effect. For, all these effects (agreeableness of one's condition, indeed even promotion of others' happiness) could have been also brought about by other causes, so that there would have been no need, for this, of the will of a rational being, in which, however, the highest and unconditional good alone can be found. Hence nothing other than the *representation of the law* in itself, *which can of course occur only in a rational being,* insofar as it and not the hoped-for effect is the determining ground of the will, can constitute the preeminent good we call moral, which is already present in the person himself who acts in accordance with this representation and need not wait upon the effect of his action. ＊＊＊

Now, all imperatives command either *hypothetically* or *categorically.* The former represent the practical necessity of a possible action as a means to achieving something else that one wills (or that it is at least possible for one to will). The categorical imperative would be that which represented an action as objectively necessary of itself, without reference to another end.

Since every practical law represents a possible action as good and thus as necessary for a subject practically determinable by reason, all imperatives are formulae for the determination of action that is necessary in accordance with the principle of a will which is good in some way. Now, if the action would be good merely as a means *to something else* the imperative is *hypothetical;* if the action is represented as *in itself* good, hence as necessary in a will in itself conforming to reason, as its principle, *then it is categorical.* ＊＊＊

＊＊＊ There is one imperative that, without being based upon and having as its condition any other purpose to be attained by certain conduct, commands this conduct immediately. This imperative is **categorical.** It has to do not with the matter of the action and what is to result from it, but with the form and the principle from which the action itself follows; and the essentially good in the action consists in the disposition, let the result be what it may. This imperative may be called the imperative of morality. ＊＊＊

When I think of a *hypothetical* imperative in general I do not know beforehand what it will contain; I do not know this until I am given the condition. But when I think of a *categorical* imperative I know at once what it contains. For, since the imperative contains, beyond the law, only the necessity that the maxim be in conformity with this law, while the law contains no condition to which it would be limited, nothing is left with which the maxim of action is to conform but the universality of a law as such; and this conformity alone is what the imperative properly represents as necessary.

There is, therefore, only a single categorical imperative and it is this: *act only in accordance with that maxim through which you can at the same time will that it become a universal law.* * * *

Since the universality of law in accordance with which effects take place constitutes what is properly called *nature* in the most general sense (as regards its form)—that is, the existence of things insofar as it is determined in accordance with universal laws—the universal imperative of duty can also go as follows: *act as if the maxim of your action were to become by your will a* **universal law of nature**.

We shall now enumerate a few duties in accordance with the usual division of them into duties to ourselves and to other human beings and into perfect and imperfect duties.

1) Someone feels sick of life because of a series of troubles that has grown to the point of despair, but is still so far in possession of his reason that he can ask himself whether it would not be contrary to his duty to himself to take his own life. Now he inquires whether the maxim of his action could indeed become a universal law of nature. His maxim, however, is: from self-love I make it my principle to shorten my life when its longer duration threatens more troubles than it promises agreeableness. The only further question is whether this principle of self-love could become a universal law of nature. It is then seen at once that a nature whose law it would be to destroy life itself by means of the same feeling whose destination is to impel toward the furtherance of life would contradict itself and would therefore not subsist as nature; thus that maxim could not possibly be a law of nature and, accordingly, altogether opposes the supreme principle of all duty.

2) Another finds himself urged by need to borrow money. He well knows that he will not be able to repay it but sees also that nothing will be lent him unless he promises firmly to repay it within a determinate time. He would like to make such a promise, but he still has enough conscience to ask himself: is it not forbidden and contrary to duty to help oneself out of need in such a way? Supposing that he still decided to do so, his maxim of action would go as follows: when I believe myself to be in need of money I shall borrow money and promise to repay it, even though I know that this will never happen. Now this principle of self-love or personal advantage is perhaps quite consistent with my whole future welfare, but the question now is whether it is right. I therefore turn the demand of self-love into a universal

law and put the question as follows: how would it be if my maxim became a universal law? I then see at once that it could never hold as a universal law of nature and be consistent with itself, but must necessarily contradict itself. For, the universality of a law that everyone, when he believes himself to be in need, could promise whatever he pleases with the intention of not keeping it would make the promise and the end one might have in it itself impossible, since no one would believe what was promised him but would laugh at all such expressions as vain pretenses.

3) A third find in himself a talent that by means of some cultivation could make him a human being useful for all sorts of purposes. However, he finds himself in comfortable circumstances and prefers to give himself up to pleasure than to trouble himself with enlarging and improving his fortunate natural predispositions. But he still asks himself whether his maxim of neglecting his natural gifts, besides being consistent with his propensity to amusement, is also consistent with what one calls duty. He now sees that a nature could indeed always subsist with such a universal law, although (as with the South Sea Islanders) the human being should let his talents rust and he concerned with devoting his life merely to idleness, amusement, procreation—in a word, to enjoyment; only he cannot possibly will that this become a universal law or be put in us as such by means of natural instinct. For, as a rational being he necessarily wills that all the capacities in him be developed, since they serve him and are given to him for all sorts of possible purposes.

Yet a *fourth*, for whom things are going well while he sees that others (whom he could very well help) have to contend with great hardships, thinks: what is it to me? let each be as happy as heaven wills or as he can make himself; I shall take nothing from him nor even envy him; only I do not care to contribute anything to his welfare or to his assistance in need! Now, if such a way of thinking were to become a universal law the human race could admittedly very well subsist, no doubt even better than when everyone prates about sympathy and benevolence and even exerts himself to practice them occasionally, but on the other hand also cheats where he can, sells the right of human beings or otherwise infringes upon it. But although it is possible that a universal law of nature could very well subsist in accordance with such a maxim, it is still impossible to will that such a principle hold everywhere as a law of nature. For, a will that decided this would conflict with itself, since many cases could occur in which one would need the love and sympathy of others and in which, by such a law of nature arisen from his own will, he would rob himself of all hope of the assistance he wishes for himself. ∗ ∗ ∗

If we now attend to ourselves in any transgression of a duty, we find that we do not really will that our maxim should become a universal law, since that is impossible for us, but that the opposite of our maxim should instead remain a universal law, only we take the liberty of making an *exception* to it for ourselves (or just for this once) to the advantage of our inclination. Consequently, if we weighed all cases from one and the same point of view, namely that of reason, we would find a contradiction in our own will, namely that a certain principle be objectively necessary as a universal law and yet subjectively not hold universally but allow exceptions. * * *

But suppose there were something the *existence of which in itself* has an absolute worth, something which as *an end in itself* could be a ground of determinate laws; then in it, and in it alone, would lie the ground of a possible categorical imperative, that is, of a practical law.

Now I say that the human being and in general every rational being *exists* as an end in itself, *not merely as a means* to be used by this or that will at its discretion; instead he must in all his actions, whether directed to himself or also to other rational beings, always be regarded *at the same time as an end.* * * * Beings the existence of which rests not on our will but on nature, if they are beings without reason, still have only a relative worth, as means, and are therefore called *things*, whereas rational beings are called *persons* because their nature already marks them out as an end in itself, that is, as something that may not be used merely as a means, and hence so far limits all choice (and is an object of respect). These, therefore, are not merely subjective ends, the existence of which as an effect of our action has a worth *for us*, but rather *objective ends*, that is, beings the existence of which is in itself an end, and indeed one such that no other end, to which they would serve *merely* as means, can be put in its place, since without it nothing of *absolute worth* would be found anywhere; but if all worth were conditional and therefore contingent, then no supreme practical principle for reason could be found anywhere.

* * * *Rational nature exists as an end in itself.* The human being necessarily represents his own existence in this way; so far it is thus a *subjective* principle of human actions. But every other rational being also represents his existence in this way consequent on just the same rational ground that also holds for me; thus it is at the same time an *objective* principle from which, as a supreme practical ground, it must be possible to derive all laws of the will. The practical imperative will therefore be the following: *So act that you use humanity, whether in your own person or in the person of any other, always*

at the same time as an end, never merely as a means. We shall see whether this can be carried out.

To keep to the preceding examples:

First, as regards the concept of necessary duty to oneself, someone who has suicide in mind will ask himself whether his action can be consistent with the idea of humanity *as an end in itself.* If he destroys himself in order to escape from a trying condition he makes use of a person *merely as a means* to maintain a tolerable condition up to the end of life. A human being, however, is not a thing and hence not something that can be used *merely* as a means, but must in all his actions always be regarded as an end in itself. I cannot, therefore, dispose of a human being in my own person by maiming, damaging or killing him. ✳ ✳ ✳

Second, as regards necessary duty to others or duty owed them, he who has it in mind to make a false promise to others sees at once that he wants to make use of another human being *merely as a means,* without the other at the same time containing in himself the end. For, he whom I want to use for my purposes by such a promise cannot possibly agree to my way of behaving toward him, and so himself contain the end of this action. This conflict with the principle of other human beings is seen more distinctly if examples of assaults on the freedom and property of others are brought forward. For then it is obvious that he who transgresses the rights of human beings intends to make use of the person of others merely as means, without taking into consideration that, as rational beings, they are always to be valued at the same time as ends, that is, only as beings who must also be able to contain in themselves the end of the very same action.

Third, with respect to contingent (meritorious) duty to oneself, it is not enough that the action does not conflict with humanity in our person as an end in itself, it must also *harmonize with it.* Now there are in humanity predispositions to greater perfection, which belong to the end of nature with respect to humanity in our subject; to neglect these might admittedly be consistent with the *preservation* of humanity as an end in itself but not with the *furtherance* of this end.

Fourth, concerning meritorious duty to others, the natural end that all human beings have is their own happiness. Now, humanity might indeed subsist if no one contributed to the happiness of others but yet did not intentionally withdraw anything from it; but there is still only a negative and not a positive agreement with *humanity as an end in itself* unless everyone also tries, as far as he can, to further the ends of others. For, the ends of a subject who is an end in itself must as far as possible be also *my* ends, if that representation is to have its *full* effect in me. ✳ ✳ ✳

The concept of every rational being as one who must regard himself as giving universal law through all the maxims of his will, so as to appraise himself and his actions from this point of view, leads to a very fruitful concept dependent upon it, namely that *of a kingdom of ends.*

By a *kingdom* I understand a systematic union of various rational beings through common laws. Now since laws determine ends in terms of their universal validity, if we abstract from the personal differences of rational beings as well as from all the content of their private ends we shall be able to think of a whole of all ends in systematic connection (a whole both of rational beings as ends in themselves and of the ends of his own that each may set himself), that is, a kingdom of ends, which is possible in accordance with the above principles.

For, all rational beings stand under the *law* that each of them is to treat himself and all others *never merely as means* but always *at the same time as ends in themselves.* But from this there arises a systematic union of rational beings through common objective laws, that is, a kingdom, which can be called a kingdom of ends (admittedly only an ideal) because what these laws have as their purpose is just the relation of these beings to one another as ends and means.

A rational being belongs as a *member* to the kingdom of ends when he gives universal laws in it but is also himself subject to these laws. He belongs to it *as sovereign* when, as lawgiving, he is not subject to the will of any other.

A rational being must always regard himself as lawgiving in a kingdom of ends possible through freedom of the will, whether as a member or as sovereign. He cannot, however, hold the position of sovereign merely by the maxims of his will but only in case he is a completely independent being, without needs and with unlimited resources adequate to his will.

Morality consists, then, in the reference of all action to the lawgiving by which alone a kingdom of ends is possible. This lawgiving must, however, be found in every rational being himself and be able to arise from his will, the principle of which is, accordingly: to do no action on any other maxim than one such that it would be consistent with it to be a universal law, and hence to act only *so that the will could regard itself as at the same time giving universal law through its maxim.* Now, if maxims are not already of their nature in agreement with this objective principle of rational beings as givers of universal law, the necessity of an action in accordance with this objective principle of rational beings as givers of universal law, the necessity of an action in accordance with this principle is called practical necessitation, that is, *duty*. Duty does not apply to the sovereign in the kingdom of ends, but it does apply to every member of it and indeed to all in equal measure. * * *

The above three ways of representing the principle of morality are at bottom only so many formulae of the very same law, and any one of them of itself unites the other two in it. * * *

We can now end where we set out from at the beginning, namely with the concept of a will unconditionally good. *That will is absolutely good* which cannot be evil, hence whose maxim, if made a universal law, can never conflict with itself. This principle is, accordingly, also its supreme law: act always on that maxim whose universality as a law you can at the same time will; this is the sole condition under which a will can never be in conflict with itself, and such an imperative is categorical. Since the validity of the will as a universal law for possible actions has an analogy with the universal connection of the existence of things in accordance with universal laws, which is the formal aspect of nature in general, the categorical imperative can also be expressed thus: *act in accordance with maxims that can at the same time have as their object themselves as universal laws of nature.* In this way, then, the formula of an absolutely good will is provided.

STUDY QUESTIONS

1. What is the distinction between hypothetical and categorical imperatives?
2. What does Kant means by "universalizing the maxim" of your action?
3. What does it mean to treat another person merely as a means?

ANNETTE BAIER
The Need for More than Justice

Annette Baier (1929–2012) was a moral philosopher who was born in New Zealand but spent her working life in the United States. She produced influential works on feminism, as well as on David Hume and other topics.

In recent decades in North American social and moral philosophy, alongside the development and discussion of widely influential theories of justice, taken as Rawls takes it as the "first virtue of social institutions,"[1] there has been

---

1   John Rawls, *A Theory of Justice* (Harvard University Press). [*Editor's note*: See selections from *A Theory of Justice* on pps. 583–590 of this reader.]

a counter-movement gathering strength, one coming from some interesting sources. For some of the most outspoken of the diverse group who have in a variety of ways been challenging the assumed supremacy of justice among the moral and social virtues are members of those sections of society whom one might have expected to be especially aware of the supreme importance of justice, namely blacks and women. Those who have only recently won recognition of their equal rights, who have only recently seen the correction or partial correction of longstanding racist and sexist injustices to their race and sex, are among the philosophers now suggesting that justice is only one virtue among many, and one that may need the presence of the others in order to deliver its own undenied value. * * * A whole group of men and women, myself included, * * * have been influenced by the writings of Harvard educational psychologist Carol Gilligan, whose book *In a Different Voice* (Harvard 1982; hereafter D.V.) caused a considerable stir both in the popular press and, more slowly, in the philosophical journals.

Let me say quite clearly at this early point that there is little disagreement that justice is *a* social value of very great importance, and injustice an evil. Nor would those who have worked on theories of justice want to deny that other things matter besides justice. Rawls, for example, incorporates the value of freedom into his account of justice, so that denial of basic freedoms counts as injustice. Rawls also leaves room for a wider theory of the right, of which the theory of justice is just a part. Still, he does claim that justice is the "first" virtue of social institutions, and it is only that claim about priority that I think has been challenged. It is easy to exaggerate the differences of view that exist, and I want to avoid that. The differences are as much in emphasis as in substance, or we can say that they are differences in tone of voice. But these differences do tend to make a difference in approaches to a wide range of topics not just in moral theory but in areas like medical ethics, where the discussion used to be conducted in terms of patients' rights, of informed consent, and so on, but now tends to get conducted in an enlarged moral vocabulary, which draws on what Gilligan calls the ethics of *care* as well as that of *justice*.

For "care" is the new buzz-word. It is not, as Shakespeare's Portia demanded, mercy that is to season justice, but a less authoritarian humanitarian supplement, a felt concern for the good of others and for community with them. The "cold jealous virtue of justice" (Hume) is found to be too cold, and it is "warmer" more communitarian virtues and social ideals that are being called in to supplement it. One might say that liberty and equality are being found inadequate without fraternity, except that "fraternity" will be quite the wrong word, if as Gilligan initially suggested, it is *women* who perceive this value most easily. "Sorority" will do no better, since it is too exclusive, and English has no gender-neuter word for the mutual concern of siblings.) She has since modified this claim, allowing that there are two perspectives on moral and social issues that we all tend to alternate between, and which are not always easy to combine, one of them what she called the justice perspective, the other the care perspective. It is increasingly obvious that there are many male philosophical spokespersons for the care perspective ∗ ∗ ∗ so that it cannot be the prerogative of women. Nevertheless Gilligan still wants to claim that women are most unlikely to take *only* the justice perspective, as some men are claimed to, at least until some mid-life crisis jolts them into "bifocal" moral vision (see D. V., ch. 6).

Gilligan in her book did not offer any explanatory theory of why there should be any difference between female and male moral outlook, but she did tend to link the naturalness to women of the care perspective with their role as primary care-takers of young children, that is with their parental and specifically maternal role. She avoided the question of whether it is their biological or their social parental role that is relevant, and some of those who dislike her book are worried precisely by this uncertainty. Some find it retrograde to hail as a special sort of moral wisdom an outlook that may be the product of the socially enforced restriction of women to domestic roles (and the reservation of such roles for them alone). For that might seem to play into the hands of those who still favor such restriction. (Marxists, presumably, will not find it so surprising that moral truths might depend for their initial clear voicing on the social oppression, and memory of it, of those who voice the truths.) Gilligan did in the first chapter of D.V. cite the theory of Nancy Chodorow (as presented in *The Reproduction of Mothering* [Berkeley 1978]) which traces what appears as gender differences in personality to early social development, in particular to the effects of the child's primary caretaker being or not being of the same gender as the child. Later, ∗ ∗ ∗ she postulates two evils that any infant may become aware of, the evil of detachment or isolation from others whose love one needs, and the evil of relative powerlessness and weakness. Two dimensions of moral development are thereby set—one aimed at achieving satisfying community with others, the other aiming at autonomy or equality of power. The relative predominance of one over the other development will depend both upon the relative salience of the two evils in early childhood, and on early and later reinforcement or discouragement in attempts made to guard against these two evils. This provides the germs of a theory about *why*, given current customs of childrearing, it should be mainly women who are not content with only the moral outlook that she calls the justice perspective, necessary though that was and is seen by them to have been to their hard won liberation from sexist oppression. They, like the blacks, used the language of rights and justice to change their own social position, but nevertheless see limitations in that language, according to Gilligan's findings as a moral psychologist. She reports their discontent with the individualist more or less Kantian moral framework that dominates Western moral theory and which influenced moral psychologists such as Lawrence Kohlberg, to whose conception of moral maturity she seeks an alternative. Since the target of Gilligan's criticism is the dominant Kantian tradition, * * * her book is of interest as much for its attempt to articulate an alternative to the Kantian justice perspective as for its implicit raising of the question of male bias in Western moral theory, especially liberal-democratic theory. For whether the supposed blind spots of that outlook are due to male bias, or to non-parental bias, or to early traumas of powerlessness or to early resignation to "detachment" from others, we need first to be persuaded that they *are* blind spots before we will have any interest in their cause and cure. Is justice blind to important social values, or at least only one-eyed? What is it that comes into view from the "care perspective" that is not seen from the "justice perspective"?

Gilligan's position here is most easily described by contrasting it with that of Kohlberg, against which she developed it. Kohlberg * * * developed a theory about typical moral development which saw it to progress from a pre-conventional level, where what is seen to matter is pleasing or not offending parental authority-figures, through a conventional level in which the child tries to fit in with a group, such as a school community, and conform to its standards and rules, to a post-conventional critical level, in which such conventional rules are subjected to tests, and where those tests are of a Utilitarian, or, eventually, a Kantian sort—namely ones that require respect for each person's individual rational will, or autonomy, and conformity to any implicit social contract such wills are deemed to have made, or to any hypothetical ones they would make if thinking clearly. What was found when Kohlberg's questionnaires (mostly by verbal response to verbally sketched moral dilemmas) were applied to female as well as male subjects, Gilligan reports, is that the girls and women not only scored generally lower than the boys and men, but tended to *revert* to the lower stage of the conventional level even after briefly (usually in adolescence) attaining the post-conventional level. Piaget's finding that girls were deficient in "the legal sense" was confirmed.

These results led Gilligan to wonder if there might not be a quite different pattern of development to be discerned, at least in female subjects. She therefore conducted interviews designed to elicit not just how far advanced the subjects were towards an appreciation of the nature and importance of Kantian autonomy, but also to find out what the subjects themselves saw as progress or lack of it, what conceptions of moral maturity they came to possess by the time they were adults. She found that although the Kohlberg version of moral maturity as respect for fellow persons, and for their rights as equals (rights including that of free association), did seem shared by many young men, the women tended to speak in a different voice about morality itself and about moral maturity. To quote Gilligan, "Since the reality of interconnexion is experienced by women as given rather than freely contracted, they arrive at an understanding of life that reflects the limits of autonomy and control. As a result, women's development delineates the path not only to a less violent life but also to a maturity realized by interdependence and taking care" (D.V., 172). She writes that there is evidence that "women perceive and construe social reality differently from men, and that these differences center around experiences of attachment and separation . . . because women's sense of integrity appears to be intertwined with an ethics of care, so that to see themselves as women is to see themselves in a relationship of connexion, the major changes in women's lives would seem to involve changes in the understanding and activities of care" (D.V., 171). She contrasts this progressive understanding of care, from merely pleasing others to helping and nurturing, with the sort of progression that is involved in Kohlberg's stages, a progression in the understanding, not of mutual care, but of mutual *respect*, where this has its Kantian overtones of distance, even of some fear for the respected, and where personal autonomy and *in*dependence, rather than more satisfactory interdependence, are the paramount values.

This contrast, one cannot but feel, is one which Gilligan might have used the Marxist language of alienation to make. For the main complaint about the Kantian version of a society with its first virtue justice—construed as respect for equal rights to formal goods such as having contracts kept, due process, equal opportunity including opportunity to participate in political activities leading to policy and law-making, to basic liberties of speech, free association and assembly, religious worship—is that none of these goods do much to ensure that the people who have and mutually respect such rights will have any other relationships to one another than the minimal relationship needed to keep such a "civil society" going. They may well be lonely, driven to suicide, apathetic about their work and about participation in political processes, find their lives meaningless and have no wish to leave offspring to face the same meaningless existence. Their rights, and respect for rights, are quite compatible with very great misery, and misery whose causes are not just individual misfortunes and psychic sickness, but social and moral impoverishment.

What Gilligan's older male subjects complain of is precisely this sort of alienation from some dimly glimpsed better possibility for human beings, some richer sort of network of relationships. As one of Gilligan's male subjects put it, "People have real emotional needs to be attached to something, and equality does not give you attachment. Equality fractures society and places on every person the burden of standing on his own two feet" (D.V., 167). It is not just the difficulty of self reliance which is complained of, but its socially "fracturing" effect. Whereas the younger men, in their college years, had seen morality as a matter of reciprocal non-interference, this older man begins to see it as reciprocal attachment. "Morality is . . . essential . . . for creating the kind of environment, interaction between people, that is a prerequisite to the fulfillment of individual goals. If you want other people not to interfere with your pursuit of whatever you are into, you have to play the game," says the spokesman for traditional liberalism (D.V. 98). But if what one is "into" is interconnexion, interdependence rather than an individual autonomy that may involve "detachment," such a version of morality will come to seem inadequate. And Gilligan stresses that the interconnexion that her mature women subjects, and some men, wanted to sustain was not merely freely chosen interconnexion, nor interconnexion between equals, but also the sort of interconnexion that can obtain between a child and her unchosen mother and father, or between a child and her unchosen older and younger siblings, or indeed between most workers and their unchosen fellow workers, or most citizens and their unchosen fellow citizens.

A model of a decent community different from the liberal one is involved in the version of moral maturity that Gilligan voices. It has in many ways more in common with the older religion-linked versions of morality and a good society than with the modern Western liberal ideal. That perhaps is why some find it so dangerous and retrograde. Yet it seems clear that it also has much in common with what we can call Hegelian versions of moral maturity and of social health and malaise, both with Marxist versions and with so-called right-Hegelian views.

Let me try to summarize the main differences, as I see them, between on the one hand Gilligan's version of moral maturity and the sort of social structures that would encourage, express and protect it, and on the other the orthodoxy she sees herself to be challenging. I shall from now on be giving my own interpretation of the significance of her challenges, not merely reporting them. The most obvious point is the challenge to the individualism of the Western tradition, to the fairly entrenched belief in the possibility and desirability of each person pursuing his own good in his own way, constrained only by a minimal formal common good, namely a working legal apparatus that enforces contracts and protects individuals from undue interference by others. Gilligan reminds us that noninterference can, especially for the relatively powerless, such as the very young, amount to neglect, and even between equals can be isolating and alienating. On her less individualist version of individuality, it becomes defined by responses to dependency and to patterns of interconnexion, both chosen and unchosen. It is not something a person *has*, and which she then chooses relationships to suit, but something that develops out of a series of dependencies and interdependencies, and responses to them. This conception of individuality is not flatly at odds with, say, Rawls' Kantian one, but there is at least a difference of tone of voice between speaking as Rawls does of each of us having our own rational life plan, which a just society's moral traffic rules will allow us to follow, and which may or may not include close association with other persons, and speaking as Gilligan does of a satisfactory life as involving "progress of affiliative relationship" (D.V., 170) where "the concept of identity expands to include the experience of interconnexion" (D.V., 173). Rawls can allow that progress to Gilligan-style moral maturity may be *a* rational life plan, but not a moral constraint on every life-pattern. The trouble is that it will not do just to say "let this version of morality be an optional extra. Let us agree on the essential minimum, that is on justice and rights, and let whoever wants to go further and cultivate this more demanding ideal of responsibility and care." For, first, it cannot be satisfactorily cultivated without closer cooperation from others than respect for rights and justice will ensure, and, second, the encouragement of some to cultivate it while others do not could easily lead to exploitation of those who do. It obviously *has* suited some in most societies well enough that others take on the responsibilities of care (for the sick, the helpless, the young) leaving them free to pursue their own less altruistic goods. Volunteer forces of those who accept an ethic of care, operating within a society where the power is exercised and the institutions designed, redesigned, or maintained by those who accept a less communal ethic of minimally constrained self-advancement, will not be the solution. The liberal individualists may be able to "tolerate" the more communally minded, if they keep the liberals' rules, but it is not so clear that the more communally minded can be content with just those rules, nor be content to be tolerated and possibly exploited.

For the moral tradition which developed the concept of rights, autonomy and justice is the same tradition that provided "justifications" of the oppression of those whom the primary right-holders depended on to do the sort of work they themselves preferred not to do. The domestic work was left to women and slaves, and the liberal morality for right-holders was surreptitiously supplemented by a different set of demands made on domestic workers. As long as women could be got to assume responsibility for the care of home and children, and to train their children to continue the sexist system, the liberal morality could continue to be the official morality, by turning its eyes away from the contribution made by those it excluded. The long unnoticed moral proletariat were the domestic workers, mostly female. Rights have usually been for the privileged. Talking about laws, and the rights those laws recognize and protect, does not in itself ensure that the group of legislators and rights-holders will not be restricted to some elite. Bills of rights have usually been proclamations of the rights of some in-group, barons, landowners, males, whites, non-foreigners. The "justice perspective," and the legal sense that goes with it, are shadowed by their patriarchal past. What did Kant, the great prophet of autonomy, say in his moral theory about women? He said they were incapable of legislation not fit to vote, that they needed the guidance of more "rational" males.[2] Autonomy was not for them, only for first class, really rational, persons. It is ironic that Gilligan's original findings in a way confirm Kant's views—it seems that autonomy really may not be for women. Many of them reject that ideal (D.V., 48), and have been found not as good at making rules as are men. But where Kant concludes—"so much the worse for women," we can conclude—"so much the worse for the male fixation on the special skill of drafting legislation, for the bureaucratic mentality of rule worship, and for the male exaggeration of the importance of independence over mutual interdependence."

---

2 Immanuel Kant, *Metaphysics of Morals*, sec. 46

It is however also true that the moral theories that made the concept of a person's rights central were not just the instruments for excluding some persons, but also the instruments used by those who demanded that more and more persons be included in the favored group. Abolitionists, reformers, women, used the language of rights to assert their claims to inclusion in the group of full members of a community. The tradition of liberal moral theory has in fact developed so as to include the women it had for so long excluded, to include the poor as well as rich, blacks and whites, and so on. Women like Mary Wollstonecraft[3] used the male moral theories to good purpose. So we should not be wholly ungrateful for those male moral theories, for all their objectionable earlier content. They were undoubtedly patriarchal, but they also contained the seeds of the challenge, or antidote, to this patriarchal poison.

But when we transcend the values of the Kantians, we should not forget the facts of history—that those values were the values of the oppressors of women. The Christian church, whose version of the moral law Aquinas codified, in his very legalistic moral theory, still insists on the maleness of the God it worships, and jealously reserves for males all the most powerful positions in its hierarchy. Its patriarchical prejudice is open and avowed. In the secular moral theories of men, the sexist patriarchal prejudice is today often less open, not as blatant as it is in Aquinas, in the later natural law tradition, and in Kant and Hegel, but is often still there. No moral theorist today would say that women are unfit to vote, to make laws, or to rule a nation without powerful male advisors (as most queens had), but the old doctrines die hard. In one of the best male theories we have, John Rawls's theory, a key role is played by the idea of the "head of a household." It is heads of households who are to deliberate behind a "veil of ignorance" of historical details, and of details of their own special situation, to arrive at the "just" constitution for a society. Now of course Rawls does not think or say that these "heads" are fathers rather than mothers. But if we have really given up the age-old myth of women needing, as Grotius put it, to be under the "eye" of a more "rational" male protector and master, then how do families come to have any one "head," except by the death or desertion of one parent? They will either be two-headed, or headless. Traces of the old patriarchal poison still remain in even the best contemporary moral theorizing. Few may actually

---

3 *Editor's note*: See selections from Mary Wollstonecraft's *A Vindication of the Rights of Woman* on pps. 212–218 of this reader.

say that women's place is in the home, but there is much muttering, when unemployment figures rise, about how the relatively recent flood of women into the work force complicates the problem, as if it would be a good thing if women just went back home whenever unemployment rises, to leave the available jobs for the men. We still do not really have a wide acceptance of the equal right of women to employment outside the home. Nor do we have wide acceptance of the equal duty of men to perform those domestic tasks which in no way depend on special female anatomy, namely cooking, cleaning, and the care of weaned children. All sorts of stories (maybe true stories), about children's need for one "primary" parent, who must be the mother if the mother breast feeds the child, shore up the unequal division of domestic responsibility between mothers and fathers, wives and husbands. If we are really to transvalue the values of our patriarchal past, we need to rethink all of those assumptions, really test those psychological theories. And how will men ever develop an understanding of the "ethics of care" if they continue to be shielded or kept from that experience of caring for a dependent child, which complements the experience we all have had of being cared for as dependent children? These experiences form the natural background for the development of moral maturity as Gilligan's women saw it.

Exploitation aside, why would women, once liberated, not be content to have their version of morality merely tolerated? Why should they not see themselves as voluntarily, for their own reasons, taking on *more* than the liberal rules demand, while having no quarrel with the content of those rules themselves, nor with their remaining the only ones that are expected to be generally obeyed? To see why, we need to move on to three more differences between the Kantian liberals (usually contractarians) and their critics. These concern the relative weight put on relationships between equals, and the relative weight put on freedom of choice, and on the authority of intellect over emotions. It is a typical feature of the dominant moral theories and traditions, since Kant, or perhaps since Hobbes, that relationships between equals or those who are deemed equal in some important sense, have been the relations that morality is concerned primarily to regulate. Relationships between those who are clearly unequal in power, such as parents and children, earlier and later generations in relation to one another, states and citizens, doctors and patients, the well and the ill, large states and small states, have had to be shunted to the bottom of the agenda, and then dealt with by some sort of "promotion" of the weaker so that an appearance of virtual equality is achieved. Citizens collectively become equal to states, children are treated as adults-to-be, the ill and dying are treated as continuers of their earlier more potent selves, so that their "rights" could be seen as the rights of equals. This pretence of an equality that is in fact absent may often lead to desirable protection of the weaker, or more dependent. But it somewhat masks the question of what our moral relationships *are* to those who are our superiors or our inferiors in power. A more realistic acceptance of the fact that we begin as helpless children, that at almost every point of our lives we deal with both the more and the less helpless, that equality of power and interdependency, between two persons or groups, is rare and hard to recognize when it does occur, might lead us to a more direct approach to questions concerning the design of institutions structuring these relationships between unequals (families, schools, hospitals, armies) and of the morality of our dealings with the more and the less powerful. One reason why those who agree with the Gilligan version of what morality is about will not want to agree that the liberals' rules are a good minimal set, the only ones we need pressure *everyone* to obey, is that these rules do little to protect the young or the dying or the starving or any of the relatively powerless against neglect, or to ensure an education that will form persons to be *capable* of conforming to an ethics of care and responsibility. Put baldly, and in a way Gilligan certainly has not put it, the liberal morality, if unsupplemented, may *unfit* people to be anything other than what its justifying theories suppose them to be, ones who have no interest in each others' interests. Yet some must take an interest in the next generation's interests. Women's traditional work, of caring for the less powerful, especially for the young, is obviously socially vital. One cannot regard any version of morality that does not ensure that it gets well done as an adequate "minimal morality," any more than we could so regard one that left any concern for more distant future generations an optional extra. ∗ ∗ ∗

∗ ∗ ∗ So far I have discussed three reasons women have not to be content to pursue their own values within the framework of the liberal morality. The first was its dubious record. The second was its inattention to relations of inequality or its pretence of equality. The third reason is its exaggeration of the scope of choice, or its inattention to unchosen relations. Showing up the partial myth of equality among actual members of a community, and of the undesirability of trying to pretend that we are treating all of them as equals, tends to go along with an exposure of the companion myth that moral obligations arise from freely *chosen* associations between such equals. Vulnerable future generations do not choose their dependence on earlier generations. The unequal infant does not choose its place in a family or nation, nor is it treated as free to do as it likes until some association is freely entered into. Nor do its parents always choose their parental role, or freely assume their parental responsibilities any more than we choose our power to affect the conditions in which later generations will live. Gilligan's attention to the version of morality and moral maturity found in women, many of whom had faced a choice of whether or not to have an abortion, and who had at some point become mothers, is attention to the perceived inadequacy of the language of rights to help in such choices or to guide them in their parental role. It would not be much of an exaggeration to call the Gilligan "different voice" the voice of the potential parents. The emphasis on care goes with a recognition of the often unchosen nature of the responsibilities of those who give care, both of children who care for their aged or infirm parents, and of parents who care for the children they in fact have. Contract soon ceases to seem the paradigm source of moral obligation once we attend to parental responsibility, and justice as a virtue of social institutions will come to seem at best only first equal with the virtue, whatever its name, that ensures that each new generation is made appropriately welcome and prepared for their adult lives.

⁂ The fourth feature of the Gilligan challenge to liberal orthodoxy is a challenge to its typical *rationalism*, or intellectualism, to its assumption that we need not worry what passions persons have, as long as their rational wills can control them. This Kantian picture of a controlling reason dictating to possibly unruly passions also tends to seem less useful when we are led to consider what sort of person we need to fill the role of parent, or indeed want in any close relationship. It might be important for father figures to have rational control over their violent urges to beat to death the children whose screams enrage them, but more than control of such nasty passions seems needed in the mother or primary parent, or parent-substitute, by most psychological theories. They need to love their children, not just to control their irritation. So the emphasis in Kantian theories on rational control of emotions, rather than on cultivating desirable forms of emotion, is challenged by Gilligan, along with the challenge to the assumption of the centrality of autonomy, or relations between equals, and of freely chosen relations. ⁂

It is clear, I think, that the best moral theory has to be a cooperative product of women and men, has to harmonize justice and care. The morality it theorizes about is after all for all persons, for men and for women, and will need their combined insights. As Gilligan said (D.V., 174), what we need now is a "marriage" of the old male and the newly articulated female insights. If she is right about the special moral aptitudes of women, it will most likely be the women who propose the marriage, since they are the ones with more natural empathy, with the better diplomatic skills, the ones more likely to shoulder responsibility and take moral initiative, and the ones who find it easiest to empathize and care about how the other party feels. Then, once there is this union of male and female moral wisdom, we maybe can teach each other the moral skills each gender currently lacks, so that the gender difference in moral outlook that Gilligan found will slowly become less marked.

STUDY QUESTIONS

1. Explain the difference between the ethics of justice and the ethics of care.
2. In what way is the ethics of justice individualistic?
3. How could the idea of the ethics of care be misused?

ARISTOTLE
Nicomachean Ethics

Aristotle (384–322 BCE) was one of the world's greatest and most influential philosophers. He was a pupil of Plato but disagreed sharply with many of Plato's doctrines. His works cover a huge variety of topics, from ethics, politics, and rhetoric to metaphysics and even biology.

BOOK I: THE HUMAN GOOD

2. If, then, there is some end of the things we do, which we desire for its own sake (everything else being desired for the sake of this), and if we do not choose everything for the sake of something else (for at that rate the process would go on to infinity, so that our desire would be empty and vain), clearly this must be the good and the chief good. Will not the knowledge of it, then, have a great influence on life? Shall we not, like archers who have a mark to aim at, be more likely to hit upon what is right? If so, we must try, in outline at least, to determine what it is, and of which of the sciences or capacities it is the object. It would seem to belong to the most authoritative art and that which is most truly the master art. ✳✳✳

3. Our discussion will be adequate if it has as much clearness as the subject-matter admits of, for precision is not to be sought for alike in all discussions,

any more than in all the products of the crafts. ✳ ✳ ✳ We must be content, then, in speaking of such subjects and with such premises to indicate the truth roughly and in outline, and in speaking about things which are only for the most part true, and with premises of the same kind, to reach conclusions that are no better. In the same spirit, therefore, should each type of statement be *received*; for it is the mark of an educated man to look for precision in each class of things just so far as the nature of the subject admits; it is evidently equally foolish to accept probable reasoning from a mathematician and to demand from a rhetorician demonstrative proofs.

Now each man judges well the things he knows, and of these he is a good judge. And so the man who has been educated in a subject is a good judge of that subject, and the man who has received an all-round education is a good judge in general. Hence a young man is not a proper hearer of lectures on political science; for he is inexperienced in the actions that occur in life, but its discussions start from these and are about these; and, further, since he tends to follow his passions, his study will be vain and unprofitable, because the end aimed at is not knowledge but action. And it makes no difference whether he is young in years or youthful in character; the defect does not depend on time, but on his living, and pursuing each successive object, as passion directs. ✳ ✳ ✳

4. Let us resume our inquiry and state, in view of the fact that all knowledge and every pursuit aims at some good, what it is that we say political science aims at and what is the highest of all goods achievable by action. Verbally there is very general agreement; for both the general run of men and people of superior refinement say that it is happiness, and identify living well and faring well with being happy; but with regard to what happiness is they differ, and the many do not give the same account as the wise. For the former think it is some plain and obvious thing, like pleasure, wealth, or honour; they differ, however, from one another—and often even the same man identifies it with different things, with health when he is ill, with wealth when he is poor; but, conscious of their ignorance, they admire those who proclaim some great thing that is above their comprehension. Now some thought that apart from these many goods there is another which is good in itself and causes the goodness of all these as well. ✳ ✳ ✳

7. Let us again return to the good we are seeking, and ask what it can be. It seems different in different actions and arts; it is different in medicine, in strategy, and in the other arts likewise. What then is the good of

each? Surely that for whose sake everything else is done. In medicine this is health, in strategy victory, in architecture a house, in any other sphere something else, and in every action and pursuit the end; for it is for the sake of this that all men do whatever else they do. Therefore, if there is an end for all that we do, this will be the good achievable by action, and if there are more than one, these will be the goods achievable by action.

* * * Clearly not all ends are final ends; but the chief good is evidently something final. Therefore, if there is only one final end, this will be what we are seeking, and if there are more than one, the most final of these will be what we are seeking. * * *

Now such a thing happiness, above all else, is held to be; for this we choose always for itself and never for the sake of something else, but honour, pleasure, reason, and every virtue we choose indeed for themselves (for if nothing resulted from them we should still choose each of them), but we choose them also for the sake of happiness, judging that through them we shall be happy. Happiness, on the other hand, no one chooses for the sake of these, nor, in general, for anything other than itself.

From the point of view of self-sufficiency the same result seems to follow; for the final good is thought to be self-sufficient. * * * The self-sufficient we now define as that which when isolated makes life desirable and lacking in nothing; and such we think happiness to be; and further we think it most desirable of all things, not a thing counted as one good thing among others. * * * Happiness, then, is something final and self-sufficient, and is the end of action.

Presumably, however, to say that happiness is the chief good seems a platitude, and a clearer account of what it is is still desired. This might perhaps be given, if we could first ascertain the function of man. For just as for a flute-player, a sculptor, or any artist, and, in general, for all things that have a function or activity, the good and the "well" is thought to reside in the function, so would it seem to be for man, if he has a function. * * * We state the function of man to be certain kind of life, and this to be an activity or actions of the soul implying a rational principle, and the function of a good man to be the good and noble performance of these, and if any action is well performed when it is performed in accordance with the appropriate virtue: if this is the case, human good turns out to be activity of soul exhibiting virtue, and if there are more than one virtue, in accordance with the best and most complete.

But we must add "in a complete life." For one swallow does not make a summer, nor does one day; and so too one day, or a short time, does not make a man blessed and happy. * * *

Some identify happiness with virtue, some with practical wisdom, others with a kind of philosophic wisdom, others with these, or one of these, accompanied by pleasure or not without pleasure; while others include also external prosperity. * * *

With those who identify happiness with virtue or some one virtue our account is in harmony; for to virtue belongs virtuous activity. But it makes, perhaps, no small difference whether we place the chief good in possession or in use, in state of mind or in activity. For the state of mind may exist without producing any good result, as in a man who is asleep or in some other way quite inactive, but the activity cannot; for one who has the activity will of necessity be acting, and acting well. And as in the Olympic Games it is not the most beautiful and the strongest that are crowned but those who compete (for it is some of these that are victorious), so those who act win, and rightly win, the noble and good things in life.

Their life is also in itself pleasant. For pleasure is a state of *soul*, and to each man that which he is said to be a lover of is pleasant. * * * Now for most men their pleasures are in conflict with one another because these are not by nature pleasant, but the lovers of what is noble find pleasant the things that are by nature pleasant; and virtuous actions are such, so that these are pleasant for such men as well as in their own nature. Their life, therefore, has no further need of pleasure as a sort of adventitious charm, but has its pleasure in itself. For, besides what we have said, the man who does not rejoice in noble actions is not even good; since no one would call a man just who did not enjoy acting justly, nor any man liberal who did not enjoy liberal actions; and similarly in all other cases. If this is so, virtuous actions must be in themselves pleasant. But they are also *good* and *noble*, and have each of these attributes in the highest degree, since the good man judges well about these attributes; his judgement is such as we have described. Happiness then is the best, noblest, and most pleasant thing in the world. * * *

Yet evidently, as we said, it needs the external goods as well; for it is impossible, or not easy, to do noble acts without the proper equipment. In many actions we use friends and riches and political power as instruments; and there are some things the lack of which takes the lustre from happiness—good birth, goodly children, beauty, for the man who is very ugly in appearance or ill-born or solitary and childless is not very likely to be happy, and perhaps a man would be still less likely if he had thoroughly bad children or friends or had lost good children or friends by death. * * *

13. Since happiness is an activity of soul in accordance with perfect virtue, we must consider the nature of virtue; for perhaps we shall thus see better the nature of happiness. The true student of politics, too, is thought to have studied virtue above all things; for he wishes to make his fellow citizens good and obedient to the laws. * * * But clearly the virtue we must study is human virtue; for the good we were seeking was human good and the happiness human happiness. By human virtue we mean not that of the body but that of the soul; and happiness also we call an activity of soul. But if this is so, clearly the student of politics must know somehow the facts about the soul. * * *

Virtue too is distinguished into kinds in accordance with this difference, for we say that some of the virtues are intellectual and others moral, philosophic wisdom and understanding and practical wisdom being intellectual, liberality and temperance moral. For in speaking about a man's character we do not say that he is wise or has understanding, but that he is good-tempered or temperate; yet we praise the wise man also with respect to his state of mind; and of states of mind we call those which merit praise virtues.

BOOK II: MORAL VIRTUE

1. Virtue, then, being of two kinds, intellectual and moral, intellectual virtue in the main owes both its birth and its growth to teaching (for which reason it requires experience and time), while moral virtue comes about as a result of habit, whence also its name (*ēthikē*) is one that is formed by a slight variation from the word *ethos* (habit). From this it is also plain that none of the moral virtues arises in us by nature; for nothing that exists by nature can form a habit contrary to its nature. For instance the stone which by nature moves downwards cannot be habituated to move upwards, not even if one tries to train it by throwing it up ten thousand times; nor can fire be habituated to move downwards, nor can anything else that by nature behaves in one way be trained to behave in another. Neither by nature, then, nor contrary to nature do the virtues arise in us; rather we are adapted by nature to receive them, and are made perfect by habit.

Again, of all the things that come to us by nature we first acquire the potentiality and later exhibit the activity (this is plain in the case of the senses; for it was not by often seeing or often hearing that we got these senses, but on the contrary we had them before we used them, and did not come to have them by using them); but the virtues we get by first exercising them, as also happens in the case of the arts as well. For the things we have to learn before we can do them, we learn by doing them, e.g. men become builders by building and lyre-players by playing the lyre; so too we become just by doing just acts, temperate by doing temperate acts, brave by doing brave acts.

This is confirmed by what happens in states; for legislators make the citizens good by forming habits in them, and this is the wish of every legislator, and those who do not effect it miss their mark, and it is in this that a good constitution differs from a bad one.

Again, it is from the same causes and by the same means that every virtue is both produced and destroyed, and similarly every art; for it is from playing the lyre that both good and bad lyre-players are produced. And the corresponding statement is true of builders and of all the rest; men will be good or bad builders as a result of building well or badly. For if this were not so, there would have been no need of a teacher, but all men would have been born good or bad at their craft. This, then, is the case with the virtues also; by doing the acts that we do in our transactions with other men we become just or unjust, and by doing the acts that we do in the presence of danger, and by being habituated to feel fear or confidence, we become brave or cowardly. The same is true of appetites and feelings of anger; some men become temperate and good-tempered, others self-indulgent and irascible, by behaving in one way or the other in the appropriate circumstances. Thus, in one word, states of character arise out of like activities. This is why the activities we exhibit must be of a certain kind; it is because the states of character correspond to the differences between these. It makes no small difference, then, whether we form habits of one kind or of another from our very youth; it makes a very great difference, or rather *all* the difference. ＊＊＊

＊＊＊ First, then, let us consider this, that it is the nature of such things to be destroyed by defect and excess, as we see in the case of strength and of health (for to gain light on things imperceptible we must use the evidence of sensible things); exercise either excessive or defective destroys the strength, and similarly drink or food which is above or below a certain amount destroys the health, while that which is proportionate both produces and increases and preserves it. So too is it, then, in the case of temperance and courage and the other virtues. For the man who flies from and fears everything and does not stand his ground against anything becomes a coward, and the man who fears nothing at all but goes to meet every danger becomes rash; and similarly the man who indulges in every pleasure and abstains from none becomes self-indulgent, while the man who shuns every pleasure, as boors do, becomes in a way insensible; temperance and courage, then, are destroyed by excess and defect, and preserved by the mean.

But not only are the sources and causes of their origination and growth the same as those of their destruction, but also the sphere of their actualization will be the same; for this is also true of the things which are more evident to sense, e.g. of strength; it is produced by taking much food and undergoing much exertion, and it is the strong man that will be most able to do these things. So too is it with the virtues; by abstaining from pleasures we become temperate, and it is when we have become so that we are most able to abstain from them; and similarly too in the case of courage; for by being habituated to despise things that are fearful and to stand our ground against them we become brave, and it is when we have become so that we shall be most able to stand our ground against them. * * *

3. We must take as a sign of states of character the pleasure or pain that supervenes upon acts; for the man who abstains from bodily pleasures and delights in this very fact is temperate, while the man who is annoyed at it is self-indulgent, and he who stands his ground against things that are terrible and delights in this or at least is not pained is brave, while the man who is pained is a coward. For moral virtue is concerned with pleasures and pains; it is on account of the pleasure that we do bad things, and on account of the pain that we abstain from noble ones. Hence we ought to have been brought up in a particular way from our very youth, as Plato says, so as both to delight in and to be pained by the things that we ought; this is the right education.

Again, if the virtues are concerned with actions and passions, and every passion and every action is accompanied by pleasure and pain, for this reason also virtue will be concerned with pleasures and pains. * * *

4. The question might be asked, what we mean by saying that we must become just by doing just acts, and temperate by doing temperate acts; for if men do just and temperate acts, they are already just and temperate, exactly as, if they do what is grammatical or musical, they are grammarians and musicians.

Or is this not true even of the arts? It is possible to do something grammatical, either by chance or under the guidance of another. A man will be a grammarian, then, only when he has both done something grammatical and done it grammatically; and this means doing it in accordance with the grammatical knowledge in himself.

Again, the case of the arts and that of the virtues are not similar; for the products of the arts have their goodness in themselves, so that it is enough that they should have a certain character, but if the acts that are in accordance with the virtues have themselves a certain character it does not follow that they are done justly or temperately. The agent also must be in a certain condition when he does them; in the first place he must have knowledge, secondly he must choose the acts, and choose them for their own sakes, and thirdly his action must proceed from a firm and unchangeable character. * * *

Actions, then, are called just and temperate when they are such as the just or the temperate man would do; but it is not the man who does these that is just and temperate, but the man who also does them *as* just and temperate men do them. * * *

But most people do not do these, but take refuge in theory and think they are being philosophers and will become good in this way, behaving somewhat like patients who listen attentively to their doctors, but do none of the things they are ordered to do. As the latter will not be made well in body by such a course of treatment, the former will not be made well in soul by such a course of philosophy. * * *

6. * * * In everything that is continuous and divisible it is possible to take more, less, or an equal amount, and that either in terms of the thing itself or relatively to us; and the equal is an intermediate between excess and defect. By the intermediate in the object I mean that which is equidistant from each of the extremes, which is one and the same for all; by the intermediate relatively to us that which is neither too much nor too little—and this is not one, nor the same for all. For instance, if ten is many and two is few, six is the intermediate, taken in terms of the object; for it exceeds and is exceeded by an equal amount; this is intermediate according to arithmetical proportion. But the intermediate relatively to us is not to be taken so; if ten pounds is too much for a particular person to eat and two too little, it does not follow that the trainer will order six pounds; for this also is perhaps too much for the person who is to take it, or too little—too little for Milo [a wrestler], too much for the beginner in athletic exercises. The same is true of running and wrestling. Thus a master of any art avoids excess and defect, but seeks the intermediate and chooses this—the intermediate not in the object but relatively to us.

If it is thus, then, that every art does its work well—by looking to the intermediate and judging its works by this standard (so that we often say of good works of art that it is not possible either to take away or to add anything, implying that excess and defect destroy the goodness of works of art, while the mean preserves it; and good artists, as we say, look to this in their work), and if, further, virtue is more exact and better than any art, as nature also is, then virtue must have the quality of aiming at the intermediate. I mean moral virtue; for it is this that is concerned with passions and actions, and in these there is excess, defect, and the intermediate. For instance, both fear and confidence and appetite and anger and pity and in general pleasure and pain may be felt both too much and too little, and in both cases not well; but to feel them at the right times, with reference to the right objects, towards the right people, with the right motive, and in the right way, is what is both intermediate and best, and this is characteristic of virtue. Similarly with regard to actions also there is excess, defect, and the intermediate. Now virtue is concerned with passions and actions, in which excess is a form of failure, and so is defect, while the intermediate is praised and is a form of success; and being praised and being successful are both characteristics of virtue. Therefore virtue is a kind of mean, since, as we have seen, it aims at what is intermediate.

Again, it is possible to fail in many ways (for evil belongs to the class of the unlimited, as the Pythagoreans conjectured, and good to that of the limited), while to succeed is possible only in one way (for which reason also one is easy and the other difficult—to miss the mark easy, to hit it difficult); for these reasons also, then, excess and defect are characteristic of vice, and the mean of virtue;

For men are good in but one way, but bad in many.

Virtue, then, is a state of character concerned with choice, lying in a mean, i.e. the mean relative to us, this being determined by reason, and by that reason by which the man of practical wisdom would determine it. Now it is a mean between two vices, that which depends on excess and that which depends on defect; and again it is a mean because the vices respectively fall short of or exceed what is right in both passions and actions, while virtue both finds and chooses that which is intermediate. Hence in respect of what it is, i.e. the definition which states its essence, virtue is a mean, with regard to what is best and right an extreme.

But not every action nor every passion admits of a mean; for some have names that already imply badness, e.g. spite, shamelessness, envy, and in the case of actions adultery, theft, murder; for all of these and suchlike things imply by their names that they are themselves bad, and not the excesses or deficiencies of them. It is not possible, then, ever to be right with regard to them; one must always be wrong. Nor does goodness or badness with regard to such things depend on committing adultery with the right woman, at the right time, and in the right way, but simply to do any of them is to go wrong. It would be equally absurd, then, to expect that in unjust, cowardly, and self-indulgent action there should be a mean, an excess, and a deficiency; for at that rate there would be a mean of excess and of deficiency, an excess of excess, and a deficiency of deficiency. But as there is no excess and deficiency of temperance and courage because what is intermediate is in a sense an extreme, so too of the actions we have mentioned there is no mean nor any excess and deficiency, but however they are done they are wrong; for in general there is neither a mean of excess and deficiency, nor excess and deficiency of a mean.

7. We must, however, not only make this general statement, but also apply it to the individual facts. For among statements about conduct those which are general apply more widely, but those which are particular are more true, since conduct has to do with individual cases, and our statements must harmonize with the facts in these cases. * * * With regard to feelings of fear and confidence courage is the mean; of the people who exceed, he who exceeds in fearlessness has no name (many of the states have no name), while the man who exceeds in confidence is rash, and he who exceeds in fear and falls short in confidence is a coward. With regard to pleasures and pains—not all of them, and not so much with regard to the pains—the mean is temperance, the excess self-indulgence. Persons deficient with regard to the pleasures are not often found; hence such persons also have received no name. But let us call them "insensible."

With regard to giving and taking of money the mean is liberality, the excess and the defect prodigality and meanness. In these actions people exceed and fall short in contrary ways; the prodigal exceeds in spending and falls short in taking, while the mean man exceeds in taking and falls short in spending. * * * With regard to money there are also other dispositions—a mean, magnificence (for the magnificent man differs from the liberal man; the former deals with large sums, the latter with small ones), an excess, tastelessness and vulgarity, and a deficiency, niggardliness; these differ from the states opposed to liberality, and the mode of their difference will be stated later.

With regard to honour and dishonour the mean is proper pride, the excess is known as a sort of "empty vanity," and the deficiency is undue humility. * * *

With regard to anger also there is an excess, a deficiency, and a mean. Although they can scarcely be said to have names, yet since we call the intermediate person good-tempered let us call the mean good temper; of the persons at the extremes let the one who exceeds be called irascible, and his vice irascibility, and the man who falls short an unirascible sort of person, and the deficiency unirascibility.

There are also three other means, which have a certain likeness to one another, but differ from one another. * * * With regard to truth, then, the intermediate is a truthful sort of person and the mean may be called truthfulness, while the pretence which exaggerates is boastfulness and the person characterized by it a boaster, and that which understates is mock modesty and the person characterized by it mock-modest. With regard to pleasantness in the giving of amusement the intermediate person is ready-witted and the disposition ready wit, the excess is buffoonery and the person characterized by it a buffoon, while the man who falls short is a sort of boor and his state is boorishness. With regard to the remaining kind of pleasantness, that which is exhibited in life in general, the man who is pleasant in the right way is friendly and the mean is friendliness, while the man who exceeds is an obsequious person if he has no end in view, a flatterer if he is aiming at his own advantage, and the man who falls short and is unpleasant in all circumstances is a quarrelsome and surly sort of person.

There are also means in the passions and concerned with the passions; since shame is not a virtue, and yet praise is extended to the modest man. For even in these matters one man is said to be intermediate, and another to exceed, as for instance the bashful man who is ashamed of everything; while he who falls short or is not ashamed of anything at all is shameless, and the intermediate person is modest. Righteous indignation is a mean between envy and spite, and these states are concerned with the pain and pleasure that are felt at the fortunes of our neighbours; the man who is characterized by righteous indignation is pained at undeserved good fortune, the envious man, going beyond him, is pained at all good fortune, and the spiteful man falls so far short of being pained that he even rejoices. * * *

9. * * * It is no easy task to be good. For in every thing it is no easy task to find the middle, e.g. to find the middle of a circle is not for everyone but for him who knows; so, too, anyone can get angry—that is easy—or give or spend money; but to do this to the right person, to the right extent, at the right time, with the right motive, and in the right way, *that* is not for everyone, nor is it easy; wherefore goodness is both rare and laudable and noble.

STUDY QUESTIONS
1. Explain the idea that a virtue is a disposition of character.
2. Why does Aristotle think it is necessary to be habituated into virtue? How is this to be done?
3. Explain the doctrine of the mean.

CONFUCIUS
Analects

Confucius (551?–479? BCE) was a Chinese philosopher, among the most influential in the Chinese tradition. His works still have wide influence and application today.

CHAPTER 4

4.1. The Master said: "It is beautiful to live amidst humanity. To choose a dwelling place destitute of humanity is hardly wise."

4.2. The Master said: "A man without humanity cannot long bear adversity and cannot long know joy. A good man rests in his humanity, a wise man profits from his humanity."

4.3. The Master said: "Only a good man can love people and can hate people."

4.4. The Master said: "Seeking to achieve humanity leaves no room for evil."

4.5. The Master said: "Riches and rank are what every man craves; yet if the only way to obtain them goes against his principles, he should desist from such a pursuit. Poverty and obscurity are what every man hates; yet if the only escape from them goes against his principles, he should accept his lot. If a gentleman forsakes humanity, how can he make a name for himself? Never for a moment does a gentleman part from humanity; he clings to it through trials, he clings to it through tribulations."

4.6. The Master said: "I have never seen a man who truly loved goodness and hated evil. Whoever truly loves goodness would put nothing above it; whoever truly hates evil would practice goodness in such a way that no evil could enter him. Has anyone ever devoted all his strength to goodness just for one day? No one ever has, and yet it is not for want of strength—there may be people who do not have even the small amount of strength it takes, but I have never seen any."

4.7. The Master said: "Your faults define you. From your very faults one can know your quality."

4.8. The Master said: "In the morning hear the Way; in the evening die content."

4.9. The Master said: "A scholar sets his heart on the Way; if he is ashamed of his shabby clothes and coarse food, he is not worth listening to."

4.10. The Master said: "In the affairs of the world, a gentleman has no parti pris: he takes the side of justice."

4.11. The Master said: "A gentleman seeks virtue; a small man seeks land. A gentleman seeks justice; a small man seeks favors."

4.12. The Master said: "He who acts out of self-interest arouses much resentment."

4.13. The Master said: "If one can govern the country by observing ritual and showing deference, there is no more to be said. If one cannot govern the country by observing ritual and showing deference, what's the use of ritual?"

4.14. The Master said: "Do not worry if you are without a position; worry lest you do not deserve a position. Do not worry if you are not famous; worry lest you do not deserve to be famous."

4.15. The Master said: "Shen, my doctrine has one single thread running through it." Master Zeng Shen replied: "Indeed."

The Master left. The other disciples asked: "What did he mean?" Master Zeng said: "The doctrine of the Master is: Loyalty and reciprocity, and that's all."

4.16. The Master said: "A gentleman considers what is just; a small man considers what is expedient."

4.17. The Master said: "When you see a worthy man, seek to emulate him. When you see an unworthy man, examine yourself."

4.18. The Master said: "When you serve your parents, you may gently remonstrate with them. If you see that they do not take your advice, be all the more respectful and do not contradict them. Let not your efforts turn to bitterness."

4.19. The Master said: "While your parents are alive, do not travel afar. If you have to travel, you must leave an address."

4.20. The Master said: "If three years after his father's death, the son does not alter his father's ways, he is a good son indeed."

4.21. The Master said: "Always keep in mind the age of your parents. Let this thought be both your joy and your worry."

4.22. The Master said: "The ancients were reluctant to speak, fearing disgrace should their deeds not match their words."

4.23. The Master said: "Self-control seldom leads astray."

4.24. The Master said: "A gentleman should be slow to speak and prompt to act."

4.25. The Master said: "Virtue is not solitary; it always has neighbors."

4.26. The Master said: "In the service of one's lord, pettiness brings disgrace; in friendly intercourse, pettiness brings estrangement." ＊＊＊

CHAPTER 12

12.1. Yan Hui asked about humanity. The Master said: "The practice of humanity comes down to this: tame the self and restore the rites. Tame the self and restore the rites for but one day, and the whole world will rally to your humanity. The practice of humanity comes from the self, not from anyone else."

Yan Hui said: "May I ask which steps to follow?" The Master said: "Observe the rites in this way: don't look at anything improper; don't listen to anything improper; don't say anything improper; don't do anything improper."

Yan Hui said: "I may not be clever, but with your permission, I shall endeavor to do as you have said."

12.2. Ran Yong asked about humanity. The Master said: "When abroad, behave as if in front of an important guest. Lead the people as if performing a great ceremony. What you do not wish for yourself, do not impose upon others. Let no resentment enter public affairs; let no resentment enter private affairs."

Ran Yong said: "I may not be clever, but with your permission I shall endeavor to do as you have said."

12.3. Sima Niu asked about humanity. The Master said: "He who practices humanity is reluctant to speak." The other said: "Reluctant to speak? And you call that humanity?" The Master said: "When the practice of something is difficult, how could one speak about it lightly?"

12.4. Sima Niu asked: "What is a gentleman?" The Master said: "A gentleman is without grief and without fear." Sima Niu said: "Without grief and without fear? And that makes a gentleman?" The Master said: "His conscience is without reproach. Why should he grieve, what should he fear?"

12.5. Sima Niu was grieving: "All men have brothers; I alone have none." Zixia said: "I have heard this: life and death are decreed by fate, riches and honors are allotted by Heaven. Since a gentleman behaves with reverence and diligence, treating people with deference and courtesy, all within the Four Seas are his brothers. How could a gentleman ever complain that he has no brothers?"

12.6. Zizhang asked about clear-sightedness. The Master said: "He who is soaked in slander and deafened with denunciations, and still does not waver, may be called clear-sighted. Actually he may also be called farsighted."

12.7. Zigong asked about government. The Master said: "Sufficient food, sufficient weapons, and the trust of the people." Zigong said: "If you had to do without one of these three, which would you give up?—"Weapons."—"If you had to do without one of the remaining two, which would you give up?"—"Food; after all, everyone has to die eventually. But without the trust of the people, no government can stand."

12.8. Ji Zicheng said: "One is a gentleman simply by his nature. What is the use of culture?" Zigong said: "Sir, what you have just said is deplorable indeed. 'A team of four horses cannot catch up with a loose tongue.' Nature is culture, culture is nature. Without its hair, the skin of a tiger or of a leopard is just the same as that of a dog or of a sheep."

12.9. Duke Ai asked You Ruo: "The crops have failed; I am running out of supplies. What should I do?" You Ruo replied: "Why not levy a tithe?" Duke Ai said: "Even the double of that would not meet my needs; what could be the use of a mere tithe?" You Ruo replied: "If the people have enough, how could their lord not have enough? If the people do not have enough, how could their lord have enough?"

12.10. Zizhang asked how to accumulate moral power and how to recognize emotional incoherence. The Master said: "Put loyalty and faith above everything, and follow justice. That is how one accumulates moral power. When you love someone, you wish him to live; when you hate someone, you wish him to die. Now, if you simultaneously wish him to live and to die, this is an instance of incoherence."

If not for the sake of wealth,
Then for the sake of change . . .

12.11. Duke Jing of Qi asked Confucius about government. Confucius replied: "Let the lord be a lord; the subject a subject; the father a father; the son a son." The Duke said: "Excellent! If indeed the lord is not a lord, the subject not a subject, the father not a father, the son not a son, I could be sure of nothing anymore—not even of my daily food."

12.12. The Master said: "To pass judgment on the mere basis of half the evidence: only Zilu can do that."

Zilu never slept over a promise.

12.13. The Master said: "I could adjudicate lawsuits as well as anyone. But I would prefer to make lawsuits unnecessary."

12.14. Zizhang asked about government. The Master said: "Ponder over it untiringly. Carry it out loyally."

12.15. The Master said: "A gentleman enlarges his learning through literature and restrains himself with ritual; therefore he is not likely to go wrong."

12.16. The Master said: "A gentleman brings out the good that is in people, he does not bring out the bad. A vulgar man does the opposite."

12.17. Lord Ji Kang asked Confucius about government. Confucius replied: "To govern is to be straight. If you steer straight, who would dare not to go straight?"

12.18. Lord Ji Kang was troubled by burglars. He consulted with Confucius. Confucius replied: "If you yourself were not covetous, they would not rob you, even if you paid them to."

12.19. Lord Ji Kang asked Confucius about government, saying: "Suppose I were to kill the bad to help the good: how about that?" Confucius replied: "You are here to govern; what need is there to kill? If you desire what is good, the people will be good. The moral power of the gentleman is wind, the moral power of the common man is grass. Under the wind, the grass must bend."

12.20. Zizhang asked: "When can one say that a scholar has attained superior perception?" The Master said: "It depends: what do you mean by 'perception'?" Zizhang replied: "To be recognized in public life, to be recognized in private life." The Master said: "This is recognition, not perception. To attain perception, a man must be cut from straight timber and love justice, examine men's words and observe their expressions, and bear in mind the necessity of deferring to others. As regards recognition, it is enough to put on an air of virtue while behaving to the contrary. Just keep up an unflappable pretense, and you will certainly achieve recognition in public life and you will certainly achieve recognition in private life."

12.21. Fan Chi was taking a walk with Confucius under the Rain Dance Terrace. He said: "May I ask how one can accumulate moral power, neutralize hostility, and recognize emotional incoherence." The Master said: "Excellent question! Always put the effort before the reward: is this not the way to accumulate moral power? To attack evil in itself and not the evil that is in people: is this not the way to neutralize hostility? To endanger oneself and one's kin in a sudden fit of anger: is this not an instance of incoherence?"

12.22. Fan Chi asked about humanity. The Master said "Love all men."

He asked about knowledge. The Master said: "Know all men." Fan Chi did not understand. The Master said: "Raise the straight and put them above the crooked, so that they may straighten the crooked."

Fan Chi withdrew. He saw Zixia and asked: "A moment ago, as I was with the Master I asked him about knowledge, and he said: 'Raise the straight and put them above the crooked, so that they may straighten the crooked.' What does this mean?" Zixia said: "Rich words indeed! When Shun ruled the world, choosing among the multitude he raised Gao Yao, and the wicked disappeared. When Tang ruled the world, choosing among the multitude he raised Yi Yin, and the wicked disappeared."

12.23. Zigong asked how to treat friends. The Master said: "Give them loyal advice and guide them tactfully. If that fails, stop: do not expose yourself to rebuff."

12.24. Master Zeng said: "A gentleman gathers friends through his culture; and with these friends, he develops his humanity."

STUDY QUESTIONS

1. How does Confucius deal with the possible clash between the acquisition of worldly goods and virtue?
2. In what way or ways does Confucius emphasize the importance of ritual and loyalty?
3. What does Confucius mean by humanity? Illustrate with examples.

VIRGINIA HELD
The Caring Person

Virginia Held (b. 1929) is an American moral and political philosopher who has produced important works of feminist philosophy.

Being caring is not one of the virtues we immediately think of when we try to recall the lists of virtues we have encountered. But most of us think that it is admirable to be caring, and we want our children to become caring persons. * * *

I argue that to be a caring person is not the same as to be a person with a virtue we call caring. But what else could it be?

Let's begin with the question of persons: Who and what are they? I start with a normative framework, asking how we should think of persons capable of wondering how they should live. Then I'll ask whether they should be caring and what that should mean.

* * * I will see persons as moral subjects, capable of action and of shaping their lives and institutions and societies over time, at least to some extent, through cultivating in themselves and others certain characteristics and practices and values.

What is a person who is a moral subject? * * *

* * * I begin with the self-awareness I think we have of being saddled with moral responsibility. * * *

* * * We experience ourselves, I take it, as moral subjects and as persons. From the normative perspective of considering how we should live, we must assume there is an I capable of responding to proposed recommendations with acceptance or rejection (even children partially grasp this) and capable of being responsible for many of our choices. * * *

Children are potentially (if not actually) moral subjects. When they fail to do what they ought, we disapprove with the intention of gradually steering them to take moral responsibility for themselves. At given stages, we may not expect them to understand the moral significance of their behavior, but we can try to cultivate in them from early ages the appropriate characteristics and bring about their participation in moral practices.

Hilde Nelson, along with various others, shows how "identities are narratively constructed," although this may not be all they are.[1] She also shows how we can change our identities through "counterstories." Diana Meyers says that "narrativity clarifies how people can be profoundly influenced by their social context and yet retain their capacity to shape self-determined moral lives—to transvalue values, reroute their own pathways, and reconfigure their social ideals."[2] This may be a helpful way of thinking about

---

1   Hilde Lindemann Nelson, "Identity and Free Agency," in *Feminists Doing Ethics*, eds. Peggy DesAutels and Joanne Waugh (Lanham, Md.: Rowman and Littlefield, 2001), p. 45.

2   Diana Tietjens Meyers, "Narrative and Moral Life," in *Setting the Moral Compass*, ed. Cheshire Calhoun (New York: Oxford University Press, 2004), p. 299.

how we shape our selves and even how we are able to go in new directions. It leaves open our questions about how we *should* continue our stories: Should we become more caring, more concerned with injustice, less assertive in pursuing our interests, more demanding of respect? And why?

I start, then, with a normative perspective. But instead of the Kantian normative perspective some things I have said might suggest, I will start with that of the ethics of care. ∗∗∗ I see the ethics of care from as fully a normative point of view as any other ethic. It addresses questions about whether and how and why we ought to engage in activities of care, questions about how such activities should be conducted and structured, and questions about the meanings of care and caring. It especially evaluates relations of care.

THE PERSON IN THE ETHICS OF CARE

It is characteristic of the ethics of care to view persons as relational and as interdependent. Deontological and consequentialist moral theories of which Kantian moral theory and utilitarianism are the leading examples concentrate their attention on the rational decisions of agents assumed to be independent, autonomous individuals. Virtue theory also focuses on individual persons and their dispositions. The ethics of care, in contrast, conceptualizes persons as deeply affected by, and involved in, relations with others; to many care theorists persons are at least partly constituted by their social ties. The ethics of care attends especially to relations between persons, evaluating such relations and valuing relations of care. It does not assume that relations relevant for morality have been entered into voluntarily by free and equal individuals, as do dominant moral theories. It appreciates as well the values of care between persons of unequal power in unchosen relations such as those between parents and children and between members of social groups of various kinds. To the ethics of care, our embeddedness in familial, social, and historical contexts is basic.

Jean Keller argues that this conception of the person is central to feminist ethics. She writes that "whatever shape feminist ethics ends up taking, it will incorporate a relational model of moral agency. That is, the insight that the moral agent is an 'encumbered self,' who is always already embedded in relations with flesh-and-blood others and is partly constituted by these relations, is here to stay."[3] I would slightly modify this position because I

3　Jean Keller, "Autonomy, Relationality, and Feminist Ethics," *Hypatia: A Journal of Feminist Philosophy* 12(2) (1997): 152–65, p. 152.

see feminist ethics as wider than care ethics, but it is largely true, I think, of the ethics of care.

Here is Marilyn Friedman's characterization of relational persons as developed by contemporary feminists:

> According to the relational approach, persons are fundamentally social beings who develop the competency of autonomy . . . in a context of values, meanings, and modes of self-reflection that cannot exist except as constituted by social practices. . . . It is now well recognized that our reflective capacities and our very identities are always partly constituted by communal traditions and norms that we cannot put entirely into question without at the same time voiding our very capacities to reflect.

> We are each reared in a social context of some sort, typically although not always that of a family, itself located in wider social networks such as community and nation. Nearly all of us remain, throughout our lives, involved in social relationships and communities, at least some of which partly define our identities and ground our highest values.[4] * * *

Diana Meyers describes what she sees as various currently influential conceptions of the self. "The feminist relational self," she writes,

> is the interpersonally bonded self. . . . As relational selves . . . people share in one another's joys and sorrows, give and receive care, and generally profit from the many rewards and cope with the many aggravations of friendship, family membership, religious or ethnic affiliation, and the like. These relationships are sources of moral identity, for people become committed to their intimates and to others whom they care about, and these commitments become central moral concerns.[5]

The concept of the relational person might solve some of the current puzzles of how it is that we feel empathy for others. In examples of small children trying to alleviate the distress of other children, we see something that appears to be direct and spontaneous sympathetic feeling with others and wanting to help them overcome their unhappiness. The idea that "human nature" is displayed in the image of toddler Hobbesian egoistically fighting all obstacles to get what he wants is seen to have another side. If small children do not yet have a sense of themselves as separate persons, perhaps they are simply feeling the pain of the other child as their own. But if they do understand themselves as individuals, what is going on? * * *

---

4 Marilyn Friedman, "Autonomy, Social Disruption, and Women," in *Relational Autonomy: Feminist Perspectives on Autonomy, Agency, and the Social Self*, eds. Catriona Mackenzie and Natalie Stoljar (New York: Oxford University Press, 2000), pp. 40–41.

5 Meyers, "Narrative and Moral Life," p. 292.

If we see the person as an embodied nexus of relations, the relations constituting one child are different from those constituting another, and even a small child can be aware that he is different from others. But when the other child is in distress, the relation between them may be upset, and he may wish it would be better. This would not be inconsistent with his feeling glee on another occasion at the pain of the other child if he felt that the other child was a threat, say, to his own possession of a toy. * * *

CARING AND AUTONOMY

Can caring persons be autonomous? * * * Autonomy is still to be sought, but it will be a quite different kind of autonomy than that of the self-sufficient, atomistic self that can be distilled, uncharitably, from traditional liberal theory. * * * Persons are shaped by a complex of intersecting social factors, including race, class, gender, ethnicity, and ties of family and community. * * *

Diana Meyers's description of autonomy as a set of competencies is persuasive: The autonomous person, she says, will have developed a "repertory of skills through which self-discovery, self-definition, and self-direction are achieved." Relational persons can develop these skills, though for some it will be harder than for others. "As with other competencies," she notes, "one learns through practice and practice augments proficiency."[6] * * *

The point, for relational persons, is that as we modify and often distance ourselves from existing relations, it is for the sake of better and often more caring relations, rather than for the splendid independence, self-sufficiency, and easy isolation of the traditional liberal ideal of the autonomous rational agent.

Are some persons just caused by their upbringings and friends, perhaps with the help of their genes, to be caring and considerate, sensitive to and respectful of the feelings of others, and adept at engaging in the practices of care, whereas others are brought up in such a way that they simply lack and can never attain these competencies? The goal of being a caring person can certainly and should be a matter of autonomous choice. A person who has merely unthinkingly and uncritically followed the caring practices into which she has been brought up can seem in outward appearance to be caring but will lack the appropriate motive of consciously and reflectively recognizing the value of care. Learning and cultivating the relevant abilities

---

6   Diana Tietjens Meyers, "Intersectional Identity and the Authentic Self; Opposites Attract!" in *Relational Autonomy*, eds. Mackenzie and Stoljar, pp. 174/1. See also Diana T. Meyers, *Self, Society, and Personal Choice* (New York: Columbia University Press, 1989), pp. 174–175.

to be a caring person will depend on many efforts by a moral agent and by others in relations with that person. Given practices should be subjected to critical scrutiny and improved. Some persons at any given time will fail to be caring persons; I doubt that any person has a permanent incapacity to become caring.

RELATIONAL PERSONS AND OVERCOMMITMENT

To some critics of the ethics of care, the conception of the person as relational with which it works is thought to be dangerously submerged in unchosen social relations. * * * The ethics of care must take account of the experience of recipients of care as well as providers, how care must not be overbearing [and] * * * the many ways caring can go wrong as well as the many ways it should be promoted. Care has been seriously undervalued in the past by dominant moral theories. Those now clarifying its value aim to correct this but do not suggest that it is the only value to which we need to attend. * * *

* * * Deficient social assistance makes * * * many of the commitments of the relational person * * * burdensome and hard to fulfill. For instance, what puts so much of the burden of caring for aged parents on their daughters is society's failure to take responsibility for the care of the elderly. And that mothers have such trouble with entanglement in their relational webs is highly related to the paucity of adequate child care arrangements. An adequately cared for and caring elderly parent can be content with an occasional phone call from a busy daughter, affirming a bond of relational closeness that includes a mutual understanding that the parent does not want her to and the adult child does not need to expend large amounts of time or energy to reaffirm the relation. Children well cared for and happy in publicly provided daycare do not need to interact constantly with their parents to understand that they are loved and valued and that their relation with their parents is strong and close.

Sometimes, certainly, the actual demands made by other persons on the relational person will seem overwhelming, and the demands may not be of the kind for which society could take responsibility, even if it included mental health services along with other health care provisions. But when relationships are so entangling that they impede free agency, they are often the kind of relationship that is in need of revision.

The difference here may often be like that between persons who feel they must constantly talk with a partner for the relationship to be close, which is not a problem if the partner feels the same way. But there can be close relationships in which mutual understanding allows both to be absent or silent for long periods and certainly to be fully independent moral agents. Many of the relationships in which we are entangled are ones we did not choose but simply found ourselves in, as with our parents and siblings. But even these relationships can be ones we strive to revise. Among the relations we choose, we can steer our lives toward those that will be harmonious with respect to the degree of entanglement they require and in terms of their level of demandingness. Friends can recognize each other as highly caring without constant demonstrations of care.

CARE AS A VIRTUE OF PERSONS

It is easy to suppose that caring is a virtue that persons can have and to interpret the virtues, as virtue theory standardly does, as *dispositions of individuals.* Some think of caring as another name for benevolence, a familiar virtue. I will show why I do not agree. * * *

* * * A caring person, in my view, will not only have the intention to care and the disposition to care effectively but will participate in caring relations. If persons lack the capacity to do so, they can be persons who are trying to be caring, but they are not yet caring persons. To be a caring person requires more than the right motives or dispositions. It requires the ability to engage in the practice of care, and the *exercise* of this ability. Care, as we saw, is *work* as well as an emotion or motive or intention. The caring person participates in this work in ways that roughly meet its standards. Care is not *only* work, however. So it is not enough that the work get done and the child get fed if done without an appropriately caring motive. But, in my view, having caring motives is not enough to make one a caring person. * * *

* * * Seeing care as simply a virtue, I think * * * misses a central feature of care: its evaluations of and recommendations concerning relations *between* persons. [Howard Curzer] says "a person is caring if he or she is disposed to make and maintain the right sort of relationships, with the right people, in the right way, at the right times, for the right motives, etc. The caring person must also feel the right level and sort of fondness and responsibility for people standing in various different relationships to him or her."[7] He acknowledges the affinities between this definition and Aristotle's of friendship.

---

7 Howard J. Curzer, "Admirable Immorality, Dirty Hands, Care Ethics, Justice Ethics, and Child Sacrifice," *Ratio* 15(3) (September 2002): 227–244, 236.

This goes a considerable way toward describing a caring person, but it is limited to evaluating an individual's dispositions and behavior, including interactions with others, but not relations themselves between persons. Descriptions of the virtues concentrate on the characteristics of persons as individuals. These individuals should "make and maintain," as Curzer puts it, various relations. But this misses the enormous reality of the relations we are already enmeshed in from the moment we are born. For many years we are *in* relations, we gradually *find* and become aware of them, we do not "make" them. Many of these relations will be highly unsatisfactory, certainly not chosen by us, and we may have to struggle to unmake them. But often where they are unsatisfactory, we can try to modify, improve, and transform them. In all these cases we need moral evaluations of *relations*, not just dispositions. And we need moral recommendations for whether to maintain or change or try to break them, though the extent to which the latter is even possible is a serious question, since they will often remain part of who we are. We will never, for instance, cease to be the child of given parents, or the person brought up with a certain group identity, even if we repudiate these. The ethics of care and our conceptions of caring persons should be able to offer these evaluations and recommendations, I think.

Some feminists find an Aristotelian approach to moral problems far more hospitable to their concerns than Kantian or utilitarian ones. Some have felt close to Hume in their moral orientations. Virtue theory, however, including that of Aristotle and Hume, has characteristically seen the virtues as attaching to individual persons. The ethics of care, in contrast, is more concerned with relations between persons. A *relation* of caring is seen as valuable or faulty, more than the dispositions of persons apart from this. Of course valuable relations between persons depend to a considerable extent on the characteristics of the persons in them, but persons with individually valuable characteristics may still fail to have good relations between them.

For all these reasons, care should not in my view be seen as just another component—hitherto neglected—in the longer lists or shorter compendiums of virtues. The ethics of care is an alternative moral approach of its own.

* * * Two individuals can be personally virtuous in the sense of having virtuous dispositions and yet have a relationship that is hostile, conflictual, and unhelpful to either. A caring relationship requires *mutuality* and the cultivation of ways of achieving this in the various contexts of interdependence in human life. Noticing interdependencies, rather than thinking only or largely in terms of independent individuals and their individual circumstances is

one of the central aspects of an ethics of care. A caring person will cultivate mutuality in the interdependencies of personal, political, economic, and global contexts. A caring person will appropriately value caring relations and will seek to modify existing relations to make them more caring. And yes, caring persons will do this in the right ways, with the right motives, and all that. But the focus will remain, for the caring person, on his or her *relations* rather than on his or her own dispositions, and on the *practice* of care. * * *

PROBLEMS WITH CARE AS A DISPOSITION

If we think of a caring person as having a virtuous disposition instead of (as I am advocating) as engaging in a caring relational practice, consider the many ways that care as a disposition can go wrong. To continue to have strong feelings of affection for someone who does not want those feelings but wants rather to be left alone, can be a failure of care in the sense of failing to constitute a caring relation. Of course one cannot simply shut off one's affectionate feelings at will, but one can cultivate distance, stop bestowing gifts or unwanted praise, and so forth. On the other hand, someone who seems to want to be left alone, such as a young person trying to distance himself from an overly concerned parent, may actually welcome continuing affection despite the appearance of disdaining it. Both parent and child may acknowledge that the caring relation is important and solid and needs only reinterpretation to allow for greater mutual autonomy.

Mutual autonomy is very different from what traditional autonomy would be, if there were such a thing. Traditionally, autonomy has been understood in terms of self-sufficiency, noninterference, self-direction, rational control, and the like. Feminist and other critics have pointed out the artificial and misleading aspects of ideals of these kinds of autonomy. We are all in fact thoroughly dependent as children and for periods of illness and deeply interdependent as inhabitants of modern societies. Holding up liberal ideals of self-sufficiency masks these facts of dependency and interdependence, and distorts the realities of, among other things, caring labor. There can certainly be lives of greater or lesser capacity to make choices in life without undue outside constraints. Choices can be interfered with by educational inadequacies, economic pressures, political and legal compulsions, and coercive persons. They can also be constrained by the psychological pressures that those to whose affections we are vulnerable can exert. To live and act as we choose requires the resources and capacities to do so. So there can be more, or less, self-direction within the interdependencies that surround us, and caring relations often contribute to such autonomy. But more self-sufficiency is not always better: Cooperative activity involves mutual dependence. The critique of domination basic to the ethics of care can contribute to fostering appropriate kinds of autonomy.

The ideal of rational control asks us to exclude emotional influence in achieving autonomy. But the emotions thus excluded would include the moral emotions of empathy, sensitivity, and mutual consideration, as well as the emotions that threaten morality. We may thus do well to question the ideal of autonomy as rational control. Through appropriate relations with caretakers and through education and practice, we can learn the competencies of thinking for ourselves and resisting undue pressure from others. Such autonomy is fully consistent with the ethics of care and should be cultivated, but does not require the suppression of emotion. * * *

Another limitation in seeing care as a virtue becomes apparent when we ask how caring we should be. The person who tries to be caring but is instead selfless to the point of lacking self-respect, can be criticized as failing to have the requisite virtue. The servile housewife, the martyr mother, aspire to virtue but miss it. We can discern the deficiencies in their dispositions, but we can discern them even more clearly when we examine the relations in which they display them. The servile housewife contributes to the macho husband and martinet father who disdain her. The martyr mother produces children who either flee from indebtedness to her or face the world presuming they are owed deference. The person who participates in an admirable practice of care will not only respect himself but will foster mutual respect and mutual sensitivity. * * *

In political and economic contexts, * * * relations of power * * * can * * * easily undermine the value of care. Differences of actual power are inevitable in public as well as in personal contexts, and we do well to recognize them rather than mask them behind liberal fictions of equality. But when we focus on relations, we can come to see how to shape good caring relations so that differences in power will not be pernicious and so that the vulnerable are empowered. Good caring relations can involve not only mutual recognition of moral equality but practices that avoid subtle as well as blatant coercion where it is disrespectful and inconsiderate. We can foster trust and mutuality in place of benevolent domination. Caring persons may often need to exercise power, but they will also understand how best to do so and especially how to avoid doing so in ways that become violent and damaging.

STUDY QUESTIONS

1. What is Held's conception of the moral subject?
2. Explain Held's distinction between "care as a virtue" and the "caring person."
3. What does Held mean by "mutual autonomy" and how does it differ from traditional conceptions of autonomy?

JEAN-PAUL SARTRE
Existentialism and Humanism

Jean-Paul Sartre (1905–1980) was a leading French philosopher, novelist, playwright, and radical public intellectual—a key figure in existentialism.

My purpose here is to offer a defence of existentialism against several reproaches that have been laid against it.

First, it has been reproached as an invitation to people to dwell in quietism of despair. For if every way to a solution is barred, one would have to regard any action in this world as entirely ineffective, and one would arrive finally at a contemplative philosophy. Moreover, since contemplation is a luxury, this would be only another bourgeois philosophy. This is, especially, the reproach made by the Communists.

From another quarter we are reproached for having underlined all that is ignominious in the human situation, for depicting what is mean, sordid or base to the neglect of certain things that possess charm and beauty and belong to the brighter side of human nature: for example, according to the Catholic critic, Mlle. Mercier, we forget how an infant smiles. Both from this side and from the other we are also reproached for leaving out of account the solidarity of mankind and considering man in isolation. And this, say the Communists, is because we base our doctrine upon pure subjectivity—upon the Cartesian "I think": which is the moment in which solitary man attains to himself; a position from which it is impossible to regain solidarity with other men who exist outside of the self. The *ego* cannot reach them through the *cogito*.

From the Christian side, we are reproached as people who deny the reality and seriousness of human affairs. For since we ignore the commandments of God and all values prescribed as eternal, nothing remains but what is strictly voluntary. Everyone can do what he likes, and will be incapable, from such a point of view, of condemning either the point of view or the action of anyone else.

It is to these various reproaches that I shall endeavour to reply to-day; that is why I have entitled this brief exposition "Existentialism and Humanism." Many may be surprised at the mention of humanism in this connection, but we shall try to see in what sense we understand it. In any case, we can begin by saying that existentialism, in our sense of the word, is a doctrine that does render human life possible; a doctrine, also, which affirms that every truth and every action imply both an environment and a human subjectivity. The essential charge laid against us is, of course, that of over-emphasis upon the evil side of human life. I have lately been told of a lady who, whenever she lets slip a vulgar expression in a moment of nervousness, excuses herself by exclaiming, "I believe I am becoming an existentialist." So it appears that ugliness is being identified with existentialism. * * *

What is alarming in the doctrine that I am about to try to explain to you is * * * that it confronts man with a possibility of choice. To verify this, let us review the whole question upon the strictly philosophic level. What, then, is this that we call existentialism? * * *

* * * What [existentialists] have in common is simply the fact that they believe that *existence* comes before *essence*—or, if you will, that we must begin from the subjective. What exactly do we mean by that?

If one considers an article of manufacture—as, for example, a book or a paper-knife—one sees that it has been made by an artisan who had a conception of it; and he has paid attention, equally, to the conception of a paper-knife and to the pre-existent technique of production which is a part of that conception and is, at bottom, a formula. Thus the paper-knife is at the same time an article producible in a certain manner and one which, on the other hand, serves a definite purpose, for one cannot suppose that a man would produce a paper-knife without knowing what it was for. Let us say, then, of the paper-knife that its essence—that is to say the sum of the formulae and the qualities which made its production and its definition possible—precedes its existence. The presence of such-and-such a paper-knife or book is thus determined before my eyes. Here, then, we are viewing the world from a technical standpoint, and we can say that production precedes existence.

When we think of God as the creator, we are thinking of him, most of the time, as a supernal artisan. * * * God * * * knows precisely what he is creating. Thus, the conception of man in the mind of God is comparable to that of the paper-knife in the mind of the artisan: God makes man according to a procedure and a conception, exactly as the artisan manufactures a paper-knife, following a definition and a formula. Thus each individual man is the realisation of a certain conception which dwells in the divine understanding. In the philosophic atheism of the eighteenth century, the notion of God is suppressed, but not, for all that, the idea that essence is prior to existence; something of that idea we still find everywhere, in Diderot, in Voltaire and even in Kant. Man possesses a human nature; that "human nature," which is the conception of human being, is found in every man; which means that each man is a particular example of an universal conception, the conception of Man. In Kant, this universality goes so far that the wild man of the woods, man in the state of nature and the bourgeois are all contained in the same definition and have the same fundamental qualities. Here again, the essence of man precedes that historic existence which we confront in experience.

Atheistic existentialism, of which I am a representative, declares with greater consistency that if God does not exist there is at least one being whose existence comes before its essence, a being which exists before it can be defined by any conception of it. That being is man or, as Heidegger has it, the human reality. What do we mean by saying that existence precedes essence? We mean that man first of all exists, encounters himself, surges up in the world—and defines himself afterwards. If man as the existentialist sees him is not definable, it is because to begin with he is nothing. He will not be anything until later, and then he will be what he makes of himself. Thus, there is no human nature, because there is no God to have a conception of it. Man simply is. Not that he is simply what he conceives himself to be, but he is what he wills, and as he conceives himself after already existing—as he wills to be after that leap towards existence. Man is nothing else but that which he makes of himself. That is the first principle of existentialism. And this is what people call its "subjectivity," using the word as a reproach against us. But what do we mean to say by this, but that man is of a greater dignity than a stone or a table? For we mean to say that man primarily exists—that man is, before all else, something which propels itself towards a future and is aware that it is doing so. Man is, indeed, a project which possesses a subjective life, instead of being a kind of moss, or a fungus or a cauliflower. Before that projection of the self nothing exists; not even in the heaven of intelligence: man will only attain existence when he is what he purposes to be. Not, however, what he may wish to be. For what we usually understand by wishing or willing is a conscious decision taken—much more often than not—after we have made ourselves what we are. I may wish to join a party, to write a book or to marry—but in such a case what is usually called my will is probably a manifestation of a prior and more spontaneous decision. If, however, it is true that existence is prior to essence, man is responsible for what he is. Thus, the first effect of existentialism is that it puts every man in possession of himself as he is, and places the entire responsibility for his existence squarely upon his own shoulders. And, when we say that man is responsible for himself, we do not mean that he is responsible only for his own individuality, but that he is responsible for all men. The word "subjectivism" is to be understood in two senses, and our adversaries play upon only one of them. Subjectivism means, on the one hand, the freedom of the individual subject and, on the other, that man cannot pass beyond human subjectivity. It is the latter which is the deeper meaning of existentialism. When we say that man chooses himself, we do mean that every one of us must choose himself; but by that we also mean that in choosing for himself he chooses for all men. For in effect, of all the actions a man may take in order to create himself as he wills to be, there is not one which is not creative, at the same time, of an image of man such as he believes he ought to be. To choose between this or that is at the same time to affirm the value of that which is chosen; for we are unable ever to choose the worse. What we choose is always the better; and nothing can be better for us unless it is better for all. If, moreover, existence precedes essence and we will to exist at the same time as we fashion our image, that image is valid for all and for the entire epoch in which we find ourselves. Our responsibility is thus much greater than we had supposed, for it concerns mankind as a whole. If I am a worker, for instance, I may choose to join a Christian rather than a Communist trade union. And if, by that membership, I choose to signify that resignation is, after all, the attitude that best becomes a man, that man's kingdom is not upon this earth, I do not commit myself alone to that view. Resignation is my will for everyone, and my action is, in consequence, a commitment on behalf of all mankind. Or if, to take a more personal case, I decide to marry and to have children, even though this decision proceeds simply from my situation, from my passion or my desire, I am thereby committing not only myself, but humanity as a whole, to the practice of monogamy. I am thus responsible for myself and for all men, and I am creating a certain image of man as I would have him to be. In fashioning myself I fashion man.

This may enable us to understand what is meant by such terms—perhaps a little grandiloquent—as anguish, abandonment and despair. As you will soon see, it is very simple. First, what do we mean by anguish? The existentialist frankly states that man is in anguish. His meaning is as follows—When a man commits himself to anything, fully realising that he is not only choosing what he will be, but is thereby at the same time a legislator deciding for the whole of mankind—in such a moment a man cannot escape from the sense of complete and profound responsibility. There are many, indeed, who show no such anxiety. But we affirm that they are merely disguising their anguish or are in flight from it. Certainly, many people think that in what they are doing they commit no one but themselves to anything: and if you ask them, "What would happen if everyone did so?" they shrug their shoulders and reply, "Everyone does not do so." But in truth, one ought always to ask oneself what would happen if everyone did as one is doing; nor can one escape from that disturbing thought except by a kind of self-deception. The man who lies in self-excuse, by saying "Everyone will not do it" must be ill at ease in his conscience, for the act of lying implies the universal value which it denies. By its very disguise his anguish reveals itself. This is the anguish that Kierkegaard called "the anguish of Abraham." You know the story: An angel commanded Abraham to sacrifice his son: and obedience was obligatory, if it really was an angel who had appeared and said, "Thou, Abraham, shalt sacrifice thy son." But anyone in such a case would wonder, first, whether it was indeed an angel and secondly, whether I am really Abraham. Where are the proofs? A certain mad woman who suffered from hallucinations said that people were telephoning to her, and giving her orders. The doctor asked, "But who is it that speaks to you?" She replied: "He says it is God." And what, indeed, could prove to her that it was God? If an angel appears to me, what is the proof that it is an angel; or, if I hear voices, who can prove that they proceed from heaven and not from hell, or from my own subconsciousness or some pathological condition? Who can prove that they are really addressed to me?

Who, then, can prove that I am the proper person to impose, by my own choice, my conception of man upon mankind? I shall never find any proof whatever; there will be no sign to convince me of it. If a voice speaks to me, it is still I myself who must decide whether the voice is or is not that of an angel. If I regard a certain course of action as good, it is only I who choose to say that it is good and not bad. There is nothing to show that I am Abraham: nevertheless I also am obliged at every instant to perform actions which are examples. Everything happens to every man as though the whole human race had its eyes fixed upon what he is doing and regulated its conduct accordingly. So every man ought to say, "Am I really a man who has the right to act in such a manner that humanity regulates itself by what I do." If a man does not say that, he is dissembling his anguish. Clearly, the anguish with which we are concerned here is not one that could lead to quietism or inaction. It is anguish pure and simple, of the kind well known to all those who have borne responsibilities. When, for instance, a military leader takes upon himself the responsibility for an attack and sends a number of men to their death, he chooses to do it and at bottom he alone chooses. No doubt he acts under a higher command, but its orders, which are more general, require interpretation by him and upon that interpretation depends the life of ten, fourteen or twenty men. In making the decision, he cannot but feel a certain anguish. All leaders know that anguish. It does not prevent their acting, on the contrary it is the very condition of their action, for the action presupposes that there is a plurality of possibilities, and in choosing one of these, they realise that it has value only because it is chosen. Now it is anguish of that kind which existentialism describes, and moreover, as we shall see, makes explicit through direct responsibility towards other men who are concerned. Far from being a screen which could separate us from action, it is a condition of action itself.

And when we speak of "abandonment"—a favourite word of Heidegger—we only mean to say that God does not exist, and that it is necessary to draw the consequences of his absence right to the end. The existentialist is strongly opposed to a certain type of secular moralism which seeks to suppress God at the least possible expense. Towards 1880, when the French professors endeavoured to formulate a secular morality, they said something like this:—God is a useless and costly hypothesis, so we will do without it. However, if we are to have morality, a society and a law-abiding world, it is essential that certain values should be taken seriously; they must have an *à priori* existence ascribed to them. It must be considered obligatory *à priori* to be honest, not to lie, not to beat one's wife, to bring up children and so forth; so we are going to do a little work on this subject, which will enable us to show that these values exist all the same, inscribed in an intelligible heaven although, of course, there is no God. In other words—and this is, I believe, the purport of all that we in France call radicalism—nothing will be changed if God does not exist; we shall re-discover the same norms of honesty, progress and humanity, and we shall have disposed of God as an out-of-date hypothesis which will die away quietly of itself. The existentialist, on the contrary, finds it extremely embarrassing that God does not exist, for there disappears with Him all possibility of finding values in an intelligible heaven. There can no longer be any good *à priori*, since there is no infinite and perfect consciousness to think it. It is nowhere written that "the good" exists, that one must be honest or must not lie, since we are now upon the plane where there are only men. Dostoievsky once wrote "If God did not exist, everything would be permitted"; and that, for existentialism, is the starting point. Everything is indeed permitted if God does not exist, and man is in consequence forlorn, for he cannot find anything to depend upon either within or outside himself. He discovers forthwith, that he is without excuse. For if indeed existence precedes essence, one will never be able to explain one's action by reference to a given and specific human nature; in other words, there is no determinism—man is free, man *is* freedom. Nor, on the other hand, if God does not exist, are we provided with any values or commands that could legitimise our behaviour. Thus we have neither behind us, nor before us in a luminous realm of values, any means of justification or excuse. We are left alone, without excuse. That is what I mean when I say that man is condemned to be free. Condemned, because he did not create himself, yet is nevertheless at liberty, and from the moment that he is thrown into this world he is responsible for everything he does. The existentialist does not believe in the power of passion. He will never regard a grand passion as a destructive torrent upon which a man is swept into certain actions as by fate, and which, therefore, is an excuse for them. He thinks that man is responsible for his passion. ✳ ✳ ✳

As an example by which you may the better understand this state of abandonment, I will refer to the case of a pupil of mine, who sought me out in the following circumstances. His father was quarrelling with his mother and was also inclined to be a "collaborator"; his elder brother had been killed in the German offensive of 1940 and this young man, with a sentiment somewhat primitive but generous, burned to avenge him. His mother was living alone with him, deeply afflicted by the semi-treason of his father and by the death of her eldest son, and her one consolation was in this young man. But he, at this moment, had the choice between going to England to join the Free French Forces or of staying near his mother and helping her to live. He fully realised that this woman lived only for him and that his disappearance—or perhaps his death—would plunge her into despair. He also realised that, concretely and in fact, every action he performed on his mother's behalf would be sure of effect in the sense of aiding her to live, where as anything he did in order to go and fight would be an ambiguous action which might vanish like water into sand and serve no purpose. For instance, to set out for England he would have to wait indefinitely in a Spanish camp on the way through Spain; or, on arriving in England or in Algiers he might be put into an office to fill up forms. Consequently, he found himself confronted by two very different modes of action; the one concrete, immediate, but directed towards only one individual; and the other an action addressed to an end infinitely greater, a national collectivity, but for that very reason ambiguous—and it might be frustrated on the way. At the same time, he was hesitating between two kinds of morality; on the one side the morality of sympathy, of personal devotion and, on the other side, a morality of wider scope but of more debatable validity. He had to choose between those two. What could help him to choose? Could the Christian doctrine? No. Christian doctrine says: Act with charity, love your neighbour, deny yourself for others, choose the way which is hardest, and so forth. But which is the harder road? To whom does one owe the more brotherly love, the patriot or the mother? Which is the more useful aim, the general one of fighting in and for the whole community, or the precise aim of helping one particular person to live? Who can give an answer to that à priori? No one. Nor is it given in any ethical scripture. The Kantian ethic says, Never regard another as a means, but always as an end. Very well; if I remain with my mother, I shall be regarding her as the end and not as a means: but by the same token I am in danger of treating as means those who are fighting on my behalf; and the converse is also true, that if I go to the aid of the combatants I shall be treating them as the end at the risk of treating my mother as a means.

If values are uncertain, if they are still too abstract to determine the particular, concrete case under consideration, nothing remains but to trust in our instincts. That is what this young man tried to do; and when I saw him he said, "In the end, it is feeling that counts; the direction in which it is really pushing me is the one I ought to choose. If I feel that I love my mother enough to sacrifice everything else for her—my will to be avenged, all my longings for action and adventure—then I stay with her. If, on the contrary, I feel that my love for her is not enough, I go." But how does one estimate the strength of a feeling? The value of his feeling for his mother was determined precisely by the fact that he was standing by her. I may say that I love a certain friend enough to sacrifice such or such a sum of money for him, but I cannot prove that unless I have done it. I may say, "I love my mother enough to remain with her," if actually I have remained with her. I can only estimate the strength of this affection if I have performed an action by which it is defined and ratified. But if I then appeal to this affection to justify my action, I find myself drawn into a vicious circle. * * *

Quietism is the attitude of people who say, "let others do what I cannot do." The doctrine I am presenting before you is precisely the opposite of this, since it declares that there is no reality except in action. It goes further, indeed, and adds, "Man is nothing else but what he purposes, he exists only in so far as he realises himself, he is therefore nothing else but the sum of his actions, nothing else but what his life is." Hence we can well understand why some people are horrified by our teaching. For many have but one resource to sustain them in their misery, and that is to think, "Circumstances have been against me, I was worthy to be something much better than I have been. I admit I have never had a great love or a great friendship; but that is because I never met a man or a woman who were worthy of it; if I have not written any very good books, it is because I had not the leisure to do so; or, if I have had no children to whom I could devote myself it is because I did not find the man I could have lived with. So there remains within me a wide range of abilities, inclinations and potentialities, unused but perfectly viable, which endow me with a worthiness that could never be inferred from the mere history of my actions." But in reality and for the existentialist, there is no love apart from the deeds of love; no potentiality of love other than that which is manifested in loving; there is no genius other than that which is expressed in works of art. The genius of Proust is the totality of the works of Proust; the genius of Racine is the series of his tragedies, outside of which there is nothing. Why should we attribute to Racine the capacity to write yet another tragedy when that is precisely what he did not write? In life, a man commits himself, draws his own portrait and there is nothing but that portrait. No doubt this thought may seem comfortless to one who has not made a success of his life. On the other hand, it puts everyone in a position to understand that reality alone is reliable; that dreams, expectations and hopes serve to define a man only as deceptive dreams, abortive hopes, expectations unfulfilled; that is to say, they define him negatively, not positively. Nevertheless, when one says, "You are nothing else but what you live," it does not imply that an artist is to be judged solely by his works of art, for a thousand other things contribute no less to his definition as a man. What we mean to say is that a man is no other than a series of undertakings, that he is the sum, the organisation, the set of relations that constitute these undertakings. * * *

What is at the very heart and centre of existentialism, is the absolute character of the free commitment, by which every man realises himself in realising a type of humanity—a commitment always understandable, to no matter whom in no matter what epoch—and its bearing upon the relativity of the cultural pattern which may result from such absolute commitment. * * *

* * * Those who hide from this total freedom, in a guise of solemnity or with deterministic excuses, I shall call cowards. Others, who try to show that their existence is necessary, when it is merely an accident of the appearance of the human race on earth,—I shall call scum. But neither cowards nor scum can be identified except upon the plane of strict authenticity. Thus, although the content of morality is variable, a certain form of this morality is universal. Kant declared that freedom is a will both to itself and to the freedom of others. Agreed: but he thinks that the formal and the universal suffice for the constitution of a morality. We think, on the contrary, that principles that are too abstract break down when we come to defining action. To take once again the case of that student; by what authority, in the name of what golden rule of morality, do you think he could have decided, in perfect peace of mind, either to abandon his mother or to remain with her? There are no means of judging. The content is always concrete, and therefore unpredictable; it has always to be invented. The one thing that counts, is to know whether the invention is made in the name of freedom. * * *

* * * There is no other universe except the human universe, the universe of human subjectivity. * * * This is humanism, because we remind man that there is no legislator but himself; that he himself, thus abandoned, must decide for himself; also because we show that it is not by turning back upon himself, but always by seeking, beyond himself, an aim which is one of liberation or of some particular realisation, that man can realise himself as truly human.

STUDY QUESTIONS

1. What does Sartre mean by "existence precedes essence"?
2. Why does Sartre believe that the human condition is one of anguish?
3. What lesson does Sartre draw from the example of the student forced to choose between staying with his mother or joining the French Resistance?

applied
ethics

art 3 of this book moves from normative ethics to topics in applied ethics. Both normative ethics and applied ethics are concerned with the practicalities of moral action. However, normative ethics concentrates on the issue of how to develop a general perspective on the requirements of morality, whereas applied ethics narrows the focus to explore particular moral questions, or a related set of concerns. Accordingly, Part 3 is split into a large number of sub-sections, each clustered on a single problem or set of problems. We start with the problem of gender equality.

GENDER EQUALITY

We have already encountered two contributions to feminist moral philosophy in this book, by Annette Baier and Virginia Held, in criticism of aspects of mainstream, male-dominated moral philosophy. We will continue to see feminist contributions later, in the discussion of pornography, sexual consent, and other topics. In this section, we will look first at two classic contributions to feminist thought and then two more which widen the debates.

We begin with the work of pioneering feminist writer Mary Wollstone-craft, the mother of novelist Mary Shelley, who was the author of *Franken-stein*. This extract, taken from her book *A Vindication of the Rights of Woman*, which she wrote shortly after another important work, *A Vindication of the Rights of Man*, sets out her understanding of the role of education in bring-ing women to be regarded as inferiors to men, and what is necessary in order to improve their position.

Wollstonecraft's main claim is that women are educated not as human beings but to prepare them to fulfill feminine, subservient roles in society. True, she says, men are typically physically stronger than women, but that alone cannot justify the many ways in which women are treated as inferiors. Women, she says, are kept in a state of "perpetual childhood," utterly depen-dent on men, existing to serve them, and, at least for the wealthy women who are Wollstonecraft's subject, kept in a state of leisure and idleness.

Instead, women need to be educated with the virtues that will allow for their independence. In addition to the good it will do for women themselves, such an education will make them better companions for their husbands. An independent woman can be a friend, rather than slave, of her husband, argues Wollstonecraft.

Simone de Beauvoir begins with a different question: "What is a woman?" In doing so she forces us to make a distinction between the biological—"she is a womb, some say"—and the social question concerning the nature of femininity. And this question is much more difficult. Is there a feminine "essence" that all woman have, or can have, perhaps to different degrees? Or is it an arbitrary classification, and should we stop considering people as men or as women, but just as human beings? For de Beauvoir, though, that suggestion goes too far, and there is no doubt that human beings divide into two groups, who wear different clothes, behave in different ways, and have different interests and occupations. Perhaps, she says, this is a superficial difference that will disappear. But its current existence cannot be denied. And it is asymmetrical, for women are defined in terms of not being men. Man is the "absolute human type"; woman is the "other." The distinction between the biological and the social can also be described as a distinction between (biological) sex and (social) gender, to describe the social roles and attributes typically taken on by women and men. Gender is often thought to be "socially constructed" and hence much more liable to change.

De Beauvoir compares the subordination of women with the situation of other groups, such as American blacks, Jews, or the proletariat. Although there are some parallels, the position of women is unique, in that it is not possible to conceive of a "before" in which women were not subordinated to men. De Beauvoir also believes that women lack opportunity for organized resistance because they are dispersed, and their interests, for example as bourgeois and proletariat women, are often opposed. De Beauvoir cites examples from religion, philosophy, and law that all express and attempt to justify women's inferiority and the need to keep women "in their place." Treating women as inferior is self-perpetuating, as women do, in a sense, become inferior, and men see themselves as superior, holding their privileged position as a matter of right.

De Beauvoir concludes this section of her writing by raising the question of how feminists can go beyond analysis to action, noting that some small victories have already been won and linking her position to the existentialist moral philosophy that she developed with Jean-Paul Sartre, included earlier in this volume. On this view, women must take charge of their own freedom, understanding what circumstances limit their freedom and what they can do to overcome those circumstances.

The next reading, from Audre Lorde, intensifies a point made by de Beauvoir by considering the many differences that divide society and what it would mean to relate across those differences as equals. These differences induce what Lorde calls "distortions" in which one side is taken to be superior and the other inferior and therefore subordinated. Instead of looking for creative change, we tend either to deny that barriers exist or to take the barriers as insurmountable.

Lorde remarks, "As a forty-nine-year-old Black lesbian feminist socialist mother of two, including one boy, and a member of an inter-racial couple, I usually find myself a part of some group defined as other, deviant, inferior, or just plain wrong." And in this role Lorde argues that she has had to educate her oppressors about the oppression she and her family suffer.

Even within an oppressed group, divisions appear; for example, white women may assume that they speak for all women, ignoring differences of class or race. Lorde points out that, at the time of writing, the literature of women of color was rarely included even in women's literature courses. Lorde explores what has become known as "intersectionality." Those who experience more than one form of oppression may suffer in a way that is distinctive and cannot be treated as the combination of the oppressions suffered by all members of the groups to which they belong. For example, black women and black men experience racism in different ways, with black women often subject to violence and sexual hostility. Black women, says Lorde, are the lowest-paid sector of the American economy. Black lesbians also face prejudice from other black women, although, of course, not only from black women.

The essay, taken from Lorde's collection *Sister Outsider*, sets out the phrase for which Lorde is best known (and which in fact is the title of another essay in the collection): "The master's tools will never dismantle the master's house." What Lorde means is that oppression in society can go so deep that the oppressing class can even control the ways in which justice and injustice are defined and understood. When this is the case, existing conceptual "tools"—theories and concepts—will not be able to express the nature and depth of the suffering experienced by those who are most oppressed, and therefore new approaches will be needed.

Finally in this section we turn to Lori Girshick's discussion "Gender Policing." It is not, in itself, offered as a contribution to moral philosophy, but rather documents some very significant ways in which people with nonbinary gender identities or presentation face significant prejudice. Girshick uses the term "gender policing" to emphasize that these practices of intimidation are often a way of trying to force people to take up conventional gender identities. The discussion, therefore, provides some powerful case studies on which we should reflect in order to consider how, from a moral point of view, society and law should respond.

Girshick's first example is the use of public bathrooms, which has become a widely contended issue. In some cases, a transgender individual has been refused access to both male and female restrooms. Rather than try to solve the problem in conventional terms, Girshick's suggestion is to de-gender restrooms, just as, some decades ago in the United States, racially segregated restrooms were abolished, despite protests. A second difficult issue concerns "women-only" events, which raises the question "who is a real woman?" Girshick points out that a rule identifying only those who are born biologically female or have gone through surgical transition would discriminate against those who identify as female but cannot afford expensive surgery.

People who do not fall into the traditional binary gender classifications often face bullying and harassment, even to the point of murder. While these are very serious crimes against individuals, Girshick argues that they also send a message that anyone who challenges gender norms is in danger. Other examples concern the response of the medical and legal establishments to gender change, in terms of medical care (including surgery), access to medical records, legal practices such as marriage, and the issuing of documents such as driving licenses.

These examples force us to consider what would genuinely count as an inclusive, equal society, given the wide variety of human difference in the world today, especially in the area of gender identity and presentation.

MARY WOLLSTONECRAFT
A Vindication of the Rights of Woman

Mary Wollstonecraft (1759–1797) was an English political philosopher, author of A Vindication of the Rights of Man, *shortly followed by* A Vindication of the Rights of Woman, *a highly influential early feminist work. She was the mother of Mary Shelley, author of* Frankenstein.

INTRODUCTION

After considering the historic page, and viewing the living world with anxious solicitude, the most melancholy emotions of sorrowful indignation have depressed my spirits, and I have sighed when obliged to confess, that either nature has made a great difference between man and man, or that the civilization which has hitherto taken place in the world has been very partial. I have turned over various books written on the subject of education, and patiently observed the conduct of parents and the management of schools; but what has been the result?—a profound conviction that the neglected education of my fellow-creatures is the grand source of the misery I deplore; and that women, in particular, are rendered weak and wretched by a variety of concurring causes, originating from one hasty conclusion. The conduct and manners of women, in fact, evidently prove that their minds are not in a healthy state; for, like the flowers which are planted in too rich a soil, strength and usefulness are sacrificed to beauty; and the flaunting leaves, after having pleased a fastidious eye, fade, disregarded on the stalk, long before the season when they ought to have arrived at maturity.—One cause of this barren blooming I attribute to a false system of education, gathered from the books written on this subject by men who, considering females rather as women than human creatures, have been more anxious to make them alluring mistresses than affectionate wives and rational mothers; and the understanding of the sex has been so bubbled by this specious homage, that the civilized women of the present century, with a few exceptions, are only anxious to inspire love, when they ought to cherish a nobler ambition, and by their abilities and virtues exact respect. * * *

* * * In the government of the physical world it is observable that the female in point of strength is, in general, inferior to the male. This is the law of nature; and it does not appear to be suspended or abrogated in favour of woman. A degree of physical superiority cannot, therefore, be denied—and it is a noble prerogative! But not content with this natural pre-eminence, men endeavour to sink us still lower, merely to render us alluring objects for a moment; and women, intoxicated by the adoration which men, under the influence of their senses, pay them, do not seek to obtain a durable interest in their hearts, or to become the friends of the fellow creatures who find amusement in their society.

I am aware of an obvious inference:—from every quarter have I heard exclamations against masculine women; but where are they to be found? If by this appellation men mean to inveigh against their ardour in hunting, shooting, and gaming, I shall most cordially join in the cry; but if it be against the imitation of manly virtues, or, more properly speaking, the attainment of those talents and virtues, the exercise of which ennobles the human character, and which raise females in the scale of animal being, when they are comprehensively termed mankind;—all those who view them with a philosophic eye must, I should think, wish with me, that they may every day grow more and more masculine. * * *

My own sex, I hope, will excuse me, if I treat them like rational creatures, instead of flattering their *fascinating* graces, and viewing them as if they were in a state of perpetual childhood, unable to stand alone. I earnestly wish to point out in what true dignity and human happiness consists—I wish to persuade women to endeavour to acquire strength, both of mind and body, and to convince them that the soft phrases, susceptibility of heart, delicacy of sentiment, and refinement of taste, are almost synonymous with epithets of weakness, and that those beings who are only the objects of pity and that kind of love, which has been termed its sister, will soon become objects of contempt.

Dismissing then those pretty feminine phrases, which the men condescendingly use to soften our slavish dependence, and despising that weak elegancy of mind, exquisite sensibility, and sweet docility of manners, supposed to be the sexual characteristics of the weaker vessel, I wish to shew that elegance is inferior to virtue, that the first object of laudable ambition is to obtain a character as a human being, regardless of the distinction of sex; and that secondary views should be brought to this simple touchstone. * * *

The education of women has, of late, been more attended to than formerly; yet they are still reckoned a frivolous sex, and ridiculed or pitied by the writers who endeavour by satire or instruction to improve them. It is acknowledged that they spend many of the first years of their lives in acquiring a smattering of accomplishments; meanwhile strength of body and mind are sacrificed to libertine notions of beauty, to the desire of establishing themselves,—the only way women can rise in the world,—by marriage. And this desire making mere animals of them, when they marry they act as such children may be expected to act:—they dress; they paint, and nickname God's creatures.—Surely these weak beings are only fit for a seraglio!—Can they be expected to govern a family with judgment, or take care of the poor babes whom they bring into the world?

If then it can be fairly deduced from the present conduct of the sex, from the prevalent fondness for pleasure which takes place of ambition and those nobler passions that open and enlarge the soul; that the instruction which women have hitherto received has only tended, with the constitution of civil society, to render them insignificant objects of desire—mere propagators of fools!—if it can be proved that in aiming to accomplish them, without cultivating their understandings, they are taken out of their sphere of duties, and made ridiculous and useless when the short-lived bloom of beauty is over, I presume that *rational* men will excuse me for endeavouring to persuade them to become more masculine and respectable. * * *

Women are, in fact, so much degraded by mistaken notions of female excellence, that I do not mean to add a paradox when I assert, that this artificial weakness produces a propensity to tyrannize, and gives birth to cunning, the natural opponent of strength, which leads them to play off those contemptible infantine airs that undermine esteem even whilst they excite desire. Let men become more chaste and modest, and if women do not grow wiser in the same ratio, it will be clear that they have weaker understandings. It seems scarcely necessary to say, that I now speak of the sex in general. Many individuals have more sense than their male relatives; and, as nothing preponderates where there is a constant struggle for an equilibrium, without it has naturally more gravity, some women govern their husbands without degrading themselves, because intellect will always govern. * * *

CHAP. II

The Prevailing Opinion of a Sexual Character Discussed

To account for, and excuse the tyranny of man, many ingenious arguments have been brought forward to prove, that the two sexes, in the acquirement of virtue, ought to aim at attaining a very different character: or, to speak explicitly, women are not allowed to have sufficient strength of mind to acquire what really deserves the name of virtue. Yet it should seem, allowing them to have souls, that there is but one way appointed by Providence to lead *mankind* to either virtue or happiness.

If then women are not a swarm of ephemeron triflers, why should they be kept in ignorance under the specious name of innocence? Men complain, and with reason, of the follies and caprices of our sex, when they do not keenly satirize our headstrong passions and groveling vices.—Behold, I should answer, the natural effect of ignorance! The mind will ever be unstable that has only prejudices to rest on, and the current will run with destructive fury when there are no barriers to break its force. Women are told from their infancy, and taught by the example of their mothers, that a little knowledge of human weakness, justly termed cunning, softness of temper, *outward* obedience, and a scrupulous attention to a puerile kind of propriety, will obtain for them the protection of man; and should they be beautiful, every thing else is needless, for, at least, twenty years of their lives. * * *

How grossly do they insult us who thus advise us only to render ourselves gentle, domestic brutes! * * * Men, indeed, appear to me to act in a very unphilosophical manner when they try to secure the good conduct of women by attempting to keep them always in a state of childhood. * * *

Consequently, the most perfect education, in my opinion, is such an exercise of the understanding as is best calculated to strengthen the body and form the heart. Or, in other words, to enable the individual to attain such habits of virtue as will render it independent. In fact, it is a farce to call any being virtuous whose virtues do not result from the exercise of its own reason. * * *

* * * In the education of women, the cultivation of the understanding is always subordinate to the acquirement of some corporeal accomplishment; even while enervated by confinement and false notions of modesty, the body is prevented from attaining that grace and beauty which relaxed half-formed limbs never exhibit. Besides, in youth their faculties are not brought forward by emulation; and having no serious scientific study, if they have natural sagacity it is turned too soon on life and manners. They dwell on effects,

and modifications, without tracing them back to causes; and complicated rules to adjust behaviour are a weak substitute for simple principles. * * *

* * * Riches and hereditary honours have made cyphers of women to give consequence to the numerical figure; and idleness has produced a mixture of gallantry and despotism into society, which leads the very men who are the slaves of their mistresses to tyrannize over their sisters, wives, and daughters. This is only keeping them in rank and file, it is true. Strengthen the female mind by enlarging it, and there will be an end to blind obedience; but, as blind obedience is ever sought for by power, tyrants and sensualists are in the right when they endeavour to keep women in the dark, because the former only want slaves, and the latter a play-thing. * * *

* * * Rousseau declares that a woman should never, for a moment, feel herself independent, that she should be governed by fear to exercise her natural cunning, and made a coquetish slave in order to render her a more alluring object of desire, a *sweeter* companion to man, whenever he chooses to relax himself. He carries the arguments, which he pretends to draw from the indications of nature, still further, and insinuates that truth and fortitude, the corner stones of all human virtue, should be cultivated with certain restrictions, because, with respect to the female character, obedience is the grand lesson which ought to be impressed with unrelenting rigour.

What nonsense! when will a great man arise with sufficient strength of mind to puff away the fumes which pride and sensuality have thus spread over the subject! If women are by nature inferior in men, their virtues must be the same in quality, if not in degree, or virtue is a relative idea; consequently, their conduct should be founded on the same principles, and have the same aim. * * *

Besides, the woman who strengthens her body and exercises her mind will, by managing her family and practising various virtues, become the friend, and not the humble dependent of her husband; and if she, by possessing such substantial qualities, merit his regard, she will not find it necessary to conceal her affection, nor to pretend to an unnatural coldness of constitution to excite her husband's passions. In fact, if we revert to history, we shall find that the women who have distinguished themselves have neither been the most beautiful nor the most gentle of their sex. * * *

* * * Gentleness, docility, and a spaniel-like affection are, on this ground, consistently recommended as the cardinal virtues of the sex; and, disregarding the arbitrary economy of nature, one writer has declared that it is masculine for a woman to be melancholy. She was created to be the toy of man, his rattle, and it must jingle in his ears whenever, dismissing reason, he chooses to be amused. ＊ ＊ ＊

＊ ＊ ＊ Do passive indolent women make the best wives? Confining our discussion to the present moment of existence, let us see how such weak creatures perform their part? Do the women who, by the attainment of a few superficial accomplishments, have strengthened the prevailing prejudice, merely contribute to the happiness of their husbands? Do they display their charms merely to amuse them? And have women, who have early imbibed notions of passive obedience, sufficient character to manage a family or educate children? So far from it, that, after surveying the history of woman, I cannot help, agreeing with the severest satirist, considering the sex as the weakest as well as the most oppressed half of the species. What does history disclose but marks of inferiority, and how few women have emancipated themselves from the galling yoke of sovereign man?—So few, that the exceptions remind me of an ingenious conjecture respecting Newton: that he was probably a being of a superior order, accidentally caged in a human body. Following the same train of thinking, I have been led to imagine that the few extraordinary women who have rushed in eccentrical directions out of the orbit prescribed to their sex, were *male* spirits, confined by mistake in female frames. But if it be not philosophical to think of sex when the soul is mentioned, the inferiority must depend on the organs; or the heavenly fire, which is to ferment the clay, is not given in equal portions.

But avoiding, as I have hitherto done, any direct comparison of the two sexes collectively, or frankly acknowledging the inferiority of woman, according to the present appearance of things, I shall only insist that men have increased that inferiority till women are almost sunk below the standard of rational creatures. Let their faculties have room to unfold, and their virtues to gain strength, and then determine where the whole sex must stand in the intellectual scale. Yet let it be remembered, that for a small number of distinguished women I do not ask a place.

It is difficult for us purblind mortals to say to what height human discoveres and improvements may arrive when the gloom of despotism subsides, which makes us stumble at every step; but, when morality shall be settled on a more solid basis, then, without being gifted with a prophetic spirit, I will venture to predict that woman will be either the friend or slave of man. We shall not, as at present, doubt whether she is a moral agent, or the link which unites man with brutes. But, should it then appear, that like the brutes they were principally created for the use of man, he will let them patiently bite the bridle, and not mock them with empty praise; or, should their rationality be proved, he will not impede their improvement merely to gratify his sensual appetites. He will not, with all the graces of rhetoric, advise them to submit implicitly their understanding to the guidance of man. He will not, when he treats of the education of women, assert that they ought never to have the free use of reason, nor would he recommend cunning and dissimulation to beings who are acquiring, in like manner as himself, the virtues of humanity.

Surely there can be but one rule of right, if morality has an eternal foundation, and whoever sacrifices virtue, strictly so called, to present convenience, or whose *duty* it is to act in such a manner, lives only for the passing day, and cannot be an accountable creature. * * *

These may be termed Utopian dreams.—Thanks to that Being who impressed them on my soul, and gave me sufficient strength of mind to dare to exert my own reason, till, becoming dependent only on him for the support of my virtue, I view, with indignation, the mistaken notions that enslave my sex. * * *

Brutal force has hitherto governed the world, and that the science of politics is in its infancy, is evident from philosophers scrupling to give the knowledge most useful to man that determinate distinction.

I shall not pursue this argument any further than to establish an obvious inference, that as sound politics diffuse liberty, mankind, including woman, will become more wise and virtuous.

STUDY QUESTIONS

1. How, according to Wollstonecraft, have women been educated?
2. What differences does Wollstonecraft acknowledge between the sexes? How have these differences been treated, and how, does she argue, should they be treated?
3. What are the advantages of educating women with the virtues needed for independence?

SIMONE DE BEAUVOIR
The Second Sex

Simone de Beauvoir (1908–1986) was a French writer and philosopher, whose book The Second Sex *is one of the classics of feminist philosophy.*

One is not born, but rather becomes, woman.

INTRODUCTION

I hesitated a long time before writing a book on woman. The subject is irritating, especially for women; and it is not new. Enough ink has flowed over the quarrel about feminism; it is now almost over: let's not talk about it any more. Yet it is still being talked about. And the volumes of idiocies churned out over this past century do not seem to have clarified the problem. Besides, is there a problem? And what is it? Are there even women? True, the theory of the eternal feminine still has its followers; they whisper, "Even in Russia, *women* are still very much women"; but other well-informed people—and also at times those same ones—lament, "Woman is losing herself, woman is lost." It is hard to know any longer if women still exist, if they will always exist, if there should be women at all, what place they hold in this world, what place they should hold. "Where are the women?" asked a short-lived magazine recently. But first, what is a woman? "*Tota mulier in utero*: she is a womb," some say. Yet speaking of certain women, the experts proclaim, "They are not women," even though they have a uterus like the others. Everyone agrees there are females in the human species; today, as in the past, they make up about half of humanity; and yet we are told that "femininity is in jeopardy"; we are urged, "Be women, stay women, become women." So not every female human being is necessarily a woman; she must take part in this mysterious and endangered reality known as femininity. Is femininity secreted by the ovaries? Is it enshrined in a Platonic heaven? Is a frilly petticoat enough to bring it down to earth? Although some women zealously strive to embody it, the model has never been patented. It is typically described in vague and shimmering terms borrowed from a clairvoyant's vocabulary. In St Thomas's time it was an essence defined with as much certainty as the sedative quality of a poppy. But conceptualism has lost ground: biological and social sciences no longer believe there are immutably determined entities that define given characteristics like those of the woman, the Jew or the black; science considers characteristics as secondary reactions to a *situation*. If there is no such thing today as femininity, it is because there never was. Does the word "woman," then, have no content? It is what advocates of Enlightenment philosophy, rationalism or nominalism vigorously assert: women are, among human beings, merely those who are arbitrarily designated by the word "woman"; American women in particular are inclined to think that woman as such no longer exists. If some backward individual still takes herself for a woman, her friends advise her to undergo psychoanalysis to get rid of this obsession. Referring to a book—a very irritating one at that—*Modern Woman: The Lost Sex*, Dorothy Parker wrote: "I cannot be fair about books that treat women as women. My idea is that all of us, men as well as women, whoever we are, should be considered as human beings." But nominalism is a doctrine that falls a bit short; and it is easy for anti-feminists to show that women *are* not men. Certainly woman like man is a human being; but such an assertion is abstract; the fact is that every concrete human being is always uniquely situated. Rejecting the notions of the eternal feminine, the black soul or the Jewish character is not to deny that there are today Jews, blacks or women: this denial is not a liberation for those concerned, but an inauthentic flight. Clearly, no woman can claim without bad faith to be situated beyond her sex. A few years ago, a well-known woman writer refused to have her portrait appear in a series of photographs devoted specifically to women writers. She wanted to be included in the men's category; but to get this privilege, she used her husband's influence. Women who assert they are men still claim masculine consideration and respect. I also remember a young Trotskyite standing on a platform during a stormy meeting, about to come to blows in spite of her obvious fragility. She was denying her feminine frailty; but it was for the love of a militant man she wanted to be equal to. The defiant position that American women occupy proves they are haunted by the feeling of their own femininity. And the truth is that anyone can clearly see that humanity is split into two categories of individuals with manifestly different clothes, faces, bodies, smiles, movements, interests and occupations; these differences are perhaps superficial; perhaps they are destined to disappear. What is certain is that for the moment they exist in a strikingly obvious way.

If the female function is not enough to define woman, and if we also reject the explanation of the "eternal feminine," but if we accept, even temporarily, that there are women on the earth, we then have to ask: what is a woman?

Merely stating the problem suggests an immediate answer to me. It is significant that I pose it. It would never occur to a man to write a book on the singular situation of males in humanity. If I want to define myself, I first have to say, "I am a woman"; all other assertions will arise from this basic truth. A man never begins by positing himself as an individual of a certain sex: that he is a man is obvious. The categories "masculine" and "feminine" appear as symmetrical in a formal way on town hall records or identification papers. The relation of the two sexes is not that of two electrical poles: the man represents both the positive and the neuter to such an extent that in French *hommes* designates human beings, the particular meaning of the word *vir* being assimilated into the general meaning of the word "homo." Woman is the negative, to such a point that any determination is imputed to her as a limitation, without reciprocity. I used to get annoyed in abstract discussions to hear men tell me: "You think such and such a thing because you're a woman." But I know my only defence is to answer, "I think it because it is true," thereby eliminating my subjectivity; it was out of the question to answer, "And you think the contrary because you are a man," because it is understood that being a man is not a particularity; a man is in his right by virtue of being man; it is the woman who is in the wrong. In fact, just as for the ancients there was an absolute vertical that defined the oblique, there is an absolute human type that is masculine. Woman has ovaries and a uterus; such are the particular conditions that lock her in her subjectivity; some even say she thinks with her hormones. Man vainly forgets that his anatomy also includes hormones and testicles. He grasps his body as a direct and normal link with the world that he believes he apprehends in all objectivity, whereas he considers woman's body an obstacle, a prison, burdened by everything that particularises it. "The female is female by virtue of a certain *lack* of qualities," Aristotle said. "We should regard women's nature as suffering from natural defectiveness." And St Thomas in his turn decreed that woman was an "incomplete man," an "incidental" being. This is what the Genesis story symbolises, where Eve appears as if drawn from Adam's "supernumerary" bone, in Bossuet's words. Humanity is male, and man defines woman, not in herself, but in relation to himself, she is not considered an autonomous being. "Woman, the relative being," writes Michelet. Thus Monsieur Benda declares in *Uriel's Report*: "A man's body has meaning by itself, disregarding the body of the woman, whereas the woman's body seems devoid of meaning without reference to the male. Man thinks himself without woman. Woman does not think herself without man." And she is nothing other than what man decides; she is thus called "the sex," meaning that the male sees her essentially as a sexed being; for him she is sex, so she is it in the absolute. She determines and differentiates herself in relation to man, and he does not in relation to her; she is the inessential in front of the essential. He is the Subject; he is the Absolute. She is the Other.

The category of *Other* is as original as consciousness itself. The duality between Self and Other can be found in the most primitive societies, in the most ancient mythologies; this division did not always fall into the category of the division of the sexes, it was not based on any empirical given: this comes out in works like Granet's on Chinese thought, and Dumézil's on India and Rome. In couples such as Varuna–Mitra, Uranos–Zeus, Sun–Moon, Day–Night, no feminine element is involved at the outset; neither in Good–Evil, auspicious and inauspicious, left and right, God and Lucifer; alterity is the fundamental category of human thought. No group ever defines itself as One without immediately setting up the Other opposite itself. It only takes three travellers brought together by chance in the same train compartment for the rest of the travellers to become vaguely hostile "others." Village people view anyone not belonging to the village as suspicious "others." For the native of a country, inhabitants of other countries are viewed as "foreigners"; Jews are the "others" for anti-Semites, blacks for racist Americans, indigenous people for colonists, proletarians for the propertied classes. After studying the diverse forms of primitive society in depth, Lévi-Strauss could conclude: "The passage from the state of Nature to the state of Culture is defined by man's ability to think biological relations as systems of oppositions; duality, alternation, opposition, and symmetry, whether occurring in defined or less clear form, are not so much phenomena to explain as fundamental and immediate givens of social reality. These phenomena could not be understood if human reality were solely a *Mitsein* based on solidarity and friendship. On the contrary, they become clear if, following Hegel, a fundamental hostility to any other consciousness is found in consciousness itself; the subject posits itself only in opposition; it asserts itself as the essential and sets up the other as inessential, as the object.

But the other consciousness has an opposing reciprocal claim: travelling, a local is shocked to realise that in neighbouring countries locals view him as a foreigner; between villages, clans, nations and classes there are wars, potlatches, agreements, treaties and struggles that remove the absolute meaning from the idea of the Other and bring out its relativity; whether one likes it or not, individuals and groups have no choice but to recognise the reciprocity of their relation. How is it, then, that between the sexes this reciprocity has not been put forward, that one of the terms has been asserted as the only essential one, denying any relativity in regard to its correlative, defining the latter as pure alterity? Why do women not contest male sovereignty? No subject posits itself spontaneously and at once as the inessential from the outset; it is not the Other who, defining itself as Other, defines the One; the Other is posited as Other by the One positing itself as One. But in order for the Other not to turn into the One, the Other has to submit to this foreign point of view. Where does this submission in woman come from?

There are other cases where, for a shorter or longer time, one category has managed to dominate another absolutely. It is often numerical inequality that confers this privilege: the majority imposes its law on or persecutes the minority. But women are not a minority like American blacks, or like Jews: there are as many women as men on the earth. Often, the two opposing groups concerned were once independent of each other; either they were not aware of each other in the past or they accepted each other's autonomy; and some historical event subordinated the weaker to the stronger: the Jewish diaspora, slavery in America, or the colonial conquests are facts with dates. In these cases, for the oppressed there was a *before*: they share a past, a tradition, sometimes a religion, or a culture. In this sense, the parallel Bebel draws between women and the proletariat would be the best founded: proletarians are not a numerical minority either and yet they have never formed a separate group. However, not *one* event but a whole historical development explains their existence as a class and accounts for the distribution of *these* individuals in this class. There have not always been proletarians: there have always been women; they are women by their physiological structure; as far back as history can be traced, they have always been subordinate to men; their dependence is not the consequence of an event or a becoming, it did not *happen*. Alterity here appears to be an absolute, partly because it falls outside the accidental nature of historical fact. A situation created over time can come undone at another time—blacks in Haiti for one are a good example; on the contrary, a natural condition seems to defy change. In truth, nature is no more an immutable given than is historical reality. If woman discovers herself as the inessential, and never turns into the essential, it is because she does not bring about this transformation herself. Proletarians say "we." So do blacks. Positing themselves as subjects, they thus transform the bourgeois or whites into "others." Women—except in certain abstract gatherings such as conferences—do not use "we"; men say "women" and women adopt this word to refer to themselves; but they do not posit themselves authentically as Subjects. The proletarians made the revolution in Russia, the blacks in Haiti, the Indo-Chinese are fighting in Indochina. Women's actions have never been more than symbolic agitation; they have won only what men have been willing to concede to them; they have taken nothing; they have received. It is that they lack the concrete means to organise themselves into a unit that could posit itself in opposition. They have no past, no history, no religion of their own; and unlike the proletariat, they have no solidarity of labour or interests; they even lack their own space that makes communities of American blacks, or the Jews in ghettos, or the workers in Saint-Denis or Renault factories. They live dispersed among men, tied by homes, work, economic interests and social conditions to certain men—fathers or husbands—more closely than to other women. As bourgeois women, they are in solidarity with bourgeois men and not with women proletarians; as white women, they are in solidarity with white men and not with black women. The proletariat could plan to massacre the whole ruling class; a fanatic Jew or black could dream of seizing the secret of the atomic bomb and turning all of humanity entirely Jewish or entirely black: but a woman could not even dream of exterminating males. The tie that binds her to her oppressors is unlike any other. The division of the sexes is a biological given, not a moment in human history. Their opposition took shape within an original *Mitsein* and she has not broken it. The couple is a fundamental unit with the two halves riveted to each other: cleavage of society by sex is not possible. This is the fundamental characteristic of woman: she is the Other at the heart of a whole whose two components are necessary to each other.

One might think that this reciprocity would have facilitated her liberation; when Hercules spins wool at Omphale's feet, his desire enchains him. Why was Omphale unable to acquire long-lasting power? Medea, in revenge against Jason, kills her children: this brutal legend suggests that the bond attaching the woman to her child could have given her a formidable upper hand. In *Lysistrata*, Aristophanes light-heartedly imagined a group of women who, uniting together for the social good, tried to take advantage of men's need for them: but it is only a comedy. The legend that claims that the ravished Sabine women resisted their ravishers with obstinate sterility also recounts that by whipping them with leather straps, the men magically won them over into submission. Biological need—sexual desire and desire for posterity—which makes the male dependent on the female, has not liberated women socially. Master and slave are also linked by a reciprocal economic need that does not free the slave. That is, in the master–slave relation, the master does not *posit* the need he has for the other; he holds the power to satisfy this need and does not mediate it; the slave, on the other hand, out of dependence, hope or fear, internalises his need for the master; however equally compelling the need may be to them both, it always plays in favour of the oppressor over the oppressed: this explains the slow pace of working-class liberation, for example. Now woman has always been, if not man's slave, at least his vassal; the two sexes have never divided the world up equally; and still today, even though her condition is changing, woman is heavily handicapped. In no country is her legal status identical to man's, and often it puts her at a considerable disadvantage. Even when her rights are recognised abstractly, long-standing habit keeps them from being concretely manifested in customs. Economically, men and women almost form two castes; all things being equal, the former have better jobs, higher wages and greater chances to succeed than their new female competitors; they occupy many more places in industry, in politics, and so on, and they hold the most important positions. In addition to their concrete power they are invested with a prestige whose tradition is reinforced by the child's whole education: the present incorporates the past, and in the past all history was made by males. At the moment that women are beginning to share in the making of the world, this world still belongs to men: men have no doubt about this, and women barely doubt it. Refusing to be the Other, refusing complicity with man, would mean renouncing all the advantages an alliance with the superior caste confers on them. Lord-man will materially protect liege-woman and will be in charge of justifying her existence: along with the economic risk, she eludes the metaphysical risk of a freedom that must invent its goals without help. Indeed, beside every individual's claim to assert himself as subject—an ethical claim—lies the temptation to flee freedom and to make himself into a thing: it is a pernicious path because the individual, passive, alienated and lost, is prey to a foreign will, cut off from his transcendence, robbed of all worth. But it is an easy path: the anguish and stress of authentically assumed existence are thus avoided. The man who sets the woman up as an *Other* will thus find in her a deep complicity. Hence woman makes no claim for herself as subject because she lacks the concrete means, because she senses the necessary link connecting her to man without positing its reciprocity, and because she often derives satisfaction from her role as *Other*.

But a question immediately arises: how did this whole story begin? It is understandable that the duality of the sexes, like all duality, be expressed in conflict. It is understandable that if one of the two succeeded in imposing its superiority, it had to establish itself as absolute. It remains to be explained how it was that man won at the outset. It seems possible that women might have carried off the victory, or that the battle might never be resolved. Why is it that this world has always belonged to men and that only today things are beginning to change? Is this change a good thing? Will it bring about an equal sharing of the world between men and women or not?

These questions are far from new; they have already had many answers; but the very fact that woman is *Other* challenges all the justifications that men have ever given: these were only too clearly dictated by their own interest. "Everything that men have written about women should be viewed with suspicion, because they are both judge and party," wrote Poulain de la Barre, a little-known seventeenth-century feminist. Males have always and everywhere paraded their satisfaction of feeling they are kings of creation. "Blessed be the Lord our God, and the Lord of all worlds that has not made me a woman," Jews say in their morning prayers; meanwhile their wives resignedly murmur: "Blessed be the Lord for creating me according to His will." Among the blessings Plato thanked the gods for was, first, being born free and not a slave, and second, a man and not a woman. But males could not have enjoyed this privilege so fully had they not considered it as founded in the absolute and in eternity: they sought to make the fact of their supremacy a right. "Those who made and compiled the laws, being men, favoured their own sex, and the jurisconsults have turned the laws into principles," Poulain de la Barre continues. Lawmakers, priests, philosophers, writers and scholars have gone to great lengths to prove that women's subordinate condition was willed in heaven and profitable on earth. Religions forged by men reflect this will for domination: they found ammunition in the legends of Eve and Pandora. They have put philosophy and theology in their service, as seen in the previously cited words of Aristotle and St Thomas. Since ancient times, satirists and moralists have delighted in depicting women's weaknesses. The violent indictments brought against them all through French literature are well known: Montherlant, with less verve, picks up the tradition from Jean de Meung. This hostility seems sometimes founded but is often gratuitous; in truth, it covers up a more or less skilfully camouflaged will to self-justification. "It is much easier to accuse one sex than to excuse the other," says Montaigne. In certain cases, the process is transparent. It is striking, for example, that the Roman code limiting a wife's rights invokes "the imbecility and fragility of the sex" just when a weakening family structure makes her a threat to male heirs. It is striking that in the sixteenth century, to keep a married woman under wardship, the authority of St Augustine affirming "the wife is an animal neither reliable nor stable" is called on, whereas the unmarried woman is recognised as capable of managing her own affairs. Montaigne well understood the arbitrariness and injustice of the lot assigned to women: "Women are not wrong at all when they reject the rules of life that have been introduced into the world, inasmuch as it is the men who have made these without them. There is a natural plotting and scheming between them and us." But he does not go so far as to champion their cause. It is only in the eighteenth century that deeply democratic men begin to consider the issue objectively. Diderot, for one, tries to prove that, like man, woman is a human being. A bit later, John Stuart Mill ardently defends women. But these philosophers are exceptional in their impartiality. In the nineteenth century the feminist quarrel once again becomes a partisan quarrel; one of the consequences of the Industrial Revolution is that women enter the labour force: at that point, women's demands leave the realm of the theoretical and find economic grounds; their adversaries become all the more aggressive; even though landed property is partially discredited, the bourgeoisie clings to the old values where family solidity guarantees private property: it insists all the more fiercely that woman's place should be in the home as her emancipation becomes a real threat; even within the working class, men tried to thwart women's liberation because women were becoming dangerous competitors—especially as women were used to working for low salaries. To prove women's inferiority, antifeminists began to draw not only, as before, on religion, philosophy and theology, but also on science: biology, experimental psychology, and so forth. At most they were willing to grant "separate but equal status" to the *other* sex. That winning formula is most significant: it is exactly that formula the Jim Crow laws put into practice with regard to black Americans; this so-called egalitarian segregation served only to introduce the most extreme forms of discrimination. This convergence is in no way pure chance: whether it is race, caste, class or sex reduced to an inferior condition, the justification process is the same. "The eternal feminine" corresponds to "the black soul" or "the Jewish character." However, the Jewish problem on the whole is very different from the two others: for the anti-Semite, the Jew is more an enemy than an inferior and no place on this earth is recognised as his own; it would be preferable to see him annihilated. But there are deep analogies between the situations of women and blacks: both are liberated today from the same paternalism, and the former master caste wants to keep them "in their place," that is, the place chosen for them; in both cases, they praise, more or less sincerely, the virtues of the "good black," the carefree, childlike, merry soul of the resigned black, and the woman who is a "true woman"—frivolous, infantile, irresponsible, the woman subjugated to man. In both cases, the ruling caste bases its argument on the state of affairs it created itself. The familiar line from George Bernard Shaw sums it up: "The white American relegates the black to the rank of shoe-shine boy, and then concludes that blacks are only good for shining shoes." The same vicious circle can be found in all analogous circumstances: when an individual or a group of individuals is kept in a situation of inferiority, the fact is that he or they *are* inferior. But the scope of the verb *to be* must be understood; bad faith means giving it a substantive value, when in fact it has the sense of the Hegelian dynamic: to *be* is to have become, to have been made as one manifests oneself. Yes, women in general *are* today inferior to men; that is, their situation provides them with fewer possibilities: the question is whether this state of affairs must be perpetuated.

Many men wish it would be: not all men have yet laid down their arms. The conservative bourgeoisie continues to view women's liberation as a danger threatening their morality and their interests. Some men feel threatened by women's competition. In *Hebdo-Latin* the other day, a student declared: "Every woman student who takes a position as a doctor or lawyer is *stealing* a place from us." That student never questioned his rights over this world. Economic interests are not the only ones in play. One of the benefits that oppression secures for the oppressor is that the humblest among them feels *superior*: in the United States, a "poor white" from the South can console himself for not being a "dirty nigger"; and more prosperous whites cleverly exploit this pride. Likewise, the most mediocre of males believes himself a demigod next to women. It was easier for M. de Montherlant to think himself a hero in front of women (handpicked, by the way) than to act the man among men, a role that many women assumed better than he did. Thus, in one of his articles in *Le Figaro Littéraire* in September 1948, M. Claude Mauriac—whom everyone admires for his powerful originality—could write about women: "*We* listen in a tone [*sic!*] of polite indifference . . . to the most brilliant one among them, knowing that her intelligence, in a more or less dazzling way, reflects ideas that come from *us*." Clearly his female interlocutor does not reflect M. Mauriac's own ideas, since he is known not to have any; that she reflects ideas originating with men is possible: among males themselves, more than one of them takes as his own opinions he did not invent; one might wonder if it would not be in M. Claude Mauriac's interest to converse with a good reflection of Descartes, Marx or Gide rather than with himself; what is remarkable is that with the ambiguous "*we*," he identifies with St Paul, Hegel, Lenin and Nietzsche, and from their heights he looks down on the herd of women who dare to speak to him on an equal footing; frankly, I know of more than one woman who would not put up with M. Mauriac's "tone of polite indifference."

I have stressed this example because of its disarming masculine naïvety. Men profit in many other more subtle ways from woman's alterity. For all those suffering from an inferiority complex, this is a miraculous liniment; no one is more arrogant towards women, more aggressive or more disdainful, than a man anxious about his own virility. Those who are not threatened by their fellow men are far more likely to recognise woman as a counterpart; but even for them the myth of the Woman, of the Other, remains precious for many reasons; they can hardly be blamed for not wanting to light-heartedly sacrifice all the benefits they derive from the myth: they know what they lose by relinquishing the woman of their dreams, but they do not know what the woman of tomorrow will bring them. It takes great abnegation to refuse to posit oneself as unique and absolute Subject. Besides, the vast majority of men do not explicitly make this position their own. They do not *posit* woman as inferior: they are too imbued today with the democratic ideal not to recognise all human beings as equals. Within the family, the male child and then the young man sees the woman as having the same social dignity as the adult male; afterwards, he experiences in desire and love the resistance and independence of the desired and loved woman; married, he respects in his wife the spouse and the mother, and in the concrete experience of married life she affirms herself opposite him as a freedom. He can thus convince himself that there is no longer a social hierarchy between the sexes and that on the whole, in spite of their differences, woman is an equal. As he nevertheless recognises some points of inferiority—professional incapacity being the predominant one—he attributes them to nature. When he has an attitude of benevolence and partnership towards a woman, he applies the principle of abstract equality; and he does not *posit* the concrete inequality he recognises. But as soon as he clashes with her, the situation is reversed. He will apply the concrete inequality theme and will even allow himself to disavow abstract equality. This is how many men affirm, with quasi-good faith, that women *are* equal to man and have no demands to make, and *at the same time* that women will never be equal to men and that their demands are in vain. It is difficult for men to measure the enormous extent of social discrimination that seems insignificant from the outside and whose moral and intellectual repercussions are so deep in woman that they appear to spring from an original nature. The man most sympathetic to women never knows her concrete situation fully. So there is no good reason to believe men when they try to defend privileges whose scope they cannot even fathom. We will not let ourselves be intimidated by the number and violence of attacks against women; nor be fooled by the self-serving praise showered on the "real woman"; nor be won over by men's enthusiasm for her destiny, a destiny they would not for the world want to share.

We must not, however, be any less mistrustful of feminists' arguments: very often their attempt to polemicise robs them of all value. If the "question of women" is so trivial, it is because masculine arrogance turned it into a "quarrel"; when people quarrel, they no longer reason well. What people have endlessly sought to prove is that woman is superior, inferior or equal to man: created after Adam, she is obviously a secondary being, some say; on the contrary, say others, Adam was only a rough draft, and God perfected the human being when he created Eve; her brain is smaller, but relatively bigger; Christ was made man: but perhaps out of humility. Every argument has its opposite and both are often misleading. To see clearly, one needs to get out of these ruts; these vague notions of superiority, inferiority and equality that have distorted all discussions must be discarded in order to start anew.

But how, then, will we ask the question? And in the first place, who are we to ask it? Men are judge and party: so are women. Can an angel be found? In fact, an angel would be ill qualified to speak, would not understand all the givens of the problem; as for the hermaphrodite, it is a case of its own: it is not both a man and a woman, but neither man nor woman. I think certain women are still best suited to elucidate the situation of women. It is a sophism to claim that Epimenides should be enclosed within the concept of Cretan and all Cretans within the concept of liar: it is not a mysterious essence that dictates good or bad faith to men and women; it is their situation that disposes them to seek the truth to a greater or lesser extent. Many women today, fortunate to have had all the privileges of the human being restored to them, can afford the luxury of impartiality: we even feel the necessity of it. We are no longer like our militant predecessors; we have more or less won the game; in the latest discussions on women's status, the UN has not ceased to imperiously demand equality of the sexes, and indeed many of us have never felt our femaleness to be a difficulty or an obstacle; many other problems seem more essential than those that concern us uniquely: this very detachment makes it possible to hope our attitude will be objective. Yet we know the feminine world more intimately than men do because our roots are in it; we grasp more immediately what the fact of being female means for a human being, and we care more about knowing it. I said that there are more essential problems; but this one still has a certain importance from our point of view: how will the fact of being women have affected our lives?

What precise opportunities have been given us and which ones have been denied? What destiny awaits our younger sisters, and in which direction should we point them? It is striking that most feminine literature is driven today by an attempt at lucidity more than by a will to make demands; coming out of an era of muddled controversy, this book is one attempt among others to take stock of the current state.

But it is no doubt impossible to approach any human problem without partiality: even the way of asking the questions, of adopting perspectives, presupposes hierarchies of interests; all characteristics comprise values; every so-called objective description is set against an ethical background. Instead of trying to conceal those principles that are more or less explicitly implied, we would be better off stating them from the start; then it would not be necessary to specify on each page the meaning given to the words "superior," "inferior," "better," "worse," "progress," "regression," and so on. If we examine some of the books on women, we see that one of the most frequently held points of view is that of public good or general interest: in reality, this is taken to mean the interest of society as each one wishes to maintain or establish it. In our opinion, there is no public good other than one that assures the citizens' private good; we judge institutions from the point of view of the concrete opportunities they give to individuals. But neither do we confuse the idea of private interest with happiness: that is another frequently encountered point of view; are women in a harem not happier than a woman voter? Is a housewife not happier than a woman worker? We cannot really know what the word "happiness" means, and still less what authentic values it covers; there is no way to measure the happiness of others, and it is always easy to call a situation that one would like to impose on others happy: in particular, we declare happy those condemned to stagnation, under the pretext that happiness is immobility. This is a notion, then, we will not refer to. The perspective we have adopted is one of existentialist morality. Every subject posits itself as a transcendence concretely, through projects; it accomplishes its freedom only by perpetual surpassing towards other freedoms; there is no other justification for present existence than its expansion towards an indefinitely open future. Every time transcendence lapses into immanence, there is degradation of existence into "in-itself," of freedom into facticity; this fall is a moral fault if the subject consents to it; if this fall is inflicted on the subject, it takes the form of frustration and oppression; in both cases it is an absolute evil. Every individual concerned with justifying his existence experiences his existence as an indefinite need to transcend himself. But what singularly defines the situation of woman is that being, like all humans, an autonomous freedom, she discovers and chooses herself in a world where men force her to assume herself as Other: an attempt is made to freeze her as an object and doom her to immanence, since her transcendence will be forever transcended by another essential and sovereign consciousness. Woman's drama lies in this conflict between the fundamental claim of every subject, which always posits itself as essential, and the demands of a situation that constitutes her as inessential. How, in the feminine condition, can a human being accomplish herself? What paths are open to her? Which ones lead to dead ends? How can she find independence within dependence? What circumstances limit women's freedom and can she overcome them? These are the fundamental questions we would like to elucidate. This means that in focusing on the individual's possibilities, we will define these possibilities not in terms of happiness but in terms of freedom.

STUDY QUESTIONS

1. Explain de Beauvoir's claim that "One is not born, but rather becomes, woman."
2. Why does de Beauvoir describe women as "the Other" to men?
3. What use does de Beauvoir make of existentialist moral philosophy?

AUDRE LORDE
Age, Race, Class, and Sex

Audre Lorde (1934–1982) was an African American poet, essayist, and activist.

Much of western european history conditions us to see human differences in simplistic opposition to each other: dominant/subordinate, good/bad, up/down, superior/inferior. In a society where the good is defined in terms of profit rather than in terms of human need, there must always be some group of people who, through systematized oppression, can be made to feel surplus, to occupy the place of the dehumanized inferior. Within this society, that group is made up of Black and Third World people, working-class people, older people, and women.

As a forty-nine-year-old Black lesbian feminist socialist mother of two, including one boy, and a member of an interracial couple, I usually find myself a part of some group defined as other, deviant, inferior, or just plain wrong. Traditionally, in american society, it is the members of oppressed, objectified groups who are expected to stretch out and bridge the gap between the actualities of our lives and the consciousness of our oppressor. For in order to survive, those of us for whom oppression is as american as apple pie have always had to be watchers, to become familiar with the language and manners of the oppressor, even sometimes adopting them for some illusion of protection. Whenever the need for some pretense of communication arises, those who profit from our oppression call upon us to share our knowledge with them. In other words, it is the responsibility of the oppressed to teach the oppressors their mistakes. I am responsible for educating teachers who dismiss my children's culture in school. Black and Third World people are expected to educate white people as to our humanity. Women are expected to educate men. Lesbians and gay men are expected to educate the heterosexual world. The oppressors maintain their position and evade responsibility for their own actions. There is a constant drain of energy which might be better used in redefining ourselves and devising realistic scenarios for altering the present and constructing the future.

Institutionalized rejection of difference is an absolute necessity in a profit economy which needs outsiders as surplus people. As members of such an economy, we have *all* been programmed to respond to the human differences between us with fear and loathing and to handle that difference in one of three ways: ignore it, and if that is not possible, copy it if we think it is dominant, or destroy it if we think it is subordinate. But we have no patterns for relating across our human differences as equals. As a result, those differences have been misnamed and misused in the service of separation and confusion.

Certainly there are very real differences between us of race, age, and sex. But it is not those differences between us that are separating us. It is rather our refusal to recognize those differences, and to examine the distortions which result from our misnaming them and their effects upon human behavior and expectation.

Racism, the belief in the inherent superiority of one race over all others and thereby the right to dominance. Sexism, the belief in the inherent superiority of one sex over the other and thereby the right to dominance. Ageism. Heterosexism. Elitism. Classism.

It is a lifetime pursuit for each one of us to extract these distortions from our living at the same time as we recognize, reclaim, and define those differences upon which they are imposed. For we have all been raised in a society where those distortions were endemic within our living. Too often, we pour the energy needed for recognizing and exploring difference into pretending those differences are insurmountable barriers, or that they do not exist at all. This results in a voluntary isolation, or false and treacherous connections. Either way, we do not develop tools for using human difference as a springboard for creative change within our lives. We speak not of human difference, but of human deviance.

Somewhere, on the edge of consciousness, there is what I call a *mythical norm*, which each one of us within our hearts knows "that is not me." In america, this norm is usually defined as white, thin, male, young, heterosexual, christian, and financially secure. It is with this mythical norm that the trappings of power reside within this society. Those of us who stand outside that power often identify one way in which we are different, and we assume that to be the primary cause of all oppression, forgetting other distortions around difference, some of which we ourselves may be practising. By and large within the women's movement today, white women focus upon their oppression as women and ignore differences of race, sexual preference, class, and age. There is a pretense to a homogeneity of experience covered by the word *sisterhood* that does not in fact exist.

Unacknowledged class differences rob women of each others' energy and creative insight. Recently a women's magazine collective made the decision for one issue to print only prose, saying poetry was a less "rigorous" or "serious" art form. Yet even the form our creativity takes is often a class issue. Of all the art forms, poetry is the most economical. It is the one which is the most secret, which requires the least physical labor, the least material, and the one which can be done between shifts, in the hospital pantry, on the subway, and on scraps of surplus paper. Over the last few years, writing a novel on tight finances, I came to appreciate the enormous differences in the material demands between poetry and prose. As we reclaim our literature, poetry has been the major voice of poor, working class, and Colored women. A room of one's own may be a necessity for writing prose, but so are reams of paper, a typewriter, and plenty of time. The actual requirements to produce the visual arts also help determine, along class lines, whose art is whose. In this day of inflated prices for material, who are our sculptors, our painters, our photographers? When we speak of a broadly based women's culture, we need to be aware of the effect of class and economic differences on the supplies available for producing art.

As we move toward creating a society within which we can each flourish, ageism is another distortion of relationship which interferes without vision.

By ignoring the past, we are encouraged to repeat its mistakes. The "genera-tion gap" is an important social tool for any repressive society. If the younger members of a community view the older members as contemptible or sus-pect or excess, they will never be able to join hands and examine the living memories of the community, nor ask the all important question, "Why?" This gives rise to a historical amnesia that keeps us working to invent the wheel every time we have to go to the store for bread.

We find ourselves having to repeat and relearn the same old lessons over and over that our mothers did because we do not pass on what we have learned, or because we are unable to listen. For instance, how many times has this all been said before? For another, who would have believed that once again our daughters are allowing their bodies to be hampered and purgatoried by girdles and high heels and hobble skirts?

Ignoring the differences of race between women and the implications of those differences presents the most serious threat to the mobilization of women's joint power.

As white women ignore their built-in privilege of whiteness and define *woman* in terms of their own experience alone, then women of Color become "other," the outsider whose experience and tradition is too "alien" to compre-hend. An example of this is the signal absence of the experience of women of Color as a resource for women's studies courses. The literature of women of Color is seldom included in women's literature courses and almost never in other literature courses, nor in women's studies as a whole. All too often, the excuse given is that the literatures of women of Color can only be taught by Colored women, or that they are too difficult to understand, or that classes cannot "get into" them because they come out of experiences that are "too different." I have heard this argument presented by white women of oth-erwise quite clear intelligence, women who seem to have no trouble at all teaching and reviewing work that comes out of the vastly different experi-ences of Shakespeare, Molière, Dostoyefsky, and Aristophanes. Surely there must be some other explanation.

This is a very complex question, but I believe one of the reasons white women have such difficulty reading Black women's work is because of their reluctance to see Black women as women and different from themselves. To examine Black women's literature effectively requires that we be seen as whole people in our actual complexities—as individuals, as women, as human—rather than as one of those problematic but familiar stereotypes provided in this society in place of genuine images of Black women. And I believe this holds true for the literatures of other women of Color who are not Black.

The literatures of all women of Color recreate the textures of our lives, and many white women are heavily invested in ignoring the real differences. For as long as any difference between us means one of us must be inferior, then the recognition of any difference must be fraught with guilt. To allow women of Color to step out of stereotypes is too guilt provoking, for it threatens the complacency of those women who view oppression only in terms of sex.

Refusing to recognize difference makes it impossible to see the different problems and pitfalls facing us as women.

Thus, in a patriarchal power system where whiteskin privilege is a major prop, the entrapments used to neutralize Black women and white women are not the same. For example, it is easy for Black women to be used by the power structure against Black men, not because they are men, but because they are Black. Therefore, for Black women, it is necessary at all times to separate the needs of the oppressor from our own legitimate conflicts within our communities. This same problem does not exist for white women. Black women and men have shared racist oppression and still share it, although in different ways. Out of that shared oppression we have developed joint defenses and joint vulnerabilities to each other that are not duplicated in the white community, with the exception of the relationship between Jewish women and Jewish men.

On the other hand, white women face the pitfall of being seduced into joining the oppressor under the pretense of sharing power. This possibility does not exist in the same way for women of Color. The tokenism that is sometimes extended to us is not an invitation to join power; our racial "otherness" is a visible reality that makes that quite clear. For white women there is a wider range of pretended choices and rewards for identifying with patriarchal power and its tools.

Today, with the defeat of ERA,[1] the tightening economy, and increased conservatism, it is easier once again for white women to believe the dangerous fantasy that if you are good enough, pretty enough, sweet enough, quiet enough, teach the children to behave, hate the right people, and marry the right men, then you will be allowed to co-exist with patriarchy in relative peace, at least until a man needs your job or the neighborhood rapist happens along. And true, unless one lives and loves in the trenches it is difficult to remember that the war against dehumanization is ceaseless.

---

1 *Editor's note*: The Equal Rights Amendment, a proposed constitutional reform which was not formally ratified within its allowed time period.

But Black women and our children know the fabric of our lives is stitched with violence and with hatred, that there is no rest. We do not deal with it only on the picket lines, or in dark midnight alleys, or in the places where we dare to verbalize our resistance. For us, increasingly, violence weaves through the daily tissues of our living—in the supermarket, in the classroom, in the elevator, in the clinic and the schoolyard, from the plumber, the baker, the saleswoman, the bus driver, the bank teller, the waitress who does not serve us.

Some problems we share as women, some we do not. You fear your children will grow up to join the patriarchy and testify against you, we fear our children will be dragged from a car and shot down in the street, and you will turn your backs upon the reasons they are dying.

The threat of difference has been no less blinding to people of Color. Those of us who are Black must see that the reality of our lives and our struggle does not make us immune to the errors of ignoring and misnaming difference. Within Black communities where racism is a living reality, differences among us often seem dangerous and suspect. The need for unity is often misnamed as a need for homogeneity, and a Black feminist vision mistaken for betrayal of our common interests as a people. Because of the continuous battle against racial erasure that Black women and Black men share, some Black women still refuse to recognize that we are also oppressed as women, and that sexual hostility against Black women is practiced not only by the white racist society, but implemented within our Black communities as well. It is a disease striking the heart of Black nationhood, and silence will not make it disappear. Exacerbated by racism and the pressures of powerlessness, violence against Black women and children often becomes a standard within our communities, one by which manliness can be measured. But these woman-hating acts are rarely discussed as crimes against Black women.

As a group, women of Color are the lowest paid wage earners in america. We are the primary targets of abortion and sterilization abuse, here and abroad. In certain parts of Africa, small girls are still being sewed shut between their legs to keep them docile and for men's pleasure. This is known as female circumcision, and it is not a cultural affair as the late Jomo Kenyatta insisted, it is a crime against Black women.

Black women's literature is full of the pain of frequent assault, not only by a racist patriarchy, but also by Black men. Yet the necessity for and history of shared battle have made us, Black women, particularly vulnerable to the false accusation that anti-sexist is anti-Black. Meanwhile, womanhating as a recourse of the powerless is sapping strength from Black communities, and our very lives. Rape is on the increase, reported and unreported, and rape is not aggressive sexuality, it is sexualized aggression. As Kalamu ya Salaam, a Black male writer points out, "As long as male domination exists, rape will exist. Only women revolting and men made conscious of their responsibility to fight sexism can collectively stop rape."[2]

Differences between ourselves as Black women are also being misnamed and used to separate us from one another. As a Black lesbian feminist comfortable with the many different ingredients of my identity, and a woman committed to racial and sexual freedom from oppression, I find I am constantly being encouraged to pluck out some one aspect of myself and present this as the meaningful whole, eclipsing or denying the other parts of self. But this is a destructive and fragmenting way to live. My fullest concentration of energy is available to me only when I integrate all the parts of who I am, openly, allowing power from particular sources of my living to flow back and forth freely through all my different selves, without the restrictions of externally imposed definition. Only then can I bring myself and my energies as a whole to the service of those struggles which I embrace as part of my living.

A fear of lesbians, or of being accused of being a lesbian, has led many Black women into testifying against themselves. It has led some of us into destructive alliances, and others into despair and isolation. In the white women's communities, heterosexism is sometimes a result of identifying with the white patriarchy, a rejection of that interdependence between women-identified women which allows the self to be, rather than to be used in the service of men. Sometimes it reflects a die-hard belief in the protective coloration of heterosexual relationships, sometimes a self-hate which all women have to fight against, taught us from birth.

Although elements of these attitudes exist for all women, there are particular resonances of heterosexism and homophobia among Black women. Despite the fact that woman-bonding has a long and honorable history in the African and African-american communities, and despite the knowledge and accomplishments of many strong and creative women-identified Black women in the political, social and cultural fields, heterosexual Black women often tend to ignore or discount the existence and work of Black lesbians.

---

2 From "Rape: A Radical Analysis, An African-American Perspective" by Kalamu ya Salaam in *Black Books Bulletin*, vol. 6, no. 4 (1980).

Part of this attitude has come from an understandable terror of Black male attack within the close confines of Black society, where the punishment for any female self-assertion is still to be accused of being a lesbian and therefore unworthy of the attention or support of the scarce Black male. But part of this need to misname and ignore Black lesbians comes from a very real fear that openly women-identified Black women who are no longer dependent upon men for their self-definition may well reorder our whole concept of social relationships.

Black women who once insisted that lesbianism was a white woman's problem now insist that Black lesbians are a threat to Black nationhood, are consorting with the enemy, are basically un-Black. These accusations, coming from the very women to whom we look for deep and real understanding, have served to keep many Black lesbians in hiding, caught between the racism of white women and the homophobia of their sisters. Often, their work has been ignored, trivialized, or misnamed, as with the work of Angelina Grimke, Alice Dunbar-Nelson, Lorraine Hansberry. Yet women-bonded women have always been some part of the power of Black communities, from our unmarried aunts to the amazons of Dahomey.

And it is certainly not Black lesbians who are assaulting women and raping children and grandmothers on the streets of our communities.

Across this country, as in Boston during the spring of 1979 following the unsolved murders of twelve Black women, Black lesbians are spearheading movements against violence against Black women.

What are the particular details within each of our lives that can be scrutinized and altered to help bring about change? How do we redefine difference for all women? It is not our differences which separate women, but our reluctance to recognize those differences and to deal effectively with the distortions which have resulted from the ignoring and misnaming of those differences.

As a tool of social control, women have been encouraged to recognize only one area of human difference as legitimate, those differences which exist between women and men. And we have learned to deal across those differences with the urgency of all oppressed subordinates. All of us have had to learn to live or work or coexist with men, from our fathers on. We have recognized and negotiated these differences, even when this recognition only continued the old dominant/subordinate mode of human relationship, where the oppressed must recognize the masters' difference in order to survive.

But our future survival is predicated upon our ability to relate within equality. As women, we must root out internalized patterns of oppression within ourselves if we are to move beyond the most superficial aspects of social change. Now we must recognize differences among women who are our equals, neither inferior nor superior, and devise ways to use each others' difference to enrich our visions and our joint struggles.

The future of our earth may depend upon the ability of all women to identify and develop new definitions of power and new patterns of relating across difference. The old definitions have not served us, nor the earth that supports us. The old patterns, no matter how cleverly rearranged to imitate progress, still condemn us to cosmetically altered repetitions of the same old exchanges, the same old guilt, hatred, recrimination, lamentation, and suspicion.

For we have, built into all of us, old blueprints of expectation and response, old structures of oppression, and these must be altered at the same time as we alter the living conditions which are a result of those structures. For the master's tools will never dismantle the master's house.

As Paulo Freire shows so well in *The Pedagogy of the Oppressed*,[3] the true focus of revolutionary change is never merely the oppressive situations which we seek to escape, but that piece of the oppressor which is planted deep within each of us, and which knows only the oppressors' tactics, the oppressors' relationships.

Change means growth, and growth can be painful. But we sharpen self-definition by exposing the self in work and struggle together with those whom we define as different from ourselves, although sharing the same goals. For Black and white, old and young, lesbian and heterosexual women alike, this can mean new paths to our survival.

> *We have chosen each other*
> *and the edge of each others battles*
> *the war is the same*
> *if we lose*
> *someday women's blood will congeal*
> *upon a dead planet*
> *if we win*
> *there is no telling*
> *we seek beyond history*
> *for a new and more possible meeting.*[4]

---

3 Seabury Press, New York, 1970.
4 From "Outlines," unpublished poem.

1. What does Lorde mean by the "distortions" that arise in respect to differences?
2. Why cannot the experience of black woman be analysed in terms of the combination of being a black person and a woman?
3. Why cannot "the master's tools dismantle the master's house"?

LORI GIRSHICK
Gender Policing

Lori Girshick (born 1953) is an American sociologist and feminist.

While transitioning, I go to the bathroom in a movie theater. The female ticket taker objects when I try to go into the ladies' room. The male ticket taker objects when I try to go into the men's room. When I confront them both and ask which I should use, they refuse to come up with an answer, both just desperately reiterating that I can't go in either "for the sake of the other patrons." Rather than call the manager, make a scene, and leave my kid sitting for a long time alone in the theater, I go out back and piss in a dumpster and then went back to the film. (Raven, transgendered FtM intersexual)

I'm frequently made uneasy by offhand comments, jokes made at the expense of cross-dressers or gays. It's not as acceptable as it used to be, at least not in the academic community I live in, but cross-dressers are still fair game, especially in the media, where almost routinely in television commercials they are employed for the sake of a guaranteed laugh. In this way, I'm reminded of the attitudes deemed appropriate by the majority. It's as if a cultural edict has been issued: Thou shalt ridicule those who cross the gender line. (BJ, male cross-dresser)

The gender binary has a little wiggle room. After all, some men are househusbands, some women are astronauts, some men have long hair, and some women sculpt their bodies, muscles bulging, through body-building. David Bowie, Boy George, Dennis Rodman, and Marilyn Manson are hugely popular. But, in general, it is a serious offense to violate gender norms.

＊ ＊ ＊ Some transgressions that are public—such as when transsexuals transition and face job loss, or when masculine women are harassed in the bathroom—give us clues as to what kinds of departures from the binary norms draw people's ire. Other transgressions that are often private— such as when males cross-dress in secrecy, or when intersex people cannot access their own medical records—indicate their importance by the shame attached. ＊ ＊ ＊

BATHROOM POLICING

Public bathrooms, with the familiar stick symbols for men and for women on the doors, are, as Dan (FtM) put it, "a perfect crystallization of all the gender norms in place. . . . It's like this amazing literalization of the more abstract binary teachings we get everyday." For Dan, bathrooms have been a "site of terror." He continued: "All it takes is one snotty person to make you feel like you don't deserve to live. I've had security guards remove me because they had quote unquote complaints from other students. And being removed from a public washroom at the University of Oxford isn't the sort of thing you want to tell your parents."

I heard from many genderqueer and butch women that women had reacted negatively to their using the women's restroom. These upset women had challenged the right of androgynous and masculine-looking female-bodied individuals to use the bathroom. But you shouldn't have to be a certain kind of woman to be entitled to use a public space; some women should not be privileged over other women. Why do feminine women feel that they have a greater right to use the bathroom, and furthermore why are they allowed to humiliate or antagonize other women? * * *

Hostile reactions to gender-nonconforming people using public bathrooms are common. * * *

For transitioning employees, use of the bathrooms at work is a contentious point. Oftentimes transpersons are either told they can't use the bathroom of their gender identification or told to use a bathroom on a different floor or in a different building. * * *

At other workplaces, management has taken a strong stand to support every employee's right to use the bathroom of self-identity. * * *

Clearly, the issue of who uses what bathroom creates anxiety for many non-trans or non-genderqueer people, and these fears do need to be addressed. Everyone, whether male or female, needs a safe place to go to the bathroom. Some women feel that a sex-segregated bathroom increases their safety, but an unlocked door that anyone can walk through doesn't really make them any safer. The stereotype that only men (and never women) are potentially violent or rapists is factually incorrect. A violent male *or* female can walk through that door. Greater safety would be achieved with either single-user bathrooms or multiple-user bathrooms with locked stall doors that go from the floor to the ceiling. * * *

A second concern of some women is that men are messy when they pee standing up. That can be ameliorated by having toilets with push-button plastic sanitary seat covers that change with each use. Businesses and public works can also have bathrooms cleaned more frequently. ⁂ Perhaps boys need stronger socialization in bathroom etiquette.

The thought of all-gender or gender-neutral public bathrooms, sometimes proposed as a way to secure everyone's right to equal access, makes many people uncomfortable. This is something they aren't used to. However, after much resistance people got used to race-desegregated public facilities, and people can get used to gender-desegregated facilities. Right now, because of the harassment they encounter, some people are denied safe access to freely use the bathrooms they need and have a right to use in public spaces, at work, or at school.

Since going to the bathroom is not in itself a safety threat, we should work on education to decrease the discomfort of people who feel that sex-segregated spaces are natural and necessary. They are neither. In fact, taking the "Men" and "Women" signs off bathroom doors and calling them "Restrooms" would go a long way toward loosening the idea of the gender binary. It would eliminate the experience of intersex individuals' having to choose which type of bathroom to enter, and of someone, such as a butch woman or male cross-dresser, not fitting in. Everyone of any gender expression fits into a restroom.

THE WOMEN'S MOVEMENT AND WHO IS A "WOMAN"

Sadly, feminist politics has its share of controversy around the boundaries of who qualifies as a man and who as a woman. Since women-only events are largely organized and attended by lesbians, lesbians have been in the forefront of debates about whether transwomen qualify as real women. A polarization opened up in 1973 when the lesbian rights organization Daughters of Bilitis splintered on the issue of whether MtF Beth Elliott, who had been the group's vice president, was a woman. She was expelled as not being one. Later that year Elliott, also a musician, was performing at the West Coast Lesbian Conference and was shouted off the stage. There was a huge split among attendees regarding Elliott's status. The next day, feminist leader Robin Morgan denounced Elliott in her keynote speech, accusing male-bodied transsexuals of "leeching off women." ⁂

One of the most contentious efforts in the lesbian community to police who is accepted as a woman is the policy of the Michigan Womyn's Music Festival (MWMF), which is open to "women who were born as women, who have lived their entire experience as women, and who identify as women" (statement by festival owner Lisa Vogel). The policy divides women along lines of "real women" and "fake women." MWMF is the oldest and largest feminist women's music festival in the country, dedicated to creating women-only space for safety, cultural renewal and production, and escape from sexism, misogyny, heterosexism, and homophobia. While it is open to women of a wide range of gender presentation (bearded, butch, androgynous, and femme), transgender and transsexual women have not been welcome. ✳ ✳ ✳

✳ ✳ ✳ By policy, MWMF workers will not question an attendee's gender, and they rely on individuals who attend to respect their policy of "womynborn womyn" only. In other words, they request that transwomen stay away for that week of women-only space. Yet their "don't ask, don't tell" policy means that transwomen, genderqueers, tranny boys, and others who don't mention they are trans or perhaps are male-identified can attend. ✳ ✳ ✳

Apparently the debate continues as to whether transwomen are real women, and the feminist community has vocal adherents to the different perspectives. To advocate only for acceptance of post-op transwomen only is classist and racist, since surgery is an option only for those with money. It is also exclusionary, since many transwomen don't choose to have surgery. To deny the self-determination of individuals who identify as women regardless of the body they were born in seems contrary to feminism. Genitals are not the only markers of femaleness or maleness—some people are born identifying in ways that do not correspond with the gender binary edict. For feminists to reject those who are marginalized by society because of gender identification is particularly unfeminist gender policing. While there are many strands of feminism, and lesbian separatists in particular may always find transwomen incompatible with their politics, ✳ ✳ ✳ genitals do not determine gender identity—nor does socialization, as important as that is in influencing gender expression and gender roles.

BULLYING, HOSTILITY, AND HATE CRIMES

Hate-motivated violence arises from a variety of sources: fear, ignorance, bigotry, misdirected anger, intolerance, and a need for control. Perpetrators of violence can be acquaintances of the victim, peers, family members, or strangers. Often, homophobic and gender identity anxieties are mixed up together, and perpetrators may not even be aware of their motivations. While statistics of harassment of and violence against transgender people are hard to come by, a 1996 survey of 397 MtFs by the San Francisco

Department of Public Health gives us one impression. Eighty-three percent suffered verbal abuse; 46 percent faced employment discrimination; 37 percent had suffered abuse within the previous twelve months (and, of those, 44 percent reported it was by a partner); and 59 percent reported a history of rape.

Only a small number of the people I interviewed said they had faced no hostility ∗ ∗ ∗

The message of this hostility is, You need to change. And while most individuals stand up to this, they do so at considerable emotional cost.

Bullying of MtFs was common. ∗ ∗ ∗ Felicia (transgendered) talked about her discomfort around men: "When I walk into a room full of men, the intimidation starts at the door. I feel intimidated. I feel I'm being bullied even before I even speak or even before they even speak. There's something about a group of men being together, there's a lot of tension in the air. Men are very intense. Highly competitive, violent, rough, coarse." Since Felicia works as a male in a macho occupation, she has been having a difficult time. She is smaller than the typical firefighter and speaks softly. "I've heard lots of comments, you're a fag, you're a sissy, you're queer."

Being yelled at on the street, or accosted by strangers laughing and asking, "Are you a man or a woman?" are not uncommon experiences. cj (transgendered) has had "strangers freak out and call me perverted and pull young kids farther from me." These insults and shaming comments are forms of gender policing, attempts to keep people who are preceived as gender transgressors in line. ∗ ∗ ∗

The verbal taunts, bullying behaviors, and harassments are preludes to the more severe physical violence inflicted on many of them. Dee (MtF) was beaten up and urinated on while in the military and stationed in Germany. A former lover who "couldn't deal with the gender situation" beat up Keven (two-spirit). Jennifer (MtF) was told by her wife before their separation that a man Jennifer's wife had slept with had offered to kill Jennifer. Laura (MtF) has been beaten up several different times by men denigrating her transsexual status.

The ultimate and irreversible gender policing involves the hate crime of murder. Hate crimes are defined as being motivated by hatred or dislike of someone because of that person's identity, perceived identity, or affiliation with a particular group. Police view a crime as bias- or hate-motivated when it involves slurs or name-calling against the particular identity or group, and/or extreme violence. Trans-identified victims of hate crimes are often called fags or queers, or hatred is expressly directed toward transsexuals. Hate crime laws address the violence that is motivated by bias and provide for the tracking of these crimes, the training of law enforcement personal, and sometimes the mandatory enhancement of penalties at sentencing for those convicted of hate crimes. * * *

A report by the Gender Public Advocacy Coalition titled 50 *under* 30 examines the murders of fifty people aged thirty and under who were targeted because of their gender presentation or identity in the previous ten years. The findings are significant: most victims were people of color (85 percent Black and Latino), most victims were poor (often unemployed and/or homeless), 88 percent of the victims were from the LGBT communities (4 percent were heterosexual, and 8 percent of identities were unknown), 92 percent of the victims were biologically male but presenting some degree of femininity, and most cases were ignored by the media even though assailants used extreme violence and the murders typically took place in major cities. Only 46 percent of these cases have been solved (compared with 69 percent of all homicides nationally). * * *

Such hate crimes have an importance beyond the loss of precious life. They are also message crimes committed against an entire group. When any transgender person is attacked, verbally and physically, because of being transgender, the message is that something is terribly wrong with all transgender identities and behaviors. Continue to be this way, the message goes, and all of you face this type of punishment—humiliation, pain, or death. It is clearly an extreme form of gender policing. I found that most participants in this study were aware of the risks they were taking just to be themselves. Because of the fears and ignorance of other people, they risked their very lives.

MEDICAL GATEKEEPING

Trans-identified individuals face many barriers in accessing medical care. Although the hormones, procedures, and surgeries that many seek are medically necessary and essential for confirming their sense of self, all too often doctors, therapists, and insurance companies view these treatments as cosmetic or elective. Health care providers may not be well informed about transgender issues, and their low level of cultural competence may result in stigmatizing behaviors, insensitivity, or denial of needed services. * * *

An FtM may have difficulty accessing gynecological care, whether for a pap smear or a hysterectomy. An MtF may need tests for prostate cancer. Non-trans men who have gynecomastia (excessive breast tissue) can have breast tissue removed and the procedure covered by insurance, but a female-bodied transman who wants his excessive breast tissue removed through double mastectomy is not covered. Hormonal imbalances are not uncommon, and people who are non-trans routinely have insurance coverage for their thyroid medication, estrogen replacement, or T prescriptions for low testosterone levels. But a transsexual's medical need for hormone replacement therapy is not generally covered by insurance. These double standards are linked to judgments of acceptable medical conditions and the view that gender is determined at birth.

Perhaps the most significant gender-policing mechanisms our society employs for transsexuals are the diagnoses of gender identity disorder (GID) and transvestic fetishism (TF) found in the current *Diagnostic and Statistical Manual of Mental Disorders* (DSM) of the American Psychiatric Association. The label "gender identity disorder" suggests that to have a gender identity different from the category a doctor assigned to one's body at birth is disordered, confused, illegitimate, or perverted. Such an individual is dysphoric, perhaps neurotic, bipolar, autogynephilic, or has a dissociative personality. The TF diagnosis labels cross-dressing by heterosexual males as a sexual fetish. Application of these diagnostic labels unnecessarily pathologizes transgender and gender-variant people.

When the DSM was updated in 1994, GID replaced the diagnosis of gender dysphoria, which referred to an intense, persistent distress with one's physical sex characteristics or their associated social role. But transsexuality should be seen as the medical condition it is and not a mental illness, since there is no illness or disease to cure. The real medical issue is more with the person's physical body than it is with the person's gender identity, but the GID label focuses on cross-gender identity as a problem, a "disorder," rather than on what can be done to alleviate the distress of the mismatch. The fact is antianxiety medications, antipsychotic medications, and electroshock do not relieve gender dysphoria. The only measure that "works" is living in the gender the person identifies as.

The university-affiliated gender identity clinics that opened in the mid-1960s were highly experimental and research-oriented. The treatment they offered was quite limited (serving a tiny fraction of the people who contacted them), and those individuals who were successful in obtaining what was then called sex change surgery told the therapists and doctors what they wanted to hear. At that time, based on little actual knowledge, therapists believed that the drag queen was the ideal model of the MtF. Those male-bodied people with exaggerated feminine looks and mannerisms, who were highly sexualized and who expressed sexual interest in men, were considered to be transsexual. Well-adjusted people who were not homeless, unemployed, or on the brink of suicide or drug addiction were not believed to be transsexual. Such individuals were denied not only surgery but also access to hormones. The concept of GID is both sexist and heterosexist in its application and its gendered expectations.

In the heyday of the gender clinics in the United States (1966–1990), transsexuals were sent away in droves without help. The clinics were not staffed to handle the numbers of people looking for treatment, and in any case the research and knowledge that would have been needed did not exist. Clinics often demanded that patients agree to research interviews and years of therapy, that they divorce spouses, or that they change jobs. Many of these demands would be seen today as unethical.

Although this "illness" of GID had no cure, therapists did become the primary gatekeepers for transsexuals who were seeking to gain access to their medical needs. ✳ ✳ ✳

Today, ✳ ✳ ✳ the protocol used by most doctors in the United States for providing medical care to transsexuals ✳ ✳ ✳ calls for a therapist's diagnosis and consequent letter that can be presented to an endocrinologist for hormones and/or a surgeon for sex reassignment or chest reconstruction surgery. A surgeon will usually require letters from two therapists. [The protocol] also calls for a transitioning individual to live full-time for one year in true gender identity (called the Real Life Experience, RLE) before having surgery. ✳ ✳ ✳ The yearlong RLE is supposed to show the patient's ability to adjust. Many see this year as a very dangerous time: the transitioning individual, now living full-time as what will often seem to others the "wrong" gender, is at higher risk for hate crimes, hostility, job loss, and family rejection because the measures (such as hormones or chest reconstruction) that might help that person be better accepted as the gender he or she is are the very measures being denied. ✳ ✳ ✳ These risks ✳ ✳ ✳ reside in social attitudes and practices. ✳ ✳ ✳

A group known as GID Reform Advocates ✳ ✳ ✳ argue[s], first, that a psychiatric diagnosis is unnecessarily stigmatizing for transsexuals, who in fact have a physical (body) problem, and, second, that calling it an "identity disorder" suggests that cross-gender identity is not legitimate. ✳ ✳ ✳ It is the *distress* of gender dysphoria that is the problem, and ✳ ✳ ✳ medical steps that make cross-living easier alleviate this distress. ✳ ✳ ✳ A different way—without stigma—must be found to provide access to needed medical services. These should be available just as prescriptions and procedures are provided for other medical conditions.

LEGAL DOCUMENTS

Medical gatekeeping influences far more than just access to medical care. It also influences legal status, since the "letters" that are written by therapists and surgeons provide access to legal change of one's gender status. This in itself is problematic. Most transgender people do not have surgery, because they either do not want it, cannot afford it, or it is medically contraindicated. Furthermore, many transgender people, including transsexuals, do not have surgery *or* therapy *or* take hormones, yet they live in their true gender. Therefore, the requirement that they need proof of such medical interventions to validate their authentic gender clearly impedes their ability to function in society. Since they are no longer living as their birth sex, they cannot freely access services (employment, housing, health care, travel, etc.) dependent on identification that indicates one's sex (passports, driver's licenses, social security cards, etc.).

One's legal status as a male or a female matters. It matters for marriage, divorce, adoption, child custody, inheritance, immigration status, employment; for access to services such as shelters, clinics and centers, health benefits; and for identity papers and personal records (name, driver's license, passport, birth certificate, school transcript, work history). For trans individuals, even those who are not transitioning (e.g., genderqueers or male cross-dressers), being stopped by police or showing a driver's license to cash a check can be stressful. The M or F on a driver's license may not jibe with what people see (or how the person identifies). Some transsexuals carry their therapist's letter in case they find themselves in precisely this kind of situation, needing to "justify" who they are. The anxiety this causes, and the ridicule or embarrassment that may follow, originate from a personal medical matter that should be no one else's business. As a medical issue (since being able to fully live one's true gender is therapeutic), trans-identified people should have an easier time getting the legal documents they need to complete their transition or live in their preferred gender—they should not have to deal with the complexity and roadblocks they now encounter.

Identity documents may seem completely reasonable documents to have, but for trans-identified people they become a form of gender policing. Required procedures for changing names and/or sex designations are time-consuming and costly. * * *

Leslie Feinberg talks about these labels:

> Why am I forced to check off an F or an M on these documents in the first place? For identification? Both a driver's license and a passport include photographs! Most cops and passport agents would feel insulted to think they needed an M or an F to determine if a person is a man or a woman. It's only those of us who cross the boundaries of sex or gender, or live ambiguously between those borders, who are harassed by this legal requirement.[1]

In fact one could argue that these designations are so often incorrect as to render them meaningless—or at least to reduce their usefulness to the point that we should not depend on them as part of a true identification. After all, intersex individuals may later realize they are not the sex and/or gender the birth certificate states, and transsexual individuals undergo surgical changes to align their identity. The records were wrong originally and need to be corrected.

Legal name change is supposed to be available to anyone as long as that person is not seeking to defraud. * * *

After name change, the driver's license is often the next item to change. * * *

Birth certificates are another key item that needs to be changed. Three states * * * do not allow a change of sex designation on birth certificates. Other states will change the M or F after receiving a letter from a surgeon stating that the individual has gone through irreversible sex change surgery. While this has generally been interpreted to mean genital surgery, some FtMs have succeeded in getting their birth certificate changed after having only chest reconstruction and being on testosterone. A court order showing the name change is also needed.

Some states amend the birth certificate; others issue a completely new document. * * *

New York City had been unique in issuing new birth certificates without a sex designation altogether. This in itself was embarrassing. It made the certificates less useful as identification, and because only transsexuals had this type of birth certificate, they were outed. In September 2006, the New York City Department of Health and Mental Hygiene proposed liberalizing the rules so that birth certificates could be changed even if individuals did not have surgery. However, in December of 2006 city officials slowed the rule-changing process in order to consider whether this proposal might conflict with new federal rules that are being developed. The Department

---

1　*Editor's note*: Leslie Feinberg, *Transgender Warriors* (Boston: Beacon Press, 1996), pp. 61–62.

of Health did, however, change its policy of eliminating gender on the certificate. Now the birth sex will be listed until a letter confirming irreversible sex change surgery has been performed. ✳ ✳ ✳

Marriage is another area where trans-identified people encounter roadblocks and risks in their pursuit of happiness. Legally, marriage is a union between a man and a woman, except for same-sex marriages ✳ ✳ ✳ and civil unions ✳ ✳ ✳. If a birth certificate establishes the legal sex of an individual, then a heterosexual transsexual who wants to be married needs to have that document changed. However, even in cases where the birth certificate has been changed, marriages involving transsexuals have been successfully challenged.

In 2002, the Kansas Supreme Court invalidated the marriage between J'Noel Gardiner (MtF) and Marshall Gardiner. After Mr. Gardiner's death, his son contested Mrs. Gardiner's inheritance, and the court ruled in his favor by refusing to recognize Mrs. Gardiner's birth certificate and what the court deemed to be a same-sex marriage. ✳ ✳ ✳

There has been some concern as to whether marriages continue to be legal after one partner transitions and changes his or her birth certificate. Does this become a same-sex marriage, which is illegal in most states?[2] It would be best if there were no restrictions on marriage—individuals who commit to each other should be able to marry regardless of how they identify. But for now, marriage laws are not trans-friendly. Transsexuals remain at the mercy of the state they were born in, and the gender-policing beliefs and prejudices of individual judges and the court process.

GENDER POLICING AND LEGAL PROTECTION

Overcoming discrimination is a long and painful process. ✳ ✳ ✳ There is an urgent need for nondiscrimination policies and laws in government jurisdictions, at workplaces, and in schools and colleges to prevent discrimination against trans-identified people. ✳ ✳ ✳

✳ ✳ ✳ Countless individuals still lack the protection they need against discrimination based on gender identity or sexual orientation. ✳ ✳ ✳

What is needed is a federal law that specifically includes gender identity and sexual orientation among the kinds of discrimination it covers. ✳ ✳ ✳

Gender policing has complicated the lives of trans-identified individuals because of the barriers it has created, the personal stress it has produced,

---

2 *Editor's note:* More recently the law has changed, and state-level bans were deemed unconstitutional in 2015.

and the physical and emotional risks it has exposed them to through rein-forcement of their presumed abnormality. Medical and legal gatekeeping, lack of legal protection, and other forms of gender policing facilitate the ongoing harassment of, and discrimination against, trans-identified people.

STUDY QUESTIONS

1. What does Girshick mean by "gender policing"?
2. Take one of Girshick's examples. What issues does it raise, and how can so-ciety adopt a fully inclusive policy?
3. How far is it possible and desirable to remove gender classification from offi-cial documents such as driving licenses and passports?

▪ Compare and Contrast Questions

1. Are there any significant differences in the arguments of Wollstonecraft and de Beauvoir?
2. Does Lorde's perspective reveal limitations in the arguments of Wollstone-craft and de Beauvoir?
3. How far do the positions of Wollstonecraft, de Beauvoir, and Lorde presup-pose a binary conception of gender? Do they have the resources to answer the problems raised by Girshick?

FREE SPEECH AND ITS LIMITS

This section contains three very different discussions of free speech. We start with the classic case for free speech by John Stuart Mill, in his book *On Liberty*. Mill begins by emphasizing the importance of the free press against tyrannical government. Mill asserts that the majority has no right to silence a minority opinion, however unpopular. The essence of his case is that society progresses, and permanently benefits, through free and open discussion. Suppose the minority view is true. Then we lose the oppor-tunity to exchange error for truth, as Mill puts it, by not listening to the new view. But even if the minority view is false, we still have good reason to let it be heard. For if we refuse to listen to opposition, we will hold our views as "dead dogma" and may forget the good reasons for which we hold them. This can be dangerous, for when we are confronted with plausible false views in the future, we might lose our ability to defend the true view. Hence, we must always allow our views to be challenged, even if we are certain we are right. Finally, if the new view is in part true, we can improve our understanding by combining the old and new views.

Mill's position is essentially utilitarian, since he argues that the consequences of freedom of expression will tend to lead to human happiness. This
contrasts with those who would argue that we have a right—perhaps even a
human right—to freedom of expression independently of the consequences.
And Mill has been criticized for making his case in the way he does, for if
it turned out that freedom of expression had bad consequences (contrary
to Mill's belief), then there would be a utilitarian justification for limiting
it. And indeed Mill does find utilitarian reason for banning freedom of
expression in some rare cases if, for example, it would incite an angry mob
to violence. In such a case, the reason for the prohibition is not the content
of the view, but the fact that, on the occasion on which it is expressed, it is
very likely to have adverse consequences.

What is to count as speech, however? Should all forms of pornography be
protected as free speech? Catharine MacKinnon, lawyer and philosopher, has
been, with Andrea Dworkin, a very powerful critic of some forms of pornography, on feminist grounds. She has thus opposed an argument that regards
pornography as a type of speech that is protected by the First Amendment of
the American Constitution. MacKinnon and Dworkin drafted a possible new
human rights ordinance on pornography for Minneapolis. Here, however,
we look primarily at the moral issues. It is important to keep in mind that
MacKinnon and Dworkin define pornography as "graphic sexually explicit
subordination of women through pictures or words that also includes women
dehumanized as sexual objects." It is distinguished from erotica, which
involves sexually explicit materials, but not subordination.

MacKinnon's main case is that pornography, so understood, oppresses
women. Hence she is not especially interested in arguments regarding
obscenity, but rather relates pornography to power and powerlessness. She
considers how pornography is made, how it is used, and the effect it has on
gender relations in society. First, her studies show that women who take
part especially in violent pornography sometimes do so under extreme
coercion, to the point of rape and even murder. Second, pornography has
been implicated in very serious sex crimes and influences the type of sex
men force on their partners. Third, and in the main argument of the paper,
pornography eroticizes dominance and submission and in doing so celebrates and reinforces gender oppression, thereby harming all women.
MacKinnon argues that a great many women have been victims of sexual
violence, harassment, and assault, but find it impossible, in general, to speak
of this abuse. This reticence is reinforced by the representation of gender

oppression as consensual in pornography. In this way, and others, pornography contributes to an atmosphere that, according to MacKinnon, silences women. Feminism can contribute to giving women the means by which they can express, oppose, and perhaps overcome their subordination. For MacKinnon, prohibiting pornography (as she defines it) is part of that process.

The third selection is a controversial and provocative piece by Greg Lukianoff and Jonathan Haidt, who describe a number of developments in U.S. universities regarding the exposure of students to views that they might find distressing, offensive, or traumatic. Many academics now offer "trigger" warnings concerning sensitive material that they may cover in class; other instructors even adopt policies of self-censorship.

Another important issue concerns "microaggressions," which are seemingly innocent comments that have nevertheless an aggressive element, such as asking Asian Americans "Where are you really from?"—implying that they are not really American. Campuses are issuing instructions to protect students from such microaggressions and other forms of offence, so that the university does not place students at risk of trauma or deep offense. The authors use the term "vindictive protectiveness" for the practice of punishing those who, by failing to give trigger warnings or using microaggressive speech, violate the rules.

Such vindictive protectiveness raises important questions of freedom of speech and expression. Lukianoff and Haidt object to the issuing of trigger warnings and similar protective practices, arguing that they are harmful to student development. They argue that it is important for people to be confronted with views they find difficult, even if they have previously suffered trauma. Only through exposure, the authors argue, can people develop the capacities that will allow them to overcome past trauma or cope with potential threats to their emotional well-being. According to Lukianoff and Haidt, protecting students from the emotional shock of confronting views that make them uncomfortable is bad for the students, bad for the university, and bad for democracy.

JOHN STUART MILL
On Liberty of Expression

John Stuart Mill (1806–1873) was born in England, of Scottish descent. Mill was initially a disciple of Bentham but branched out to develop his own distinctive and highly influential moral views. He wrote on a very wide range of moral, political, philosophical and economic issues, including arguing for the emancipation of women.

OF THE LIBERTY OF THOUGHT AND DISCUSSION

The time, it is to be hoped, is gone by, when any defence would be necessary of the "liberty of the press" as one of the securities against corrupt or tyrannical government. No argument, we may suppose, can now be needed, against permitting a legislature or an executive, not identified in interest with the people, to prescribe opinions to them, and determine what doctrines or what arguments they shall be allowed to hear. This aspect of the question, besides, has been so often and so triumphantly enforced by preceding writers, that it needs not be specially insisted on in this place. Though the law of England, on the subject of the press, is as servile to this day as it was in the time of the Tudors, there is little danger of its being actually put in force against political discussion, except during some temporary panic, when fear of insurrection drives ministers and judges from their propriety; and, speaking generally, it is not, in constitutional countries, to be apprehended, that the government, whether completely responsible to the people or not, will often attempt to control the expression of opinion, except when in doing so it makes itself the organ of the general intolerance of the public. Let us suppose, therefore, that the government is entirely at one with the people, and never thinks of exerting any power of coercion unless in agreement with what it conceives to be their voice. But I deny the right of the people to exercise such coercion, either by themselves or by their government. The power itself is illegitimate. The best government has no more title to it than the worst. It is as noxious, or more noxious, when exerted in accordance with public opinion, than when in opposition to it. If all mankind minus one were of one opinion, and only one person were of the contrary opinion, mankind would be no more justified in silencing that one person, than he, if he had the power, would be justified in silencing mankind. Were an opinion a personal possession of no value except to the owner; if to be obstructed in the enjoyment of it were simply a private injury, it would make some difference whether the injury was inflicted only on a few persons or on many. But the peculiar evil of silencing the expression of an opinion is that it is robbing the human race; posterity as well as the existing generation; those who dissent from the opinion, still more than those who hold it. If the opinion is right, they are deprived of the opportunity of exchanging error for truth: if wrong, they lose, what is almost as great a benefit, the clearer perception and livelier impression of truth, produced by its collision with error.

It is necessary to consider separately these two hypotheses, each of which has a distinct branch of the argument corresponding to it. We can never be sure that the opinion we are endeavouring to stifle is a false opinion; and if we were sure, stifling it would be an evil still.

First: the opinion which it is attempted to suppress by authority may possibly be true. Those who desire to suppress it, of course deny its truth; but they are not infallible. They have no authority to decide the question for all mankind, and exclude every other person from the means of judging. To refuse a hearing to an opinion, because they are sure that it is false, is to assume that *their* certainty is the same thing as *absolute* certainty. All silencing of discussion is an assumption of infallibility. Its condemnation may be allowed to rest on this common argument, not the worse for being common.

Unfortunately for the good sense of mankind, the fact of their fallibility is far from carrying the weight in their practical judgment which is always allowed to it in theory; for while every one well knows himself to be fallible, few think it necessary to take any precautions against their own fallibility, or admit the supposition that any opinion, of which they feel very certain, may be one of the examples of the error to which they acknowledge themselves to be liable. Absolute princes, or others who are accustomed to unlimited deference, usually feel this complete confidence in their own opinions on nearly all subjects. People more happily situated, who sometimes hear their opinions disputed, and are not wholly unused to be set right when they are wrong, place the same unbounded reliance only on such of their opinions as are shared by all who surround them, or to whom they habitually defer; for in proportion to a man's want of confidence in his own solitary judgment, does he usually repose, with implicit trust, on the infallibility of "the world" in general. And the world, to each individual, means the part of it with which he comes in contact; his party, his sect, his church, his class of society; the man may be called, by comparison, almost liberal and large-minded to whom it means anything so comprehensive as his own country or his own age. Nor is his faith in this collective authority at all shaken by his being aware that other ages, countries, sects, churches, classes, and parties have thought, and even now think, the exact reverse. He devolves upon his own world the responsibility of being in the right against the dissentient worlds of other people; and it never troubles him that mere accident has decided which of these numerous worlds is the object of his reliance, and that the same causes which make him a Churchman in London, would have made him a Buddhist or a Confucian in Pekin. Yet it is as evident in itself, as any amount of argument can make it, that ages are no more infallible than individuals; every age having held many opinions which subsequent ages have deemed not only false but absurd: and it is as certain that many opinions now general will be rejected by future ages, as it is that many, once general, are rejected by the present.

The objection likely to be made to this argument would probably take some such form as the following. There is no greater assumption of infallibility in forbidding the propagation of error, than in any other thing which is done by public authority on its own judgment and responsibility. Judgment is given to men that they may use it. Because it may be used erroneously, are men to be told that they ought not to use it at all? To prohibit what they think pernicious, is not claiming exemption from error, but fulfilling the duty incumbent on them, although fallible, of acting on their conscientious conviction. If we were never to act on our opinions, because those opinions may be wrong, we should leave all our interests uncared for, and all our duties unperformed. An objection which applies to all conduct can be no valid objection to any conduct in particular. It is the duty of governments, and of individuals, to form the truest opinions they can; to form carefully, and never impose them upon others unless they are quite sure of being right. But when they are sure (such reasoners may say), it is not conscientiousness but cowardice to shrink from acting on their opinions, and allow doctrines which they honestly think dangerous to the welfare of mankind, either in this life or in another, to be scattered abroad without restraint, because other people, in less enlightened times, have persecuted opinions now believed to be true. Let us take care, it may be said, not to make the same mistake: but governments and nations have made mistakes in other things, which are not denied to be fit subjects for the exercise of authority: they have laid on bad taxes, made unjust wars. Ought we therefore to lay on no taxes, and, under whatever provocation. make no wars? Men and governments, must act to the best of their ability. There is no such thing as absolute certainty, but there is assurance sufficient for the purposes of human life. We may, and must, assume our opinion to be true for the guidance of our own conduct: and it is assuming no more when we forbid bad men to pervert society by the propagation of opinions which we regard as false and pernicious.

I answer, that it is assuming very much more. There is the greatest difference between presuming an opinion to be true, because, with every opportunity for contesting it, it has not been refuted, and assuming its truth for the purpose of not permitting its refutation. Complete liberty of contradicting and disproving our opinion is the very condition which justifies us in assuming its truth for purposes of action; and on no other terms can a being with human faculties have any rational assurance of being right. * * *

In the present age—which has been described as "destitute of faith, but terrified at scepticism"—in which people feel sure, not so much that their opinions are true, as that they should not know what to do without them—the claims of an opinion to be protected from public attack are rested not so much on its truth, as on its importance to society. There are, it is alleged, certain beliefs so useful, not to say indispensable, to well-being that it is as much the duty of governments to uphold those beliefs, as to protect any other of the interests of society. In a case of such necessity, and so directly in the line of their duty, something less than infallibility may, it is maintained, warrant, and even bind, governments to act on their own opinion, confirmed by the general opinion of mankind. It is also often argued, and still oftener thought, that none but bad men would desire to weaken these salutary beliefs; and there can be nothing wrong, it is thought, in restraining bad men, and prohibiting what only such men would wish to practise. This mode of thinking makes the justification of restraints on discussion not a question of the truth of doctrines, but of their usefulness; and flatters itself by that means to escape the responsibility of claiming to be an infallible judge of opinions. But those who thus satisfy themselves, do not perceive that the assumption of infallibility is merely shifted from one point to another. The usefulness of an opinion is itself matter of opinion: as disputable, as open to discussion, and requiring discussion as much as the opinion itself. There is the same need of an infallible judge of opinions to decide an opinion to be noxious, as to decide it to be false, unless the opinion condemned has full opportunity of defending itself. And it will not do to say that the heretic may be allowed to maintain the utility or harmlessness of his opinion, though forbidden to maintain its truth. The truth of an opinion is part of its utility. If we would know whether or not it is desirable that a proposition should be believed, is it possible to exclude the consideration of whether or not it is true? In the opinion, not of bad men, but of the best men, no belief which is contrary to truth can be really useful: and can you prevent such men from urging that plea, when they are charged with culpability for denying some doctrine which they are told is useful, but which they believe to be false? Those who are on the side of received opinions never fail to take all possible advantage of this plea: you do not find *them* handling the question of utility as if it could be completely abstracted from that of truth: on the contrary, it is, above all, because their doctrine is "the truth," that the knowledge or the belief of it is held to be so indispensable. There can be no fair discussion of the question of usefulness when an argument so vital may be employed on one side, but not on the other. And in point of fact, when law or public feeling do not permit the truth of an opinion to be disputed, they are just as little tolerant of a denial of its usefulness. The utmost they allow is an extenuation of its absolute necessity, or of the positive guilt of rejecting it.

In order more fully to illustrate the mischief of denying a hearing to opinions because we, in our own judgment, have condemned them, it will be desirable to fix down the discussion to a concrete case; and I choose, by preference, the cases which are least favourable to me—in which the argument against freedom of opinion, both on the score of truth and on that of utility, is considered the strongest. Let the opinions impugned be the belief in a God and in a future state, or any of the commonly received doctrines of morality. To fight the battle on such ground gives a great advantage to an unfair antagonist; since he will be sure to say (and many who have no desire to be unfair will say it internally), Are these the doctrines which you do not deem sufficiently certain to be taken under the protection of law? Is the belief in a God one of the opinions to feel sure of which you hold to be assuming infallibility? But I must be permitted to observe, that it is not the feeling sure of a doctrine (be it what it may) which I call an assumption of infallibility. It is the undertaking to decide that question *for others*, without allowing them to hear what can be said on the contrary side. And I denounce and reprobate this pretension not the less, if put forth on the side of my most solemn convictions. However positive any one's persuasion may be, not only of the falsity but of the pernicious consequences—not only of the pernicious consequences, but (to adopt expressions which I altogether condemn) the immorality and impiety of an opinion; yet if, in pursuance of that private judgment, though backed by the public judgment of his country or his cotemporaries, he prevents the opinion from being heard in its defence, he assumes infallibility. And so far from the assumption being less objectionable or less dangerous because the opinion is called immoral or impious, this is the case of all others in which it is most fatal. These are exactly the occasions on which the men of one generation commit those dreadful mistakes which excite the astonishment and horror of posterity. It is among such that we find the instances memorable in history, when the arm of the law has been employed to root out the best men and the noblest doctrines; with deplorable success as to the men, though some of the doctrines have survived to be (as if in mockery) invoked in defence of similar conduct towards those who dissent from *them*, or from their received interpretation.

Mankind can hardly be too often reminded, that there was once a man named Socrates, between whom and the legal authorities and public opinion of his time there took place a memorable collision. Born in an age and country abounding in individual greatness, this man has been handed down to us by those who best knew both him and the age, as the most virtuous man in it; while *we* know him as the head and prototype of all subsequent teachers of virtue, the source equally of the lofty inspiration of Plato and the judicious utilitarianism of Aristotle, "*i maëstri di color che sanno*," the two headsprings of ethical as of all other philosophy. This acknowledged master of all the eminent thinkers who have since lived—whose fame, still growing after more than two thousand years, all but outweighs the whole remainder of the names which make his native city illustrious—was put to death by his countrymen, after a judicial conviction, for impiety and immorality. Impiety, in denying the gods recognised by the State; indeed his accuser asserted (see the "Apologia") that he believed in no gods at all. Immorality, in being, by his doctrines and instructions, a "corruptor of youth." Of these charges the tribunal, there is every ground for believing, honestly found him guilty, and condemned the man who probably of all then born had deserved best of mankind to be put to death as a criminal.

To pass from this to the only other instance of judicial iniquity, the mention of which, after the condemnation of Socrates, would not be an anticlimax: the event which took place on Calvary rather more than eighteen hundred years ago. The man who left on the memory of those who witnessed his life and conversation such an impression of his moral grandeur that eighteen subsequent centuries have done homage to him as the Almighty in person, was ignominiously put to death, as what? As a blasphemer. Men did not merely mistake their benefactor; they mistook him for the exact contrary of what he was, and treated him as that prodigy of impiety which they themselves are now held to be for their treatment of him. The feelings with which mankind now regard these lamentable transactions, especially the later of the two, render them extremely unjust in their judgment of the unhappy actors. These were, to all appearance, not bad men—not worse than men commonly are, but rather the contrary; men who possessed in a full, or somewhat more than a full measure, the religious, moral and patriotic feelings of their time and people: the very kind of men who, in all times, our own included, have every chance of passing through life blameless and respected. ∗ ∗ ∗

But, indeed, the dictum that truth always triumphs over persecution is one of those pleasant falsehoods which men repeat after one another till they pass into commonplaces, but which all experience refutes. History teems with instances of truth put down by persecution. If not suppressed for ever, it may be thrown back for centuries. To speak only of religious opinions: the Reformation broke out at least twenty times before Luther, and was put down, Arnold of Brescia was put down. Fra Dolcino was put down. Savonarola was put down. The Albigeois were put down. The Vaudois were put down. The Lollards were put down. The Hussites were put down. Even after the era of Luther, wherever persecution was persisted in, it was successful. In Spain, Italy, Flanders, the Austrian empire, Protestantism was rooted out; and, most likely, would have been so in England, had Queen Mary lived, or Queen Elizabeth died. Persecution has always succeeded, save where the heretics were too strong a party to be effectually persecuted. No reasonable person can doubt that Christianity might have been extirpated in the Roman Empire. It spread, and became predominant, because the persecutions were only occasional, lasting but a short time, and separated by long intervals of almost undisturbed propagandism. It is a piece of idle sentimentality that truth, merely as truth, has any inherent power denied to error of prevailing against the dungeon and the stake. Men are not more zealous for truth than they often are for error, and a sufficient application of legal or even of social penalties will generally succeed in stopping the propagation of either. The real advantage which truth has consists in this, that when an opinion is true, it may be extinguished once, twice, or many times, but in the course of ages there will generally be found persons to rediscover it, until some one of its reappearances falls on a time when from favourable circumstances it escapes persecution until it has made such head as to withstand all subsequent attempts to suppress it. ∗ ∗ ∗

Let us now pass to the second division of the argument, and dismissing the supposition that any of the received opinions may be false, let us assume them to be true, and examine into the worth of the manner in which they are likely to be held, when their truth is not freely and openly canvassed. However unwillingly a person who has a strong opinion may admit the possibility that his opinion may be false, he ought to be moved by the consideration that, however true it may be, if it is not fully, frequently, and fearlessly discussed, it will be held as a dead dogma, not a living truth.

There is a class of persons (happily not quite so numerous as formerly) who think it enough if a person assents undoubtingly to what they think true, though he has no knowledge whatever of the grounds of the opinion, and could not make a tenable defence of it against the most superficial objections. Such persons, if they can once get their creed taught from authority, naturally think that no good, and some harm, comes of its being allowed to be questioned. Where their influence prevails, they make it nearly impossible for the received opinion to be rejected wisely and considerately, though it may still be rejected rashly and ignorantly; for to shut out discussion entirely is seldom possible, and when it once gets in, beliefs not grounded on conviction are apt to give way before the slightest semblance of an argument. Waiving, however, this possibility—assuming that the true opinion abides in the mind, but abides as a prejudice, a belief independent of, and proof against, argument—this is not the way in which truth ought to be held by a rational being. This is not knowing the truth. Truth, thus held, is but one superstition the more, accidentally clinging to the words which enunciate a truth.

If the intellect and judgment of mankind ought to be cultivated, a thing which Protestants at least do not deny, on what can these faculties be more appropriately exercised by any one, than on the things which concern him so much that it is considered necessary for him to hold opinions on them? If the cultivation of the understanding consists in one thing more than in another, it is surely in learning the grounds of one's own opinions. Whatever people believe, on subjects on which it is of the first importance to believe rightly, they ought to be able to defend against at least the common objections. But, some one may say, "Let them be *taught* the grounds of their opinions. It does not follow that opinions must be merely parroted because they are never heard controverted. Persons who learn geometry do not simply commit the theorems to memory, but understand and learn likewise the demonstrations; and it would be absurd to say that they remain ignorant of the grounds of geometrical truths, because they never hear any one deny, and attempt to disprove them." Undoubtedly: and such teaching suffices on a subject like mathematics, where there is nothing at all to he said on the wrong side of the question. The peculiarity of the evidence of mathematical truths is that all the argument is on one side. There are no objections, and no answers to objections. But on every subject on which difference of opinion is possible, the truth depends on a balance to be struck between two sets of conflicting reasons. Even in natural philosophy, there is always some other explanation possible of the same facts; some geocentric theory instead of heliocentric, some phlogiston instead of oxygen; and it has to be shown why that other theory cannot be the true one: and until this is shown, and until we know how it is shown, we do not understand the grounds of our opinion. But when we turn to subjects infinitely more complicated, to morals, religion, politics, social relations, and the business of life, three-fourths of the arguments for every disputed opinion consist in dispelling the appearances which favour some opinion different from it. The greatest orator, save one, of antiquity, has left it on record that he always studied his adversary's case with as great, if not still greater, intensity than even his own. What Cicero practised as the means of forensic success requires to be imitated by all who study any subject in order to arrive at the truth. He who knows only his own side of the case, knows little of that. His reasons may be good, and no one may have been able to refute them. But if he is equally unable to refute the reasons on the opposite side; if he does not so much as know what they are, he has no ground for preferring either opinion. The rational position for him would be suspension of judgment, and unless he contents himself with that, he is either led by authority, or adopts, like the generality of the world, the side to which he feels most inclination. Nor is it enough that he should hear the arguments of adversaries from his own teachers, presented as they state them, and accompanied by what they offer as refutations. That is not the way to do justice to the arguments, or bring them into real contact with his own mind. He must be able to hear them from persons who actually believe them; who defend them in earnest, and do their very utmost for them. He must know them in their most plausible and persuasive form; he must feel the whole force of the difficulty which the true view of the subject has to encounter and dispose of; else he will never really possess himself of the portion of truth which meets and removes that difficulty. Ninety-nine in a hundred of what are called educated men are in this condition; even of those who can argue fluently for their opinions. Their conclusion may be true, but it might be false for anything they know: they have never thrown themselves into the mental position of those who think differently from them, and considered what such persons may have to say; and consequently they do not, in any proper sense of the word, know the doctrine which they themselves profess. They do not know those parts of it which explain and justify the remainder; the considerations which show that a fact which seemingly conflicts with another is reconcilable with it, or that, of two apparently strong reasons, one and not the other ought to be preferred. All that part of the truth which turns the scale, and decides the judgment of a completely informed mind, they are strangers to; nor is it ever really known, but to those who have attended equally and impartially to both sides, and endeavoured to see the reasons of both in the strongest light. So essential is this discipline to a real understanding of moral and human subjects, that if opponents of all important truths do not exist, it is indispensable to imagine them, and supply them with the strongest arguments which the most skilful devil's advocate can conjure up. ✳ ✳ ✳

If, however, the mischievous operation of the absence of free discussion, when the received opinions are true, were confined to leaving men ignorant of the grounds of those opinions, it might be thought that this, if an intellectual, is no moral evil, and does not affect the worth of the opinions, regarded in their influence on the character. The fact, however, is, that not only the grounds of the opinion are forgotten in the absence of discussion, but too often the meaning of the opinion itself. The words which convey it cease to suggest ideas, or suggest only a small portion of those they were originally employed to communicate. Instead of a vivid conception and a living belief there remain only a few phrases retained by rote; or, if any part, the shell and husk only of the meaning is retained, the finer essence being lost. The great chapter in human history which this fact occupies and fills, cannot be too earnestly studied and meditated on.

It is illustrated in the experience of almost all ethical doctrines and religious creeds. They are all full of meaning and vitality to those who originate them, and to the direct disciples of the originators. Their meaning continues to be felt in undiminished strength, and is perhaps brought out into even fuller consciousness, so long as the struggle lasts to give the doctrine or creed an ascendancy over other creeds. At last it either prevails, and becomes the general opinion, or its progress stops; it keeps possession of the ground it has gained, but ceases to spread further. When either of these results has become apparent, controversy on the subject flags, and gradually dies away. The doctrine has taken its place, if not as a received opinion, as one of the admitted sects or divisions of opinion: those who hold it have generally inherited, not adopted it; and conversion from one of these doctrines to another, being now an exceptional fact, occupies little place in the thoughts their professors. Instead of being, as at first, constantly on the alert either to defend themselves against the world, or to bring the world over to them, they have subsided into acquiescence, and neither listen, when they can help it, to arguments against their creed, nor trouble dissentients (if there be such) with arguments in its favour. From this time may usually be dated the decline in the living power of the doctrine. We often bear the teachers of all creeds lamenting the difficulty of keeping up in the minds of believers a lively apprehension of the truth which they nominally recognise, so that it may penetrate the feelings, and acquire a real mastery over the conduct. No such difficulty is complained of while the creed is still fighting for its existence: even the weaker combatants then know and feel what they are fighting for, and the difference between it and other doctrines: and in that period of every creed's existence, not a few persons may be found, who have realised its fundamental principles in all the forms of thought, have weighed and considered them in all their important bearings, and have experienced the full effect on the character which belief in that creed ought to produce in a mind thoroughly imbued with it. But when it has come to be an hereditary creed, and to be received passively, not actively—when the mind is no longer compelled, in the same degree as at first, to exercise its vital powers on the questions which its belief presents to it, there is a progressive tendency to forget all of the belief except the formularies, or to give it a dull and torpid assent, as if accepting it on trust dispensed with the necessity of realising it in consciousness, or testing it by personal experience, until it almost ceases to connect itself at all with the inner life of the human being. Then are seen the cases, so frequent in this age of the world as almost to form the majority, in which the creed remains as it were outside the mind, incrusting and petrifying it against all other influences addressed to the higher parts of our nature; manifesting its power by not suffering any fresh and living conviction to get in, but itself doing nothing for the mind or heart, except standing sentinel over them to keep them vacant.

* * * Both teachers and learners go to sleep at their post, as soon as there is no enemy in the field.

* * * It is the fashion of the present time to disparage negative logic— that which points out weaknesses in theory or errors in practice, without establishing positive truths. Such negative criticism would indeed be poor enough as an ultimate result; but as a means to attaining any positive knowledge or conviction worthy the name, it cannot be valued too highly; and until people are again systematically trained to it, there will be few great thinkers, and a low general average of intellect, in any but the mathematical and physical departments of speculation. On any other subject no one's opinions deserve the name of knowledge, except so far as he has either had forced upon him by others, or gone through of himself, the same mental process which would have been required of him in carrying on an active controversy with opponents. That, therefore, which when absent, it is so indispensable, but so difficult, to create, how worse than absurd it is to forego, when spontaneously offering itself! If there are any persons who contest a received opinion, or who will do so if law or opinion will let them, let us thank them for it, open our minds to listen to them, and rejoice that there is some one to do for us what we otherwise ought, if we have any regard for either the certainty or the vitality of our convictions, to do with much greater labour for ourselves.

* * * We have hitherto considered only two possibilities: that the received opinion may be false, and some other opinion, consequently, true; or that, the received opinion being true, a conflict with the opposite error is essential to a clear apprehension and deep feeling of its truth. But there is a commoner case than either of these; when the conflicting doctrines, instead of being one true and the other false, share the truth between them; and the nonconforming opinion is needed to supply the remainder of the truth, of which the received doctrine embodies only a part. Popular opinions, on subjects not palpable to sense, are often true, but seldom or never the whole truth. They are a part of the truth; sometimes a greater, sometimes a smaller part, but exaggerated, distorted, and disjointed from the truths by which they ought to be accompanied and limited. Heretical opinions, on the other hand, are generally some of these suppressed and neglected truths, bursting the bonds which kept them down, and either seeking reconciliation with the truth contained in the common opinion, or fronting it as enemies, and setting themselves up, with similar exclusiveness, as the whole truth. The latter case is hitherto the most frequent, as, in the human mind, one-sidedness has always been the rule, and many-sidedness the exception. Hence, even in revolutions of opinion, one part of the truth usually sets while another rises. Even progress, which ought to superadd, for the most part only substitutes, one partial and incomplete truth for another; improvement consisting chiefly in this, that the new fragment of truth is more wanted, more adapted to the needs of the time, than that which it displaces. Such being the partial character of prevailing opinions, even when resting on a true foundation, every opinion which embodies somewhat of the portion of truth which the common opinion omits, ought to be considered precious, with whatever amount of error and confusion that truth may be blended. No sober judge of human affairs will feel bound to be indignant because those who force on our notice truths which we

should otherwise have overlooked, overlook some of those which we see. Rather, he will think that so long as popular truth is one-sided, it is more desirable than otherwise that unpopular truth should have one-sided assertors too; such being usually the most energetic, and the most likely to compel reluctant attention to the fragment of wisdom which they proclaim as if it were the whole. ✳ ✳ ✳

We have now recognised the necessity to the mental well-being of mankind (on which all their other well-being depends) of freedom of opinion, and freedom of the expression of opinion, on four distinct grounds; which we will now briefly recapitulate.

First, if any opinion is compelled to silence, that opinion may, for aught we can certainly know, be true. To deny this is to assume our own infallibility.

Secondly, though the silenced opinion be an error, it may, and very commonly does, contain a portion of truth; and since the general or prevailing opinion on any subject is rarely or never the whole truth, it is only by the collision of adverse opinions that the remainder of the truth has any chance of being supplied.

Thirdly, even if the received opinion be not only true, but the whole truth; unless it is suffered to be, and actually is, vigorously and earnestly contested, it will, by most of those who receive it, be held in the manner of a prejudice, with little comprehension or feeling of its rational grounds. And not only this, but, fourthly, the meaning of the doctrine itself will be in danger of being lost, or enfeebled, and deprived of its vital effect on the character and conduct; the dogma becoming a mere formal profession, inefficacious for good, but cumbering the ground, and preventing the growth of any real and heartfelt conviction, from reason or personal experience.

Before quitting the subject of freedom of opinion, it is fit to take some notice of those who say that the free expression of all opinions should be permitted, on condition that the manner be temperate, and do not pass the bounds of fair discussion. Much might be said on the impossibility of fixing where these supposed bounds are to be placed; for if the test be offence to those whose opinions are attacked, I think experience testifies that this offence is given whenever the attack is telling and powerful, and that every opponent who pushes them hard, and whom they find it difficult to answer, appears to them, if he shows any strong feeling on the subject, an intemperate opponent. But this, though an important consideration in a practical point of view, merges in a more fundamental objection. Undoubtedly the manner of asserting an opinion, even though it be a true one, may be very objectionable, and may justly incur severe censure. * * *

* * * An opinion that corn-dealers are starvers of the poor, or that private property is robbery, ought to be unmolested when simply circulated through the press, but may justly incur punishment when delivered orally to an excited mob assembled before the house of a corn-dealer, or when handed about among the same mob in the form of a placard. Acts, of whatever kind, which, without justifiable cause, do harm to others, may be, and in the more important cases absolutely require to be, controlled by the unfavourable sentiments, and, when needful, by the active interference of mankind. The liberty of the individual must be thus far limited; he must not make himself a nuisance to other people. But if he refrains from molesting others in what concerns them, and merely acts according to his own inclination and judgment in things which concern himself, the same reasons which show that opinion should be free, prove also that he should be allowed, without molestation, to carry his opinions into practice at his own cost.

STUDY QUESTIONS

1. What is lost, according to Mill, if we ban the expression of a false view?
2. Is Mill's utilitarian defense the best basis for arguing for free expression?
3. Under what circumstances, according to Mill, can free expression rightly be limited? Is his position defensible?

CATHARINE MACKINNON
Pornography, Civil Rights, and Speech

Catharine MacKinnon (b. 1946) is an American lawyer, radical feminist, and activist. She is known especially for her work with Andrea Dworkin on pornography.

I will first situate a critique of pornography within a feminist analysis of the condition of women. I will speak of what pornography means for the social status and treatment of women. * * *

* * * Once power constructs social reality, as I will show pornography constructs social reality of gender, the force behind sexism, the subordination in gender inequality, is made invisible; dissent from it becomes inaudible as well as rare. What a woman is, is defined in pornographic terms; this is what pornography *does*. If the law then looks neutrally on the reality of gender

so produced, the harm that has been done *will not be perceptible as harm.* It becomes just the way things are. * * *

In the philosophical terms of classical liberalism, an equality-freedom dilemma is produced: Freedom to make or consume pornography weighs against the equality of the sexes. Some people's freedom hurts other people's equality. * * * Equality for women is incompatible with a definition of men's freedom that is at our expense. What can freedom for women mean, so long as we remain unequal? Why should men's freedom to use us in this way be purchased with our second-class civil status?

I.

There is a belief that this is a society in which women and men are basically equals. Room for marginal corrections is conceded, flaws are known to exist, attempts are made to correct what are conceived as occasional lapses from the basic condition of sex equality. Sex discrimination law has centered most of its focus on these occasional lapses. It is difficult to overestimate the extent to which this belief in equality is an article of faith to most people, including most women, who wish to live in self-respect in an internal universe, even (perhaps especially) if not in the world. It is also partly an expression of natural law thinking: If we are inalienably equal, we can't "really" be degraded.

This is a world in which it is worth trying. In this world of presumptive equality, people make money based on their training or abilities or diligence or qualifications. They are employed and advanced on the basis of merit. In this world of just deserts, if someone is abused, it is thought to violate the basic rules of the community. If it doesn't, that person is seen to have done something she could have chosen to do differently, by exercise of will or better judgment. Maybe such people have placed themselves in a situation of vulnerability to physical abuse. Maybe they have done something provocative. Or maybe they were just unusually unlucky. In such a world, if such a person has an experience, there are words for it. When they speak and say it, they are listened to. If they write about it, they will be published. If there are certain experiences that are never spoken, or certain people or issues seldom heard from, it is supposed that silence has been chosen. The law, including much of the law of sex discrimination and the first amendment, operates largely within the realm of these beliefs.

Feminism is the discovery that women do not live in this world, that the person occupying this realm is a man, so much more a man if he is white and wealthy. This world of potential credibility, authority, security, and just rewards, recognition of one's identity and capacity, is a world that some people do inhabit as a condition of birth, with variations *among them*. It is not a basic condition accorded humanity in this society, but a prerogative of status, a privilege, among other things, of gender.

I call this a discovery because it has not been an assumption. Feminism is the first theory, the first practice, the first movement, to take seriously the situation of all women from the point of view of all women, both on our situation and on social life as a whole. * * *

Looking at the world from this point of view, a whole shadow world of previously invisible silent abuse has been discerned. Rape, battery, sexual harassment, forced prostitution, and the sexual abuse of children emerge as common and systematic. We find rape happens to women in all contexts, from the family, including rape of girls and babies, to students and women in the workplace, on the streets, at home, in their own bedrooms by men that they do not know, and by men that they do know, by men they are married to, men they have had a social conversation with, or, least often, men they have never seen before. Overwhelmingly, rape is something that men do or attempt to do to women (forty-four percent according to a recent study) at some point in our lives. Sexual harassment of women by men is common in workplaces and educational institutions. Up to eighty-five percent of women in one study report it, many in physical forms. Between a quarter and a third of women are battered in their homes by men. Thirty-eight percent of little girls are sexually molested inside or outside the family. Until women listened to women, this world of sexual abuse was *not spoken* of. It was the unspeakable. What I am saying is, if you *are* the tree falling in the epistemological forest, your demise doesn't make a sound if no one is listening. Women did not "report" these events, and overwhelmingly do not today, because no one is listening, because no one believes us. This silence does not mean nothing happened, and it does not mean consent. * * *

Men *are* damaged by sexism. (By men, I am referring to the status of masculinity which is accorded to males on the basis of their biology, but is not itself biological.) But whatever the damage of sexism is to men, the condition of being a man is not defined as subordinate to women by force. Looking at the facts of the abuses of women all at once, you see that a woman is socially defined as a person who, whether or not she is or has been, *can at any time* be treated in these ways by men, and little, if anything, will be done about it. This is what it means when feminists say that maleness is a form of power and femaleness is a form of powerlessness. * * *

I could describe this but I couldn't explain it until I started studying a lot of pornography. In pornography, there it is, in one place, all of the abuses that women had to struggle so long even to begin to articulate, all the *unspeakable* abuse: the rape, the battery, the sexual harassment, the prostitution, and the sexual abuse of children. Only in the pornography it is called something else: sex, sex, sex, sex, and sex, respectively. Pornography sexualizes rape, battery, sexual harassment, prostitution, and child sexual abuse; it thereby celebrates, promotes, authorizes, and legitimizes them. More generally, it eroticizes the dominance and submission that is the dynamic common to them all. It makes hierarchy sexy. * * *

* * * Pornography's world of equality is a harmonious and balanced place. Men and women are perfectly complementary and perfectly bipolar. Women's desire to be fucked by men is equal to men's desire to fuck women. All the ways men love to take and violate women, women love to be taken and violated. The women who most love this are most men's equals, the most liberated; the most participatory child is the most grown-up, the most equal to an adult. Their consent merely expresses or ratifies these preexisting facts.

* * * Women are there to be violated and possessed, men to violate and possess us either on screen or by camera or pen on behalf of the consumer. On a simple descriptive level, the inequality of hierarchy, of which gender is the primary one, seems necessary for the sexual arousal to work. * * *

What pornography *does* goes beyond its content: It eroticizes hierarchy, it sexualizes inequality. It makes dominance and submission sex. Inequality is its central dynamic; the illusion of freedom coming together with the reality of force is central to its working. * * *

From this perspective, pornography is neither harmless fantasy nor a corrupt and confused misrepresentation of an otherwise natural and healthy sexual situation. It institutionalizes the sexuality of male supremacy, fusing the erotization of dominance and submission with the social construction of male and female. To the extent that gender is sexual, pornography is part of constituting the meaning of that sexuality. Men treat women as who they see women as being. Pornography constructs who that is. Men's power over women means that the way men see women defines who women can be. Pornography is that way. * * *

* * * Pornography *participates* in its audience's eroticism through creating an accessible sexual object, the possession and consumption of which *is* male sexuality, as socially constructed; to be consumed and possessed as

which, *is* female sexuality, as socially constructed; and pornography is a process that constructs it that way.

✳✳✳ Pornography defines women by how we look according to how we can be sexually used. Pornography codes how to look at women, so you know what you can do with one when you see one. Gender is an assignment made visually, both originally and in everyday life. A sex object is defined on the basis of its looks, in terms of its usability for sexual pleasure, such that both the looking—the quality of the gaze, including its point of view—and the definition according to use become eroticized as part of the sex itself. This is what the feminist concept "sex object" means. In this sense, sex in life is no less mediated than it is in art. One could say men have sex with *their image* of a woman. It is not that life and art imitate each other; in this sexuality, they *are* each other.

✳✳✳ To defend pornography as consistent with the equality of the sexes is to defend the subordination of women to men as sexual equality. What in the pornographic view is love and romance looks a great deal like hatred and torture to the feminist. Pleasure and eroticism become violation. Desire appears as lust for dominance and submission. The vulnerability of women's projected sexual availability, that acting we are allowed (i.e. asking to be acted upon), is victimization. Play conforms to scripted roles. Fantasy expresses ideology, is not exempt from it. Admiration of natural physical beauty becomes objectification. Harmlessness becomes harm. Pornography is a harm of male supremacy made difficult to see because of its pervasiveness, potency, and, principally, because of its success in making the world a pornographic place. ✳✳✳

II.

Obscenity law provides a very different analysis and conception of the problem. In 1973, the legal definition of obscenity became that which

> the average person, applying contemporary community standards, would find that, taken as a whole, appeals to the prurient interest; that which depicts and describes in a patently offensive way [You feel like you're a cop reading someone's *Miranda* rights] sexual conduct as defined by the applicable state law; and that which, taken as a whole, lacks serious literary, artistic, political or scientific value.[1]

Feminism doubts whether the average gender-neutral person exists; has more questions about the content and process of defining what community standards are than it does about deviations from them; wonders why prurience counts but powerlessness does not, and why sensibilities are better

---

1   Miller v. California, 413 U.S. 15, 24 (1973).

protected from offense than women are from exploitation; defines sexuality, and thus its violation and expropriation, more broadly than does state law; and questions why a body of law which has not in practice been able to tell rape from intercourse should, without further guidance, be entrusted with telling pornography from anything less. Taking the work "as a whole" ignores that which the victims of pornography have long known: Legitimate settings diminish the injury perceived to be done to those whose trivialization and objectification it contextualizes. Besides, and this is a heavy one, if a woman is subjected, why should it matter that the work has other value? Maybe what redeems the work's value is what enhances its injury to women, not to mention that existing standards of literature, art, science, and politics, examined in a feminist light, are remarkably consonant with pornography's mode, meaning, and message. And finally—first and foremost, actually— although the subject of these materials is overwhelmingly women, their contents almost entirely comprised of women's bodies, our invisibility has been such, our equation as a sex *with* sex has been such, that the law of obscenity has never even considered pornography a woman's issue.

Obscenity, in this light, is a moral idea; an idea about judgments of good and bad. Pornography, by contrast, is a political practice, a practice of power and powerlessness. Obscenity is ideational and abstract; pornography is concrete and substantive. The two concepts represent two entirely different things. Nudity, excess of candor, arousal or excitement, prurient appeal, illegality of the acts depicted, and unnaturalness or perversion are all qualities that bother obscenity law when sex is depicted or portrayed. Sex forced on real women so that it can be sold at a profit to be forced on other real women; women's bodies trussed and maimed and raped and made into things to be hurt and obtained and accessed and this presented as the nature of women in a way that is acted on and acted out over and over; the coercion that is visible and the coercion that has become invisible—this and more bothers feminists about pornography. Obscenity as such probably does little harm. Pornography is integral to attitudes and behaviors of violence and discrimination which define the treatment and status of half the population.

III.

At the request of the city of Minneapolis, Andrea Dworkin and I conceived and designed a local human rights ordinance in accordance with our approach to the pornography issue. We define pornography as a practice of sex discrimination, a violation of women's civil rights, the opposite of sexual equality. Its point is to hold accountable, to those who are injured, those who profit from and benefit from that injury. It means that women's injury—our damage, our pain, our enforced inferiority—should outweigh their pleasure and their profits, or sex equality is meaningless.

We define pornography as the graphic sexually explicit subordination of women through pictures or words that also includes women dehumanized as sexual objects, things, or commodities, enjoying pain or humiliation or rape, being tied up, cut up, mutilated, bruised, or physically hurt, in postures of sexual submission or servility or display, reduced to body parts, penetrated by objects or animals, or presented in scenarios of degradation, injury, torture, shown as filthy or inferior, bleeding, bruised, or hurt in a context that makes these conditions sexual. Erotica, defined by distinction as not this, might be sexually explicit materials premised on equality. We also provide that the use of men, children or transsexuals in the place of women is pornography. The definition is substantive in that it is sex-specific, but it covers everyone in a sex-specific way, so is gender neutral in overall design. * * *

This law aspires to guarantee women's rights consistent with the first amendment by making visible a conflict of rights between the equality guaranteed to all women and what, in some legal sense, is now the freedom of the pornographers to make and sell, and their consumers to have access to, the materials this ordinance defines. Judicial resolution of this conflict, if they do for women what they have done for others, is likely to entail a balancing of the rights of women arguing that our lives and opportunities, including our freedom of speech and action, are constrained by—and in many cases flatly precluded by, in, and through—pornography, against those who argue that the pornography is harmless, or harmful only in part but not in the whole of the definition; or that it is more important to preserve the pornography than it is to prevent or remedy whatever harm it does.

* * * Pornography is a practice of discrimination on the basis of sex, on one level because of its role in creating and maintaining sex as a basis for discrimination. It harms many women one at a time and helps keep all women in an inferior status by defining our subordination as our sexuality and equating that with our gender. It is also sex discrimination because its victims, including men, are selected for victimization on the basis of their gender. But for their sex, they would not be so treated. * * *

Pornography does treat the sexes differently, so the case for sex differentiation can be made here. Men as a group do not tend to be (although some individuals may be) treated like women are treated in pornography. But as a social group, men are not hurt by pornography the way women as a social group are. ✳ ✳ ✳

The first victims of pornography are the ones in it. ✳ ✳ ✳ This is particularly true in visual media, where it takes a real person doing each act to make what you see. This is the double meaning in a statement one ex-prostitute made at our hearing: "[E]very single thing you see in pornography is happening to a real woman right now." Linda Marchiano, in her book *Ordeal*, recounts being coerced as "Linda Lovelace" into performing for "Deep Throat," a fabulously profitable film, by abduction, systematic beating, being kept prisoner, watched every minute, threatened with her life and the lives of her family if she left, tortured, and kept under constant psychological intimidation and duress. ✳ ✳ ✳

The further fact that prostitution and modeling are structurally women's best economic options should give pause to those who would consider women's presence there a true act of free choice. ✳ ✳ ✳ I will leave you wondering, with me, why it is that when a woman spreads her legs for a camera, what she is assumed to be exercising is free will. Women's freedom is rather substantively defined here. And as you think about the assumption of consent that follows women into pornography, look closely some time for the skinned knees, the bruises, the welts from the whippings, the scratches, the gashes. Many of them are not simulated. ✳ ✳ ✳

Coerced pornography models encounter devastating problems of lack of credibility because of a cycle of forced acts in which coercion into pornography is central. For example, children are typically forced to perform the acts in the pornography that is forced on them; photographs are taken of these rapes, photographs which are used to coerce the children into prostitution or into staying in prostitution, telling them that if they try to leave, the pictures will be shown to the authorities, their parents, their teachers, (whoever is *not* coercing them at the time) and no one will believe them. This gets them into prostitution and keeps them there. Understand, the documentation of the harm as it is being done is taken as evidence that no harm was done. Partly, desire for the abuse is attributed to the victim's nature from the fact of the abuse: She's a natural born whore; see, there she is chained to a bed. ✳ ✳ ✳

✳ ✳ ✳ Marchiano now tells that it took kidnapping and death threats and hypnosis to put her there, [and] that is found *difficult to believe*. The point is not only that when women can be coerced with impunity the results, when mass-produced, set standards that are devastating and dangerous for all women. The point is also that the assumptions that the law of the first amendment makes about adults—that adults are autonomous, self-defining, freely-acting, *equal* individuals—are exactly those qualities which pornography systematically denies and undermines for women. ✳✳✳ It is ✳✳✳ vicious to suggest, as many have, that women like Linda Marchiano should remedy their situations through the exercise of more speech. Pornography makes their speech impossible and where possible, worthless. Pornography makes women into objects. Objects do not speak. When they do, they are by then regarded as objects, not as humans, which is what it means to have no credibility. ✳✳✳

✳✳✳ Under the obscenity rubric, much legal and psychological scholarship has centered on a search for the elusive link between pornography defined as obscenity and harm. They have looked high and low—in the mind of the male consumer, in society or in its "moral fabric," in correlations between variations in levels of anti-social acts and liberalization of obscenity laws. The only harm they have found has been one they have attributed to "the social interest in order and morality." Until recently, no one looked very persistently for harm to women, particularly harm to women through men. The rather obvious fact that the sexes *relate* has been overlooked in the inquiry into the male consumer and his mind. The pornography doesn't just drop out of the sky, go into his head and stop there. Specifically, men rape, batter, prostitute, molest, and sexually harass women. Under conditions of inequality, they also hire, fire, promote, and grade women, decide how much or whether or not we are worth paying and for what, define and approve and disapprove of women in ways that count, that determine our lives. ✳✳✳

✳✳✳ Recent experimental research on pornography shows that the materials covered by our definition cause measurable harm to women through increasing men's attitudes and behaviors of discrimination in both violent and nonviolent forms. Exposure to some of the pornography in our definition increases normal men's immediately subsequent willingness to aggress against women under laboratory conditions. It makes normal men more closely resemble convicted rapists attitudinally, although as a group they don't look all that different from them to start with. It also significantly increases attitudinal measures known to correlate with rape and self-reports of aggressive acts, measures such as hostility toward women, propensity to rape, condoning rape, and predicting that one would rape or force sex on a woman if one knew one would not get caught. This latter measure, by the way, begins with rape at about a third of all men and moves to half with "forced sex."

As to that pornography covered by our definition in which normal research subjects seldom perceive violence, long-term exposure still makes them see women as more worthless, trivial, non-human, and object-like, i.e., the way those who are discriminated against are seen by those who discriminate against them. Crucially, all pornography by our definition acts dynamically over time to diminish one's ability to distinguish sex from violence. The materials work behaviorally to diminish the capacity of both men and women to perceive that an account of a rape is an account of a rape. X-only materials, in which subjects perceive no force, also increase perceptions that a rape victim is worthless and decrease the perception she was harmed. * * * Women are rendered fit for use and targeted for abuse. * * *

In our hearings, women spoke, to my knowledge for the first time in history in public, about the damage pornography does to them. We learned that pornography is used to break women, to train women to sexual submission, to season women, to terrorize women, and to silence their dissent. It is this that has previously been termed "having no effect." Men inflict on women the sex that they experience through the pornography in a way that gives women no choice about seeing the pornography or doing the sex. Asked if anyone ever tried to inflict sex acts on them they did not want that they knew came from pornography, ten percent of women in a recent random study said yes. Twenty-four percent of married women said yes. That is a lot of women. A lot more don't know. * * *

Pornography also hurts men's capacity to relate to women. * * *

* * * Substantively, pornography defines the meaning of what a woman is by connecting access to her sexuality with masculinity through orgasm. * * *

* * * Exceptions to the first amendment * * * exist. The reason they exist is that the harm done by some speech outweighs its expressive value, if any. * * * One can say—and I have—that pornography is a causal factor in violations of women; one can also say that women will be violated so long as pornography exists; but one can also say simply that pornography violates women. Perhaps this is what the woman had in mind who testified at our hearings that whether or not pornography causes violent acts to be perpetrated against some women is not her only issue. "Porn is already a violent act against women. It is our mothers, our daughters, our sisters, and our wives that are for sale for pocket change at the newsstands in this country." *Chaplinsky v. New Hampshire* recognizes the ability to restrict as "fighting words" speech which, "by [its] very utterance inflicts injury. . . . " Perhaps the only reason that pornography has not been "fighting words"—in the sense of words which by their utterance tend to incite immediate breach of the peace—is that women have seldom fought back, yet. * * *

The most basic assumption underlying first amendment adjudication is that, socially, speech is free. The first amendment says Congress shall not abridge the freedom of speech. Free speech, get it, *exists*. Those who wrote the first amendment *had* speech—they wrote the Constitution. *Their* problem was to keep it free from the only power that realistically threatened it: the federal government. They designed the first amendment to prevent government from constraining that which if unconstrained by government was free, meaning *accessible to them*. At the same time, we can't tell much about the intent of the Framers with regard to the question of women's speech, because I don't think we crossed their minds. It is consistent with this analysis that their posture to freedom of speech tends to presuppose that whole segments of the population are not systematically silenced, socially, prior to government action. If everyone's power were equal to theirs, if this were a non-hierarchical society, that might make sense. But the place of pornography in the inequality of the sexes makes the assumption of equal power untrue.

This is a hard question. It involves risks. Classically, opposition to censorship has involved keeping government off the backs of people. Our law is about getting some people off the backs of other people. The risks that it will be misused have to be measured against the risks of the status quo. Women will never have that dignity, security, compensation that is the promise of equality so long as the pornography exists as it does now. The situation of women suggests that the urgent issue of our freedom of speech is not primarily the avoidance of state intervention as such, but getting affirmative access to speech for those to whom it has been denied.

STUDY QUESTIONS

1. How does MacKinnon distinguish her critique of pornography from objections based on obscenity?
2. What, for MacKinnon, is the relation between pornography and powerlessness?
3. In what way, according to MacKinnon, does pornography silence women?

GREG LUKIANOFF AND JONATHAN HAIDT
The Coddling of the American Mind

Greg Lukianoff (b. 1974) is an American attorney and the president and CEO of the Foundation for Individual Rights in Education (FIRE). Jonathan Haidt (b. 1963) is an American social psychologist.

Something strange is happening at America's colleges and universities. A movement is arising, undirected and driven largely by students, to scrub campuses clean of words, ideas, and subjects that might cause discomfort or give offense. Last December, Jeannie Suk wrote in an online article for *The New Yorker* about law students asking her fellow professors at Harvard not to teach rape law—or, in one case, even use the word *violate* (as in "that violates the law") lest it cause students distress. In February, Laura Kipnis, a professor at Northwestern University, wrote an essay in *The Chronicle of Higher Education* describing a new campus politics of sexual paranoia—and was then subjected to a long investigation after students who were offended by the article and by a tweet she'd sent filed Title IX complaints against her. In June, a professor protecting himself with a pseudonym wrote an essay for Vox describing how gingerly he now has to teach. "I'm a Liberal Professor, and My Liberal Students Terrify Me," the headline said. A number of popular comedians, including Chris Rock, have stopped performing on college campuses. Jerry Seinfeld and Bill Maher have publicly condemned the oversensitivity of college students, saying too many of them can't take a joke.

Two terms have risen quickly from obscurity into common campus parlance. *Microaggressions* are small actions or word choices that seem on their face to have no malicious intent but that are thought of as a kind of violence nonetheless. For example, by some campus guidelines, it is a microaggression to ask an Asian American or Latino American "Where were you born?," because this implies that he or she is not a real American. *Trigger warnings* are alerts that professors are expected to issue if something in a course might cause a strong emotional response. For example, some students have called for warnings that Chinua Achebe's *Things Fall Apart* describes racial violence and that F. Scott Fitzgerald's *The Great Gatsby* portrays misogyny and physical abuse, so that students who have been previously victimized by racism or domestic violence can choose to avoid these works, which they believe might "trigger" a recurrence of past trauma.

Some recent campus actions border on the surreal. In April, at Brandeis University, the Asian American student association sought to raise awareness of microaggressions against Asians through an installation on the steps of an academic hall. The installation gave examples of microaggressions such as "Aren't you supposed to be good at math?" and "I'm colorblind! I don't see race." But a backlash arose among other Asian American students, who felt that the display itself was a microaggression. The association removed the installation, and its president wrote an e-mail to the entire student body apologizing to anyone who was "triggered or hurt by the content of the microaggressions."

This new climate is slowly being institutionalized, and is affecting what can be said in the classroom, even as a basis for discussion. During the 2014–15 school year, for instance, the deans and department chairs at the 10 University of California system schools were presented by administrators at faculty leader-training sessions with examples of microaggressions. The list of offensive statements included: "America is the land of opportunity" and "I believe the most qualified person should get the job."

The press has typically described these developments as a resurgence of political correctness. That's partly right, although there are important differences between what's happening now and what happened in the 1980s and '90s. That movement sought to restrict speech (specifically hate speech aimed at marginalized groups), but it also challenged the literary, philosophical, and historical canon, seeking to widen it by including more-diverse perspectives. The current movement is largely about emotional well-being. More than the last, it presumes an extraordinary fragility of the collegiate psyche, and therefore elevates the goal of protecting students from psychological harm. The ultimate aim, it seems, is to turn campuses into "safe spaces" where young adults are shielded from words and ideas that make some uncomfortable. And more than the last, this movement seeks to punish anyone who interferes with that aim, even accidentally. You might call this impulse *vindictive protectiveness*. It is creating a culture in which everyone must think twice before speaking up, lest they face charges of insensitivity, aggression, or worse.

* * * What are the effects of this new protectiveness *on the students themselves?* Does it benefit the people it is supposed to help? What exactly are students learning when they spend four years or more in a community that polices unintentional slights, places warning labels on works of classic literature, and in many other ways conveys the sense that words can be forms of violence that require strict control by campus authorities, who are expected to act as both protectors and prosecutors?

There's a saying common in education circles: Don't teach students *what* to think; teach them *how* to think. The idea goes back at least as far as Socrates. Today, what we call the Socratic method is a way of teaching that fosters critical thinking, in part by encouraging students to question their own unexamined beliefs, as well as the received wisdom of those around them. Such questioning sometimes leads to discomfort, and even to anger, on the way to understanding.

But vindictive protectiveness teaches students to think in a very different way. It prepares them poorly for professional life, which often demands intellectual engagement with people and ideas one might find uncongenial or wrong. The harm may be more immediate, too. A campus culture devoted to policing speech and punishing speakers is likely to engender patterns of thought that are surprisingly similar to those long identified by cognitive behavioral therapists as causes of depression and anxiety. The new protectiveness may be teaching students to think pathologically.

HOW DID WE GET HERE?

It's difficult to know exactly why vindictive protectiveness has burst forth so powerfully in the past few years. The phenomenon may be related to recent changes in the interpretation of federal antidiscrimination statutes (about which more later). But the answer probably involves generational shifts as well. Childhood itself has changed greatly during the past generation. Many Baby Boomers and Gen Xers can remember riding their bicycles around their home-towns, unchaperoned by adults, by the time they were 8 or 9 years old. In the hours after school, kids were expected to occupy themselves, getting into minor scrapes and learning from their experiences. But "free range" childhood be-came less common in the 1980s. The surge in crime from the '60s through the early '90s made Baby Boomer parents more protective than their own parents had been. Stories of abducted children appeared more frequently in the news, and in 1984, images of them began showing up on milk cartons. In response, many parents pulled in the reins and worked harder to keep their children safe.

The flight to safety also happened at school. Dangerous play structures were removed from playgrounds; peanut butter was banned from student lunches. After the 1999 Columbine massacre in Colorado, many schools cracked down on bullying, implementing "zero tolerance" policies. In a variety of ways, children born after 1980—the Millennials—got a consistent message from adults: life is dangerous, but adults will do everything in their power to protect you from harm, not just from strangers but from one another as well.

These same children grew up in a culture that was (and still is) becoming more politically polarized. Republicans and Democrats have never particu-larly liked each other, but survey data going back to the 1970s show that on average, their mutual dislike used to be surprisingly mild. Negative feelings have grown steadily stronger, however, particularly since the early 2000s. Political scientists call this process "affective partisan polarization," and it is a very serious problem for any democracy. As each side increasingly demonizes the other, compromise becomes more difficult. A recent study shows that implicit or unconscious biases are now at least as strong across political parties as they are across races.

So it's not hard to imagine why students arriving on campus today might be more desirous of protection and more hostile toward ideological opponents than in generations past. This hostility, and the self-righteousness fueled by strong partisan emotions, can be expected to add force to any moral crusade. A principle of moral psychology is that "morality binds and blinds." Part of what we do when we make moral judgments is express allegiance to a team. But that can interfere with our ability to think critically. Acknowledging that the other side's viewpoint has any merit is risky—your teammates may see you as a traitor.

Social media makes it extraordinarily easy to join crusades, express solidarity and outrage, and shun traitors. Facebook was founded in 2004, and since 2006 it has allowed children as young as 13 to join. This means that the first wave of students who spent all their teen years using Facebook reached college in 2011, and graduated from college only this year.

These first true "social-media natives" may be different from members of previous generations in how they go about sharing their moral judgments and supporting one another in moral campaigns and conflicts. We find much to like about these trends; young people today are engaged with one another, with news stories, and with prosocial endeavors to a greater degree than when the dominant technology was television. But social media has also fundamentally shifted the balance of power in relationships between students and faculty; the latter increasingly fear what students might do to their reputations and careers by stirring up online mobs against them.

We do not mean to imply simple causation, but rates of mental illness in young adults have been rising, both on campus and off, in recent decades. ⁂ Students seem to be reporting more emotional crises; many seem fragile, and this has surely changed the way university faculty and administrators interact with them. The question is whether some of those changes might be doing more harm than good.

THE THINKING CURE

For millennia, philosophers have understood that we don't see life as it is; we see a version distorted by our hopes, fears, and other attachments. The Buddha said, "Our life is the creation of our mind." Marcus Aurelius said, "Life itself is but what you deem it." The quest for wisdom in many traditions begins with this insight. Early Buddhists and the Stoics, for example, developed practices for reducing attachments, thinking more clearly, and finding release from the emotional torments of normal mental life.

Cognitive behavioral therapy is a modern embodiment of this ancient wisdom. It is the most extensively studied nonpharmaceutical treatment of mental illness, and is used widely to treat depression, anxiety disorders, eating disorders, and addiction. It can even be of help to schizophrenics. No other form of psychotherapy has been shown to work for a broader range of problems. Studies have generally found that it is as effective as antidepressant drugs (such as Prozac) in the treatment of anxiety and depression. The therapy is relatively quick and easy to learn; after a few months of training, many patients can do it on their own. Unlike drugs, cognitive behavioral therapy keeps working long after treatment is stopped, because it teaches thinking skills that people can continue to use.

The goal is to minimize distorted thinking and see the world more accurately. You start by learning the names of the dozen or so most common cognitive distortions (such as overgeneralizing, discounting positives, and emotional reasoning). Each time you notice yourself falling prey to one of them, you name it, describe the facts of the situation, consider alternative interpretations, and then choose an interpretation of events more in line with those facts. Your emotions follow your new interpretation. In time, this process becomes automatic. When people improve their mental hygiene in this way—when they free themselves from the repetitive irrational thoughts that had previously filled so much of their consciousness—they become less depressed, anxious, and angry.

The parallel to formal education is clear: cognitive behavioral therapy teaches good critical-thinking skills, the sort that educators have striven for so long to impart. By almost any definition, critical thinking requires grounding one's beliefs in evidence rather than in emotion or desire, and learning how to search for and evaluate evidence that might contradict one's initial hypothesis. But does campus life today foster critical thinking? Or does it coax students to think in more-distorted ways? * * *

HIGHER EDUCATION'S EMBRACE OF "EMOTIONAL REASONING"

* * * Emotional reasoning dominates many campus debates and discussions. A claim that someone's words are "offensive" is not just an expression of one's own subjective feeling of offendedness. It is, rather, a public charge

that the speaker has done something objectively wrong. It is a demand that the speaker apologize or be punished by some authority for committing an offense.

There have always been some people who believe they have a right not to be offended. Yet throughout American history—from the Victorian era to the free-speech activism of the 1960s and '70s—radicals have pushed boundaries and mocked prevailing sensibilities. Sometime in the 1980s, however, college campuses began to focus on preventing offensive speech, especially speech that might be hurtful to women or minority groups. The sentiment underpinning this goal was laudable, but it quickly produced some absurd results.

Among the most famous early examples was the so-called water-buffalo incident at the University of Pennsylvania. In 1993, the university charged an Israeli-born student with racial harassment after he yelled "Shut up, you water buffalo!" to a crowd of black sorority women that was making noise at night outside his dorm-room window. Many scholars and pundits at the time could not see how the term *water buffalo* (a rough translation of a Hebrew insult for a thoughtless or rowdy person) was a racial slur against African Americans, and as a result, the case became international news.

Claims of a right not to be offended have continued to arise since then, and universities have continued to privilege them. In a particularly egregious 2008 case, for instance, Indiana University-Purdue University at Indianapolis found a white student guilty of racial harassment for reading a book titled *Notre Dame vs. the Klan*. The book honored student opposition to the Ku Klux Klan when it marched on Notre Dame in 1924. Nonetheless, the picture of a Klan rally on the book's cover offended at least one of the student's co-workers (he was a janitor as well as a student), and that was enough for a guilty finding by the university's Affirmative Action Office.

These examples may seem extreme, but the reasoning behind them has become more commonplace on campus in recent years. Last year, at the University of St. Thomas, in Minnesota, an event called Hump Day, which would have allowed people to pet a camel, was abruptly canceled. Students had created a Facebook group where they protested the event for animal cruelty, for being a waste of money, and for being insensitive to people from the Middle East. The inspiration for the camel had almost certainly come from a popular TV commercial in which a camel saunters around an office on a Wednesday, celebrating "hump day"; it was devoid of any reference to Middle Eastern peoples. Nevertheless, the group organizing the event announced on its Facebook page that the event would be canceled because the "program [was] dividing people and would make for an uncomfortable and possibly unsafe environment."

Because there is a broad ban in academic circles on "blaming the victim," it is generally considered unacceptable to question the reasonableness (let alone the sincerity) of someone's emotional state, particularly if those emotions are linked to one's group identity. The thin argument "I'm offended" becomes an unbeatable trump card. This leads to what [journalist] Jonathan Rauch ∗ ∗ ∗ calls the "offendedness sweepstakes," in which opposing parties use claims of offense as cudgels. In the process, the bar for what we consider unacceptable speech is lowered further and further.

Since 2013, new pressure from the federal government has reinforced this trend. Federal antidiscrimination statutes regulate on-campus harassment and unequal treatment based on sex, race, religion, and national origin. Until recently, the Department of Education's Office for Civil Rights acknowledged that speech must be "objectively offensive" before it could be deemed actionable as sexual harassment—it would have to pass the "reasonable person" test. To be prohibited, the office wrote in 2003, allegedly harassing speech would have to go "beyond the mere expression of views, words, symbols or thoughts that some person finds offensive."

But in 2013, the Departments of Justice and Education greatly broadened the definition of sexual harassment to include verbal conduct that is simply "unwelcome." Out of fear of federal investigations, universities are now applying that standard—defining unwelcome speech as harassment—not just to sex, but to race, religion, and veteran status as well. Everyone is supposed to rely upon his or her own subjective feelings to decide whether a comment by a professor or a fellow student is unwelcome, and therefore grounds for a harassment claim. Emotional reasoning is now accepted as evidence.

If our universities are teaching students that their emotions can be used effectively as weapons—or at least as evidence in administrative proceedings—then they are teaching students to nurture a kind of hypersensitivity that will lead them into countless drawn-out conflicts in college and beyond. Schools may be training students in thinking styles that will damage their careers and friendships, along with their mental health.

FORTUNE-TELLING AND TRIGGER WARNINGS

Burns defines *fortune-telling* as "anticipat[ing] that things will turn out badly" and feeling "convinced that your prediction is an already-established fact." Leahy, Holland, and McGinn define it as "predict[ing] the future negatively" or seeing potential danger in an everyday situation. The recent spread of demands for trigger warnings on reading assignments with provocative content is an example of fortune-telling.

The idea that words (or smells or any sensory input) can trigger searing memories of past trauma—and intense fear that it may be repeated—has been around at least since World War I, when psychiatrists began treating soldiers for what is now called post-traumatic stress disorder. But explicit trigger warnings are believed to have originated much more recently, on message boards in the early days of the Internet. Trigger warnings became particularly prevalent in self-help and feminist forums, where they allowed readers who had suffered from traumatic events like sexual assault to avoid graphic content that might trigger flashbacks or panic attacks. Search-engine trends indicate that the phrase broke into mainstream use online around 2011, spiked in 2014, and reached an all-time high in 2015. The use of trigger warnings on campus appears to have followed a similar trajectory; seemingly overnight, students at universities across the country have begun demanding that their professors issue warnings before covering material that might evoke a negative emotional response.

In 2013, a task force composed of administrators, students, recent alumni, and one faculty member at Oberlin College, in Ohio, released an online resource guide for faculty (subsequently retracted in the face of faculty pushback) that included a list of topics warranting trigger warnings. These topics included classism and privilege, among many others. The task force recommended that materials that might trigger negative reactions among students be avoided altogether unless they "contribute directly" to course goals, and suggested that works that were "too important to avoid" be made optional.

It's hard to imagine how novels illustrating classism and privilege could provoke or reactivate the kind of terror that is typically implicated in PTSD. Rather, trigger warnings are sometimes demanded for a long list of ideas and attitudes that some students find politically offensive, in the name of preventing other students from being harmed. This is an example of what psychologists call "motivated reasoning"—we spontaneously generate arguments for conclusions we want to support. Once *you* find something hateful, it is easy to argue that exposure to the hateful thing could trauma-tize some *other* people. You believe that you know how others will react, and that their reaction could be devastating. Preventing that devastation becomes a moral obligation for the whole community. Books for which students have called publicly for trigger warnings within the past couple of years include Virginia Woolf's *Mrs. Dalloway* (at Rutgers, for "suicidal inclinations") and Ovid's *Metamorphoses* (at Columbia, for sexual assault).

Jeannie Suk's *New Yorker* essay described the difficulties of teaching rape law in the age of trigger warnings. Some students, she wrote, have pressured their professors to avoid teaching the subject in order to protect themselves and their classmates from potential distress. Suk compares this to trying to teach "a medical student who is training to be a surgeon but who fears that he'll become distressed if he sees or handles blood."

However, there is a deeper problem with trigger warnings. According to the most-basic tenets of psychology, the very idea of helping people with anxiety disorders avoid the things they fear is misguided. A person who is trapped in an elevator during a power outage may panic and think she is going to die. That frightening experience can change neural connections in her amygdala, leading to an elevator phobia. If you want this woman to retain her fear for life, you should help her avoid elevators.

But if you want to help her return to normalcy, you should take your cues from Ivan Pavlov and guide her through a process known as expo-sure therapy. You might start by asking the woman to merely look at an elevator from a distance—standing in a building lobby, perhaps—until her apprehension begins to subside. If nothing bad happens while she's standing in the lobby—if the fear is not "reinforced"—then she will begin to learn a new association: elevators are not dangerous. (This reduction in fear during exposure is called habituation.) Then, on subsequent days, you might ask her to get closer, and on later days to push the call button, and eventually to step in and go up one floor. This is how the amygdala can get rewired again to associate a previously feared situation with safety or normalcy.

Students who call for trigger warnings may be correct that some of their peers are harboring memories of trauma that could be reactivated by course readings. But they are wrong to try to prevent such reactivations. Students with PTSD should of course get treatment, but they should not try to avoid normal life, with its many opportunities for habituation. Classroom discus-sions are safe places to be exposed to incidental reminders of trauma (such as the word *violate*). A discussion of violence is unlikely to be followed by actual violence, so it is a good way to help students change the associations that are causing them discomfort. And they'd better get their habituation done in college, because the world beyond college will be far less willing to accommodate requests for trigger warnings and opt-outs.

The expansive use of trigger warnings may also foster unhealthy mental habits in the vastly larger group of students who do not suffer from PTSD or other anxiety disorders. People acquire their fears not just from their own past experiences, but from social learning as well. If everyone around you acts as though something is dangerous—elevators, certain neighborhoods, novels depicting racism—then you are at risk of acquiring that fear too. The psychiatrist Sarah Roff pointed this out last year in an online article for *The Chronicle of Higher Education*. "One of my biggest concerns about trigger warnings," Roff wrote, "is that they will apply not just to those who have experienced trauma, but to all students, creating an atmosphere in which they are encouraged to believe that there is something dangerous or damaging about discussing difficult aspects of our history."

In an article published last year by *Inside Higher Ed*, seven humanities professors wrote that the trigger-warning movement was "already having a chilling effect on [their] teaching and pedagogy." They reported their colleagues' receiving "phone calls from deans and other administrators investigating student complaints that they have included 'triggering' material in their courses, with or without warnings." A trigger warning, they wrote, "serves as a guarantee that students will not experience unexpected discomfort and implies that if they do, a contract has been broken." When students come to *expect* trigger warnings for any material that makes them uncomfortable, the easiest way for faculty to stay out of trouble is to avoid material that might upset the most sensitive student in the class. ✳ ✳ ✳

WHAT CAN WE DO NOW?

Attempts to shield students from words, ideas, and people that might cause them emotional discomfort are bad for the students. They are bad for the workplace, which will be mired in unending litigation if student expectations of safety are carried forward. And they are bad for American democracy, which is already paralyzed by worsening partisanship. When the ideas, values, and speech of the other side are seen not just as wrong but as willfully aggressive toward innocent victims, it is hard to imagine the kind of mutual respect, negotiation, and compromise that are needed to make politics a positive-sum game.

Rather than trying to protect students from words and ideas that they will inevitably encounter, colleges should do all they can to equip students to thrive in a world full of words and ideas that they cannot control. One of the great truths taught by Buddhism (and Stoicism, Hinduism, and many other traditions) is that you can never achieve happiness by making the world conform to your desires. But you can master your desires and habits of thought. This, of course, is the goal of cognitive behavioral therapy. With this in mind, here are some steps that might help reverse the tide of bad thinking on campus.

The biggest single step in the right direction does not involve faculty or university administrators, but rather the federal government, which should release universities from their fear of unreasonable investigation and sanctions by the Department of Education. Congress should define peer-on-peer harassment according to the Supreme Court's definition in the 1999 case *Davis v. Monroe County Board of Education*. The *Davis* standard holds that a single comment or thoughtless remark by a student does not equal harassment; harassment requires a pattern of objectively offensive behavior by one student that interferes with another student's access to education. Establishing the *Davis* standard would help eliminate universities' impulse to police their students' speech so carefully.

Universities themselves should try to raise consciousness about the need to balance freedom of speech with the need to make all students feel welcome. Talking openly about such conflicting but important values is just the sort of challenging exercise that any diverse but tolerant community must learn to do. Restrictive speech codes should be abandoned.

Universities should also officially and strongly discourage trigger warnings. They should endorse the American Association of University Professors' report on these warnings, which notes, "The presumption that students need to be protected rather than challenged in a classroom is at once infantilizing and anti-intellectual." Professors should be free to use trigger warnings if they choose to do so, but by explicitly discouraging the practice, universities would help fortify the faculty against student requests for such warnings.

Finally, universities should rethink the skills and values they most want to impart to their incoming students. At present, many freshman-orientation programs try to raise student sensitivity to a nearly impossible level. Teaching students to avoid giving unintentional offense is a worthy goal, especially when the students come from many different cultural backgrounds. But students should also be taught how to live in a world full of potential offenses. Why not teach incoming students how to practice cognitive behavioral therapy? Given high and rising rates of mental illness, this simple step would be among the most humane and supportive things a university could do. The cost and time commitment could be kept low: a few group training sessions could be supplemented by Web sites or apps. But the outcome could pay dividends in many ways. For example, a shared vocabulary about reasoning, common distortions, and the appropriate use of evidence to draw conclusions would facilitate critical thinking and real debate. It would also tone down the perpetual state of outrage that seems to engulf some colleges these days, allowing students' minds to open more widely to new ideas and new people. A greater commitment to formal, public debate on campus—and to the assembly of a more politically diverse faculty—would further serve that goal.

Thomas Jefferson, upon founding the University of Virginia, said:

> This institution will be based on the illimitable freedom of the human mind. For here we are not afraid to follow truth wherever it may lead, nor to tolerate any error so long as reason is left free to combat it.

We believe that this is still—and will always be—the best attitude for American universities. Faculty, administrators, students, and the federal government all have a role to play in restoring universities to their historic mission.

STUDY QUESTIONS

1. What do the authors mean by "trigger warnings" and "microaggressions"?
2. What is "vindictive protectiveness"?
3. Why might overprotectiveness be harmful to those who are protected?

■ Compare and Contrast Questions

1. Does John Stuart Mill's argument for freedom of expression mean that it would be wrong to prohibit pornography in the sense in which Catharine MacKinnon defines it?
2. Does Lukianoff and Haidt's argument have the consequence that individuals opposed to pornography ought to be exposed to it?
3. Would John Stuart Mill agree with Lukianoff and Haidt's arguments?

SEXUAL MORALITY

The three papers in this section consider the distinction between fully consensual sex and sex that crosses the line into a form of assault. There are of course very clear cases of sexual assault, but these papers are more concerned with cases at the margins. We start with Lois Pineau's attempt to understand the circumstances in the gray area between fully consensual sex and aggressive rape, commonly known as "date rape"; nonconsensual sex that does not involve violence, physical pressure, or its threat. Conventionally, whether an act counts as date rape has been regarded as a matter of whether valid consent was given. Yet silent submission is often taken as consent, and what really amounts to assault can sometimes be confused with seduction. A woman might "go along with" a man's overbearingness because her resistance is worn down and she fears worse if she doesn't, but it would be highly problematic to count her acquiescence as consent. Furthermore, Pineau also argues that a woman who has engaged in sexually provocative behavior has not, simply in virtue of that behavior, in effect consented to sex. Such beliefs, she thinks, generate a series of myths that often wrongly excuse men's behavior, through a "she asked for it" defense.

Pineau argues that for sex to go well it is important that both parties should understand, and take on as their own, the other person's ends and desires, without paternalism or manipulation. This suggests that communication needs to be at the heart of sexual relations. Sex, therefore, must be conceived of as a communicative activity. Pineau argues that the notion of consent relevant to sex should be understood in this communicative fashion, rather than modeled on the negotiation and bargaining typical of a commercial contract. Pineau calls this "communicative sexuality." It means that genuine conversation and discussion will typically be part of a communicative sexual act, and the question of whether date rape took place should focus not on the simple yes/no of consent but on the nature of the entire communication between the parties.

Nicholas Dixon builds on Pineau's analysis to consider the role of alcohol and sexual consent. The *actus reus*—guilty act—of rape is sex without consent. The *mens rea*, or guilty mind, requires that the act took place "intentionally, knowingly, recklessly, or negligently." The question Dixon considers is how a woman's consumption of alcohol can affect both the *actus reus* and the *mens rea*. At one extreme, a woman could be so incapacitated by alcohol that she is unable to give meaningful consent, and to have sex with someone in that condition should normally count as rape. At the other extreme, a woman may have her inhibitions relaxed by drinking a little more than she is used to; she therefore consents but later regrets it. This should not count as rape. But where is the line to be drawn? Dixon uses the term "impaired sex" for an intermediate case in which a woman is significantly under the effects of alcohol but still able to act for herself. If the man deliberately got her drunk, then arguably the case meets the conditions for rape, but is less clear in examples where this is not the case. Dixon argues that Pineau's notion of communicative sexuality shows that impaired sex can be sexual assault, for merely saying "yes" when drunk cannot always be taken as a sign of real consent.

Dixon then moves on to ask whether a man should be punished for engaging in impaired sex, discussing a range of different circumstances. He notes the great difficulties in framing a law that can define what it is for a woman to be so intoxicated that she is not able to give meaningful consent but is still able to act. It can also be very difficult for a man to be able to judge how much a woman has drunk, and as a result laws in this area would be fraught with difficulty and the possibility of false conviction. Hence Dixon argues that impaired sex should be dealt with by strong moral disapproval rather than legal punishment.

Conor Kelly's topic is the "hookup culture": the practice, said to be increasingly prevalent on U.S. campuses, of sexual activity with no expectation of a longer-term relationship. Reactions range from appalled moralism to enthusiastic endorsement of the practice as an expression of female liberation. Approaching the issues from the standpoint of feminist theory, Kelly argues that typical features of the hookup culture reveal its sexist nature.

According to Kelly, four features of the hookup culture work against the interests of women. The first is a lack of commitment. This is welcomed by many participants because early emotional attachment to a partner may well stand in the way of ambition and pursuit of a career. The second is an acceptance of ambiguity. What, after all, is a "hookup"? It could mean anything from "fairly chaste making out" to sexual intercourse. Hence when two people report that they have hooked up, they can be understood in different ways by their different audiences. The third is a role for alcohol, which often allows people to take the view that they were less responsible for their actions than they would otherwise be. And finally, there is social pressure to conform, which makes it very difficult to have any type of relationship that does not follow the hookup culture's "script."

While the hookup culture may seem to offer freedom and independence, Kelly argues that a feminist perspective reveals several problems. It is argued that, despite appearances, it is impossible to remove emotional attachment completely and the pretense of doing so is damaging. Further, many women, over time, would wish to develop longer-term relationships, but the hookup culture stands in the way. The use of alcohol and ambiguous language also are said to work against women's interests. Together, Kelly argues, these features combine so that the hookup culture is a form of sexism that produces the perception of freedom but without the reality.

LOIS PINEAU
Date Rape: A Feminist Analysis

Lois Pineau was formerly a professor of philosophy at Kansas State University.

Date rape is nonaggravated sexual assault, nonconsensual sex that does not involve physical injury, or the explicit threat of physical injury. But because it does not involve physical injury, and because physical injury is often the only criterion that is accepted as evidence that the *actus reas* is nonconsensual, what is really sexual assault is often mistaken for seduction. * * *

* * * The criteria for consent continues to be the central concern of discourse on sexual assault. * * *

THE PROBLEM OF THE CRITERION

The reasoning that underlies the present criterion of consent is entangled in a number of mutually supportive mythologies which see sexual assault as masterful seduction, and silent submission as sexual enjoyment. * * * This * * * has given rise to a network of rationalizations that support the conflation of assault with seduction, submission with enjoyment. I therefore want to begin my argument by providing an example which shows both why it is so difficult to make this distinction, and that it exists. * * *

> The woman I have in mind agrees to see someone because she feels an initial attraction to him and believes that he feels that same way about her. She goes out with him in the hope that there will be mutual enjoyment and in the

course of the day or evening an increase of mutual interest. Unfortunately, these hopes of *mutual* and *reciprocal* interest are not realized. We do not know how much interest she has in him by the end of their time together, but whatever her feelings she comes under pressure to have sex with him, and she does not want to have the kind of sex he wants. She may desire to hold hands and kiss, to engage in more intense caresses or in some form of foreplay, or she may not want to be touched. She may have reasons unrelated to desire for not wanting to engage in the kind of sex he is demanding. She may have religious reservations, concerns about pregnancy or disease, a disinclination to be just another conquest. She may be engaged in a seduction program of her own which sees abstaining from sexual activity as a means of building an important emotional bond. She feels she is desirable to him, and she knows, and he knows that he will have sex with her if he can. And while she feels she doesn't owe him anything, and that it is her prerogative to refuse him, this feeling is partly a defensive reaction against a deeply held belief that if he is in need, she should provide. If she buys into the myth of insistent male sexuality she may feel he is suffering from sexual frustration and that she is largely to blame.

We do not know how much he desires her, but we do know that his desire for erotic satisfaction can hardly be separated from his desire for conquest. He feels no dating obligation, but has a strong commitment to scoring. He uses the myth of "so hard to control" male desire as a rhetorical tactic, telling her how frustrated she will leave him. He becomes overbearing. She resists, voicing her disinclination. He alternates between telling her how desirable she is and taking a hostile stance, charging her with misleading him, accusing her of wanting him, and being coy, in short of being deceitful, all the time engaging in rather aggressive body contact. It is late at night, she is tired and a bit queasy from too many drinks, and he is reaffirming her suspicion that perhaps she has misled him. She is having trouble disengaging his body from hers, and wishes he would just go away. She does not adopt a strident angry stance, partly because she thinks he is acting normally and does not deserve it, partly because she feels she is partly to blame, and partly because there is always the danger that her anger will make him angry, possibly violent. It seems that the only thing to do, given his aggression, and her queasy fatigue, is to go along with him and get it over with, but this decision is so entangled with the events in process it is hard to know if it is not simply a recognition of what is actually happening. She finds the whole encounter a thoroughly disagreeable experience, but he does not take any notice, and wouldn't have changed course if he had. He congratulates himself on his sexual prowess and is confirmed in his opinion that aggressive tactics pay off. Later she feels that she has been raped, but paradoxically tells herself that she let herself be raped.

The paradoxical feelings of the woman in our example indicate her awareness that what she feels about the incident stands in contradiction to the prevailing cultural assessment of it. She knows that she did not want to have sex with her date. She is not so sure, however, about how much her own desires count, and she is uncertain that she has made her desires clear. Her uncertainty is reinforced by the cultural reading of this incident as an ordinary seduction.

As for us, we assume that the woman did not want to have sex, but just like her, we are unsure whether her mere reluctance, in the presence of high-pressure tactics, constitutes nonconsent. We suspect that submission to an overbearing and insensitive lout is no way to go about attaining sexual enjoyment, and we further suspect that he felt no compunction about providing it, so that on the face of it, from the outside looking in, it looks like a pretty unreasonable proposition for her.

Let us look at this reasoning more closely. Assume that she was not attracted to the kind of sex offered by the sort of person offering it. Then it would be *prima facie* unreasonable for her to agree to have sex, unreasonable, that is, unless she were offered some pay-off for her stoic endurance, money perhaps, or tickets to the opera. The reason is that in sexual matters, agreement is closely connected to attraction. Thus, where the presumption is that she was not attracted, we should at the same time presume that she did not consent. Hence, the burden of proof should be on her alleged assailant to show that she had good reasons for consenting to an unattractive proposition.

This is not, however, the way such situations are interpreted. In the unlikely event that the example I have described should come before the courts, there is little doubt that the law would interpret the woman's eventual acquiescence or "going along with" the sexual encounter as consent. But along with this interpretation would go the implicit understanding that she had consented because when all was said and done, when the "token" resistances to the "masterful advances" had been made she had wanted to after all. Once the courts have constructed this interpretation, they are then forced to conjure up some horror story of feminine revenge in order to explain why she should bring charges against her "seducer."

In the even more unlikely event that the courts agreed that the woman had not consented to the above encounter, there is little chance that her assailant would be convicted of sexual assault. The belief that the man's aggressive tactics are a normal part of seduction means that *mens rea* cannot be established. Her eventual "going along" with his advances constitutes reasonable grounds for his believing in her consent. These "reasonable" grounds attest to the sincerity of his belief in her consent. ✳✳✳ The sympathy of the court is more likely to lie with the rapist than with his victim, since, if the court is typical, it will be strongly inclined to believe that the victim had in some way "asked for it."

The position of the courts is supported by the widespread belief that male aggression and female reluctance are normal parts of seduction. Given their acceptance of this model, the logic of their response must be respected. For if sexual aggression is a part of ordinary seduction, then it cannot be inconsistent with the legitimate consent of the person allegedly seduced by this means. And if it is normal for a woman to be reluctant, then this reluctance must be consistent with her consent as well. The position of the courts is not inconsistent just so long as they allow that some sort of protest on the part of a woman counts as a refusal. As we have seen, however, it frequently happens that no sort of a protest would count as a refusal. Moreover, if no sort of protest, or at least if precious few count, then the failure to register these protests will amount to "asking for it," it will amount, in other words, to agreeing. ✳✳✳

RAPE MYTHS

The claim that the victim provoked a sexual incident, that "she asked for it," is by far the most common defence given by men who are accused of sexual assault. Feminists, rightly incensed by this response, often treat it as beneath contempt. ✳✳✳

The least sophisticated of the "she asked for it" rationales, and in a sense, the easiest to deal with, appeals to an injunction against sexually provocative behaviour on the part of women. If women should not be sexually provocative, then, from this standpoint, a woman who is sexually provocative deserves to suffer the consequences. Now it will not do to respond that women get raped even when they are not sexually provocative, or that it is men who get to interpret (unfairly) what counts as sexually provocative. The question should be: Why shouldn't a woman be sexually provocative? Why should this behaviour warrant any kind of aggressive response whatsoever?

Attempts to explain that women have a right to behave in sexually provocative ways without suffering dire consequences still meet with surprisingly tough resistance. Even people who find nothing wrong or sinful with sex itself, in any of its forms, tend to suppose that women must not behave sexually unless they are prepared to carry through on some fuller course of sexual interaction. The logic of this response seems to be that at some point a woman's behaviour commits her to following through on the full course of a sexual encounter as it is defined by her assailant. At some point she has made an agreement, or formed a contract, and once that is done, her contractor is entitled to demand that she satisfy the terms of that contract. ✳ ✳ ✳ But we do not normally suppose that casual nonverbal behaviour generates agreements. Nor do we normally grant private persons the right to enforce contracts. What rationale would support our conclusion in this case?

The rationale, I believe, comes in the form of a belief in the especially insistent nature of male sexuality, an insistence which lies at the root of natural male aggression, and which is extremely difficult, perhaps impossible to contain. At a certain point in the arousal process, it is thought, a man's rational will gives way to the prerogatives of nature. His sexual need can and does reach a point where it is uncontrollable, and his natural masculine aggression kicks in to assure that this need is met. Women, however, are naturally more contained, and so it is their responsibility not to provoke the irrational in the male. If they do go so far as that, they have both failed in their responsibilities, and subjected themselves to the inevitable. One does not go into the lion's cage and expect not to be eaten. ✳ ✳ ✳

This belief about the normal aggressiveness of male sexuality is complemented by common knowledge about female gender development. Once, women were taught to deny their sexuality and to aspire to ideals of chastity. Things have not changed so much. Women still tend to eschew conquest mentalities in favour of a combination of sex and affection. Insofar as this is thought to be merely a cultural requirement, however, there is an expectation that women will be coy about their sexual desire. The assumption that women both want to indulge sexually, and are inclined to sacrifice this desire for higher ends, gives rise to the myth that they want to be raped. After all, doesn't rape give them the sexual enjoyment they *really* want, at the same time that it relieves them of the responsibility for admitting to and acting upon what they want? And how then can we blame men, who have been socialized to be aggressively seductive precisely for the purpose of overriding female reserve? If we find fault at all, we are inclined to cast our suspicions on the motives of the woman. For it is on her that the contradictory roles of sexual desirer and sexual denier has been placed. ✳ ✳ ✳

But if women really want sexual pleasure, what inclines us to think that they will get it through rape? This conclusion logically requires a theory about the dynamics of sexual pleasure that sees that pleasure as an emergent property of overwhelming male insistence. For the assumption that a raped female experiences sexual pleasure implies that the person who rapes her knows how to cause that pleasure independently of any information she might convey on that point. Since her ongoing protest is inconsistent with requests to be touched in particular ways in particular places, to have more of this and less of that, then we must believe that the person who touches her knows these particular ways and places instinctively, without any directives from her.

Thus we find, underlying and reinforcing this belief in incommunicative male prowess, a conception of sexual pleasure that springs from wordless interchanges, and of sexual success that occurs in a place of meaningful silence. The language of seduction is accepted as a tacit language: eye contact, smiles, blushes, and faintly discernible gestures. It is, accordingly, imprecise and ambiguous. It would be easy for a man to make mistakes about the message conveyed, understandable that he should mistakenly think that a sexual invitation has been made, and a bargain struck. But honest mistakes, we think, must be excused.

In sum, the belief that women should not be sexually provocative is logically linked to several other beliefs, some normative, some empirical. The normative beliefs are that (1) people should keep the agreements they make (2) that sexually provocative behaviour, taken beyond a certain point, generates agreements (3) that the peculiar nature of male and female sexuality places such agreements in a special category, one in which the possibility of retracting an agreement is ruled out, or at least made highly unlikely, (4) that women are not to be trusted, in sexual matters at least. The empirical belief, which turns out to be false, is that male sexuality is not subject to rational and moral control.

DISPELLING THE MYTHS

The "she asked for it" justification of sexual assault incorporates a conception of a contract that would be difficult to defend in any other context and the presumptions about human sexuality which function to reinforce sympathies rooted in the contractual notion of just deserts are not supported by empirical research.

The belief that a woman generates some sort of contractual obligation whenever her behaviour is interpreted as seductive is the most indefensible part of the mythology of rape. In law, contracts are not legitimate just because a promise has been made. In particular, the use of pressure tactics to extract agreement is frowned upon. Normally, an agreement is upheld only if the contractors were clear on what they were getting into, and had sufficient time to reflect on the wisdom of their doing so. ✳ ✳ ✳

∗ ∗ ∗ Even if we assume that a woman has initially agreed to an encounter, her agreement does not automatically make all subsequent sexual activity to which she submits legitimate. If during coitus a woman should experience pain, be suddenly overcome with guilt or fear of pregnancy, or simply lose her initial desire, those are good reasons for her to change her mind. Having changed her mind, neither her partner nor the state has any right to force her to continue. But then if she is forced to continue she is assaulted. Thus, establishing that consent occurred at a particular point during a sexual encounter should not conclusively establish the legitimacy of the encounter. ∗ ∗ ∗

If the "she asked for it" contractual view of sexual interchange has any validity, it is because there is a point at which there is no stopping a sexual encounter, a point at which that encounter becomes the inexorable outcome of the unfolding of natural events. If a sexual encounter is like a slide on which I cannot stop halfway down, it will be relevant whether I enter the slide of my own free will, or am pushed.

But there is no evidence that the entire sexual act is like a slide. While there may be a few seconds in the "plateau" period just prior to orgasm in which people are "swept" away by sexual feelings to the point where we could justifiably understand their lack of heed for the comfort of their partner, the greater part of a sexual encounter comes well within the bounds of morally responsible control of our own actions. Indeed, the available evidence shows that most of the activity involved in sex has to do with building the requisite level of desire, a task that involves the proper use of foreplay, the possibility of which implies control over the form that foreplay will take. ∗ ∗ ∗ Sexologists are unanimous ∗ ∗ ∗ in holding that mutual sexual enjoyment requires an atmosphere of comfort and communication, a minimum of pressure, and an ongoing check-up on one's partner's state. They maintain that different people have different predilections, and that what is pleasurable for one person is very often anathema to another. These findings show that the way to achieve sexual pleasure, at any time at all, let alone with a casual acquaintance, decidedly does not involve overriding the other person's express reservations and providing them with just any kind of sexual stimulus. ∗ ∗ ∗

If aggressive seduction does not lead to good sex, if women do not like it or want it, then it is not rational to think that they would agree to it. Where such sex takes place, it is therefore rational to presume that the sex was not consensual.

The myth that women like to be raped, is closely connected, as we have seen, to doubt about their honesty in sexual matters, and this suspicion is exploited by defence lawyers when sexual assault cases make it to the court-room. It is an unfortunate consequence of the presumption of innocence that rape victims who end up in court frequently find that it is they who are on trial. For if the defendant is innocent, then either he did not intend to do what he was accused of, or the plaintiff is mistaken about his identity, or she is lying. Often the last alternative is the only plausible defence, and as a result, the plaintiff's word seldom goes unquestioned. Women are frequently accused of having made a false accusation, either as a defensive mechanism for dealing with guilt and shame, or out of a desire for revenge.

٭ ٭ ٭ We can now establish a logical connection between the evidence that a woman was subjected to high-pressure aggressive "seduction" tactics, and her claim that she did not consent to that encounter. Where the kind of encounter is not the sort to which it would be reasonable to consent, there is a logical presumption that a woman who claims that she did not consent is telling the truth. Where the kind of sex involved is not the sort of sex we would expect a woman to like, the burden of proof should not be on the woman to show that she did not consent, but on the defendant to show that contrary to every reasonable expectation she did consent. The defendant should be required to convince the court that the plaintiff persuaded him to have sex with her even though there are no visible reasons why she should.

In conclusion, there are no grounds for the "she asked for it" defence. Sexually provocative behaviour does not generate sexual contracts. ٭ ٭ ٭ Secondly, all the evidence suggests that neither women nor men find sexual enjoyment in rape or in any form of non-communicative sexuality. Thirdly, male sexual desire is containable, and can be subjected to moral and rational control. Fourthly, since there is no reason why women should not be sexually provocative, they do not "deserve" any sex they do not want. This last is a welcome discovery. The taboo on sexual provocativeness in women is a taboo both on sensuality and on teasing. But sensuality is a source of delight, and teasing is playful and inspires wit. What a relief to learn that it is not sexual provocativeness, but its enemies, that constitutes a danger to the world.

COMMUNICATIVE SEXUALITY: REINTERPRETING THE KANTIAN IMPERATIVE

In thinking about sex we must keep in mind its sensual ends, and the facts show that aggressive high-pressure sex contradicts those ends. ٭ ٭ ٭

٭ ٭ ٭ If a man wants to be sure that he is not forcing himself on a woman, he has an obligation either to ensure that the encounter really is mutually enjoyable, or to know the reasons why she would want to continue the encounter in spite of her lack of enjoyment. A closer investigation of the nature of this obligation will enable us to construct a more rational and a more plausible norm of sexual conduct.

Onora O'Neill has argued that in intimate situations we have an obligation to take the ends of others as our own, and to promote those ends in a non-manipulative and non-paternalistic manner.[1] Now it seems that in honest sexual encounters just this is required. Assuming that each person enters the encounter in order to seek sexual satisfaction, each person engaging in the encounter has an obligation to help the other seek his or her ends. To do otherwise is to risk acting in opposition to what the other desires, and hence to risk acting without the other's consent.

But the obligation to promote the sexual ends of one's partner implies the obligation to know what those ends are, and also the obligation to know how those ends are attained. Thus, the problem comes down to a problem of epistemic responsibility, the responsibility to know. The solution, in my view, lies in the practice of a communicative sexuality, one which combines the appropriate knowledge of the other with respect for the dialectics of desire.

So let us, for a moment, conceive of sexual interaction on a communicative rather than a contractual model. * * *

* * * The difference is this: typically, where contracts are concerned, cooperation is primarily required as a means to some further end set by the contract. In proper conversations, as I shall define them here, cooperation is sought as an end in itself.

It is not inimical to most contracts that the cooperation necessary for achieving its ends be reluctant, or even hostile. Although we can find fault with a contractor for failing to deliver goods or services, we do not normally criticize her for her attitude. And although there are situations where we employ people on the condition that they be congenial, even then we do not require that their congeniality be the real thing. When we are having a proper conversation, however, we do, typically, want the real thing. In conversation, the cooperation with the other is not just a means to an interesting conversation; it is one of the ends we seek, without which the conversation ceases to satisfy.

The communicative interaction involved in conversation is concerned with a good deal more than didactic content and argument. Good

---

1   O'Neill, "Between Consenting Adults," *Philosophy and Public Affairs* 14, 252–277.

conversationalists are intuitive, sympathetic, and charitable. Intuition and charity aid the conversationalist in her effort to interpret the words of the other correctly and sympathy enables her to enter into the other's point of view. Her sensitivity alerts her to the tone of the exchange. Has her point been taken good-humouredly or resentfully? Aggressively delivered responses are taken as a sign that *ad hominems* are at work, and that the respondent's self-worth has been called into question. Good conversationalists will know to suspend further discussion until this sense of self-worth has been reestablished. Angry responses, resentful responses, bored responses, even over-enthusiastic responses require that the emotional ground be cleared before the discussion be continued. Often it is better to change the topic, or to come back to it on another day under different circumstances. Good conversationalists do not overwhelm their respondents with a barrage of their own opinions. While they may be persuasive, the forcefulness of their persuasion does not lie in their being over-bearing, but rather in their capacity to see the other's point of view, to understand what it depends on, and so to address the essential point, but with tact and clarity.

Just as communicative conversationalists are concerned with more than didactic content, persons engaged in communicative sexuality will be concerned with more than achieving coitus. They will be sensitive to the responses of their partners. They will, like good conversationalists, be intuitive, sympathetic, and charitable. Intuition will help them to interpret their partner's responses; sympathy will enable them to share what their partner is feeling; charity will enable them to care. Communicative sexual partners will not overwhelm each other with the barrage of their own desires. They will treat negative, bored, or angry responses, as a sign that the erotic ground needs to be either cleared or abandoned. Their concern with fostering the desire of the other must involve an ongoing state of alertness in interpreting her responses.

Just as a conversationalist's prime concern is for the mutuality of the discussion, a person engaged in communicative sexuality will be most concerned with the mutuality of desire. As such, both will put into practice a regard for their respondent that is guaranteed no place in the contractual language of rights, duties, and consent. The dialectics of both activities reflect the dialectics of desire insofar as each person's interest in continuing is contingent upon the other person wishing to do so too, and each person's interest is as much fueled by the other's interest as it is by her own. Each respects the subjectivity of the other not just by avoiding treading on it, but by fostering and protecting the quality of that subjectivity. Indeed, the requirement to avoid treading on the subjectivity of the other entails the obligation to respect the dialectics of desire. For in intimacy there is no passing by on the other side. To be intimate just is to open up in emotional and personal ways, to share personal knowledge, and to be receptive to the openness of the other. This openness and sharing normally takes place only in an atmosphere of confidence and trust. But once availed of this knowledge, and confidence, and trust, one has, as it were, responsibility thrust upon one, the responsibility not to betray the trust by misusing the knowledge. And only by respecting the dialectics of desire can we have any confidence that we have not misused our position of trust and knowledge. * * *

CULTURAL PRESUMPTIONS

* * * Traditionally, the decision to date indicates that two people have an initial attraction to each other, that they are disposed to like each other, and look forward to enjoying each other's company. Dating derives its implicit meaning from this tradition. It retains this meaning unless other aims are explicitly stated, and even then it may not be possible to alienate this meaning. It is a rare woman who will not spurn a man who states explicitly, right at the onset, that he wants to go out with her solely on the condition that he have sexual intercourse with her at the end of the evening, and that he has no interest in her company apart from gaining that end, and no concern for mutual satisfaction.

* * * As long as we are operating under the auspices of a dating relationship, it requires that we behave in the mode of friendship and trust. But if a date is more like a friendship than a business contract, then clearly respect for the dialectics of desire is incompatible with the sort of sexual pressure that is inclined to end in date rape. And clearly, also, a conquest mentality which exploits a situation of trust and respect for purely selfish ends is morally pernicious. Failure to respect the dialectics of desire when operating under the auspices of friendship and trust is to act in flagrant disregard of the moral requirement to avoid manipulative, coercive, and exploitive behaviour. Respect for the dialectics of desire is *prima facie* inconsistent with the satisfaction of one person at the expense of the other. The proper end of friendship relations is mutual satisfaction. * * *

* * * The evidence of sexologists strongly indicates that women whose partners are aggressively uncommunicative have little chance of experiencing sexual pleasure. But it is not reasonable for women to consent to what

they have little chance of enjoying. Hence it is not reasonable for women to consent to aggressive noncommunicative sex. Nor can we reasonably suppose that women have consented to sexual encounters which we know and they know they do not find enjoyable. With the communicative model as the norm, the aggressive contractual model should strike us as a model of deviant sexuality, and sexual encounters patterned on that model should strike us as encounters to which *prima facie* no one would reasonably agree. But if acquiescence to an encounter counts as consent only if the acquiescence is reasonable, something to which a reasonable person, in full possession of knowledge relevant to the encounter, would agree, then acquiescence to aggressive noncommunicative sex is not reasonable. Hence, acquiescence under such conditions should not count as consent. * * *

* * * All that is needed then, in order to provide women with legal protection from "date rape" is to make both reckless indifference and willful ignorance a sufficient condition of *mens rea* and to make communicative sexuality the accepted norm of sex to which a reasonable woman would agree. Thus, the appeal to communicative sexuality as a norm for sexual encounters accomplishes two things. It brings the aggressive sex involved in "date rape" well within the realm of sexual assault, and it locates the guilt of date rapists in the failure to approach sexual relations on a communicative basis.

THE EPISTEMOLOGICAL IMPLICATIONS

* * * On the new model of communicative sexuality what we want is evidence of an ongoing positive and encouraging response on the part of the plaintiff. This new goal will require quite different tactics on the part of the cross-examiners, and quite different expectations on the part of juries and judges. Where communicative sexuality is taken as the norm, and aggressive sexual tactics as a presumption against consent, the outcome for the example that I described above would be quite different. It would be regarded as sexual assault rather than seduction.

Let us then consider a date rape trial in which a man is cross-examined. He is asked whether he was presuming mutual sexual enjoyment. Suppose he answers in the negative. Then he would have to account for why he persisted in the face of her voiced reluctance. He cannot give as an excuse that he thought she liked it, because he believes that she did not. If he thought that she had consented even though she didn't like it, then it seems to me that the burden of proof would lie with him to say why it was reasonable to think this. Clearly, her initial resistance, her presumed lack of enjoyment, and the pressure tactics involved in getting her to "go along" would not support a reasonable belief in consent, and his persisting in the face of her dissatisfaction would surely cast doubt on the sincerity of his belief in her consent.

But suppose he answers in the affirmative. Then the cross-examiner would not have to rely on the old criteria for non-consent. He would not have to show either that she had resisted him, or that she was in a fearful or intimidated state of mind. Instead he could use a communicative model of sexuality to discover how much respect there had been for the dialectics of desire. Did he ask her what she liked? If she was using contraceptives? If he should? What tone of voice did he use? How did she answer? Did she make any demands? Did she ask for penetration? How was that desire conveyed? Did he ever let up the pressure long enough to see if she was really that interested? Did he ask her which position she preferred? Assuming that the defendant does not perjure himself, he would lack satisfactory answers to these questions. But even where the defendant did lie, a skilled cross-examiner who was willing to go into detail could probably establish easily enough when the interaction had not been communicative. It is extraordinarily difficult to keep up a consistent story when you are not telling the truth. ✳ ✳ ✳

CONCLUSION

In sum, using communicative sexuality as a model of normal sex has several advantages over the "aggressive-acquiescence" model of seduction. The new model ties the presumption that consensual sex takes place in the expectation of mutual desire much more closely to the facts about how that desire actually functions. Where communicative sex does not occur, this establishes a presumption that there was no consent. The importance of this presumption is that we are able, in criminal proceedings, to shift the burden of proof from the plaintiff, who on the contractual model must show that she resisted or was threatened, to the defendant who must then give some reason why she should consent after all. The communicative model of sexuality also enables us to give a different conceptual content to the concept of consent. It sees consent as something more like an ongoing cooperation than the one-shot agreement which we are inclined to see it as on the contractual model. Moreover, it does not matter, on the communicative model, whether a woman was sexually provocative, what her reputation is, what went on before the sex began. All that matters is the quality of communication with regard to the sex itself.

But most importantly, the communicative model of normal sexuality gives us a handle on a solution to the problem of date-rape. If noncommunicative sexuality establishes a presumption of nonconsent, then where there are no overriding reasons for thinking that consent occurred, we have a criterion for a category of sexual assault that does not require evidence of physical violence or threat. If we are serious about date rape, then the next step is to take this criterion as objective grounds for establishing that a date rape has occurred. The proper legislation is the shortest route to establishing this criterion.

STUDY QUESTIONS

1. How is date rape to be distinguished from other forms of rape?
2. What does Pineau find wrong with the "she asked for it" defense?
3. How does Pineau think consent should be managed in order to avoid the possibility of date rape?

NICHOLAS DIXON
Alcohol and Rape

Nicholas Dixon is professor of philosophy at Alma College, Michigan.

Many date or acquaintance rapes, especially those that occur in a college setting, involve the use of alcohol by both rapist and victim. To what extent, if any, should the fact that a woman has been drinking alcohol before she has sexual relations affect our determination of whether or not she has been raped? I will consider the impact of the woman's intake of alcohol on both the *actus reus* ("guilty act") and *mens rea* ("guilty mind") elements of rape. A man is guilty of rape only if he not only commits the *actus reus* of rape—sex without his partner's consent—but does so with the requisite guilty mind, that is, intentionally, knowingly, recklessly, or negligently. I will take for granted that, regardless of a woman's alcoholic intake, she has been raped whenever a man forces himself on her after she says "no" or otherwise resists. I will focus instead on situations when women who have been drinking provide varying levels of acquiescence to sex. Let us begin by considering two relatively straightforward examples, which we can use as limiting cases, of sexual encounters involving alcohol.

I. TWO LIMITING CASES

A. Fraternity Gang Rape

In 1988 four Florida State University fraternity members allegedly had sex with an 18-year-old female student after she had passed out with an almost lethal blood alcohol level of .349 percent. Afterwards, she was allegedly "dumped" in a different fraternity house.

If these events, which led to a five-year ban on the fraternity chapter, really happened, the woman was certainly raped. Since a woman who is unconscious after heavy drinking is unable to consent, the fraternity members committed the *actus reus* of rape. Moreover, any claim that they were unaware of her lack of consent, thus potentially negating the *mens rea* requirement, would ring hollow. We may extrapolate beyond this extreme case to situations where a person is so drunk that, while she is conscious, she is barely aware of where she is and who her partner is, and she has no recollection of what has happened the following day. She may acquiesce and give the physiological responses that indicate consent, and she may even say "yes" when asked whether she wants to have sex, but her mental state is so impaired by alcohol that she cannot give a sufficiently meaningful level of consent to rebut rape charges against the man with whom she has sexual relations.

B. A Regretted Sexual Encounter

A male and female college student go on a dinner date, and both drink a relatively small amount of alcohol, say a glass of wine or beer. The conversation flows freely, and she agrees to go back to his place to continue the evening. They have one more drink there, start kissing and making out, and he asks her to spend the night. She is not drunk and, impressed by his gentle and communicative manner, accepts his offer. However, she is not used to drinking, and, although she is not significantly cognitively impaired—her speech is not slurred and her conversation is lucid—her inhibitions have been markedly lowered by the alcohol. When she wakes up alongside him the following morning, she bitterly regrets their lovemaking.

No rape has occurred. While she now regrets having spent the night with her date, and would quite likely not have agreed to do so had she not drunk any alcohol, her consent at the time was sufficiently voluntary to rule out any question of rape. While their sexual encounter violated her more lasting values, this no more entails that she did not "really" consent than the fact that my overeating at dinner violates my long-term plan to diet entails that my indulgence was not an autonomous action. Moreover, even if we granted for the sake of argument the far fetched claim that the *actus reus* of rape occurred, his belief that she did consent was perfectly reasonable, so he would still fail to exhibit the requisite *mens rea*. * * * A distinction exists between rape and bad sex. Unwisely having sex after unwisely drinking alcohol is not necessarily rape. We do a lot of unwise things when drinking, like *continuing to drink* too long and getting a bad hangover, and staying up too late when we have to work the next day. In neither case would we question our consent to our act of continuing to drink or staying up late. Why should a person's consent to sex after moderate amounts of drinking be any more suspect?

II. PROBLEMATIC INTERMEDIATE CASES: IMPAIRED SEX

Real sexual encounters involving alcohol tend to fall in between these two limiting cases. Imagine, for instance, a college student who gets very drunk at a party. Her blood alcohol level is well above the legal limit for driving. She is slurring her words and is unsteady on her feet, but she knows where she is and with whom she is speaking or dancing. She ends up spending the night with a guy at the party—perhaps someone she has just met, perhaps an acquaintance, but no one with whom she is in an ongoing relationship. She willingly responds to his sexual advances, but, like the woman in case IB, horribly regrets her sexual encounter the next day. Although she remembers going home with the guy from the party, she cannot recall much else from the evening and night. Let us call this intermediate case, in which the woman's judgment is significantly impaired by alcohol, "impaired sex." Has she been raped?

In the next two subsections I will examine two competing analyses of impaired sex, each one suggested by one of the limiting cases in section I. First, though, I pause to consider how relevant the degree to which the man has helped to bring about the woman's impaired state is to the question of whether rape has occurred. Suppose that he has deliberately got her drunk, cajoling her to down drink after drink, with the intention of lowering her resistance to his planned sexual advances? The very fact that he uses such a strategy implies that he doubts that she would agree to have sex with him if she were sober. Should she bring rape charges, on the ground that her acquiescence to sex when she was drunk was invalid, his claim that he believed that she voluntarily consented would appear disingenuous. His recklessness in disregarding doubts about the voluntariness of her consent arguably meets the *mens rea* requirement. * * *

For the remainder of this paper, I will focus instead on the more difficult variant of impaired sex in which the man does not use alcohol as a tool for seduction. Instead, he meets the woman when she is already drunk, or else he drinks with her with no designs on getting her drunk. In either case, he spontaneously takes advantage of the situation in which he finds himself. Is he guilty of rape?

A. Women's Responsibility for Their Own Actions

Few would deny that the woman in section IB is responsible for her own unwise decision to engage in a sexual encounter that she now regrets. Katie Roiphe and Camille Paglia would extend this approach to impaired sex, involving a woman who is very drunk but not incoherent. Roiphe insists that women are autonomous adults who are responsible for the consequences of their use of alcohol and other drugs.[1] And Paglia argues that sex is an inherently risky business, in which rape is an ever-present danger. Rather than complain about sexual assault, women who desire to be sexually active should take steps to minimize its danger, by being alert to warning signs, learning self-defense, and avoiding getting drunk when doing so would put them at risk for rape.[2]

Both Roiphe and Paglia are vulnerable to powerful criticisms. For instance, Roiphe's blanket dismissal of the extensive date rape literature is based on her own flimsy anecdotal evidence and a superficial reading of the studies. And, among multiple outrageous, offensive comments about uncontrollable male sexuality and women's desire to be with abusive he-men, Paglia is especially guilty of blatant victim-blaming. Even if it does result from a woman's recklessness, rape is still rape and the rapist is primarily to blame. We would not dream of exonerating a Central Park mugger because the victim was foolish to go there at 4 a.m. Indeed, the whole point of "Take Back the Night" marches is precisely that the burden is on *aggressors* to stop their violence, not on women to change their behavior to accommodate aggressors.

However, we can isolate from their more dubious views a relatively uncontroversial underlying principle, which is surely congenial to liberal and most other types of feminists: namely, that we should respect women's status as agents, and we should not degrade them by treating them as incapable

---

1   The relevant passage from Roiphe's book *The Morning After* is reprinted in Robert Trevas, Arthur Zucker, and Donald Borchert (eds.), *Philosophy of Sex and Love: A Reader* (Upper Saddle River, N.J.: Prentice Hall, 1997), p. 365.

2   Camille Paglia, "Date Rape: Another Perspective," William H. Shaw (ed.), *Social and Personal Ethics*, 2nd edition (Belmont, Calif.: Wadsworth Publishing Co., 1996).

of making autonomous decisions about alcohol and sexuality. We should, instead, hold women at least partly responsible for the consequences of their voluntary decision to drink large amounts of alcohol, made in full knowledge that it may result in choices that they will later regret. This principle would count against regarding impaired sex as rape. A plausible corollary of this principle is that women, as autonomous beings, have a duty to make their wishes about sex clear to their partners. When a woman drinks heavily and ends up having a sexual encounter that she later regrets she has failed to exercise this positive duty of autonomous people. Her actions have sent the wrong message to her partner, and to blame him for the sex in which she willingly engages but that she later regrets seems unfair. Even if we allow that her consent is so impaired that the *actus reus* of rape has occurred, on this view he does not fulfill the *mens rea* element of the crime of rape. The onus is on the woman to communicate her lack of consent and, in the absence of such communication, his belief in her consent is quite reasonable. In sum, proponents of this approach hesitate to regard impaired sex as rape, because doing so suggests that women are unable to make autonomous decisions about alcohol and sexuality, and because it ignores women's positive duty to exercise their autonomy by clearly communicating their considered preferences (and not just their momentary passion) about sex.

B. Communicative Sexuality: Men's Duty to Ensure that Women Consent

The "women's responsibility for sex" approach is very plausible in case IB, where a woman later regrets sex in which she willingly engaged after moderate drinking. However, men's accountability for unwanted sex becomes unavoidable in the gang rape described in subsection IA. Granted, the female student may have voluntarily and very unwisely chosen to drink massive amounts of alcohol, but once she had passed out, the four fraternity members who allegedly had intercourse with her had absolutely no reason to believe that she consented to sex. Regardless of whether they deliberately got her drunk or, on the other hand, took advantage of her after finding her in this condition, they are guilty of recklessly ignoring the evident risk that she did not consent, and hence fulfill the *mens rea* requirement for rape.

In cases such as this, Lois Pineau's model of "communicative sexuality" becomes enormously plausible.[3] While Pineau's view does not preclude

---

3   Lois Pineau, "Date Rape: A Feminist Analysis," *Law and Philosophy* 8 (1989). [*Editor's note*: See selections from "Date Rape: A Feminist Analysis" on pp. 293–306 of this reader.]

regarding women as having a duty to clearly communicate their wishes regarding sexual intimacy—indeed, such a duty may be an integral part of communicative sexuality—its central tenet is that men too are responsible for ensuring that effective communication occurs. In particular, the burden is on men to ensure that their female partners really do consent to sexual intimacy, and they should refrain from sexual activity if they are not sure of this consent. A reasonable belief that a woman consented to sex will still count as a defense against rape, but the reasonableness of this belief will itself be judged on whether it would have been reasonable, from the woman's point of view, to consent to sex. Since virtually no woman would want four men to have sex with her after she has passed into an alcoholic coma, in the absence of some miraculous evidence that the female student actually wanted sex in such unpleasant circumstances, the four fraternity members blatantly violated their duty to be sure of the woman's consent, and are indeed guilty of rape.

More generally, Pineau argues that it is never reasonable to assume that a woman consents to "aggressive noncommunicative sex." Not only does her approach regard the extreme case of sex with an unconscious person as rape, but it would put any man who fails to take reasonable precautions to ensure that a woman consents to sex at risk for a rape conviction should she later declare that she did not consent. When doubt exists about consent, the burden is on the man to *ask*. The much-discussed Antioch University "Sexual Offense Policy," which requires explicit consent to each new level of sexual intimacy every time it occurs, is a quasi-legal enactment of Pineau's model of communicative sexuality.[4]

Pineau's approach entails a very different analysis of our central case of impaired sex than the "women's responsibility for sex" model discussed in the previous section. At first blush, one might think that all that Pineau would require of a man would be to ask the woman whether she is really sure that she wants to continue with sexual intimacy. If he boldly forges ahead without even asking the woman this question, and if the woman later claims that she was too drunk for her acquiescence to sex to constitute genuine consent, he risks being found guilty of Pineau's proposed category of "nonaggravated sexual assault," which would carry a lighter penalty than "standard" rape when a woman communicates her lack of consent by saying "no" or otherwise resisting.

---

4   See Alan Soble, "Antioch's 'Sexual Offense Policy': A Philosophical Exploration," *Journal of Social Philosophy*, vol. 28, no. 1 (Spring 1997) for an excellent analysis and critique of Antioch's policy.

But even explicitly asking the woman for consent may be insufficient to protect him from blame and liability under the communicative sexuality model. The issue is precisely whether the word "yes," when spoken by a woman who is very drunk, is sufficient evidence of her consent. Being very drunk means that her judgment is impaired, as is evident from her horror and regret the following morning when she realizes what she has done. Given that we are only too aware of our propensity to do things that we later regret when we are very drunk, the man in this situation has good reason to doubt whether the woman's acquiescence to his advances and her "yes" to his explicit question is a fully autonomous reflection of lasting values and desires. Since he cannot be reasonably sure that the woman consents, he should refrain from sexual intercourse. Even if he is unaware of the danger that she does not consent, he *should* be aware and is, therefore, guilty of negligence. His belief that she consents may be sincere, but it is unreasonable and does not provide a defense to charges of nonaggravated sexual assault. On Pineau's "communicative sexuality" model, then, the man who proceeds with impaired sex meets both the *actus reus* and *mens rea* requirements of nonaggravated sexual assault.

III. SHOULD WE PUNISH MEN FOR IMPAIRED SEX?

Pineau's claim that men have a *moral obligation* to ensure that their partners consent to sex is very plausible. Given alcohol's tendency to cloud people's judgment, men should be especially careful to ensure that a woman consents to sex when she is very drunk. In most circumstances, this requires simply refraining from sexual activity. Imposing this relatively minor restriction on men's sexual freedom seems amply justified by the goal of preventing the enormous harm of rape. However, whether we should find men who fail to meet this duty and proceed to have sex with very drunk women guilty of rape—or even of nonaggravated sexual assault or a similar felony carrying a lighter penalty than "standard" rape—is much more controversial.

A. The Importance of Context

Alan Soble criticizes the Antioch University policy on the ground that it fails to distinguish between different types of sexual encounter.[5] Its demand that people obtain explicit verbal consent to each new level of sexual activity during each sexual encounter may be appropriate for one night stands with strangers. However, it seems unduly intrusive in the context of an ongoing, committed relationship, when the partners may well

---

5 Ibid., pp. 30–32.

be sufficiently well attuned to one another's body language to be reasonably sure that both people consent to sex. Under Antioch's policy, "[t]he history of the relationship, let alone the history of the evening, counts for nothing."[6]

A similar criticism applies to the demand that men always refrain from impaired sex. While the existence of a long-term, committed relationship does not provide a man with immunity from charges of sexual misconduct—marital rape, after all, can occur—men may reasonably proceed with sexual intimacy with long-term partners who are very drunk when doing so with a stranger would be wrong. In the case of a stranger, the only clue to her wishes that he has is her current, drunken acquiescence, whereas his history of consenting lovemaking with his partner, presumably often when both are sober, gives him every reason to believe that her current consent is fully voluntary and reflective of her ongoing desires. Another exception that could apply even in the case of one-night stands would be when a woman, while sober, gives her advance consent to consuming large amounts of alcohol followed by sexual activity. So if we do criminalize sex with women whose judgment is impaired by large amounts of alcohol, we need to build in exceptions for ongoing relationships and advance consent. * * *

C. Imprecise Distinctions and Fairness to Men

Because of the risk of the substantial harm of sex without a woman's fully voluntary consent, men should normally not have impaired sex. And, provided that we widely publicize the change in rape law and allow exceptions for established relationships and advance consent, criminalizing impaired sex would not be inherently unfair to men. The strongest reason against doing so is that implementing such a law would be a logistical nightmare that would indeed create the risk of unjustly convicting men.

Distinctions that are morally significant are difficult to translate into law. For instance, whether a man deliberately encourages a woman to drink large amounts of alcohol in order to make her more responsive to his sexual advances or, on the other hand, encounters her when she is already drunk or else innocently drinks with her with no intention of taking advantage of her, is relevant to our judgment of his actions. However, proving such subtle differences in intention would be extremely difficult, especially when the prosecution's star witness, the woman who was allegedly assaulted, was drunk at the crucial time.

---

6 Ibid., p. 30.

The biggest logistical problem of all concerns drawing boundaries. The only clear cases are of the type discussed in section I: sex with a woman who is unconscious or incoherent due to alcohol (rape), and communicative sex with a lucid, slightly tipsy woman who later regrets it (no rape). In between these limiting cases is a vast array of situations, whose diversity is concealed by my use of the blanket category of impaired sex. Just how impaired does a woman's judgment have to be to fall into this category? At what point does a woman progress from being merely tipsy, and responsible for any poor judgments that she makes as a result of her condition, to being so impaired that a man who proceeds to have sex with her recklessly or negligently runs the risk of sex without her fully voluntary consent? * * * But the vagueness of the meaning of "significantly impaired" does indeed create doubts about whether men would have fair warning about how to conform their behavior to this new law. Saying that when in doubt, men should err on the side of caution is fair enough, but the only way to be completely sure of avoiding conviction for this felony would be to completely abstain from sex with women who have drunk any alcohol, and this would be an unreasonable restriction on sexual freedom. A law that gives fair warning requires a certain amount of precision about forbidden behavior, and this is hard to come by in matters of impairment due to alcohol. Setting a certain blood alcohol level as the cutoff point seems arbitrary, and requiring a man to be aware of his partner's reading on this scale seems unreasonable and even absurd.

In defense of criminalizing impaired sex, one might argue that making judgment calls about how a legal rule applies to a particular case is precisely what courts are supposed to do. This approach works well when courts are asked to determine how a clear-cut rule applies to the often messy details of a case. The problem here, though, is that the distinction on which impaired sex is based is itself fuzzy, making judgments about whether rape has occurred doubly difficult.

Those who would make impaired sex a felony might point out the analogy with drunk driving laws, in which we set a more or less arbitrary blood alcohol level as the legally acceptable limit, in full knowledge that this limit corresponds only approximately with drivers' level of impairment. The overwhelmingly good overall consequences of a law that deters drunk driving help us to accept the occasional minor injustice of convicting a person whose driving ability was, despite his or her illegal blood alcohol level, not significantly affected. In this light, my dismissal of a blood alcohol level as a cutoff point for impaired sex may have been premature. Such a law would give men a strong incentive to refrain from sex when they have any doubts that their potential partner may be too impaired to give fully voluntary consent.

However, criminalizing impaired sex when the woman's blood alcohol level is above a certain limit is unacceptable for several reasons. First, it places an onerous burden on the man to know his partner's blood alcohol level, in contrast to drunk driving laws, which require us to monitor our *own* intake of intoxicants. Even a man who accompanies his partner throughout her drinking may be unaware of her tolerance level, which may be unusually low. Men who meet women who have already been drinking would have even less reason to be sure that their blood alcohol level is within the legal limit. To be sure of escaping conviction for rape, men in these circumstances would have to either administer portable breathalyzer tests to their partners or else simply abstain from sex. Now showing such restraint may be precisely the kind of caring, thoughtful behavior that we, following Pineau's communicative sexuality model, want to encourage. But to require men to do so, on pain of criminal sanctions (typically imprisonment), seems to be an unduly heavy-handed intrusion into the sex lives of two adults. ✳ ✳ ✳

IV. CONCLUSION

Existing rape laws probably suffice to convict men for clear cases of sexual misconduct involving alcohol, such as sex with unconscious women or with women who are drunk to the point of incoherence. In jurisdictions where such laws do not exist, we should create a category of rape—on the lines of "sex with a partner who is incapable of consent"—that would criminalize such cases. Granted, complications would arise. We would probably have to allow for exceptions for advance consent and for ongoing relationships. And, as in all rape cases, proving guilt may often be difficult, often reducing to "her word against his." But the harm done by men who take advantage of women in such circumstances is great enough to justify taking on these problems.

However, we would do better to deal with impaired sex by means of moral disapproval and educational measures rather than legal sanctions. The dangers of unjustly convicting men on the basis of unworkable distinctions, and of simultaneously degrading women (however inadvertently) and being unfair to men by underestimating women's ability to take responsibility for their alcohol intake and sexuality, are too great. Instead, we should regard impaired sex as a moral wrong on the lines of obtaining sexual gratification by means of trickery, such as concealing the fact that one has a spouse or significant other, or declaring one's undying love when all one wants is a brief fling. In the case of both impaired sex and trickery, one's partner is prevented from making a fully autonomous decision about her sexual activity: either because her judgment is clouded by alcohol, or because she has been denied vital information. Both are wrong, and both are better dealt with by informal sanctions than by inevitably heavy-handed and sometimes unfair legal interventions.

STUDY QUESTIONS

1. What does Dixon mean by "impaired sex"?
2. How does Pineau's theory of "communicative sexuality" help us judge whether impaired sex is sexual assault?
3. Why does Dixon think that normally the sexual assault involved in impaired sex should not be criminalized?

CONOR KELLY
Feminist Ethics: Evaluating the Hookup Culture[1]

Conor Kelly (1987) teaches and researches in theological ethics at Marquette University.

Hooking up—the practice of pursuing sexual activity without any expectation of a relationship—has become a fixture of the U.S. college experience. * * * Sociological research reveals that this practice appeals to college students by ostensibly providing greater independence than traditional relationships. An outside analysis of these claims, however, demonstrates that the heterosexual hookup culture operates in a decidedly sexist fashion. In fact, the four common features of this culture: lack of commitment, ambiguous language, alcohol use, and social pressure to conform, all undermine the freedom, equality, and safety of women on campus. An intentionally feminist perspective is in a unique position to highlight and critique these faults and the additional resources of feminist theology and ethics have the potential to help change this sexism in practice.

* * * Pursuit of some level of sexual activity without the constraints and expectations of a relationship is a common element of the U.S. college experience. * * * While some parents, faculty, and administrators view it as the

---

1   *Editor's note*: For the purposes of this volume a number of detailed citations have been omitted. For full details, see the original publication: Conor Kelly, "Feminist Ethics: Evaluating the Hookup Culture," *Journal of Feminist Studies in Religion* vol. 28, no. 2 (1992), 27–48.

end of morality, a number of the students involved embrace hooking up as the epitome of freedom and equality. Common sense suggests that neither generalization is sufficient, and encourages a closer examination to grasp the situation more accurately. * * *

THE HOOKUP CULTURE: WHAT IS IT?

As college students will reveal from their own experiences, there simply is not one definition of "hooking up." Sociologist Kathleen Bogle acknowledges that "it can mean kissing, sexual intercourse, or any form of sexual interaction generally seen as falling in between those two extremes." * * * In general usage, then, hooking up commonly refers to some form of sexual activity without the expectation of a consequent relationship between the parties. * * * In actual practice, it appears that the random hookup between total strangers is very rare. Usually, hookup partners have had some previous contact, even if it is something as simple as sharing a common class. * * * Four common elements—a lack of commitment, an acceptance of ambiguity, a role for alcohol, and a social pressure to conform—make it possible to speak of an identifiable hookup culture across the collegiate landscape in the United States, * * * although * * * diversity of race, ethnicity, socioeconomic status, the type of institution one attends, and a host of other variables converge to create different experiences for different people. * * *

The most striking common feature among various understandings of hooking up is the lack of commitment: * * * a divorce between one's sexual activity and one's emotions. * * *

The primary commitment that men and women seek to avoid in the hookup culture is a long-term relationship. * * *

* * * Research shows that those who hook up identify the removal of relationships as one of the hookup culture's chief advantages because it preserves autonomy. Specifically, they view hooking up as a way to get sexual gratification without compromising their freedom. This is hardly a surprising by-product of U.S. culture, which traditionally places great emphasis on independence. High-achieving college students have been encouraged by both parents and peers to lead multitasking lives in which their success in academics and extracurricular activities is touted as their ticket to a bright future. Women in particular are placing higher burdens of perfection upon themselves, and assume that they can have a successful career or a love life, but never both. Love actually appears as a stumbling block to the independent, successful lives these students have been raised to expect. * * *

A 2001 study discovered that only two kinds of relationships existed on campus in actuality: either interested parties were "hanging out" in groups, without any real one-on-one time, or in "joined at the hip' relationships," in which a sexually active couple chose to be exclusive and would immediately begin spending all their time, including every night, together. There is little to no space in the college atmosphere for slowly progressing relationships that might begin on an emotional level before moving to physical intimacy and even less space for traditional dating relationships.

∗ ∗ ∗ In the hookup framework, though, there are no clear steps to a relationship and there are few examples of what a relationship can or ought to look like in the aberrant situation when one should arise. As a result, students often imagine that a relationship is an overwhelming commitment that will completely consume their lives. They have no means to envision something between hookups and weddings. So, on campuses all across America, students choose hookups now and postpone marriage for later.

While the decline of dating has indeed been a contributing factor in the rise of the hookup culture, research on this link at least implies that a return to dating would be preferable. ∗ ∗ ∗ Such a claim deserves critical analysis from a feminist perspective because the history of dating suggests its return would hardly be a boon for women. In fact, dating gave a preponderance of power to men, especially in contrast with previous systems for courtship. Traditionally, men were expected to provide the financial means for each date, which gave them control over a number of factors from venues to initiative. This system often led men to believe that their payments entitled them to sexual favors in return. Meanwhile, women were expected to limit sexual activity to such an extent that blame even fell upon the victims of rape. While some have suggested that dating left both men and women open to the possibility of exploitation—men being able to exploit women sexually and women being able to exploit men for their money—these respective potentials cannot be equated fairly. Additionally, equal capacity for exploitation would hardly be considered the basis of a system that promotes full human flourishing. In historical practice, dating functioned far from its romantic idealization, facilitating the commodification of women rather than promoting genuine relationships between men and women. Thus, there is little to suggest that dating would be a positive alternative to the hookup culture, but even less to characterize hooking up as an improvement. ∗ ∗ ∗

∗ ∗ ∗ When students choose to hook up, the ambiguous nature of language in the hookup culture appears as another benefit. ∗ ∗ ∗ Hooking up can mean anything from "fairly chaste making out" to sexual intercourse. ∗ ∗ ∗ Researchers have found this to be the value of the phrase in the first place, with the ambiguity serving a curious double duty in female and male circles. In general, the imprecision provides women the opportunity to speak about hooking up without revealing the sorts of specifics that might damage reputations, while allowing men to suggest to their friends that they engaged in more sexual activity than they actually did.

The very purpose of the ambiguity seems to be the creation of a level of privacy in what most college students assume to be a public element of their lives. * * * Like the avoidance of committed relationships, the vague language allows for the preservation of one of a college student's most important assets: independence.

* * * A third common feature across the hookup culture is its connection with the party culture, specifically alcohol use. * * *

Significantly, even at the schools where most students self-reported that their hookup habits did not involve alcohol, these same students still identified drinking as a key component of the hookup culture on their campus. Regardless of what students self-report, it seems that alcohol is a central component in the social expectations of the hookup culture, even if it is not always an element in isolated practices. * * *

* * * Students choose alcohol because, like other aspects of the hookup culture, it allows them greater freedom—in this case freedom from complete responsibility for their choices. It helps them handle rejection, allowing young adults to tell themselves, in retrospect, that they did not put their best self forward because of the alcohol. Additionally, drinking also allows them to dismiss activity that they would normally regret, like going too far sexually or even hooking up with someone with whom they would not normally choose to partner. * * *

* * * The social pressure to conform to the hookup culture is so great that * * * no one has the liberty to avoid the system altogether. Certainly, abstaining from the hookup scene is possible, but this decision is rife with social consequences that all contribute to the perpetuation of the hookup culture.

The first element ensuring the hookup culture's power and prevalence is the potential for social marginalization. * * * Students who wish to avoid the hookup culture leave themselves with few alternatives for forming intimate and romantic relationships while at college. * * * Most of the students who choose to opt out of the hookup culture are already in committed relationships, usually with long-distance boyfriends or girlfriends.

The second element arises from the fact that the hookup culture is the dominant form for relating between the sexes, with the result that every heterosexual college student seems to expect all his or her peers to follow its script. * * *

Consequently, for individuals choosing to leave the hookup culture after they enter an exclusive relationship with someone else, the temptation to continue hooking up with individuals back on campus is always present and the general presumption against commitment offers no real reason to pursue strict fidelity. * * * Additionally, due to the prevalence of the hookup script, men and women who remove themselves from the hookup culture run into difficulties should they attempt to have social lives on campus because other classmates presume that any interest—from dancing to talking—is a signal for a hookup. Truly, then, it is impossible to completely sever oneself from the hookup culture, no matter how distasteful one might find it.

The oppressive nature of the hookup culture's dominance is also evident in the effects it can have on dating in the lesbian gay bisexual transgender and queer (LGBTQ) community. In a profound example, LGBTQ students report that the heterosexist assumptions of the hookup culture make it difficult for them to build their own, nonheterosexual relationships. * * * Suffice to say that the experience of the LGBTQ community on campus reveal that the hookup culture not only promotes sexist values but heterosexist ones as well.

* * * The hookup culture serves students longing for independence and balancing busy lives. On this basis, one could argue that the hookup culture is a beneficial element of today's college experience for those who want to pursue it. The social pressure to conform problematizes this interpretation some, although this too could be explained as a necessary evil that should be mitigated, if not removed, in order to allow the willful participants of the hookup culture to preserve their freedom.

THE HOOKUP CULTURE: WHY SHOULD IT BE CONCERNING?

* * * Elements of the hookup culture * * * that afford participants freedom are more complex and more hazardous than the culture acknowledges. Bogle summarizes the situation quite succinctly, noting that "in many ways, the hookup system creates an illusion of choice. Although students may have many options about how they conduct themselves within the hookup culture, they cannot change the fact that hooking up is the dominant script on campus."[1] * * *

---

1   Kathleen A. Bogle, *Hooking Up: Sex, Dating, and Relationships on Campus* (New York. New York University Press, 2008), 184.

✳ ✳ ✳ Feminism's pro-women stance is attuned to the sexism that other points of view might easily miss. ✳ ✳ ✳ Oftentimes a tradition will be unable to see the problematic aspects of its common practices. This opposition to criticism ✳ ✳ ✳ can obscure the real issues and prevent necessary challenges from arising because most people within the system will never conceive of questioning their normal activities in the first place. In such instances, it is the "view from the victims" that has the capacity to ✳ ✳ ✳ get to the true nature of the matter. ✳ ✳ ✳

✳ ✳ ✳ A feminist perspective is necessary to critique each element of hooking up, as it occurs in practice, in order to illuminate the bigger picture. ✳ ✳ ✳

To begin, removing commitment from the interactions between men and women produces three ✳ ✳ ✳ challenge[s]. ✳ ✳ ✳ First, a true expulsion of commitment requires a separation of emotions from physical activity that is challenging to accomplish. A number of students report feeling awkwardness toward their partners in the days after a hookup and both individuals appear unsure of how to proceed without any sense of obligation to each other. ✳ ✳ ✳

Second, researchers have found that however much young men and women value freedom, they do not actually wish to eschew all relationships. Admittedly, the extent to which this is a problem seems to vary by sex and age. Bogle observed that when men and women arrive on campus, both seem to want the same freedom to play the field, so to speak.[2] As time goes on, though, women quickly become disenchanted with the hookup culture, hoping for something more. In its 2001 survey, the IAV [Institute for American Values] found that 83 percent of women envisioned marriage as "a very important goal" in their lives and 63 percent of young women expected to meet their future spouse in college.[3] Young men, however, do not seek marriage to the same extent. ✳ ✳ ✳

While none of this is to say that no men want to marry and all women do, this sort of discussion still raises concerns about stereotyping and generalizing women's (and men's) experience. At the same time, acknowledging diversity does not make it impossible to speak about commonalities across human experiences. ✳ ✳ ✳ It is still significant that the majority of men and women in the thirty-year study maintained that marriage is important to them, making it possible to identify the hookup culture as a disservice to

---

2 Bogle, *Sex, Dating, and Relationships,* 97.
3 Norval Glenn and Elizabeth Marquardt, *Hooking Up, Hanging Out, and Hoping for Mr. Right: College Women on Dating and Mating Today* (New York: Institute for American Values, 2001), quotation on 42, 59.

both sexes in this regard. * * * However, * * * scholars still generally acknowledge that men are more willing to engage in the hookup culture for sexual gratification alone while women are more likely to be seeking relationships from their hookups.

* * * Compounding the sexist operation of this arrangement, the IAV study uncovered that the decision to turn a hookup interaction into an actual relationship hinged on the male partner. * * * College women are quite aware of the unlikelihood of achieving their goals within the hookup framework, but they still settle for hooking up, either in hopes that they will be the ones to buck the trend or because a "relationship" based on steadily hooking up with one individual appears better than no relationship at all. All this points to the disturbing conclusion that the hookup culture's lack of commitment serves male goals while limiting female agency.

* * * Scholars have also raised concerns about the challenges an abandonment of commitment poses for future relationships. * * * The skills the hookup culture encourages young men and women to develop—specifically a detachment from emotion in relationships and an aversion to commitment—are not only unhelpful for creating and sustaining relationships and marriages later in life, they are antithetical. * * * The only "norm" operative in the hookup culture is that individuals should avoid hooking up with someone with whom they might be interested in pursuing a relationship, and if they were to hook up, they should limit the extent of sexual activity as much as possible. This reveals that women and men in the hookup culture realize on some level that hooking up is a habit that is detrimental to relationships. * * *

* * * The reliance on ambiguous language further contests the perceived benefits of the hookup culture in much the same vein.

* * * The ambiguity in language has the potential to stifle the development of character traits that would promote healthy interactions between the sexes. * * * Relationships, and the trust upon which they are built, require frank conversations. This task is hardly aided by years of employing ambiguous language. The fact that this vagueness develops around relationships and sexual activity only serves to increase the possibility for future challenges.

In addition, one of the most beneficial traits of the ambiguity embedded in the term *hooking up* is its ability to leave as much as possible to the imagination of the listener. Intentionally or otherwise, this has the end result of fostering some level of misperception about the sorts of practices in which college students are actually choosing to engage. * * * In a culture with few rules to guide students' behavior, perceptions about what one's peers are doing play a huge role in determining how far individuals are willing to go sexually with a hookup partner. In general, college students believe their classmates are all engaging in more promiscuous activity than they themselves have experienced, a view that the research does not support. This belief is at least facilitated, if not directly caused, by the ambiguous nature of the language surrounding hooking up and only serves to encourage individuals to pursue riskier activities than they might choose on their own. * * *

* * * The supposed assets of alcohol's role in the hookup culture are also challenged by a negative potential to facilitate risky behavior. To begin, a belief that one's drunkenness will exculpate bad decisions can, and ostensibly does, lead individuals to make more perilous choices in deciding with whom to hook up and how far to go. Of primary concern, however, is the way in which an inebriation-induced lack of control puts women at risk for rape and sexual assault. This is particularly dangerous for women who may want to hook up but not have intercourse. * * * Women will often drink in order to lower their inhibitions when they begin this process, and a woman's capacity to offer resistance can be further limited. What is just as troubling * * * is the notion taught to and accepted by some females that it is a woman's responsibility to look after herself and not get into a position where she is uncomfortable or loses control. A more critical analysis from a feminist perspective shows, however, that the hookup culture and this view both avoid addressing how much control a woman really has in a system of pressure so geared toward fulfilling societal expectations of male sexuality.

Lack of control in the hookup culture is * * * [also] created by * * * the prevalence of social pressure to hook up, and the lack of viable alternatives. * * * Once again, for a variety of reasons, it affects women more than men. For example, women must deal with a separate set of social pressures than men do: the legacy of the feminist movement. It may seem counterintuitive, but * * * the initial message of female empowerment and total equality has been interpreted to say that women should participate in the hookup culture in order to match the freedom of men, who have (as a sex, on the whole) traditionally pursued sexual activity for individual gratification without worrying about consequences. As a result, women are told, and sometimes accept, that enjoying the freedoms of the hookup culture is supposed to be an empowering experience. * * * To this end, some would say that the hookup culture helps women.

The claim ＊ ＊ ＊ demands critical analysis. ＊ ＊ ＊ Established traditions are not intrinsically ordered toward equality and flourishing for all members. ＊ ＊ ＊ In ＊ ＊ ＊ application to hooking up, this starts with the assumption that the structures of the hookup culture are not neutrally geared toward everyone's benefit. The appropriate challenge for each feature, then, is to ask [for whose benefit?] and to give women a chance to answer. In the case of social pressure to conform, the large number of women who report negative hookup experiences challenges the narrative of empowerment. The feminist movement may be a source of pressure for women, but this does not mean that the pressure benefits women. In a disturbing twist, men seem to be benefiting the most, and the women involved express this on the basis of their own experience. "Most girls," admitted one female student in hindsight, "eventually realize that getting a guy to sleep with you is just a fancy way of 'letting' a guy sleep with you."

＊ ＊ ＊ A double standard clearly exists with regard to conduct. ＊ ＊ ＊ Female students have to walk a fine line between playing the social games of the hookup culture enough to maintain status while avoiding the "slut" label for participating too much. ＊ ＊ ＊ Unlike women, men in the hookup culture quickly learn that promiscuity on their part is either identified jokingly or for the sake of praise. ＊ ＊ ＊ Should their reputations be damaged, women can expect either social marginalization or a shrinking pool of viable hookup partners, since few men would be willing to hook up with a known "slut."

From a feminist perspective, the mere existence of these contrary sets of standards is enough to reveal discrimination in the hookup culture. Using this fact to conclude that the hookup culture is pro-men and anti-women would be too simplistic, however. Certainly, the hookup culture serves the relationship goals of the general male population (sex without relationships) and not those of the general female population (commitment). Additionally, as Stepp discovered, "guys frequently create the social environment in which hooking up flourishes and set the expectations about what girls will do."[4] Yet the fact that men derive benefits from the system does not make it truly pro-men. Freitas reveals that the same structures that are stacked against women also pressure men to prove their sexuality by having sex with multiple partners, and any dissent from this pattern becomes a denial of their masculinity.[5] It is important to be attentive to this fact

---

4   Laura Sessions Stepp, *Unhooked: How Young Women Pursue Sex, Delay Love, and Lose at Both* (New York: Riverhead Books, 2007), 34.
5   Donna Freitas, *Sex and the Soul: Juggling Sexuality, Spirituality, Romance, and Religion on America's College Campuses* (Oxford: Oxford University Press, 2008), 101–2.

because the point of a feminist perspective is not to ignore men and focus on women. ∗ ∗ ∗ The goal is full human flourishing. It would be most appropriate, then, to speak of the hookup culture as being biased against women rather than unequivocally biased toward men.

Strengthening the conclusion that the hookup culture is biased against women, the limited alternatives to hooking up are similarly oppressive. First, the "friends with benefits" structure purportedly helps women avoid damaging their reputation without abdicating their sexual license because it limits their sexual encounters to one man. This hardly constitutes a relationship, though. More important from a feminist perspective concerned with challenging discrimination, this system is just as biased against women because neither commitment nor exclusivity is expected of the male partner. ∗ ∗ ∗

Combining all these negative implications identified by a feminist analysis, the conclusion is clearly that the four central elements of the hookup culture offer only the perception of freedom. While this is arguably true for both sexes, it is indisputably the case for women. The removal of commitment places an undue burden upon all students to separate their emotions, deny their actual desires, and inhibit their potential for future relationships. The ambiguous language encourages them to avoid frank conversations with their friends and leaves them with little guidance beyond a constant pressure to go further sexually, while the presence of alcohol as a crutch puts women at greater risk for assault. Last, the social pressures to participate in the hookup culture are magnified for women, and work more for men's interests. ∗ ∗ ∗

FEMINIST THEOLOGY AND ETHICS: ADDRESSING THE SEXISM

In light of its flaws, a desire for some viable solutions to the sexism of the hookup culture is certainly reasonable, especially for concerned outsiders adopting a feminist perspective. ∗ ∗ ∗ While there are numerous places to turn for potential resources, three of the more fundamental concerns of feminist theology represent excellent tools for this process because they can address one of the most important, yet least considered, questions behind the shortcomings of the hookup culture: "Why?" ∗ ∗ ∗

[The] three fundamental concerns from feminist theology that can help facilitate this evaluation are the role of language in the constitution of the self, the link between autonomy and relationality, and the importance of structural analysis. The first notion, that language plays a role in constituting the self, is essential because it explains why students should bother talking about a hookup culture that seems so impossible to change. As feminist theologian Rebecca Chopp describes, language is political and the act of giving voice to those who have been silenced has the potential for "emancipatory transformation."[6] The ultimate goal is to transform the structures of oppression, but even when falling short of this goal the project is not a failure because there is something self-actualizing about expressing one's own experience. *** The act of speaking allows individuals not only to reflect on their experiences but also to have power over their own identity. *** This should *** be the first step in responding to the hookup culture, for allowing men and women to voice their own concerns in a culture that functions to silence frank conversation is itself a subversive act. As the notion that language is constitutive of the self suggests, the result will be first an empowerment of these students and then, hopefully, an emancipatory transformation of structures.

Similarly, the link between autonomy and relationality in feminist theology can help explain why the pursuit of independence in the hookup culture will necessarily be insufficient. Admittedly, feminism in a multitude of forms has long promoted freedom and autonomy, especially for women. *** What feminist theology has stressed alongside this, however, is that freedom must be properly understood not as complete license, but as interdependence. An excellent critique of the tendency to understand independence in isolation has come from Brazilian ecofeminist theologian Ivone Gebara, who *** has criticized Western notions of autonomy for being excessively individualistic. Due to the fact that individual autonomy "was promoted in a dogmatic, absolute, univocal, and unlimited way," she laments, "what was originally affirmed as a value seems to have turned into an antivalue."[7] *** To counter this possibility, a foundational assumption of feminist theology and ethics expressed by Elizabeth Johnson stresses "that the self is rightly structured not in dualistic opposition to the other but in intrinsic relationship with the other."[8] There is an additional caution raised by Elisabeth Schüssler Fiorenza, however, that an exclusive emphasis on relationality can undermine women's agency, making it difficult for women to recognize

---

6   Rebecca S. Chopp, *The Power to Speak: Feminism, Language, God* (New York: Crossroads, 1989), 3, quotation on 18.

7   Ivone Gebara, *Longing for Running Water: Ecofeminism and Liberation* (Minneapolis: Fortress Press, 1999), 72.

8   Elizabeth A. Johnson, *She Who Is. The Mystery of God in Feminist Theological Discourse* (New York. Herder and Herder, 2002), 68.

their own individual value apart from their relational identity as daughters, mothers, sisters, and friends.[9] Keeping independence and interdependence together in tension, though, helps relieve some of these concerns. Thus the message * * * is not that autonomy is a false human good, but that authentic independence cannot be understood apart from a relational conception of the human person. * * *

A third basic concern from feminist theology and ethics, the importance of structural analysis, addresses why the social pressures perpetuating the hookup culture are so damaging. In feminist theology, structural analysis has accompanied an attentiveness to social context that has helped identify and combat injustice. * * *

* * * Structural analysis highlights the troubling fact that the hookup culture is built upon a coercive pressure to conform and that women bear the brunt of this burden. From such a perspective, the perpetuation of the double standard exemplified in reserving derogatory labels for women alone serves as an additional example of the injustices inherent in the structures that promote hooking up. * * *

* * * The role of language in constituting the self, the link between relationality and autonomy, and the concern for structural analysis will not lead to a sudden displacement of hooking up, but they can help change the practice. * * *

Given the sexism inherent in the hookup culture, maintenance of the status quo is an untenable outcome. * * * While it may be tempting to provide solutions for wholesale transformation of the hookup culture, there can be no one-size-fits-all answer to a phenomenon that has become a problem precisely because it assumed everyone should have the same thing. True change must come from within and the only way to support it is to help young adults think through the problems and alternatives. * * * The main significance of these three resources lies in * * * facilitating this conversation. * * * I hope this discussion will allow students to move to the next step of creating a space and system for relationships more conducive to human flourishing and * * * to chip away at a hookup culture that for all its supposed benefits [the hookup culture] is really nothing more than sexism in practice.

---

9 See Elisabeth Schüssler Fiorenza, *Jesus: Miriam's Child, Sophia's Project, Critical Issues in Feminist Christology* (New York: Continuum, 1995), 55.

STUDY QUESTIONS

1. Explain the role of "ambiguous language" within the hookup culture.
2. Why does Kelly think that the hookup culture offers the perception of freedom but not the reality?
3. Why does Kelly think that the hookup culture is "sexism in practice"?

■ Compare and Contrast Questions

1. How would Pineau respond to Dixon's argument that some forms of assault involved in impaired sex should not be subject to the criminal law?
2. Does Kelly's argument show that there can be a form of mutual coercion into sex?
3. Can Kelly's arguments about the problems with the hookup culture be extended to sexual activity that takes place under other circumstances?

ABORTION

This section contains four papers on the critically important question of the moral standing of abortion. We start with Judith Jarvis Thomson's famous paper "A Defense of Abortion." Thomson suggests that typically the question of the morality of abortion has been thought to turn on whether a fetus is or is not a human being or person. However, Thomson argues that even if we assume that the fetus is a person, it could still be the case that abortion is morally permissible in certain circumstances. At the heart of her analysis is an argument from analogy. Suppose you wake up one day and find that you have been surgically connected to a famous violinist who needs the use of your kidneys for nine months and will die if disconnected. What obligations do you have to remain connected?

Thomson argues that you do not violate anyone's rights if you disconnect, even though you are disconnecting from a person who will die. This, she argues, shows that abortion can be morally acceptable even if the fetus is a person and will die as a result of abortion. She is aware, of course, that there are complicating factors that render many pregnancies not analogous to the violinist case, such as the fact that most pregnancies are the result of intentional action. She appeals to a range of other examples to explore our intuitions about different cases. Nevertheless, if we accept that in the violinist case you do have the right to disconnect yourself, the general point is established. Even if a fetus is a person, there can be circumstances in which abortion is permissible, contrary to the "extreme view" that abortion is never permissible.

Thomson also discusses what it means to have "a right to life." It cannot, she thinks, mean to have a right for others to come to your assistance to keep you alive under all circumstances. Rather, she says, it is the "right not to be killed unjustly." We then need a different set of arguments to consider when an abortion does involve an unjust killing. Thomson accepts that there are cases in which abortion would be morally indecent, for example if a very late abortion is requested simply to avoid the nuisance of postponing a foreign trip. But even in these cases she denies that the fetus has a right to be kept alive, for Thomson insists that even if abortion (or some other action) is morally wrong in a particular case, it still does not always follow that the fetus has the right that the abortion not take place.

Mary Anne Warren replies to Thomson that, although she has set out a strong case for the permissibility of abortion for pregnancy following rape, the violinist analogy does not apply to the normal case in which pregnancy follows from intentional sexual intercourse. In the normal case, a woman can be regarded as in some way responsible for her pregnancy. In order to defend the more general permissibility of abortion, Warren sets out to argue that the fetus is not a person with a "strong moral right to life."

It is central to Warren's case to make a distinction between the "moral sense" of the term *human being* and the "genetic sense." It is true, she argues, that a fetus is a human being in the genetic sense, but it does not follow that it is a human being in the moral sense of being a person who is a member of the moral community. The characteristics that are central to the concept of personhood, argues Warren, are sentience, emotionality, reason, the capacity to communicate, self-awareness, and moral agency. Although these characteristics are not all strictly necessary for personhood and the possession of rights, on Warren's view the more that are present, the stronger the claim to personhood. If sentience is lacking, many others will be too, and Warren claims that an early fetus lacks sentience and hence, while genetically human, lacks personhood. This will also be true of an adult who permanently lacks consciousness.

While it is persons who create rights, argues Warren, they can extend rights to those who are not persons. But in doing so, they should take care not to burden persons with overly demanding duties. And this is the danger, argues Warren, if we give the fetus a right to life, for there are times when to do so would create very onerous duties for pregnant women. Warren concedes that a fetus may gradually develop a stronger right to life as it develops, and a seven-month fetus is very different from an early fetus. And while it is true that a fetus deserves special consideration because it is a potential person, nevertheless Warren insists that the rights of actual persons take precedence when there is a conflict.

It has been objected that Warren's account would also permit infanticide, as a newborn baby lacks many of the features of personhood. Warren points out that the justification for abortion rests on the argument that the rights of the pregnant woman are a reason not to extend very strong rights to the fetus, but once the baby is born no such conflict exists. Hence she does not regard the objection as convincing.

In opposition to the views of Thomson and Warren, Don Marquis sets out to argue that the great majority of deliberate abortions are seriously immoral. After arguing that the standard arguments in the literature on both sides of the debate are inadequate, Marquis turns to the question of why killing is wrong. It is, he suggests, because killing deprives someone of the activities, projects, experiences, and enjoyments that would have constituted the person's future life. This theory explains why it can be wrong to kill beings who are not biologically human, such as, possibly, alien forms of life or some nonhuman mammals. And, of course, the theory also entails that it is wrong to kill a fetus by means of abortion, since the fetus would thus be deprived of a valuable future. Marquis is aware that in some cases there can be arguments on the other side. Marquis's argument, if successful, shows that abortion is "prima facie" wrong, but it could be that, all things considered, abortion is acceptable in some cases, if there are even more important moral considerations to weigh on the other side.

Marquis argues that the most promising way of replying to his argument is to find some other basis to explain why ordinary killing is wrong. He considers two alternatives, the "desire" account and the "discontinuation" account. The desire account says that it is wrong to kill because people have a strong desire to remain alive. However, because it would be problematic to attribute a strong desire to remain alive to a fetus, arguably abortion would not be wrong on this account. However, Marquis argues that the account is defective, since it is wrong to kill even those people who have no desire to live. The discontinuation account is based on the idea that there is value in the continuation of experience. As the fetus has no past experience, there is nothing to discontinue and hence, once more, abortion would not be wrong. Marquis argues, however, that what matters is the value of the future, not what happened in the past, and so the discontinuation account collapses into his own "value of the future" theory and hence does not provide an alternative.

Rosalind Hursthouse's contribution to the debate concerning the morality of abortion draws heavily on Aristotelian virtue ethics and hence can also be seen as an illustration of how virtue ethics can be applied to a serious moral problem. Unlike other authors, Hursthouse does not think it fruitful to consider metaphysical questions about whether or not a fetus is a person, for the issue is too urgent to wait for a resolution of that question. She also denies that the most important question is whether a woman should have a legal right to abortion. Even if there is a legal right, that on its own does not provide an answer to the question of what a woman facing the decision of whether to have an abortion should do.

Hursthouse also resists the idea that it should be possible to derive a formula or universal moral principle that will provide sufficient guidance to answer the question of whether it is right or wrong for a particular woman to have an abortion. Rather, virtue ethics suggests that what matters is that a woman deliberates the right way: taking all relevant issues into account and avoiding doing something "cruel, or callous, or selfish, light-minded, self-righteous, stupid, inconsiderate, disloyal [or] dishonest." Hence a virtuous woman (which Hursthouse points out does not mean a "chaste" woman) exhibits certain strengths or virtues of character in her reflections.

Hursthouse reminds us that pregnancy is an event with a unique biological nature, embedded in human relations and wrapped up with particular emotional responses. Much writing on abortion takes place at a level of abstraction that does not capture this nature, and that, in itself, is a type of the "vice" of not giving the matter proper seriousness. Hursthouse takes us through a number of examples, including comparing abortion to miscarriage in a variety of circumstances, to bring out the point that different considerations can be relevant in different cases.

JUDITH JARVIS THOMSON
A Defense of Abortion

Judith Jarvis Thomson (b. 1929) is an American philosopher, especially noted for her contributions to moral and political philosophy.

Most opposition to abortion relies on the premise that the fetus is a human being, a person, from the moment of conception. * * *

* * * I am inclined to think * * * that we shall probably have to agree that the fetus has already become a human person well before birth. * * * The fetus is not a person from the moment of conception. A newly fertilized ovum, a newly implanted clump of cells, is no more a person than an acorn is an oak tree. But I shall not discuss any of this. For it seems to me to be of great interest to ask what happens if, for the sake of argument, we allow the premise. How, precisely, are we supposed to get from there to the conclusion that abortion is morally impermissible? Opponents of abortion commonly spend most of their time establishing that the fetus is a person, and hardly any time explaining the step from there to the impermissibility of abortion. Perhaps they think the step too simple and obvious to require much comment. Or perhaps instead they are simply being economical in argument. Many of those who defend abortion rely on the premise that the fetus is not a person, but only a bit of tissue that will become a person at birth; and why pay out more arguments than you have to? Whatever the explanation, I suggest that the step they take is neither easy nor obvious, that it calls for closer examination than it is commonly given, and that when we do give it this closer examination we shall feel inclined to reject it.

I propose, then, that we grant that the fetus is a person from the moment of conception. How does the argument go from here? Something like this, I take it. Every person has a right to life. So the fetus has a right to life. No doubt the mother has a right to decide what shall happen in and to her body; everyone would grant that. But surely a person's right to life is stronger and more stringent than the mother's right to decide what happens in and to her body, and so outweighs it. So the fetus may not be killed; and abortion may not be performed.

It sounds plausible. But now let me ask you to imagine this. You wake up in the morning and find yourself back to back in bed with an unconscious violinist. A famous unconscious violinist. He has been found to have a fatal kidney ailment, and the Society of Music Lovers has canvassed all the available medical records and found that you alone have the right blood type to help. They have therefore kidnapped you, and last night the violinist's circulatory system was plugged into yours, so that your kidneys can be used to extract poisons from his blood as well as your own. The director of the hospital now tells you, "Look, we're sorry the Society of Music Lovers did this to you—we would never have permitted it if we had known. But still, they did it, and the violinist now is plugged into you. To unplug you would be to kill him. But never mind, it's only for nine months. By then he will have recovered from his ailment, and can safely be unplugged from you." Is it morally incumbent on you to accede to this situation? No doubt it would be very nice of you if you did, a great kindness. But do you *have* to accede to it? What if it were not nine months, but nine years? Or longer still? What if the director of the hospital says, "Tough luck, I agree, but you've now got to stay in bed, with the violinist plugged into you, for the rest of your life. Because remember this. All persons have a right to life, and violinists are persons. Granted you have a right to decide what happens in and to your body, but a person's right to life outweighs your right to decide what happens in and to your body. So you cannot ever be unplugged from him." I imagine you would regard this as outrageous, which suggests that something really is wrong with that plausible-sounding argument I mentioned a moment ago.

In this case, of course, you were kidnapped; you didn't volunteer for the operation that plugged the violinist into your kidneys. Can those who oppose abortion on the ground I mentioned make an exception for a pregnancy due to rape? Certainly. They can say that persons have a right to life only if they didn't come into existence because of rape; or they can say that all persons have a right to life, but that some have less of a right to life than others, in particular, that those who came into existence because of rape have less. But these statements have a rather unpleasant sound. Surely the question of whether you have a right to life at all, or how much of it you have, shouldn't turn on the question of whether or not you are the product of a rape. And in fact the people who oppose abortion on the ground I mentioned do not make this distinction, and hence do not make an exception in case of rape.

Nor do they make an exception for a case in which the mother has to spend the nine months of her pregnancy in bed. They would agree that would be a great pity, and hard on the mother; but all the same, all persons have a right to life, the fetus is a person, and so on. I suspect, in fact, that they would not make an exception for a case in which, miraculously enough, the pregnancy went on for nine years, or even the rest of the mother's life.

Some won't even make an exception for a case in which continuation of the pregnancy is likely to shorten the mother's life; they regard abortion as impermissible even to save the mother's life. Such cases are nowadays very rare, and many opponents of abortion do not accept this extreme view. All the same, it is a good place to begin: a number of points of interest come out in respect to it.

Let us call the view that abortion is impermissible even to save the mother's life "the extreme view." I want to suggest first that it does not issue from the argument I mentioned earlier without the addition of some fairly powerful premises. Suppose a woman has become pregnant, and now learns that she has a cardiac condition such that she will die if she carries the baby to term. What may be done for her? The fetus, being a person, has a right to life, but as the mother is a person too, so has she a right to life. Presumably they have an equal right to life. How is it supposed to come out that an abortion may not be performed? If mother and child have an equal right to life, shouldn't we perhaps flip a coin? Or should we add to the mother's right to life her right to decide what happens in and to her body, which everybody seems to be ready to grant—the sum of her rights now outweighing the fetus' right to life? ✳ ✳ ✳

✳ ✳ ✳ If directly killing an innocent person is murder, and thus is impermissible, then the mother's directly killing the innocent person inside her is murder, and thus is impermissible. But it cannot seriously be thought to be murder if the mother performs an abortion on herself to save her life. It cannot seriously be said that she *must* refrain, that she *must* sit passively by and wait for her death. Let us look again at the case of you and the violinist. There you are, in bed with the violinist, and the director of the hospital says to you, "It's all most distressing, and I deeply sympathize, but you see this is putting an additional strain on your kidneys, and you'll be dead within the month. But you *have* to stay where you are all the same. Because unplugging you would be directly killing an innocent violinist, and that's murder, and that's impermissible." If anything in the world is true, it is that you do not commit murder, you do not do what is impermissible, if you reach around to your back and unplug yourself from that violinist to save your life.

✳ ✳ ✳ Suppose you find yourself trapped in a tiny house with a growing child. I mean a very tiny house, and a rapidly growing child—you are already up against the wall of the house and in a few minutes you'll be crushed to death. The child on the other hand won't be crushed to death; if nothing is done to stop him from growing he'll be hurt, but in the end he'll simply burst open the house and walk out a free man. Now I could well understand it if a bystander were to say, "There's nothing we can do for you. We cannot choose between your life and his, we cannot be the ones to decide who is to live, we cannot intervene." But it cannot be concluded that you too can do nothing, that you cannot attack it to save your life. However innocent the child may be, you do not have to wait passively while it crushes you to death. ✳ ✳ ✳

I should perhaps stop to say explicitly that I am not claiming that people have a right to do anything whatever to save their lives. I think, rather, that there are drastic limits to the right of self-defense. If someone threatens you with death unless you torture someone else to death, I think you have not the right, even to save your life, to do so. But the case under consideration here is very different. In our case there are only two people involved, one whose life is threatened, and one who threatens it. Both are innocent: the one who is threatened is not threatened because of any fault, the one who threatens does not threaten because of any fault. For this reason we may feel that we bystanders cannot intervene. But the person threatened can.

In sum, a woman surely can defend her life against the threat to it posed by the unborn child, even if doing so involves its death. And this shows ✳ ✳ ✳ that the extreme view of abortion is false, and so we need not canvass any other possible ways of arriving at it from the argument I mentioned at the outset. ✳ ✳ ✳

Where the mother's life is not at stake, the argument I mentioned at the outset seems to have a much stronger pull. "Everyone has a right to life, so the unborn person has a right to life." And isn't the child's right to life weightier than anything other than the mother's own right to life, which she might put forward as ground for an abortion?

This argument treats the right to life as if it were unproblematic. It is not, and this seems to me to be precisely the source of the mistake.

For we should now, at long last, ask what it comes to, to have a right to life. In some views having a right to life includes having a right to be given at least the bare minimum one needs for continued life. But suppose that what in fact *is* the bare minimum a man needs for continued life is something he has no right at all to be given? If I am sick unto death, and the only thing that will save my life is the touch of Henry Fonda's cool hand on my fevered brow, then all the same, I have no right to be given the touch of Henry Fonda's cool hand on my fevered brow. It would be frightfully nice of him to fly in from the West Coast to provide it. It would be less nice, though no doubt well meant, if my friends flew out to the West Coast and carried Henry Fonda back with them. But I have no right at all against anybody that he should do this for me. Or again, to return to the story I told earlier, the fact that for continued life that violinist needs the continued use of your kidneys does not establish that he has a right to be given the continued use of your kidneys. He certainly has no right against you that *you* should give him continued use of your kidneys. For nobody has any right to use your kidneys unless you give him this right—if you do allow him to go on using your kidneys, this is a kindness on your part, and not something he can claim from you as his due. Nor has he any right against anybody else that *they* should give him continued use of your kidneys. Certainly he had no right against the Society of Music Lovers that they should plug him into you in the first place. And if you now start to unplug yourself, having learned that you will otherwise have to spend nine years in bed with him, there is nobody in the world who must try to prevent you, in order to see to it that he is given something he has a right to be given. ✳✳✳

✳✳✳ I would stress that I am not arguing that people do not have a right to life—quite to the contrary, it seems to me that the primary control we must place on the acceptability of an account of rights is that it should turn out in that account to be a truth that all persons have a right to life. I am arguing only that having a right to life does not guarantee having either a right to be given the use of or a right to be allowed continued use of another person's body—even if one needs it for life itself. So the right to life will not serve the opponents of abortion in the very simple and clear way in which they seem to have thought it would. ✳✳✳

✳✳✳ The right to life consists not in the right not to be killed, but rather in the right not to be killed unjustly. This runs a risk of circularity, but never mind: it would enable us to square the fact that the violinist has a right to life with the fact that you do not act unjustly toward him in unplugging yourself, thereby killing him. For if you do not kill him unjustly, you do not violate his right to life, and so it is no wonder you do him no injustice.

But if this emendation is accepted, the gap in the argument against abortion stares us plainly in the face: it is by no means enough to show that the fetus is a person, and to remind us that all persons have a right to life—we need to be shown also that killing the fetus violates its right to life, i.e., that abortion is unjust killing. And is it?

I suppose we may take it as a datum that in a case of pregnancy due to rape the mother has not given the unborn person a right to the use of her body for food and shelter. Indeed, in what pregnancy could it be supposed that the mother has given the unborn person such a right? It is not as if there were unborn persons drifting about the world, to whom a woman who wants a child says "I invite you in."

But it might be argued that there are other ways one can have acquired a right to the use of another person's body than by having been invited to use it by that person. Suppose a woman voluntarily indulges in intercourse, knowing of the chance it will issue in pregnancy, and then she does become pregnant; is she not in part responsible for the presence, in fact the very existence, of the unborn person inside her? No doubt she did not invite it in. But doesn't her partial responsibility for its being there itself give it a right to the use of her body? If so, then her aborting it * * * would be doing it an injustice.

And then, too, it might be asked whether or not she can kill it even to save her own life: If she voluntarily called it into existence, how can she now kill it, even in self-defense?

The first thing to be said about this is that it is something new. Opponents of abortion have been so concerned to make out the independence of the fetus, in order to establish that it has a right to life, just as its mother does, that they have tended to overlook the possible support they might gain from making out that the fetus is *dependent* on the mother, in order to establish that she has a special kind of responsibility for it, a responsibility that gives it rights against her which are not possessed by any independent person—such as an ailing violinist who is a stranger to her.

On the other hand, this argument would give the unborn person a right to its mother's body only if her pregnancy resulted from a voluntary act, undertaken in full knowledge of the chance a pregnancy might result from it. It would leave out entirely the unborn person whose existence is due to rape. Pending the availability of some further argument, then, we would be left with the conclusion that unborn persons whose existence is due to rape have no right to the use of their mothers' bodies, and thus that aborting them is not depriving them of anything they have a right to and hence is not unjust killing.

And we should also notice that it is not at all plain that this argument really does go even as far as it purports to. For there are cases and cases, and the details make a difference. If the room is stuffy, and I therefore open a window to air it, and a burglar climbs in, it would be absurd to say, "Ah, now he can stay, she's given him a right to the use of her house—for she is partially responsible for his presence there, having voluntarily done what enabled him to get in, in full knowledge that there are such things as burglars, and that burglars burgle." It would be still more absurd to say this if I had had bars installed outside my windows, precisely to prevent burglars from getting in, and a burglar got in only because of a defect in the bars. It remains equally absurd if we imagine it is not a burglar who climbs in, but an innocent person who blunders or falls in. Again, suppose it were like this: people-seeds drift about in the air like pollen, and if you open your windows, one may drift in and take root in your carpets or upholstery. You don't want children, so you fix up your windows with fine mesh screens, the very best you can buy. As can happen, however, and on very, very rare occasions does happen, one of the screens is defective; and a seed drifts in and takes root. Does the person-plant who now develops have a right to the use of your house? Surely not—despite the fact that you voluntarily opened your windows, you knowingly kept carpets and upholstered furniture, and you knew that screens were sometimes defective. Someone may argue that you are responsible for its rooting, that it does have a right to your house, because after all you *could* have lived out your life with bare floors and furniture, or with sealed windows and doors. But this won't do—for by the same token anyone can avoid a pregnancy due to rape by having a hysterectomy, or anyway by never leaving home without a (reliable!) army.

It seems to me that the argument we are looking at can establish at most that there are *some* cases in which the unborn person has a right to the use of its mother's body, and therefore *some* cases in which abortion is unjust killing. There is room for much discussion and argument as to precisely which, if any. But I think we should sidestep this issue and leave it open, for at any rate the argument certainly does not establish that all abortion is unjust killing.

There is room for yet another argument here, however. We surely must all grant that there may be cases in which it would be morally indecent to detach a person from your body at the cost of his life. Suppose you learn that what the violinist needs is not nine years of your life, but only one hour: all you need do to save his life is to spend one hour in that bed with him. Suppose also that letting him use your kidneys for that one hour would not affect your health in the slightest. Admittedly you were kidnapped. Admittedly you did not give anyone permission to plug him into you. Nevertheless it seems to me plain you *ought* to allow him to use your kidneys for that hour—it would be indecent to refuse.

Again, suppose pregnancy lasted only an hour, and constituted no threat to life or health. And suppose that a woman becomes pregnant as a result of rape. Admittedly she did not voluntarily do anything to bring about the existence of a child. Admittedly she did nothing at all which would give the unborn person a right to the use of her body. All the same it might well be said, as in the newly emended violinist story, that she *ought* to allow it to remain for that hour—that it would be indecent in her to refuse. * * *

* * * My own view is that even though you ought to let the violinist use your kidneys for the one hour he needs, we should not conclude that he has a right to do so—we should say that if you refuse, you are * * * self-centered and callous, indecent in fact, but not unjust. And similarly, that even supposing a case in which a woman pregnant due to rape ought to allow the unborn person to use her body for the hour he needs, we should not conclude that he has a right to do so; we should conclude that she is self-centered, callous, indecent, but not unjust, if she refuses. The complaints are no less grave; they are just different. * * *

My argument will be found unsatisfactory on two counts by many of those who want to regard abortion as morally permissible. First, while I do argue that abortion is not impermissible, I do not argue that it is always permissible. * * * I am inclined to think it a merit of my account precisely that it does *not* give a general yes or a general no. It allows for and supports our sense that, for example, a sick and desperately frightened fourteen-year-old schoolgirl, pregnant due to rape, may *of course* choose abortion, and that any law which rules this out is an insane law. And it also allows for and supports our sense that in other cases resort to abortion is even positively indecent. It would be indecent in the woman to request an abortion, and indecent in a doctor to perform it, if she is in her seventh month, and wants the abortion just to avoid the nuisance of postponing a trip abroad. The very fact that the arguments I have been drawing attention to treat all cases of abortion, or even all cases of abortion in which the mother's life is not at stake, as morally on a par ought to have made them suspect at the outset.

Secondly, while I am arguing for the permissibility of abortion in some cases, I am not arguing for the right to secure the death of the unborn child. It is easy to confuse these two things in that up to a certain point in the life of the fetus it is not able to survive outside the mother's body; hence removing it from her body guarantees its death. But they are importantly different. I have argued that you are not morally required to spend nine months in bed, sustaining the life of that violinist; but to say this is by no means to say that if, when you unplug yourself, there is a miracle and he survives, you then have a right to turn round and slit his throat. You may detach yourself even if this costs him his life; you have no right to be guaranteed his death, by some other means, if unplugging yourself does not kill him. There are some people who will feel dissatisfied by this feature of my argument. A woman may be utterly devastated by the thought of a child, a bit of herself, put out for adoption and never seen or heard of again. She may therefore want not merely that the child be detached from her, but more, that it die. Some opponents of abortion are inclined to regard this as beneath contempt—thereby showing insensitivity to what is surely a powerful source of despair. All the same, I agree that the desire for the child's death is not one which anybody may gratify, should it turn out to be possible to detach the child alive.

At this place, however, it should be remembered that we have only been pretending throughout that the fetus is a human being from the moment of conception. A very early abortion is surely not the killing of a person, and so is not dealt with by anything I have said here.

STUDY QUESTIONS

1. What does Thomson hope to achieve with the example of the violinist?
2. Are there possible cases of abortion that would be morally wrong, even if we accept Thomson's arguments?
3. How can Thomson argue that there can be cases in which an abortion is morally indecent, but nevertheless the fetus has no right not to be aborted?

MARY ANNE WARREN
On the Moral and Legal Status of Abortion

Mary Anne Warren (1946–2010) was an American philosopher and a pioneering figure in the field of applied ethics.

For our purposes, abortion may be defined as the act a woman performs in deliberately terminating her pregnancy before it comes to term, or in allowing another person to terminate it. Abortion usually entails the death of a fetus. Nevertheless, I will argue that it is morally permissible, and should be neither legally prohibited nor made needlessly difficult to obtain, e.g. by obstructive legal regulations.

∗ ∗ ∗ The advocates of prohibition believe that ∗ ∗ ∗ abortion is ∗ ∗ ∗ the moral equivalent of murder, and must be prohibited in all or most cases. (Some would make an exception where the woman's life is in danger, or when the pregnancy is due to rape or incest; others would prohibit abortion even in those cases.)

In response, advocates of a right to choose abortion point to the terrible consequences of prohibiting it, especially while contraception is still unreliable, and is financially beyond the reach of much of the world's population. Worldwide, hundreds of thousands of women die each year from illegal abortions, and many more suffer from complications that may leave them injured or infertile. Women who are poor, underage, disabled, or otherwise vulnerable, suffer most from the absence of safe and legal abortion. Advocates of choice also argue that to deny a woman access to abortion is to deprive her of the right to control her own body. ∗ ∗ ∗

Abortion opponents ∗ ∗ ∗ regard the deliberate killing of fetuses as even more tragic. Nor do appeals to the right to control one's own body impress them, since they deny that this right includes the right to destroy a fetus. We cannot hope to persuade those who equate abortion with murder that they are mistaken, unless we can refute the standard anti-abortion argument: that because fetuses are human beings, they have a right to life equal to that of any other human being. Unfortunately, confusion has prevailed with respect to the two important questions which that argument raises: (1) Is a human fetus really a human being at all stages of prenatal development? and (2) If so, what (if anything) follows about the moral and legal status of abortion?

∗ ∗ ∗ [Some philosophers assume that] if a fetus is a human being then abortion is almost always immoral.

Judith Thomson has questioned this assumption. She argues that, even if we grant the anti-abortionist the claim that a fetus is a human being with the same right to life as any other human being, we can still demonstrate that women are not morally obliged to complete every unwanted pregnancy. ∗ ∗ ∗

Even if Thomson's argument does not hold up, her essential insight—that it requires argument to show that if fetuses are human beings then abortion is murder—is a valuable one. The assumption that she attacks is invidious, for it requires that in our deliberations about the ethics of abortion we must ignore almost entirely the needs of the pregnant woman and other persons for whom she is responsible. This will not do; determining what moral rights a fetus has is only one step in determining the moral status of abortion. The next step is finding a just solution to conflicts between whatever rights the fetus has, and the rights and responsibilities of the woman who is unwillingly pregnant. * * *

I

Judith Thomson argues that, even if a fetus has a right to life, abortion is often morally permissible. Her argument is based upon an imaginative analogy. She asks you to picture yourself waking up one day in bed with a famous violinist, who is a stranger to you. Imagine that you have been kidnapped, and your bloodstream connected to that of the violinist, who has an ailment that will kill him unless he is permitted to share your kidneys for nine months. No one else can save him, since you alone have the right type of blood. Consequently the Society of Music Lovers has arranged for you to be kidnapped, and hooked up. If you unhook yourself, he will die. But if you remain in bed with him, then after nine months he will be cured and able to survive without further assistance from you.

Now, Thomson asks, what are your obligations in this situation? To be consistent, the anti-abortionist must say that you are obliged to stay in bed with the violinist: for violinists are human beings, and all human beings have a right to life. But this is outrageous; thus there must be something very wrong with the same argument when it is applied to abortion. It would be extremely generous of you to agree to stay in bed with the violinist; but it is absurd to suggest that your refusal to do so would be the moral equivalent of murder. The violinist's right to life does not oblige you to do whatever is required to keep him alive; still less does it justify anyone else in forcing you to do so. * * *

Thomson concludes * * * one has no duty to keep another human being alive at a great personal cost, unless one has somehow contracted a special obligation toward that individual; and a woman who is pregnant may have done nothing that morally obliges her to make the burdensome personal sacrifices necessary to preserve the life of the fetus.

This argument is plausible, and in the case of pregnancy due to rape it is probably conclusive. Difficulties arise, however, when we attempt to specify the larger range of cases in which abortion can be justified on the basis of this argument. Thomson considers it a virtue that her argument does not imply that abortion is always morally permissible. It would, she says, be indecent for a woman in her seventh month of pregnancy to have an abortion in order to embark on a trip to Europe. On the other hand, the violinist analogy shows that, "a sick and desperately frightened fourteen-year-old schoolgirl, pregnant due to rape, may *of course* choose abortion, and that any law which rules this out is an insane law." So far, so good; but what are we to say about the woman who becomes pregnant not through rape but because she and her partner did not use available forms of contraception, or because their attempts at contraception failed? What about a woman who becomes pregnant intentionally, but then re-evaluates the wisdom of having a child? In such cases, the violinist analogy is considerably less useful to advocates of the right to choose abortion.

It is perhaps only when a woman's pregnancy is due to rape, or some other form of coercion, that the situation is sufficiently analogous to the violinist case for our moral intuitions to transfer convincingly from the one case to the other. One difference between a pregnancy caused by rape and most unwanted pregnancies is that only in the former case is it perfectly clear that the woman is in no way responsible for her predicament. In the other cases, she *might* have been able to avoid becoming pregnant, e.g., by taking birth control pills (more faithfully), or insisting upon the use of high-quality condoms, or even avoiding heterosexual intercourse altogether throughout her fertile years. In contrast, if you are suddenly kidnapped by strange music lovers and hooked up to a sick violinist, then you are in no way responsible for your situation, which you could not have foreseen or prevented. And responsibility does seem to matter here. If a person behaves in a way which she could have avoided, and which she knows might bring into existence a human being who will depend upon her survival, then it is not entirely clear that if and when that happens she may rightly refuse to do what she must in order to keep that human being alive.

This argument shows that the violinist analogy provides a persuasive defense of a woman's right to choose abortion only in cases where she is in no way morally responsible for her own pregnancy. In all other cases, the assumption that a fetus has a strong right to life makes it necessary to look carefully at the particular circumstances in order to determine the extent of the woman's responsibility, and hence the extent of her obligation. ✳ ✳ ✳

A supporter of the violinist analogy might reply that it is absurd to suggest that forgetting her pill one day might be sufficient to morally oblige a woman to complete an unwanted pregnancy. And indeed it is absurd to suggest this. As we will see, a woman's moral right to choose abortion does not depend upon the extent to which she might be thought to be morally responsible for her own pregnancy. But once we allow the assumption that a fetus has a strong right to life, we cannot avoid taking this absurd suggestion seriously. On this assumption, it is a vexing question whether and when abortion is morally justifiable. * * *

My conviction is * * * a fetus is not yet a person, and therefore does not yet have a strong moral right to life. Although the truth of this conviction may not be self-evident, it does, I believe, follow from some highly plausible claims about the appropriate grounds for ascribing moral rights. * * *

II

The question we must answer in order to determine the moral status of abortion is, How are we to define the moral community, the set of beings with full and equal moral rights? What sort of entity has the inalienable moral rights to life, liberty, and the pursuit of happiness? Thomas Jefferson attributed these rights to all men, and he may have intended to attribute them only to men. Perhaps he ought to have attributed them to all human beings. If so, then we arrive first, at [the] problem of defining what makes an entity a human being, and second, at the question * * * : what reason is there for identifying the moral community with the set of all human beings, in whatever way we have chosen to define that term?

ON THE DEFINITION OF "HUMAN"

The term "human being" has two distinct, but not often distinguished, senses. This results in a slide of meaning, which serves to conceal the fallacy in the traditional argument that, since (1) it is wrong to kill innocent human beings, and (2) fetuses are innocent human beings, therefore (3) it is wrong to kill fetuses. For if "human being" is used in the same sense in both (1) and (2), then whichever of the two senses is meant, one of these premises is question-begging. And if it is used in different senses then the conclusion does not follow.

Thus, (1) is a generally accepted moral truth, and one that does not beg the question about abortion, only if "human being" is used to mean something like "a full-fledged member of the moral community, who is also a member of the human species." I will call this the *moral* sense of "human being." It is not to be confused with what I will call the *genetic* sense, i.e., the sense in which any individual entity that belongs to the human species is a human being, regardless of whether or not it is rightly considered to be an equal member of the moral community. Premise (1) avoids begging the question only if the moral sense is intended, while premise (2) avoids it only if what is intended is the genetic sense.

[Some] argue for the classification of fetuses with human beings by pointing, first, to the presence of the human genome in cell nuclei of the human conceptus from conception onwards; and secondly, to the potential capacity for rational thought. But [what must be shown], in order to support ∗ ∗ ∗ this version of the traditional anti-abortion argument, is that fetuses are human beings in the moral sense—the sense in which all human beings have full equal moral rights. In the absence of any argument showing that whatever is genetically human is also morally human ∗ ∗ ∗ nothing more than genetic humanity can be demonstrated by the presence of human chromosomes in the fetus's cell nuclei. And, as we will see, the strictly potential capacity for rational thought can at most show that the fetus may later *become* human in the moral sense.

DEFINING THE MORAL COMMUNITY

Is genetic humanity sufficient for moral humanity? There are good reasons for not defining the moral community in this way. I would suggest that the moral community consists, in the first instance, of all persons, rather than all genetically human entities. It is *persons* who invent moral rights, and who are (sometimes) capable of respecting them. It does not follow from this that only persons can have moral rights. However, persons are wise not to ascribe to entities that clearly are not persons moral rights that cannot in practice be respected without severely undercutting the fundamental moral rights of those who clearly are.

What characteristics entitle an entity to be considered a person? This is not the place to attempt a complete analysis of the concept of personhood; but we do not need such an analysis to explain why a fetus is not a person. All we need is an approximate list of the most basic criteria of personhood. In searching for these criteria, it is useful to look beyond the set of people with whom we are acquainted, all of whom are human. Imagine then, a space traveller who lands on a new planet, and encounters organisms unlike any she has ever seen or heard of. If she wants to behave morally toward these organisms, she has somehow to determine whether they are people and thus have full moral rights, or whether they are things that she need not feel guilty about treating, for instance, as a source of food.

How should she go about making this determination? * * *

I suggest that among the characteristics which are central to the concept of personhood are the following:

1. *sentience*—the capacity to have conscious experiences, usually including the capacity to experience pain and pleasure;
2. *emotionality*—the capacity to feel happy, sad, angry, loving, etc.;
3. *reason*—the capacity to solve new and relatively complex problems;
4. *the capacity to communicate*, by whatever means, messages of an indefinite variety of types; that is, not just with an indefinite number of possible contents but on indefinitely many possible topics;
5. *self-awareness*—having a concept of oneself as an individual and/or as a member of a social group; and finally
6. *moral agency*—the capacity to regulate one's own actions through moral principles or ideals.

* * * Let us assume that our explorer knows approximately what these six characteristics mean, and that she is able to observe whether or not the extraterrestrials possess these mental and behavioral capacities. How should she use her findings to decide whether or not they are persons?

An entity need not have *all* of these attributes to be a person and perhaps none of them is absolutely necessary. For instance, the absence of emotion would not disqualify a being that was person-like in all other ways. * * * Some people are unemotional; some cannot communicate well; some lack self-awareness; and some are not moral agents. It should not surprise us that many people do not meet all of the criteria of personhood. Criteria for the applicability of complex concepts are often like this: none may be logically necessary, but the more criteria that are satisfied, the more confident we are that the concept is applicable. Conversely, the fewer criteria are satisfied, the less plausible it is to hold that the concept applies. And if none of the relevant criteria are met, then we may be confident that it does not.

Thus, to demonstrate that a fetus is not a person, all I need to claim is that an entity that has none of these six characteristics is not a person. Sentience is the most basic mental capacity, and the one that may have the best claim to being a necessary (though not sufficient) condition for personhood. Sentience can establish a claim to moral considerability, since sentient beings can be harmed in ways that matter to them; for instance, they can be caused to feel pain, or deprived of the continuation of a life that is pleasant to them. It is unlikely that an entirely insentient organism could develop the other mental behavioral capacities that are characteristic of persons. Consequently, it is odd to claim that an entity that is not sentient, and that has never been sentient, is nevertheless a person. Persons who have permanently and irreparably lost all capacity for sentience, but who remain biologically alive, arguably still have strong moral rights by virtue of what they have been in the past. But small fetuses, which have not yet begun to have experiences, are not persons yet and do not have the rights that persons do. * * *

If (1)–(6) are the primary criteria of personhood, then genetic humanity is neither necessary nor sufficient for personhood. Some genetically human entities are not persons, and there may be persons who belong to other species. A man or woman whose consciousness has been permanently obliterated but who remains biologically alive is a human entity who may no longer be a person; and some unfortunate humans, who have never had any sensory or cognitive capacities at all, may not be people either. Similarly, an early fetus is a human entity which is not yet a person. It is not even minimally sentient, let alone capable of emotion, reason, sophisticated communication, self-awareness, or moral agency. Thus, while it may be greatly valued as a future child, it does not yet have the claim to moral consideration that it may come to have later. * * *

Although only those persons who are moral agents can participate directly in the shaping and enforcement of moral rights, they need not and usually do not ascribe moral rights only to themselves and other moral agents. Human beings are social creatures who naturally care for small children, and other members of the social community who are not currently capable of moral agency. Moreover, we are all vulnerable to the temporary or permanent loss of the mental capacities necessary for moral agency. Thus, we have self-interested as well as altruistic reasons for extending basic moral rights to infants and other sentient human beings who have already been born, but who currently lack some of these other mental capacities. These human beings, despite their current disabilities, are persons and members of the moral community.

But in extending moral rights to beings (human or otherwise) that have few or none of the morally significant characteristics of persons, we need to be careful not to burden human moral agents with obligations that they cannot possibly fulfill, except at an unacceptably great cost to their own well-being and that of those they care about. Women often cannot complete unwanted pregnancies, except at intolerable mental, physical, and economic cost to themselves and their families. And heterosexual intercourse is too important a part of the social lives of most men and women to be reserved for times when pregnancy is an acceptable outcome. Furthermore, the world cannot afford the continued rapid population growth which is the inevitable consequence of prohibiting abortion, so long as contraception is neither very reliable nor available to everyone. If fetuses were persons, then they would have rights that must be respected, even at great social or personal cost. But given that early fetuses, at least, are unlike persons in the morally relevant respects, it is unreasonable to insist that they be accorded exactly the same moral and legal status.

FETAL DEVELOPMENT AND THE RIGHT TO LIFE

Two questions arise regarding the application of these suggestions to the moral status of the fetus. First, if indeed fetuses are not yet persons, then might they nevertheless have strong moral rights based upon the degree to which they *resemble* persons? Secondly, to what extent, if any does a fetus's potential to *become* a person imply that we ought to accord to it some of the same moral rights? * * *

It is reasonable to suggest that the more like a person something is—the more it appears to meet at least some of the criteria of personhood—the stronger is the case for according it a right to life and perhaps the stronger its right to life is. That being the case, perhaps the fetus gradually gains a stronger right to life as it develops. * * *

A seven-month fetus can apparently feel pain and can respond to such stimuli as light and sound. Thus it may have a rudimentary form of consciousness. Nevertheless, it is probably not as conscious, or as capable of emotion, as even a very young infant is; and it has as yet little or no capacity for reason, sophisticated intentional communication, or self-awareness. In these respects, even a late-term fetus is arguably less like a person than are many nonhuman animals. Many animals (e.g., large-brained mammals such as elephants, cetaceans, or apes) are not only sentient, but clearly possessed of a degree of reason, and perhaps even of self-awareness. Thus on the basis of its resemblance to a person, even a late-term fetus can have no more right to life than do these animals.

Animals may, indeed, plausibly be held to have some moral rights and perhaps rather strong ones. But it is impossible in practice to accord full and equal rights to all animals. When an animal poses a serious threat to the life or well-being of a person, we do not, as a rule, greatly blame the person for killing it; and there are good reasons for this species-based discrimination. Animals, however intelligent in their own domains, are generally not beings with whom we can reason; we cannot persuade mice not to invade our dwellings or consume our food. That is why their rights are necessarily weaker than those of a being who can understand and respect the rights of other beings.

But the probable sentience of late-term fetuses is not the only argument in favor of treating late abortion as a morally more serious matter than early abortion. Many—perhaps most—people are repulsed by the thought of needlessly aborting a late-term fetus. The late-term fetus has features which cause it to arouse in us almost the same powerful protective instinct as does a small infant.

This response needs to be taken seriously. If it were impossible to perform abortions early in pregnancy, then we might have to tolerate the mental and physical trauma that would be occasioned by the routine resort to late abortion. But where early abortion is safe, legal, and readily available to all women, it is not unreasonable to expect most women who wish to end a pregnancy to do so prior to the third trimester. Most women strongly prefer early to late abortion, because it is far less physically painful and emotionally traumatic. Other things being equal, it is better for all concerned that pregnancies that are not to be completed should be ended as early as possible. Few women would consider ending a pregnancy in the seventh month in order to take a trip to Europe. If, however, a woman's own life or health is at stake, or if the fetus has been found to be so severely abnormal as to be unlikely to survive or to have a life worth living, then late abortion may be the morally best choice. For even a late-term fetus is not a person yet, and its rights must yield to those of the woman whenever it is impossible for both to be respected.

POTENTIAL PERSONHOOD AND THE RIGHT TO LIFE

We have seen that a presentient fetus does not yet resemble a person in ways which support the claim that it has strong moral rights. But what about its *potential*, the fact that if nurtured and allowed to develop it may eventually become a person? Doesn't that potential give it at least some right to life? The fact that something is a potential person may be a reason for not destroying it; but we need not conclude from this that potential people have a strong right to life. It may be that the feeling that it is better not to destroy a potential person is largely due to the fact that potential people are felt to be an invaluable resource, not to be lightly squandered. If every speck of dust were a potential person, we would be less apt to suppose that all potential persons have a right to become actual.

We do not need to insist that a potential person has no right to life whatever. There may be something immoral, and not just imprudent about wantonly destroying potential people, when doing so isn't necessary. But even if a potential person does have some right to life, that right could not outweigh the right of a woman to obtain an abortion; for the basic moral rights of an actual person outweigh the rights of a merely potential person, whenever the two conflict. * * *

THE OBJECTION FROM INFANTICIDE

One objection to my argument is that it appears to justify not only abortion, but also infanticide. A newborn infant is not much more person-like than a nine-month fetus, and thus it might appear that if late-term abortion is sometimes justified then infanticide must also sometimes be justified. Yet most people believe that infanticide is a form of murder, and virtually never justified.

This objection is less telling than it may seem. There are many reasons why infanticide is more difficult to justify than abortion, even though neither fetuses nor newborn infants are clearly persons. In this period of history, the deliberate killing of newborns is virtually never justified. This is in part because newborns are so close to being persons that to kill them requires a very strong moral justification—as does the killing of dolphins, chimpanzees, and other highly person-like creatures. It is certainly wrong to kill such beings for the sake of convenience, or financial profit, or "sport." Only the most vital human needs, such as the need to defend one's own life and physical integrity, can provide a plausible justification for killing such beings.

In the case of an infant, there is no such vital need, since in the contemporary world there are usually other people who are eager to provide a good home for an infant whose own parents are unable or unwilling to care for it. Many people wait years for the opportunity to adopt a child, and some are unable to do so, even though there is every reason to believe that they would be good parents. The needless destruction of a viable infant not only deprives a sentient human being of life, but also deprives other persons of a source of great satisfaction, perhaps severely impoverishing *their* lives.

Even if an infant is unadoptable (e.g., because of some severe physical disability), it is still wrong to kill it. For most of us value the lives of infants, and would greatly prefer to pay taxes to support foster care and state institutions for disabled children, rather than to allow them to be killed or abandoned. So long as most people feel this way, and so long as it is possible to provide care for infants who are wanted, or who have special needs that their parents cannot meet without assistance, it is wrong to let any infant die who has a chance of living a reasonably good life.

If these arguments show that infanticide is wrong, at least in today's world, then why don't they also show that late-term abortion is always wrong? After all, third-trimester fetuses are almost as person-like as infants, and many people value them and would prefer that they be preserved. As a potential source of pleasure to some family, a fetus is just as valuable as an infant. But there is an important difference between these two cases: once the infant is born, its continued life cannot pose any serious threat to the woman's life or health, since she is free to put it up for adoption or to place it in foster care. While she might, in rare cases, prefer that the child die rather than being raised by others, such a preference would not establish a right on her part.

In contrast, a pregnant woman's right to protect her own life and health outweighs other people's desire that the fetus be preserved—just as, when a person's desire for life or health is threatened by an animal, and when the threat cannot be removed without killing the animal, that person's right to self-defense outweighs the desires of those who would prefer that the animal not be killed. Thus, while the moment of birth may mark no sharp discontinuity in the degree to which an infant resembles a person, it does mark the end of the mother's right to determine its fate. Indeed, if a late abortion can be safely performed without harming the fetus, the mother has in most cases no right to insist upon its death, for the same reason that she has no right to insist that a viable infant be killed or allowed to die.

It remains true that, on my view, neither abortion nor the killing of newborns is obviously a form of murder. Perhaps our legal system is correct in its classification of infanticide as murder, since no other legal category adequately expresses the force of our disapproval of this action. But some moral distinction remains, and it has important consequences. When a society cannot possibly care for all of the children who are born, without endangering the survival of adults and older children, allowing some infants to die may be the best of a bad set of options. Throughout history, most societies—from those that lived by gathering and hunting to the highly civilized Chinese, Japanese, Greeks, and Romans—have permitted infanticide under such unfortunate circumstances, regarding it as a necessary evil. It shows a lack of understanding to condemn these societies as morally benighted for this reason alone, since in the absence of safe and effective means of contraception and abortion, parents must some times have had no morally better options.

CONCLUSION

*** Because women are persons, and fetuses are not, women's rights to life, liberty, and physical integrity morally override whatever right to life it may be appropriate to ascribe to a fetus. Consequently, laws that deny women the right to obtain abortions, or that make safe early abortions difficult or impossible for some women to obtain, are an unjustified violation of basic moral and constitutional rights.

STUDY QUESTIONS

1. Why does Warren feel the need to extend Thomson's argument?
2. What use does Warren make of the distinction between genetic human beings and moral human beings?
3. Does Warren's argument also justify infanticide?

DON MARQUIS
Why Abortion Is Immoral

Don Marquis (b. 1935) is an American philosopher best known for his writing on abortion.

*** This essay sets out an argument that purports to show, as well as any argument in ethics can show, that abortion is, except possibly in rare cases, seriously immoral, that it is in the same moral category as killing an innocent adult human being.

The argument is based on a major assumption. Many of the most insightful and careful writers on the ethics of abortion *** believe that whether or not abortion is morally permissible stands or falls on whether or not a fetus is the sort of being whose life it is seriously wrong to end. The argument of this essay will assume, but not argue, that they are correct.

* * * The purpose of this essay is to develop a general argument for the claim that the overwhelming majority of deliberate abortions are seriously immoral.

I.

* * * Consider the way a typical anti-abortionist argues. She will argue or assert that life is present from the moment of conception or that fetuses look like babies or that fetuses possess a characteristic such as a genetic code that is both necessary and sufficient for being human. Anti–abortionists seem to believe that (1) the truth of all of these claims is quite obvious, and (2) establishing any of these claims is sufficient to show that abortion is morally akin to murder.

A standard pro-choice strategy exhibits similarities. The pro-choicer will argue or assert that fetuses are not persons or that fetuses are not rational agents or that fetuses are not social beings. Pro-choicers seem to believe that (1) the truth of any of these claims is quite obvious, and (2) establishing any of these claims is sufficient to show that an abortion is not a wrongful killing.

In fact, both the pro-choice and the anti-abortion claims do seem to be true * * * We seem to have a standoff. How can it be resolved?

* * * If any of these arguments concerning abortion is a good argument, it requires not only some claim characterizing fetuses, but also some general moral principle that ties a characteristic of fetuses to having or not having the right to life or to some other moral characteristic that will generate the obligation or the lack of obligation not to end the life of a fetus. Accordingly, the arguments of the anti-abortionist and the pro-choicer need a bit of filling in to be regarded as adequate.

Note what each partisan will say. The anti-abortionist will claim that her position is supported by such generally accepted moral principles as "It is always prima facie seriously wrong to take a human life" or "It is always prima facie seriously wrong to end the life of a baby." Since these are generally accepted moral principles, her position is certainly not obviously wrong. The pro-choicer will claim that her position is supported by such plausible moral principles as "Being a person is what gives an individual intrinsic moral worth" or "It is only seriously prima facie wrong to take the life of a member of the human community." Since these are generally accepted moral principles, the pro-choice position is certainly not obviously wrong. Unfortunately, we have again arrived at a standoff.

Now, how might one deal with this standoff? The standard approach is to try to show how the moral principles of one's opponent lose their plausibility under analysis. It is easy to see how this is possible. On the one hand, the anti-abortionist will defend a moral principle concerning the wrongness of killing which tends to be broad in scope in order that even fetuses at an early stage of pregnancy will fall under it. The problem with broad principles is that they often embrace too much. In this particular instance, the principle "It is always prima facie wrong to take a human life" seems to entail that it is wrong to end the existence of a living human cancer-cell culture, on the grounds that the culture is both living and human. Therefore, it seems that the anti-abortionist's favored principle is too broad.

On the other hand, the pro-choicer wants to find a moral principle concerning the wrongness of killing which tends to be narrow in scope in order that fetuses will *not* fall under it. The problem with narrow principles is that they often do not embrace enough. Hence, the needed principles such as "It is prima facie seriously wrong to kill only persons" or "It is prima facie wrong to kill only rational agents" do not explain why it is wrong to kill infants or young children or the severely retarded or even perhaps the severely mentally ill. Therefore, we seem again to have a standoff. The anti-abortionist charges, not unreasonably, that pro–choice principles concerning killing are too narrow to be acceptable; the pro-choicer charges, not unreasonably, that anti-abortionist principles concerning killing are too broad to be acceptable.

Attempts by both sides to patch up the difficulties in their positions run into further difficulties. The anti-abortionist will try to remove the problem in her position by reformulating her principle concerning killing in terms of human beings. Now we end up with: "It is always prima facie seriously wrong to end the life of a human being." This principle has the advantage of avoiding the problem of the human cancer-cell culture counterexample. But this advantage is purchased at a high price. For although it is clear that a fetus is both human and alive, it is not at all clear that a fetus is a human *being*. There is at least something to be said for the view that something becomes a human being only after a process of development, and that therefore first trimester fetuses and perhaps all fetuses are not yet human beings. Hence, the anti-abortionist, by this move, has merely exchanged one problem for another.

The pro-choicer fares no better. She may attempt to find reasons why killing infants, young children, and the severely retarded is wrong which are independent of her major principle that is supposed to explain the wrongness of taking human life, but which will not also make abortion immoral. This is no easy task. Appeals to social utility will seem satisfactory only to those who resolve not to think of the enormous difficulties with a utilitarian account of the wrongness of killing and the significant social costs of preserving the lives of the unproductive. A pro-choice strategy that extends the definition of "person" to infants or even to young children seems just as arbitrary as an anti-abortion strategy that extends the definition of "human being" to fetuses. Again, we find symmetries in the two positions and we arrive at a standoff. * * *

There is a way out of this apparent dialectical quandary. The moral generalizations of both sides are not quite correct. The generalizations hold for the most part, for the usual cases. This suggests that they are all *accidental* generalizations, that the moral claims made by those on both sides of the dispute do not touch on the *essence* of the matter.

* * * A necessary condition of resolving the abortion controversy is a more theoretical account of the wrongness of killing. After all, if we merely believe, but do not understand, why killing adult human beings such as ourselves is wrong, how could we conceivably show that abortion is either immoral or permissible?

II.

In order to develop such an account, we can start from the following unproblematic assumption concerning our own case: it is wrong to kill *us*. Why is it wrong? * * *

* * * The loss of one's life is one of the greatest losses one can suffer. The loss of one's life deprives one of all the experiences, activities, projects, and enjoyments that would otherwise have constituted one's future. Therefore, killing someone is wrong, primarily because the killing inflicts (one of) the greatest possible losses on the victim. To describe this as the loss of life can be misleading, however. The change in my biological state does not by itself make killing me wrong. The effect of the loss of my biological life is the loss to me of all those activities, projects, experiences, and enjoyments which would otherwise have constituted my future personal life. These activities, projects, experiences, and enjoyments are either valuable for their own sakes or are means to something else that is valuable for its own sake. Some parts of my future are not valued by me now, but will come to be valued by me as I grow older and as my values and capacities change. When I am killed,

I am deprived both of what I now value which would have been part of my future personal life, but also what I would come to value. Therefore, when I die, I am deprived of all of the value of my future. Inflicting this loss on me is ultimately what makes killing me wrong. * * *

The claim * * * is directly supported by two considerations. In the first place, this theory explains why we regard killing as one of the worst of crimes. Killing is especially wrong, because it deprives the victim of more than perhaps any other crime. In the second place, people with AIDS or cancer who know they are dying believe, of course, that dying is a very bad thing for them. * * *

The view that what makes killing wrong is the loss to the victim of the value of the victim's future gains additional support when some of its implications are examined. In the first place, it is incompatible with the view that it is wrong to kill only beings who are biologically human. It is possible that there exists a different species from another planet whose members have a future like ours. * * * This theory entails that it would be wrong to kill members of such a species. * * *

In the second place, the claim that the loss of one's future is the wrong-making feature of one's being killed entails the possibility that the futures of some actual nonhuman mammals on our own planet are sufficiently like ours that it is seriously wrong to kill them also. * * *

In the third place, the claim that the loss of one's future is the wrong-making feature of one's being killed does not entail, as sanctity of human life theories do, that active euthanasia is wrong. Persons who are severely and incurably ill, who face a future of pain and despair, and who wish to die will not have suffered a loss if they are killed. It is, strictly speaking, the value of a human's future which makes killing wrong in this theory. This being so, killing does not necessarily wrong some persons who are sick and dying. * * *

In the fourth place, the account of the wrongness of killing defended in this essay does straightforwardly entail that it is prima facie seriously wrong to kill children and infants, for we do presume that they have futures of value. Since we do believe that it is wrong to kill defenseless little babies, it is important that a theory of the wrongness of killing easily account for this. Personhood theories of the wrongness of killing, on the other hand, cannot straightforwardly account for the wrongness of killing infants and young children. * * *

The claim that the primary wrong-making feature of a killing is the loss to the victim of the value of its future has obvious consequences for the ethics of abortion. The future of a standard fetus includes a set of experiences, projects, activities, and such which are identical with the futures of adult human beings and are identical with the futures of young children. Since the reason that is sufficient to explain why it is wrong to kill human beings after the time of birth is a reason that also applies to fetuses, it follows that abortion is prima facie seriously morally wrong.

This argument does not rely on the invalid inference that, since it is wrong to kill persons, it is wrong to kill potential persons also. The category that is morally central to this analysis is the category of having a valuable future like ours; it is not the category of personhood. * * *

The structure of this anti-abortion argument can be both illuminated and defended by comparing it to what appears to be the best argument for the wrongness of the wanton infliction of pain on animals. This latter argument is based on the assumption that it is prima facie wrong to inflict pain on me (or you, reader). What is the natural property associated with the infliction of pain which makes such infliction wrong? The obvious answer seems to be that the infliction of pain causes suffering and that suffering is a misfortune. The suffering caused by the infliction of pain is what makes the wanton infliction of pain on me wrong. The wanton infliction of pain on other adult humans causes suffering. The wanton infliction of pain on animals causes suffering. Since causing suffering is what makes the wanton infliction of pain wrong and since the wanton infliction of pain on animals causes suffering, it follows that the wanton infliction of pain on animals is wrong.

This argument * * * shares a number of structural features with the argument for the serious prima facie wrongness of abortion. Both arguments start with an obvious assumption concerning what it is wrong to do to me (or you, reader). Both then look for the characteristic or the consequence of the wrong action which makes the action wrong. Both recognize that the wrong–making feature of these immoral actions is a property of actions sometimes directed at individuals other than postnatal human beings. If the structure of the argument for the wrongness of the wanton infliction of pain on animals is sound, then the structure of the argument for the prima facie serious wrongness of abortion is also sound, for the structure of the two arguments is the same. The structure common to both is the key to the explanation of how the wrongness of abortion can be demonstrated without recourse to the category of person. In neither argument is that category crucial. * * *

Of course, this value of a future-like-ours argument, if sound, shows only that abortion is prima facie wrong, not that it is wrong in any and all circumstances. Since the loss of the future to a standard fetus, if killed, is, however, at least as great a loss as the loss of the future to a standard adult human being who is killed, abortion, like ordinary killing, could be justified only by the most compelling reasons. The loss of one's life is almost the greatest misfortune that can happen to one. Presumably abortion could be justified in some circumstances, only if the loss consequent on failing to abort would be at least as great. Accordingly, morally permissible abortions will be rare indeed unless, perhaps, they occur so early in pregnancy that a fetus is not yet definitely an individual. Hence, this argument should be taken as showing that abortion is presumptively very seriously wrong, where the presumption is very strong—as strong as the presumption that killing another adult human being is wrong.

III.

* * * This account does not have to be an account of the necessary conditions for the wrongness of killing. Some persons in nursing homes may lack valuable human futures, yet it may be wrong to kill them for other reasons. Furthermore, this account does not obviously have to be the sole reason killing is wrong where the victim did have a valuable future. This analysis claims only that, for any killing where the victim did have a valuable future like ours, having that future by itself is sufficient to create the strong presumption that the killing is seriously wrong.

One way to overturn the value of a future-like-ours argument would be to find some account of the wrongness of killing which is at least as intelligible and which has different implications for the ethics of abortion. Two rival accounts possess at least some degree of plausibility. One account is based on the obvious fact that people value the experience of living and wish for that valuable experience to continue. Therefore, it might be said, what makes killing wrong is the discontinuation of that experience for the victim. Let us call this the *discontinuation account*. Another rival account is based upon the obvious fact that people strongly desire to continue to live. This suggests that what makes killing us so wrong is that it interferes with the fulfillment of a strong and fundamental desire, the fulfillment of which is necessary for the fulfillment of any other desires we might have. Let us call this the *desire account*. * * *

One problem with the desire account is that we do regard it as seriously wrong to kill persons who have little desire to live or who have no desire to live or, indeed, have a desire not to live. We believe it is seriously wrong to kill the unconscious, the sleeping, those who are tired of life, and those who are suicidal. The value-of-a-human-future account renders standard morality intelligible in these cases; these cases appear to be incompatible with the desire account.

The desire account is subject to a deeper difficulty. We desire life, because we value the goods of this life. The goodness of life is not secondary to our desire for it. If this were not so, the pain of one's own premature death could be done away with merely by an appropriate alteration in the configuration of one's desires. This is absurd. Hence, it would seem that it is the loss of the goods of one's future, not the interference with the fulfillment of a strong desire to live, which accounts ultimately for the wrongness of killing. * * *

It is also worth noting that, if future desires have moral force in a modified desire account of the wrongness of killing, one can find support for an anti-abortion ethic even in the absence of a value of a future-like-ours account. If one decides that a morally relevant property, the possession of which is sufficient to make it wrong to kill some individual, is the desire at some future time to live—one might decide to justify one's refusal to kill suicidal teenagers on these grounds, for example—then, since typical fetuses will have the desire in the future to live, it is wrong to kill typical fetuses. Accordingly, it does not seem that a desire account of the wrongness of killing can provide a justification of a pro-choice ethic of abortion which is nearly as adequate as the value of a human-future justification of an anti-abortion ethic.

The discontinuation account looks more promising as an account of the wrongness of killing. It seems just as intelligible as the value of a future-like-ours account, but it does not justify an anti-abortion position. Obviously, if it is the continuation of one's activities, experiences, and projects, the loss of which makes killing wrong, then it is not wrong to kill fetuses for that reason, for fetuses do not have experiences, activities, and projects to be continued or discontinued. Accordingly, the discontinuation account does not have the anti-abortion consequences that the value of a future-like-ours account has. Yet, it seems as intelligible as the value of a future-like-ours account, for when we think of what would be wrong with our being killed, it does seem as if it is the discontinuation of what makes our lives worthwhile which makes killing us wrong.

Is the discontinuation account just as good an account as the value of a future-like-ours account? The discontinuation account will not be adequate at all, if it does not refer to the *value* of the experience that may be discontinued. One does not want the discontinuation account to make it wrong to kill a patient who begs for death and who is in severe pain that cannot be relieved short of killing. (I leave open the question of whether it is wrong for other reasons.) Accordingly, the discontinuation account must be more than a bare discontinuation account. It must make some reference to the positive value of the patient's experiences. But, by the same token, the value of a future-like-ours account cannot be a bare future account either. Just having a future surely does not itself rule out killing the above patient. This account must make some reference to the value of the patient's future experiences and projects also. Hence, both accounts involve the value of experiences, projects, and activities. So far we still have symmetry between the accounts.

The symmetry fades, however, when we focus on the time period of the value of the experiences, etc., which has moral consequences. Although both accounts leave open the possibility that the patient in our example may be killed, this possibility is left open only in virtue of the utterly bleak future for the patient. It makes no difference whether the patient's immediate past contains intolerable pain, or consists in being in a coma (which we can imagine is a situation of indifference), or consists in a life of value. If the patient's future is a future of value, we want our account to make it wrong to kill the patient. If the patient's future is intolerable, whatever his or her immediate past, we want our account to allow killing the patient. Obviously, then, it is the value of that patient's future which is doing the work in rendering the morality of killing the patient intelligible.

This being the case, it seems clear that whether one has immediate past experiences or not does no work in the explanation of what makes killing wrong. The addition the discontinuation account makes to the value of a human future account is otiose. Its addition to the value-of-a-future account plays no role at all in rendering intelligible the wrongness of killing. Therefore, it can be discarded with the discontinuation account of which it is a part. ∗∗∗

VI.

The purpose of this essay has been to set out an argument for the serious presumptive wrongness of abortion subject to the assumption that the moral permissibility of abortion stands or falls on the moral status of the fetus. ∗∗∗

* * * This analysis can be viewed as resolving a standard problem—indeed, *the* standard problem—concerning the ethics of abortion. Clearly, it is wrong to kill adult human beings. Clearly, it is not wrong to end the life of some arbitrarily chosen single human cell. Fetuses seem to be like arbitrarily chosen human cells in some respects and like adult humans in other respects. The problem of the ethics of abortion is the problem of determining the fetal property that settles this moral controversy. The thesis of this essay is that the problem of the ethics of abortion, so understood, is solvable.

STUDY QUESTIONS

1. Explain Marquis's "value of the future" account of the wrongness of killing and its consequences for the permissibility of abortion.
2. What does Marquis find wrong with the "desire" account of the wrongness of killing?
3. What does Marquis find wrong with the "discontinuation" account of the wrongness of killing?

ROSALIND HURSTHOUSE
Virtue Theory and Abortion

Rosalind Hursthouse (b. 1943) is a philosopher from New Zealand and an important figure in the revival of virtue ethics.

As everyone knows, the morality of abortion is commonly discussed in relation to just two considerations: first, and predominantly, the status of the fetus and whether or not it is the sort of thing that may or may not be innocuously or justifiably killed; and second, and less predominantly (when, that is, the discussion concerns the *morality* of abortion rather than the question of permissible legislation in a just society), women's rights. If one thinks within this familiar framework, one may well be puzzled about what virtue theory, as such, could contribute. Some people assume the discussion will be conducted solely in terms of what the virtuous agent would or would not do. * * * Others assume that only justice, or at most justice and charity, will be applied to the issue, generating a discussion very similar to Judith Jarvis Thomson's.[1]

---

1 Judith Jarvis Thomson, "A Defense of Abortion." One could indeed regard this article as proto-virtue theory (no doubt to the surprise of the author) if the concepts of callousness and kindness were allowed more weight. [*Editor's note*: See selections from "A Defense of Abortion" on pp. 332–340 of this reader.]

Now if this is the way the virtue theorist's discussion of abortion is imagined to be, no wonder people think little of it. It seems obvious in advance that in any such discussion there must be either a great deal of extremely tendentious application of the virtue terms *just, charitable*, and so on or a lot of rhetorical appeal to "this is what only the virtuous agent knows." But these are caricatures; they fail to appreciate the way in which virtue theory quite transforms the discussion of abortion by dismissing the two familiar dominating considerations as, in a way, fundamentally irrelevant. In what way or ways, I hope to make both clear and plausible.

Let us first consider women's rights. Let me emphasize again that we are discussing the *morality* of abortion, not the rights and wrongs of laws prohibiting or permitting it. If we suppose that women do have a moral right to do as they choose with their own bodies, or, more particularly, to terminate their pregnancies, then it may well follow that a *law* forbidding abortion would be unjust. Indeed, even if they have no such right, such a law might be, as things stand at the moment, unjust, or impractical, or inhumane: on this issue I have nothing to say in this article. But, putting all questions about the justice or injustice of laws to one side, and supposing only that women have such a moral right, *nothing* follows from this supposition about the morality of abortion, according to virtue theory, once it is noted (quite generally, not with particular reference to abortion) that in exercising a moral right I can do something cruel, or callous, or selfish, light-minded, self-righteous, stupid, inconsiderate, disloyal, dishonest—that is, act viciously. Love and friendship do not survive their parties' constantly insisting on their rights, nor do people live well when they think that getting what they have a right to is of preeminent importance; they harm others, and they harm themselves. So whether women have a moral right to terminate their pregnancies is irrelevant within virtue theory, for it is irrelevant to the question "In having an abortion in these circumstances, would the agent be acting virtuously or viciously or neither?"

What about the consideration of the status of the fetus—what can virtue theory say about that? One might say that this issue is not in the province of *any* moral theory; it is a metaphysical question, and an extremely difficult one at that. Must virtue theory then wait upon metaphysics to come up with the answer?

At first sight it might seem so. For virtue is said to involve knowledge, and part of this knowledge consists in having the *right* attitude to things. "Right" here does not just mean "morally right" or "proper" or "nice" in the modern sense; it means "accurate, true." One cannot have the right or correct attitude to something if the attitude is based on or involves false beliefs. And this suggests that if the status of the fetus is relevant to the rightness or wrongness of abortion, its status must be known, as a truth, to the fully wise and virtuous person.

But the sort of wisdom that the fully virtuous person has is not supposed to be recondite; it does not call for fancy philosophical sophistication, and it does not depend upon, let alone wait upon, the discoveries of academic philosophers. And this entails the following, rather startling, conclusion: that the status of the fetus—that issue over which so much ink has been spilt—is, according to virtue theory, simply not relevant to the rightness or wrongness of abortion (within, that is, a secular morality).

Or rather, since that is clearly too radical a conclusion, it is in a sense relevant, but only in the sense that the familiar biological facts are relevant. By "the familiar biological facts" I mean the facts that most human societies are and have been familiar with—that, standardly (but not invariably), pregnancy occurs as the result of sexual intercourse, that it lasts about nine months, during which time the fetus grows and develops, that standardly it terminates in the birth of a living baby, and that this is how we all come to be.

It might be though that this distinction—between the familiar biological facts and the status of the fetus—is a distinction without a difference. But this is not so. To attach relevance to the status of the fetus, in the sense in which virtue theory claims it is not relevant, is to be gripped by the conviction that we must go beyond the familiar biological facts, deriving some sort of conclusion from them, such as that the fetus has rights, or is not a person, or something similar. It is also to believe that this exhausts the relevance of the familiar biological facts, that all they are relevant to is the status of the fetus and whether or not it is the sort of thing that may or may not be killed.

These convictions, I suspect, are rooted in the desire to solve the problem of abortion by getting it to fall under some general rule such as "You ought not to kill anything with the right to life but may kill anything else." But they have resulted in what should surely strike any nonphilosopher as a most bizarre aspect of nearly all the current philosophical literature on abortion, namely, that, far from treating abortion as a unique moral problem, markedly unlike any other, nearly everything written on the status of the fetus and its bearing on the abortion issue would be consistent with the human reproductive facts (to say nothing of family life) being totally different from what they are. Imagine that you are an alien extraterrestrial anthropologist who does not know that the human race is roughly 50 percent female and 50 percent male, or that our only (natural) form of reproduction involves heterosexual intercourse, viviparous birth, and the female's (and only the female's) being pregnant for nine months, or that females are capable of childbearing from late childhood to late middle age, or that childbearing is painful, dangerous, and emotionally charged—do you think you would pick up these facts from the hundreds of articles written on the status of the fetus? I am quite sure you would not. And that, I think, shows that the current philosophical literature on abortion has got badly out of touch with reality.

Now if we are using virtue theory, our first question is not "What do the familiar biological facts show—what can be derived from them about the status of the fetus?" but "How do these facts figure in the practical reasoning, actions and passions, thoughts and reactions, of the virtuous and the nonvirtuous? What is the mark of having the right attitude to these facts and what manifests having the wrong attitude to them?" This immediately makes essentially relevant not only all the facts about human reproduction I mentioned above, but a whole range of facts about our emotions in relation to them as well. I mean such facts as that human parents, both male and female, tend to care passionately about their offspring, and that family relationships are among the deepest and strongest in our lives—and, significantly, among the longest-lasting.

These facts make it obvious that pregnancy is not just one among many other physical conditions; and hence that anyone who genuinely believes that an abortion is comparable to a haircut or an appendectomy is mistaken. The fact that the premature termination of a pregnancy is, in some sense, the cutting off of a new human life, and thereby, like the procreation of a new human life, connects with all our thoughts about human life and death, parenthood, and family relationships, must make it a serious matter. To disregard this fact about it, to think of abortion as nothing but the killing of something that does not matter, or as nothing but the exercise of some right or rights one has, or as the incidental means to some desirable state of affairs, is to do something callous and light-minded, the sort of thing that no virtuous and wise person would do. It is to have the wrong attitude not only to fetuses, but more generally to human life and death, parenthood, and family relationships.

Although I say that the facts make this obvious, I know that this is one of my tendentious points. In partial support of it I note that even the most dedicated proponents of the view that deliberate abortion is just like an appendectomy or haircut rarely hold the same view of spontaneous abortion, that is, miscarriage. It is not so tendentious of me to claim that to react to people's grief over miscarriage by saying, or even thinking, "What a fuss about nothing!" would be callous and light-minded, whereas to try to laugh someone out of grief over an appendectomy scar or a botched haircut would not be. It is hard to give this point due prominence within act-centered theories, for the inconsistency is an inconsistency in attitude about the seriousness of loss of life, not in beliefs about which acts are right or wrong. Moreover, an act-centered theorist may say, "Well, there is nothing wrong with *thinking* 'What a fuss about nothing!' as long as you do not say it and hurt the person who is grieving. And besides, we cannot be held responsible for our thoughts, only for the intentional actions they give rise to." But the character traits that virtue theory emphasizes are not simply dispositions to intentional actions, but a seamless disposition to certain actions and passions, thoughts and reactions.

To say that the cutting off of a human life is always a matter of some seriousness, at any stage, is not to deny the relevance of gradual fetal development. Notwithstanding the well-worn point that clear boundary lines cannot be drawn, our emotions and attitudes regarding the fetus do change as it develops, and again when it is born, and indeed further as the baby grows. Abortion for shallow reasons in the later stages is much more shocking than abortion for the same reasons in the early stages in a way that matches the fact that deep grief over miscarriage in the later stages is more appropriate than it is over miscarriage in the earlier stages (when, that is, the grief is solely about the loss of *this* child, not about, as might be the case, the loss of one's only hope of having a child or of having one's husband's child). Imagine (or recall) a woman who already has children; she had not intended to have more, but finds herself unexpectedly pregnant. Though contrary to her plans, the pregnancy, once established as a fact, is welcomed—and then she loses the embryo almost immediately. If this were bemoaned as a tragedy, it would, I think, be a misapplication of the concept of what is tragic. But it may still properly be mourned as a loss. The grief is expressed in such terms as "I shall always wonder how she or he would have turned out" or "When I look at the others, I shall think, 'How different their lives would have been if this other one had been part of them.'" It would, I take it, be callous and light-minded to say, or think, "Well, she has already *got* four children; what's the problem?"; it would be neither, nor arrogantly intrusive in the case of a close friend, to try to correct prolonged mourning by saying, "I know it's sad, but it's not a tragedy; rejoice in the ones you have." The application of *tragic* becomes more appropriate as the fetus grows, for the mere fact that one has lived with it for longer, conscious of its existence, makes a difference. To shrug off an early abortion is understandable just because it is very hard to be fully conscious of the fetus's existence in the early stages and hence hard to appreciate that an early abortion is the destruction of life. It is particularly hard for the young and inexperienced to appreciate this, because appreciation of it usually comes only with experience.

I do not mean "with the experience of having an abortion" (though that may be part of it) but, quite generally, "with the experience of life." Many women who have borne children contrast their later pregnancies with their first successful one, saying that in the later ones they were conscious of a new life growing in them from very early on. And, more generally, as one reaches the age at which the next generation is coming up close behind one, the counterfactuals "If I, or she, had had an abortion, Alice, or Bob, would not have been born" acquire a significant application, which casts a new light on the conditionals "If I or Alice have an abortion then some Caroline or Bill will not be born."

The fact that pregnancy is not just one among many physical conditions does not mean that one can never regard it in that light without manifesting a vice. When women are in very poor physical health, or worn out from childbearing, or forced to do very physically demanding jobs, then they cannot be described as self-indulgent, callous, irresponsible, or light-minded if they seek abortions mainly with a view to avoiding pregnancy as the physical condition that it is. To go through with a pregnancy when one is utterly exhausted, or when one's job consists of crawling along tunnels hauling coal, as many women in the nineteenth century were obliged to do, is perhaps heroic, but people who do not achieve heroism are not necessarily vicious. That they can view the pregnancy only as eight months of misery, followed by hours if not days of agony and exhaustion, and abortion only as the blessed escape from this prospect, is entirely understandable and does not manifest any lack of serious respect for human life or a shallow attitude to motherhood. What it does show is that something is terribly amiss in the conditions of their lives, which make it so hard to recognize pregnancy and childbearing as the good that they can be.

In relation to this last point I should draw attention to the way in which virtue theory has a sort of built-in indexicality. Philosopher arguing against

anything remotely resembling a belief in the sanctity of life (which the above claims clearly embody) frequently appeal to the existence of other communities in which abortion and infanticide are practiced. We should not automatically assume that it is impossible that some other communities could be morally inferior to our own; maybe some are, or have been, precisely insofar as their members are, typically, callous or light-minded or unjust. But in communities in which life is a great deal tougher for everyone than it is in ours, having the right attitude to human life and death, parenthood, and family relationships might well manifest itself in ways that are unlike ours. When it is essential to survival that most members of the community fend for themselves at a very young age or work during most of their waking hours, selective abortion or infanticide might be practiced either as a form of genuine euthanasia or for the sake of the community and not, I think, be thought callous or light-minded. But this does not make everything all right; as before, it shows that there is something amiss with the conditions of their lives, which are making it impossible for them to live really well.[2]

The foregoing discussion, insofar as it emphasizes the right attitude to human life and death, parallels to a certain extent those standard discussions of abortion that concentrate on it solely as an issue of killing. But it does not, as those discussions do, gloss over the fact, emphasized by those who discuss the morality of abortion in terms of women's rights, that abortion, wildly unlike any other form of killing, is the termination of a pregnancy, which is a condition of a woman's body and results in *her* having a child if it is not aborted. This fact is given due recognition not by appeal to women's rights but by emphasizing the relevance of the familiar biological and psychological facts and their connection with having the right attitude to parenthood and family relationships. But it may well be thought that failing to bring in women's rights still leaves some important aspects of the problem of abortion untouched.

Speaking in terms of women's rights, people sometimes say things like, "Well, it's her life you're talking about too, you know; she's got a right to her own life, her own happiness." And the discussion stops there. But in the context of virtue theory, given that we are particularly concerned with what constitutes a good human life, with what true happiness or *eudaimonia* is, this is no place to stop. We go on to ask, "And is this life of hers a good one? Is she living well?"

---

2 For another example of the way in which "tough conditions" can make a difference to what is involved in having the right attitude to human life and death and family relationships, see the concluding sentences of Foot's "Euthanasia." [*Editor's note:* See selections from "Euthanasia" on pp. 379–388 of this reader.]

If we are to go on to talk about good human lives, in the context of abortion, we have to bring in our thoughts about the value of love and family life, and our proper emotional development through a natural life cycle. The familiar facts support the view that parenthood in general, and motherhood and childbearing in particular, are intrinsically worthwhile, are among the things that can be correctly thought to be partially constitutive of a flourishing human life. If this is right, then a woman who opts for not being a mother (at all, or again, or now) by opting for abortion may thereby be manifesting a flawed grasp of what her life should be, and be about—a grasp that is childish, or grossly materialistic, or shortsighted, or shallow.

I said "*may* thereby": this *need* not be so. Consider, for instance, a woman who has already had several children and fears that to have another will seriously affect her capacity to be a good mother to the ones she has—she does not show a lack of appreciation of the intrinsic value of being a parent by opting for abortion. Nor does a woman who has been a good mother and is approaching the age at which she may be looking forward to being a good grandmother. Nor does a woman who discovers that her pregnancy may well kill her, and opts for abortion and adoption. Nor, necessarily, does a woman who has decided to lead a life centered around some other worthwhile activity or activities with which motherhood would compete.

People who are childless by choice are sometimes described as "irresponsible," or "selfish," or "refusing to grow up," or "not knowing what life is about." But one can hold that having children is intrinsically worthwhile without endorsing this, for we are, after all, in the happy position of there being more worthwhile things to do than can be fitted into one lifetime. Parenthood, and motherhood in particular, even if granted to be intrinsically worthwhile, undoubtedly take up a lot of one's adult life, leaving no room for some other worthwhile pursuits. But some women who choose abortion rather than have their first child, and some men who encourage their partners to choose abortion, are not avoiding parenthood for the sake of other worthwhile pursuits, but for the worthless one of "having a good time," or for the pursuit of some false vision of the ideals of freedom or self-realization. And some others who say "I am not ready for parenthood yet" are making some sort of mistake about the extent to which one can manipulate the circumstances of one's life so as to make it fulfill some dream that one has. Perhaps one's dream is to have two perfect children, a girl and a boy, within a perfect marriage, in financially secure circumstances, with

an interesting job of one's own. But to care too much about that dream, to demand of life that it give it to one and act accordingly, may be both greedy and foolish, and is to run the risk of missing out on happiness entirely. Not only may fate make the dream impossible, or destroy it, but one's own attachment to it may make it impossible. Good marriages, and the most promising children, can be destroyed by just one adult's excessive demand for perfection.

Once again, this is not to deny that girls may quite properly say "I am not ready for motherhood yet," especially in our society, and, far from manifesting irresponsibility or light-mindedness, show an appropriate modesty or humility, or a fearfulness that does not amount to coward-ice. However, even when the decision to have an abortion is the right decision—one that does not itself fall under a vice-related term and thereby one that the perfectly virtuous could recommend—it does not follow that there is no sense in which having the abortion is wrong, or guilt inappropriate. For, by virtue of the fact that a human life has been cut short, some evil has probably been brought about, and that circumstances make the decision to bring about some evil the right decision will be a ground for guilt if getting into those circumstances in the first place itself manifested a flaw in character.

What "gets one into those circumstances" in the case of abortion is, except in the case of rape, one's sexual activity and one's choices, or the lack of them, about one's sexual partner and about contraception. The virtuous woman (which here of course does not mean simply "chaste woman" but "woman with the virtues") has such character traits as strength, indepen-dence, resoluteness, decisiveness, self-confidence, responsibility, serious-mindedness, and self-determination—and no one, I think, could deny that many women become pregnant in circumstances in which they cannot welcome or cannot face the thought of having *this* child precisely because they lack one or some of these character traits. So even in the cases where the decision to have an abortion is the right one, it can still be the reflec-tion of a moral failing—not because the decision itself is weak or cowardly or irresolute or irresponsible or light-minded, but because lack of the req-uisite opposite of these failings landed one in the circumstances in the first place. Hence the common universalized claim that guilt and remorse are never appropriate emotions about an abortion is denied. They may be appropriate, and appropriately inculcated, even when the decision was the right one.

Another motivation for bringing women's rights into the discussion may be to attempt to correct the implication, carried by the killing-centered approach, that insofar as abortion is wrong, it is a wrong that only women do, or at least (given the preponderance of male doctors) that only women instigate. I do not myself believe that we can thus escape the fact that nature bears harder on women than it does on men, but virtue theory can certainly correct many of the injustices that the emphasis on women's rights is rightly concerned about. With very little amendment, everything that has been said above applies to boys and men too. Although the abortion decision is, in a natural sense, the women's decision, proper to her, boys and men are often party to it, for well or ill, and even when they are not, they are bound to have been party to the circumstances that brought it up. No less than girls and women, boys and men can, in their actions, manifest self-centeredness, callousness, and light-mindedness about life and parenthood in relation to abortion. They can be self-centered or courageous about the possibility of disability in their offspring; they need to reflect on their sexual activity and their choices, or the lack of them, about their sexual partner and contraception; they need to grow up and take responsibility for their own actions and life in relation to fatherhood. If it is true, as I maintain, that insofar as motherhood is intrinsically worthwhile, being a mother is an important purpose in women's lives, being a father (rather than a mere generator) is an important purpose in men's lives as well, and it is adolescent of men to turn a blind eye to this and pretend that they have many more important things to do.

STUDY QUESTIONS

1. Virtue ethics has been accused of having nothing to say to help us settle the question of the morality of abortion. Is this a fair criticism?
2. Why does Hursthouse think that the moral question of abortion is not primarily the question of whether abortion should be legally available?
3. Why does Hursthouse think it is wrong to seek a general principle to guide us in our thinking about abortion?

■ Compare and Contrast Questions

1. Does Warren convincingly show that Thomson's account can only justify abortion in a very limited range of cases?
2. Does Marquis show that Warren and Thomson are mistaken in their arguments in defence of abortion?
3. How would Hursthouse judge the arguments given by Thomson, Warren, and Marquis?

EUTHANASIA

This section contains two papers on euthanasia, the practice of hastening the death of someone for whom life has become a burden. The second paper, by Philippa Foot, was written at least in part in response to the first, by James Rachels. Rachels brings out an important distinction between active euthanasia, in which steps are taken to end a life, through the administration of a drug, for example, and passive euthanasia, in which someone is allowed to die, even though prolonging the person's life would have been medically possible. It is commonly thought that in some circumstances passive euthanasia can be morally acceptable but that active euthanasia is simply a form of murder.

Rachels's aim in this discussion is to overturn this common view. One argument is that active euthanasia will typically bring about death more rapidly than passive euthanasia and hence would do more to reduce suffering. Another argument confronts the common view that killing is morally worse than letting die. Rachels offers an example in which there seems to be a moral equivalence between the two. Rachels acknowledges, of course, that it is generally true that cases of killing are morally worse than cases of letting die. But it does not follow that this is always true, and in respect to euthanasia, Rachels argues that active and passive euthanasia are morally equivalent.

Philippa Foot makes clear that the question of the moral permissibility of euthanasia is distinct from the question of its legal standing. The moral question is whether it is ever a sufficient justification for the choice of a death of another that the death can be counted a benefit rather than a harm. Foot addresses this question from the perspective of virtue ethics, specifically the virtues of justice and charity. Justice concerns what we owe to each other, through assistance or noninterference, whereas charity directs us to other people's good, whether or not, formally speaking, we owe them anything. Having made this distinction, Foot is able to consider Rachels's discussion of active and passive euthanasia. From her perspective, Rachels is quite wrong to deny that there is a significant moral difference between killing and letting die. For killing is a failure of justice: we owe it to people not to kill them. Letting someone die, if it is a moral failing at all, is a failure of charity, to act for the sake of their own good.

Foot does not argue that killing, being a failure of justice, is always worse than letting die, a failure of charity. Rather her point is that because they are distinct virtues, it is likely that there will be occasions when one applies and the other does not; for example, while letting die would be acceptable, killing would be a grave wrong.

She then moves on to discuss potential cases of nonvoluntary euthanasia, when we are unable to ascertain people's wishes about whether they would prefer to live or die, but when death would be in their interests. This is distinct from voluntary cases, when the person requests their own death. Foot argues that active nonvoluntary euthanasia is ruled out because people have, in justice, a right to noninterference unless they waive it. But she does believe that such rights can be waived, which means that, in her view, active, as well as passive, voluntary euthanasia should in at least some cases be permitted. However, there can be moral arguments, from charity, against voluntary euthanasia, where, for example, people have taken an unduly pessimistic view of their prospects and are asking to be killed or let die on the basis of false beliefs. Nonvoluntary passive euthanasia can sometimes be morally legitimate as an act of charity, as long as it is done for the good of the person who is to be allowed to die. This is very important, because Foot concludes her discussion by reminding us that some people would wish to get rid of their ailing, elderly relatives to make their own lives easier and not for the sake of the person involved. Because of this selfish motive, active euthanasia could be very badly abused if it were made legal, whatever the moral circumstances in any particular case.

JAMES RACHELS
Active and Passive Euthanasia

James Rachels (1941–2003) was an American philosopher especially known for his writings in ethics.

The distinction between active and passive euthanasia is thought to be crucial for medical ethics. The idea is that it is permissible, at least in some cases, to withhold treatment and allow a patient to die, but it is never permissible to take any direct action designed to kill the patient. This doctrine seems to be accepted by most doctors, and it is endorsed in a statement adopted by the House of Delegates of the American Medical Association on December 4, 1973:

> The intentional termination of the life of one human being by another—mercy killing—is contrary to that for which the medical profession stands and is contrary to the policy of the American Medical Association.

> The cessation of the employment of extraordinary means to prolong the life of the body when there is irrefutable evidence that biological death is imminent is the decision of the patient and/or his immediate family. The advice and judgment of the physician should be freely available to the patient and/or his immediate family.

However, a strong case can be made against this doctrine. In what follows I will set out some of the relevant arguments, and urge doctors to reconsider their views on this matter.

To begin with a familiar type of situation, a patient who is dying of incurable cancer of the throat is in terrible pain, which can no longer be satisfactorily alleviated. He is certain to die within a few days, even if present treatment is continued, but he does not want to go on living for those days since the pain is unbearable. So he asks the doctor for an end to it, and his family joins in the request.

Suppose the doctor agrees to withhold treatment, as the conventional doctrine says he may. The justification for his doing so is that the patient is in terrible agony, and since he is going to die anyway, it would be wrong to prolong his suffering needlessly. But now notice this. If one simply withholds treatment, it may take the patient longer to die, and so he may suffer more than he would if more direct action were taken and a lethal injection given. This fact provides strong reason for thinking that, once the initial decision not to prolong his agony has been made, active euthanasia is actually preferable to passive euthanasia, rather than the reverse. To say otherwise is to endorse the option that leads to more suffering rather than less, and is contrary to the humanitarian impulse that prompts the decision not to prolong his life in the first place.

Part of my point is that the process of being "allowed to die" can be relatively slow and painful, whereas being given a lethal injection is relatively quick and painless. Let me give a different sort of example. In the United States about one in 600 babies is born with Down's syndrome. Most of these babies are otherwise healthy—that is, with only the usual pediatric care, they will proceed to an otherwise normal infancy. Some, however, are born with congenital defects such as intestinal obstructions that require operations if they are to live. Sometimes, the parents and the doctor will decide not to operate, and let the infant die. Anthony Shaw describes what happens then:

> . . . When surgery is denied (the doctor) must try to keep the infant from suffering while natural forces sap the baby's life away. As a surgeon whose natural inclination is to use the scalpel to fight off death, standing by and watching a salvageable baby die is the most emotionally exhausting experience I know.

It is easy at a conference, in a theoretical discussion, to decide that such infants should be allowed to die. It is altogether different to stand by in the nursery and watch as dehydration and infection wither a tiny being over hours and days. This is a terrible ordeal for me and the hospital staff—much more so than for the parents who never set foot in the nursery.[1]

I can understand why some people are opposed to all euthanasia, and insist that such infants must be allowed to live. I think I can also understand why other people favor destroying these babies quickly and painlessly. But why should anyone favor letting "dehydration and infection wither a tiny being over hours and days"? The doctrine that says that a baby may be allowed to dehydrate and wither, but may not be given an injection that would end its life without suffering, seems so patently cruel as to require no further refutation. The strong language is not intended to offend, but only to put the point in the clearest possible way.

My second argument is that the conventional doctrine leads to decisions concerning life and death made on irrelevant grounds.

Consider again the case of the infants with Down's syndrome who need operations for congenital defects unrelated to the syndrome to live. Sometimes, there is no operation, and the baby dies, but when there is no such defect, the baby lives on. Now, an operation such as that to remove an intestinal obstruction is not prohibitively difficult. The reason why such operations are not performed in these cases is, clearly, that the child has Down's syndrome and the parents and doctor judge that because of that fact it is better for the child to die.

But notice that this situation is absurd, no matter what view one takes of the lives and potentials of such babies. If the life of such an infant is worth preserving, what does it matter if it needs a simple operation? Or, if one thinks it better that such a baby should not live on, what difference does it make that it happens to have an unobstructed intestinal tract? In either case, the matter of life and death is being decided on irrelevant grounds. It is the Down's syndrome, and not the intestines, that is the issue. The matter should be decided, if at all, on that basis, and not be allowed to depend on the essentially irrelevant question of whether the intestinal tract is blocked.

What makes this situation possible, of course, is the idea that when there is an intestinal blockage, one can "let the baby die," but when there

---

[1] Shaw Anthony, "Doctor, Do We Have a Choice?" *The New York Times Magazine*, January 30, 1972, p. 54.

is no such defect there is nothing that can be done, for one must not "kill" it. The fact that this idea leads to such results as deciding life or death on irrelevant grounds is another good reason why the doctrine should be rejected.

One reason why so many people think that there is an important moral difference between active and passive euthanasia is that they think killing someone is morally worse than letting someone die. But is it? Is killing, in itself, worse than letting die? To investigate this issue, two cases may be considered that are exactly alike except that one involves killing whereas the other involves letting someone die. Then, it can be asked whether this difference makes any difference to the moral assessments. It is important that the cases be exactly alike, except for this one difference, since otherwise one cannot be confident that it is this difference and not some other that accounts for any variation in the assessments of the two cases. So, let us consider this pair of cases:

In the first, Smith stands to gain a large inheritance if anything should happen to his six-year-old cousin. One evening while the child is taking his bath, Smith sneaks into the bathroom and drowns the child, and then arranges things so that it will look like an accident.

In the second, Jones also stands to gain if anything should happen to his six-year-old cousin. Like Smith, Jones sneaks in planning to drown the child in his bath. However, just as he enters the bathroom Jones sees the child slip and hit his head, and fall face down in the water. Jones is delighted; he stands by, ready to push the child's head back under if it is necessary, but it is not necessary. With only a little thrashing about, the child drowns all by himself, "accidentally," as Jones watches and does nothing.

Now Smith killed the child, whereas Jones "merely" let the child die. That is the only difference between them. Did either man behave better, from a moral point of view? If the difference between killing and letting die were in itself a morally important matter, one should say that Jones's behavior was less reprehensible than Smith's. But does one really want to say that? I think not. In the first place, both men acted from the same motive, personal gain, and both had exactly the same end in view when they acted. It may be inferred from Smith's conduct that he is a bad man, although that judgment may be withdrawn or modified if certain further facts are learned about him—for example, that he is mentally deranged. But would not the very same thing be inferred about Jones from his conduct? And would not the same further considerations also be relevant to any modification of this judgment? Moreover, suppose Jones pleaded, in his own defense, "After all, I didn't do anything except just stand there and watch the child drown. I didn't kill him; I only let him die." Again, if letting die were in itself less bad than killing, this defense should have at least some weight. But it does not. Such a "defense" can only be regarded as a grotesque perversion of moral reasoning. Morally speaking, it is no defense at all.

Now, it may be pointed out, quite properly, that the cases of euthanasia with which doctors are concerned are not like this at all. They do not involve personal gain or the destruction of normal healthy children. Doctors are concerned only with cases in which the patient's life is of no further use to him, or in which the patient's life has become or will soon become a terrible burden. However, the point is the same in these cases: the bare difference between killing and letting die does not, in itself, make a moral difference. If a doctor lets a patient die, for humane reasons, he is in the same moral position as if he had given the patient a lethal injection for humane reasons. If his decision was wrong—if, for example, the patient's illness was in fact curable—the decision would be equally regrettable no matter which method was used to carry it out. And if the doctor's decision was the right one, the method used is not in itself important.

The AMA policy statement isolates the crucial issue very well; the crucial issue is "the intentional termination of the life of one human being by another." But after identifying this issue, and forbidding "mercy killing," the statement goes on to deny that the cessation of treatment is the intentional termination of a life. This is where the mistake comes in, for what is the cessation of treatment, in these circumstances, if it is not "the intentional termination of the life of one human being by another"? Of course it is exactly that, and if it were not, there would be no point to it.

Many people will find this judgment hard to accept. One reason, I think, is that it is very easy to conflate the question of whether killing is, in itself, worse than letting die, with the very different question of whether most actual cases of killing are more reprehensible than most actual cases of letting die. Most actual cases of killing are clearly terrible (think, for example, of all the murders reported in the newspapers), and one hears of such cases every day. On the other hand, one hardly ever hears of a case of letting die, except for the actions of doctors who are motivated by humanitarian reasons. So one learns to think of killing in a much worse light than of letting die. But this does not mean that there is something about killing that makes it in itself worse than letting die, for it is not the bare difference between killing and letting die that makes the difference in these cases. Rather, the other factors—the murderer's motive of personal gain, for example, contrasted with the doctor's humanitarian motivation—account for different reactions to the different cases.

I have argued that killing is not in itself any worse than letting die; if my contention is right, it follows that active euthanasia is not any worse than passive euthanasia. What arguments can be given on the other side? The most common, I believe, is the following:

"The important difference between active and passive euthanasia is that, in passive euthanasia, the doctor does not do anything to bring about the patient's death. The doctor does nothing, and the patient dies of whatever ills already afflict him. In active euthanasia, however, the doctor does something to bring about the patient's death: he kills him. The doctor who gives the patient with cancer a lethal injection has himself caused his patient's death; whereas if he merely ceases treatment, the cancer is the cause of the death."

A number of points need to be made here. The first is that it is not exactly correct to say that in passive euthanasia the doctor does nothing, for he does do one thing that is very important: he lets the patient die. "Letting someone die" is certainly different, in some respects, from other types of action—mainly in that it is a kind of action that one may perform by way of not performing certain other actions. For example, one may let a patient die by way of not giving medication, just as one may insult someone by way of not shaking his hand. But for any purpose of moral assessment, it is a type of action nonetheless. The decision to let a patient die is subject to moral appraisal in the same way that a decision to kill him would be subject to moral appraisal: it may be assessed as wise or unwise, compassionate or sadistic, right or wrong. If a doctor deliberately let a patient die who was suffering from a routinely curable illness, the doctor would certainly be to blame for what he had done, just as he would be to blame if he had needlessly killed the patient. Charges against him would then be appropriate. If so, it would be no defense at all for him to insist that he didn't "do anything." He would have done something very serious indeed, for he let his patient die.

Fixing the cause of death may be very important from a legal point of view, for it may determine whether criminal charges are brought against the doctor. But I do not think that this notion can be used to show a moral difference between active and passive euthanasia. The reason why it is considered bad to be the cause of someone's death is that death is regarded as a great evil—and so it is. However, if it has been decided that euthanasia—even passive euthanasia—is desirable in a given case, it has also been decided that in this instance death is no greater an evil than the patient's continued existence. And if this is true, the usual reason for not wanting to be the cause of someone's death simply does not apply.

Finally, doctors may think that all of this is only of academic interest—the sort of thing that philosophers may worry about but that has no practical bearing on their own work. After all, doctors must be concerned about the legal consequences of what they do, and active euthanasia is clearly forbidden by the law. But even so, doctors should also be concerned with the fact that the law is forcing upon them a moral doctrine that may well be indefensible, and has a considerable effect on their practices. Of course, most doctors are not now in the position of being coerced in this matter, for they do not regard themselves as merely going along with what the law requires. Rather, in statements such as the AMA policy statement that I have quoted, they are endorsing this doctrine as a central point of medical ethics. In that statement, active euthanasia is condemned not merely as illegal but as "contrary to that for which the medical profession stands," whereas passive euthanasia is approved. However, the preceding considerations suggest that there is really no moral difference between the two, considered in themselves (there may be important moral differences in some cases in their *consequences*, but, as I pointed out, these differences may make active euthanasia, and not passive euthanasia, the morally preferable option). So, whereas doctors may have to discriminate between active and passive euthanasia to satisfy the law, they should not do any more than that. In particular, they should not give the distinction any added authority and weight by writing it into official statements of medical ethics.

STUDY QUESTIONS

1. Why does Rachels regard active euthanasia as sometimes more humane than passive euthanasia in the same circumstances?
2. Does Rachels show that there is no important moral distinction between killing and letting die?
3. What should be the consequences of Rachels's discussion for the medical profession?

PHILIPPA FOOT
Euthanasia

Philippa Foot (1920–2010) was an English moral philosopher who helped bring about the revival of virtue ethics.

When we talk about euthanasia we are talking about a death understood as a good or happy event for the one who dies. * * * By an act of euthanasia we mean one of inducing or otherwise opting for death for the sake of the one who is to die.

* * * It must be said that the word "act" is not to be taken to exclude omission: we shall speak of an act of euthanasia when someone is deliberately allowed to die, for his own good, and not only when positive measures are taken to see that he does. * * *

* * * The question * * * to be asked is whether acts of euthanasia are ever justifiable. But there are two topics here rather than one. For it is one thing to say that some acts of euthanasia considered only in themselves and their results are morally unobjectionable, and another to say that it would be all right to legalize them. Perhaps the practice of euthanasia would allow too many abuses, and perhaps there would be too many mistakes. Moreover the practice might have very important and highly undesirable side effects, because it is unlikely that we could change our principles about the treatment of the old and the ill without changing fundamental emotional attitudes and social relations. The topics must, therefore, be treated separately. In the next part of the discussion, nothing will be said about the social consequences and possible abuses of the practice of euthanasia, but only about acts of euthanasia considered in themselves.

What we want to know is whether * * * it is ever sufficient justification of the choice of death for another that death can be counted a benefit rather than harm, and that this is why the choice is made.

It will be impossible to get a clear view of the area to which this topic belongs without first marking the distinct grounds on which objection may lie when one man opts for the death of another. There are two different virtues whose requirements are, in general, contrary to such actions. An unjustified act of killing, or allowing to die, is contrary to justice or to charity, or to both virtues, and the moral failings are distinct. Justice has to do with what men *owe* each other in the way of noninterference and positive service. When used in this wide sense, which has its history in the doctrine of the cardinal virtues, justice is not especially connected with, for instance, law courts but with the whole area of rights, and duties corresponding to rights. Thus murder is one form of injustice, dishonesty another, and wrongful failure to keep contracts a third; chicanery in a law court or defrauding someone of his inheritance are simply other cases of injustice. Justice as such is not directly linked to the good of another, and may require that something be rendered to him even where it will do him harm, as Hume pointed out when he remarked that a debt must be paid even to a profligate debauchee who "would rather receive harm than benefit from large possessions."[1] Charity, on the other hand, is the virtue which attaches us to the good of others. An act of charity is in question only where something is not demanded by justice, but a lack of charity and of justice can be shown where a man is denied something which he both needs and has a right to; both charity and justice demand that widows and orphans are not defrauded, and the man who cheats them is neither charitable nor just.

It is easy to see that the two grounds of objection to inducing death are distinct. A murder is an act of injustice. A culpable failure to come to the aid of someone whose life is threatened is normally contrary, not to justice, but to charity. But where one man is under contract, explicit or implicit, to come to the aid of another injustice too will be shown. Thus injustice may be involved either in an act or an omission, and the same is true of a lack of charity; charity may demand that someone be aided, but also that an unkind word not be spoken. ＊ ＊ ＊

Let us now ask how the right to life affects the morality of acts of euthanasia. Are such acts sometimes or always ruled out by the right to life? This is certainly a possibility; for although an act of euthanasia is, by our definition, a matter of opting for death for the good of the one who is to die, there is ＊ ＊ ＊ no direct connection between that to which a man has a right and that which is for his good. ＊ ＊ ＊ A man may have the right to something which he himself would be better off without; where rights exist it is a man's will that counts, not his or anyone else's estimate of benefit or harm. So the duties complementary to the right to life—the general duty of noninterference and the duty of service incurred by certain persons—are not affected by the quality of a man's life or by his prospects. Even if it is true that he would be, as we say, "better off dead," so long as he wants to live this does not justify us in killing him and may not justify us in deliberately allowing him to die. All of us have the duty of noninterference, and some of us may have the duty to sustain his life. Suppose, for example, that a retreating army

---

1 David Hume, *Treatise*, Book III, Part II, Section 1.

has to leave behind wounded or exhausted soldiers in the wastes of an arid or snowbound land where the only prospect is death by starvation or at the hands of an enemy notoriously cruel. It has often been the practice to accord a merciful bullet to men in such desperate straits. But suppose that one of them demands that he should be left alive? It seems clear that his comrades have no right to kill him, though it is a quite different question as to whether they should give him a life-prolonging drug. The right to life can sometimes give a duty of positive service, but does not do so here. What it does give is the right to be left alone.

Interestingly enough we have arrived by way of a consideration of the right to life at the distinction normally labeled "active" versus "passive" euthanasia, and often thought to be irrelevant to the moral issue.[2] Once it is seen that the right to life is a distinct ground of objection to certain acts of euthanasia, and that this right creates a duty of noninterference more widespread than the duties of care there can be no doubt about the relevance of the distinction between passive and active euthanasia. Where everyone may have the duty to leave someone alone, it may be that no one has the duty to maintain his life, or that only some people do.

Where then do the boundaries of the "active" and "passive" lie? In some ways the words are themselves misleading, because they suggest the difference between act and omission which is not quite what we want. Certainly the act of shooting someone is the kind of thing [that counts as] "interference," and omitting to give him a drug a case of refusing care. But the act of turning off a respirator should surely be thought of as no different from the decision not to start it; if doctors had decided that a patient should be allowed to die, either course of action might follow, and both should be counted as passive rather than active euthanasia if euthanasia were in question. The point seems to be that interference in a course of treatment is not the same as other interference in a man's life, and particularly if the same body of people are responsible for the treatment and for its discontinuance. In such a case we could speak of the disconnecting of the apparatus as killing the man, or of the hospital as allowing him to die. By and large, it is the act of killing that is ruled out under the heading of noninterference, but not in every case.

Doctors commonly recognize this distinction, and the grounds on which some philosophers have denied it seem untenable. James Rachels,

---

2   See, for example, James Rachels, "Active and Passive Euthanasia." [*Editor's note*: See "Active and Passive Euthanasia" on pp. 372–378 of this reader.]

for instance, believes that if the difference between active and passive is relevant anywhere, it should be relevant everywhere, and he has pointed to an example in which it seems to make no difference which is done. If someone saw a child drowning in a bath it would seem just as bad to let it drown as to push its head under water.[3] If "it makes no difference" means that one act would be as iniquitous as the other this is true. It is not that killing is *worse* than allowing to die, but that the two are contrary to distinct virtues, which gives the possibility that in some circumstances one is impermissible and the other permissible. In the circumstances invented by Rachels, both are wicked: it is contrary to justice to push the child's head under the water—something one has no right to do. To leave it to drown is not contrary to justice, but it is a particularly glaring example of lack of charity. Here it makes no practical difference because the requirements of justice and charity coincide; but in the case of the retreating army they did not: charity would have required that the wounded soldier be killed had not justice required that he be left alive. In such a case it makes all the difference whether a man opts for the death of another in a positive action, or whether he allows him to die. ＊＊＊

We see then that the distinction between active and passive, important as it is elsewhere, has a special importance in the area of euthanasia. It should also be clear why James Rachels' other argument, that it is often "more humane" to kill than to allow to die, does not show that the distinction between active and passive euthanasia is morally irrelevant. It might be "more humane" in this sense to deprive a man of the property that brings evils on him, or to refuse to pay what is owed to Hume's profligate debauchee; but if we say this we must admit that an act which is "more humane" than its alternative may be morally objectionable because it infringes rights. ＊＊＊

Perhaps few will deny what has so far been said about the impermissibility of acts of euthanasia simply because we have so far spoken about the case of one who positively wants to live, and about his rights, whereas those who advocate euthanasia are usually thinking either about those who wish to die or about those whose wishes cannot be ascertained either because they cannot properly be said to have wishes or because, for one reason or another, we are unable to form a reliable estimate of what they are. The question that must now be asked is whether the latter type of case, where

---

3   Ibid.

euthanasia ∗ ∗ ∗ would again be nonvoluntary, is different from the one discussed so far. Would we have the right to kill someone for his own good so long as we had no idea that he positively wished to live? And what about the life-prolonging duties of doctors in the same circumstances? This is a very difficult problem. On the one hand, it seems ridiculous to suppose that a man's right to life is something which generates duties only where he has signaled that he wants to live; as a borrower does indeed have a duty to return something lent on indefinite loan only if the lender indicates that he wants it back. On the other hand, it might be argued that there is something illogical about the idea that a right has been infringed if someone incapable of saying whether he wants it or not is deprived of something that is doing him harm rather than good. Yet on the analogy of property we would say that a right has been infringed. Only if someone had earlier told us that in such circumstances he would not want to keep the thing could we think that his right had been waived. Perhaps if we could make confident judgments about what anyone in such circumstances would wish, or what he would have wished beforehand had he considered the matter, we could agree to consider the right to life as "dormant," needing to be asserted if the normal duties were to remain. But as things are we cannot make any such assumption; we simply do not know what most people would want, or would have wanted, us to do unless they tell us. This is certainly the case so far as active measures to end life are concerned. Possibly it is different, or will become different, in the matter of being kept alive, so general is the feeling against using sophisticated procedures on moribund patients, and so much is this dreaded by people who are old or terminally ill. Once again the distinction between active and passive euthanasia has come on the scene, but this time because most people's attitudes to the two are so different. It is just possible that we might presume, in the absence of specific evidence, that someone would not wish, beyond a certain point, to be kept alive; it is certainly not possible to assume that he would wish to be killed.

In the last paragraph we have begun to broach the topic of voluntary euthanasia, and this we must now discuss. What is to be said about the case in which there is no doubt about someone's wish to die: either he has told us beforehand that he would wish it in circumstances such as he is now in, and has shown no sign of a change of mind, or else he tells us now, being in possession of his faculties and of a steady mind. We should surely say that the objections previously urged against acts of euthanasia, which it must be remembered were all on the ground of rights, had disappeared. It does not seem that one would infringe someone's right to life in killing him with his permission and in fact at his request. Why should someone not be able to waive his right to life, or rather, as would be more likely to happen, to cancel some of the duties of noninterference that this right entails? (He is more likely to say that he should be killed by this man at this time in this manner, than to say that anyone may kill him at any time and in any way.) Similarly someone may give permission for the destruction of his property, and request it. The important thing is that he gives a critical permission, and it seems that this is enough to cancel the duty normally associated with the right. If someone gives you permission to destroy his property it can no longer be said that you have no right to do so, and I do not see why it should not be the case with taking a man's life. An objection might be made on the ground that only God has the right to take life, but in this paper religious as opposed to moral arguments are being left aside. Religion apart, there seems to be no case to be made out for an infringement of rights if a man who wishes to die is allowed to die or even killed. But of course it does not follow that there is no moral objection to it. Even with property, which is after all a relatively small matter, one might be wrong to destroy what one had the right to destroy. For, apart from its value to other people, it might be valuable to the man who wanted it destroyed, and charity might require us to hold our hand where justice did not.

Let us review the conclusion of this part of the argument, which has been about euthanasia and the right to life. It has been argued that from this side come stringent restrictions on the acts of euthanasia that could be morally permissible. Active nonvoluntary euthanasia is ruled out by that part of the right to life which creates the duty of noninterference though passive nonvoluntary euthanasia is not ruled out, except where the right to life-preserving action has been created by some special condition such as a contract between a man and his doctor, and it is not always certain just what such a contract involves. Voluntary euthanasia is another matter: as the preceding paragraph suggested, no right is infringed if a man is allowed to die or even killed at his own request.

Turning now to the other objection that normally holds against inducing the death of another, that it is against charity, or benevolence, we must tell a very different story. Charity is the virtue that gives attachment to the good of others, and because life is normally a good, charity normally demands that it should be saved or prolonged. But as we so defined an act of euthanasia that it seeks a man's death for his own sake—for his good—charity will normally speak in favor of it. This is not, of course, to say that charity can require an act of euthanasia which justice forbids, but if an act of euthanasia is not contrary to justice—that is, it does not infringe rights—charity will rather be in its favor than against.

Once more the distinction between nonvoluntary and voluntary euthanasia must be considered. Could it ever be compatible with charity to seek a man's death although he wanted to live, or at least had not let us know that he wanted to die? It has been argued that in such circumstances active euthanasia would infringe his right to life, but passive euthanasia would not do so, unless he had some special right to life-preserving service from the one who allowed him to die. What would charity dictate? Obviously when a man wants to live there is a presumption that he will be benefited if his life is prolonged, and if it is so the question of euthanasia does not arise. But it is, on the other hand, possible that he wants to live where it would be better for him to die: perhaps he does not realize the desperate situation he is in, or perhaps he is afraid of dying. So, in spite of a very proper resistance to refusing to go along with a man's own wishes in the matter of life and death, someone might justifiably refuse to prolong the life even of someone who asked him to prolong it, as in the case of refusing to give the wounded soldier a drug that would keep him alive to meet a terrible end. And it is even more obvious that charity does not always dictate that life should be prolonged where a man's own wishes, hypothetical or actual, are not known.

So much for the relation of charity to nonvoluntary passive euthanasia, which was not, like nonvoluntary active euthanasia, ruled out by the right to life. Let us now ask what charity has to say about voluntary euthanasia both active and passive. It was suggested in the discussion of justice that if of sound mind and steady desire a man might give others the *right* to allow him to die or even to kill him, where otherwise this would be ruled out. But it was pointed out that this would not settle the question of whether the act was morally permissible, and it is this that we must now consider. Could not charity speak against what justice allowed? Indeed it might do so. For while the fact that a man wants to die suggests that his life is wretched, and while his rejection of life may itself tend to take the good out of the things he might have enjoyed, nevertheless his wish to die might here be opposed for his own sake just as it might be if suicide were in question. Perhaps there is hope that his mental condition will improve. Perhaps he is mistaken in thinking his disease incurable. Perhaps he wants to die for the sake of someone else on whom he feels he is a burden, and we are not ready to accept this sacrifice whether for ourselves or others. In such cases, and there will surely be many of them, it could not be for his own sake that we kill him or allow him to die, and therefore euthanasia as defined in this paper would not be in question. But this is not to deny that there could be acts of voluntary euthanasia both passive and active against which neither justice nor charity would speak.

We have now considered the morality of euthanasia both voluntary and nonvoluntary, and active and passive. The conclusion has been that nonvoluntary active euthanasia (roughly, killing a man against his will or without his consent) is never justified; that is to say, that a man's being killed for his own good never justifies the act unless he himself has consented to it. A man's rights are infringed by such an action, and it is therefore contrary to justice. However, all the other combinations, nonvoluntary passive euthanasia, voluntary active euthanasia, and voluntary passive euthanasia are sometimes compatible with both justice and charity. But the strong condition carried in the definition of euthanasia adopted in this paper must not be forgotten; an act of euthanasia as here understood is one whose purpose is to benefit the one who dies.

In the light of this discussion let us look at our present practices. Are they good or are they bad? And what changes might be made, thinking now not only of the morality of particular acts of euthanasia but also of the indirect effects of instituting different practices, of the abuses to which they might be subject and of the changes that might come about if euthanasia became a recognized part of the social scene.

The first thing to notice is that it is wrong to ask whether we should introduce the practice of euthanasia as if it were not something we already had. In fact we do have it. For instance it is common, where the medical prognosis is very bad, for doctors to recommend against measures to prolong life, and particularly where a process of degeneration producing one medical emergency after another has already set in. If these doctors are not certainly within their legal rights this is something that is apt to come as a surprise to them as to the general public. It is also obvious that euthanasia is often practiced where old people are concerned. If someone very old and soon to die is attacked by a disease that makes his life wretched, doctors do not always come in with life-prolonging drugs. Perhaps poor patients are more fortunate in this respect than rich patients, being more often left to die in peace; but it is in any case a well recognized piece of medical practice, which is a form of euthanasia.

No doubt the case of infants with mental or physical defects will be suggested as another example of the practice of euthanasia as we already have it, since such infants are sometimes deliberately allowed to die. That they are deliberately allowed to die is certain; children with severe spina bifida malformations are not always operated on even where it is thought that without the operation they will die; and even in the case of children with Down's Syndrome who have intestinal obstructions the relatively simple operation that would make it possible to feed them is sometimes not performed. Whether this is euthanasia in our sense or only as the Nazis understood it is another matter. We must ask the crucial question, "Is it for the sake of the child himself that the doctors and parents choose his death?" In some cases the answer may really be yes, and what is more important it may really be true that the kind of life which is a good is not possible or likely for this child, and that there is little but suffering and frustration in store for him. But this must presuppose that the medical prognosis is wretchedly bad, as it may be for some spina bifida children. With children who are born with Down's Syndrome it is, however, quite different. Most of these are able to live on for quite a time in a reasonably contented way, remaining like children all their lives but capable of affectionate relationships and able to play games and perform simple tasks. The fact is, of course, that the doctors who recommend against life-saving procedures for handicapped infants are usually thinking not of them but rather of their parents and of other children in the family or of the "burden on society" if the children survive. So it is not for their sake but to avoid trouble to others that they are allowed to die. When brought out into the open this seems unacceptable: at least we do not easily accept the principle that adults who need special care should be counted too burdensome to be kept alive. ✳ ✳ ✳

What we must consider, even if only briefly, is the possibility that euthanasia, genuine euthanasia, and not contrary to the requirements of justice or charity, should be legalized over a wider area. Here we are up against the really serious problem of abuse. Many people want, and want very badly, to be rid of their elderly relatives and even of their ailing husbands or wives. Would any safeguards ever be able to stop them describing as euthanasia what was really for their own benefit? And would it be possible to prevent the occurrence of acts which were genuinely acts of euthanasia but morally impermissible because infringing the rights of a patient who wished to live?

Perhaps the furthest we should go is to encourage patients to make their own contracts with a doctor by making it known whether they wish him to prolong their life in case of painful terminal illness or of incapacity. A document such as the Living Will seems eminently sensible, and should surely be allowed to give a doctor following the previously expressed wishes of the patient immunity from legal proceedings by relatives. Legalizing active euthanasia is, however, another matter. Apart from the special repugnance doctors feel towards the idea of a lethal injection, it may be of the very greatest importance to keep a psychological barrier up against killing. Moreover it is active euthanasia which is the most liable to abuse. Hitler would not have been able to kill 275,000 people in his "euthanasia" program if he had had to wait for them to need life-saving treatment. But there are other objections to active euthanasia, even voluntary active euthanasia. In the first place it would be hard to devise procedures that would protect people from being persuaded into giving their consent. And secondly the possibility of active voluntary euthanasia might change the social scene in ways that would be very bad. As things are, people do, by and large, expect to be looked after if they are old or ill. This is one of the good things that we have, but we might lose it, and be much worse off without it. It might come to be expected that someone likely to need a lot of looking after should call for the doctor and demand his own death. Something comparable could be good in an extremely poverty-stricken community where the children genuinely suffered from lack of food; but in rich societies such as ours it would surely be a spiritual disaster. Such possibilities should make us very wary of supporting large measures of euthanasia, even where moral principle applied to the individual act does not rule it out.

STUDY QUESTIONS

1. How does Foot distinguish the virtues of justice and charity?
2. When, in Foot's view, is nonvoluntary euthanasia permitted?
3. In what ways would a legalized practice of voluntary active euthanasia be liable to abuse?

■ Compare and Contrast Question

1. Does Foot show that Rachels is wrong to argue for the moral equivalence of active and passive euthanasia?

THE DEATH PENALTY

This section contains two selections concerning the death penalty. The first, from John Stuart Mill, defending capital punishment, is a huge surprise since Mill is known as one of the great defenders of liberalism. But

Mill uses a utilitarian argument to insist that capital punishment is morally acceptable in the worst cases of murder. Mill's assumption, appropriate for the age in which he wrote, is that if aggravated murder was not punished by death, the only alternative would be life imprisonment with hard labor. Mill argues that, in fact, this would be a worse outcome for the criminal than death, but death would be a greater fear. Hence the utilitarian argument for the death penalty is made: It is the greater fear, and hence greater deterrent, but the lesser harm. Society, overall, would be better off for the death penalty. And, Mill claims, given the alternative of life imprisonment with hard labor, the death penalty is the humane outcome for the criminal.

Mill is aware of objections to the death penalty. One is that we are no better than the murderer if we take a life in punishment. Mill is not impressed with this argument, pointing out that if we fine people for theft the same argument could be made, but it is not thought a serious objection. Another is that, because death is irreversible, we had better not execute criminals in case the conviction is made on a false basis. Mill accepts this problem could occur, but argues that for this reason the death penalty must be reserved for cases where there is absolutely no doubt.

In considering the morality of the death penalty, especially in relation to the contemporary United States, Hugo Bedau begins by raising some empirical questions comparing the death penalty to its most likely alternative, a lengthy period of incarceration. On a range of measures, the evidence is not conclusive one way or another; hence arguments about the death penalty must move to other grounds, not only because the evidence is marginal, but also because there is a logical gap between facts and moral conclusions.

Essentially, for Bedau, arguments about the death penalty should focus on two types of questions: What are the social goals of punishment, and what normative principles should guide or constrain our practices? There are two social goals on which everyone can agree: that crime should be reduced and that it should be done in the most economical fashion. Other possible goals, such as that punishment should communicate moral indignation, are more contestable.

Bedau lists a range of normative principles, such as the more severe a punishment, the more important it is that it should be imposed only on those who truly deserve it. Bedau concedes that none of the principles directly rules out the death penalty. He argues, though, that together they favor the abolition of the death penalty. This is a slightly surprising argumentative strategy in an area where theorists often seek to argue that a single principle, such as the sanctity of life, rules out the death penalty. Bedau, however, presents a more subtle and complex picture in which the argument is conducted on the basis of the balance of reasoning rather than a single decisive argument.

JOHN STUART MILL
Speech in Defense of Capital Punishment

John Stuart Mill (1806–1873) was born in England, of Scottish descent. Mill was initially a disciple of Bentham but branched out to develop his own distinctive and highly influential moral views. He wrote on a very wide range of moral, political, philosophical, and economic issues, including arguing for the emancipation of women.

. . . It would be a great satisfaction to me if I were able to support this Motion. It is always a matter of regret to me to find myself, on a public question, opposed to those who are called—sometimes in the way of honour, and sometimes in what is intended for ridicule—the philanthropists. Of all persons who take part in public affairs, they are those for whom, on the whole, I feel the greatest amount of respect; for their characteristic is, that they devote their time, their labour, and much of their money to objects purely public, with a less admixture of either personal or class selfishness, than any other class of politicians whatever. On almost all the great questions, scarcely any politicians are so steadily and almost uniformly to be found on the side of right; and they seldom err, but by an exaggerated application of some just and highly important principle. On the very subject that is now occupying us we all know what signal service they have rendered. It is through their efforts that our criminal laws—which within my memory hanged people for stealing in a dwelling house to the value of 40s.—laws by virtue of which rows of human beings might be seen suspended in front of Newgate by those who ascended or descended Ludgate Hill—have so greatly relaxed their most revolting and most impolitic ferocity, that aggravated murder is now practically the only crime which is punished with death by any of our lawful tribunals; and we are even now deliberating whether the extreme penalty should be retained in that solitary case. This vast gain, not only to humanity, but to the ends of penal justice, we owe to the philanthropists; and if they are mistaken, as I cannot but think they are, in the present instance, it is only in not perceiving the right time and place for stopping in a career hitherto so eminently beneficial. Sir, there is a point at which, I conceive, that career ought to stop. When there has been brought home to any one, by conclusive evidence, the greatest crime known to the law; and when the attendant circumstances suggest no palliation of the guilt, no hope that the culprit may even yet not be unworthy to live among mankind, nothing to make it probable that the crime was an exception to his general character rather than a consequence of it, then I confess it appears to me that to deprive the criminal of the life of which he has proved himself to be unworthy—solemnly to blot him out from the fellowship of mankind and from the catalogue of the living—is the most appropriate, as it is certainly the most impressive, mode in which society can attach to so great a crime the penal consequences which for the security of life it is indispensable to annex to it. I defend this penalty, when confined to atrocious cases, on the very ground on which it is commonly attacked—on that of humanity to the criminal; as beyond comparison the least cruel mode in which it is possible adequately to deter from the crime. If, in our horror of inflicting death, we endeavour to devise some punishment for the living criminal which shall act on the human mind with a deterrent force at all comparable to that of death, we are driven to inflictions less severe indeed in appearance, and therefore less efficacious, but far more cruel in reality. Few, I think, would venture to propose, as a punishment for aggravated murder, less than imprisonment with hard labour for life; that is the fate to which a murderer would be consigned by the mercy which shrinks from putting him to death. But has it been sufficiently considered what sort of a mercy this is, and what kind of life it leaves to him? If, indeed, the punishment is not really inflicted—if it becomes the sham which a few years ago such punishments were rapidly becoming—then, indeed, its adoption would be almost tantamount to giving up the attempt to repress murder altogether. But if it really is what it professes to be, and if it is realized in all its rigour by the popular imagination, as it very probably would not be, but as it must be if it is to be efficacious, it will be so shocking that when the memory of the crime is no longer fresh, there will be almost insuperable difficulty in executing it. What comparison can there really be, in point of severity, between consigning a man to the short pang of a rapid death, and immuring him in a living tomb, there to linger out what may be a long life in the hardest and most monotonous toil, without any of its alleviations or rewards—debarred from all pleasant sights and sounds, and cut off from all earthly hope, except a slight mitigation of bodily restraint, or a small improvement of diet? Yet

even such a lot as this, because there is no one moment at which the suffering is of terrifying intensity, and, above all, because it does not contain the
element, so imposing to the imagination, of the unknown, is universally
reputed a milder punishment than death—stands in all codes as a mitigation of the capital penalty, and is thankfully accepted as such. For it is characteristic of all punishments which depend on duration for their efficacy—
all, therefore, which are not corporal or pecuniary—that they are more
rigorous than they seem; while it is, on the contrary, one of the strongest
recommendations a punishment can have, that it should seem more rigorous than it is; for its practical power depends far less on what it is than on
what it seems. There is not, I should think, any human infliction which
makes an impression on the imagination so entirely out of proportion to its
real severity as the punishment of death. The punishment must be mild
indeed which does not add more to the sum of human misery than is necessarily or directly added by the execution of a criminal. As my hon. Friend
the Member for Northampton (Mr Gilpin) has himself remarked, the most
that human laws can do to anyone in the matter of death is to hasten it; the
man would have died at any rate; not so very much later, and on the average,
I fear, with a considerably greater amount of bodily suffering. Society is
asked, then, to denude itself of an instrument of punishment which, in the
grave cases to which alone it is suitable, effects its purposes at a less cost of
human suffering than any other; which, while it inspires more terror, is
less cruel in actual fact than any punishment that we should think of substituting for it. My hon. Friend says that it does not inspire terror, and that
experience proves it to be a failure. But the influence of a punishment is not
to be estimated by its effect on hardened criminals. Those whose habitual
way of life keeps them, so to speak, at all times within sight of the gallows,
do grow to care less about it; as, to compare good things with bad, an old
soldier is not much affected by the chance of dying in battle. I can afford to
admit all that is often said about the indifference of professional criminals
to the gallows. Though of that indifference one-third is probably bravado
and another third confidence that they shall have the luck to escape, it is
quite probable that the remaining third is real. But the efficacy of a punishment which acts principally through the imagination, is chiefly to be measured by the impression it makes on those who are still innocent; by the
horror with which it surrounds the first promptings of guilt; the restraining influence it exercises over the beginning of the thought which, if
indulged, would become a temptation; the check which it exerts over the

graded declension towards the state—never suddenly attained—in which crime no longer revolts, and punishment no longer terrifies. As for what is called the failure of death punishment, who is able to judge of that? We partly know who those are whom it has not deterred; but who is there who knows whom it has deterred, or how many human beings it has saved who would have lived to be murderers if that awful association had not been thrown round the idea of murder from their earliest infancy? Let us not forget that the most imposing fact loses its power over the imagination if it is made too cheap. When a punishment fit only for the most atrocious crimes is lavished on small offences until human feeling recoils from it, then, indeed, it ceases to intimidate, because it ceases to be believed in. The failure of capital punishment in cases of theft is easily accounted for; the thief did not believe that it would be inflicted. He had learnt by experience that jurors would perjure themselves rather than find him guilty; that Judges would seize any excuse for not sentencing him to death, or for recommending him to mercy; and that if neither jurors nor Judges were merciful, there were still hopes from an authority above both. When things had come to this pass it was high time to give up the vain attempt. When it is impossible to inflict a punishment, or when its infliction becomes a public scandal, the idle threat cannot too soon disappear from the statute book. And in the case of the host of offences which were formerly capital, I heartily rejoice that it did become impracticable to execute the law. If the same state of public feeling comes to exist in the case of murder; if the time comes when jurors refuse to find a murderer guilty; when Judges will not sentence him to death, or will recommend him to mercy; or when, if juries and Judges do not flinch from their duty, Home Secretaries, under pressure of deputations and memorials, shrink from theirs, and the threat becomes, as it became in the other cases, a mere *brutum fulmen*; then, indeed, it may become necessary to do in this case what has been done in those—to abrogate the penalty. That time may come—my hon. Friend thinks that it has nearly come. I hardly know whether he lamented it or boasted of it; but he and his Friends are entitled to the boast; for if it comes it will be their doing, and they will have gained what I cannot but call a fatal victory, for they will have achieved it by bringing about, if they will forgive me for saying so, an enervation, an effeminancy, in the general mind of the country. For what else than effeminancy is it to be so much more shocked by taking a man's life than by depriving him of all that makes life desirable or valuable? Is death, then, the greatest of all earthly ills? *Usque adeone mori miserum est?* Is it, indeed, so dreadful a thing to die? Has it not been from of old one chief part of a manly education to make us despise death—teaching us to account it, if an evil at all, by no means high in the list of evils; at all events, as an inevitable one, and to hold, as it were, our lives in our hands, ready to be given or risked at any moment, for a sufficiently worthy object? I am sure that my hon. Friends know all this as well, and have as much of all these feelings as any of the rest of us; possibly more. But I cannot think that this is likely to be the effect of their teaching on the general mind. I cannot think that the cultivating of a peculiar sensitiveness of conscience on this one point, over and above what results from the general cultivation of the moral sentiments, is permanently consistent with assigning in our own minds to the fact of death no more than the degree of relative importance which belongs to it among the other incidents of our humanity. The men of old cared too little about death, and gave their own lives or took those of others with equal recklessness. Our danger is of the opposite kind, lest we should be so much shocked by death, in general and in the abstract, as to care too much about it in individual cases, both those of other people and our own, which call for its being risked. And I am not putting things at the worst, for it is proved by the experience of other countries that horror of the executioner by no means necessarily implies horror of the assassin. The stronghold, as we all know, of hired assassination in the 18th century was Italy; yet it is said that in some of the Italian populations the infliction of death by sentence of law was in the highest degree offensive and revolting to popular feeling. Much has been said of the sanctity of human life, and the absurdity of supposing that we can teach respect for life by ourselves destroying it. But I am surprised at the employment of this argument, for it is one which might be brought against any punishment whatever. It is not human life only, not human life as such, that ought to be sacred to us, but human feelings. The human capacity of suffering is what we should cause to be respected, not the mere capacity of existing. And we may imagine somebody asking how we can teach people not to inflict suffering by ourselves inflicting it? But to this I should answer—all of us would answer—that to deter by suffering from inflicting suffering is not only possible, but the very purpose of penal justice. Does fining a criminal show want of respect for property, or imprisoning him, for personal freedom? Just as unreasonable is it to think that to take the life of a man who has taken that of another is to show want of regard for human life. We show, on the contrary, most emphatically our regard for it, by the adoption of a rule that he who violates that right in another forfeits it for himself, and that while no other crime that he can commit deprives him of his right to live, this shall. There is one argument against capital punishment, even in extreme cases, which I cannot deny to have weight—on which my hon. Friend justly laid great stress, and which never can be entirely got rid of. It is this—that if by an error of justice an innocent person is put to death, the mistake can never be corrected; all compensation, all reparation for the wrong is impossible. This would be indeed a serious objection if these miserable mistakes—among the most tragical occurrences in the whole round of human affairs—could not be made extremely rare. The argument is invincible where the mode of criminal procedure is dangerous to the innocent, or where the Courts of Justice are not trusted. And this probably is the reason why the objection to an irreparable punishment began (as I believe it did) earlier, and is more intense and more widely diffused, in some parts of the Continent of Europe than it is here. There are on the Continent great and enlightened countries, in which the criminal procedure is not so favourable to innocence, does not afford the same security against erroneous conviction, as it does among us; countries where the Courts of Justice seem to think they fail in their duty unless they find somebody guilty; and in their really laudable desire to hunt guilt from its hiding places, expose themselves to a serious danger of condemning the innocent. If our own procedure and Courts of Justice afforded ground for similar apprehension, I should be the first to join in withdrawing the power of inflicting irreparable punishment from such tribunals. But we all know that the defects of our procedure are the very opposite. Our rules of evidence are even too favourable to the prisoner; and juries and Judges carry out the maxim, 'It is better that ten guilty should escape than that one innocent person should suffer', not only to the letter, but beyond the letter. Judges are most anxious to point out, and juries to allow for, the barest possibility of the prisoner's innocence. No human judgement is infallible; such sad cases as my hon. Friend cited will sometimes occur; but in so grave a case as that of murder, the accused, in our system, has always the benefit of the merest shadow of a doubt. And this suggests another consideration very germane to the question. The very fact that death punishment is more shocking than any other to the imagination, necessarily renders the Courts of Justice more scrupulous in requiring the fullest evidence of guilt. Even that which is the greatest objection to capital punishment, the impossibility of correcting an error once committed, must make, and does make, juries and Judges more careful in forming their opinion, and more jealous in their scrutiny of the evidence. If the substitution of penal servitude for death in cases of murder should cause any declaration in this conscientious scrupulosity, there would be a great evil to set against the real, but I hope rare, advantage of being able to make reparation to a condemned person who was afterwards discovered to be innocent. In order that the possibility of correction may be kept open wherever the chance of this sad contingency is more than infinitesimal, it is quite right that the Judge should recommend to the Crown a commutation of the sentence, not solely when the proof of guilt is open to the smallest suspicion, but whenever there remains anything unexplained and mysterious in the case, raising a desire for more light, or making it likely that further information may at some future time be obtained. I would also suggest that whenever the sentence is commuted the grounds of the commutation should, in some authentic form, be made known to the public. Thus much I willingly concede to my hon. Friend; but on the question of total abolition I am inclined to hope that the feeling of the country is not with him, and that the limitation of death punishment to the cases referred to in the Bill of last year will be generally considered sufficient. The mania which existed a short time ago for paring down all our punishments seems to have reached its limits, and not before it was time. We were in danger of being left without any effectual punishment, except for small offences. What was formerly our chief secondary punishment—transportation—before it was abolished, had become almost a reward. Penal servitude, the substitute for it, was becoming, to the classes who were principally subject to it, almost nominal, so comfortable did we make our prisons, and so easy had it become to get quickly out of them. Flogging—a most objectionable punishment in ordinary cases, but a particularly appropriate ones for crimes of brutality, especially crimes against women—we would not hear of, except, to be sure, in the case of garrotters, for whose peculiar benefit we re-established it in a hurry, immediately after a Member of Parliament had been garrotted. With this exception, offences, even of an atrocious kind, against the person, as my hon. and learned Friend the Member for Oxford (Mr Neate) well remarked, not only were, but still are, visited with penalties so ludicrously inadequate, as to be almost an encouragement to the crime. I think, Sir, that in the case of most offences, except those against property, there is more need of strengthening our punishments than of weakening them; and that severer sentences, with an apportionment of them to the different kinds of offences which shall approve itself better than at present to the moral sentiments of the community, are the kind of reform of which our penal system now stands in need. I shall therefore vote against the Amendment.

STUDY QUESTIONS

1. Outline Mill's argument for capital punishment.
2. How does Mill respond to the argument that in taking a life we are no better than the murderer?
3. Is the fact that capital punishment is irreversible a good reason for making sure that it is never used?

HUGO ADAM BEDAU
How to Argue About the Death Penalty

Hugo Bedau (1926–2012) was an American political philosopher especially noted for his work on the death penalty.

I.

Argument over the death penalty—especially in the United States during the past generation—has been concentrated in large part on trying to answer various disputed *questions of fact*. Among them two have been salient: is the death penalty a better deterrent to crime (especially murder) than the alternative of imprisonment? Is the death penalty administered in a discriminatory way—in particular, are black or other nonwhite offenders (or offenders whose victims are white) more likely to be tried, convicted, sentenced to death, and executed than whites (or than offenders whose victims are nonwhite)? Other questions of fact have also been explored, including these two: what is the risk that an innocent person could actually be executed for a crime he did not commit? What is the risk that a person convicted of a capital felony but not executed will commit another capital felony?

* * * I * * * think anyone who studies the evidence today must conclude that the best current answers to these four questions are as follows: (1) There is little or no evidence that the death penalty is a better deterrent to murder than is imprisonment: on the contrary, most evidence shows that these two punishments are about equally (in)effective as deterrents to murder. * * * (2) There is evidence that the death penalty has been and continues to be administered, whether intentionally or not, in a manner that produces

arbitrary and racially discriminatory results in sentencing. * * * (3) It is impossible to calculate the risk that an innocent person will be executed—but the risk is not zero, as the record of convicted, sentenced, and executed innocents shows. (4) Recidivism data show that some convicted murderers have killed again, either in prison or after release, so there is a risk that others will do so as well.

* * * The first thing to notice is that even if everyone accepted these answers, this would not by itself settle the dispute over whether to keep, expand, reduce, or abolish the death penalty. * * *

There are two reasons for this. The facts as they currently stand and as seen from the abolitionist perspective do not point strongly and overwhelmingly to the futility of the death penalty or to the harm it does. * * * Nor do the facts show that the alternative of life imprisonment is on balance a noticeably superior punishment. The evidence of racial discrimination in the administration of the death penalty, while incontestable, may be no worse than racial discrimination where lesser crimes and punishments are concerned. * * * Besides, it is always possible to argue that such discrimination is diminishing, or will diminish over time, and that in any case since the fault lies not in the capital statutes themselves—they are color-blind on their face—the remedy does not lie in repealing them. Nor is it clear that a life sentence in prison without the possibility of release is an enormous improvement from the offender's point of view over death.

But the marginal impact of the empirical evidence is not the major factor in explaining why settling disputes over matters of fact does not and cannot settle the larger controversy over the death penalty itself. As a matter of sheer logic, it is not possible to deduce a policy conclusion (such as the desirability of abolishing the death penalty) from any set of factual premises however general and well supported. Any argument intended to recommend continuing or reforming current policy on the death penalty must include among its premises one or more normative propositions. Unless disputants over the death penalty can agree about these normative propositions, their argument on the empirical facts will never suffice to resolve their dispute.

II.

* * * Logically prior to the idea of punishment is the idea of a crime. What counts as a criminal harm depends in part on our conception of persons as bearers of rights deserving respect and protection. In this setting, liability to punishment and its actual infliction serve the complex function of re-

inforcing compliance with a set of laws deemed necessary to protect the fundamental equal rights of all members of society. The normative propositions relevant to the death penalty controversy are interwoven with the basic purposes and principles of liberal society, including the recognition and protection of individual rights to life and liberty, and to security of person and property.

These norms can be divided into two groups: those that express relevant and desirable *social goals or purposes*, and those that express relevant and respectable *moral principles*. Punishment is thus a practice or institution defined through various policies—such as the death penalty for murder—intended to be the means or instrument whereby certain social goals are achieved within the constraints imposed by acknowledged moral principles.

Reduction of crime, or at least prevention of increase in crime, is an example of such a goal. This goal influences the choice of punishments because of their (hypothesized, verified) impact on the crime rate. ＊ ＊ ＊ Because it is assumed to be relevant there is continuing interest in the outcome of research on the question of the differential deterrent efficacy of death vs. imprisonment. The only questions normally in dispute are what that research shows ＊ ＊ ＊ and how important this goal is (for some it is decisive).

Similarly, that no one should be convicted and sentenced to death without a fair trial (i.e., in violation of "due process of law") is a principle of law and morality generally respected. Its general acceptance explains the considerable reformation in the laws governing the death penalty in the United States that have been introduced since 1972 in response to the Supreme Court's decisions in *Furman* v. *Georgia.* The Court argued in *Furman* that capital trials and death sentencing were in practice unfair (in constitutional jargon, they were in violation of the Eighth and Fourteenth Amendments, which bar "cruel and unusual punishments" and require "equal protection of the laws," respectively). State legislatures and thoughtful observers agreed. Here again the only questions concern how important it is to comply with this principle (for some it is decisive) and the extent to which the death penalty currently violates it. ＊ ＊ ＊

＊ ＊ ＊ Identifying the relevant goals, acknowledging the force of the relevant principles, and agreeing on the relevant general facts, will still not suffice to resolve the dispute. Disagreement over the relative importance of achieving a given goal or disagreement over the relative weight of a given principle is likely to show up in disagreement over the justification of the death penalty itself. * * *

III.

Where choice of punishments is concerned, the relevant social goals, I suggest, are few. Two in particular generally commend themselves:

(G1) Punishment ought to contribute to the reduction of crime: accordingly, the punishment for a crime ought not to be so idle a threat or so slight a deprivation that it has little or no deterrent or incapacitative effects; and it certainly ought not to contribute to the increase of crime.

(G2) Punishments ought to be "economical"—they ought not to waste valuable social resources in futile or unnecessarily costly endeavours.

The instrumental character of these purposes and goals is evident. They reflect the fact that society does not institute and maintain the practice of punishment for its own sake, as though it were a good in itself. Rather, punishment is and is seen to be a means to an end or ends. The justification of a society's punitive policies and practices, therefore, must involve two steps: first, it must be assumed or argued that these ends are desirable; second, it must be shown that the practice of punishment is a necessary means to these ends. What is true of the justification of punishment generally is true *a fortiori* of justifying the death penalty.

Endorsement of these two policy goals tends to encourage support for the death penalty. Opponents of capital punishment need not reject these goals, however, and its defenders cannot argue that accepting these goals vindicates their preferred policy. Traditionally, it is true, the death penalty has often been supported on the ground that it provides the best social defence and is extremely cheap to administer. But * * * these empirical claims have been challenged, and rightly so. If support for the death penalty today in a country such as the United States were thought to rest on the high priority of achieving these goals, then there is much (some would say compelling) evidence to undermine this support. The most that can be said solely by reference to these goals is that recognition of their importance can always be counted on to kindle interest in capital punishment, and to that extent force its opponents on the defensive.

Whether punishment is intended to serve only the two goals so far identified is disputable. An argument can be made that there are two or three further goals, as follows:

(G3) Punishment ought to rectify the harm and injustice caused by crime.

(G4) Punishment ought to serve as a recognized channel for the release of public indignation and anger at the offender over crime.

(G5) Punishment ought to make convicted offenders into better persons rather than leave them as they are or make them worse.

Obviously, anyone who accepts the fifth goal must reject the death penalty. I shall not try here to argue the merits of this goal, either in itself or relative to the other goals of punishment. * * *

The third proposed goal of punishment is open to the objection that rectification of injustice is not really a goal of punishment, even if it is a desirable goal whenever injustice is discovered. * * * Imprisonment as typically practiced in the United States rectifies nothing. Since mere incarceration by itself does not provide any direct and unique benefit to the victims of crime or to society generally, there is no way it can rectify the unjust harms that crime causes. Nonetheless, this goal is at least indirectly important for the death penalty controversy. To the extent that one believes punishments ought to serve this goal, and that there is no possible way to rectify the crime of murder, one may come to believe the fourth goal is of even greater importance than would otherwise be the case. Indeed, striving to achieve this fourth goal and embracing the death penalty as a consequence is quite parallel to striving to achieve the fifth goal and consequently embracing abolition.

Does this fourth goal have a greater claim on our support than I have allowed is true of the fifth goal, so obviously incompatible with it? Many would say that it does. Some * * * would even argue that it is this goal, not any of the others, that is the paramount purpose of the practice of punishment under law. Whatever else punishment does, its threat and infliction are to be seen as the expression of legitimate social indignation at deliberate harm to the innocent. Preserving a socially acceptable vehicle for the expression of anger at offenders is absolutely crucial to the health of a just society.

There are in principle three ways to respond to this claim insofar as it is part of an argument for capital punishment. One is to reject it out of hand as a false proposition from start to finish. A second is to concede that the goal of providing a visible and acceptable channel for the emotion of anger is legitimate, but to argue that this goal can justify the death penalty only in a very small number of rare cases (the occasional Adolf Eichmann, for example), or only if its importance is vastly exaggerated. A third is to concede both the legitimacy and relative importance of this goal, but to point out that its pursuit, like that of all other goals, is nonetheless constrained by moral principles (yet to be examined), and that once these principles are properly employed, the death penalty ceases to be a permissible method of achieving this goal. I think both the second and third objections are sound, and a few further words here about each are appropriate.

First of all, resentment or indignation is not the same as anger, since the former feeling or emotion can be aroused only through the perceived violation of some moral principle, whereas the latter does not have this constraint. But the question whether the feeling aroused by awareness of a horrible murder really is indignation rather than only anger just is the question whether the principles of justice have been severely violated or not. Knowing that the accused offender has no legal excuse or justification for his criminal conduct is not yet knowing enough to warrant the inference that he and his conduct are appropriate objects of our unqualified moral hostility. More about the context of the offence and its causation must be supplied; it may well be that in ordinary criminal cases one rarely or never knows enough to reach such a condemnatory judgment with confidence. Even were this not so, one has no reason to suppose that justified anger at offenders is of overriding importance, and that all countervailing considerations must yield to its claims. ＊ ＊ ＊

Quite apart from such objections, there is a certain anomaly, even irony, in the defence of the death penalty by appeal to this goal. On the one hand, we are told that a publicly recognized ritual for extermination of convicted murderers is a necessary vent for otherwise unchanneled disruptive public emotions. On the other hand our society scrupulously rejects time-honoured methods of execution that truly do express hatred and anger at offenders—beheading, crucifixion, dismemberment are unheard of today, and even hanging and the electric chair are disappearing. Execution by lethal injection, increasingly the popular option, hardly seems appropriate as the outlet of choice for such allegedly volatile energies. And is it not bizarre that this technique, invented to facilitate life-saving surgery, now turns out to be the preferred channel for the expression of moral indignation?

IV.

If the purpose or goals of punishment lend a utilitarian quality to the practice of punishment, the moral principles relevant to the death penalty operate as deontological constraints on the pursuit of these goals. Stating all and only the principles relevant to the death penalty controversy is not easy, and the list that follows is no more than the latest approximation to the task. With some overlap here and there, these principles are seven:

(P1) No one's life may be deliberately and intentionally taken by another unless there is no feasible alternative to protect the latter's own life.

(P2) The more severe a penalty is, the more important it is that it be imposed only on those who truly deserve it.

(P3) The more severe a penalty is, the weightier the justification required to warrant its imposition on anyone.

(P4) Whatever the criminal offence, the accused or convicted offender does not forfeit his rights and dignity as a person.

(P5) There is an upper limit to the severity—cruelty, destructiveness, finality—of permissible punishments, regardless of the offence.

(P6) Fairness requires that punishments should be graded in their severity according to the gravity of the offence.

(P7) If human lives are to be risked, the risk should fall more heavily on wrong-doers (the guilty) than on the others (the innocent).

I cannot argue here for all these principles, but they really need no argument from me. Each is recognized implicitly or explicitly in our practice; each can be seen to constrain our conduct as individuals and as officers in democratic institutions. Outright repudiation or cynical disregard of any of these principles would disqualify one from engaging in serious discourse and debate over punishment in a liberal society. All can be seen as corollaries or theorems of the general principle that life, limb, and security of person—of *all* persons—are of paramount value. Thus, only minimal interference (in the jargon of the law, "the least restrictive means") is warranted with anyone's life, limb, and security in order to protect the rights of others.

How do these principles direct or advise us in regard to the permissibility or desirability of the death penalty? The first thing to note is that evidently none directly rules it out. I know of no moral principle that is both sufficiently precise and sufficiently well established for us to point to it and say "the practice of capital punishment is flatly contradictory to the requirements of this moral principle." * * * This should not be surprising; few if any of the critics or the defenders of the death penalty have supposed otherwise. Second, several of these principles do reflect the heavy burden that properly falls on anyone who advocates that certain human beings be deliberately killed by others, even though those to be killed are not at the time a danger to anyone. For example, whereas the first principle may justify lethal force in self-defence and other circumstances, it directly counsels against the death penalty in *all* cases without exception. The second and third principles emphasize the importance of "due process" and "equal protection" as the finality and incompensability of punishments increase. The fourth principle draws attention to the nature and value of persons, even those convicted of terrible crimes. The fifth reminds us that even if crimes have no upper limit in their wantonness, cruelty, destructiveness, and horror, punishments under law in a civilized society may not imitate crimes in this regard. Punishment does operate under limits, and these limits are not arbitrary.

The final two principles, however, seem to be exceptions to the generalization that the principles as a group tend to favour punishments other than death. The sixth principle entails that if murder is the gravest crime, then it must receive the severest punishment. This does not, of course, *require* a society to invoke the death penalty for murder—unless one accepts *lex talionis* ("a life for a life, an eye for an eye") in a singularly literal-minded manner. But *lex talionis* is not a sound principle on which to construct the penalty schedule generally, and so appealing to that interpretation of the sixth principle here simply begs the question. Nevertheless, the principle that punishments should be graded to fit the crime does encourage consideration of the death penalty, especially if it seems there is no other way to punish murder with utmost permissible severity.

Rather of more interest is the seventh principle. Some * * * make it the cornerstone of their defence of the death penalty. They argue that it is better to execute all convicted murderers, lest on some future occasion some of them murder again, than it is to execute none of them in order to avert the risk of executing the few who may be innocent. For, so the argument goes, a policy of complete abolition would result in thousands of convicted killers (only a few of whom are innocent) being held behind bars. This cohort constitutes a permanent risk to the safety of many millions of innocent citizens. The sole gain to counterbalance this risk is the guarantee that no lives—innocent or guilty—will be lost through legal executions. The practice of executions thus is argued to protect far more innocent citizens than the same practice puts in jeopardy.

This argument is far less conclusive than it may, at first, seem. Even if we grant it full weight, it is simply unreasonable to use it (or any other argument) as a way of dismissing the relevance of principles that counsel a different result, or as a tactic to imply the subordinate importance of all other relevant principles. Used in this objectionable manner, what I have called the seventh principle has been transformed. It has become a disguised version of the first policy goal (viz., Reduce crime!) and in effect elevates that goal to pre-eminence over every competing and constraining consideration. It has also ceased to be a constraint on policy. Second, the argument fosters the illusion that we can, in fact, reasonably estimate, if not actually calculate, the number of lives risked by a policy of abolition vs. a policy of capital punishment. This is false; we do not and cannot reasonably hope to know what the risk is of convicting the innocent, even if we could estimate the risk of recidivist murder. We therefore cannot really compare the two risks with any precision. ∗ ∗ ∗

What has our examination of the relevant goals and principles shown about the possibility of resolving the death penalty controversy on purely rational grounds? First, the death penalty is primarily a means to one or more ends (goals), but it is not the only and probably not the best means to those ends. Second, several principles familiar to us in many areas of punitive policy favour (although they do not demand) abolition of the death penalty. Third, there is no principle that constitutes a conclusive reason favouring either side in the dispute—except, of course, for conclusive reasons (like the fifth goal, or the sixth principle interpreted as *lex talionis*) that either one side or the other simply need not accept. ∗ ∗ ∗

Despite the absence of any conclusive reasons or decisive ranking of principles, we may take refuge ∗ ∗ ∗ in the thought that a preponderance of reasons does favour one side rather than the other. Such a preponderance emerges, however, only when the relevant goals and principles of punishment are seen in a certain light, or from a particular angle of vision. This perhaps amounts to one rather than another weighting of goals and principles but without reliance upon any manifest theory. One relies instead on other considerations. I shall mention three whose importance may be decisive.

The first and by far the most important is the role and function of *power* in the hands of government. It is preferable, *ceteris paribus*, that such power over individuals shrink rather than expand. Where such power must be used, it is better to use it for constructive rather than destructive purposes—enhancing the autonomy and liberty of those persons directly affected by it. The death penalty is government power used in a dramatically destructive manner upon individuals in the absence of any compelling social necessity. No wonder it is the ultimate symbol of such power.

A second consideration * * * is an orientation to the *future* rather than to the past. We cannot do anything to benefit the dead victims of crime. (How many of those who oppose the death penalty would continue to do so if, *mirabile dictu*, executing the murderer brought the victim back to life?) But we can—or at least we can try to—do something for the living: we can protect the innocent, console those in despair, and try to prevent future crimes. None of these constructive tasks presuppose or involve the expressive, vindictive, and retributive roles of punishment. The more we stress these roles to the neglect of all else, the more we orient our punitive policies toward the past—toward trying to use government power over the lives of a few as a socially approved instrument of moral bookkeeping.

Finally, the death penalty projects a false and misleading picture of man and society. Its professed message for those who support it is this: justice requires killing the convicted murderer. So we focus on the death that all murderers supposedly deserve, and overlook our inability to give a rational account of why so few actually get what they allegedly deserve. Hence the lesson taught by the practice of capital punishment is not what its retributivist defenders infer from their theory. Far from being a symbol of justice it is a symbol of brutality and stupidity. Perhaps if we lived in a world of autonomous Kantian moral agents, where even the criminals freely and rationally express their will in the intention to kill others without their consent or desert, then death for the convicted murderer might be just. * * * But a closer look at the convicts who actually are on our death rows shows that these killers are a far cry from the rational agents of Kant's metaphysical imagination. We fool ourselves if we think a system of ideal retributive justice designed for such persons is the appropriate model for the penal system in our society.

STUDY QUESTIONS

1. Why does Bedau think that the argument about the death penalty cannot be settled on empirical grounds?
2. What social goals does Bedau think the practice of punishment should fulfill? Is he right?
3. Why does Bedau think that the normative principles he lists favor the abolition of the death penalty?

■ Compare and Contrast Question

1. How would Bedau respond to Mill's arguments for the death penalty?

THE CRIMINALIZATION OF DRUGS

This section contains two selections, the second of which, by George Sher, was written as a direct response to the first, by Douglas Husak. Husak, who has written many books and articles in favor of drug decriminalization, sets out to defend the decriminalization of drug use, leaving the topics of production and sale to one side. After outlining some of the striking facts about the number of people in the United States who have used illicit drugs and the number of people currently in prison for doing so, Husak attempts to invert the debate by asking what are the reasons for criminalizing drug use in the first place. Husak thinks that if we cannot find any good arguments for criminalization, then the case for decriminalization is made.

Husak admits that his methodology puts him in a somewhat uncomfortable position. Some writers think that there is a single principle that opposes criminalization, such as that each of us has an absolute right over what we put into our own bodies. Husak, however, does not accept that principle and does not believe that there is any other deep reason to defend drug use. Rather his strategy is to counter arguments for criminalization and hence is largely responsive.

Husak points out that much debate about criminalization in general relies on the harm principle: that people should be punished for inflicting harm on others. This cannot explain why society prohibits drug use, for if drug use harms anyone, it will generally only be the person who takes the drug.

The main argument that Husak discusses is that if we were to decriminalize drug use, then use would soar. Husak carefully weighs the arguments on both sides and argues that the evidence is inconclusive. Yet, he says, even if it were true that drug use would rise, that would only matter if we already had reasons to oppose drug use. But, he says, he has been unable to find any reason. Decriminalizing drug use would improve the lives of the very many people who would otherwise be caught and punished for using drugs.

George Sher directly responds to Douglas Husak's argument by presenting three arguments for criminalization, and he then compares drug and alcohol use. Sher's first argument is "paternalistic"; because the use of some drugs such as heroin or cocaine harms the user, governments have a reason to criminalize such use to protect people from serious injury. The second argument is "protective" and returns to the harm principle that Husak dismissed. Drug users do harm third parties, such as people caught up in drug-related crime and, tragically, unborn fetuses. Finally, a third argument is called "perfectionist," which means that it appeals to the idea of a good life or good society. Sher argues that those who spend much of their life under the influence of drugs do not lead a good life.

Husak had accepted that the arguments just given are reasons for people not to take drugs. But it is a further step to say that they are reasons for people to be punished if they take them. Sher, however, takes the view that the state is permitted to act to reduce risk of harm, which is what it does when it prohibits drunk driving. Because drug use, so Sher argues, can lead to harm, it is legitimate for the state to punish its use.

One reply to Sher is that all the arguments for criminalizing drug use apply with equal or greater force to alcohol. Sher accepts the comparison but argues that the fact that we allow one harmful thing does not mean that we should allow another, even if the harm is smaller, for the small harm may take us over a critical threshold. To help see Sher's point, consider pollution. The fact that one factory in our neighborhood pours out pollution is not a good reason for allowing another, smaller factory to pollute too, even if the pollution is less. If anything, the existing large amount of pollution is a reason for prohibiting extra pollution.

DOUGLAS HUSAK
Four Points About Drug Decriminalization

Douglas Husak (b. 1948) is an American political philosopher who specializes in the philosophy of the criminal law.

Philosophers have been strangely silent about the topic of illicit drugs. * * * Approximately 80 to 90 million people have used illicit drugs at some point in their lives. There are well over 400,000 drug offenders in jail, about 130,000 for possession alone. * * * It is plausible to suppose that drug users should not be punished at all, and this is what I want to argue here. * * *

Yet without the input of philosophers, the field has been left largely to scholars in criminal justice, nearly all of whom profess to have no theory of criminalization, but seem mostly to be consequentialists. They prepare cost-benefit analyses of the relative merits of criminalization and decriminalization. Many have concluded that our current drug laws are ineffective and counterproductive. They are probably correct, but that is not the line of inquiry I want to pursue here. As philosophers, I think we should be more interested in examining arguments of *principle*.

I THE MEANING OF DECRIMINALIZATION

∗∗∗ What I mean by the use of the term "decriminalization" in this context is that the *use* of a given drug would not be a criminal offense. I take it to be a conceptual truth for which I will not argue here that criminal offenses render persons liable to state punishment. Thus anyone who thinks that the use of a given drug should be decriminalized believes that persons should not be punished merely for using that drug. ∗∗∗

For a number of reasons, this definition of decriminalization is deceptively simple. First, there really is little punishment for use today. In most but not all jurisdictions, what is punished is possession rather than use. Technically, then, drug use is generally not criminalized. But I take the fact that statutes punish possession rather than use to be relatively unimportant. Possession is punished rather than use because it is easier to prove. In what follows, I ignore this complication and continue to suppose that decriminalization pertains to drug use. Except perhaps in fantastic cases, no one can use a drug without possessing it.

Second, there is no clear understanding of what kinds of state responses amount to punishments. Many reformers argue that drug users should be fined rather than imprisoned, and they call this idea decriminalization. Others argue that drug users should be made to undergo treatment, and they also call this idea decriminalization. ∗∗∗ Simply put, whatever you take punishment to be, that is what decriminalization forbids the state from doing to people who merely use drugs.

Third, decriminalization as I propose to define it has no implications for what should be done to persons who *produce* or *sell* drugs. Therefore, it is not really a comprehensive drug policy that can rival the status quo. The considerations that I think work in favor of decriminalizing use are somewhat different from those that apply to the decriminalization of production and sale, so I propose to put production and sale aside in this essay. This is bound to disappoint some people. Many thinkers are attracted to decriminalization, or reluctantly driven to support it, because they hope to end the violence, black market, and involvement of organized crime in drug transactions today. These sound like worthwhile objectives, but drug decriminalization per se does not achieve them. I think we should start by clarifying what should happen to drug users, and *then* move to the issue of whether or how production and sale should be regulated. Again, I am aware that many thoughtful people believe that these topics should all be tackled simultaneously, but I think it is easier to proceed one step at a time.

Finally, I admit that there is something odd about my understanding of decriminalization. What I call decriminalization in the context of drugs is comparable to what was called prohibition in the context of alcohol from 1920 to 1933. During those memorable years, production and sale were banned, but not the use or mere possession of alcohol. If we replicated that approach in our drug policy, I would call it decriminalization. That is admittedly odd, but it underscores the fact that our response to illicit drug users today is far more punitive than anything we ever did to drinkers.

II THE BEST REASON TO DECRIMINALIZE DRUG USE

With these preliminaries out of the way, let me proceed to the basic question to be addressed. In my judgment, the fundamental issue is not whether to *de*criminalize the use of any or all drugs, but whether to *criminalize* the use of any or all drugs. The status quo must be defended. If this is the right question to ask, I would now like to offer what I believe to be the most plausible answer to it: The best reason *not* to criminalize drug use is that no argument in favor of criminalizing drug use is any good—no argument is good enough to justify criminalization. I want to make three points about this general strategy for decriminalization.

First, I recognize that this approach is not very exciting. My reason to oppose criminalization does not invoke any deep principle worth fighting about like freedom of speech or religion. I am not sure that there is any deep principle that *all* drug prohibitions violate. In particular, my approach does not invoke the principle that some libertarians cite: the "freedom to do whatever you want to your own body." I do not invoke this principle because I do not believe it is true. I am not a libertarian. Whether you have a right to do something you want to your body depends on what happens when you do it.

Then again, *some* drug prohibitions seem to violate deep principles that philosophers should care about. This becomes more apparent when you pause to consider exactly what it is that drug proscriptions are designed to prevent. Most drugs have a legitimate use, so drug consumption per se is rarely prohibited. Instead, the use of most drugs is prohibited only for a given purpose. To get directly to the heart of the matter, the proscribed purpose is usually to produce a state of intoxication or a drug "high." In case there is any doubt, let me cite the California criminal statute regulating nitrous oxide. This statute makes it a crime for "any person [to possess] nitrous oxide . . . with the intent to breathe [or] inhale . . . for purposes of causing a condition of intoxication, elation, euphoria, dizziness, stupefaction, or dulling of the senses or for the purpose of, in any manner, changing . . . mental processes."[1] The ultimate objective of this statute is to prevent persons from breathing something in order to change their mental processes. It is hard to see why this objective is legitimate in a state committed to freedom of thought and expression. I am not sure that *all* drug prohibitions so transparently jeopardize our right to freedom of thought. In any event, I do not believe we need to appeal to any deep principle to resist drug prohibitions generally.

Second, my case is necessarily inconclusive. I am in the unenviable position of trying to prove a negative. How can I hope to show that no argument in favor of criminalizing drug use is good enough? All I can ever aspire to do is to respond to the best arguments that have been given. I am reminded of a remark made by Hume. "'Tis impossible to refute a system, which has never been explain'd. In such a manner of fighting in the dark, a man loses his blows in the air, and often places them where the enemy is not present."[2] This is the predicament someone faces in trying to defend drug decriminalization. * * *

Third, my case for decriminalization has the advantage of making minimal assumptions about justice. I assume that no one should be punished unless there are excellent reasons for doing so. Punishment, after all, is the worst thing our state can do to us. The imposition of punishment must satisfy a very demanding standard of justification. It is hard to imagine that anyone would reject this assumption.

Thus my case against criminalization depends on the claim that no case for criminalization has been adequately defended. It is utterly astounding, I think, that no very good argument for drug prohibitions has ever been given. When I am asked to recommend the best book or article that makes a philosophically plausible case for punishing drug users, I am embarrassed to say that I have little to suggest.

Let me then cut directly to my own conclusions. No single argument for decriminalization responds to all arguments for criminalization. We must respond argument-by-argument, and, I think, drug-by-drug. We may have good reasons to criminalize some drugs, but not others. For example, I do not know anyone who wants to punish persons who use caffeine. Surely this is because of empirical facts about caffeine—how it affects those who use

---

1   *Cal. State Penal Code*, §381 (b) (2002).
2   David Hume, *A Treatise of Human Nature* (Selby-Bigge ed., 1968), Book III Section 1 p. 464.

it and society in general. I can certainly *imagine* a drug that people should be punished for using. Such drugs are easy to describe; they are vividly portrayed in great works of fiction. Consider the substance that transformed Dr. Jekyll into Mr. Hyde. If a drug literally turned users into homicidal monsters, we would have excellent reasons to prohibit its consumption. Fortunately, no such drug actually exists. In fact, I have never seen a persuasive argument for punishing persons who use any drug that I am aware is widely used for recreational purposes.

III CRIMINALIZATION

∗ ∗ ∗ The most distinguished criminal theorists of our day ∗ ∗ ∗ mostly continue to argue about the *harm principle*. But debates about whether to accept the harm principle in our theory of criminalization do not get us very far when trying to decide whether to punish drug users. We have excellent reasons to punish people who commit theft or rape. These offenses harm others by violating their rights. But this rationale cannot explain why drug users should be punished. I do not think there is any sense of harm or any theory of rights that can be invoked to show that I harm someone or violate his rights when I inject heroin or smoke crack. At most, I risk harm to myself or to others when I use a drug. I conceptualize offenses that create only a *risk* of harm that may or may not materialize as *inchoate* offenses—similar to attempt, solicitation, or conspiracy. If I am correct, the criteria we should apply to assess the justifiability of drug proscriptions are those we should apply to assess the justifiability of inchoate offenses. Unfortunately, we have no such criteria. Almost no theorist has tried very hard to extend a theory of criminalization to conduct that creates a risk of harm rather than harm itself.

Notice, however, the enormous burden an argument for criminalization would have to bear. As I have said, there are about 80 or 90 million Americans who have used an illicit drug at some point in their lives. That is approximately 42 percent of our population aged 12 and over. About 15 million Americans used an illicit drug last year, on literally billions of occasions. Very few of these occasions produced any harm. Longitudinal studies do not indicate that the population of persons who ever have used illicit drugs is very different from the population of lifetime abstainers in any ways that seem relevant to criminalization. So any argument for punishment would have to justify punishing the many, whose behavior is innocuous, for the sake of some objective that results in a very tiny percentage of cases. Many attempted murders result in successful murders, which are harms, but very few instances of drug use bring about any result we should describe as significantly harmful.

When you cannot possibly punish *all* of the people who commit a crime, you can only punish *some*. Inevitably, those who get arrested, prosecuted, and sentenced are the least powerful. Drug prohibition would have vanished long ago had whites been sent to prison for drug offenses at the same rate as blacks. Although minorities are no more likely to use illicit drugs, they are far more likely to be arrested, prosecuted, and punished when they do. This is one of the features of drug prohibitions that should outrage us all. Some people try to package drug prohibitions as a benefit to minorities, but there is plenty of evidence that they devastate minority communities and will continue to do so as long as enforcement is so selective. And yet enforcement will always be selective, since every offender cannot possibly be punished.

If drug prohibitions are so bad for minority communities, one may wonder why minority leaders are not more outspoken about the drug war. In fact, blacks are more ambivalent than whites about drug policy.[3] Overall, blacks tend to have more negative opinions about drugs (both licit and illicit) than whites. At the same time, blacks are less likely than whites to believe that the solution to the problem is to enforce prohibition with severe punishments. Black mothers who are staunchly anti-drug are not enthusiastic about policies that lock up their sons and daughters for lengthy periods of time. But why are blacks not even more critical of the status quo? No one explanation can be given. But my own hypothesis cites the role of religion on attitudes about drugs. Although opinions about drug policy vary somewhat with age, education, income, and gender, no variable correlates with anti-drug attitudes more closely than religion and, at least in the United States, protestant Christianity in particular.

IV PREDICTIONS: A BAD REASON TO CRIMINALIZE

I have space to provide a brief critique of only *one* argument, and I apologize in advance if I neglect the reader's own candidate for the best reason to criminalize drug use. I will not comment on drugs and kids, drugs and health, drugs and crime, or drugs and morality. But I think the argument I discuss here may be the most common. It rests on predictions that the use of drugs would soar if we stopped punishing persons who use them. This argument, I think, flounders on both empirical and normative grounds.

---

3 U.S. Department of Justice, Bureau of Justice Statistics: *Sourcebook of Criminal Justice* (29th ed., 2001), Table 2.49.

I begin with the empirical considerations. My conclusion is that we simply do not have any good basis to predict how the amount of harm caused by drugs would change if we did not punish those who use them. Many persons find my uncertainty to be unwarranted. Economic models indicate that the frequency of use is a function of costs: decriminalize use, and the monetary and non-monetary costs of drugs will go down. The trouble is that all predictions about how rates of consumption will rise after use is decriminalized assume that nothing else will change. One thing we can predict is that many other things will change if drug use is decriminalized. Let me mention just a few things that might very well change, and that make all such predictions perilous.

I begin by challenging the claim that decriminalization will cause the monetary price of drugs to plummet. Why assume that decriminalization will make illicit drugs significantly more affordable? Decriminalization itself, as I have emphasized, need not allow illicit drugs to be sold with impunity. If decriminalization does not extend to sale, it need not have much affect on the monetary cost of drugs. But even were sale decriminalized, illicit drugs would become subject to taxation. I will not try to estimate the optimal rate of taxation. Whatever the exact amount, we can be sure that taxes would add enormously to the price of newly decriminalized drugs.

However uncertain we may be about how decriminalization will affect the monetary price of drugs, it will clearly eliminate the non-monetary cost of use. People will no longer fear arrest and prosecution. To the extent that this fear has helped to keep illicit drug use in check, we can anticipate that decriminalization would cause the incidence of drug use to rise. But to what extent? How will consumption change if drug users need not worry about punishment? No single piece of evidence on this point is decisive. But several factors suggest that the threat of punishment is not especially effective in curbing drug use. In what follows, I will describe a number of reasons to doubt that the removal of criminal penalties would cause a significant increase in the use of illicit drugs.

One source of evidence is obtained through surveys. People who have never used drugs are asked to explain their reasons for abstaining, and to speculate about how their willingness to experiment would be affected by a change in the law. Very few respondents cite their fear of punishment as a substantial factor in their decision not to try drugs.[4] The more dangerous the

---

4 See Robert J. MacCoun and Peter Reuter, *Drug War Heresies*, Cambridge: Cambridge University Press, 2001, pp. 82–84.

drug is perceived to be, the smaller the number of respondents who mention the law when asked to explain their reluctance to use it. Other surveys ask former users why they decided to quit. Those who once used drugs are asked why they do not continue to do so today, and to explain why their behavior has changed. Very few respondents report that fear of arrest and prosecution led them to stop using drugs. They cite a bad experience with a drug or some new responsibility, like a job or a newborn, but rarely mention the risk of punishment.[5] Of course, the value of these kinds of surveys is questionable. We may doubt that people have accurate insights into why they behave as they do, or what might lead them to behave differently. Surely, however, these surveys provide better evidence than mere conjecture. These surveys suggest that the fear of punishment is not a major factor in explaining why drug use is not more pervasive than it is.

For further evidence about how the fear of punishment affects the incidence of drug use, we might examine how trends in illicit drug use over the past thirty years are correlated with changes in law enforcement. If the fear of punishment were a significant factor in deterring illicit drug use, one would expect that rates of consumption would decline as punishments increased in frequency and severity. There is no correlation, however, between the frequency and severity of punishment and trends in drug use. * * * States with greater rates of incarceration for drug offenders tend to experience higher rates of drug use. Prohibitionists who predict a massive increase in drug use after decriminalization must struggle to explain these data. If punitive drug policies keep drug use in check, why do actual trends in drug consumption prove so resistant to the massive efforts we have made to punish drug users?

Additional evidence can be gleaned from the experience of other countries, where the fear of arrest and prosecution for the use of given drugs is practically nonexistent. Most European countries have lower rates of illicit drug use, even though given drugs are often higher in quality, lower in price, and less likely to result in punishments. American teenagers consume more marijuana and most other illicit drugs than their European counterparts, although European teens are more likely to smoke cigarettes and drink alcohol. Consider the Netherlands, which is known for its relatively permissive drug laws. Although marijuana prevalence rates are roughly comparable in

---

5   See Mitch Earlywine, *Understanding Marijuana*, New York: Oxford University Press, 2002, p. 247.

the two countries, about twice as many residents of the United States have experimented with other kinds of illicit drugs. In general, data from other parts of the world provide better evidence for an inverse than for a positive correlation between severities of punishments and rates of illicit drug use. Admittedly, however, this evidence is inconclusive. No country in the world has implemented decriminalization as I have defined it here.

The history of the United States provides further reason to doubt that fear of punishment plays a major role in reducing the use of illicit drugs. We must keep in mind that, for all practical purposes, drug prohibition did not begin until the early part of the twentieth century. In the nineteenth century, purchases of opium, morphine, cocaine, and marijuana were subject to almost no restrictions. Americans could buy these drugs in many different varieties from several different sources, including by mail order. But even though criminal penalties were not imposed for the use of opiates and cocaine, these drugs were probably less popular than today. Admittedly, however, the verdict of history is mixed. Most Americans agree that our era of alcohol prohibition was a dismal failure. By most accounts, however, per capita consumption of alcohol decreased throughout prohibition, and did not return to pre-prohibition levels for many years. This finding has led some social scientists to conclude that prohibition "worked" after all—if a reduction in use is the most important criterion of success. Others are skeptical. Curiously, however, even those social scientists who insist that alcohol prohibition was effective almost never recommend that our country should reinstate that policy.

Trends in the use of *licit* drugs provide yet another source of evidence. Prohibitionists tend to point to a reduction in illicit drug use over the last twenty years as a reason to believe that severe punishments have been effective in curbing drug use. Comparable declines in the use of alcohol and tobacco, however, have taken place over this same period of time, even without the threat of criminal liability. Rates of monthly illicit drug use in the United States peaked at about 14 percent in 1979, steadily declined to a low of just above 5 percent in 1992, and slowly increased thereafter to about 6 percent in 2001. Trends in alcohol and tobacco use exhibit more similarities than dissimilarities with these patterns. The overall use of alcohol and tobacco declined throughout the 1980s, and rebounded somewhat during the 1990s. We have ample evidence that the use of licit drugs can be decreased without the need to resort to criminal sanctions. We should assume that the same is true of illicit drugs.

If changes in the certainty and severity of punishment are not major factors in explaining trends in illicit drug use, what *does* account for these patterns? This is one of the most fascinating and difficult questions that arises about drug use, and I confess to having no good answer to it. Trends in the use of both licit and illicit drugs are as baffling and mysterious as trends in fashion. Unless we have better theories to explain why people use drugs, our forecasts about the future are bound to be simplistic. No one has a convincing explanation of why the use of a given drug increases or decreases within a given group in a given place at a given time. By 2001, the popularity of crack in inner cities had waned enormously. Crack is no longer regarded as "cool" or "hip." Why? No simple answer can be given. Most experts believe that a heightened consciousness about health contributed to the reduction in the use of licit drugs during the 1980s. But what caused this growing concern about health, and why did it not lead rates of drug use to fall still further throughout the 1990s? Again, no answer is clearly correct. But credibility is strained if we suppose that a factor is important in accounting for decreases in the consumption of alcohol and tobacco but unimportant in accounting for decreases in the consumption of illicit drugs, especially when the patterns of these decreases are roughly comparable. In any event, we have little reason to believe that punishments play a central role in explaining trends in drug use.

I have provided several reasons to doubt that punishment is needed to keep rates of illicit drug use within reasonable bounds. But skepticism about the efficacy of punishment as a deterrent to drug use is only a small part of the reason why predictions about drug use after decriminalization are so tenuous. Recall the terms of decriminalization that I have offered here. The only change that this policy requires is that the state would not *punish* anyone simply for using a drug for recreational purposes. The state may adopt any number of devices to discourage drug use, as long as these devices are not punitive. Even more important, institutions other than the state can and do play a significant role in discouraging drug use. After decriminalization, some of these institutions might exert even more influence. Private businesses, schools, insurance companies, and universities, to cite just a few examples, might adopt policies that discriminate against drug users. Suppose that employers fired or denied promotions to workers who use cocaine. Suppose that schools barred students who drink alcohol from participating in extracurricular activities. Suppose that insurance companies charged higher premiums to policy holders who smoke tobacco. Suppose that colleges denied loans and grants to undergraduates who use marijuana. I do not endorse any of these ideas; many seem unwise and destined to backfire.

Removing drug-using kids from schools, for example, seems destined to *increase* their consumption. I simply point out that such institutions could have a far greater impact than our criminal justice system on people's decisions to use drugs.

Predictions about drug use after decriminalization are confounded by yet another phenomenon—the "forbidden fruit" effect. Many people, adolescents in particular, are attracted to an activity precisely because it is forbidden or perceived as dangerous. Much of the thrill of illicit drug use stems from its illegality and the culture of deviance that surrounds it. Might the use of some illicit drugs actually *decrease* because they are no longer forbidden? If we change the law, the appeal of illicit drugs will be changed as well. To what extent? No one knows. Although many scholars have noted the forbidden fruit effect, serious research has yet to demonstrate its real significance.

Alarming predictions about future use assume that the drugs of tomorrow will resemble the drugs of today. This assumption seems extraordinarily naïve. The development of new and different substances makes predictions about consumption enormously speculative. Even though many illicit drugs—heroin and LSD, for example—were originally created by pharmaceutical companies, reputable corporations have tried hard to disassociate their drug products from illicit drugs. Decriminalization may lead pharmaceutical companies to expend their talent and ingenuity to create better and safer recreational drugs. One can only wonder about the products that might be developed if the best minds were put to the task. If more enjoyable and less dangerous drugs could be perfected, consumption might boom. But the development of better and safer drugs would make the increase in consumption less of a problem.

Whether or not better drugs appear on the market, no one can predict how users will substitute newly decriminalized drugs for existing licit drugs. After decriminalization, consumers will have lawful alternatives that we take for granted in other contexts. We simply do not know whether and to what extent users will substitute newly decriminalized drugs for those licit drugs they now tend to prefer. If a great deal of substitution takes place, the enormous social harm presently caused by tobacco and alcohol might decline considerably. So the total amount of harm caused by *all* categories of drugs might actually *decrease*, even if the consumption of illicit drugs were to *increase*. I do not find this conjecture so implausible. Over time, one would expect that users would tend to gravitate toward those drugs that could be integrated more easily into their lifestyles. In particular, we should welcome a possible reduction in alcohol use. As any college administrator knows, alcohol is the drug implicated in most of the date rapes, property damage, and violent behavior on campus. A possible decrease in alcohol consumption is one of the silver linings on the feared black cloud of drug decriminalization.

For all of these reasons, we should avoid predictions about how the decriminalization of drugs will affect rates of consumption. An even more important point is that these empirical conjectures are not especially relevant to the topic at hand. We are looking for a respectable reason to criminalize drug use. Predictions about how decriminalization will cause an increase in drug use simply do not provide such a reason. Indeed, this reason could be given against repealing virtually any law, however unjustified it may be. Let me illustrate this point by providing an example of an imaginary crime that I assume everyone would agree to be unjustified. Suppose that the state sought to curb obesity by prohibiting people from eating pizza. * * * Suppose that a group of philosophers convened to discuss whether we should change this law and decriminalize pizza consumption. Someone would be likely to protest that repealing this law would cause the consumption of pizza to increase. I imagine they would be correct. But surely this prediction would not serve to justify retaining this imaginary prohibition. If we lacked a good reason to attack the problem of obesity by punishing pizza eaters in the first place, the effects of repeal on pizza consumption would not provide such a reason. And so with drugs. Unless we already *have* a reason to punish pizza consumption, the prediction does not provide a good reason to *continue* to punish it.

If there is a good reason to criminalize illicit drug use, we have yet to find it. We need a better reason to criminalize something other than predictions about how its frequency would increase if punishments were not imposed. These predictions are dubious both normatively and (in this case) empirically. Despite my uncertainty about the future, there is *one* prediction about which we can be absolutely confident. After decriminalization, those who use illicit drugs will not face arrest and prosecution. The lives of drug users would not be devastated by a state that is committed to waging war against them. Punishment, we must always be reminded, is the worst thing a state can do to us. The single prediction we can safely make about decriminalization is that it will improve the lives of the hundreds of thousands of people who otherwise would be punished for the crime of using drugs for recreational purposes.

STUDY QUESTIONS

1. Why does Husak concentrate on arguments for criminalization, rather than arguments for decriminalization?
2. Can the harm principle be used to defend the criminalization of drugs?
3. Assess Husak's response to the argument that if drug use was decriminalized, usage would soar.

GEORGE SHER
On the Decriminalization of Drugs

George Sher (b. 1942) is an American moral and political philosopher.

In his lively and provocative paper, "Four Points About Drug Decriminalization," Douglas Husak advances two main claims: first, that none of the standard arguments for criminalizing drugs are any good, and, second, that there is little evidence that drug laws deter drug use. In these comments, I will not take up the second claim (though I must admit to some skepticism), but I do want to take issue with the first. My strategy will be, first, to sketch three pro-criminalization arguments that I take to have real weight; second, to respond to an objection of Husak's that, if sound, would tell against all three of my arguments; and, third, to confront the related objection that we cannot consistently support the criminalization of narcotics without also supporting the criminalization of alcohol.

I THREE ARGUMENTS FOR CRIMINALIZATION

I begin with two ritual disclaimers. When I say that there is a good case for continuing to attach criminal penalties to the use of narcotics, I do not mean that that case extends to any particular schedule of penalties or to any special list of drugs. I am sure that many drug sentences, both past and present, are far too harsh. I am also willing to concede that the harms and bads associated with some drugs—marijuana is the obvious example—may not be significant enough to justify attaching even minor penalties to their use. I do think, however, that the harms and bads associated with many other drugs are sufficiently weighty to justify their continued criminalization. The drugs of which I take this to be true include heroin, cocaine, methamphetamine, LSD, and ecstasy, among others.

What, then, are the main arguments for criminalizing these drugs? They are, I think, just the familiar ones: drug users harm themselves, they harm others, and they do not live good lives. At the risk of sounding like an eighth-grade teacher, or a drug czar, I will briefly sketch each argument.

(1) The paternalistic argument

The nature of the harms that drug users risk is of course a function of the drugs they use. ∗ ∗ ∗ Heroin harms the user by sapping his motivation and initiative. Also, because heroin is addictive, using it now forecloses the option of comfortably not using it later. By contrast, cocaine and methamphetamine do not have only these effects (though "crack" is by all accounts highly addictive), but their regular use also significantly increases the risk of heart attack and stroke. Furthermore, by drastically enhancing self-confidence, aggression, and libido, these drugs elicit behavior that predictably culminates in high-speed collisions, shootouts in parking lots, and destroyed immune systems. Other drugs have still other destructive effects: LSD can trigger lasting psychosis; ecstasy harms the brain, impairs the memory, and, taken with alcohol, damages the liver; and so on. Thus, one obvious reason to continue to criminalize these drugs is simply that many persons deterred by the law from using them will thereby be spared serious injury.

(2) The protective argument

Just as drug use can harm the user, so, too, can it harm others. Drug use harms strangers by involving them in the collisions, shootouts, and other catastrophes to which the impaired and overly aggressive are prone. It harms family members by depriving them of the steady companionship and income of their addicted partners. It harms fetuses by exposing them to a toxic and permanently damaging prenatal environment. It harms children by subjecting them to the neglect and abuse of their drug-addled parents. Thus, a second obvious reason to continue criminalizinng drugs is that many persons deterred by the law from using drugs will thereby be prevented from harming others.

(3) The perfectionist argument

Just as there is broad agreement about what constitutes harm, so, too, is there broad agreement about many factors determining both good and bad lives. Most would agree that it is bad when people stumble through life with a blurred and distorted view of reality; bad when they cannot hold a thought from one moment to the next or follow a simple chain of reasoning; bad when they drift passively with no interest in pursuing worthwhile goals;

and bad when they care more about the continued repetition of pleasant sensations than about the needs and interests of those who love and depend on them. Many would agree, too, that it is doubly bad when the reason people live this way is simply because they have squandered the chance to live better. Thus, a third main argument for retaining the drug laws is that many persons whom they deter are thereby prevented from wasting their lives.

II CRIMINALIZATION AND THE RISK OF HARM

There may be other arguments for continuing to criminalize drugs, but the three just mentioned are surely among the most influential. However, although Husak concedes that some such arguments may indeed explain "why rational persons might well decide not to use illicit drugs, or why the state may have good reasons to discourage people from using drugs," he denies that any of them "provide a justification for *punishing* drug users." Why, exactly, does he deny this?

As Husak agreeably acknowledges, his opposition to criminalization is not a matter of deep principle. He emphasizes that he is not a libertarian, and allows that he can easily imagine drugs so harmful that they should be criminalized: "[i]f a drug literally literally turned users into homicidal monsters, we would have excellent reasons to prohibit its consumption." However, according to Husak, no actual drug satisfies this description because no drug causes harm in more than a small proportion of cases. As Husak points out, "[a]bout 15 million Americans used an illicit drug last year, on literally billions of occasions," but "[v]ery few of these occasions produced any harm." Because the antecedent likelihood of harm is small on any given occasion, Husak maintains that there is no "sense of harm . . . that can be invoked to show that I harm someone . . . when I inject heroin or smoke crack. At most, I risk harm to myself or to others when I use a drug." This is said to undermine the case for criminalization because "[a]lmost no theorist has tried very hard to extend a theory of criminalization to conduct that creates a risk of harm rather than harm itself."

Although Husak's official aim in these passages is only to cast doubt on those defenses of the drug laws that appeal to the harm principle, his reasoning can also be extended to the paternalistic and perfectionist arguments. To extend it, we need note only that just as no single occasion of drug use is likely to harm anyone other than the user, so, too, is no single occasion likely either to harm the user himself or to reduce significantly the goodness of his life. Because the (un)likelihood of each effect is roughly equal, the threats that Husak's reasoning poses to our three arguments seem roughly equal as well. This, of course, makes it all the more urgent to ask whether the reasoning can in fact be sustained.

Whatever else we say, we surely must insist that all reasonable theories of criminalization *do* allow governments to criminalize behavior simply on the grounds that it is too risky. We must insist on this not only for the boring reason that all reasonable theories permit governments to attach criminal penalties to drunk driving, discharging firearms in public places, and innumerable other forms of endangerment, but also for the more interesting reason that any decision to criminalize a form of behavior must be made *before* any occurrence of that behavior for which anyone can be punished. Such a decision must be based on an *ex ante* judgment about how risky the behavior is. Husak can hardly be unaware of this, and so his point can hardly be that we are *never* justified in criminalizing behavior merely on the grounds that it is risky. Instead, I take him to be making only the more modest (but still relevant) point that we are not justified in criminalizing behavior merely on the grounds that it imposes a risk of harm *that is as small as the risk imposed by a single instance of drug use.*

Should we accept this version of Husak's claim? We might have reason to accept it if the relevant forms of low-risk behavior could all be assumed to be rare, for then the amounts of harm we would tolerate by tolerating them would also be small. However, drug use is of course not rare—Husak puts its frequency at billions of occurrences per year—so even if the risk on any given occasion is small, the total amount of harm must still be large. Even if, say, cocaine users harm no one but themselves in 999 out of 1000 cases, ten million uses of cocaine will still harm non-users ten thousand times. If there is any reason to take this number of harms less seriously when they result from ten million uses of cocaine than when they result from only ten thousand uses of some more reliably harmful drug, I must confess that I do not see what it is. Thus, if criminalizing the more reliably harmful drug to prevent this number of harms to non-users is legitimate—as it surely would be if each harm were on average as severe as the average harm done by cocaine—then criminalizing cocaine to prevent this number of harms must be legitimate too.

Even were prevention of harm to others the only legitimate rationale for criminalizing any form of behavior, the aggregative nature of the harms associated with drug use would pose a serious problem for Husak's claim about risk. However, if, as I believe, the state may also legitimately criminalize behavior for paternalistic and perfectionist reasons, then aggregation will pose problems for his claim in at least four more ways. First, just as the infrequent but serious harms that drug users do to others are bound to add up, so are the infrequent but serious harms they do to themselves. Second, if each use of a given drug does a small amount of harm to the user's brain or heart, then his frequent and repetitive use of that drug is likely to do his brain or heart a lot of harm. Third, even if no single instance of drug use has much impact on the goodness of a person's life, a life entirely given over to drug use may be very bad indeed. And, fourth, just as there can be aggregation within each category of harm or bad, so, too, can there be aggregation across the categories. If the cumulative harm that drug users do to themselves is one reason to criminalize drugs, and the cumulative harm they do to others is another, and the cumulative badness of their lives is still another, then the cumulative weight of the three cumulative reasons must surely be greater than the weight of any single one alone.

III IF NARCOTICS, WHY NOT ALCOHOL?

Given all this, I am unconvinced by Husak's suggestion that the risks associated with drugs are too small to warrant their criminalization. However, another objection to their criminalization—an objection which Husak does not make explicit but which hovers near the edge of much of what he says—bothers me more. This is the objection that every argument that speaks for the criminalization of drugs speaks with equal strength for the criminalization of alcohol. If this objection can be sustained, then those who favor criminalizing drugs but not alcohol—as I do—are simply giving their preferred intoxicant a free pass.

Although the parallels between drugs and alcohol are pretty obvious, it may be useful to make a few of them explicit. To bring these out, we need only remind ourselves that alcohol, too, is famous for causing people to do things that culminate in fiery collisions, parking-lot shootouts, and destroyed immune systems; that alcoholics are well known for neglecting their partners and abusing their children; that alcohol creates an environment that is toxic and permanently damaging to fetuses; that being drunk cuts a person off from reality and prevents him from thinking clearly; and that alcohol harms the brain, impairs the memory, and, taken with ecstasy, damages the liver. We may remind ourselves, as well, that although most instances of alcohol use have no such effects, its use is so common—Americans drink alcohol billions of times per year—that the overall amount of harm and degradation that it causes is very large indeed.

Given these impressive similarities, the arguments for criminalizing the two intoxicants appear to stand or fall together. Thus, having claimed that the arguments succeed for drug criminalization, I may seem also committed to the view that they succeed for alcohol. However, because I find a world without beer too grim to contemplate, I want to resist this conclusion if possible. Is there any wiggle room here?

Given the structure of the pro-criminalization arguments, I think there may be. The salient feature of each argument is that it appeals to a kind of harm or bad that is (relatively) infrequent but whose overall total exceeds some crucial threshhold. Thus, all three of my arguments leave open the possibility that the reason drugs take us past the threshhold is that alcohol has already gotten us part of the way there. It may be the case, in other words, that either alcohol or the use of drugs by itself would *not* produce more harms or bads than a reasonable society can tolerate, but that in combination they would produce harms and bads that surpass the threshhold. If anything like this is true, then it will not be at all inconsistent to advocate the criminalization of drugs but not alcohol. The reason for treating drugs and alcohol differently will be that we can hold the relevant harms and bads below the threshhold by legally permitting one or the other but not by permitting both; the reason for continuing to criminalize drugs but not alcohol will be that this is easier and less costly than switching—easier because it avoids divisive legislative battles and the uprooting of entrenched traditions, less costly because it does not require the dismantling of a multi-million-dollar industry.

Is what I have just described anything more than a bare logical possibility? Would the decriminalization of drugs, together with the continued non-criminalization of alcohol, really take us beyond some crucial threshhold of harm and badness? I must admit that I do not know. I do not know how to conceptualize the relevant threshhold, how to quantify the harms and bads to which it applies, or (therefore) how to decide whether drugs plus alcohol would add up to one legal intoxicant too many. But although I am sure that I do not know these things, I am also sure that those who favor drug decriminalization do not know them either. Thus, as long as there is *some* level of harmfulness and badness beyond which criminalization becomes reasonable, the question of whether we should legalize both intoxicants, or one of the two, or neither will remain unsettled. Although the status quo is not easy to defend, it is not clear that Husak's relaxed alternative is really any easier.

STUDY QUESTIONS

1. What arguments does Sher give for criminalizing drug use?
2. How does Sher respond to the claim that the reasons he has given are reasons not to take drugs, but not reasons to criminalize drug use?
3. How does Sher respond to the claim that his arguments should also lead to the criminalization of alcohol use?

■ Compare and Contrast Question

1. How should Husak respond to Sher's arguments?

ANIMAL RIGHTS

This section contains three highly contrasting perspectives on human relations to animals. The first is a very short piece by Immanuel Kant. Kant believes that animals are not self-conscious and therefore, according to his theory, do not have moral standing as ends in themselves. Nevertheless, he argues that human beings should treat animals well, not because of any intrinsic right or dignity possessed by animals, but because by treating them badly we brutalize our own humanity. This is bad in itself, but could also lead us to act badly to other human beings. Hence, for Kant, our duties to animals are, in fact, really duties to ourselves and to other people. He describes them as indirect duties.

Peter Singer, in direct contrast, argues that we should extend to other animals the basic principle of equality that we apply to human beings. Although there are many differences between humans and other animals, all are owed equal consideration. Just as equality condemns racism and sexism, it also condemns the exploitation of one species by another, which Singer calls "speciesism." The basis for equal consideration, argues Singer, following Jeremy Bentham, is capacity to suffer, which animals have as well as human beings. Singer argues that many human practices toward animals violate our moral duties, in that they treat animals as having a lesser status. Examples include eating meat, intensive farming, and scientific experiments on animals.

Singer notes that most people, taking for granted that there is a moral difference between human beings and animals, assume that this difference justifies the way we treat other species. Yet what is the argument to defend the current position? Singer points out that human privilege has often been defended by appeal to the "intrinsic worth" or "intrinsic dignity" of human beings. Yet Singer regards these terms merely as high-blown phrases with no real meaning, pointing out that similar arguments have been used to defend the privileged position of whites vis-à-vis blacks or men vis-à-vis women. Hence Singer regards many of our current practices toward animals as quite unjustified and arguments purporting to defend those practices as a screen for prejudice.

Roger Scruton's contribution to the debate on animal ethics, from a conservative standpoint, pays much more attention to the lives of animals than is common in the discussion. Scruton argues that if animals were persons then we should treat them as we do human beings, but they are not, and consequently they do not have rights. Approaching animal ethics through a framework of rights is to falsify our relation to animals. While Scruton accepts Singer's argument that we have moral duties to animals because animals are capable of suffering, he does not regard the considerations raised by Singer as sufficient to justify equality with animals, as there are other moral aspects to take into account too.

Scruton argues that the nature of our relations with animals affects our duties toward them: Some animals are pets; others are kept for human purposes; and others are wild. Each requires separate treatment, as animals that have been raised to depend on us are in a different position from those that have not. However, morally the most important question is whether we should raise animals for the purpose of eating them. Here Scruton notes different religious and cultural practices regarding the eating of meat and argues for toleration of diverse practices. He argues that it is only because they are raised to be eaten that many animals exist, living a comfortable life. As an animal lover, he claims that it is right to eat meat because this allows more animals to live a good life. He contrasts the quick death of a farm animal with the painful, lingering death of a human being, kept alive by modern medicine. However, Scruton does not wish to defend all current farming practices, and he accepts that some cruel methods should be reformed, while noting that to do so will be likely to raise the price of food, to the particular detriment of the poor. He ends by discussing the role of animals in scientific experiments, noting the indispensability of experiments to scientific progress, but at the same time raising a question of the value of scientific progress itself.

IMMANUEL KANT
Duties Towards Animals

Immanuel Kant (1724–1804) was an exceptionally significant and influential philosopher who wrote on many topics. He was born and lived in Konigsberg, Germany. He is particularly noted for his fundamental but difficult writings on metaphysics, especially his Critique of Pure Reason, *but equally renowned for his rigorous, principled approach to moral philosophy.*

Baumgarten[1] speaks of duties towards beings which are beneath us and beings which are above us. But so far as animals are concerned, we have no direct duties. Animals are not self-conscious and are there merely as a means to an end. That end is man. We can ask, "Why do animals exist?" But to ask, "Why does man exist?" is a meaningless question. Our duties towards animals are merely indirect duties towards humanity. Animal nature has analogies to human nature, and by doing our duties to animals in respect of manifestations which correspond to manifestations of human nature, we indirectly do our duty towards humanity. Thus, if a dog has served his master long and faithfully, his service, on the analogy of human service, deserves reward, and when the dog has grown too old to serve, his master ought to keep him until he dies. Such action helps to support us in our duties towards human beings, where they are bounden duties. If then any acts of animals are analogous to human acts and spring from the same principles, we have duties towards the animals because thus we cultivate the corresponding duties towards human beings. If a man shoots his dog because the animal is no longer capable of service, he does not fail in his duty to the dog, for the dog cannot judge, but his act is inhuman and damages in himself that humanity which it is his duty to show towards mankind. If he is not to stifle his human feelings, he must practise kindness towards animals, for he who is cruel to animals becomes hard also in his dealings with men. We can judge the heart of a man by his treatment of animals. Hogarth[2] depicts this in his engravings. He shows how cruelty grows and develops. He shows the child's cruelty to animals, pinching the tail of a dog or a cat; he then depicts the grown man in his cart running over

---

1   *Editor's note:* Alexander Gottlieb Baumgarten (1714–1762). German philosopher who wrote on ethics and metaphysics.

2   Hogarth's four engravings, "The Stages of Cruelty" 1751. [*Editor's note:* William Hogarth (1697–1764). English painter and engraver, especially known for his use of art as a form of social criticism.]

a child; and lastly, the culmination of cruelty in murder. He thus brings home to us in a terrible fashion the rewards of cruelty, and this should be an impressive lesson to children. The more we come in contact with animals and observe their behaviour, the more we love them, for we see how great is their care for their young. It is then difficult for us to be cruel in thought even to a wolf. Leibnitz[3] used a tiny worm for purposes of observation, and then carefully replaced it with its leaf on the tree so that it should not come to harm through any act of his. He would have been sorry—a natural feeling for a humane man—to destroy such a creature for no reason. Tender feelings towards dumb animals develop humane feelings towards mankind. In England butchers and doctors do not sit on a jury because they are accustomed to the sight of death and hardened. Vivisectionists, who use living animals for their experiments, certainly act cruelly, although their aim is praiseworthy, and they can justify their cruelty, since animals must be regarded as man's instruments; but any such cruelty for sport cannot be justified. A master who turns out his ass or his dog because the animal can no longer earn its keep manifests a small mind. * * * Our duties towards animals, then, are indirect duties towards mankind.

STUDY QUESTIONS

1. Why does Kant think that animals exist merely as means to an end?
2. What is the basis, for Kant, of our "indirect duties" to animals?
3. How plausible is Kant's argument that we have indirect duties to animals?

PETER SINGER
All Animals Are Equal

Peter Singer (b. 1946) is a contemporary Australian utilitarian philosopher, known for his uncompromising views on many issues of contemporary morality, such as animal liberation and the moral necessity to address global poverty.

A liberation movement demands an expansion of our moral horizons and an extension or reinterpretation of the basic moral principle of equality. Practices that were previously regarded as natural and inevitable come to be seen as the result of an unjustifiable prejudice. Who can say with confidence that all his or her attitudes and practices are beyond criticism? If we wish

---

3   *Editor's note*: Gottfried Wilhelm Leibniz (1646–1716). German philosopher, mathematician, and scientist. Dominant figure in German philosophy prior to Kant.

to avoid being numbered amongst the oppressors, we must be prepared to re-think even our most fundamental attitudes. We need to consider them from the point of view of those most disadvantaged by our attitudes, and the practices that follow from these attitudes. If we can make this unaccustomed mental switch we may discover a pattern in our attitudes and practices that consistently operates so as to benefit one group—usually the one to which we ourselves belong—at the expense of another. In this way we may come to see that there is a case for a new liberation movement. My aim is to advocate that we make this mental switch in respect of our attitudes and practices towards a very large group of beings: members of species other than our own—or, as we popularly though misleadingly call them, animals. In other words, I am urging that we extend to other species the basic principle of equality that most of us recognise should be extended to all members of our own species. * * *

* * * There *are* important differences between humans and other animals, and these differences must give rise to *some* differences in the rights that each have. Since a pig can't vote, it is meaningless to talk of its right to vote. There is no reason why * * * Animal Liberation should get involved in such nonsense. The extension of the basic principle of equality from one group to another does not imply that we must treat both groups in exactly the same way, or grant exactly the same rights to both groups. Whether we should do so will depend on the nature of the members of the two groups. The basic principle of equality, I shall argue, is equality of consideration; and equal consideration for different beings may lead to different treatment and different rights.

* * * There is * * * nothing absurd in the idea that the basic principle of equality applies to so-called "brutes." I believe that we reach this conclusion if we examine the basis on which our opposition to discrimination on grounds of race or sex ultimately rests. We will then see that we would be on shaky ground if we were to demand equality for blacks, women, and other groups of oppressed humans while denying equal consideration to non-humans. * * *

* * * The claim to equality does not depend on intelligence, moral capacity, physical strength, or similar matters of fact. Equality is a moral ideal, not a simple assertion of fact. There is no logically compelling reason for assuming that a factual difference in ability between two people justifies any difference in the amount of consideration we give to satisfying their needs and interests. The principle of the equality of human beings is not a description of an alleged actual equality among humans: it is a prescription of how we should treat humans.

Jeremy Bentham incorporated the essential basis of moral equality into his utilitarian system of ethics in the formula: "Each to count for one and none for more than one." In other words, the interests of every being affected by an action are to be taken into account and given the same weight as the like interests of any other being. A later utilitarian, Henry Sidgwick, put the point in this way: "The good of any one individual is of no more importance, from the point of view (if I may say so) of the Universe, than the good of any other."[1] More recently, the leading figures in contemporary moral philosophy have shown a great deal of agreement in specifying as a fundamental presupposition of their moral theories some similar requirement which operates so as to give everyone's interests equal consideration—although they cannot agree on how this requirement is best formulated.

It is an implication of this principle of equality that our concern for others ought not to depend on what they are like, or what abilities they possess—although precisely what this concern requires us to do may vary according to the characteristics of those affected by what we do. It is on this basis that the case against racism and the case against sexism must both ultimately rest; and it is in accordance with this principle that speciesism is also to be condemned. If possessing a higher degree of intelligence does not entitle one human to use another for his own ends, how can it entitle humans to exploit non-humans?

Many philosophers have proposed the principle of equal consideration of interests, in some form or other, as a basic moral principle; but, as we shall see in more detail shortly, not many of them have recognised that this principle applies to members of other species as well as to our own. Bentham was one of the few who did realize this. In a forward-looking passage, written at a time when black slaves in the British dominions were still being treated much as we now treat non-human animals, Bentham wrote:

> The day *may* come when the rest of the animal creation may acquire those rights which never could have been witholden from them but by the hand of tyranny. The French have already discovered that the blackness of the skin is no reason why a human being should be abandoned without redress to the caprice of a tormentor. It may one day come to be recognised that the number of the legs, the villosity of the skin, or the termination of the *os sacrum*, are reasons equally insufficient for abandoning a sensitive being to the same fate. What else is it that should trace the insuperable line? Is it the faculty of reason, or perhaps the faculty of discourse? But a full-grown horse or dog is beyond comparison a more rational, as well as a more conversable animal,

---

1   *The Methods of Ethics* (7th Ed.) p. 382.

than an infant of a day, or a week, or even a month, old. But suppose they were otherwise, what would it avail? The question is not, Can they reason? nor Can they *talk*? but, *Can they suffer?*[2]

In this passage Bentham points to the capacity for suffering as the vital characteristic that gives a being the right to equal consideration. The capacity for suffering—or more strictly, for suffering and/or enjoyment or happiness—is not just another characteristic like the capacity for language, or for higher mathematics. Bentham is not saying that those who try to mark "the insuperable line" that determines whether the interests of a being should be considered happen to have selected the wrong characteristic. The capacity for suffering and enjoying things is a pre-requisite for having interests at all, a condition that must be satisfied before we can speak of interests in any meaningful way. It would be nonsense to say that it was not in the interests of a stone to be kicked along the road by a schoolboy. A stone does not have interests because it cannot suffer. Nothing that we can do to it could possibly make any difference to its welfare. A mouse, on the other hand, does have an interest in not being tormented, because it will suffer if it is.

If a being suffers, there can be no moral justification for refusing to take that suffering into consideration. No matter what the nature of the being, the principle of equality requires that its suffering be counted equally with the like suffering—in so far as rough comparisons can be made—of any other being. If a being is not capable of suffering, or of experiencing enjoyment or happiness, there is nothing to be taken into account. This is why the limit of sentience (using the term as a convenient, if not strictly accurate, shorthand for the capacity to suffer or experience enjoyment or happiness) is the only defensible boundary of concern for the interests of others. To mark this boundary by some characteristic like intelligence or rationality would be to mark it in an arbitrary way. Why not choose some other characteristic, like skin color?

The racist violates the principle of equality by giving greater weight to the interests of members of his own race, when there is a clash between their interests and the interests of those of another race. Similarly the speciesist allows the interests of his own species to override the greater interests of members of other species. The pattern is the same in each case. Most human beings are speciesists. I shall now very briefly describe some of the practices that show this.

For the great majority of human beings, especially in urban, industrialized societies, the most direct form of contact with members of other species

---

2 *Introduction to the Principles of Morals and Legislation*, ch. XVII.

is at meal-times: we eat them. In doing so we treat them purely as means to our ends. We regard their life and well-being as subordinate to our taste for a particular kind of dish. I say "taste" deliberately—this is purely a matter of pleasing our palate. There can be no defence of eating flesh in terms of satisfying nutritional needs, since it has been established beyond doubt that we could satisfy our need for protein and other essential nutrients far more efficiently with a diet that replaced animal flesh by soy beans, or products derived from soy beans, and other high-protein vegetable products.

It is not merely the act of killing that indicates what we are ready to do to other species in order to gratify our tastes. The suffering we inflict on the animals while they are alive is perhaps an even clearer indication of our speciesism than the fact that we are prepared to kill them. In order to have meat on the table at a price that people can afford, our society tolerates methods of meat production that confine sentient animals in cramped, unsuitable conditions for the entire durations of their lives. Animals are treated like machines that convert fodder into flesh, and any innovation that results in a higher "conversion ratio" is liable to be adopted. As one authority on the subject has said, "cruelty is acknowledged only when profitability ceases."[3] * * *

Since, as I have said, none of these practices cater for anything more than our pleasures of taste, our practice of rearing and killing other animals in order to eat them is a clear instance of the sacrifice of the most important interests of other beings in order to satisfy trivial interests of our own. To avoid speciesism we must stop this practice, and each of us has a moral obligation to cease supporting the practice. Our custom is all the support that the meat-industry needs. The decision to cease giving it that support may be difficult, but it is no more difficult than it would have been for a white Southerner to go against the traditions of his society and free his slaves; if we do not change our dietary habits, how can we censure those slaveholders who would not change their own way of living?

The same form of discrimination may be observed in the widespread practice of experimenting on other species in order to see if certain substances are safe for human beings, or to test some psychological theory about the effect of severe punishment on learning, or to try out various new compounds just in case something turns up. * * *

---

3   Ruth Harrison, *Animal Machines* (Stuart, London, 1964). This book provides an eye-opening account of intensive farming methods for those unfamiliar with the subject.

In the past, argument about vivesection has often missed this point, because it has been put in absolutist terms: would the abolitionist be prepared to let thousands die if they could be saved by experimenting on a single animal? The way to reply to this purely hypothetical question is to pose another: would the experimenter be prepared to perform his experiment on an orphaned human infant, if that were the only way to save many lives? (I say "orphan" to avoid the complication of parental feelings, although in doing so I am being overfair to the experimenter, since the nonhuman subjects of experiments are not orphans.) If the experimenter is not prepared to use an orphaned human infant, then his readiness to use nonhumans is simple discrimination, since adult apes, cats, mice and other mammals are more aware of what is happening to them, more self-directing and, so far as we can tell, at least as sensitive to pain, as any human infant. There seems to be no relevant characteristic that human infants possess that adult mammals do not have to the same or a higher degree. (Someone might try to argue that what makes it wrong to experiment on a human infant is that the infant will, in time and if left alone, develop into more than the nonhuman, but one would then, to be consistent, have to oppose abortion, since the fetus has the same potential as the infant—indeed, even contraception and abstinence might be wrong on this ground, since the egg and sperm, considered jointly, also have the same potential. In any case, this argument still gives us no reason for selecting a nonhuman, rather than a human with severe and irreversible brain damage, as the subject for our experiments.)

The experimenter, then, shows a bias in favor of his own species whenever he carries out an experiment on a nonhuman for a purpose that he would not think justified him in using a human being at an equal or lower level of sentience, awareness, ability to be self-directing, etc. * * *

Faced with a situation in which they see a need for some basis for the moral gulf that is commonly thought to separate humans and animals, but can find no concrete difference that will do the job without undermining the equality of humans, philosophers tend to waffle. They resort to high-sounding phrases like "the intrinsic dignity of the human individual"; they talk of the "intrinsic worth of all men" as if men (humans?) had some worth that other beings did not or they say that humans, and only humans, are "ends in themselves," while "everything other than a person can only have value for a person."

This idea of a distinctive human dignity and worth has a long history; it can be traced back directly to the Renaissance humanists, for instance to Pico della Mirandola's *Oration on the Dignity of Man*. Pico and other humanists based their estimate of human dignity on the idea that man possessed the central, pivotal position in the "Great Chain of Being" that led from the lowliest forms of matter to God himself; this view of the universe, in turn, goes back to both classical and Judeo-Christian doctrines. Contemporary philosophers have cast off these metaphysical and religious shackles and freely invoke the dignity of mankind without needing to justify the idea at all. Why should we not attribute "intrinsic dignity" or "intrinsic worth" to ourselves? Fellow-humans are unlikely to reject the accolades we so generously bestow on them, and those to whom we deny the honor are unable to object. Indeed, when one thinks only of humans, it can be very liberal, very progressive, to talk of the dignity of all human beings. In so doing, we implicitly condemn slavery, racism, and other violations of human rights. We admit that we ourselves are in some fundamental sense on a par with the poorest, most ignorant members of our own species. It is only when we think of humans as no more than a small sub-group of all the beings that inhabit our planet that we may realize that in elevating our own species we are at the same time lowering the relative status of all other species.

The truth is that the appeal to the intrinsic dignity of human beings appears to solve the egalitarian's problems only as long as it goes unchallenged. Once we ask *why* it should be that all humans—including infants, mental defectives, psychopaths, Hitler, Stalin and the rest—have some kind of dignity or worth that no elephant, pig or chimpanzee can ever achieve, we see that this question is as difficult to answer as our original request for some relevant fact that justifies the inequality of humans and other animals. In fact, these two questions are really one: talk of intrinsic dignity or moral worth only takes the problem back one step, because any satisfactory defence of the claim that all and only humans have intrinsic dignity would need to refer to some relevant capacities or characteristics that all and only humans possess. Philosophers frequently introduce ideas of dignity, respect and worth at the point at which other reasons appear to be lacking, but this is hardly good enough. Fine phrases are the last resource of those who have run out of arguments.

STUDY QUESTIONS

1. What does Singer mean by "speciesism"?
2. What, for Singer, is the moral basis of equal consideration? What does it mean in practice?
3. Is Singer right to dismiss the idea that human beings possess a worth or dignity not possessed by other animals?

ROGER SCRUTON
Animal Rights and Wrongs

Roger Scruton (b. 1942) is an English philosopher known especially for his work in aesthetics and for his defense of conservative political positions.

NON-MORAL BEINGS

I shall use the term "animal" to mean those animals that lack the distinguishing features of the moral being—rationality, self-consciousness, personality, and so on. If there are non-human animals who are rational and self-conscious, then they, like us, are persons, and should be described and treated accordingly. If *all* animals are persons, then there is no longer a problem as to how we should treat them. They would be full members of the moral community, with rights and duties like the rest of us. But it is precisely because there are animals who are not persons that the moral problem exists. And to treat these non-personal animals as persons is not to grant to them a privilege nor to raise their chances of contentment. It is to ignore what they essentially are and so to fall out of relation with them altogether.

The concept of the person belongs to the ongoing dialogue which binds the moral community. Creatures who are by nature incapable of entering into this dialogue have neither rights nor duties nor personality. If animals had rights, then we should require their consent before taking them into captivity, training them, domesticating them or in any way putting them to our uses. But there is no conceivable process whereby this consent could be delivered or withheld. Furthermore, a creature with rights is duty-bound to respect the rights of others. The fox would be duty-bound to respect the right to life of the chicken and whole species would be condemned out of hand as criminal by nature. Any law which compelled persons to respect the rights of non-human species would weigh so heavily on the predators as to drive them to extinction in a short while. Any morality which really attributed rights to animals would therefore constitute a gross and callous abuse of them.

Those considerations are obvious, but by no means trivial. For they point to a deep difficulty in the path of any attempt to treat animals as our equals. By ascribing rights to animals, and so promoting them to full membership of the moral community, we tie them in obligations that they can neither fulfil nor comprehend. Not only is this senseless cruelty in itself; it effectively destroys all possibility of cordial and beneficial relations between us and them. Only by refraining from personalising animals do we behave towards them in ways that they can understand. And even the most sentimental animal lovers know this, and confer "rights" on their favourites in a manner so selective and arbitrary as to show that they are not really dealing with the ordinary moral concept. When a dog savages a sheep no one believes that the dog, rather than its owner, should be sued for damages. Sei Shonagon, in *The Pillow Book*, tells of a dog breaching some rule of court etiquette and being horribly beaten, as the law requires.[1] The scene is most disturbing to the modern reader. Yet surely, if dogs have rights, punishment is what they must expect when they disregard their duties.

But the point does not concern rights only. It concerns the deep and impassable difference between personal relations, founded on dialogue, criticism and the sense of justice, and animal relations, founded on affections and needs. The moral problem of animals arises because they cannot enter into relations of the first kind, while we are so much bound by those relations that they seem to tie us even to creatures who cannot themselves be bound by them.

Defenders of "animal liberation" have made much of the fact that animals suffer as we do: they feel pain, hunger, cold and fear and therefore, as Singer puts it, have "interests" which form, or ought to form, part of the moral equation.[2] While this is true, it is only part of the truth. There is more to morality than the avoidance of suffering: to live by no other standard than this one is to avoid life, to forgo risk and adventure, and to sink into a state of cringing morbidity. Moreover, while our sympathies ought to be—and unavoidably will be—extended to the animals, they should not be indiscriminate. Although animals have no rights, we still have duties and responsibilities towards them, or towards some of them. These will cut across the utilitarian equation, distinguishing the animals who are close to us and who have a claim on our protection from those towards whom our duties fall under the broader rule of charity.

This is important for two reasons. Firstly, we relate to animals in three distinct situations, which define three distinct kinds of responsibility: as pets, as domestic animals reared for human purposes and as wild creatures.

---

1 *Editor's note*: Sei Shonogan (c. 966–1017/1025) was a Japanese poet and writer. She was a court lady to the Empress Teishi.

2 *Editor's note*: See Selections from Peter Singer's "All Animals Are Equal" on pp. 429–435 of this reader.

Secondly, the situation of animals is radically and often irreversibly changed as soon as human beings take an interest in them. Pets and other domestic animals are usually entirely dependent on human care for their survival and well-being; and wild animals, too, are increasingly dependent on human measures to protect their food supplies and habitats.

Some shadow version of the moral law therefore emerges in our dealings with animals. I cannot blithely count the interests of my dog as on a par with the interests of any other dog, wild or domesticated, even though they have an equal capacity for suffering and an equal need for help. My dog has a special claim on me, not wholly dissimilar from the claim of my child. I caused it to be dependent on me precisely by leading it to expect that I would cater for its needs.

The situation is further complicated by the distinction between species. Dogs form life-long attachments and a dog brought up by one person may be incapable of living comfortably with another. A horse may be bought or sold many times, with little or no distress, provided it is properly cared for by each of its owners. Sheep maintained in flocks are every bit as dependent on human care as dogs and horses; but they do not notice it and regard their shepherds and guardians as little more than aspects of the environment, which rise like the sun in the morning and depart like the sun at night. ∗ ∗ ∗

LIVESTOCK AND THE EATING OF MEAT

It is impossible to consider the question of farm animals without discussing an issue which for many people is of pressing concern: whether we should consume animal products in general and meat in particular. To what sphere of moral debate does this question belong? Not, surely, to the moral law, which offers no decisive answer to the question of whether it is wrong to eat a *person*, provided he or she is already dead. Nor to the sphere of sympathy, which gives few unambiguous signals as to how we should treat the dead remains of living creatures. Our only obvious guide in this area is piety which, because it is shaped by tradition, provides no final court of appeal. In the Judaeo-Hellenic tradition, animals were sacrificed to the deity and it was considered an act of piety to share a meal prepared for such a distinguished guest. In the Hindu tradition, by contrast, animal life is sacred and the eating of meat is as impious as the eating of people.

In the face of this clash of civilisations there is little that the sceptical conscience can affirm, apart from the need for choice and toleration. At the same time, I cannot believe that a lover of animals would be favourably impressed by their fate in Hindu society, where they are so often neglected, ill-fed and riddled with disease. Having opted for the Western approach, I find myself driven by my love of animals to favour eating them. Most of the animals which graze in our fields are there because we eat them. Sheep and beef cattle are, in the conditions which prevail in English pastures, well-fed, comfortable and protected, cared for when disease afflicts them and, after a quiet life among their natural companions, despatched in ways which human beings, if they are rational, must surely envy. There is nothing immoral in this. On the contrary, it is one of the most vivid triumphs of comfort over suffering in the entire animal world. It seems to me, therefore, that it is not just permissible, but positively right, to eat these animals whose comforts depend upon our doing so.

I am more inclined to think in this way when I consider the fate of human beings under the rule of modern medicine. In comparison with the average farm animal, a human being has a terrible end. Kept alive too long by processes like the organ transplant, which nature never intended, we can look forward to years of suffering and alienation, the only reward for which is death—a death which, as a rule, comes too late for anyone else to regret it. Well did the Greeks say that those whom the gods love die young. It is not only divine love but also human love that expires as the human frame declines. Increasingly, many human beings end their lives unloved, unwanted and in pain. This, the greatest achievement of modern science, should remind us of the price that is due for our impieties. How, in the face of this, can we believe that the fate of the well-cared for cow or sheep is a cruel one?

Two questions trouble the ordinary conscience, however. First, under what conditions should farm animals be raised? Secondly, at what age ought they to be killed? Both questions are inevitably bound up with economics, since the animals in question would not exist at all if they could not be sold profitably as food. If it is uneconomical to rear chickens for the table, except in battery farms, should they therefore not be reared at all? The answer to such a question requires us to examine the balance of comfort over discomfort available to a chicken, cooped up in those artificial conditions. But it is not settled by utilitarian considerations alone. There is the further and deeper question, prompted by both piety and natural sympathy, as to whether it is right to keep animals, however little they may suffer, in conditions so unnatural and so destructive of the appetite for life. Most people find the sight of pigs or chickens, reared under artificial light in tiny cages, in conditions more appropriate to vegetables than to animals, deeply disturbing and this feeling ought surely to be respected, as stemming from the primary sources of moral emotion.

Those who decide this question merely by utilitarian calculation have no real understanding of what it means. Sympathy and piety are indispensable motives in the moral being and their voices cannot be silenced by a mere calculation. Someone who was indifferent to the sight of pigs confined in batteries, who did not feel some instinctive need to pull down these walls and barriers and let in light and air, would have lost sight of what it is to be a living animal. His sense of the value of his own life would be to that extent impoverished by his indifference to the sight of life reduced to a stream of sensations. It seems to me, therefore, that a true morality of animal welfare ought to begin from the premise that this way of treating animals is wrong, even if legally permissible. Most people in Britain agree with that verdict, although most do not feel so strongly that they will pay the extra price for a free-range chicken or for free-range eggs. To some extent, of course, people are the victims of well-organised deception. By describing chickens and eggs as "farm fresh," producers effectively hide the living death upon which their profits depend. But customers who are easily deceived lack one important part of human virtue. Travellers in the former communist countries of Eastern Europe, for example, would do well to ask themselves why meat is so readily available in shops and restaurants, even though no animals whatsoever are visible in the fields. A Czech *samizdat* cartoon from the communist years shows two old women staring sadly into a vast factory farm, full of cows. One of them remarks to her companion: "I remember the days when cows had souls"; to which her companion replies "yes, and so did we." The cartoon was intended as a comment on communism; but it points to the deep connection that exists between our way of treating animals and our way of treating ourselves.

Suppose we agree that farm animals should be given a measure of their natural freedom. The question remains as to when they should be killed. To feed an animal beyond the point at which it has ceased to grow is to increase the cost to the consumer, and therefore to jeopardise the practice to which its life is owed. There is no easy solution to this problem, even if, when it comes to calves, whose mournful liquid eyes have the capacity to raise a cloud of well-meaning sentiment, the solution may seem deceptively simple. Calves are an unavoidable by-product of the milk industry. Male calves are useless to the industry and represent, in existing conditions, an unsustainable cost if they are not sold for slaughter. If we decide that it really is wrong to kill them so young, then we must also accept that the price of milk—on which human children depend for much of their nourishment—is at present far too low. We must, in other words, be prepared to accept considerable human hardship, in particular among poorer people, in order to satisfy this moral demand. It is therefore very important to know whether the demand is well-grounded.

Young animals have been slaughtered without compunction from the beginning of history. The lamb, the sucking pig, the calf and the leveret have been esteemed as delicacies and eaten in preference to their parents, who are tough, coarse and over-ripe by comparison. Only if there is some other use for an animal than food is it economical to keep it past maturity. Mutton makes sense as food only in countries where wool is a commodity. Elsewhere sheep are either kept for breeding or eaten as lambs. Beef cattle, too, await an early death, as do porkers. We could go on feeding these animals beyond the usual date for slaughter but this would so increase the price of meat as to threaten the habit of producing it and therefore the lives of the animals themselves.

In the face of this, we surely cannot regard the practice of slaughtering young animals as intrinsically immoral. Properly cared for, the life of a calf or lamb is a positive addition to the sum of joy, and there can be no objection in principle to a humane and early death, provided the life is a full and active one. It is right to give herbivores the opportunity to roam out of doors on grass, in the herds and flocks which are their natural society; it is right to allow pigs to rootle and rummage in the open air, and chickens to peck and squawk in the farmyard, before meeting their end. But when that end should be is more a question of economics than of morals.

In short, once it is accepted that animals may be eaten, that many of them exist only *because* they are eaten, and that there are ways of giving them a fulfilled life and an easy death on their way to the table, I cannot see that we can find fault with the farmer who adopts these ways when producing animals for food. Those who criticise farmers may often have reason on their side; but there is also a danger of self-righteousness in criticisms offered from a comfortable armchair by people who do not have the trouble of looking after farm animals and see only their soft and endearing side. Farmers are human beings and no less given to sympathy than the rest of us. And a good farmer, rearing sheep and cattle on pasture, keeping dogs, cats and horses as domestic animals, and free-range chickens for eggs, contributes more to the sum of animal welfare than a thousand suburban dreamers, stirred into emotion by a documentary on television. Such people may easily imagine that all animals are as easy to deal with as the cat which purrs on their knees, and whose food comes prepared in tins, offering no hint of the other animals whose death was required to manufacture it. It would be lamentable if the moral highground in the debate over livestock were conceded to those who have neither the capacity nor the desire to look after the animals whose fate they bewail, and not to the farmers who do their best to ensure that these animals exist in the first place.

EXPERIMENTS ON ANIMALS

There is no humane person who believes that we are free to use animals as we will just because the goal is knowledge. But there are many who argue that experiments on live animals are nevertheless both necessary for the advance of science (and of medical science in particular), and also permissible when suitably controlled.

It seems to me that we must consider this question in the same spirit as we have considered that of livestock. We should study the entire practice of experimentation on live animals, the function it performs and the good that it produces. We should consider the fate of the animals who are the subject of experiment and the special duty of care that might be owed to them. Finally, we should lay down principles concerning what cannot be done, however beneficial the consequences—and here our reasoning must derive from sympathy, piety and the concept of virtue, and cannot be reduced to utilitarian principles alone.

Medical research requires live experimentation and the subjects cannot be human, except in the cases where their consent can reasonably be offered and sought. It is not only humans who benefit from medical research: all animals within our care have an interest in it, and the assumption must be that it is so conducted that the long-term benefits to all of us, human and animal, outweigh the short-term costs in pain and discomfort.

The duty of care owed to animals used in medical research is to ensure that their lives are worth living and their suffering minimised. Even within these constraints, however, there are certain things that a decent person will not do, since they offend too heavily against sympathy or piety. The sight of the higher mammals, subject to operations that destroy or interfere with their capacities to move, perceive or understand, is so distressing that a certain measure of callousness is required if these operations are to be conducted. And that which can be done only by a callous person, ought not to be done. The case is comparable to the battery farm. But it is also crucially different. For an experiment is typically conducted on a healthy animal, which is *singled out* for this misfortune and the life of which may be deliberately destroyed in the process. The relentless course of science will always ensure that these experiments occur. But that is part of what is wrong with the relentless course of science.

And here we touch on a question so deep that I doubt that ordinary moral thinking can supply the answer to it. As I hinted above, the advance of medical science is by no means an unmixed blessing. The emerging society of joyless geriatrics is not one at which the human spirit spontaneously rejoices. And although discoveries cannot be undiscovered, nor knowledge deliberately undone, there is truth in the saying that ignorance—or at least ignorance of a certain kind—is bliss. Piety once set obstacles in the path of knowledge—and these obstacles had a function; for they prevented the present generation from seizing control of the earth's resources, and bending them to the cause of its own longevity. Medical science may have benefited the living; but it threatens the resources which the dead laid by for us, and on which the unborn depend. Animals were once sacrificed to the gods by people who cheerfully accepted that they would soon follow their victims to oblivion. Now they are sacrificed to science by people who nurture the impious hope that they can prolong their tenancy forever. This may be morally acceptable. But something in the human heart rebels against it.

STUDY QUESTIONS

1. Why does Scruton reject the idea that animals have rights?
2. Why, according to Scruton, isn't the question of how humans should treat animals settled by the fact that animals are capable of suffering?
3. Why does Scruton argue that as an animal lover he is right to eat meat?

■ Compare and Contrast Questions

1. How should Singer reply to Kant's arguments?
2. How should Scruton reply to Kant's arguments?
3. Does Scruton show that Singer's arguments are mistaken?

THE ENVIRONMENT

This section contains two selections on different, though related topics in environmental ethics. Aldo Leopold's *A Sand County Almanac*, from which "The Land Ethic" is taken, was first published in 1949. Leopold was one of the first theorists to try to find a way of connecting the emerging ecological movement to philosophical ethics. Leopold starts from a premise about the nature of ethics, that it concerns the relations between members of a community of interdependent parts. The next step is to argue that the land, by which he means soils, waters, plants, and animals, is part of a system of interdependency with human beings. Leopold uses the image of the "biotic pyramid" to show levels of dependency between different elements. From these premises, it follows that human beings are in a moral relationship with the land. Leopold does not develop a land ethic in detail, suggesting it needs much more work and thought, but he does suggest that it gives the land the right to continue to exist in a natural state.

Leopold contrasts his approach with a form of instrumentalism in which human beings treat the land as existing purely to serve human purposes. Leopold is clearly opposed to this view, arguing that by these means human beings act as if they are conquerors of the land instead of citizens with duties of conservation. He also argues that the instrumental approach will ultimately be self-defeating. For if we continue to exploit the land as we do, failing to appreciate the extent of our dependence on it, we will overuse it to a point where we will harm ourselves. When the government intervenes, it has tended to try to attach economic incentives to pro-conservation behavior. But this effort will inevitably be limited in its effects. In the final passage included here, Leopold uses the example of the elimination of wolves to show how human intervention in nature can lead to unexpected and undesirable consequences.

In the next essay, Darrel Moellendorf tackles what many people believe is the greatest challenge facing humanity today, human-caused climate change. Moellendorf believes that it is now beyond doubt that carbon emissions have caused, and will continue to cause, the warming of the surface of the earth, and if this continues there will be devastating effects, some of which we are already beginning to see.

Moellendorf distinguishes three types of response: mitigation, to reduce carbon emissions; adaptation, to prepare for climate change; and geoengineering, which seeks technological solutions to lessen the effects of emissions. Mitigation is now a matter of urgency, to be achieved especially by ending the burning of fossil fuels and increasing the use of renewables. However, mitigation will be very expensive, at least in the short term, and threatens to hold back the development of some of the least developed countries, as development is heavily dependent on energy use. Hence questions of global justice arise, and also intergenerational justice, since what we do now will affect future generations.

Moellendorf discusses three principles of justice for distributing the costs of mitigation. The first is the Polluter-Pays principle, which requires those that have caused the greatest harm to take on the largest burden. A second is the Beneficiary-Pays, which says that those who have received the greatest benefits should pay the most. The third is the Ability-to-Pay principle, which asks those who can afford it most easily to make the contribution. Moellendorf argues that this last principle is the most defensible, as it allows for the sustainable development of poor countries. However, mitigation will take time to have an effect, and in the meantime, Moellendorf argues, policies of adaptation and possibly geo-engineering will be required.

ALDO LEOPOLD
The Land Ethic

Aldo Leopold (1887–1948) was an American environmentalist especially known for the best-selling A Sand County Almanac, *from which this extract is taken.*

When god-like Odysseus returned from the wars in Troy, he hanged all on one rope a dozen slave-girls of his household whom he suspected of misbehavior during his absence.

This hanging involved no question of propriety. The girls were property. The disposal of property was then, as now, a matter of expediency, not of right and wrong.

Concepts of right and wrong were not lacking from Odysseus' Greece: witness the fidelity of his wife through the long years before at last his black-prowed galleys clove the wine-dark seas for home. The ethical structure of that day covered wives, but had not yet been extended to human chattels. During the three thousand years which have since elapsed, ethical criteria have been extended to many fields of conduct, with corresponding shrinkages in those judged by expediency only.

THE ETHICAL SEQUENCE

This extension of ethics, so far studied only by philosophers, is actually a process in ecological evolution. Its sequences may be described in ecological as well as in philosophical terms. An ethic, ecologically, is a limitation on freedom of action in the struggle for existence. An ethic, philosophically,

is a differentiation of social from anti-social conduct. These are two definitions of one thing. The thing has its origin in the tendency of interdependent individuals or groups to evolve modes of co-operation. The ecologist
calls these symbioses. Politics and economics are advanced symbioses in
which the original free-for-all competition has been replaced, in part, by
co-operative mechanisms with an ethical content.

The complexity of co-operative mechanisms has increased with population density, and with the efficiency of tools. It was simpler, for example, to
define the anti-social uses of sticks and stones in the days of the mastodons
than of bullets and billboards in the age of motors.

The first ethics dealt with the relation between individuals; the Mosaic
Decalogue is an example. Later accretions dealt with the relation between
the individual and society. The Golden Rule tries to integrate the individual
to society; democracy to integrate social organization to the individual.

There is as yet no ethic dealing with man's relation to land and to the
animals and plants which grow upon it, Land, like Odysseus' slave-girls, is
still property. The land-relation is still strictly economic, entailing privileges
but not obligations.

The extension of ethics to this third element in human environment is,
if I read the evidence correctly, an evolutionary possibility and an ecological
necessity. It is the third step in a sequence. The first two have already been
taken. Individual thinkers since the days of Ezekiel and Isaiah have asserted
that the despoliation of land is not only inexpedient but wrong. Society,
however, has not yet affirmed their belief. I regard the present conservation
movement as the embryo of such an affirmation.

An ethic may be regarded as a mode of guidance for meeting ecological
situations so new or intricate, or involving such deferred reactions, that
the path of social expediency is not discernible to the average individual.
Animal instincts are modes of guidance for the individual in meeting such
situations. Ethics are possibly a kind of community instinct in-the-making.

THE COMMUNITY CONCEPT

All ethics so far evolved rest upon a single premise: that the individual is a
member of a community of interdependent parts. His instincts prompt him
to compete for his place in that community, but his ethics prompt him also
to co-operate (perhaps in order that there may be a place to compete for).

The land ethic simply enlarges the boundaries of the community to
include soils, waters, plants, and animals, or collectively: the land.

This sounds simple: do we not already sing our love for and obligation to the land of the free and the home of the brave? Yes, but just what and whom do we love? Certainly not the soil, which we are sending helter-skelter downriver. Certainly not the waters, which we assume have no function except to turn turbines, float barges, and carry off sewage. Certainly not the plants, of which we exterminate whole communities without batting an eye. Certainly not the animals, of which we have already extirpated many of the largest and most beautiful species. A land ethic of course cannot prevent the alteration, management, and use of these "resources," but it does affirm their right to continued existence, and, at least in spots, their continued existence in a natural state.

In short, a land ethic changes the role of *Homo sapiens* from conqueror of the land-community to plain member and citizen of it. It implies respect for his fellow-members, and also respect for the community as such.

In human history, we have learned (I hope) that the conqueror role is eventually self-defeating. Why? Because it is implicit in such a role that the conqueror knows, *ex cathedra*, just what makes the community clock tick, and just what and who is valuable, and what and who is worthless, in community life. It always turns out that he knows neither, and this is why his conquests eventually defeat themselves.

In the biotic community, a parallel situation exists. Abraham knew exactly what the land was for: it was to drip milk and honey into Abraham's mouth. At the present moment, the assurance with which we regard this assumption is inverse to the degree of our education.

The ordinary citizen today assumes that science knows what makes the community clock tick; the scientist is equally sure that he does not. He knows that the biotic mechanism is so complex that its workings may never be fully understood. ✳ ✳ ✳

THE ECOLOGICAL CONSCIENCE

Conservation is a state of harmony between men and land. Despite nearly a century of propaganda, conservation still proceeds at a snail's pace; progress still consists largely of letterhead pieties and convention oratory. On the back forty we still slip two steps backward for each forward stride.

The usual answer to this dilemma is "more conservation education." No one will debate this, but is it certain that only the *volume* of education needs stepping up? Is something lacking in the *content* as well?

It is difficult to give a fair summary of its content in brief form, but, as I understand it, the content is substantially this: obey the law, vote right, join some organizations, and practice what conservation is profitable on your own land; the government will do the rest.

Is not this formula too easy to accomplish anything worth-while? It defines no right or wrong, assigns no obligation, calls for no sacrifice, implies no change in the current philosophy of values. In respect of land-use, it urges only enlightened self-interest. Just how far will such education take us? An example will perhaps yield a partial answer.

By 1930 it had become clear to all except the ecologically blind that south-western Wisconsin's topsoil was slipping seaward. In 1933 the farmers were told that if they would adopt certain remedial practices for five years, the public would donate CCC labor to install them, plus the necessary machinery and materials. The offer was widely accepted, but the practices were widely forgotten when the five-year contract period was up. The farmers continued only those practices that yielded an immediate and visible economic gain for themselves. ＊＊＊

The puzzling aspect of such situations is that the existence of obligations over and above self-interest is taken for granted in such rural community enterprises as the betterment of roads, schools, churches, and baseball teams. Their existence is not taken for granted, nor as yet seriously discussed, in bettering the behavior of the water that falls on the land, or in the preserving of the beauty or diversity of the farm landscape. Land-use ethics are still governed wholly by economic self-interest, just as social ethics were a century ago. ＊＊＊

No important change in ethics was ever accomplished without an internal change in our intellectual emphasis, loyalties, affections, and convictions. The proof that conservation has not yet touched these foundations of conduct lies in the fact that philosophy and religion have not yet heard of it. In our attempt to make conservation easy, we have made it trivial.

SUBSTITUTES FOR A LAND ETHIC

When the logic of history hungers for bread and we hand out a stone, we are at pains to explain how much the stone resembles bread. I now describe some of the stones which serve in lieu of a land ethic.

One basic weakness in a conservation system based wholly on economic motives is that most members of the land community have no economic value. Wildflowers and songbirds are examples. Of the 22,000 higher plants and animals native to Wisconsin, it is doubtful whether more than 5 per cent can be sold, fed, eaten, or otherwise put to economic use. Yet these creatures are members of the biotic community, and if (as I believe) its stability depends on its integrity, they are entitled to continuance.

When one of these non-economic categories is threatened, and if we happen to love it, we invent subterfuges to give it economic importance. At the beginning of the century song-birds were supposed to be disappearing. Ornithologists jumped to the rescue with some distinctly shaky evidence to the effect that insects would eat us up if birds failed to control them. The evidence had to be economic in order to be valid.

It is painful to read these circumlocutions today. We have no land ethic yet, but we have at least drawn nearer the point of admitting that birds should continue as a matter of biotic right, regardless of the presence or absence of economic advantage to us.

A parallel situation exists in respect of predatory mammals, raptorial birds, and fish-eating birds. Time was when biologists somewhat overworked the evidence that these creatures preserve the health of game by killing weaklings, or that they control rodents for the farmer, or that they prey only on "worthless" species. Here again, the evidence had to be economic in order to be valid. It is only in recent years that we hear the more honest argument that predators are members of the community, and that no special interest has the right to exterminate them for the sake of a benefit, real or fancied, to itself. Unfortunately this enlightened view is still in the talk stage. In the field the extermination of predators goes merrily on: witness the impending erasure of the timber wolf by fiat of Congress, the Conservation Bureaus, and many state legislatures.

Some species of trees have been "read out of the party" by economics-minded foresters because they grow too slowly, or have too low a sale value to pay as timber crops: white cedar, tamarack, cypress, beech, and hemlock are examples. In Europe, where forestry is ecologically more advanced, the non-commercial tree species are recognized as members of the native forest community, to be preserved as such, within reason. Moreover some (like beech) have been found to have a valuable function in building up soil fertility. The interdependence of the forest and its constituent tree species, ground flora, and fauna is taken for granted.

Lack of economic value is sometimes a character not only of species or groups, but of entire biotic communities: marshes, bogs, dunes, and "deserts" are examples. Our formula in such cases is to relegate their conservation to government as refuges, monuments, or parks. The difficulty is that these communities are usually interspersed with more valuable private lands; the government cannot possibly own or control such scattered parcels. The net effect is that we have relegated some of them to ultimate extinction over large areas. If the private owner were ecologically minded, he would be proud to be the custodian of a reasonable proportion of such areas, which add diversity and beauty to his farm and to his community.

In some instances, the assumed lack of profit in these "waste" areas has proved to be wrong, but only after most of them had been done away with. The present scramble to reflood muskrat marshes is a case in point.

There is a clear tendency in American conservation to relegate to government all necessary jobs that private land-owners fail to perform. Government ownership, operation, subsidy, or regulation is now widely prevalent in forestry, range management, soil and watershed management, park and wilderness conservation, fisheries management, and migratory bird management, with more to come. Most of this growth in governmental conservation is proper and logical, some of it is inevitable. That I imply no disapproval of it is implicit in the fact that I have spent most of my life working for it. Nevertheless the question arises: What is the ultimate magnitude of the enterprise? Will the tax base carry its eventual ramifications? At what point will governmental conservation, like the mastodon, become handicapped by its own dimensions? The answer, if there is any, seems to be in a land ethic, or some other force which assigns more obligation to the private landowner.

Industrial landowners and users, especially lumbermen and stockmen, are inclined to wail long and loudly about the extension of government ownership and regulation to land, but (with notable exceptions) they show little disposition to develop the only visible alternative: the voluntary practice of conservation on their own lands. * * *

THE LAND PYRAMID

An ethic to supplement and guide the economic relation to land presupposes the existence of some mental image of land as a biotic mechanism. We can be ethical only in relation to something we can see, feel, understand, love, or otherwise have faith in.

The image commonly employed in conservation education is "the balance of nature." For reasons too lengthy to detail here, this figure of speech fails to describe accurately what little we know about the land mechanism. A much truer image is the one employed in ecology: the biotic pyramid. * * *

Plants absorb energy from the sun. This energy flows through a circuit called the biota, which may be represented by a pyramid consisting of layers.

The bottom layer is the soil. A plant layer rests on the soil, an insect layer on the plants, a bird and rodent layer on the insects, and so on up through various animal groups to the apex layer, which consists of the larger carnivores. * * *

The lines of dependency for food and other services are called food chains. Thus soil-oak-deer-Indian is a chain that has now been largely converted to soil-corn-cow-farmer. Each species, including ourselves, is a link in many chains. The deer eats a hundred plants other than oak, and the cow a hundred plants other than corn. Both, then, are links in a hundred chains. The pyramid is a tangle of chains so complex as to seem disorderly, yet the stability of the system proves it to be a highly organized structure. Its functioning depends on the co-operation and competition of its diverse parts. * * *

Land, then, is not merely soil; it is a fountain of energy flowing through a circuit of soils, plants, and animals. Food chains are the living channels which conduct energy upward; death and decay return it to the soil. The circuit is not closed; some energy is dissipated in decay, some is added by absorption from the air, some is stored in soils, peats, and long-lived forests; but it is a sustained circuit, like a slowly augmented revolving fund of life. There is always a net loss by downhill wash, but this is normally small and offset by the decay of rocks. It is deposited in the ocean and, in the course of geological time, raised to form new lands and new pyramids. * * *

When a change occurs in one part of the circuit, many other parts must adjust themselves to it. Change does not necessarily obstruct or divert the flow of energy; evolution is a long series of self-induced changes, the net result of which has been to elaborate the flow mechanism and to lengthen the circuit. Evolutionary changes, however, are usually slow and local. Man's invention of tools has enabled him to make changes of unprecedented violence, rapidity, and scope. * * *

This thumbnail sketch of land as an energy circuit conveys three basic ideas:

(1) That land is not merely soil.

(2) That the native plants and animals kept the energy circuit open; others may or may not.

(3) That man-made changes are of a different order than evolutionary changes, and have effects more comprehensive than is intended or foreseen.

These ideas, collectively, raise two basic issues: Can the land adjust itself to the new order? Can the desired alterations be accomplished with less violence? * * *

The combined evidence of history and ecology seems to support one general deduction: the less violent the man-made changes, the greater the probability of successful readjustment in the pyramid. Violence, in turn, varies with human population density; a dense population requires a more violent conversion. In this respect, North America has a better chance for permanence than Europe, if she can contrive to limit her density.

This deduction runs counter to our current philosophy, which assumes that because a small increase in density enriched human life, an indefinite increase will enrich it indefinitely. Ecology knows of no density relationship that holds for indefinitely wide limits. All gains from density are subject to a law of diminishing returns.

Whatever may be the equation for men and land, it is improbable that we as yet know all its terms. Recent discoveries in mineral and vitamin nutrition reveal unsuspected dependencies in the up-circuit: incredibly minute quantities of certain substances determine the value of soils to plants, of plants to animals. What of the down-circuit? What of the vanishing species, the preservation of which we now regard as an esthetic luxury? They helped build the soil; in what unsuspected ways may they be essential to its maintenance? Professor Weaver[1] proposes that we use prairie flowers to reflocculate the wasting soils of the dust bowl; who knows for what purpose cranes and condors, otters and grizzlies may some day be used?

LAND HEALTH AND THE A-B CLEAVAGE

A land ethic, then, reflects the existence of an ecological conscience, and this in turn reflects a conviction of individual responsibility for the health of the land. Health is the capacity of the land for self-renewal. Conservation is our effort to understand and preserve this capacity.

Conservationists are notorious for their dissensions. Superficially these seem to add up to mere confusion, but a more careful scrutiny reveals a single plane of cleavage common to many specialized fields. In each field one group (A) regards the land as soil, and its function as commodity-production; another group (B) regards the land as a biota, and its function as something broader. How much broader is admittedly in a state of doubt and confusion.

In my own field, forestry, group A is quite content to grow trees like cabbages, with cellulose as the basic forest commodity. It feels no inhibition

---

1   *Editor's note:* John Ernest Weaver (1884–1966) was an American botanist.

against violence; its ideology is agronomic. Group B, on the other hand, sees forestry as fundamentally different from agronomy because it employs natural species, and manages a natural environment rather than creating an artificial one. Group B prefers natural reproduction on principle. It worries on biotic as well as economic grounds about the loss of species like chestnut, and the threatened loss of the white pines. It worries about a whole series of secondary forest functions: wildlife, recreation, watersheds, wilderness areas. To my mind, Group B feels the stirrings of an ecological conscience.

In the wildlife field, a parallel cleavage exists. For Group A the basic commodities are sport and meat; the yardsticks of production are ciphers of take in pheasants and trout. Artificial propagation is acceptable as a permanent as well as a temporary recourse—if its unit costs permit. Group B, on the other hand, worries about a whole series of biotic side-issues. What is the cost in predators of producing a game crop? Should we have further recourse to exotics? How can management restore the shrinking species, like prairie grouse, already hopeless as shootable game? How can management restore the threatened rarities, like trumpeter swan and whooping crane? Can management principles be extended to wildflowers? Here again it is clear to me that we have the same A-B cleavage as in forestry.

In the larger field of agriculture I am less competent to speak, but there seem to be somewhat parallel cleavages. Scientific agriculture was actively developing before ecology was born, hence a slower penetration of ecological concepts might be expected. Moreover the farmer, by the very nature of his techniques, must modify the biota more radically than the forester or the wildlife manager. Nevertheless, there are many discontents in agriculture which seem to add up to a new vision of "biotic farming."

Perhaps the most important of these is the new evidence that poundage or tonnage is no measure of the food-value of farm crops; the products of fertile soil may be qualitatively as well as quantitatively superior. We can bolster poundage from depleted soils by pouring on imported fertility, but we are not necessarily bolstering food-value. The possible ultimate ramifications of this idea are so immense that I must leave their exposition to abler pens.

The discontent that labels itself "organic farming," while bearing some of the earmarks of a cult, is nevertheless biotic in its direction, particularly in its insistence on the importance of soil flora and fauna. * * *

THE OUTLOOK

It is inconceivable to me that an ethical relation to land can exist without love, respect, and admiration for land, and a high regard for its value. By value, I of course mean something far broader than mere economic value; I mean value in the philosophical sense.

Perhaps the most serious obstacle impeding the evolution of a land ethic is the fact that our educational and economic system is headed away from, rather than toward, an intense consciousness of land. Your true modern is separated from the land by many middlemen, and by innumerable physical gadgets. He has no vital relation to it; to him it is the space between cities on which crops grow. Turn him loose for a day on the land, and if the spot does not happen to be a golf links or a "scenic" area, he is bored stiff. If crops could be raised by hydroponics instead of farming, it would suit him very well. Synthetic substitutes for wood, leather, wool, and other natural land products suit him better than the originals. In short, land is something he has "outgrown."

Almost equally serious as an obstacle to a land ethic is the attitude of the farmer for whom the land is still an adversary, or a taskmaster that keeps him in slavery. Theoretically, the mechanization of farming ought to cut the farmer's chains, but whether it really does is debatable.

One of the requisites for an ecological comprehension of land is an understanding of ecology, and this is by no means co-extensive with "education"; in fact, much higher education seems deliberately to avoid ecological concepts. An understanding of ecology does not necessarily originate in courses bearing ecological labels; it is quite as likely to be labeled geography, botany, agronomy, history, or economics. This is as it should be, but whatever the label, ecological training is scarce.

The case for a land ethic would appear hopeless but for the minority which is in obvious revolt against these "modern" trends.

The "key-log" which must be moved to release the evolutionary process for an ethic is simply this: quit thinking about decent land-use as solely an economic problem. Examine each question in terms of what is ethically and esthetically right, as well as what is economically expedient. A thing is right when it tends to preserve the integrity, stability, and beauty of the biotic community. It is wrong when it tends otherwise.

It of course goes without saying that economic feasibility limits the tether of what can or cannot be done for land. It always has and it always will. The fallacy the economic determinists have tied around our collective neck, and which we now need to cast off, is the belief that economics determines *all* land-use. This is simply not true. An innumerable host of actions and attitudes, comprising perhaps the bulk of all land relations, is determined by the land-users' tastes and predilections, rather than by his purse. The bulk of all land relations hinges on investments of time, forethought, skill, and faith rather than on investments of cash. As a land-user thinketh, so is he.

I have purposely presented the land ethic as a product of social evolution because nothing so important as an ethic is ever "written." Only the most superficial student of history supposes that Moses "wrote" the Decalogue; it evolved in the minds of a thinking community, and Moses wrote a tentative summary of it for a "seminar." I say tentative because evolution never stops.

The evolution of a land ethic is an intellectual as well as emotional process. Conservation is paved with good intentions which prove to be futile, or even dangerous, because they are devoid of critical understanding either of the land, or of economic land-use. I think it is a truism that as the ethical frontier advances from the individual to the community, its intellectual content increases.

The mechanism of operation is the same for any ethic: social approbation for right actions: social disapproval for wrong actions.

By and large, our present problem is one of attitudes and implements. We are remodeling the Alhambra with a steam-shovel, and we are proud of our yardage. We shall hardly relinquish the shovel, which after all has many good points, but we are in need of gentler and more objective criteria for its successful use. * * *

THINKING LIKE A MOUNTAIN

A deep chesty bawl echoes from rimrock to rimrock, rolls down the mountain, and fades into the far blackness of the night. It is an outburst of wild defiant sorrow, and of contempt for all the adversities of the world.

Every living thing (and perhaps many a dead one as well) pays heed to that call. To the deer it is a reminder of the way of all flesh, to the pine a forecast of midnight scuffles and of blood upon the snow, to the coyote a promise of gleanings to come, to the cowman a threat of red ink at the bank, to the hunter a challenge of fang against bullet. Yet behind these obvious and immediate hopes and fears there lies a deeper meaning, known only to the mountain itself. Only the mountain has lived long enough to listen objectively to the howl of a wolf.

Those unable to decipher the hidden meaning know nevertheless that it is there, for it is felt in all wolf country, and distinguishes that country from all other land. It tingles in the spine of all who hear wolves by night, or who scan their tracks by day. Even without sight or sound of wolf, it is implicit in a hundred small events: the midnight whinny of a pack horse, the rattle of rolling rocks, the bound of a fleeing deer, the way shadows lie under the spruces. Only the ineducable tyro can fail to sense the presence or absence of wolves, or the fact that mountains have a secret opinion about them.

My own conviction on this score dates from the day I saw a wolf die. We were eating lunch on a high rimrock, at the foot of which a turbulent river elbowed its way. We saw what we thought was a doe fording the torrent, her breast awash in white water. When she climbed the bank toward us and shook out her tail, we realized our error: it was a wolf. A half-dozen others, evidently grown pups, sprang from the willows and all joined in a welcoming mêlée of wagging tails and playful maulings. What was literally a pile of wolves writhed and tumbled in the center of an open flat at the foot of our rimrock.

In those days we had never heard of passing up a chance to kill a wolf. In a second we were pumping lead into the pack, but with more excitement than accuracy: how to aim a steep downhill shot is always confusing. When our rifles were empty, the old wolf was down, and a pup was dragging a leg into impassable slide-rocks.

We reached the old wolf in time to watch a fierce green fire dying in her eyes. I realized then, and have known ever since, that there was something new to me in those eyes—something known only to her and to the mountain. I was young then, and full of trigger-itch; I thought that because fewer wolves meant more deer, that no wolves would mean hunters' paradise. But after seeing the green fire die, I sensed that neither the wolf nor the mountain agreed with such a view.

• • •

Since then I have lived to see state after state extirpate its wolves. I have watched the face of many a newly wolfless mountain, and seen the south-facing slopes wrinkle with a maze of new deer trails. I have seen every edible bush and seedling browsed, first to anaemic desuetude, and then to death. I have seen every edible tree defoliated to the height of a saddlehorn. Such a mountain looks as if someone had given God a new pruning shears, and forbidden Him all other exercise. In the end the starved bones of the hoped-for deer herd, dead of its own too-much, bleach with the bones of the dead sage, or molder under the high-lined junipers.

I now suspect that just as a deer herd lives in mortal fear of its wolves, so does a mountain live in mortal fear of its deer. And perhaps with better cause, for while a buck pulled down by wolves can be replaced in two or three years, a range pulled down by too many deer may fail of replacement in as many decades.

So also with cows. The cowman who cleans his range of wolves does not realize that he is taking over the wolf's job of trimming the herd to fit the range. He has not learned to think like a mountain. Hence we have dust-bowls, and rivers washing the future into the sea.

. . .

We all strive for safety, prosperity, comfort, long life, and dullness. The deer strives with his supple legs, the cowman with trap and poison, the statesman with pen, the most of us with machines, votes, and dollars, but it all comes to the same thing: peace in our time. A measure of success in this is all well enough, and perhaps is a requisite to objective thinking, but too much safety seems to yield only danger in the long run. Perhaps this is behind Thoreau's dictum: In wildness is the salvation of the world. Perhaps this is the hidden meaning in the howl of the wolf, long known among mountains, but seldom perceived among men.

STUDY QUESTIONS

1. Explain Leopold's argument that there is a moral relation between human beings and the land.
2. What, according to Leopold, is wrong with the instrumental approach to nature?
3. What duties does Leopold's land ethic give to human beings?

DARREL MOELLENDORF
Justice and Climate Change

Darrel Moellendorf is an American political philosopher, now working at Goethe University in Frankfurt, Germany.

Climate change caused by the behavior of human beings (known as anthropogenic climate change) affects the lives and well-being of hundreds of millions of people now and into the foreseeable future. The change is driven by the use of greenhouse gases, most importantly CO_2. According to recent scientific projections surveyed by the Intergovernmental Panel on

Climate Change (IPCC), if we carry on as we are, the mean equilibrium surface temperature of Earth by the end of this century is likely to be 2.6 to 4.8°C higher than the temperature during recent preindustrial times.

Warming at that rate is unprecedented in human history. Its effects are likely to be devastating, including widespread species loss and destruction of ecosystems, heat waves, extreme precipitation and tropical storms, and large and irreversible sea-level rise from terrestrial ice sheet loss. The rise in sea level will swamp low-lying island nations, such as Kiribati and the Maldives, and will threaten major coastal cities including New York, Mumbai, and Shanghai. Some parts of Africa and Asia would no longer be habitable. Food and water supplies would become much less secure, and there would be increased risks from food- and water-borne as well as vector-borne diseases such as malaria, increased displacement due to migration, increased risks of violent conflicts, slowed economic growth, and increased poverty.

Human life and civilization depend on a stable climate system and the means to protect against extreme weather. Three classes of climate change policies are particularly important in that regard. First, there are mitigation policies that seek to reduce overall climate change by phasing out greenhouse gas emissions and stabilizing their atmospheric concentrations. Mitigation policies do not primarily address the present effects of climate change. Instead, they mostly serve the health and well-being of people in the future. Because a transition to renewable energy seems to require short-term costs, mitigation policies raise the issue of the distribution of these costs between generations. How much should we pay now and in the near future to secure the health and well-being of people in the more distant future? This is a question of intergenerational justice.

Because the costs of mitigation policies must be shared around the world, the distribution of those costs raises other concerns, questions of global justice. How should the costs of mitigation be distributed among nations? Should nations have differential burdens? These are especially important questions because human development is impossible without energy use, and therefore increasing the price of energy, which mitigation could do, would threaten to slow human development.

In addition to mitigation policies to reduce emissions, we need also to consider a second class of policies that seek to reduce the impact of climate change on human communities by adapting to its effects. These policies of adaptation take various forms, including sea-wall and levee construction, crop diversification, infrastructure reinforcement, and the relocation of communities. The question of how the costs of adaptation should be distributed around the world is also a question of global justice.

A third class of policies is known as geo-engineering strategies. These are technological solutions that do not, in themselves, reduce emissions but rather aim to lessen their effects. One possible technique is carbon capture, which attempts to take CO_2 out of the atmosphere. Another is solar radiation management, which tries to reflect back some of the energy from the sun and hence bring down temperatures.

THE 2°C LIMIT

International negotiations on climate change under the auspices of the United Nations Framework Convention on Climate Change (UNFCCC) have adopted the goal of limiting warming to 2°C. In order to have a better than 66 percent chance of limiting warming to 2°C, total human emissions must not exceed one trillion tons of carbon. From the beginning of the industrial revolution to the present, humanity has emitted approximately 579,500,000 tons of carbon. I will say more about justice and the 2°C target presently, but what is important to note for now is that there is a cumulative carbon budget for any particular temperature target, whether it is 1.5°C, 2°C, 3°C, or whatever. This suggests that as a matter of intergenerational justice, we must bring about a global transition to a zero-carbon economy, regardless of the temperature goal we adopt.

Does intergenerational justice recommend the 2°C limit? Or would a higher limit be reasonable? It is difficult to give an unequivocal answer to that question for three reasons. First, the primary means by which warming will be limited will be by transitioning to renewable energy, and the costs of doing so over the course of this century are uncertain. It is encouraging that the cost of energy produced by photovoltaic cells, for example, is dropping quickly. That reduction helps to reduce the cost of the 2°C goal. The costs of mitigation are relevant to the question of intergenerational justice because we think about this issue in part as a matter of intergenerational cost sharing. As the costs sink, it becomes more plausible to think that fair cost sharing requires the current generation to do more. Additionally, if it really is possible to supplement mitigation with a safe, relatively inexpensive, and temporary deployment of solar radiation management, then the case for a low warming limit would be even stronger because the low costs would make it easier to keep the temperature within the 2°C limit. But whether we could have such an option is unknown.

A second reason why it is hard to know whether justice calls for a 2°C limit is that many of the most worrying negative effects of climate change, such as rapid sea-level rise caused by the abrupt collapse of the Greenland and Antarctic ice sheets, or superwarming caused by a massive release of methane from Arctic waters, are uncertain in the technical sense that there is simply insufficient evidence to develop objective probabilities of these catastrophic events. Consequently, it seems we should err on the side of caution. This is a reason to aim for a low temperature increase, perhaps even below 2°C if that were possible.

Finally, what justice requires with respect to limiting warming depends on how effective and expensive climate change adaptation, such as new forms of agriculture or sea defenses, will be. The less mitigation and geo-engineering we undertake, the more important adaptation becomes. As our technological capacity increases, presumably our ability to adapt will also develop, and the costs of adapting will decrease. We would thus worry less about hitting a very low warming limit. But we should be aware that the magnitude of the climate impacts might outstrip our capacity to adapt, even if that capacity grows along with technological sophistication, because among the possible events are catastrophic ones. The three considerations just mentioned on the whole support a low warming target, and 2°C might be about as low as we could feasibly hit.

There is, however, a possible drawback to the 2°C goal. The climate scientist Kevin Anderson and the popular writer Naomi Klein have argued that achieving the 2°C limit on global warming would require economies in industrialized countries to "degrow." Indeed, they both urge such degrowth policies. But "degrowth" is a euphemism for managed recession. We know from the experience of the recent Great Recession that recessions do reduce emissions. In 2009, global emissions of CO_2 fell slightly. But recessions are also very costly, and the costs rarely fall only to industrialized countries. Often recessions are transmitted to developing and least developed countries, as was the case of the Great Recession. There was a massive drop in foreign investment in the developing world, a large loss of income due to a reduction in the transfer of money remitted from people working in the developed world to their relatives in the developing world, and exports from least developed countries fell significantly as demand in wealthier nations dropped. If the only means of achieving the 2°C goal requires degrowth in the industrialized world, the hardships faced by poor countries as a result of a global recession argue against it.

The necessity of degrowth to hit 2°C is, however, very controversial among economists. Some economists, such as Nicolas Stern of the United Kingdom, emphasize rather that the costs of renewable energy are falling and that there are significant health costs to the current generation due to the use of fossil fuels. These economists argue that economic growth and robust climate change mitigation are compatible. This position gives credibility to the 2°C limit. Still, it is important not to hold to that limit as if it were a scientifically precise measure of justice. We should not suppose that 2.1°C warming, for example, would necessarily involve grave injustice to future generations. The climate scientist Mike Hulme has argued that its lack of scientific credentials is a compelling reason to abandon the 2°C goal in favor of a goal based on atmospheric concentrations of CO_2. In contrast, there are two strong reasons not to give up on the goal. First, because the risks of climate change increase as warming increases, a temperature goal of higher than 2°C poses greater risks of catastrophic change. In an effort to reduce such risks, we should maintain a policy of keeping the temperature increase as low as possible without triggering recession. Second, tremendous international attention and diplomatic effort have been focused on the 2°C limit. It is sensible to utilize this enthusiasm to get a strong mitigation regime, especially since it might be impossible to maintain an even lower temperature goal without incurring the costs of long-term global recession.

MITIGATION POLICIES

The costs of mitigating climate change, regardless of the particular temperature limit, however, must be distributed internationally. How should the architecture of an international treaty regime assign costs to nations for the project of transitioning to a zero-carbon global economy? Three principles have been much discussed. The first of these is the Polluter-Pays principle, which holds that countries should be assigned shares of the costs of climate change mitigation in proportion to their historic contribution to the problem. Intuitively this seems very plausible, for it appears to be a principle of natural justice that those who have caused a problem have a special responsibility for clearing it up. But there are complications. First, in applying this principle, the decision when to start counting contributions makes an enormous difference. From 1850 to 2011, about 27 percent of all emissions were produced by the United States and about 11 percent by China. From 1990 to 2011, the United States' share declined to 16 percent and China's increased to 15 percent.

Should the Polluter-Pays principle be applied to all emissions since the beginning of the industrial revolution or only to more recent emissions? There are two main ways to justify the Polluter-Pays principle and neither seems to work for emissions from the distant past. The first justification is that those who pollute are at fault for polluting. Assignment of fault in the law standardly requires that people either know or could reasonably be expected to know the consequences of their actions and they fail to take due care in light of that knowledge. But it would be unreasonable to assert that prior to the second half of the 20th century nations should have known that CO_2 emissions would cause climate change. The science simply was not well enough established.

The second justification for Polluter-Pays incorporates strict liability. Here the idea is that regardless of whether people take due care in light of their knowledge of the consequences of an action, they are responsible for the costs of the action. Assignment of strict responsibility is relatively rare in the law, and it is employed typically when activities are particularly important to human well-being, such as milk production, or particularly dangerous, such as transporting explosives. It might seem unfair to assign costs to a party who took care to avoid an accident, but strict liability is justified on two grounds. One ground is that agents are put on notice of their liability so they can decide whether or not to assume the risk of liability when deciding how to act. The second ground is that the knowledge that they will be held strictly liable encourages agents to take greater than normal care in acting. Both grounds make sense only if the agents are aware that they will be held strictly liable when they decide to act. In other words, it makes no sense retrospectively to claim a strict liability justification for the assignment of costs. Since we cannot now put nations in the late 19th and early 20th century on prior notice that they will be held strictly liable for their emissions, we lack the justification for employing strict liability.

Any employment of the Polluter-Pays principle thus would have to cover only relatively recent emissions, when knowledge of the causal relationship between fossil fuels and global warming was relatively well established. If emissions only since 1990 were to be considered, then the United States and China would bear an almost equal share of the responsibility for the costs of global climate change mitigation. Would it be fair to treat their contributions as morally equivalent? From the period of 1990 to 2011, the Human Development Index (HDI) (a measure of life expectancy, education, and income) for China rose from 0.501 to 0.707. The HDI for the

United States by comparison rose from 0.859 to 0.911. In short, the United States improved little but remained one of the most highly developed countries, whereas China improved significantly, moving out of a fairly underdeveloped condition as measured by the HDI.

Although an international mitigation regime must aim for the rapid transition to a zero-carbon global economy, it is reasonable to expect it to do so without slowing the morally mandatory project of eradicating global poverty. As the example of China suggests, appropriate national development plans can be a fairly effective means of combating poverty. According to the World Bank, the rate of poverty in China from 1981 to 2001 dropped from 53 to 8 percent. But now the problem with applying the Polluter-Pays principle only to relatively recent emissions becomes obvious. Laying responsibility for recent emissions on rapidly developing countries could significantly slow poverty-eradicating development strategies by assigning new costs to development. And compared to a lack of such responsibility for now developed countries back when they were at a similar early stage of development, it appears unfair. The Polluter-Pays principle is less morally appealing than at first it may have seemed.

A second principle for assigning to countries the costs of transitioning toward a zero-carbon economy is the Beneficiary-Pays principle. According to some accounts, citizens of industrialized countries are responsible for assuming the costs of climate change mitigation not because they produced the emissions that caused climate change, but because these people have benefited from those emissions by the high standard of living that they produced. The idea behind Beneficiary-Pays is that people who have benefited from an injustice, even if they did not commit the injustice, bear a responsibility for paying to rectify the injustice. The principle has been used to defend the claim that citizens of a state that in the past engaged in unjust conquest bear war reparations, as well as the claim that those who receive stolen art bear a responsibility to return the artwork.

It is important to underscore that the moral plausibility of Beneficiary-Pays seems to depend in part on the injustice of the action that produces the benefit. Students are not normally thought to bear a responsibility to pay for some of the educational expenses of classmates who have benefited them by making insightful contributions to class discussions. This is because making insightful comments in class discussions is hardly unjust. However, if students inadvertently benefit from a classmate's hacking into the university finance system to reduce everyone's fees, there is a strong case that the students who benefit are morally required to repay the university even though they did not cause the injustice. This brings us to the central problem in the application of Beneficiary-Pays to the costs of climate change mitigation. Although present generations living in industrialized nations may have benefited from previous emissions, the attribution of injustice to these emissions is difficult to sustain. If it is unreasonable to claim either fault-based or strict liability-based responsibility for the past emissions of nations, then it is unclear in what sense previous emissions were unjust. Failing the attribution of injustice to the earlier emissions, the Beneficiary-Pays principle seems unjustified.

The third principle for the distribution of the costs of transitioning to a zero-carbon global economy under a mitigation regime is the Ability-to-Pay principle. According to this principle, when the costs of certain kinds of activities must be distributed among parties, the costs should be assigned on the basis of the parties' ability to assume the costs. This is a familiar way to assign the costs of the provision of certain public goods within nations, such as when highway construction, public safety, and defense are paid for by means of a progressive income tax. The premise is not that the rich are at fault or that they benefit more from the provision of these goods; it is simply that the rich are able to pay a higher percentage of their income to cover the costs. It seems fair that the poor should pay much less or even nothing at all for the provision of these goods.

Ability-to-Pay might also seem applicable in the case of providing for the global public good of climate change mitigation. The idea would be that provision of a stable climate will be enjoyed by all countries, but achieving it requires some form of international cooperation, and fairness in the provision of the common benefit should lay lighter burdens on those nations less able to bear the burden. That idea seems especially plausible when assuming a burden might set back the development prospects of a nation since the eradication of poverty is plausibly a morally mandatory aim. One way to measure a nation's ability to pay that would be consistent with this line of thought would be by the nation's rank on the HDI. For example, it might be decided that only the most highly human developed nations should pay for the transition to a zero-carbon global economy. A virtue of this proposal is that it would protect the development ambitions of less developed nations by allowing their own resources to be assigned to development rather than mitigation. Assigning responsibility in that way aligns the principle of responsibility with the right to sustainable development.

There is an additional reason to think that the distribution of the costs of climate change mitigation among nations should conform to the right of sustainable development. In ratifying the UNFCCC, which expressly recognizes the right to sustainable development, member nations have agreed to respect it, regardless of whether they in fact accept its merits. The architecture of the assignment of responsibility in an international mitigation regime, then, should ensure that developing and least developed nations are able to exercise their rights to sustainable development.

The right to sustainable development establishes a justified claim for increased energy consumption in developing and least developed countries. In light of that claim, two policy options for mitigation are available. If increasing energy consumption in the developing world were to involve increased consumption of fossil fuels over the short term, due to their lower costs in most energy markets, then developed countries would need to reduce their emissions enough to offset the emissions increase since the aim must be an overall reduction in CO_2 emissions. Alternatively, if the increased consumption is to be of renewable energy, then developed countries would be required to subsidize the purchase of that energy as long as fossil fuels remain cheaper, since assuming the burden of mitigation should not slow the process of poverty eradication.

ADAPTATION POLICIES

As mentioned above, although mitigation is vitally important, it is not enough on its own to deal with all aspects of climate change. The mean surface temperature of the planet is already almost 0.8°C higher than during the middle of the nineteenth century. Because of lags in the climate system, the temperature will continue to increase for a very long time, even once net CO_2 emissions reach zero. This makes adaptation policies necessary. Adaptation policies such as the construction of flood defenses, moving residences from vulnerable lands, and developing new lands of agriculture may offer assistance in coping with climate change to people in the present as well as in the future. Unlike mitigation policies, adaptation policies can be directed toward specific groups of people who are especially vulnerable to climate change. Vulnerability to climate change is the product of exposure to the risks of climate change and the lack of capacity to cope with the negative outcomes. The first of these is a matter of geography, the second mainly of poverty. For many of the most vulnerable people, both geography and poverty conspire to render them vulnerable. Although relocation will sometimes be unavoidable, more often the aim of adaptation should be to address vulnerabilities that can be dealt with through infrastructural development and agricultural investment.

Adaptation spending globally should track vulnerability. Since, unlike mitigation, adaptation policies target specific people, the distribution of the burden to fund adaptation could in principle be assigned to states in whose territory the vulnerable live. But this would place much heavier adaptation burdens on poor countries with especially vulnerable populations. The right to sustainable development is also relevant to adaptation policies. The increasing costs of adapting to climate change should not reduce from investment in other development projects. The additional costs of development due to adaptation spending should not be borne by the developing and least developed countries. In other words, developing countries should not be left in a worse position with respect to their development agenda because of the need to adapt to climate change. Developing and least developed states, then, have a claim of justice to assistance in financing adaptation.

GEO-ENGINEERING STRATEGIES

Even with ambitious global reductions in greenhouse gas emissions, limiting warming to 2°C or less is unlikely without the employment of additional strategies. Most of the models surveyed by the IPCC that aim to restrict warming that much assume the use of a form of technology that removes CO_2 from the atmosphere. That technology is at an early stage of development and at present would barely make any contribution to reducing CO_2, so there is a question mark hanging over those efforts. Another form of technology, known as stratospheric aerosol sulphate injection, involves spraying particles of sulphur into the stratosphere to filter out some sunlight. This method is relatively inexpensive and has been proposed as a bridging technology. This technology, or other kinds of technology that would serve the same end by different means, might ease the transition to a zero-carbon economy by providing time to develop and to deploy renewable energy technologies and CO_2 capture-and-removal technologies. Solar radiation management technology, however, is also not fully tested and refined. Until it is, its side effects are difficult to predict.

Sulphate aerosol injections would not in any case address all the problems of climate change. As long as the concentration of CO_2 in the atmosphere continues to increase, ocean acidification will worsen, threatening coral reefs and delicate marine ecosystems. The case for mitigation (or CO_2 removal) would therefore remain even given a feasible solar radiation management program with acceptable side effects. One suggestion made by the climate scientist David Keith is that the amount of aerosol sulphate injected could be reduced as emissions fall. Insofar as emissions have an end point, so too would sulphate aerosol injections. Such technology might provide a means by which a lower warming limit and a slower rate of warming could be achieved without overburdening nations. Technology of this sort is attractive in light of intergenerational justice: A lower warming limit and slower warming rate would be better for future generations. This technology is also attractive on grounds of global justice because if the costs of limiting warming can be kept down, there is less pressure on developing countries to assume costs that might harm their development objectives.

Nevertheless, much more research is needed into the possible serious side effects of these injections, including ozone depletion and regional droughts. Additionally, the projected relative lack of expense of such solar radiation management is in one way worrying. If it were developed, the incentive to use it could be expected to be high. This suggests the strong possibility of international conflict about its unauthorized use. A system of global governance would be needed to put the brakes on its use. It would be important to ensure procedural international legitimacy for any decision to use it. Whether the international state system is capable of developing such a high degree of cooperation regarding the deployment of the technology is an open question.

Questions of justice arise with respect to a variety of climate change policies. And two main categories of justice stand out. The need to mitigate climate change is a requirement of intergenerational justice. The distribution of the costs of mitigation and adaptation are matters of global justice. And although we do not know enough yet to say for sure, geo-engineering could be attractive on grounds of both intergenerational and global justice.

STUDY QUESTIONS
1. Explain the difference between mitigation, adaptation, and geo-engineering.
2. Why does Moellendorf think that Ability-to-Pay is a preferable principle to the Polluter-Pays and the Beneficiary-Pays principles for distributing the costs of mitigation?
3. What risks and benefits should be taken into account when considering policies of geo-engineering to reduce climate change?

▪ Compare and Contrast Question
1. Can Leopold's land ethic be applied to questions of climate change?

WAR

The two selections in this section are both concerned with conduct during warfare. The first was written by John Rawls in 1995, 50 years after the devastating atomic bombing of Hiroshima and Nagaskai in Japan. Rawls describes the bombing as a very great wrong, as was, he says, the fire-bombing of Japanese cities. To support this judgment, he draws on just-war theory, setting out six principles that explain the circumstances under which a democratic country is justified in going to war and the way it should conduct itself during war.

In the present context, the most important of the principles that Rawls lists concerns the idea that the war that the country fights should be a model for the type of peace that will follow. For this reason, among others, a country should exercise restraint in the methods it uses. A statesman—looking to the next generation and not only the next election—should fight the war with these considerations in mind, wishing to guarantee the losing side a decent future. The only exception is in conditions of extreme crisis, such as early in World War II when Britain was fighting alone and had to do everything in its power to ensure that the Nazis did not win. In Rawls's view, the United States was never in this position in relation to Japan. The motivation of the American leaders was to save American lives, which is obviously a very reasonable goal, but not at the cost of the mass destruction of the lives of Japanese civilians, especially as the war would have been won even by other means. Hence the deliberate mass targeting of civilians was unjustified and a great evil.

Nagel is also interested in the question of the morality of conduct in war. The general issue arises because even when a general goal—an end—is legitimate, such as the defeat of a terrorist campaign, there still may be questions about the legitimate means of achieving those ends. Nagel expresses the dilemma in terms of a conflict between utilitarianism, which would justify an action if its positive outcomes outweigh the negative, and absolutism, which says that there are simply some actions that should never be done. Most of us, says Nagel, feel the force of both of these types of reasoning.

The particular focus of the discussion is the killing of civilians and other noncombatants in war. A utilitarian would justify doing so if the total consequences are better than those of any alternative—for example, if killing civilians will lead to the surrender of a hostile power with less loss of life than other strategies. An absolutist, focusing on actions rather than outcomes, might argue that nevertheless civilians should never be deliberately killed. Nagel then considers how such a view might be justified.

Nagel points out that absolutist restrictions are of two types: who can be subjected to hostilities and the form that action against them may take. He uses the analogy of the distinction between fighting clean and fighting dirty to illustrate the point that even when we are in conflict with another we feel we have a moral obligation to treat the other as a person, with at least minimal respect. To fight dirty is to fail to do this by addressing our aggression to something that is not the proper target. Any action undertaken in a conflict, Nagel says, should be aimed at the other party as a subject, and it should be direct and relevant to the conflict. We can test this by imagining whether it would be possible to justify to the victim what is being done to him or her. Nagel thinks that, for example, firing a machine gun at someone about to throw a hand grenade can be justified in this way, but shooting the attacker's wife and children cannot. This reasoning, Nagel argues, also rules out actions such as the bombing of Hiroshima, which treated no one with minimal respect. Nagel then adds that there are restrictions on what can be done even to combatants. For example, weapons specifically designed to maim or disfigure, rather than stop, enemy soldiers attack them as human beings, not soldiers, and hence do not respect them as persons. However, Nagel ends by giving only a qualified acceptance of absolutism, for when the stakes are very high, utilitarian reasoning can seem to outweigh absolutism. But Nagel doubts whether a formula is available to explain what reasoning should predominate in every circumstance.

JOHN RAWLS
50 Years After Hiroshima

John Rawls (1921–2002) was an American philosopher, regarded as the most important political philosopher writing in English in the twentieth century. He is best known for his A Theory of Justice (1971).

The fiftieth year since the bombing of Hiroshima is a time to reflect about what one should think of it. Is it really a great wrong, as many now think, and many also thought then, or is it perhaps justified after all? I believe that both the fire-bombing of Japanese cities beginning in the spring of 1945 and the later atomic bombing of Hiroshima on August 6 were very great wrongs, and rightly seen as such. In order to support this opinion, I set out what I think to be the principles governing the conduct of war—*jus in bello*—of democratic peoples. These peoples have different ends of war than nondemocratic, especially totalitarian, states, such as Germany and Japan, which sought the domination and exploitation of subjected peoples, and in Germany's case, their enslavement if not extermination.

Although I cannot properly justify them here, I begin by setting out six principles and assumptions in support of these judgments. I hope they seem not unreasonable; and certainly they are familiar, as they are closely related to much traditional thought on this subject.

1. The aim of a just war waged by a decent democratic society is a just and lasting peace between peoples, especially with its present enemy.

2. A decent democratic society is fighting against a state that is not democratic. This follows from the fact that democratic peoples do not wage war against each other;[1] and since we are concerned with the rules of war as they apply to such peoples, we assume the society fought against is nondemocratic and that its expansionist aims threatened the security and free institutions of democratic regimes and caused the war.

3. In the conduct of war, a democratic society must carefully distinguish three groups: the state's leaders and officials, its soldiers, and its civilian population. The reason for these distinctions rests on the principle of responsibility: since the state fought against is not democratic, the civilian members of the society cannot be those who organized and brought on the war. This was done by its leaders and officials assisted by other elites who control and staff the state apparatus. They are responsible, they willed the war, and for doing that, they are criminals. But civilians, often kept in ignorance and swayed by state propaganda, are not. And this is so even if some civilians knew better and were enthusiastic for the war. In a nation's conduct of war many such marginal cases may exist, but they are irrelevant. As for soldiers, they, just as civilians, and leaving aside the upper ranks of an officer class, are not responsible for the war, but are conscripted or in other ways forced into it, their patriotism often cruelly and cynically exploited. The grounds on which they may be attacked directly are not that they are responsible for

---

1 I assume that democratic peoples do not go to war against each other. There is considerable evidence of this important idea. See Michael Doyle's two part article, "Kant, Liberal Legacies, and Foreign Affairs," *Philosophy and Public Affairs*, Vol. 12, Summer and Fall 1983. See his summary of the evidence in the first part, pp. 206-232.

the war but that a democratic people cannot defend itself in any other way, and defend itself it must do. About this there is no choice.

4. A decent democratic society must respect the human rights of the members of the other side, both civilians and soldiers, for two reasons. One is because they simply have these rights by the law of peoples. The other reason is to teach enemy soldiers and civilians the content of those rights by the example of how they hold in their own case. In this way their significance is best brought home to them. They are assigned a certain status, the status of the members of some human society who possess rights as human persons. In the case of human rights in war the aspect of status as applied to civilians is given a strict interpretation. This means, as I understand it here, that they can never be attacked directly except in times of extreme crisis, the nature of which I discuss below.

5. Continuing with the thought of teaching the content of human rights, the next principle is that just peoples by their actions and proclamations are to foreshadow during war the kind of peace they aim for and the kind of relations they seek between nations. By doing so, they show in an open and public way the nature of their aims and the kind of people they are. These last duties fall largely on the leaders and officials of the governments of democratic peoples, since they are in the best position to speak for the whole people and to act as the principle applies. Although all the preceding principles also specify duties of statesmanship, this is especially true of 4 and 5. The way a war is fought and the actions ending it endure in the historical memory of peoples and may set the stage for future war. This duty of statesmanship must always be held in view.

6. Finally, we note the place of practical means-end reasoning in judging the appropriateness of an action or policy for achieving the aim of war or for not causing more harm than good. This mode of thought—whether carried on by (classical) utilitarian reasoning, or by cost-benefit analysis, or by weighing national interests, or in other ways—must always be framed within and strictly limited by the preceding principles. The norms of the conduct of war set up certain lines that bound just action. War plans and strategies, and the conduct of battles, must lie within their limits. (The only exception, I repeat, is in times of extreme crisis.)

In connection with the fourth and fifth principles of the conduct of war, I have said that they are binding especially on the leaders of nations. They are in the most effective position to represent their people's aims and obligations, and sometimes they become statesmen. But who is a statesman? There is no office of statesman, as there is of president, or chancellor, or prime minister. The statesman is an ideal, like the ideal of the truthful or virtuous individual. Statesmen are presidents or prime ministers who become statesmen through their exemplary performance and leadership in their office in difficult and trying times and manifest strength, wisdom, and courage. They guide their people through turbulent and dangerous periods for which they are esteemed always, as one of their great statesmen.

The ideal of the statesman is suggested by the saying: the politician looks to the next election, the statesman to the next generation. It is the task of the student of philosophy to look to the permanent conditions and the real interests of a just and good democratic society. It is the task of the statesman, however, to discern these conditions and interests in practice; the statesman sees deeper and further than most others and grasps what needs to be done. The statesman must get it right, or nearly so, and hold fast to it. Washington and Lincoln were statesmen. Bismarck was not. He did not see Germany's real interests far enough into the future and his judgment and motives were often distorted by his class interests and his wanting himself alone to be chancellor of Germany. Statesmen need not be selfless and may have their own interests when they hold office, yet they must be selfless in their judgments and assessments of society's interests and not be swayed, especially in war and crisis, by passions of revenge and retaliation against the enemy.

Above all, they are to hold fast to the aim of gaining a just peace, and avoid the things that make achieving such a peace more difficult. Here the proclamations of a nation should make clear (the statesman must see to this) that the enemy people are to be granted an autonomous regime of their own and a decent and full life once peace is securely reestablished. Whatever they may be told by their leaders, whatever reprisals they may reasonably fear, they are not to be held as slaves or serfs after surrender, or denied in due course their full liberties; and they may well achieve freedoms they did not enjoy before, as the Germans and the Japanese eventually did. The statesman knows, if others do not, that all descriptions of the enemy people (not their rulers) inconsistent with this are impulsive and false.

Turning now to Hiroshima and the fire-bombing of Tokyo, we find that neither falls under the exemption of extreme crisis. One aspect of this is that since (let's suppose) there are no absolute rights—rights that must be respected in all circumstances—there are occasions when civilians can be attacked directly by aerial bombing. Were there times during the war when

Britain could properly have bombed Hamburg and Berlin? Yes, when Britain was alone and desperately facing Germany's superior might; moreover, this period would extend until Russia had clearly beat off the first German assault in the summer and fall of 1941, and would be able to fight Germany until the end. Here the cutoff point might be placed differently, say the summer of 1942, and certainly by Stalingrad. I shan't dwell on this, as the crucial matter is that under no conditions could Germany be allowed to win the war, and this for two basic reasons: first, the nature and history of constitutional democracy and its place in European culture; and second, the peculiar evil of Nazism and the enormous and uncalculable moral and political evil it represented for civilized society.

The peculiar evil of Nazism needs to be understood, since in some circumstances a democratic people might better accept defeat if the terms of peace offered by the adversary were reasonable and moderate, did not subject them to humiliation and looked forward to a workable and decent political relationship. Yet characteristic of Hitler was that he accepted no possibility at all of a political relationship with his enemies. They were always to be cowed by terror and brutality, and ruled by force. From the beginning the campaign against Russia, for example, was a war of destruction against Slavic peoples, with the original inhabitants remaining, if at all, only as serfs. When Goebbels and others protested that the war could not be won that way, Hitler refused to listen.

Yet it is clear that while the extreme crisis exemption held for Britain in the early stages of the war, it never held at any time for the United States in its war with Japan. The principles of the conduct of war were always applicable to it. Indeed, in the case of Hiroshima many involved in higher reaches of the government recognized the questionable character of the bombing and that limits were being crossed. Yet during the discussions among allied leaders in June and July 1945, the weight of the practical means-end reasoning carried the day. Under the continuing pressure of war, such moral doubts as there were failed to gain an express and articulated view. As the war progressed, the heavy fire-bombing of civilians in the capitals of Berlin and Tokyo and elsewhere was increasingly accepted on the allied side. Although after the outbreak of war Roosevelt had urged both sides not to commit the inhuman barbarism of bombing civilians, by 1945 allied leaders came to assume that Roosevelt would have used the bomb on Hiroshima. The bombing grew out of what had happened before.

The practical means-end reasons to justify using the atomic bomb on Hiroshima were the following:

The bomb was dropped to hasten the end of the war. It is clear that Truman and most other allied leaders thought it would do that. Another reason was that it would save lives where the lives counted are the lives of American soldiers. The lives of Japanese, military or civilian, presumably counted for less. Here the calculations of least time and most lives saved were mutually supporting. Moreover, dropping the bomb would give the Emperor and the Japanese leaders a way to save face, an important matter given Japanese samurai culture. Indeed, at the end a few top Japanese leaders wanted to make a last sacrificial stand but were overruled by others supported by the Emperor, who ordered surrender on August 12, having received word from Washington that the Emperor could stay provided it was understood that he had to comply with the orders of the American military commander. The last reason I mention is that the bomb was dropped to impress the Russians with American power and make them more agreeable with our demands. This reason is highly disputed but urged by some critics and scholars as important.

The failure of these reasons to reflect the limits on the conduct of war is evident, so I focus on a different matter: the failure of statesmanship on the part of allied leaders and why it might have occurred. Truman once described the Japanese as beasts and to be treated as such; yet how foolish it sounds now to call the Germans or the Japanese barbarians and beasts! Of the Nazis and Tojo militarists, yes, but they are not the German and the Japanese people. Churchill later granted that he carried the bombing too far, led by passion and the intensity of the conflict. A duty of statesmanship is not to allow such feelings, natural and inevitable as they may be, to alter the course a democratic people should best follow in striving for peace. The statesman understands that relations with the present enemy have special importance: for as I have said, war must be openly and publicly conducted in ways that make a lasting and amicable peace possible with a defeated enemy, and prepares its people for how they may be expected to be treated. Their present fears of being subjected to acts of revenge and retaliation must be put to rest; present enemies must be seen as associates in a shared and just future peace.

These remarks make it clear that, in my judgment, both Hiroshima and the fire-bombing of Japanese cities were great evils that the duties of statesmanship require political leaders to avoid in the absence of the crisis exemption. I also believe this could have been done at little cost in further casualties. An invasion was unnecessary at that date, as the war was effectively over.

However, whether that is true or not makes no difference. Without the crisis exemption, those bombings are great evils. Yet it is clear that an articulate expression of the principles of just war introduced at that time would not have altered the outcome. It was simply too late. A president or prime minister must have carefully considered these questions, preferably long before, or at least when they had the time and leisure to think things out. Reflections on just war cannot be heard in the daily round of the pressure of events near the end of the hostilities; too many are anxious and impatient, and simply worn out.

Similarly, the justification of constitutional democracy and the basis of the rights and duties it must respect should be part of the public political culture and discussed in the many associations of civic society as part of one's education. It is not clearly heard in day-to-day ordinary politics, but must be presupposed as the background, not the daily subject of politics, except in special circumstances. In the same way, there was not sufficient prior grasp of the fundamental importance of the principles of just war for the expression of them to have blocked the appeal of practical means-end reasoning in terms of a calculus of lives, or of the least time to end the war, or of some other balancing of costs and benefits. This practical reasoning justifies too much, too easily, and provides a way for a dominant power to quiet any moral worries that may arise. If the principles of war are put forward at that time, they easily become so many more considerations to be balanced in the scales. ＊ ＊ ＊

＊ ＊ ＊ It is sometimes said that questioning the bombing of Hiroshima is an insult to the American troops who fought the war. This is hard to understand. We should be able to look back and consider our faults after fifty years. We expect the Germans and the Japanese to do that—"*Vergangenheitsverarbeitung*"—as the Germans say. Why shouldn't we? It can't be that we think we waged the war without moral error!

None of this alters Germany's and Japan's responsibility for the war nor their behavior in conducting it. Emphatically to be repudiated are two nihilist doctrines. One is expressed by Sherman's remark, "War is hell," so anything goes to get it over with as soon as one can. The other says that we are all guilty so we stand on a level and no one can blame anyone else. These are both superficial and deny all reasonable distinctions; they are invoked falsely to try to excuse our misconduct or to plead that we cannot be condemned.

The moral emptiness of these nihilisms is manifest in the fact that just and decent civilized societies—their institutions and laws, their civil life and background culture and mores—all depend absolutely on making significant moral and political distinctions in all situations. Certainly war is a kind of hell, but why should that mean that all moral distinctions cease to hold? And granted also that sometimes all or nearly all may be to some degree guilty, that does not mean that all are equally so. There is never a time when we are free from all moral and political principles and restraints. These nihilisms are pretenses to be free of those principles and restraints that always apply to us fully.

STUDY QUESTIONS

1. Explain Rawls's position that in the conduct of war the nature of the resulting peace should always be kept in mind.
2. What does Rawls mean by "extreme crisis" and how does it affect what might be done in war?
3. Why does Rawls appeal to the idea of the "statesman" in his discussion of just war?

THOMAS NAGEL
War and Massacre

Thomas Nagel (b. 1937) is an American philosopher known for his writings in moral and political philosophy as well as epistemology and the philosophy of mind.

When restrictions on the conduct of warfare are defended, it is usually on legal grounds alone: their moral basis is often poorly understood. I wish to argue that certain restrictions are neither arbitrary nor merely conventional, and that their validity does not depend simply on their usefulness. There is, in other words, a moral basis for the rules of war, even though the conventions now officially in force are far from giving it perfect expression.

I

* * * I propose to discuss the most general moral problem raised by the conduct of warfare: the problem of means and ends. In one view, there are limits on what may be done even in the service of an end worth pursuing—and even when adherence to the restriction may be very costly. A person who acknowledges the force of such restrictions can find himself in acute moral dilemmas. He may believe, for example, that by torturing a prisoner he can obtain information necessary to prevent a disaster, or that by obliterating one village with bombs he can halt a campaign of terrorism. If he believes that the gains from a certain measure will clearly outweigh its costs, yet still suspects that he ought not to adopt it, then he is in a dilemma produced by the conflict between two disparate categories of moral reason: categories that may be called *utilitarian* and *absolutist*.

Utilitarianism gives primacy to a concern with what will *happen*. Absolutism gives primacy to a concern with what one is *doing*. The conflict between them arises because the alternatives we face are rarely just choices between *total outcomes*: they are also choices between alternative pathways or measures to be taken. When one of the choices is to do terrible things to another person, the problem is altered fundamentally; it is no longer merely a question of which outcome would be worse.

Few of us are completely immune to either of these types of moral intuition, though in some people, either naturally or for doctrinal reasons, one type will be dominant and the other suppressed or weak. But it is perfectly possible to feel the force of both types of reason very strongly; in that case the moral dilemma in certain situations of crisis will be acute, and it may appear that every possible course of action or inaction is unacceptable for one reason or another. * * *

II

* * * Utilitarianism says that one should try, either individually or through institutions, to maximize good and minimize evil * * * and that if faced with the possibility of preventing a great evil by producing a lesser, one should choose the lesser evil. * * *

Utilitarianism certainly justifies *some* restrictions on the conduct of warfare. There are strong utilitarian reasons for adhering to any limitation which seems natural to most people—particularly if the limitation is widely accepted already. An exceptional measure which seems to be justified by its results in a particular conflict may create a precedent with disastrous long-term effects. * * * But I shall not consider these arguments, for my concern is with reasons of a different kind, which may remain when reasons of utility and interest fail.

In the final analysis, I believe that the dilemma cannot always be resolved. While not every conflict between absolutism and utilitarianism creates an insoluble dilemma, and while it is certainly right to adhere to absolutist restrictions unless the utilitarian considerations favoring violation are overpoweringly weighty and extremely certain—nevertheless, when that special condition is met, it may become impossible to adhere to an absolutist position.

What I shall offer, therefore, is a somewhat qualified defense of absolutism. I believe it underlies a valid and fundamental type of moral judgment—which cannot be reduced to or overridden by other principles. And while there may be other principles just as fundamental, it is particularly important not to lose confidence in our absolutist intuitions, for they are often the only barrier before the abyss of utilitarian apologetics for large-scale murder.

III

One absolutist position that creates no problems of interpretation is pacifism: the view that one may not kill another person under any circumstances, no matter what good would be achieved or evil averted thereby. The type of absolutist position that I am going to discuss is different. Pacifism draws the conflict with utilitarian considerations very starkly. But there are other views according to which violence may be undertaken, even on a large scale, in a clearly just cause, so long as certain absolute restrictions on the character and direction of that violence are observed. The line is drawn somewhat closer to the bone, but it exists.

The philosopher who has done most to advance contemporary philosophical discussion of such a view, and to explain it to those unfamiliar with its extensive treatment in Roman Catholic moral theology, is G.E.M. Anscombe. In 1958 Miss Anscombe published a pamphlet entitled *Mr. Truman's Degree*, on the occasion of the award by Oxford University of an honorary doctorate to Harry Truman. The pamphlet explained why she had opposed the decision to award that degree, recounted the story of her unsuccessful opposition, and offered some reflections on the history of Truman's decision to drop atom bombs on Hiroshima and Nagasaki, and on the difference between murder and allowable killing in warfare. She pointed out that the policy of deliberately killing large numbers of civilians either as a means or as an end in itself did not originate with Truman, and was common practice among all parties during World War II for some time before Hiroshima. The Allied area bombings of German cities by conventional explosives included raids which killed more civilians than did the atomic attacks; the same is true of certain fire-bomb raids on Japan.

The policy of attacking the civilian population in order to induce an enemy to surrender, or to damage his morale, seems to have been widely accepted in the civilized world, and seems to be accepted still, at least if the stakes are high enough. It gives evidence of a moral conviction that the deliberate killing of noncombatants—women, children, old people—is permissible if enough can be gained by it. This follows from the more general position that any means can in principle be justified if it leads to a sufficiently worthy end. Such an attitude is evident not only in the more spectacular current weapons systems but also in the day-to-day conduct of the nonglobal war in Indochina: the indiscriminate destructiveness of antipersonnel weapons, napalm, and aerial bombardment; cruelty to prisoners; massive relocation of civilians; destruction of crops; and so forth. An absolutist position opposes to this the view that certain acts cannot be justified no matter what the consequences. Among those acts is murder—the deliberate killing of the harmless: civilians, prisoners of war, and medical personnel. ✳ ✳ ✳

Many people feel, without being able to say much more about it, that something has gone seriously wrong when certain measures are admitted into consideration in the first place. The fundamental mistake is made there, rather than at the point where the overall benefit of some monstrous measure is judged to outweigh its disadvantages, and it is adopted. An account of absolutism might help us to understand this. If it is not allowable to *do* certain things, such as killing unarmed prisoners or civilians, then no argument about what will happen if one doesn't do them can show that doing them would be all right.

Absolutism does not, of course, require one to ignore the consequences of one's acts. It operates as a limitation on utilitarian reasoning, not as a substitute for it. An absolutist can be expected to try to maximize good and minimize evil, so long as this does not require him to transgress an absolute prohibition like that against murder. But when such a conflict occurs, the prohibition takes complete precedence over any consideration of consequences. Some of the results of this view are clear enough. It requires us to forgo certain potentially useful military measures, such as the slaughter of hostages and prisoners or indiscriminate attempts to reduce the enemy civilian population by starvation, epidemic infectious diseases like anthrax and bubonic plague, or mass incineration. It means that we cannot deliberate on whether such measures are justified by the fact that they will avert still greater evils, for as intentional measures they cannot be justified in terms of any consequences whatever. ✳ ✳ ✳

✳ ✳ ✳ Once the door is opened to calculations of utility and national interest, the usual speculations about the future of freedom, peace, and economic prosperity can be brought to bear to ease the consciences of those responsible for a certain number of charred babies. ✳ ✳ ✳

IV

* * * What absolutism forbids is *doing* certain things to people, rather than bringing about certain *results*. Not everything that happens to others as a result of what one does is something that one has *done* to them. * * *

* * * The absolutist focus on actions rather than outcomes does not merely introduce a new, outstanding item into the catalogue of evils. That is, it does not say that the worst thing in the world is the deliberate murder of an innocent person. For if that were all, then one could presumably justify one such murder on the ground that it would prevent several others, or ten thousand on the ground that they would prevent a hundred thousand more. That is a familiar argument. But if this is allowable, then there is no absolute prohibition against murder after all. Absolutism requires that we *avoid* murder at all costs, not that we *prevent* it at all costs.

* * * Let me remark on a frequent criticism of absolutism that depends on a misunderstanding. It is sometimes suggested that such prohibitions depend on a kind of moral self-interest, a primary obligation to preserve one's own moral purity, to keep one's hands clean no matter what happens to the rest of the world. If this were the position, it might be exposed to the charge of self-indulgence. After all, what gives one man a right to put the purity of his soul or the cleanness of his hands above the lives or welfare of large numbers of other people? * * *

But there are two confusions behind the view that moral self-interest underlies moral absolutism. First, it is a confusion to suggest that the need to preserve one's moral purity might be the *source* of an obligation. For if by committing murder one sacrifices one's moral purity or integrity, that can only be because there is *already* something wrong with murder. The general reason against committing murder cannot therefore be merely that it makes one an immoral person. Secondly, the notion that one might sacrifice one's moral integrity justifiably, in the service of a sufficiently worthy end, is an incoherent notion. For if one were justified in making such a sacrifice (or even morally required to make it), then one would not be sacrificing one's moral integrity by adopting that course: one would be preserving it. * * *

V

It is easier to dispose of false explanations of absolutism than to produce a true one. A positive account of the matter must begin with the observation that war, conflict, and aggression are relations between persons. The view that it can be wrong to consider merely the overall effect of one's actions on the general welfare comes into prominence when those actions involve relations with others. A man's acts usually affect more people than he deals with directly, and those effects must naturally be considered in his decisions. But if there are special principles governing the manner in which he should *treat* people, that will require special attention to the particular persons toward whom the act is directed, rather than just to its total effect.

Absolutist restrictions in warfare appear to be of two types: restrictions on the class of persons at whom aggression or violence may be directed and restrictions on the manner of attack, given that the object falls within that class. These can be combined, however, under the principle that hostile treatment of any person must be justified in terms of something *about that person* which makes the treatment appropriate. Hostility is a personal relation, and it must be suited to its target. One consequence of this condition will be that certain persons may not be subjected to hostile treatment in war at all, since nothing about them justifies such treatment. Others will be proper objects of hostility only in certain circumstances, or when they are engaged in certain pursuits. And the appropriate manner and extent of hostile treatment will depend on what is justified by the particular case.

A coherent view of this type will hold that extremely hostile behavior toward another is compatible with treating him as a person—even perhaps as an end in himself. This is possible only if one has not automatically stopped treating him as a person as soon as one starts to fight with him. If hostile, aggressive, or combative treatment of others always violated the condition that they be treated as human beings, it would be difficult to make further distinctions on that score *within* the class of hostile actions. That point of view, on the level of international relations, leads to the position that if complete pacifism is not accepted, no holds need be barred at all, and we may slaughter and massacre to our hearts' content, if it seems advisable. Such a position is often expressed in discussions of war crimes.

But the fact is that ordinary people do not believe this about conflicts, physical or otherwise, between individuals, and there is no more reason why it should be true of conflicts between nations. There seems to be a perfectly natural conception of the distinction between fighting clean and fighting dirty. To fight dirty is to direct one's hostility or aggression not at its proper object, but at a peripheral target which may be more vulnerable, and through which the proper object can be attacked indirectly. This applies in a fist fight, an election campaign, a duel, or a philosophical argument.

If the concept is general enough to apply to all these matters, it should apply to war—both to the conduct of individual soldiers and to the conduct of nations.

Suppose that you are a candidate for public office, convinced that the election of your opponent would be a disaster, that he is an unscrupulous demagogue who will serve a narrow range of interests and seriously infringe the rights of those who disagree with him; and suppose you are convinced that you cannot defeat him by conventional means. Now imagine that various unconventional means present themselves as possibilities: you possess information about his sex life which would scandalize the electorate if made public; or you learn that his wife is an alcoholic or that in his youth he was associated for a brief period with a proscribed political party, and you believe that this information could be used to blackmail him into withdrawing his candidacy; or you can have a team of your supporters flatten the tires of a crucial subset of his supporters on election day; or you are in a position to stuff the ballot boxes; or, more simply, you can have him assassinated. What is wrong with these methods, given that they will achieve an overwhelmingly desirable result?

There are, of course, many things wrong with them: some are against the law; some infringe the procedures of an electoral process to which you are presumably committed by taking part in it; very importantly, some may backfire, and it is in the interest of all political candidates to adhere to an unspoken agreement not to allow certain personal matters to intrude into a campaign. But that is not all. We have in addition the feeling that these measures, these methods of attack are *irrelevant* to the issue between you and your opponent, that in taking them up you would not be directing yourself to that which makes him an object of your opposition. You would be directing your attack not at the true target of your hostility, but at peripheral targets that happen to be vulnerable.

The same is true of a fight or argument outside the framework of any system of regulations or law. In an altercation with a taxi driver over an excessive fare, it is inappropriate to taunt him about his accent, flatten one of his tires, or smear chewing gum on his windshield; and it remains inappropriate even if he casts aspersions on your race, politics, or religion, or dumps the contents of your suitcase into the street.

The importance of such restrictions may vary with the seriousness of the case; and what is unjustifiable in one case may be justified in a more extreme one. But they all derive from a single principle: that hostility or aggression should be directed at its true object. This means both that it should be directed at the person or persons who provoke it and that it should aim more specifically at what is provocative about them. The second condition will determine what form the hostility may appropriately take.

It is evident that some idea of the relation in which one should stand to other people underlies this principle, but the idea is difficult to state. I believe it is roughly this: whatever one does to another person intentionally must be aimed at him as a subject, with the intention that he receive it as a subject. It should manifest an attitude to *him* rather than just to the situation, and he should be able to recognize it and identify himself as its object. The procedures by which such an attitude is manifested need not be addressed to the person directly. ＊＊＊

＊＊＊ Hostile acts can serve as the expression or implementation of only a limited range of attitudes to the person who is attacked. Those attitudes in turn have as objects certain real or presumed characteristics or activities of the person which are thought to justify them. When this background is absent, hostile or aggressive behavior can no longer be intended for the reception of the victim as a subject. Instead it takes on the character of a purely bureaucratic operation. This occurs when one attacks someone who is not the true object of one's hostility—the true object may be someone else, who can be attacked through the victim; or one may not be manifesting a hostile attitude toward anyone, but merely using the easiest available path to some desired goal. One finds oneself not facing or addressing the victim at all, but operating on him. ＊＊＊

If absolutism is to defend its claim to priority over considerations of utility, it must hold that the maintenance of a direct interpersonal response to the people one deals with is a requirement which no advantages can justify one in abandoning. The requirement is absolute only if it rules out any calculation of what would justify its violation. ＊＊＊ There may be circumstances so extreme that they render an absolutist position untenable. One may find then that one has no choice but to do something terrible. Nevertheless, even in such cases absolutism retains its force in that one cannot claim *justification* for the violation. It does not become *all right*.

As a tentative effort to explain this, let me try to connect absolutist limitations with the possibility of justifying *to the victim* what is being done to him. If one abandons a person in the course of rescuing several others from a fire or a sinking ship, one *could* say to him, "You understand, I have to leave you to save the others." Similarly, if one subjects an unwilling child to a painful surgical procedure, one can say to him, "If you could understand, you would realize that I am doing this to help you." One could *even* say, as one bayonets an enemy soldier, "It's either you or me." But one cannot really say while torturing a prisoner, "You understand, I have to pull out your fingernails because it is absolutely essential that we have the names of your confederates"; nor can one say to the victims of Hiroshima, "You understand, we have to incinerate you to provide the Japanese government with an incentive to surrender."

∗ ∗ ∗ To treat someone else horribly puts you in a special relation to him, which may have to be defended in terms of other features of your relation to him. ∗ ∗ ∗ If the justification for what one did to another person had to be such that it could be offered to him specifically, rather than just to the world at large, that would be a significant source of restraint. ∗ ∗ ∗

VI

Some of the restrictions on methods of warfare which have been adhered to from time to time are to be explained by the mutual interests of the involved parties: restrictions on weaponry, treatment of prisoners, etc. But that is not all there is to it. The conditions of directness and relevance which I have argued apply to relations of conflict and aggression apply to war as well. I have said that there are two types of absolutist restrictions on the conduct of war: those that limit the legitimate targets of hostility and those that limit its character, even when the target is acceptable. I shall say something about each of these. As will become clear, the principle I have sketched does not yield an unambiguous answer in every case.

First let us see how it implies that attacks on some people are allowed, but not attacks on others. It may seem paradoxical to assert that to fire a machine gun at someone who is throwing hand grenades at your emplacement is to treat him as a human being. Yet the relation with him is direct and straight-forward. The attack is aimed specifically against the threat presented by a dangerous adversary, and not against a peripheral target through which he happens to be vulnerable but which has nothing to do with that threat. For example, you might stop him by machine-gunning his wife and children, who are standing nearby, thus distracting him from his aim of blowing you up and enabling you to capture him. But if his wife and children are not threatening your life, that would be to treat them as means with a vengeance.

This, however, is just Hiroshima on a smaller scale. One objection to weapons of mass annihilation—nuclear, thermonuclear, biological, or chemical—is that their indiscriminateness disqualifies them as direct instruments for the expression of hostile relations. In attacking the civilian population, one treats neither the military enemy nor the civilians with that minimal respect which is owed to them as human beings. This is clearly true of the direct attack on people who present no threat at all. But it is also true of the character of the attack on those who *are* threatening you, viz., the government and military forces of the enemy. Your aggression is directed against an area of vulnerability quite distinct from any threat presented by them which you may be justified in meeting. You are taking aim at them through the mundane life and survival of their countrymen, instead of aiming at the destruction of their military capacity. And of course it does not require hydrogen bombs to commit such crimes.

This way of looking at the matter also helps us to understand the importance of the distinction between combatants and noncombatants, and the irrelevance of much of the criticism offered against its intelligibility and moral significance. According to an absolutist position, deliberate killing of the innocent is murder, and in warfare the role of the innocent is filled by noncombatants. * * *

* * * In the absolutist position, the operative notion of innocence is not moral innocence, and it is not opposed to moral guilt. If it were, then we would be justified in killing a wicked but noncombatant hairdresser in an enemy city who supported the evil policies of his government, and unjustified in killing a morally pure conscript who was driving a tank toward us with the profoundest regrets and nothing but love in his heart. But moral innocence has very little to do with it, for in the definition of murder "innocent" means "currently harmless," and it is opposed not to "guilty" but to "doing harm." It should be noted that such an analysis has the consequence that in war we may often be justified in killing people who do not deserve to die, and unjustified in killing people who do deserve to die, if anyone does.

So we must distinguish combatants from noncombatants on the basis of their immediate threat or harmfulness. I do not claim that the line is a sharp one, but it is not so difficult as is often supposed to place individuals on one side of it or the other. Children are not combatants even though they may join the armed forces if they are allowed to grow up. Women are not combatants just because they bear children or offer comfort to the soldiers. More problematic are the supporting personnel, whether in or out of uniform, from drivers of munitions trucks and army cooks to civilian munitions workers and farmers. I believe they can be plausibly classified by applying the condition that the prosecution of conflict must direct itself to the cause of danger, and not to what is peripheral. The threat presented by an army and its members does not consist merely in the fact that they are men, but in the fact that they are armed and are using their arms in the pursuit of certain objectives. Contributions to their arms and logistics are contributions to this threat; contributions to their mere existence as men are not. It is therefore wrong to direct an attack against those who merely serve the combatants' needs as human beings, such as farmers and food suppliers, even though survival as a human being is a necessary condition of efficient functioning as a soldier.

This brings us to the second group of restrictions: those that limit what may be done even to combatants. * * *

Consider first a case which involves both a protected class of non-combatants and a restriction on the measures that may be used against combatants. One provision of the rules of war which is universally recognized, though it seems to be turning into a dead letter in Vietnam, is the special status of medical personnel and the wounded in warfare. It might be more efficient to shoot medical officers on sight and to let the enemy wounded die rather than be patched up to fight another day. But someone with medical insignia is supposed to be left alone and permitted to tend and retrieve the wounded. I believe this is because medical attention is a species of attention to completely general human needs, not specifically the needs of a combat soldier, and our conflict with the soldier is not with his existence as a human being.

By extending the application of this idea, one can justify prohibitions against certain particularly cruel weapons: starvation, poisoning, infectious diseases (supposing they could be inflicted on combatants only), weapons designed to maim or disfigure or torture the opponent rather than merely to stop him. It is not, I think, mere casuistry to claim that such weapons attack the men, not the soldiers. * * *

* * * The same condition of appropriateness to the true object of hostility should limit the scope of attacks on an enemy country: its economy, agriculture, transportation system, and so forth. Even if the parties to a military conflict are considered to be not armies or governments but entire nations (which is usually a grave error), that does not justify one nation in warring against every aspect or element of another nation. That is not justified in a conflict between individuals, and nations are even more complex than individuals, so the same reasons apply. Like a human being, a nation is engaged in countless other pursuits while waging war, and it is not in those respects that it is an enemy. * * *

VII

Having described the elements of the absolutist position, we must now return to the conflict between it and utilitarianism. Even if certain types of dirty tactics become acceptable when the stakes are high enough, the most serious of the prohibited acts, like murder and torture, are not just supposed to require unusually strong justification. They are supposed *never* to be done, because no quantity of resulting benefit is thought capable of *justifying* such treatment of a person.

The fact remains that when an absolutist knows or believes that the utilitarian cost of refusing to adopt a prohibited course will be very high, he may hold to his refusal to adopt it, but he will find it difficult to feel that a moral dilemma has been satisfactorily resolved. The same may be true of someone who rejects an absolutist requirement and adopts instead the course yielding the most acceptable consequences. In either case, it is possible to feel that one has acted for reasons insufficient to justify violation of the opposing principle. In situations of deadly conflict, particularly where a weaker party is threatened with annihilation or enslavement by a stronger one, the argument for resorting to atrocities can be powerful, and the dilemma acute.

There may exist principles, not yet codified, which would enable us to resolve such dilemmas. But then again there may not. We must face the pessimistic alternative that these two forms of moral intuition are not capable of being brought together into a single, coherent moral system, and that the world can present us with situations in which there is no honorable or moral course for a man to take, no course free of guilt and responsibility for evil. ✳ ✳ ✳

Given the limitations on human action, it is naïve to suppose that there is a solution to every moral problem with which the world can face us. We have always known that the world is a bad place. It appears that it may be an evil place as well.

STUDY QUESTIONS

1. Explain the distinction Nagel makes between utilitarian and absolutist approaches to the killing of noncombatants in war.
2. How does Nagel characterize the distinction between fighting clean and fighting dirty, and how can it be applied in the case of war?
3. What restrictions does Nagel place on hostilities to enemy combatants in war?

▪ Compare and Contrast Question

1. Could the use of devastating methods of targeting civilians, such as the atomic bomb, ever be justified on the arguments of Rawls and Nagel?

TERROR AND TORTURE

These two selections concern one of the most pressing questions faced by political authorities today: how to respond to terrorist campaigns. Much philosophical discussion centers on "ticking bomb" cases. Suppose that the authorities know that a bomb has been placed that will cause mass death. They know it is timed to go off within the next 24 hours. They have in custody one of the terrorists who knows the location of the bomb. Are the authorities morally permitted to torture the terrorist to reveal the location of the bomb, so precautions can be taken and lives saved? The utilitarian case for torture in this case seems overwhelming. But is that a sufficient justification? Should we not also have respect for the civil liberties and human rights of all, including terrorists?

Sometimes it is argued that torture never works. In the first selection, lawyer Alan Dershowitz replies that there is evidence that torture sometimes works. He also argues that it is widespread throughout the world, although is often conducted in secret, with the complicity of countries where it is banned, such as the United States. Considering this duplicity problematic, Dershowitz argues that nonlethal torture should be permitted in ticking bomb cases, but only under judicial supervision, when it is part of an official, open process, rather than hypocritically hidden away. This procedure would respect values of accountability.

One counterargument against is that, even if we try to restrict torture only to ticking bomb cases, it is unlikely that we could contain it (Dershowitz regards this argument as "rule utilitarian" reasoning). Another is that, if a country like the United States announces that torture is justified, albeit restricted to a narrow class of cases, other countries around the world would take this as a license to engage in much wider and more barbaric practices of torture. Nevertheless, Dershowitz argues that when confronted with a real-life ticking bomb case, the best way out of the moral dilemma is to allow nonlethal torture, but only when approved by judicial warrant, which would require a very high standard of evidence that there is a ticking bomb, and the real chance that torture could avert the danger.

Michael Walzer turns his attention more closely to the nature of terrorism and the moral justifications that are sometimes attempted for it. The point of terrorism is not only to kill the innocent but also to spread fear among people trying to go about their normal daily life. Walzer begins by pointing out that no one, not even terrorists, advocates terrorism. Nevertheless, ideological excuses are commonly given. The purpose of his discussion is to try to undermine a number of common excuses.

The first excuse discussed is that terrorism is a last resort. It is chosen only when all else has failed. Walzer questions whether it is ever the case that everything has been tried and failed. A second excuse is that nothing else is possible against a strong state. But why then would terrorism work? A third is that terrorism is justified by its results, on consequentialism grounds. But empirically it is probably not true that terrorism has beneficial results. Walzer also points out that this argument presupposes one of the first two, for if other ways of bringing about change were possible, then they would be preferable on consequentialist grounds. Finally, some argue that all political action, even that of the legitimate government, is terrorism, and so the actions of terrorists are no different. This, Walzer says, is too cynical a view of politics. A more defensible view is that oppression is terrorism, and so terrorists are repaying like with like. But, Walzer suggests, the choice of terrorism as the weapon shows it is unlikely that the terrorists really do oppose oppression.

Walzer moves on to discuss how states should respond to terrorism, making clear that he believes that counterterrorism, while requiring repression and retaliation, should not repeat the wrongs of terrorism. The authorities must target the terrorists but must not victimize the people that the terrorists claim to represent. The authorities should also examine the causes of the terrorist action and, where the cause is oppression, consider how to overcome it, although there are good reasons to do this independently of the terrorism. Walzer ends by considering the ways in which oppressive states have used terrorism to reinforce their tyranny.

ALAN DERSHOWITZ
Should the Ticking Bomb Terrorist Be Tortured?

Alan Dershowitz (b. 1938) is an American civil rights lawyer and academic.

HOW THE CURRENT TORTURE DEBATE BEGAN

Before September 11, 2001, no one thought the issue of torture would ever reemerge as a topic of serious debate in this country. Yet shortly after that watershed event, FBI agents began to leak stories suggesting that they might have to resort to torture to get some detainees, who were suspected of complicity in al-Qaeda terrorism, to provide information necessary to prevent a recurrence. An FBI source told the press that because "we are known for humanitarian treatment" of arrestees, we have been unable to get any terrorist suspects to divulge information about possible future plans. ∗ ∗ ∗ A senior FBI aide warned that "it could get to the spot where we could go to pressure, . . . where *we won't have a choice,* and we are probably getting there."[1] But in a democracy there is *always* a choice.

In 1978 a terrorist group kidnapped Italy's former prime minister Aldo Moro and threatened to kill him. A summary of the case described the decision not to resort to torture: "During the hunt for the kidnappers of Aldo Moro, an investigator for the Italian security services proposed to General Carlo Della Chiesa [of the State Police] that a prisoner who seemed to have information on the case be tortured. The General rejected the idea, replying, 'Italy can survive the loss of Aldo Moro, but it cannot survive the introduction of torture.' " The terrorists eventually murdered Moro.

∗ ∗ ∗ The Geneva Convention Against Torture prohibits all forms of torture and provides for no exceptions. It defines torture so broadly as to include many techniques that are routinely used around the world, including in Western democracies:

> For the purposes of this Convention, the term "torture" means any act by which severe pain or suffering, whether physical or mental, is intentionally inflicted on a person for such purposes as obtaining from him or a third person information or a confession, punishing him for an act he or a third person has committed or is suspected of having committed, or intimidating or coercing him or a third person, or for any reason based on discrimination of any kind, when such pain or suffering is inflicted by or at the instigation of or with the consent or acquiescence of a public official or other person acting in an official capacity.[2]

Many nations that routinely practice the most brutal forms of torture are signatories to this convention, but they hypocritically ignore it. ∗ ∗ ∗

∗ ∗ ∗ There are legal steps we could take, if we chose to resort to torture, that would make it possible for us to use this technique for eliciting information in dire circumstances. Neither the presence nor the absence of legal constraints answers the fundamental moral question: should we? This is a choice that almost no one wants to have to make. Torture has

---

1 Walter Pincus, "Silence of 4 Terror Probe Suspects Poses a Dilemma for FBI," *Washington Post,* 10/21/2001 (emphasis added).

2 "Convention Against Torture and Other Cruel, Inhuman or Degrading Treatment or Punishment," adopted by the U.N. General Assembly, 12/10/1984, and in effect since 6/26/1987, after it was ratified by twenty nations.

been off the agenda of civilized discourse for so many centuries that it is a subject reserved largely for historians rather than contemporary moralists (though it remains a staple of abstract philosophers debating the virtues and vices of absolutism). I have been criticized for even discussing the issue, on the ground that academic discussion confers legitimacy on a practice that deserves none. I have also been criticized for raising a red herring, since it is "well known" that torture does not work—it produces many false confessions and useless misinformation, because a person will say anything to stop being tortured.

* * * The tragic reality is that torture sometimes works, much though many people wish it did not. There are numerous instances in which torture has produced self-proving, truthful information that was necessary to prevent harm to civilians. The *Washington Post* has recounted a case from 1995 in which Philippine authorities tortured a terrorist into disclosing information that may have foiled plots to assassinate the pope and to crash eleven commercial airliners carrying approximately four thousand passengers into the Pacific Ocean, as well as a plan to fly a private Cessna filled with explosives into CIA headquarters. For sixty-seven days, intelligence agents beat the suspect "with a chair and a long piece of wood [breaking most of his ribs], forced water into his mouth, and crushed lighted cigarettes into his private parts"—a procedure that the Philippine intelligence service calls "tactical interrogation." After successfully employing this procedure they turned him over to American authorities, along with the lifesaving information they had beaten out of him.[3]

It is impossible to avoid the difficult moral dilemma of choosing among evils by denying the empirical reality that torture *sometimes* works, even if it does not always work. No technique of crime prevention always works. * * *

It is precisely because torture sometimes does work and can sometimes prevent major disasters that it still exists in many parts of the world and has been totally eliminated from none. It also explains why the U.S. government sometimes "renders" terrorist suspects to nations like Egypt and Jordan, "whose intelligence services have close ties to the CIA and where they can be subjected to interrogation tactics—including torture and threats to families—that are illegal in the United States," as the *Washington Post*

---

3 Matthew Brzezinski, "Bust and Boom: Six Years Before the September 11 Attacks, Philippine Police Took Down an al Qaeda Cell That Had Been Plotting, Among Other Things, to Fly Explosives-Laden Planes into the Pentagon—and Possibly Some Skyscrapers," *Washington Post*, 12/30/2001.

has reported. ✳ ✳ ✳ Our government has a "don't ask, don't tell" policy when it comes to obtaining information from other governments that practice torture. All such American complicity in foreign torture violates the plain language of the Geneva Convention Against Torture, which explicitly prohibits torture from being inflicted not only by signatory nations but also "at the instigation of or with the consent or acquiescence of" any person "acting in an official capacity." ✳ ✳ ✳

HOW I BEGAN THINKING ABOUT TORTURE

In the late 1980s I traveled to Israel to conduct some research and teach a class at Hebrew University on civil liberties during times of crisis. In the course of my research I learned that the Israeli security services were employing what they euphemistically called "moderate physical pressure" on suspected terrorists to obtain information deemed necessary to prevent future terrorist attacks. ✳ ✳ ✳ In most cases the suspect would be placed in a dark room with a smelly sack over his head. Loud, unpleasant music or other noise would blare from speakers. The suspect would be seated in an extremely uncomfortable position and then shaken vigorously until he disclosed the information. ✳ ✳ ✳

In my classes and public lectures in Israel, I strongly condemned these methods as a violation of core civil liberties and human rights. The response that people gave, across the political spectrum from civil libertarians to law-and-order advocates, was essentially the same: but what about the "ticking bomb" case?

The ticking bomb case refers to a scenario that has been discussed by many philosophers, including Michael Walzer, Jean-Paul Sartre, and Jeremy Bentham. Walzer described such a hypothetical case in an article titled "Political Action: The Problem of Dirty Hands." In this case, a decent leader of a nation plagued with terrorism is asked "to authorize the torture of a captured rebel leader who knows or probably knows the location of a number of bombs hidden in apartment buildings across the city, set to go off within the next twenty-four hours. He orders the man tortured, convinced that he must do so for the sake of the people who might otherwise die in the explosions— even though he believes that torture is wrong, indeed abominable, not just sometimes, but always."[4]

---

4   Michael Walzer, "Political Action: The Problem of Dirty Hands," *Philosophy and Public Affairs*, 1973.

In Israel, the use of torture to prevent terrorism was not hypothetical; it was very real and recurring. I soon discovered that virtually no one was willing to take the "purist" position against torture in the ticking bomb case: namely, that the ticking bomb must be permitted to explode and kill dozens of civilians, even if this disaster could be prevented by subjecting the captured terrorist to nonlethal torture and forcing him to disclose its location. I realized that the extraordinarily rare situation of the hypothetical ticking bomb terrorist was serving as a moral, intellectual, and legal justification for a pervasive *system* of coercive interrogation, which, though not the paradigm of torture, certainly bordered on it. It was then that I decided to challenge this system by directly confronting the ticking bomb case. I presented the following challenge to my Israeli audience: If the reason you permit nonlethal torture is based on the ticking bomb case, why not limit it exclusively to that compelling but rare situation? Moreover, if you believe that nonlethal torture is justifiable in the ticking bomb case, why not require advance judicial approval—a "torture warrant"? That was the origin of a controversial proposal that has received much attention, largely critical, from the media. Its goal was, and remains, to reduce the use of torture to the smallest amount and degree possible, while creating public accountability for its rare use. I saw it not as a compromise with civil liberties but rather as an effort to maximize civil liberties in the face of a realistic likelihood that torture would, in fact, take place below the radar screen of accountability.

THE CASE FOR TORTURING THE TICKING BOMB TERRORIST

The arguments in favor of using torture as a last resort to prevent a ticking bomb from exploding and killing many people are both simple and simpleminded. Bentham constructed a compelling hypothetical case to support his utilitarian argument against an absolute prohibition on torture:

> Suppose an occasion were to arise, in which a suspicion is entertained, as strong as that which would be received as a sufficient ground for arrest and commitment as for felony—a suspicion that at this very time a considerable number of individuals are actually suffering, by illegal violence inflictions equal in intensity to those which if inflicted by the hand of justice, would universally be spoken of under the name of torture. For the purpose of rescuing from torture these hundred innocents, should any scruple be made of applying equal or superior torture, to extract the requisite information from the mouth of one criminal, who having it in his power to make known the place where at this time the enormity was practising or about to be practised,

should refuse to do so? To say nothing of wisdom, could any pretence be made so much as to the praise of blind and vulgar humanity, by the man who to save one criminal, should determine to abandon 100 innocent persons to the same fate?[5]

If the torture of one guilty person would be justified to prevent the torture of a hundred innocent persons, it would seem to follow—certainly to Bentham—that it would also be justified to prevent the murder of thousands of innocent civilians in the ticking bomb case. Consider two hypothetical situations that are not, unfortunately, beyond the realm of possibility. In fact, they are both extrapolations on actual situations we have faced.

Several weeks before September 11, 2001, the Immigration and Naturalization Service detained Zacarias Moussaoui after flight instructors reported suspicious statements he had made while taking flying lessons and paying for them with large amounts of cash.[6] The government decided not to seek a warrant to search his computer. Now imagine that they had, and that they discovered he was part of a plan to destroy large occupied buildings, but without any further details. They interrogated him, gave him immunity from prosecution, and offered him large cash rewards and a new identity. He refused to talk. They then threatened him, tried to trick him, and employed every lawful technique available. He still refused. They even injected him with sodium pentothal and other truth serums, but to no avail. The attack now appeared to be imminent, but the FBI still had no idea what the target was or what means would be used to attack it. We could not simply evacuate all buildings indefinitely. An FBI agent proposes the use of nonlethal torture—say, a sterilized needle inserted under the fingernails to produce unbearable pain without any threat to health or life, or the method used in the film *Marathon Man*, a dental drill through an unanesthetized tooth.

The simple cost-benefit analysis for employing such nonlethal torture seems overwhelming: it is surely better to inflict nonlethal pain on one guilty terrorist who is illegally withholding information needed to prevent an act of terrorism than to permit a large number of innocent victims to die. Pain is a lesser and more remediable harm than death; and the lives of a thousand innocent people should be valued more than the bodily integrity of one guilty person. If the variation on the Moussaoui case is not sufficiently compelling to make

---

5   Quoted in W. L. Twining and P. E. Twining, "Bentham on Torture," *Northern Ireland Legal Quarterly*, Autumn 1973, p. 347. Bentham's hypothetical question does not distinguish between torture inflicted by private persons and by governments.

6   David Johnston and Philip Shenon, "F.B.I. Curbed Scrutiny of Man Now a Suspect in the Attacks," *New York Times*, 10/6/2001.

this point, we can always raise the stakes. Several weeks after September 11, our government received reports that a ten-kiloton nuclear weapon may have been stolen from Russia and was on its way to New York City, where it would be detonated and kill hundreds of thousands of people. The reliability of the source, code named Dragonfire, was uncertain, but assume for purposes of this hypothetical extension of the actual case that the source was a captured terrorist—like the one tortured by the Philippine authorities—who knew precisely how and where the weapon was being brought into New York and was to be detonated. Again, everything short of torture is tried, but to no avail. It is not absolutely certain torture will work, but it is our last, best hope for preventing a cataclysmic nuclear devastation in a city too large to evacuate in time. Should nonlethal torture be tried? Bentham would certainly have said yes.

The strongest argument against any resort to torture, even in the ticking bomb case, also derives from Bentham's utilitarian calculus. Experience has shown that if torture, which has been deemed illegitimate by the civilized world for more than a century, were now to be legitimated—even for limited use in one extraordinary type of situation—such legitimation would constitute an important symbolic setback in the worldwide campaign against human rights abuses. Inevitably, the legitimation of torture by the world's leading democracy would provide a welcome justification for its more widespread use in other parts of the world. Two Bentham scholars, W. L. Twining and P. E. Twining, have argued that torture is unacceptable even if it is restricted to an extremely limited category of cases:

> There is at least one good practical reason for drawing a distinction between justifying an isolated act of torture in an extreme emergency of the kind postulated above and justifying the *institutionalisation* of torture as a regular practice. The circumstances are so extreme in which most of us would be prepared to justify resort to torture, if at all, the conditions we would impose would be so stringent, the practical problems of devising and enforcing adequate safeguards so difficult and the risks of abuse so great that it would be unwise and dangerous to entrust any government, however enlightened, with such a power. Even an out-and-out utilitarian can support an absolute prohibition against institutionalised torture on the ground that no government in the world can be trusted not to abuse the power and to satisfy in practice the conditions he would impose.[7]

Bentham's own justification was based on *case* or *act* utilitarianism—a demonstration that in a *particular case*, the benefits that would flow from the

---

7 Twining and Twining, "Bentham on Torture," pp. 348–49. The argument for the limited use of torture in the ticking bomb case falls into a category of argument known as "argument from the extreme case," which is a useful heuristic to counter arguments for absolute principles.

limited use of torture would outweigh its costs. The argument against any use of torture would derive from *rule* utilitarianism—which considers the implications of establishing a precedent that would inevitably be extended beyond its limited case utilitarian justification to other possible evils of lesser magnitude. Even terrorism itself could be justified by a case utilitarian approach. Surely one could come up with a singular situation in which the targeting of a small number of civilians could be thought necessary to save thousands of other civilians—blowing up a German kindergarten by the relatives of inmates in a Nazi death camp, for example, and threatening to repeat the targeting of German children unless the death camps were shut down.

The reason this kind of single-case utilitarian justification is simpleminded is that it has no inherent limiting principle. If nonlethal torture of one person is justified to prevent the killing of many important people, then what if it were necessary to use lethal torture—or at least torture that posed a substantial risk of death? What if it were necessary to torture the suspect's mother or children to get him to divulge the information? What if it took threatening to kill his family, his friends, his entire village? Under a simple-minded quantitative case utilitarianism, anything goes as long as the number of people tortured or killed does not exceed the number that would be saved. This is morality by numbers, unless there are other constraints on what we can properly do. These other constraints can come from rule utilitarianisms or other principles of morality, such as the prohibition against deliberately punishing the innocent. Unless we are prepared to impose some limits on the use of torture or other barbaric tactics that might be of some use in preventing terrorism, we risk hurtling down a slippery slope into the abyss of amorality and ultimately tyranny. Dostoevsky captured the complexity of this dilemma in *The Brothers Karamazov* when he had Ivan pose the following question to Alyosha: "Imagine that you are creating a fabric of human destiny with the object of making men happy in the end, giving them peace at least, but that it was essential and inevitable to torture to death only one tiny creature—that baby beating its breast with its fist, for instance—and to found that edifice on its unavenged tears, would you consent to be the architect on those conditions? Tell me the truth."

A willingness to kill an innocent child suggests a willingness to do anything to achieve a necessary result. Hence the slippery slope.

It does not necessarily follow from this understandable fear of the slippery slope that we can never consider the use of nonlethal infliction of pain, if its use were to be limited by acceptable principles of morality. After all, imprisoning a witness who refuses to testify after being given immunity is designed to be punitive—that is painful. Such imprisonment can, on occasion, produce more pain and greater risk of death than nonlethal torture. Yet we continue to threaten and use the pain of imprisonment to loosen the tongues of reluctant witnesses.

It is commonplace for police and prosecutors to threaten recalcitrant suspects with prison rape. As one prosecutor put it: "You're going to be the boyfriend of a very bad man." The slippery slope is an argument of caution, not a debate stopper, since virtually every compromise with an absolutist approach to rights carries the risk of slipping further. An appropriate response to the slippery slope is to build in a principled break. For example, if nonlethal torture were legally limited to convicted terrorists who had knowledge of future massive terrorist acts, were given immunity, and still refused to provide the information, there might still be objections to the use of torture, but they would have to go beyond the slippery slope argument.

In debating the issue of torture, the first question I am often asked is, "Do you want to take us back to the Middle Ages?" The association between any form of torture and gruesome death is powerful in the minds of most people knowledgeable of the history of its abuses. This understandable association makes it difficult for many people to think about nonlethal torture as a technique for *saving* lives.

＊＊＊ Raising the issue of torture makes Americans think about a brutalizing and unaesthetic phenomenon that has been out of our consciousness for many years.

＊＊＊ It is clear that if the preventable act of terrorism was of the magnitude of the attacks of September 11, there would be a great outcry in any democracy that had deliberately refused to take available preventive action, even if it required the use of torture. ＊＊＊

The real issue, therefore, is not whether some torture would or would not be used in the ticking bomb case—it would. The question is whether it would be done openly, pursuant to a previously established legal procedure, or whether it would be done secretly, in violation of existing law.

Several important values are pitted against each other in this conflict. The first is the safety and security of a nation's citizens. Under the ticking bomb scenario this value may require the use of torture, if that is the only way to prevent the bomb from exploding and killing large numbers of civilians. The second value is the preservation of civil liberties and human rights. This value requires that we not accept torture as a legitimate part of our legal system. In my debates with two prominent civil libertarians, Floyd Abrams and Harvey Silverglate, both have acknowledged that they would want nonlethal torture to be used if it could prevent thousands of deaths, but they did not want torture to be officially recognized by our legal system. As Abrams put it: "In a democracy sometimes it is necessary to do things off the books and below the radar screen." Former presidential candidate Alan Keyes took the position that although torture might be *necessary* in a given situation it could never be *right*. He suggested that a president *should* authorize the torturing of a ticking bomb terrorist, but that this act should not be legitimated by the courts or incorporated into our legal system. He argued that wrongful and indeed unlawful acts might sometimes be necessary to preserve the nation, but that no aura of legitimacy should be placed on these actions by judicial imprimatur.

This understandable approach is in conflict with the third important value: namely, open accountability and visibility in a democracy. "Off-the-book actions below the radar screen" are antithetical to the theory and practice of democracy. Citizens cannot approve or disapprove of governmental actions of which they are unaware. We have learned the lesson of history that off-the-book actions can produce terrible consequences. Richard Nixon's creation of a group of "plumbers" led to Watergate, and Ronald Reagan's authorization of an off-the-books foreign policy in Central America led to the Iran-Contra scandal. And these are only the ones we know about! * * *

In a democracy governed by the rule of law, we should never want our soldiers or our president to take any action that we deem wrong or illegal. A good test of whether an action should or should not be done is whether we are prepared to have it disclosed—perhaps not immediately, but certainly after some time has passed. No legal system operating under the rule of law should ever tolerate an "off-the-books" approach to necessity. Even the defense of necessity must be justified lawfully. The road to tyranny has always been paved with claims of necessity made by those responsible for the security of a nation. Our system of checks and balances requires that all presidential actions, like all legislative or military actions, be consistent with governing law. If it is necessary to torture in the ticking bomb case, then our governing laws must accommodate this practice. If we refuse to change our law to accommodate any particular action, then our government should not take that action.

Only in a democracy committed to civil liberties would a triangular conflict of this kind exist. Totalitarian and authoritarian regimes experience no such conflict, because they subscribe to neither the civil libertarian nor the democratic values that come in conflict with the value of security. The hard question is: which value is to be preferred when an inevitable clash occurs? One or more of these values must inevitably be compromised in making the tragic choice presented by the ticking bomb case. If we do not torture, we compromise the security and safety of our citizens. If we tolerate torture, but keep it off the books and below the radar screen, we compromise principles of democratic accountability. If we create a legal structure for limiting and controlling torture, we compromise our principled opposition to torture in all circumstances and create a potentially dangerous and expandable situation.

In 1678, the French writer François de La Rochefoucauld said that "hypocrisy is the homage that vice renders to virtue." In this case we have two vices: terrorism and torture. We also have two virtues: civil liberties and democratic accountability. Most civil libertarians I know prefer hypocrisy, precisely because it appears to avoid the conflict between security and civil liberties, but by choosing the way of the hypocrite these civil libertarians compromise the value of democratic accountability. Such is the nature of tragic choices in a complex world. As Bentham put it more than two centuries ago: "Government throughout is but a choice of evils." In a democracy, such choices must be made, whenever possible, with openness and democratic accountability, and subject to the rule of law.[8]

* * * It seems logical that a formal, visible, accountable, and centralized system is somewhat easier to control than an ad hoc, off-the-books, and under-the-radar-screen nonsystem. I believe, though I certainly cannot prove, that a formal requirement of a judicial warrant as a prerequisite to nonlethal torture would decrease the amount of physical violence directed against suspects. At the most obvious level, a double check is always more protective than a single check. In every instance in which a warrant is requested, a field officer has already decided that torture is justified and, in the absence of a warrant requirement, would simply proceed with the torture. Requiring that decision to be approved by a judicial officer will result in fewer instances of torture even if the judge rarely turns down a request. Moreover, I believe that most judges would require compelling evidence before they would authorize so extraordinary a departure from our constitutional norms, and law enforcement officials would be reluctant to seek a warrant unless they had compelling evidence that the suspect had

---

8   Quoted in Twining and Twining, "Bentham on Torture," p. 345.

information needed to prevent an imminent terrorist attack. A record would be kept of every warrant granted, and although it is certainly possible that some individual agents might torture without a warrant, they would have no excuse, since a warrant procedure would be available. They could not claim "necessity," because the decision as to whether the torture is indeed necessary has been taken out of their hands and placed in the hands of a judge. In addition, even if torture were deemed totally illegal without any exception, it would still occur, though the public would be less aware of its existence.

I also believe that the rights of the suspect would be better protected with a warrant requirement. He would be granted immunity, told that he was now compelled to testify, threatened with imprisonment if he refused to do so, and given the option of providing the requested information. Only if he refused to do what he was legally compelled to do—provide necessary information, which could not incriminate him because of the immunity—would he be threatened with torture. Knowing that such a threat was authorized by the law, he might well provide the information. If he still refused to, he would be subjected to judicially monitored physical measures designed to cause excruciating pain without leaving any lasting damage. * * *

I * * * believe that in a democracy it is always preferable to decide controversial issues in advance, rather than in the heat of battle. I would apply this rule to other tragic choices as well, including the possible use of a nuclear first strike, or retaliatory strikes—so long as the discussion was sufficiently general to avoid giving our potential enemies a strategic advantage by their knowledge of our policy.

Even if government officials decline to discuss such issues, academics have a duty to raise them and submit them to the marketplace of ideas. There may be danger in open discussion, but there is far greater danger in actions based on secret discussion, or no discussion at all.

Whatever option our nation eventually adopts—no torture even to prevent massive terrorism, no torture except with a warrant authorizing nonlethal torture, or no "officially" approved torture but its selective use beneath the radar screen—the choice is ours to make in a democracy. We do have a choice, and we should make it—before local FBI agents make it for us on the basis of a false assumption that we do not really "have a choice."

STUDY QUESTIONS

1. What values does Dershowitz think come into conflict in the "ticking bomb" case?

2. How do the act utilitarian and the rule utilitarian approaches to the ticking bomb differ?

3. Why does Dershowitz think that the most defensible policy is to allow non-lethal torture in clear ticking bomb cases, but only when given judicial authorization?

MICHAEL WALZER
Terrorism: A Critique of Excuses

Michael Walzer (b. 1935) is an American political philosopher, known especially for his work on just war and on distributive justice and social criticism.

No one these days advocates terrorism, not even those who regularly practice it. The practice is indefensible now that it has been recognized, like rape and murder, as an attack upon the innocent. In a sense, indeed, terrorism is worse than rape and murder commonly are, for in the latter cases the victim has been chosen for a purpose; he or she is the direct object of attack, and the attack has some reason, however twisted or ugly it may be. The victims of a terrorist attack are third parties, innocent bystanders; there is no special reason for attacking them; anyone else within a large class of (unrelated) people will do as well. The attack is directed indiscriminately against the entire class. Terrorists are like killers on a rampage, except that their rampage is not just expressive of rage or madness; the rage is purposeful and programmatic. It aims at a general vulnerability: Kill these people in order to terrify those. A relatively small number of dead victims makes for a very large number of living and frightened hostages.

This, then, is the peculiar evil of terrorism—not only the killing of innocent people but also the intrusion of fear into everyday life, the violation of private purposes, the insecurity of public spaces, the endless coerciveness of precaution. A crime wave might, I suppose, produce similar effects, but no one plans a crime wave; it is the work of a thousand individual decision-makers, each one independent of the others, brought together only by the invisible hand. Terrorism is the work of visible hands; it is an organizational project, a strategic choice, a conspiracy to murder and intimidate . . . you and me. No wonder the conspirators have difficulty defending, in public, the strategy they have chosen.

The moral difficulty is the same, obviously, when the conspiracy is directed not against you and me but against *them*—Protestants, say, not

Catholics, Israelis, not Italians or Germans; blacks, not whites. These "limits" rarely hold for long; the logic of terrorism steadily expands the range of vulnerability. The more hostages they hold, the stronger the terrorists are. No one is safe once whole populations have been put at risk. Even if the risk were contained, however, the evil would be no different. So far as individual Protestants or Israelis or blacks are concerned, terrorism is random, degrading, and frightening. That is its hallmark, and that, again, is why it cannot be defended.

But when moral justification is ruled out, the way is opened for ideological excuse and apology. We live today in a political culture of excuses. This is far better than a political culture in which terrorism is openly defended and justified, for the excuse at least acknowledges the evil. But the improvement is precarious, hard won, and difficult to sustain. It is not the case, even in this better world, that terrorist organizations are without supporters. The support is indirect but by no means ineffective. It takes the form of apologetic descriptions and explanations, a litany of excuses that steadily undercuts our knowledge of the evil. Today that knowledge is insufficient unless it is supplemented and reinforced by a systematic critique of excuses. That is my purpose in this chapter. I take the principle for granted: that every act of terrorism is a wrongful act. The wrongfulness of the excuses, however, cannot be taken for granted; it has to be argued. The excuses themselves are familiar enough, the stuff of contemporary political debate. I shall state them in stereotypical form. There is no need to attribute them to this or that writer, publicist, or commentator; my readers can make their own attributions.

THE EXCUSES FOR TERRORISM

The most common excuse for terrorism is that it is a last resort, chosen only when all else fails. The image is of people who have literally run out of options. One by one, they have tried every legitimate form of political and military action, exhausted every possibility, failed everywhere, until no alternative remains but the evil of terrorism. They must be terrorists or do nothing at all. The easy response is to insist that, given this description of their case, they should do nothing at all; they have indeed exhausted their possibilities. But this response simply reaffirms the principle, ignores the excuse; this response does not attend to the terrorists' desperation. Whatever the cause to which they are committed, we have to recognize that, given the commitment, the one thing they cannot do is "nothing at all."

But the case is badly described. It is not so easy to reach the "last resort." To get there, one must indeed try everything (which is a lot of things) and not just once, as if a political party might organize a single demonstration, fail to win immediate victory, and claim that it was now justified in moving on to murder. Politics is an art of repetition. Activists and citizens learn from experience, that is, by doing the same thing over and over again. It is by no means clear when they run out of options, but even under conditions of oppression and war, citizens have a good run short of that. The same argument applies to state officials who claim that they have tried "everything" and are now compelled to kill hostages or bomb peasant villages. Imagine such people called before a judicial tribunal and required to answer the question, What exactly did you try? Does anyone believe that they could come up with a plausible list? "Last resort" has only a notional finality; the resort to terror is ideologically last, not last in an actual series of actions, just last for the sake of the excuse. In fact, most state officials and movement militants who recommend a policy of terrorism recommend it as a first resort; they are for it from the beginning, although they may not get their way at the beginning. If they are honest, then, they must make other excuses and give up the pretense of the last resort.

The second excuse is designed for national liberation movements struggling against established and powerful states. Now the claim is that nothing else is possible, that no other strategy is available except terrorism. This is different from the first excuse because it does not require would-be terrorists to run through all the available options. Or, the second excuse requires terrorists to run through all the options in their heads, not in the world; notional finality is enough. Movement strategists consider their options and conclude that they have no alternative to terrorism. They think that they do not have the political strength to try anything else, and thus they do not try anything else. Weakness is their excuse.

But two very different kinds of weakness are commonly confused here: the weakness of the movement vis-à-vis the opposing state and the movement's weakness vis-à-vis its own people. This second kind of weakness, the inability of the movement to mobilize the nation, makes terrorism the "only" option because it effectively rules out all the others: nonviolent resistance, general strikes, mass demonstrations, unconventional warfare, and so on.

These options are only rarely ruled out by the sheer power of the state, by the pervasiveness and intensity of oppression. Totalitarian states may be immune to nonviolent or guerrilla resistance, but all the evidence suggests that they are also immune to terrorism. Or, more exactly, in totalitarian states state terror dominates every other sort. Where terrorism is a possible strategy for the oppositional movement (in liberal and democratic states, most obviously), other strategies are also possible if the movement has some significant degree of popular support. In the absence of popular support, terrorism may indeed be the one available strategy, but it is hard to see how its evils can then be excused. For it is not weakness alone that makes the excuse, but the claim of the terrorists to represent the weak; and the particular form of weakness that makes terrorism the only option calls that claim into question.

One might avoid this difficulty with a stronger insistence on the actual effectiveness of terrorism. The third excuse is simply that terrorism works (and nothing else does); it achieves the ends of the oppressed even without their participation. "When the act accuses, the result excuses."[1] This is a consequentialist argument, and given a strict understanding of consequentialism, this argument amounts to a justification rather than an excuse. In practice, however, the argument is rarely pushed so far. More often, the argument begins with an acknowledgment of the terrorists' wrongdoing. Their hands are dirty, but we must make a kind of peace with them because they have acted effectively for the sake of people who could not act for themselves. But, in fact, have the terrorists' actions been effective? I doubt that terrorism has ever achieved national liberation—no nation that I know of owes its freedom to a campaign of random murder—although terrorism undoubtedly increases the power of the terrorists within the national liberation movement. Perhaps terrorism is also conducive to the survival and notoriety (the two go together) of the movement, which is now dominated by terrorists. But even if we were to grant some means-end relationship between terror and national liberation, the third excuse does not work unless it can meet the further requirements of a consequentialist argument. It must be possible to say that the desired end could not have been achieved through any other, less wrongful, means. The third excuse depends, then, on the success of the first or second, and neither of these look likely to be successful.

The fourth excuse avoids this crippling dependency. This excuse does not require the apologist to defend either of the improbable claims that

---

1 Machiavelli, *The Discourses* I:ix. As yet, however, there have been no results that would constitute a Machiavellian excuse.

terrorism is the last resort or that it is the only possible resort. The fourth excuse is simply that terrorism is the universal resort. All politics is (really) terrorism. The appearance of innocence and decency is always a piece of deception.

This argument has the same form as the maxim "All's fair in love and war." Love is always fraudulent, war is always brutal, and political action is always terrorist in character. Political action works (as Thomas Hobbes long ago argued) only by generating fear in innocent men and women. Terrorism is the politics of state officials and movement militants alike. This argument does not justify either the officials or the militants, but it does excuse them all. We hardly can be harsh with people who act the way everyone else acts. Only saints are likely to act differently, and sainthood in politics is super-erogatory, a matter of grace, not obligation.

But this fourth excuse relies too heavily on our cynicism about political life, and cynicism only sometimes answers well to experience. In fact, legitimate states do not need to terrorize their citizens, and strongly based movements do not need to terrorize their opponents. Officials and militants who live, as it were, on the margins of legitimacy and strength sometimes choose terrorism and sometimes do not. Living in terror is not a universal experience. The world the terrorists create has its entrances and exits.

If we want to understand the choice of terror, the choice that forces the rest of us through the door, we have to imagine what in fact always occurs, although we often have no satisfactory record of the occurrence: A group of men and women, officials or militants, sits around a table and argues about whether or not to adopt a terrorist strategy. Later on, the litany of excuses obscures the argument. But at the time, around the table, it would have been no use for defenders of terrorism to say, "Everybody does it," because there they would be face to face with people proposing to do something else. Nor is it historically the case that the members of this last group, the opponents of terrorism, always lose the argument. They can win, however, and still not be able to prevent a terrorist campaign; the would-be terrorists (it does not take very many) can always split the movement and go their own way. Or, they can split the bureaucracy or the police or officer corps and act in the shadow of state power. Indeed, terrorism often has its origin in such splits. The first victims are the terrorists' former comrades or colleagues. What reason can we possibly have, then, for equating the two? If we value the politics of the men and women who oppose terrorism, we must reject the excuses of their murderers. Cynicism at such a time is unfair to the victims.

The fourth excuse can also take, often does take, a more restricted form. Oppression, rather than political rule more generally, is always terroristic in character, and thus, we must always excuse the opponents of oppression. When they choose terrorism, they are only reacting to someone else's previous choice, repaying in kind the treatment they have long received. Of course, their terrorism repeats the evil—innocent people are killed, who were never themselves oppressors—but repetition is not the same as initiation. The oppressors set the terms of the struggle. But if the struggle is fought on the oppressors' terms, then the oppressors are likely to win. Or, at least, oppression is likely to win, even if it takes on a new face. The whole point of a liberation movement or a popular mobilization is to change the terms. We have no reason to excuse the terrorism reactively adopted by opponents of oppression unless we are confident of the sincerity of their opposition, the seriousness of their commitment to a nonoppressive politics. But the choice of terrorism undermines that confidence. * * *

* * * We can tell a story (like the story that Richard Wright tells in *Native Son*, for example) that might lead us, not to justify terrorism, but to excuse this or that individual terrorist. We can provide a personal history, a psychological study, of compassion destroyed by fear, moral reason by hatred and rage, social inhibition by unending violence—the product, an individual driven to kill or readily set on a killing course by his or her political leaders. But the force of this story will not depend on any of the four general excuses, all of which grant what the storyteller will have to deny: that terrorism is the deliberate choice of rational men and women. Whether they conceive it to be one option among others or the only one available, they nevertheless argue and choose. Whether they are acting or reacting, they have made a decision. The human instruments they subsequently find to plant the bomb or shoot the gun may act under some psychological compulsion, but the men and women who choose terror as a policy act "freely." They could not act in any other way, or accept any other description of their action, and still pretend to be the leaders of the movement or the state. We ought never to excuse such leaders.

THE RESPONSE TO TERRORISM

What follows from the critique of excuses? There is still a great deal of room for argument about the best way of responding to terrorism. Certainly resistance will never be sufficient. In this sort of struggle, the offense is always ahead. The technology of terror is simple; the weapons are readily produced and easy to deliver. It is virtually impossible to protect people against random and indiscriminate attack. Thus, resistance will have to be supplemented by some combination of repression and retaliation. This is a dangerous business because repression and retaliation so often take terroristic forms and there are a host of apologists ready with excuses that sound remarkably like those of the terrorists themselves. It should be clear by now, however, that counterterrorism cannot be excused merely because it is reactive. Every new actor, terrorist or counterterrorist, claims to be reacting to someone else, standing in a circle and just passing the evil along. But the circle is ideological in character; in fact, every actor is a moral agent and makes an independent decision.

Therefore, repression and retaliation must not repeat the wrongs of terrorism, which is to say that repression and retaliation must be aimed systematically at the terrorists themselves, never at the people for whom the terrorists claim to be acting. That claim is in any case doubtful, even when it is honestly made. The people do not authorize the terrorists to act in their name. Only a tiny number actually participate in terrorist activities; they are far more likely to suffer than to benefit from the terrorist program. Even if they supported the program and hoped to benefit from it, however, they would still be immune from attack—exactly as civilians in time of war who support the war effort but are not themselves part of it are subject to the same immunity. Civilians may be put at risk by attacks on military targets, as by attacks on terrorist targets, but the risk must be kept to a minimum, even at some cost to the attackers. The refusal to make ordinary people into targets, whatever their nationality or even their politics, is the only way to say no to terrorism. Every act of repression and retaliation has to be measured by this standard.

But what if the "only way" to defeat the terrorists is to intimidate their actual or potential supporters? It is important to deny the premise of this question: that terrorism is a politics dependent on mass support. In fact, it is always the politics of an elite, whose members are dedicated and fanatical and more than ready to endure, or to watch others endure, the devastations of a counterterrorist campaign. Indeed, terrorists will welcome counterterrorism; it makes the terrorists' excuses more plausible and is sure to bring them, however many people are killed or wounded, however many are terrorized, the small number of recruits needed to sustain the terrorist activities.

Repression and retaliation are legitimate responses to terrorism only when they are constrained by the same moral principles that rule out terrorism itself. But there is an alternative response that seeks to avoid the violence that these two entail. The alternative is to address directly, ourselves, the oppression the terrorists claim to oppose. Oppression, they say, is the cause of terrorism. But that is merely one more excuse. The real cause of terrorism is the decision to launch a terrorist campaign, a decision made by that group of people sitting around a table whose deliberations I have already described. However, terrorists do exploit oppression, injustice, and human misery generally and look to these at least for their excuses. There can hardly be any doubt that oppression strengthens their hand. Is that a reason for us to come to the defense of the oppressed? It seems to me that we have our own reasons to do that, and do not need this one, or should not, to prod us into action. We might imitate those movement militants who argue against the adoption of a terrorist strategy—although not, as the terrorists say, because these militants are prepared to tolerate oppression. They already are opposed to oppression and now add to that opposition, perhaps for the same reasons, a refusal of terror. So should we have been opposed before, and we should now make the same addition.

But there is an argument, put with some insistence these days, that we should refuse to acknowledge any link at all between terrorism and oppression—as if any defense of oppressed men and women, once a terrorist campaign has been launched, would concede the effectiveness of the campaign. Or, at least, a defense of oppression would give terrorism the appearance of effectiveness and so increase the likelihood of terrorist campaigns in the future. Here we have the reverse side of the litany of excuses; we have turned over the record. First oppression is made into an excuse for terrorism, and then terrorism is made into an excuse for oppression. The first is the excuse of the far left; the second is the excuse of the neoconservative right. I doubt that genuine conservatives would think it a good reason for defending the status quo that it is under terrorist attack; they would have independent reasons and would be prepared to defend the status quo against any attack. Similarly, those of us who think that the status quo urgently requires change have our own reasons for thinking so and need not be intimidated by terrorists or, for that matter, antiterrorists.

If one criticizes the first excuse, one should not neglect the second. But I need to state the second more precisely. It is not so much an excuse for oppression as an excuse for doing nothing (now) about oppression. The claim is that the campaign against terrorism has priority over every other political activity. If the people who take the lead in this campaign are the old oppressors, then we must make a kind of peace with them—temporarily, of course, until the terrorists have been beaten. This is a strategy that denies the possibility of a two-front war. So long as the men and women who pretend to lead the fight against oppression are terrorists, we can concede nothing to their demands. Nor can we oppose their opponents.

But why not? It is not likely in any case that terrorists would claim victory in the face of a serious effort to deal with the oppression of the people they claim to be defending. The effort would merely expose the hollowness of their claim, and the nearer it came to success, the more they would escalate their terrorism. They would still have to be defeated, for what they are after is not a solution to the problem but rather the power to impose their own solution. No decent end to the conflict in Ireland, say, or in Lebanon, or in the Middle East generally, is going to look like a victory for terrorism—if only because the different groups of terrorists are each committed, by the strategy they have adopted, to an indecent end. By working for our own ends, we expose the indecency.

OPPRESSION AND TERRORISM

It is worth considering at greater length the link between oppression and terror. To pretend that there is no link at all is to ignore the historical record, but the record is more complex than any of the excuses acknowledge. The first thing to be read out of it, however, is simple enough: Oppression is not so much the cause of terrorism as terrorism is one of the primary means of oppression. This was true in ancient times, as Aristotle recognized, and it is still true today. Tyrants rule by terrorizing their subjects; unjust and illegitimate regimes are upheld through a combination of carefully aimed and random violence. If this method works in the state, there is no reason to think that it will not work, or that it does not work, in the liberation movement. Wherever we see terrorism, we should look for tyranny and oppression. Authoritarian states, especially in the moment of their founding, need a terrorist apparatus—secret police with unlimited power, secret prisons into which citizens disappear, death squads in unmarked cars. Even democracies may use terror, not against their own citizens, but at the margins, in their colonies, for example, where colonizers also are likely to rule tyrannically. Oppression is sometimes maintained by a steady and discriminate pressure, sometimes by intermittent and random violence— what we might think of as terrorist melodrama—designed to render the subject population fearful and passive.

This latter policy, especially if it seems successful, invites imitation by opponents of the state. But terrorism does not spread only when it is imitated. If it can be invented by state officials, it can also be invented by movement militants. Neither one need take lessons from the other; the circle has no single or necessary starting point. Wherever it starts, terrorism in the movement is tyrannical and oppressive in exactly the same way as is terrorism in the state. The terrorists aim to rule, and murder is their method. They have their own internal police, death squads, disappearances. They begin by killing or intimidating those comrades who stand in their way, and they proceed to do the same, if they can, among the people they claim to represent. If terrorists are successful, they rule tyrannically, and their people bear, without consent, the costs of the terrorists' rule. (If the terrorists are only partly successful, the costs to the people may be even greater: What they have to bear now is a war between rival terrorist gangs.) But terrorists cannot win the ultimate victory they seek without challenging the established regime or colonial power and the people it claims to represent, and when terrorists do that, they themselves invite imitation. The regime may then respond with its own campaign of aimed and random violence. Terrorist tracks terrorist, each claiming the other as an excuse.

The same violence can also spread to countries where it has not yet been experienced; now terror is reproduced not through temporal succession but through ideological adaptation. State terrorists wage bloody wars against largely imaginary enemies: army colonels, say, hunting down the representatives of "international communism." Or movement terrorists wage bloody wars against enemies with whom, but for the ideology, they could readily negotiate and compromise: nationalist fanatics committed to a permanent irredentism. These wars, even if they are without precedents, are likely enough to become precedents, to start the circle of terror and counterterror, which is endlessly oppressive for the ordinary men and women whom the state calls its citizens and the movement its "people."

The only way to break out of the circle is to refuse to play the terrorist game. Terrorists in the state and the movement warn us, with equal vehemence, that any such refusal is a sign of softness and naiveté. The self-portrait of the terrorists is always the same. They are tough-minded and realistic; they know their enemies (or privately invent them for ideological purposes); and they are ready to do what must be done for victory. Why then do terrorists turn around and around in the same circle? It is true: Movement terrorists win support because they pretend to deal energetically and effectively with the brutality of the state. It also is true: State terrorists win support because they pretend to deal energetically and effectively with the brutality of the movement. Both feed on the fears of brutalized and oppressed people. But there is no way of overcoming brutality with terror. At most, the burden is shifted from these people to those; more likely, new burdens are added for everyone. Genuine liberation can come only through a politics that mobilizes the victims of brutality and takes careful aim at its agents, or by a politics that surrenders the hope of victory and domination and deliberately seeks a compromise settlement. In either case, once tyranny is repudiated, terrorism is no longer an option. For what lies behind all the excuses, of officials and militants alike, is the predilection for a tyrannical politics.

STUDY QUESTIONS

1. Why does Walzer think that the consequentialist excuse must presuppose one or other of the last resort or the weakness excuse?
2. What reply does Walzer make to the excuse that political authority itself is a form of terrorism?
3. How does Walzer think that political authorities should respond to terrorism?

■ Compare and Contrast Question

1. Would Walzer accept Dershowitz's limited defense of torture?

RESISTANCE

This section includes three essays written in defense of forms of civil disobedience. The first, Henry David Thoreau's "Civil Disobedience," published in 1849, was written during the Mexican–American War, before the abolition of slavery in the United States. Thoreau was greatly opposed to both the war and to slavery, and he refused to pay his poll tax to a government that acted in what he regarded as a manifestly unjust fashion.

Considering whether he has a moral obligation to follow the laws set out by a democratically elected government, Thoreau argues that the power of the majority rests simply on its greater strength over the minority and that the only obligation that citizens have is to follow their conscience and do what they think is right. Thoreau criticizes those who protest against the government's action but do nothing to oppose it. He proposes that the right thing to do is to disobey the law and not pay the tax. Not paying tax is less violent and bloody than paying tax, given what the tax will be spent on. Thoreau rejects the argument that in a democracy the correct course of action is to try to convince the majority to change the law, as that is time-consuming and uncertain. Thoreau does not oppose the state in general; he thinks that a good state is possible but that, in the particular circumstances in which he lived and wrote, the honest person has no option but to disobey and to suffer the consequences.

The next selection is a letter written by Martin Luther King while he was held in jail after being arrested for taking part in a political protest for racial equality in Alabama. It is a response to a group of clergymen who had written an open letter criticizing his actions.

Noting that "injustice anywhere is a threat to justice everywhere," King sets out the steps necessary in a nonviolent campaign. First, gather facts; second, negotiate; third, self-purify, in the sense of preparing for action; and finally, engage in direct action itself. King argues that the facts show that Birmingham is one of the most segregated cities in the United States. He accepts the point of his critics that negotiation is better than direct action, but it had made little progress. The purpose of nonviolent direct action is to create a background of crisis and tension in order to generate meaningful negotiation the second time around.

King is critical of the argument that the movement must be more patient, insisting that "justice delayed is justice denied." He presents a moving account of the injustice suffered by people of color in the United States. Drawing on St. Augustine's doctrine that an unjust law is no law and Aquinas's account of natural law, King argues that people of color face many unjust laws. This is particularly the case when the laws are made under circumstances in which people of color are in effect unable to register to vote. King is careful, though, to argue that his position does not justify disobedience to all laws, but only those that are unjust. Disobedience to an unjust law should be done openly and lovingly, with a willingness to pay the penalty, and is an appeal to the conscience of the community. This, he argues, shows the highest respect for law.

King is disappointed by the lack of support from white moderates, who place the value of order over justice and thereby hinder the movement for freedom. King ends by reaffirming his commitment to Christian values and his conviction that the struggle for freedom will only gain in force.

The final reading is taken from Nelson Mandela's defense speech in what was known as the Rivonia trial, in South Africa in 1964, in which he and others were accused of conspiracy to sabotage and other offenses.

Mandela was found guilty and sentenced to life imprisonment, which led to his incarceration on Robben Island. Mandela served 18 years there, and 9 elsewhere, until his famous and moving release in 1990. In this speech Mandela puts his actions in the context of the struggle against apartheid in South Africa. He argues that all legal and nonviolent routes to liberation and equality had been closed, and therefore illegal violence was the only option. The African National Congress, to which Mandela belonged, had been declared an illegal organization in 1960, although, rather than disband, it went underground, with its leaders, including Mandela, either in hiding or exile. Black Africans had no vote and hence no say in the laws that bound them, and thus many oppressive laws were thought to lack legitimacy in relation to black Africans.

The speech provides a rich description of the way in which black South Africans were cruelly forced into poverty-stricken lives with no hope of advancement or respite. Enforcement of oppressive and unfair laws led to the breakup of families and further deprivation. At the root of the system was the ideology of "white supremacy," in which all laws and policies were aimed at reinforcing white power and privilege to the cost of other races. In response, Mandela and his ANC colleagues chose sabotage to harm the economy in order to avoid terrorism, racial war, or open revolution. Mandela's goal was to replace white supremacy with a democratic system of justice for all. And for this, he says, he was prepared to die.

HENRY DAVID THOREAU
On Civil Disobedience

Henry David Thoreau (1817–1862) was an American philosopher, essayist, and poet, best known for the text "Civil Disobedience," extracted here, and his book Walden, *which recommends simple living.*

I heartily accept the motto,—"That government is best which governs least"; and I should like to see it acted up to more rapidly and systematically. Carried out, it finally amounts to this, which also I believe,—"That government is best which governs not at all"; and when men are prepared for it, that will be the kind of government which they will have. Government is at best but an expedient; but most governments are usually, and all governments are sometimes, inexpedient. * * *

This American government,—what is it but a tradition, though a recent one, endeavoring to transmit itself unimpaired to posterity, but each instant losing some of its integrity? It has not the vitality and force of a single living man; for a single man can bend it to his will. It is a sort of wooden gun to the people themselves. But it is not the less necessary for this; for the people must have some complicated machinery or other, and hear its din, to satisfy that idea of government which they have. Governments show thus how successfully men can be imposed on, even impose on themselves, for their own advantage. It is excellent, we must all allow. Yet this government never of itself furthered any enterprise, but by the alacrity with which it got out of its way. It does not keep the country free. It does not settle the West. It does not educate. The character inherent in the American people has done all that has been accomplished; and it would have done somewhat more, if the government had not sometimes got in its way. * * *

But, to speak practically and as a citizen, unlike those who call themselves no-government men, I ask for, not at once no government, but *at once* a better government. Let every man make known what kind of government would command his respect, and that will be one step toward obtaining it.

After all, the practical reason why, when the power is once in the hands of the people, a majority are permitted, and for a long period continue, to rule, is not because they are most likely to be in the right, nor because this seems fairest to the minority, but because they are physically the strongest. But a government in which the majority rule in all cases cannot be based on justice, even as far as men understand it. Can there not be a government in which majorities do not virtually decide right and wrong, but conscience?—in which majorities decide only those questions to which the rule of expediency is applicable? Must the citizen ever for a moment, or in the least degree, resign his conscience to the legislator? Why has every man a conscience, then? I think that we should be men first, and subjects afterward. It is not desirable to cultivate a respect for the law, so much as for the right. The only obligation which I have a right to assume, is to do at any time what I think right. It is truly enough said, that a corporation has no conscience; but a corporation of conscientious men is a corporation *with* a conscience. Law never made men a whit more just; and, by means of their respect for it, even the well-disposed are daily made the agents of injustice. A common and natural result of an undue respect for law is, that you may see a file of soldiers, colonel, captain, corporal, privates, powder-monkeys, and all, marching in admirable order over hill and dale to the wars, against their wills, ay, against their common sense and consciences, which makes it very steep marching indeed, and produces a palpitation of the heart. They have no doubt that it is a damnable business in which they are concerned; they are all peaceably inclined. Now, what are they? Men at all? or small movable forts and magazines, at the service of some unscrupulous man in power? * * *

How does it become a man to behave toward this American government to-day? I answer, that he cannot without disgrace be associated with it. I cannot for an instant recognize that political organization as *my* government which is the *slave's* government also.

* * * When a sixth of the population of a nation which has undertaken to be the refuge of liberty are slaves, and a whole country is unjustly overrun and conquered by a foreign army, and subjected to military law, I think that it is not too soon for honest men to rebel and revolutionize. What makes this duty the more urgent is the fact, that the country so overrun is not our own, but ours is the invading army.

* * * If I have unjustly wrested a plank from a drowning man, I must restore it to him though I drown myself. * * * This people must cease to hold slaves, and to make war on Mexico, though it cost them their existence as a people.

* * * There are thousands who are *in opinion* opposed to slavery and to the war, who yet in effect do nothing to put an end to them; who, esteeming themselves children of Washington and Franklin, all down with their hands in their pockets, and say that they know not what to do, and do nothing; who even postpone the question of freedom to the question of free-trade, and quietly read the prices-current along with the latest advices from Mexico, after dinner, and, it may be, fall asleep over them both. What is the price-current of an honest man and patriot to-day? They hesitate, and they regret, and sometimes they petition; but they do nothing in earnest and with effect. They will wait, well disposed, for others to remedy the evil, that they may no longer have it to regret. At most, they give only a cheap vote, and a feeble countenance and God-speed, to the right, as it goes by them. There are nine hundred and ninety-nine patrons of virtue to one virtuous man. * * *

It is not a man's duty, as a matter of course, to devote himself to the eradication of any, even the most enormous wrong; he may still properly have other concerns to engage him; but it is his duty, at least, to wash his hands of it, and, if he gives it no thought longer, not to give it practically his support. If I devote myself to other pursuits and contemplations, I must first see, at least, that I do not pursue them sitting upon another man's shoulders. I must get off him first, that he may pursue his contemplations too. See what gross inconsistency is tolerated. I have heard some of my townsmen say, "I should like to have them order me out to help put down an insurrection of the slaves, or to march to Mexico;—see if I would go"; and yet these very men have each, directly by their allegiance, and so indirectly, at least, by their money, furnished a substitute. The soldier is applauded who refuses to serve in an unjust war by those who do not refuse to sustain the unjust government which makes the war. * * *

* * * Those who, while they disapprove of the character and measures of a government, yield to it their allegiance and support, are undoubtedly its most conscientious supporters, and so frequently the most serious obstacles to reform. Some are petitioning the State to dissolve the Union, to disregard the requisitions of the President. Why do they not dissolve it themselves,— the union between themselves and the State,—and refuse to pay their quota into its treasury? Do not they stand in the same relation to the State, that the State does to the Union? And have not the same reasons prevented the State from resisting the Union, which have prevented them from resisting the State? * * *

Unjust laws exist: shall we be content to obey them, or shall we endeavor to amend them, and obey them until we have succeeded, or shall we transgress them at once? Men generally, under such a government as this, think that they ought to wait until they have persuaded the majority to alter them. They think that, if they should resist, the remedy would be worse than the evil. But it is the fault of the government itself that the remedy *is* worse than the evil. *It* makes it worse. Why is it not more apt to anticipate and provide for reform? Why does it not cherish its wise minority? Why does it cry and resist before it is hurt? Why does it not encourage its citizens to be on the alert to point out its faults, and *do* better than it would have them? Why does it always crucify Christ, and excommunicate Copernicus and Luther, and pronounce Washington and Franklin rebels?

One would think, that a deliberate and practical denial of its authority was the only offence never contemplated by government; else, why has it not assigned its definite, its suitable and proportionate penalty? If a man who has no property refuses but once to earn nine shillings for the State, he is put in prison for a period unlimited by any law that I know, and determined only by the discretion of those who placed him there; but if he should steal ninety times nine shillings from the State, he is soon permitted to go at large again.

If the injustice is part of the necessary friction of the machine of government, let it go, let it go: perchance it will wear smooth,—certainly the machine will wear out. If the injustice has a spring, or a pulley, or a rope, or a crank, exclusively for itself, then perhaps you may consider whether the remedy will not be worse than the evil; but if it is of such a nature that it requires you to be the agent of injustice to another, then, I say, break the law. Let your life be a counter friction to stop the machine. What I have to do is to see, at any rate, that I do not lend myself to the wrong which I condemn.

As for adopting the ways which the State has provided for remedying the evil, I know not of such ways. They take too much time, and a man's life will be gone. I have other affairs to attend to. I came into this world, not chiefly to make this a good place to live in, but to live in it, be it good or bad. A man has not everything to do, but something; and because he cannot do *everything*, it is not necessary that he should do *something* wrong. It is not my business to be petitioning the Governor or the Legislature any more than it is theirs to petition me; and, if they should not hear my petition, what should I do then? But in this case the State has provided no way: its very Constitution is the evil. This may seem to be harsh and stubborn and unconciliatory; but it is to treat with the utmost kindness and consideration the only spirit that can appreciate or deserves it. So is all change for the better, like birth and death, which convulse the body.

I do not hesitate to say, that those who call themselves Abolitionists should at once effectually withdraw their support, both in person and property, from the government of Massachusetts, and not wait till they constitute a majority of one, before they suffer the right to prevail through them. I think that it is enough if they have God on their side, without waiting for that other one. Moreover, any man more right than his neighbors constitutes a majority of one already. * * *

Under a government which imprisons any unjustly, the true place for a just man is also a prison. The proper place to-day, the only place which Massachusetts has provided for her freer and less desponding spirits, is in her prisons, to be put out and locked out of the State by her own act, as they have already put themselves out by their principles. It is there that the fugitive slave, and the Mexican prisoner on parole, and the Indian come to plead the wrongs of his race, should find them; on that separate, but more free and honorable ground, where the State places those who are not *with* her, but *against* her,—the only house in a slave State in which a free man can abide with honor. If any think that their influence would be lost there, and their voices no longer afflict the ear of the State, that they would not be as an enemy within its walls, they do not know by how much truth is stronger than error, nor how much more eloquently and effectively he can combat injustice who has experienced a little in his own person. Cast your whole vote, not a strip of paper merely, but your whole influence. A minority is powerless while it conforms to the majority; it is not even a minority then; but it is irresistible when it clogs by its whole weight. If the alternative is to keep all just men in prison, or give up war and slavery, the State will not hesitate which to choose. If a thousand men were not to pay their tax-bills this year, that would not be a violent and bloody measure, as it would be to pay them, and enable the State to commit violence and shed innocent blood. This is, in fact, the definition of a peaceable revolution, if any such is possible. If the tax-gatherer, or any other public officer, asks me, as one has done, "But what shall I do?" my answer is, "If you really wish to do anything, resign your office." When the subject has refused allegiance, and the officer has resigned his office, then the revolution is accomplished. But even suppose blood should flow. Is there not a sort of blood shed when the conscience is wounded? Through this wound a man's real manhood and immortality flow out, and he bleeds to an everlasting death. I see this blood flowing now. ＊＊＊

When I converse with the freest of my neighbors, I perceive that, what-ever they may say about the magnitude and seriousness of the question, and their regard for the public tranquillity, the long and the short of the matter is, that they cannot spare the protection of the existing government, and they dread the consequences to their property and families of disobedience to it. For my own part, I should not like to think that I ever rely on the pro-tection of the State. But, if I deny the authority of the State when it presents its tax-bill, it will soon take and waste all my property, and so harass me and my children without end. This is hard. This makes it impossible for a man to live honestly, and at the same time comfortably, in outward respects. It will not be worth the while to accumulate property; that would be sure to go again. You must hire or squat somewhere, and raise but a small crop, and eat that soon. You must live within yourself, and depend upon yourself always tucked up and ready for a start, and not have many affairs. * * * Confucius said: "If a state is governed is the principles of reason, poverty and misery are subjects of shame; if a state is not governed by the principles of reason, riches and honors are the subjects of shame." * * * It costs me less in every sense to incur the penalty of disobedience to the State, than it would to obey. I should feel as if I were worth less in that case.

Some years ago, the State met me in behalf of the Church, and commanded me to pay a certain sum toward the support of a clergyman whose preaching my father attended, but never I myself. "Pay," it said, "or be locked up in the jail." I declined to pay. But, unfortunately, another man saw fit to pay it. I did not see why the schoolmaster should be taxed to support the priest, and not the priest the schoolmaster; for I was not the State's schoolmaster, but I supported myself by voluntary subscription. I did not see why the lyceum should not present its tax-bill, and have the State to back its demand, as well as the Church. However, at the request of the selectmen, I condescended to make some such statement as this in writing:—"Know all men by these presents, that I, Henry Thoreau, do not wish to be regarded as a member of any incorporated society which I have not joined." This I gave to the town clerk; and he has it. The State, having thus learned that I did not wish to be regarded as a member of that church, has never made a like demand on me since; though it said that it must adhere to its original presumption that time. If I had known how to name them, I should then have signed off in detail from all the societies which I never signed on to; but I did not know where to find a complete list.

I have paid no poll-tax for six years. I was put into a jail once on this account, for one night; and, as I stood considering the walls of solid stone, two or three feet thick, the door of wood and iron, a foot thick, and the iron grating which strained the light, I could not help being struck with the foolishness of that institution which treated me as if I were mere flesh and blood and bones, to be locked up. I wondered that it should have concluded at length that this was the best use it could put me to, and had never thought to avail itself of my services in some way. I saw that, if there was a wall of stone between me and my townsmen, there was a still more difficult one to climb or break through, before they could get to be as free as I was. I did not for a moment feel confined, and the walls seemed a great waste of stone and mortar. I felt as if I alone of all my townsmen had paid my tax. They plainly did not know how to treat me, but behaved like persons who are underbred. In every threat and in every compliment there was a blunder; for they thought that my chief desire was to stand the other side of that stone wall. I could not but smile to see how industriously they locked the door on my meditations, which followed them out again without let or hindrance, and *they* were really all that was dangerous. As they could not reach me, they had resolved to punish my body; just as boys, if they cannot come at some person against whom they have a spite, will abuse his dog. I saw that the State was half-witted, that it was timid as a lone woman with her silver spoons, and that it did not know its friends from its foes, and I lost all my remaining respect for it, and pitied it.

Thus the State never intentionally confronts a man's sense, intellectual or moral, but only his body, his senses. It is not armed with superior wit or honesty, but with superior physical strength. I was not born to be forced. I will breathe after my own fashion. Let us see who is the strongest. What force has a multitude? They only can force me who obey a higher law than I. They force me to become like themselves. I do not hear of *men* being *forced* to live this way or that by masses of men. What sort of life were that to live? When I meet a government which says to me, "Your money or your life," why should I be in haste to give it my money? It may be in a great strait, and not know what to do: I cannot help that. It must help itself; do as I do. It is not worth the while to snivel about it. I am not responsible for the successful working of the machinery of society. ✳ ✳ ✳

I have never declined paying the highway tax, because I am as desirous of being a good neighbor as I am of being a bad subject; and, as for supporting schools, I am doing my part to educate my fellow-countrymen now. It is for no particular item in the tax-bill that I refuse to pay it. I simply wish to refuse allegiance to the State, to withdraw and stand aloof from it effectually. I do not care to trace the course of my dollar, if I could, till it buys a man or a musket to shoot one with,—the dollar is innocent,—but I am concerned to trace the effects of my allegiance. In fact, I quietly declare war with the State, after my fashion, though I will still make what use and get what advantage of her I can, as is usual in such cases. ✳ ✳ ✳

✳ ✳ ✳ Seen from a lower point of view, the Constitution, with all its faults, is very good; the law and the courts are very respectable; even this State and this American government are, in many respects, very admirable and rare things, to be thankful for, such as a great many have described them; but seen from a point of view a little higher, they are what I have described them; seen from a higher still, and the highest, who shall say what they are, or that they are worth looking at or thinking of at all? * * *

The authority of government, even such as I am willing to submit to,— for I will cheerfully obey those who know and can do better than I, and in many things even those who neither know nor can do so well,—is still an impure one: to be strictly just, it must have the sanction and consent of the governed. It can have no pure right over my person and property but what I concede to it. The progress from an absolute to a limited monarchy, from a limited monarchy to a democracy, is a progress toward a true respect for the individual. Even the Chinese philosopher was wise enough to regard the individual as the basis of the empire. Is a democracy, such as we know it, the last improvement possible in government? Is it not possible to take a step further towards recognizing and organizing the rights of man? There will never be a really free and enlightened State, until the State comes to recognize the individual as a higher and independent power, from which all its own power and authority are derived, and treats him accordingly. I please myself with imagining a State at last which can afford to be just to all men, and to treat the individual with respect as a neighbor; which even would not think it inconsistent with its own repose, if a few were to live aloof from it, not meddling with it, nor embraced by it, who fulfilled all the duties of neighbors and fellow-men. A State which bore this kind of fruit, and suffered it to drop off as fast as it ripened, would prepare the way for a still more perfect and glorious State, which also I have imagined, but not yet anywhere seen.

STUDY QUESTIONS

1. Why does Thoreau reject the argument that reform should take place via democratic processes?
2. Why does Thoreau regard withholding tax as less violent and bloody than paying it?
3. Does Thoreau's position lead to the total rejection of all forms of state?

MARTIN LUTHER KING JR.
Letter From Birmingham Jail

Martin Luther King (1929–1968) was a leader of the American civil rights movement. For his advocacy of nonviolent resistance, he won the Nobel Peace Prize in 1964. He was assassinated in Memphis, Tennessee, in 1968.

I am cognizant of the interrelatedness of all communities and states. * * * Injustice anywhere is a threat to justice everywhere. We are caught in an inescapable network of mutuality, tied in a single garment of destiny. Whatever affects one directly, affects all indirectly. * * *

In any nonviolent campaign there are four basic steps: collection of the facts to determine whether injustices exist; negotiation; self purification; and direct action. We have gone through all these steps in Birmingham. There can be no gainsaying the fact that racial injustice engulfs this community. Birmingham is probably the most thoroughly segregated city in the United States. Its ugly record of brutality is widely known. Negroes have experienced grossly unjust treatment in the courts. There have been more unsolved bombings of Negro homes and churches in Birmingham than in any other city in the nation. These are the hard, brutal facts of the case. On the basis of these conditions, Negro leaders sought to negotiate with the city fathers. But the latter consistently refused to engage in good faith negotiation.

Then, last September, came the opportunity to talk with leaders of Birmingham's economic community. In the course of the negotiations, certain promises were made by the merchants—for example, to remove the stores' humiliating racial signs. On the basis of these promises, the Reverend Fred Shuttlesworth and the leaders of the Alabama Christian Movement for Human Rights agreed to a moratorium on all demonstrations. As the weeks and months went by, we realized that we were the victims of a broken promise. A few signs, briefly removed, returned; the others remained.

As in so many past experiences, our hopes had been blasted, and the shadow of deep disappointment settled upon us. We had no alternative except to prepare for direct action, whereby we would present our very bodies as a means of laying our case before the conscience of the local and the national community. Mindful of the difficulties involved, we decided to undertake a process of self-purification. We began a series of workshops on nonviolence, and we repeatedly asked ourselves: "Are you able to accept blows without retaliating?" "Are you able to endure the ordeal of jail?" * * *

You may well ask, "Why direct action? Why sit-ins, marches and so forth? Isn't negotiation a better path?" You are quite right in calling for negotiation. Indeed, this is the very purpose of direct action. Nonviolent direct action seeks to create such a crisis and foster such a tension that a community which has constantly refused to negotiate is forced to confront the issue. It seeks so to dramatize the issue that it can no longer be ignored. My citing the creation of tension as part of the work of the nonviolent resister may sound rather shocking. But I must confess that I am not afraid of the word "tension." I have earnestly opposed violent tension, but there is a type of constructive, nonviolent tension which is necessary for growth. Just as Socrates felt that it was necessary to create a tension in the mind so that individuals could rise from the bondage of myths and half-truths to the unfettered realm of creative analysis and objective appraisal, so must we see the need for nonviolent gadflies to create the kind of tension in society that will help men rise from the dark depths of prejudice and racism to the majestic heights of understanding and brotherhood.

The purpose of our direct action program is to create a situation so crisis-packed that it will inevitably open the door to negotiation. I therefore concur with you in your call for negotiation. Too long has our beloved Southland been bogged down in a tragic effort to live in monologue rather than dialogue.

* * * My friends, I must say to you that we have not made a single gain in civil rights without determined legal and nonviolent pressure. Lamentably, it is an historical fact that privileged groups seldom give up their privileges voluntarily. Individuals may see the moral light and voluntarily give up their unjust posture; but, as Reinhold Niebuhr[1] has reminded us, groups tend to be more immoral than individuals.

We know through painful experience that freedom is never voluntarily given by the oppressor; it must be demanded by the oppressed. Frankly, I have yet to engage in a direct action campaign that was "well timed" in the view of those who have not suffered unduly from the disease of segregation. For years now I have heard the word "Wait!" It rings in the ear of every Negro with piercing familiarity. This "Wait" has almost always meant "Never." We must come to see, with one of our distinguished jurists, that "justice too long delayed is justice denied."

---

1 *Editor's note*: Reinhold Niebuhr, American theologian, 1892–1971.

We have waited for more than 340 years for our constitutional and God-given rights. The nations of Asia and Africa are moving with jetlike speed toward gaining political independence, but we still creep at horse-and-buggy pace toward gaining a cup of coffee at a lunch counter. Perhaps it is easy for those who have never felt the stinging darts of segregation to say, "Wait." But when you have seen vicious mobs lynch your mothers and fathers at will and drown your sisters and brothers at whim; when you have seen hate-filled policemen curse, kick, and even kill your black brothers and sisters; when you see the vast majority of your twenty million Negro brothers smothering in an airtight cage of poverty in the midst of an affluent society; when you suddenly find your tongue twisted and your speech stammering as you seek to explain to your six-year-old daughter why she can't go to the public amusement park that has just been advertised on television, and see tears welling up in her eyes when she is told that Funtown is closed to colored children, and see ominous clouds of inferiority beginning to form in her little mental sky, and see her beginning to distort her personality by developing an unconscious bitterness toward white people; when you have to concoct an answer for a five-year-old son who is asking, "Daddy, why do white people treat colored people so mean?"; when you take a cross-country drive and find it necessary to sleep night after night in the uncomfortable corners of your automobile because no motel will accept you; when you are humiliated day in and day out by nagging signs reading "white" and "colored"; when your first name becomes "nigger," your middle name becomes "boy" (however old you are) and your last name becomes "John," and your wife and mother are never given the respected title "Mrs."; when you are harried by day and haunted by night by the fact that you are a Negro, living constantly at tiptoe stance, never quite knowing what to expect next, and are plagued with inner fears and outer resentments; when you are forever fighting a degenerating sense of "nobodiness"—then you will understand why we find it difficult to wait. There comes a time when the cup of endurance runs over, and men are no longer willing to be plunged into the abyss of despair. * * *

* * * Since we so diligently urge people to obey the Supreme Court's decision of 1954 outlawing segregation in the public schools, at first glance it may seem rather paradoxical for us consciously to break laws. One may well ask: "How can you advocate breaking some laws and obeying others?" The answer lies in the fact that there are two types of laws: just and unjust. I would be the first to advocate obeying just laws. One has not only a legal but a moral responsibility to obey just laws. Conversely, one has a moral

responsibility to disobey unjust laws. I would agree with St. Augustine that "an unjust law is no law at all."

Now, what is the difference between the two? How does one determine whether a law is just or unjust? A just law is a man-made code that squares with the moral law or the law of God. An unjust law is a code that is out of harmony with the moral law. To put it in the terms of St. Thomas Aquinas: An unjust law is a human law that is not rooted in eternal law and natural law. Any law that uplifts human personality is just. Any law that degrades human personality is unjust. All segregation statutes are unjust because segregation distorts the soul and damages the personality. It gives the segregator a false sense of superiority and the segregated a false sense of inferiority. Segregation, to use the terminology of the Jewish philosopher Martin Buber, substitutes an "I-it" relationship for an "I-thou" relationship and ends up relegating persons to the status of things. Hence segregation is not only politically, economically, and sociologically unsound, it is morally wrong and sinful. Paul Tillich[2] has said that sin is separation. Is not segregation an existential expression of man's tragic separation, his awful estrangement, his terrible sinfulness? Thus it is that I can urge men to obey the 1954 decision of the Supreme Court, for it is morally right; and I can urge them to disobey segregation ordinances, for they are morally wrong.

Let us consider a more concrete example of just and unjust laws. An unjust law is a code that a numerical or power majority group compels a minority group to obey but does not make binding on itself. This is *difference* made legal. By the same token, a just law is a code that a majority compels a minority to follow and that it is willing to follow itself. This is *sameness* made legal.

Let me give another explanation. A law is unjust if it is inflicted on a minority that, as a result of being denied the right to vote, had no part in enacting or devising the law. Who can say that the legislature of Alabama which set up that state's segregation laws was democratically elected? Throughout Alabama all sorts of devious methods are used to prevent Negroes from becoming registered voters, and there are some counties in which, even though Negroes constitute a majority of the population, not a single Negro is registered. Can any law enacted under such circumstances be considered democratically structured?

2   *Editor's note:* Paul Tillich, German theologian, 1886–1965.

Sometimes a law is just on its face and unjust in its application. For instance, I have been arrested on a charge of parading without a permit. Now, there is nothing wrong in having an ordinance which requires a permit for a parade. But such an ordinance becomes unjust when it is used to maintain segregation and to deny citizens the First-Amendment privilege of peaceful assembly and protest.

I hope you are able to see the distinction I am trying to point out. In no sense do I advocate evading or defying the law, as would the rabid segregationist. That would lead to anarchy. One who breaks an unjust law must do so openly, lovingly, and with a willingness to accept the penalty. I submit that an individual who breaks a law that conscience tells him is unjust, and who willingly accepts the penalty of imprisonment in order to arouse the conscience of the community over its injustice, is in reality expressing the highest respect for law. ∗ ∗ ∗

We should never forget that everything Adolf Hitler did in Germany was "legal" and everything the Hungarian freedom fighters did in Hungary was "illegal." It was "illegal" to aid and comfort a Jew in Hitler's Germany. Even so, I am sure that, had I lived in Germany at the time, I would have aided and comforted my Jewish brothers. If today I lived in a Communist country where certain principles dear to the Christian faith are suppressed, I would openly advocate disobeying that country's anti-religious laws.

I must make two honest confessions to you, my Christian and Jewish brothers. First, I must confess that over the past few years I have been gravely disappointed with the white moderate. I have almost reached the regrettable conclusion that the Negro's great stumbling block in his stride toward freedom is not the White Citizen's Counciler or the Ku Klux Klanner, but the white moderate, who is more devoted to "order" than to justice; who prefers a negative peace which is the absence of tension to a positive peace which is the presence of justice; who constantly says, "I agree with you in the goal you seek, but I cannot agree with your methods of direct action"; who paternalistically believes he can set the timetable for another man's freedom; who lives by a mythical concept of time and who constantly advises the Negro to wait for a "more convenient season." Shallow understanding from people of good will is more frustrating than absolute misunderstanding from people of ill will. Lukewarm acceptance is much more bewildering than outright rejection.

I had hoped that the white moderate would understand that law and order exist for the purpose of establishing justice and that when they fail in this purpose they become the dangerously structured dams that block the flow of social progress. I had hoped that the white moderate would understand that the present tension in the South is a necessary phase of the transition from an obnoxious negative peace, in which the Negro passively accepted his unjust plight, to a substantive and positive peace, in which all men will respect the dignity and worth of human personality. Actually, we who engage in nonviolent direct action are not the creators of tension. We merely bring to the surface the hidden tension that is already alive. We bring it out in the open, where it can be seen and dealt with. Like a boil that can never be cured so long as it is covered up but must be opened with all its ugliness to the natural medicines of air and light, injustice must be exposed, with all the tension its exposure creates, to the light of human conscience and the air of national opinion before it can be cured. ✻ ✻ ✻

✻ ✻ ✻ We will have to repent in this generation not merely for the hateful words and actions of the bad people but for the appalling silence of the good people. Human progress never rolls in on wheels of inevitability; it comes through the tireless efforts of men willing to be co-workers with God, and without this hard work, time itself becomes an ally of the forces of social stagnation. We must use time creatively, in the knowledge that the time is always ripe to do right. Now is the time to make real the promise of democracy and transform our pending national elegy into a creative psalm of brotherhood. Now is the time to lift our national policy from the quicksand of racial injustice to the solid rock of human dignity.

✻ ✻ ✻ At first I was rather disappointed that fellow clergymen would see my nonviolent efforts as those of an extremist. I began thinking about the fact that I stand in the middle of two opposing forces in the Negro community. One is a force of complacency, made up in part of Negroes who, as a result of long years of oppression, are so drained of self-respect and a sense of "somebodiness" that they have adjusted to segregation; and in part of a few middle-class Negroes who, because of a degree of academic and economic security and because in some ways they profit by segregation, have become insensitive to the problems of the masses. The other force is one of bitterness and hatred, and it comes perilously close to advocating violence. It is expressed in the various black nationalist groups that are springing up across the nation, the largest and best-known being Elijah Muhammad's Muslim movement. Nourished by the Negro's frustration over the continued existence of racial discrimination, this movement is made up of people who have lost faith in America, who have absolutely repudiated Christianity, and who have concluded that the white man is an incorrigible "devil."

I have tried to stand between these two forces, saying that we need emulate neither the "do-nothingism" of the complacent nor the hatred and despair of the black nationalist. For there is the more excellent way of love and nonviolent protest. I am grateful to God that, through the influence of the Negro church, the way of nonviolence became an integral part of our struggle.

If this philosophy had not emerged, by now many streets of the South would, I am convinced, be flowing with blood. And I am further convinced that if our white brothers dismiss as "rabble-rousers" and "outside agitators" those of us who employ nonviolent direct action, and if they refuse to support our nonviolent efforts, millions of Negroes will, out of frustration and despair, seek solace and security in black nationalist ideologies—a development that would inevitably lead to a frightening racial nightmare.

Oppressed people cannot remain oppressed forever. The yearning for freedom eventually manifests itself, and that is what has happened to the American Negro. Something within has reminded him of his birthright of freedom, and something without has reminded him that it can be gained. Consciously or unconsciously, he has been caught up by the *Zeitgeist*, and with his black brothers of Africa and his brown and yellow brothers of Asia, South America, and the Caribbean, the United States Negro is moving with a sense of great urgency toward the promised land of racial justice. If one recognizes this vital urge that has engulfed the Negro community, one should readily understand why public demonstrations are taking place. The Negro has many pent-up resentments and latent frustrations, and he must release them. So let him march; let him make prayer pilgrimages to the city hall; let him go on freedom rides—and try to understand why he must do so. If his repressed emotions are not released in nonviolent ways, they will seek expression through violence; this is not a threat but a fact of history. So I have not said to my people, "Get rid of your discontent." Rather, I have tried to say that this normal and healthy discontent can be channeled into the creative outlet of nonviolent direct action. And now this approach is being termed extremist.

✳ ✳ ✳ So the question is not whether we will be extremists, but what kind of extremists we will be. Will we be extremists for hate or for love? Will we be extremists for the preservation of injustice or for the extension of justice? ✳ ✳ ✳

I had hoped that the white moderate would see this need. Perhaps I was too optimistic; perhaps I expected too much. I suppose I should have realized that few members of the oppressor race can understand the deep groans and passionate yearnings of the oppressed race, and still fewer have the vision to see that injustice must be rooted out by strong, persistent, and determined action. * * *

* * * I have no despair about the future. I have no fear about the outcome of our struggle in Birmingham, even if our motives are at present misunderstood. We will reach the goal of freedom in Birmingham and all over the nation, because the goal of America is freedom. Abused and scorned though we may be, our destiny is tied up with America's destiny. Before the pilgrims landed at Plymouth, we were here. Before the pen of Jefferson etched the majestic words of the Declaration of Independence across the pages of history, we were here. For more than two centuries our forebears labored in this country without wages; they made cotton king; they built the homes of their masters while suffering gross injustice and shameful humiliation—and yet out of a bottomless vitality they continued to thrive and develop. If the inexpressible cruelties of slavery could not stop us, the opposition we now face will surely fail. We will win our freedom because the sacred heritage of our nation and the eternal will of God are embodied in our echoing demands. * * *

* * * One day the South will recognize its real heroes. They will be the James Merediths,[3] with the noble sense of purpose that enables them to face jeering and hostile mobs, and with the agonizing loneliness that characterizes the life of the pioneer. They will be old, oppressed, battered Negro women, symbolized in a seventy-two-year-old woman in Montgomery, Alabama, who rose up with a sense of dignity and with her people decided not to ride segregated buses, and who responded with ungrammatical profundity to one who inquired about her weariness: "My feets is tired, but my soul is at rest." They will be the young high school and college students, the young ministers of the gospel and a host of their elders, courageously and nonviolently sitting in at lunch counters and willingly going to jail for conscience's sake. One day the South will know that when these disinherited children of God sat down at lunch counters, they were in reality standing up for what is best in the American dream and for the most sacred values in our Judaeo-Christian heritage, thereby bringing our nation back to those great wells of democracy which were dug deep by the founding

---

3   *Editor's note*: James Meredith, born in 1933, was the first African American to be admitted to the University of Mississippi.

fathers in their formulation of the Constitution and the Declaration of Independence. ∗∗∗

∗∗∗ Let us all hope that the dark clouds of racial prejudice will soon pass away and the deep fog of misunderstanding will be lifted from our fear-drenched communities, and in some not too distant tomorrow the radiant stars of love and brotherhood will shine over our great nation with all their scintillating beauty.

STUDY QUESTIONS

1. What, for King, is the purpose of direct action?
2. Why does disobeying an unjust law show respect for the law, according to King?
3. What fault does King find with the white moderates?

NELSON MANDELA
I Am Prepared to Die

Nelson Mandela (1918–2013) was the first president of South Africa in the postapartheid era. He was a leading figure in the African National Congress (ANC), which during the apartheid era opposed the white supremacist government, ultimately through acts of sabotage. He was imprisoned for 27 years following the Rivonia trial. The extract below is taken from his defense speech at that trial. He won the Nobel Peace Prize in 1993.

My Lord, I am the First Accused.

I hold a Bachelor's Degree in Arts and practised as an attorney in Johannesburg for a number of years in partnership with Mr. Oliver Tambo, a co-conspirator in this case. I am a convicted prisoner serving five years for leaving the country without a permit and for inciting people to go on strike. ∗∗∗

In my youth in the Transkei I listened to the elders of my tribe telling stories of the old days. ∗∗∗ I hoped then that life might offer me the opportunity to serve my people and make my own humble contribution to their freedom struggle. This is what has motivated me in all that I have done in relation to the charges made against me in this case.

∗∗∗ I do not ∗∗∗ deny that I planned sabotage. I did not plan it in a spirit of recklessness, nor because I have any love for violence. I planned it as a result of a calm and sober assessment of the political situation that had arisen after many years of tyranny, exploitation, and oppression of my people by the whites. ∗ ∗ ∗

∗ ∗ ∗ I was one of the persons who helped to form Umkhonto. I, and the others who started the organisation, did so for two reasons. Firstly, we believed that as a result of Government policy, violence by the African people had become inevitable, and that unless responsible leadership was given to canalise and control the feelings of our people, there would be outbreaks of terrorism which would produce an intensity of bitterness and hostility between the various races of the country which is not produced even by war.

Secondly, we felt that without sabotage there would be no way open to the African people to succeed in their struggle against the principle of white supremacy. All lawful modes of expressing opposition to this principle had been closed by legislation, and we were placed in a position in which we had either to accept a permanent state of inferiority, or to defy the Government. We chose to defy the Government. We first broke the law in a way which avoided any recourse to violence; when this form was legislated against, and when the Government resorted to a show of force to crush opposition to its policies, only then did we decide to answer violence with violence.

But the violence which we chose to adopt was not terrorism. We who formed Umkhonto were all members of the African National Congress, and had behind us the ANC tradition of non-violence and negotiation as a means of solving political disputes. We believed that South Africa belonged to all the people who lived in it, and not to one group, be it black or white. We did not want an interracial war, and tried to avoid it to the last minute. ∗ ∗ ∗

Even after 1949, the ANC remained determined to avoid violence. At this time, however, there was a change from the strictly constitutional means of protest which had been employed in the past. The change was embodied in a decision which was taken to protest against apartheid legislation by peaceful, but unlawful, demonstrations against certain laws. Pursuant to this policy the ANC launched the Defiance Campaign, in which I was placed in charge of volunteers. This campaign was based on the principles of passive resis-tance. More than 8,500 people defied apartheid laws and went to jail. Yet there was not a single instance of violence in the course of this campaign. I, and nineteen colleagues, were convicted for the role and this conviction was under the Suppression of Communism Act although our campaign had nothing to do with communism, but our sentences were suspended, mainly because the Judge found that discipline and non-violence had been stressed throughout. This was the time when the volunteer section of the

ANC was established, and when the word "Amadelakufa" was first used; this was the time when the volunteers were asked to take a pledge to uphold certain principles. Evidence dealing with volunteers and their pledges has been introduced into this case, but completely out of context. The volunteers were not, and are not, the soldiers of a Black army pledged to fight a civil war against whites. They were, and are, dedicated workers who are prepared to lead campaigns initiated by the ANC to distribute leaflets, to organise strikes, or to do whatever the particular campaign required. They are called volunteers because they volunteer to face the penalties of imprisonment and whipping which are now prescribed by the legislature for such acts.

During the Defiance Campaign, the Public Safety Act and the Criminal Law Amendment Act were passed. These statutes provided harsher penalties for offences committed by way of protests against laws. Despite this, the protests continued and the ANC adhered to its policy of non-violence.

In 1956, 156 leading members of the Congress Alliance, including myself, were arrested on a charge of High Treason and charges under the Suppression of Communism Act. The non-violent policy of the ANC was put in issue by the State, but when the Court gave judgement some five years later, it found that the ANC did not have a policy of violence. We were acquitted on all counts. * * *

In 1960 there was the shooting at Sharpeville, which resulted in the proclamation of a State of Emergency and the declaration of the ANC as an unlawful organisation. My colleagues and I, after careful consideration, decided that we would not obey this decree. The African people were not part of the Government and did not make the laws by which they were governed. We believed in the words of the Universal Declaration of Human Rights, that "the will of the people shall be the basis of authority of the Government," and for us to accept the banning was equivalent to accepting the silencing of the African people for all time. The ANC refused to dissolve, but instead went underground. We believed it was our duty to preserve this organisation which had been built up with almost fifty years of unremitting toil. I have no doubt that no self-respecting white political organisation would disband itself if declared illegal by a government in which it had no say. * * *

We had no doubt that we had to continue the fight. Anything else would have been abject surrender. Our problem, My Lord, was not whether to fight, but was how to continue the fight. We of the ANC had always stood for a non-racial democracy, and we shrank from any action which might drive the races further apart than they already were. But the hard facts were that fifty years of non-violence had brought the African people nothing but more and more repressive legislation, and fewer and fewer rights. * * *

It must not be forgotten * * * that by this time violence had, in fact, become a feature of the South African political scene. There had been violence in 1957 when the women of Zeerust were ordered to carry passes; there was violence in 1958 with the enforcement of Bantu Authorities and cattle culling in Sekhukhuneland; there was violence in 1959 when the people of Cato Manor protested against pass raids; there was violence in 1960 when the Government attempted to impose Bantu Authorities in Pondoland. Thirty-nine Africans died in these Pondoland disturbances. In 1961 there had been riots in Warmbaths, and all this time, My Lord, the Transkei had been a seething mass of unrest. Each disturbance pointed clearly to the inevitable growth amongst Africans of the belief that violence was the only way out—it showed that a Government which uses force to maintain its rule teaches the oppressed to use force to oppose it. * * *

At the beginning of June 1961, after a long and anxious assessment of the South African situation, I, and some colleagues, came to the conclusion that as violence * * * was inevitable, it would be unrealistic and wrong for African leaders to continue preaching peace and non-violence at a time when the Government met our peaceful demands with force.

This conclusion * * * was not easily arrived at. It was when all, only when all else had failed, when all channels of peaceful protest had been barred to us, that the decision was made to embark on violent forms of struggle, and to form Umkhonto we Sizwe. We did so not because we desired such a course, but solely because the Government had left us with no other choice. * * *

As a result of this decision, Umkhonto was formed in 1961, in November 1961. When we took this decision, and subsequently formulated our plans, the ANC heritage of non-violence and racial harmony was very much with us. We felt that the country was drifting towards a civil war in which blacks and whites would fight each other. [We viewed] the situation with alarm. Civil war would mean the destruction of what the ANC stood for; with civil war, racial peace would be more difficult than ever to achieve. We already had examples in South African history of the results of war. It has taken more than fifty years for the scars of the South African War to disappear. How much longer would it take to eradicate the scars of interracial civil war, which could not be fought without a great loss of life on both sides? * * *

Four forms of violence are possible. There is sabotage, there is guerrilla warfare, there is terrorism, and there is open revolution. We chose to adopt the first method and to test it fully before taking any other decision.

In the light of our political background the choice was a logical one. Sabotage did not involve loss of life, and it offered the best hope for future race relations. Bitterness would be kept to a minimum and, if the policy bore fruit, democratic government could become a reality. * * *

The initial plan was based on a careful analysis of the political and economic situation of our country. We believed that South Africa depended to a large extent on foreign capital and foreign trade. We felt that planned destruction of power plants, and interference with rail and telephone communications would tend to scare away capital from the country, make it more difficult for goods from the industrial areas to reach the seaports on schedule, and would in the long run be a heavy drain on the economic life of the country, thus compelling the voters of the country to reconsider their position.

Attacks on the economic life lines of the country were to be linked with sabotage on Government buildings and other symbols of apartheid. These attacks would serve as a source of inspiration to our people and encourage them to participate in non-violent mass action such as strikes. In addition, they would provide an outlet for those people who were urging the adoption of violent methods and would enable us to give concrete proof to our followers that we had adopted a stronger line, and we were fighting back against Government violence.

In addition, if mass action were successfully organised, and mass reprisals taken, we felt that sympathy for our cause would be roused in other countries, and that greater pressure would be brought to bear on the South African Government.

This then, My Lord, was the plan. Umkhonto was to perform sabotage, and strict instructions were given to its members right from the start, that on no account were they to injure or kill people in planning or carrying out operations. * * *

Umkhonto had its first operation on the 16th of December 1961, when Government buildings in Johannesburg, Port Elizabeth and Durban were attacked. The selection of targets is proof of the policy to which I have referred. Had we intended to attack life, we would have selected targets where people congregated and not empty buildings and power stations. * * *

* * * The response of the Africans was one of encouragement. Suddenly there was hope again. Things were happening. People in the townships became eager for political news. A great deal of enthusiasm was generated

by the initial successes, and people began to speculate on how soon freedom would be obtained.

But we in Umkhonto weighed up the whites' response with anxiety. The lines were being drawn. The whites and blacks were moving into separate camps, and the prospects of avoiding a civil war were diminishing. The white newspapers carried reports that sabotage would be punished by death. If this was so, how could we continue to keep Africans away from terrorism?

* * * By 1961 scores of Africans had died as a result of racial friction. In 1920 when the famous leader, Masabalala, was held in Port Elizabeth jail, twenty-four of a group of Africans who had gathered to demand his release were killed by the police and white civilians. More than one hundred Africans died in the Bulhoek affair. In 1924 over two hundred Africans were killed when the Administrator of South-West Africa led a force against a group which had rebelled against the imposition of dog tax. On the 1st of May 1950, eighteen Africans died as a result of police shootings during the strike. On the 21st of March 1960, sixty-nine unarmed Africans died at Sharpeville.

How many more Sharpevilles would there be in the history of our country? And how many more Sharpevilles could the country stand without violence and terror becoming the order of the day? And what would happen to our people when that stage was reached? In the long run we felt certain we must succeed, but at what cost to ourselves and the rest of the country? And if this happened, how could black and white ever live together again in peace and harmony? These were the problems that faced us, and these were our decisions.

* * * I left South Africa to proceed to [the Conference of the Pan-African Freedom Movement in] Addis Ababa as a delegate of the ANC. My tour was successful beyond all our hopes. Wherever I went I met sympathy for our cause and promises of help. All Africa was united against the stand of white South Africa, and even in London I was received with great sympathy by political leaders. * * *

I had already started to make a study of the art of war and revolution and, whilst abroad, underwent a course in military training. If there was to be guerrilla warfare, I wanted to be able to stand and fight with my people and to share the hazards of war with them. * * *

* * * On my return I found that there had been little alteration in the political scene save that the threat of a death penalty for sabotage had now become a fact. * * *

The ideological creed of the ANC is, and always has been, the creed of African Nationalism. It is not the concept of African Nationalism expressed in the cry, "Drive the White man into the sea." The African Nationalism for which the ANC stands is the concept of freedom and fulfilment for the African people in their own land. The most important political document ever adopted by the ANC is the Freedom Charter. It is by no means a blue-print for a socialist state. It calls for redistribution, but not nationalisation, of land; it provides for nationalisation of mines, banks, and monopoly industry, because monopolies, big monopolies are owned by one race only, and with-out such nationalisation racial domination would be perpetuated despite the spread of political power. * * *

Today I am attracted by the idea of a classless society, an attraction which springs in part from Marxist reading and, in part, from my admiration of the structure and organisation of early African societies in this country. The land, then the main means of production, belonged to the tribe. There was no rich or poor and there was no exploitation.

It is true, as I have already stated that I have been influenced by Marxist thought. But this is also true of many of the leaders of the new independent states. Such widely different persons as Gandhi, Nehru, Nkrumah, and Nasser all acknowledge this fact. We all accept the need for some form of socialism to enable our people to catch up with the advanced countries of the world and to overcome their legacy of extreme poverty. But this does not mean we are Marxists. * * *

* * * From my reading of Marxist literature and from conversations with Marxists, I have gained the impression that communists regard the parlia-mentary system * * * of the West as undemocratic and reactionary. But, on the contrary, I am an admirer of such a system.

The Magna Carta, the Petition of Rights, the Bill of Rights are documents which are held in veneration by democrats throughout the world. * * *

* * * Basically * * * we fight against two features which are the hallmarks of African life in South Africa and which are entrenched by legislation which we seek to have repealed. These features are poverty and lack of human dignity, and we do not need communists or so-called "agitators" to teach us about these things.

South Africa is the richest country in Africa, and could be one of the richest countries in the world. But it is a land of extremes and remarkable contrasts. The whites enjoy what may well be the highest standard of living in the world, whilst Africans live in poverty and misery. Forty per cent of the Africans live in hopelessly overcrowded and, in some cases, drought-stricken reserves, where soil erosion and the overworking of the soil makes it impossible for them to live properly off the land. Thirty per cent are labourers, labour tenants, and squatters on white farms and work and live under conditions similar to those of the serfs of the Middle Ages. The other thirty per cent live in towns where they have developed economic and social habits which bring then closer in many respects to white standards. Yet most Africans, even in this group, are impoverished by low incomes and the high cost of living.

The highest-paid and the most prosperous section of urban African life is in Johannesburg. Yet their actual position is desperate. The latest figures were given on the 25th of March 1964 by Mr. Carr, Manager of the Johannesburg Non-European Affairs Department. * * * He showed that forty-six per cent of all African families in Johannesburg do not earn enough to keep them going.

Poverty goes hand in hand with malnutrition and disease. The incidence of malnutrition and deficiency diseases is very high amongst Africans. Tuberculosis, pellagra, kwashiorkor, gastroenteritis, and scurvy bring death and destruction of health. The incidence of infant mortality is one of the highest in the world. According to the Medical Officer of Health for Pretoria, it is estimated that tuberculosis kills forty people a day, almost all Africans, and in 1961 there were 58,491 new cases reported. These diseases, My Lord, not only destroy the vital organs of the body, but they result in retarded mental conditions and lack of initiative, and reduce powers of concentration. The secondary results of such conditions affect the whole community and the standard of work performed by Africans.

The complaint of Africans, however, is not only that they are poor and whites are rich, but that the laws which are made by the whites are designed to preserve this situation.

There are two ways to break out of poverty. The first is by formal education, and the second is by the worker acquiring a greater skill at his work and thus higher wages. As far as Africans are concerned, both these avenues of advancement are deliberately curtailed by legislation.

I ask the Court to remember that the present Government has always sought to hamper Africans in their search for education. One of their early acts, after coming into power, was to stop subsidies for African school feeding. Many African children who attended schools depended on this supplement to their diet. This was a cruel act.

There is compulsory education for all white children at virtually no cost to their parents, be they rich or poor. Similar facilities are not provided for the African children, though there are some who receive such assistance.

African children, however, generally have to pay more for their schooling than whites.

According to figures quoted by the South African Institute of Race Relations in its 1963 journal, approximately forty per cent of African children in the age group between seven and fourteen do not attend school. For those who do attend school, the standards are vastly different from those afforded to white children. * * *

According to the Bantu Educational Journal, only 5,660 African children in the whole of South Africa passed their Junior Certificate in 1962, and in that year only 362 passed matric. This is presumably consistent with the policy of Bantu Education about which the present Prime Minister said, during the debate on the Bantu Education Bill in 1953 when he was Minister of Native Affairs, I quote:

"When I have control of Native Education I will reform it so that Natives will be taught from childhood to realise that equality with Europeans is not for them. People who believe in equality are not desirable teachers for Natives. When my Department controls Native education it will know for what class of higher education a Native is fitted, and whether he will have a chance in life to use his knowledge."

The other main obstacle to the economic advancement of the African is the Industrial Colour Bar under which all the better paid, better jobs of industry are reserved for whites only. Moreover, Africans in the unskilled and semi-skilled occupations which are open to them are not allowed to form trade unions which have recognition under the Industrial Conciliation Act. This means that strikes of African workers are illegal, and that they are denied the right of collective bargaining which is permitted to the better-paid white workers. The discrimination in the policy of successive South African Governments towards African workers is demonstrated by the so-called "civilized labour policy" under which sheltered, unskilled Government jobs are found for those white workers who cannot make the grade in industry, at wages * * * which far exceed the earnings of the average African employee in industry. * * *

The lack of human dignity experienced by Africans is the direct result of the policy of white supremacy. White supremacy implies black inferiority. Legislation designed to preserve white supremacy entrenches this notion. Menial tasks in South Africa are invariably performed by Africans. When anything has to be carried or cleaned the white man will look around for an African to do it for him, whether the African is employed by him or not.

Because of this sort of attitude, whites tend to regard Africans as a separate breed. They do not look upon them as people with families of their own; they do not realise that we have emotions—that we fall in love like white people do; that we want to be with our wives and children like white people want to be with theirs; that we want to earn money, enough money to support our families properly, to feed and clothe them and send them to school. And what "house-boy" or "garden-boy" or labourer can ever hope to do this?

Pass laws, which to the Africans are among the most hated bits of legislation in South Africa, render any African liable to police surveillance at any time. I doubt whether there is a single African male in South Africa who has not at some stage had a brush with the police over his pass. Hundreds and thousands of Africans are thrown into jail each year under pass laws. Even worse than this is the fact that pass laws keep husband and wife apart and lead to the breakdown of family life.

Poverty and the breakdown of family life have secondary effects. Children wander about the streets of the townships because they have no schools to go to, or no money to enable them to go to school, or no parents at home to see that they go to school, because both parents, if there be two, have to work to keep the family alive. This leads to a breakdown in moral standards, to an alarming rise in illegitimacy, and to growing violence which erupts not only politically, but everywhere. Life in the townships is dangerous. There is not a day that goes by without somebody being stabbed or assaulted. And violence is carried out of the townships into the white living areas. People are afraid to walk alone in the streets after dark. Housebreakings and robberies are increasing, despite the fact that the death sentence can now be imposed for such offences. Death sentences cannot cure the festering sore.

The only cure is to alter the conditions under which Africans are forced to live and to meet their legitimate grievances. Africans want to be paid a living wage. Africans want to perform work which they are capable of doing, and not work which the Government declares them to be capable of. We want to be allowed to live where we obtain work, and not be endorsed out of an area because we were not born there. We want to be allowed [to own our own homes] and not to be obliged to live in rented houses which we can never call our own. We want to be part of the general population, and not confined to living in our ghettoes. African men want to have their wives and children to live with them where they work, and not to be forced into an unnatural existence in men's hostels. Our women want to be with their men folk and not to be left permanently widowed in the reserves. We want to be allowed out after eleven o'clock at night and not to be confined to our rooms like little children. We want to be allowed to travel in our own country and to seek work where we want to, ∗ ∗ ∗ and not where the Labour Bureau tells us to. We want a just share in the whole of South Africa; we want security and a stake in society.

Above all, My Lord, we want equal political rights, because without them our disabilities will be permanent. I know this sounds revolutionary to the whites in this country, because the majority of voters will be Africans. This makes the white man fear democracy.

But this fear cannot be allowed to stand in the way of the only solution which will guarantee racial harmony and freedom for all. It is not true that the enfranchisement of all will result in racial domination. Political division, based on colour, is entirely artificial and, when it disappears, so will the domination of one colour group by another. The ANC has spent half a century fighting against racialism. When it triumphs as it certainly must, it will not change that policy.

This then is what the ANC is fighting. Our struggle is a truly national one. It is a struggle of the African people, inspired by our own suffering and our own experience. It is a struggle for the right to live.

During my lifetime I have dedicated my life to this struggle of the African people. I have fought against white domination, and I have fought against black domination. I have cherished the ideal of a democratic and free society in which all persons will live together in harmony and with equal opportunities. It is an ideal for which I hope to live for and to see realised. But, My Lord, if it needs be, it is an ideal for which I am prepared to die.

STUDY QUESTIONS

1. How is sabotage distinguished from other forms of violent protest?
2. How does Mandela justify taking part in acts of sabotage against the government?
3. What does Mandela mean by "white supremacy"?

■ Compare and Contrast Questions

1. Would Thoreau or King have rejected Mandela's use of violence?
2. What similarities and differences are there in Thoreau's and King's approaches to civil disobedience?
3. What similarities and differences are there in Mandela's and King's approaches to civil disobedience?

RACIAL JUSTICE

The problem of the twentieth century, says W. E. B. Du Bois, is the problem of the "color-line." The selections in this section show that the problem is still with us in the 21st century, although the picture in 1903, when Du Bois's *The Souls of Black Folk* was published, was especially bleak.

After discussing the dawning of his own feeling of being different, indeed an outcast, Du Bois introduces his important theory of double consciousness. Black people see themselves through the eyes of white people, and in the America of the time, those eyes beheld black people in contempt and pity. This becomes a primary aspect of black people's experience of life. Hence the recognition of themselves as black, in addition to their identity as American, forms a double consciousness. Yet black identity also draws on and incorporates the values of African culture, art, and history. The spiritual struggle for all black Americans is to reconcile the positive black and American aspects of their nature in order to create a new type of identity and to reach their full potential.

Du Bois notes that there had been high hopes that the ending of slavery would lead to real emancipation for black Americans. But black people remain subject to prejudice and systematic humiliation, forced into inadequate education and low-grade employment, and excluded from political power. Emancipation remains a distant goal.

In more recent decades the attempt to achieve greater racial equality has led to a number of policy initiatives in the United States, including affirmative action, which gives priority in recruitment to those of a previously disadvantaged group, especially women or those of a minority race. Elizabeth Anderson's focus is policies of affirmative action for black people in the United States in education, the workplace, and government contracting. In a systematic examination, she explores four different models of affirmative action, each with its own justifications.

The compensatory model justifies affirmative action in terms of compensation for past wrongs, while the diversity model aims to increase the range of outlooks and knowledge available to an organization. The discrimination-blocking model sees affirmative action as a response to the fact that laws against discrimination do not always manage to eliminate it, so affirmative action can be seen as a further means to end discrimination. Finally, the integrative model conceives of affirmative action as a way of integrating society and avoiding the semivoluntary segregation that often leads to race-based injustice.

Anderson argues that while the first two justifications are the best known, the last two are, in fact, stronger. The weakness of the compensatory model is that those who benefit and those who bear the cost are not generally those who were victims and perpetrators of past injustice. The diversity model works better in some areas, such as employment, than in others, such as government contracting, and thus is of limited application. But both the discrimination-blocking and the more future-oriented integrative models have considerable merit, thinks Anderson, in justifying policies of affirmative action. In particular, the integrative model aims to overcome the effects of a segregated society and to dismantle the causes of racial injustice.

A different view is taken by Shelby Steele, an African American writer and documentary filmmaker, who explains his unease with policies of affirmative action (which he also calls "racial preference") on the grounds that, despite its good intentions, it does more harm than good for the very people it is supposed to benefit. Part of Steele's argument is that affirmative action for black Americans has not shown significant benefits. As social engineering, it has failed.

Steele points out that the real aim of justice would be to develop the capacities of a formerly oppressed group so that they can compete on equal terms for desired places. Affirmative action "leaps over" the hard work, offering racial representation without racial development. Steele argues that affirmative action reinforces feelings of self-doubt or inferiority, compounding the myth of racial inferiority. On mainly white campuses, black students drop out at much higher rates than white students. Policies are needed to ensure equal opportunity and to oppose discrimination, but this is not the same as affirmative action.

Steele also argues that affirmative action encourages a victim-focused identity for black people, sending a message that what is most important about black people is what happened in the past, rather than what they can contribute now. The vital task, suggests Steele, is to root out discrimination in all its forms.

In the final selection in this section, George Yancy, an African American philosopher, interviews feminist philosopher Judith Butler, who is best known for her work on gender but has also produced important work on race. The context of the discussion is the alarming number of unarmed black men and women who have been killed by the police in recent years in the United States. In the most typical cases, a police officer, mistakenly thinking that a black person poses a threat, acts in presumed self-defense. Yet later investigation shows that the victim was unarmed, so it is assumed that an unconscious racism led the police officer to see a threat where there was none. In many cases, institutional racism leads the investigating authorities or courts to accept that the police officer acted in self-defense.

In response, a campaign has grown up around the phrase "Black Lives Matter" as a reminder that, sometimes, black people, horrifically, are treated as disposable. In the name of justice and equality, this trend must stop. The phrase also brings to mind the history of the discrimination, oppression, and maltreatment that black people have suffered in the United States and elsewhere.

Some critics think that "Black Lives Matter" implies "Black lives matter more than other lives" and hence the campaign is inflammatory and divisive. The correct slogan, some say, should be "All Lives Matter." In response, Judith Butler points out that although it is obviously true that all lives matter, the tragedy is that it has almost been forgotten that black lives fall within the scope of "all lives." Hence it is vitally important at the present time to emphasize that black lives matter, in order to correct a mistake.

Yancy and Butler go on to discuss how "whiteness" is seen as a social norm and hence blackness as a deviation or even a threat. Whiteness represents not merely the color of some people's skin but a social power: a practice of superiority over minorities, which can reinforce inequality and diminish the standing of black people. It is this set of assumptions that is so damaging to black people in many aspects of their lives, including black women and girls who, historically, have disproportionately been victims of harassment and violence. Butler calls for a cross-race struggle against racism to establish the point that all lives do indeed matter.

W. E. B. DU BOIS
The Souls of Black Folk

W. E. B. Du Bois (1868–1963) was a highly influential African American philosopher and the author of many important works, including The Souls of Black Folk *(1903), from which this extract is taken.*

Herein lie buried many things which if read with patience may show the strange meaning of being black here in the dawning of the Twentieth Century. This meaning is not without interest to you, Gentle Reader; for the problem of the Twentieth Century is the problem of the color-line. * * *

Between me and the other world there is ever an unasked question: unasked by some through feelings of delicacy; by others through the difficulty of rightly framing it. All, nevertheless, flutter round it. They approach me in a half-hesitant sort of way, eye me curiously or compassionately, and then, instead of saying directly, How does it feel to be a problem? they say, I know an excellent colored man in my town; or, I fought at Mechanicsville; or, Do not these Southern outrages make your blood boil? At these I smile, or am interested, or reduce the boiling to a simmer, as the occasion may require. To the real question, How does it feel to be a problem? I answer seldom a word.

And yet, being a problem is a strange experience,—peculiar even for one who has never been anything else, save perhaps in babyhood and in Europe. It is in the early days of rollicking boyhood that the revelation first bursts upon one, all in a day, as it were. I remember well when the shadow swept across me. I was a little thing, away up in the hills of New England, where the dark Housatonic winds between Hoosac and Taghkanic to the sea. In a wee wooden schoolhouse, something put it into the boys' and girls' heads to buy gorgeous visiting-cards—ten cents a package—and exchange. The exchange was merry, till one girl, a tall newcomer, refused my card,—refused it peremptorily, with a glance. Then it dawned upon me with a certain suddenness that I was different from the others; or like, mayhap, in heart and life and longing, but shut out from their world by a vast veil. I had thereafter no desire to tear down that veil, to creep through; I held all beyond it in common contempt, and lived above it in a region of blue sky and great wandering shadows. That sky was bluest when I could beat my mates at examination-time, or beat them at a foot-race, or even beat their stringy heads. Alas, with the years all this fine contempt began to fade; for the worlds I longed for, and all their dazzling opportunities, were theirs, not mine. But they should not keep these prizes, I said; some, all, I would wrest from them. Just how I would do it I could never decide: by reading law, by healing the sick, by telling the wonderful tales that swam in my head,—some way. With other black boys the strife was not so fiercely sunny: their youth shrunk into tasteless sycophancy, or into silent hatred of the pale world about them and mocking distrust of everything white; or wasted itself in a bitter cry, Why did God make me an outcast and a stranger in mine own house? The shades of the prison-house closed round about us all: walls strait and stubborn to the whitest, but relentlessly narrow, tall, and unscalable to sons of night who must plod darkly on in resignation, or beat unavailing palms against the stone, or steadily, half hopelessly, watch the streak of blue above.

After the Egyptian and Indian, the Greek and Roman, the Teuton and Mongolian, the Negro is a sort of seventh son, born with a veil, and gifted with second-sight in this American world,—a world which yields him no true self-consciousness, but only lets him see himself through the revelation of the other world. It is a peculiar sensation, this double-consciousness, this sense of always looking at one's self through the eyes of others, of measuring one's soul by the tape of a world that looks on in amused contempt and pity. One ever feels his two-ness,—an American, a Negro; two souls, two thoughts, two unreconciled strivings; two warring ideals in one dark body, whose dogged strength alone keeps it from being torn asunder.

The history of the American Negro is the history of this strife,—this longing to attain self-conscious manhood, to merge his double self into a better and truer self. In this merging he wishes neither of the older selves to be lost. He would not Africanize America, for America has too much to teach the world and Africa. He would not bleach his Negro soul in a flood of white Americanism, for he knows that Negro blood has a message for the world. He simply wishes to make it possible for a man to be both a Negro and an American, without being cursed and spit upon by his fellows, without having the doors of Opportunity closed roughly in his face.

This, then, is the end of his striving: to be a co-worker in the kingdom of culture, to escape both death and isolation, to husband and use his best powers and his latent genius. These powers of body and mind have in the past been strangely wasted, dispersed, or forgotten. The shadow of a mighty Negro past flits through the tale of Ethiopia the Shadowy and of Egypt the Sphinx. Throughout history, the powers of single black men flash here and there like falling stars, and die sometimes before the world has rightly gauged their brightness. Here in America, in the few days since Emancipation, the black man's turning hither and thither in hesitant and doubtful striving has often made his very strength to lose effectiveness, to seem like absence of power, like weakness. And yet it is not weakness,—it is the contradiction of double aims. The double-aimed struggle of the black artisan— on the one hand to escape white contempt for a nation of mere hewers of wood and drawers of water, and on the other hand to plough and nail and dig for a poverty-stricken horde—could only result in making him a poor craftsman, for he had but half a heart in either cause. By the poverty and ignorance of his people, the Negro minister or doctor was tempted toward quackery and demagogy; and by the criticism of the other world, toward ideals that made him ashamed of his lowly tasks. The would-be black *savant* was confronted by the paradox that the knowledge his people needed was a twice-told tale to his white neighbors, while the knowledge which would teach the white world was Greek to his own flesh and blood. The innate love of harmony and beauty that set the ruder souls of his people a-dancing and a-singing raised but confusion and doubt in the soul of the black artist; for the beauty revealed to him was the soul-beauty of a race which his larger audience despised, and he could not articulate the message of another people. This waste of double aims, this seeking to satisfy two unreconciled ideals, has wrought sad havoc with the courage and faith and deeds of ten thousand thousand people,—has sent them often wooing false gods and invoking false means of salvation, and at times has even seemed about to make them ashamed of themselves.

Away back in the days of bondage they thought to see in one divine event the end of all doubt and disappointment; few men ever worshipped Freedom with half such unquestioning faith as did the American Negro for two centuries. To him, so far as he thought and dreamed, slavery was indeed the sum of all villainies, the cause of all sorrow, the root of all prejudice; Emancipation was the key to a promised land of sweeter beauty than ever stretched before the eyes of wearied Israelites. In song and exhortation swelled one refrain—Liberty; in his tears and curses the God he implored had Freedom in his right hand. At last it came,—suddenly, fearfully, like a dream. With one wild carnival of blood and passion came the message in his own plaintive cadences:—

> *"Shout, O children!*
> *Shout, you're free!*
> *For God has bought your liberty!"*

Years have passed away since then,—ten, twenty, forty; forty years of national life, forty years of renewal and development, and yet the swarthy spectre sits in its accustomed seat at the Nation's feast. In vain do we cry to this our vastest social problem:—

> *"Take any shape but that, and my firm nerves*
> *Shall never tremble!"*

The Nation has not yet found peace from its sins; the freedman has not yet found in freedom his promised land. Whatever of good may have come in these years of change, the shadow of a deep disappointment rests upon the Negro people,—a disappointment all the more bitter because the unattained ideal was unbounded save by the simple ignorance of a lowly people.

The first decade was merely a prolongation of the vain search for freedom, the boon that seemed ever barely to elude their grasp,—like a tantalizing will-o'-the-wisp, maddening and misleading the headless host. The holocaust of war, the terrors of the Ku-Klux Klan, the lies of carpet-baggers, the disorganization of industry, and the contradictory advice of friends and foes, left the bewildered serf with no new watch-word beyond the old cry for freedom. As the time flew, however, he began to grasp a new idea. The ideal of liberty demanded for its attainment powerful means, and these the Fifteenth Amendment gave him. The ballot, which before he had looked upon as a visible sign of freedom, he now regarded as the chief means of gaining and perfecting the liberty with which war had partially endowed him. And why not? Had not votes made war and emancipated millions? Had not votes enfranchised the freedmen? Was anything impossible to a power that had done all this? A million black men started with renewed zeal to vote themselves into the kingdom. So the decade flew away, the revolution of 1876 came, and left the half-free serf weary, wondering, but still inspired. Slowly but steadily, in the following years, a new vision began gradually to replace the dream of political power,—a powerful movement, the rise of another ideal to guide the unguided, another pillar of fire by night after a clouded day. It was the ideal of "book-learning"; the curiosity, born of compulsory ignorance, to know and test the power of the cabalistic letters of the white man, the longing to know. Here at last seemed to have been discovered the mountain path to Canaan; longer than the highway of Emancipation and law, steep and rugged, but straight, leading to heights high enough to overlook life.

Up the new path the advance guard toiled, slowly, heavily, doggedly; only those who have watched and guided the faltering feet, the misty minds, the dull understandings, of the dark pupils of these schools know how faithfully, how piteously, this people strove to learn. It was weary work. The cold statistician wrote down the inches of progress here and there, noted also where here and there a foot had slipped or some one had fallen. To the tired climbers, the horizon was ever dark, the mists were often cold, the Canaan was always dim and far away. If, however, the vistas disclosed as yet no goal, no resting-place, little but flattery and criticism, the journey at least gave leisure for reflection and self-examination; it changed the child of Emancipation to the youth with dawning self-consciousness, self-realization, self-respect. In those sombre forests of his striving his own soul rose before him, and he saw himself,—darkly as through a veil; and yet he saw in himself some faint revelation of his power, of his mission. He began to have a dim feeling that, to attain his place in the world, he must be himself, and not another. For the first time he sought to analyze the burden he bore upon his back, that dead-weight of social degradation partially masked behind a half-named Negro problem. He felt his poverty; without a cent, without a home, without land, tools, or savings, he had entered into competition with rich, landed, skilled neighbors. To be a poor man is hard, but to be a poor race in a land of dollars is the very bottom of hardships. He felt the weight of his ignorance,—not simply of letters, but of life, of business, of the humanities; the accumulated sloth and shirking and awkwardness of decades and centuries shackled his hands and feet. Nor was his burden all poverty and ignorance. The red stain of bastardy, which two centuries of systematic legal defilement of Negro women had stamped upon his race, meant not only the loss of ancient African chastity, but also the hereditary weight of a mass of corruption from white adulterers, threatening almost the obliteration of the Negro home.

A people thus handicapped ought not to be asked to race with the world, but rather allowed to give all its time and thought to its own social problems. But alas! while sociologists gleefully count his bastards and his prostitutes, the very soul of the toiling, sweating black man is darkened by the shadow of a vast despair. Men call the shadow prejudice, and learnedly explain it as the natural defence of culture against barbarism, learning against ignorance, purity against crime, the "higher" against the "lower" races. To which the Negro cries Amen! and swears that to so much of this strange prejudice as is founded on just homage to civilization, culture, righteousness, and prog-ress, he humbly bows and meekly does obeisance. But before that nameless prejudice that leaps beyond all this he stands helpless, dismayed, and well-nigh speechless; before that personal disrespect and mockery, the ridicule and systematic humiliation, the distortion of fact and wanton license of fancy, the cynical ignoring of the better and the boisterous welcoming of the worse, the all-pervading desire to inculcate disdain for everything black, from Toussaint to the devil,—before this there rises a sickening despair that would disarm and discourage any nation save that black host to whom "discouragement" is an unwritten word.

But the facing of so vast a prejudice could not but bring the inevitable self-questioning, self-disparagement, and lowering of ideals which ever accompany repression and breed in an atmosphere of contempt and hate. Whisperings and portents came borne upon the four winds: Lo! we are diseased and dying, cried the dark hosts; we cannot write, our voting is vain; what need of education, since we must always cook and serve? And the Nation echoed and enforced this self-criticism, saying: Be content to be servants, and nothing more; what need of higher culture for half-men? Away with the black man's ballot, by force or fraud,—and behold the suicide of a race! Nevertheless, out of the evil came something of good,—the more careful adjustment of education to real life, the clearer perception of the Negroes' social responsibilities, and the sobering realization of the meaning of progress.

So dawned the time of *Sturm und Drang:* storm and stress to-day rocks our little boat on the mad waters of the world-sea; there is within and without the sound of conflict, the burning of body and rending of soul; inspiration strives with doubt, and faith with vain questionings. The bright ideals of the past,—physical freedom, political power, the training of brains and the training of hands,—all these in turn have waxed and waned, until even the last grows dim and overcast. Are they all wrong,—all false? No, not that, but each alone was over-simple and incomplete,—the dreams of a credulous race-childhood, or the fond imaginings of the other world which does not know and does not want to know our power. To be really true, all these ideals must be melted and welded into one. The training of the schools we need to-day more than ever,—the training of deft hands, quick eyes and ears, and above all the broader, deeper, higher culture of gifted minds and pure hearts. The power of the ballot we need in sheer self-defence,—else what shall save us from a second slavery? Freedom, too, the long-sought, we still seek,—the freedom of life and limb, the freedom to work and think, the freedom to love and aspire. Work, culture, liberty,—all these we need, not singly but together, not successively but together, each growing and aiding each, and all striving toward that vaster ideal that swims before the Negro people, the ideal of human brotherhood, gained through the unifying ideal of Race; the ideal of fostering and developing the traits and talents of the Negro, not in opposition to or contempt for other races, but rather in large conformity to the greater ideals of the American Republic, in order that some day on American soil two world-races may give each to each those characteristics both so sadly lack. We the darker ones come even now not altogether empty-handed: there are to-day no truer exponents of the pure human spirit of the Declaration of Independence than the American Negroes; there is no true American music but the wild sweet melodies of the Negro slave; the American fairy tales and folk-lore are Indian and African; and, all in all, we black men seem the sole oasis of simple faith and reverence in a dusty desert of dollars and smartness. Will America be poorer if she replace her brutal dyspeptic blundering with light-hearted but determined Negro humility? or her coarse and cruel wit with loving jovial good-humor? or her vulgar music with the soul of the Sorrow Songs?

Merely a concrete test of the underlying principles of the great republic is the Negro Problem, and the spiritual striving of the freedmen's sons is the travail of souls whose burden is almost beyond the measure of their strength, but who bear it in the name of an historic race, in the name of this the land of their fathers' fathers, and in the name of human opportunity.

STUDY QUESTIONS

1. Why does Du Bois say that the problem of the 20th century is the problem of the color-line?
2. What does Du Bois mean by "double consciousness"?
3. Why didn't the abolition of slavery lead to genuine emancipation?

ELIZABETH ANDERSON
Racial Integration Remains an Imperative

Elizabeth Anderson (b. 1959) is a contemporary philosopher known for her contributions to political philosophy, feminist philosophy, and philosophy of race.

FOUR MODELS OF AFFIRMATIVE ACTION

By "affirmative action," I refer to any policy that aims to increase the participation of a disadvantaged social group in mainstream institutions, either through "outreach" (targeting the group for publicity and invitations to participate) or "preference" (using group membership as criteria for selecting participants). In the United States, affirmative action is practiced in three domains: employment, education, and government contracting.

This chapter compares four models of race-based affirmative action in the United States: compensatory, diversity, discrimination-blocking, and integrative. The compensatory model represents racial preferences as a way to compensate for the effects of past discrimination. Since blacks have suffered discrimination, they are entitled to compensation in the form of access to the opportunities that discrimination has unjustly denied them. Compensatory affirmative action is backward looking: it aims to restore justice by undoing wrongs of the past. * * *

The diversity model represents racial preferences as a means to increase the cultural and epistemic diversity of the institution practicing it. In this view, blacks, by virtue of their historical and cultural differences from other groups, have diverse ideas and perspectives from other racial groups. This epistemic diversity enriches the educational mission of schools, the public discourse needed to advance democracy, and the ability of corporations to design and market products and services that appeal to diverse consumers. This is a present-oriented and forward-looking rationale: it views the participation of racially diverse individuals as advancing institutional objectives. * * *

The discrimination-blocking model represents affirmative action as a tool for counteracting continuing discrimination. It is founded on the fact that, without pressure on institutions to meet race-conscious goals, antidiscrimination laws fail to produce race-neutral hiring and promotion in the face of entrenched and often unconscious discriminatory habits. This is a present-oriented rationale: hiring goals and timetables are means to force institutions to stop discriminating. * * *

The integrative model represents racial preferences as a means to racially integrate the main institutions of civil society. Segregation is the linchpin of unjust systematic race-based disadvantage because it blocks blacks' access to public and consumer goods, employment, and financial, human, social, and cultural capital and causes pervasive antiblack racial stigmatization and discrimination. Integration helps dismantle these underlying causes of race-based injustice. Integration is also needed to advance a democratic culture, by providing opportunities for citizens from all walks of life to communicate on matters of public interest, forge cooperative relationships, and construct an integrated collective identity, and to advance democratic governance, by creating an integrated and thereby more competent and accountable elite, better disposed and able to honor the rights and serve the interests of all members of society, regardless of their group identities. This is a forward-looking rationale: it views the integration of mainstream institutions as essential to advancing justice and democracy. * * *

Public discourse about affirmative action is dominated by the compensatory and diversity models. The discrimination-blocking and integrative models are not well understood. I shall argue that the latter models have several virtues not shared by the former: they better fit the practice of affirmative action, do not foster racial myths or lend themselves to stigmatizing interpretations, do a better job explaining the continuing causes of race-based disadvantage, and answer or avoid the objections that undermine the other two models.

Affirmative action enjoys strong elite support. ∗ ∗ ∗ Yet affirmative action is in peril. ∗ ∗ ∗ Advancing a better rationale for affirmative action will not by itself overcome popular opposition. The integrationist rationale predicts that opposition will be overcome mainly through practical experience with integration, not through abstract arguments. Nevertheless, a policy under popular assault in a democracy is at additional risk if its practitioners do not fully grasp the principles that make sense of it, if their rationales feed racial myths and stigmas, if they fail to educate the population about the continuing causes of race-based disadvantage, and if they have only weak answers to fundamental objections.

THE COMPENSATORY MODEL

Every model of race-based affirmative action offers an account of its purpose, which determines (1) which agents may practice affirmative action, (2) who should be a targeted beneficiary, and why, (3) how much weight may be given to group preferences, (4) who should bear the costs of affirmative action, and (5) the meaning and relevance of race to the purpose of affirmative action. In addition, if the model is based on considerations of justice, it also presupposes (6) an account of the causes of race-based injustice.

The compensatory rationale typically draws on an individualized model of compensatory justice. In this model, if a person has suffered from wrongdoing, she is entitled to compensation from the wrongdoer, to the extent of the damages the wrong inflicted on her. This implies that (1) the agents who should practice affirmative action are those who had previously engaged in racial discrimination; (2) the beneficiaries are targeted by virtue of being the victims of past racial discrimination by the agents; (3) they should be compensated to the extent of the harm they suffered, and (4) the agents who had engaged in discrimination should bear the costs. Membership in a disadvantaged racial group is a relevant basis for targeting beneficiaries for affirmative action, on the assumption that (5) membership serves as an accurate proxy for the morally relevant characteristic of having been victimized by racial discrimination. This model supposes that (6) past racial discrimination is the main cause of current race-based injustice.

Critics object that the practice of affirmative action does not fit the compensatory rationale very well. Schools, government bodies, and employers practice affirmative action even if they have not been found guilty of discrimination. They do not attempt to identify and compensate the victims of their own discrimination but target their benefits to others on the basis of their shared racial identity with those presumed to be victims of their own or others' discrimination. They do not adjust the degree of benefit to any measure of damages that targets suffered from discrimination. Those who bear the costs of the policy are not its practitioners, but innocent whites and Asians who are displaced by racial preferences. Finally, race is an imperfect proxy for victimization-by-discrimination. It is overinclusive, in selecting some individuals in the target groups who have not experienced discrimination, and underinclusive, in excluding individuals outside the targeted groups who have suffered discrimination.

Because affirmative action fails to meet the exacting standards of individualized remedies, the compensatory model is sometimes cast in terms of group compensation. In this view, society is fundamentally divided into racial groups who constitute the relevant units of moral agency and considerability. A discriminatory act by one white constitutes whites as a debtor class, creating a group obligation to compensate that could be discharged by any other white. A discriminatory injury to any black constitutes blacks as a creditor class, creating a group entitlement in which an injury to one black can be made up by a preference to any other. This group model does a better job fitting the practice of affirmative action to a rationale. But it is unacceptable. Individuals, not racial groups, are the relevant units of moral entitlement. In addition, the group rationale advances a divisive conception of society that undermines the democratic aspiration to unite all citizens under a common identity.

The compensatory model must therefore address the objections lodged against it within an individualist conception of justice. Start with the agents practicing affirmative action. Whether an agent has discriminated in the past is relevant only to the question of whether they are *obligated* to compensate, not whether they are *permitted* to do so. There is nothing morally objectionable about an agent compensating for damage caused by others' wrongdoing. Americans committed no wrong in donating money to help the victims of 9/11.

Now consider the targets of affirmative action and the amount of their damages. The individualized ideal of case-by-case adjudication makes little sense where it is known that there are victims, but it is too costly, difficult, or impossible to precisely identify who they are or how much they were damaged. Individuals usually do not know whether a particular agent has discriminated against them because they do not know how that agent has treated others. Moreover, people have a cognitive bias against seeing themselves as victims, even when they know they belong to a group often subject to discrimination. Discriminating agents also may not know who their victims are. A firm notorious for discrimination cannot know who was discouraged from applying for a job because they knew they would get no consideration. A firm that publicizes job openings only to its all-white staff may know that no blacks will learn of its opportunities. But there is no answer to the question of which blacks would have applied, had the firm adopted a nondiscriminatory publicity policy. There are many fair policies it could have adopted, each of which would have led to a different black applicant pool.

In such cases, we know that people have been unjustly disadvantaged because of their race but we cannot identify who they are. Many discriminatory policies inflict their damage probabilistically, like air pollution. In pollution cases, that the causal connection is statistical and not provable in any single instance does not undermine the case for compensation in a class action suit. Racial discrimination often works the same way and is often similarly settled under Title VII of the 1964 Civil Rights Act through class actions that offer affirmative action as a remedy.

The "innocent white" objection to who bears the costs of affirmative action also has little normative force. Some defenders of affirmative action argue that whites enjoy unjust enrichment, in the form of competitive advantages due to past antiblack discrimination, and thus have no valid complaint against affirmative action programs that take this advantage away from them. I am disinclined to press this divisive argument. It is enough to observe that *all* compensatory projects undertaken by corporate bodies place burdens on innocents. Whenever a corporation helps the victims of some wrongdoing, the costs are borne by innocent individuals who are or would like to be associated with it. Firms that offered jobs as compensation to the survivors of 9/11 victims denied these jobs to other innocent job applicants. We observe no protests about such compensatory acts, nor should we.

The "innocent white" objection also neglects the fact that as long as discrimination or its effects persist, there will be innocent victims suffering unjust burdens. The only question is whether these burdens should be borne exclusively by disadvantaged racial groups or more widely shared. There is no injustice in sharing the costs of widespread injustice. A main point of government is to share the costs of injustice by sharing the costs of protection from and punishment of crime. That one has neither committed nor benefited from any crime constitutes no claim against paying the taxes used to help the victims of crime.

These considerations support a compensatory model of race-based affirmative action as a kind of "rough justice." * * *

Thus, the compensatory model of affirmative action can be defended against common objections. Yet it suffers from an inadequate conception of the wrongs its beneficiaries suffer. In focusing on past discrimination, it suggests that discrimination is only in the past, and that current group disadvantage consists only of the inherited effects of past events. This inspires impatience about the continuation of the policy once antidiscrimination laws have been in place for decades since it does not explain why the current beneficiaries of affirmative action have been unable to overcome the legacy of discrimination against their ancestors, unlike many groups, such as Asians and Irish, who have suffered severe discrimination in the past.

The compensatory model also does not offer a satisfactory explanation of why affirmative action, which is practiced only by selective colleges, large corporations, and governments, is an appropriate form of compensation. It benefits only a small proportion of the members of such groups, often the best-off among them—those who already have enough education to handle the work at a selective college, enough qualifications to function in a corporate job, and enough assets to own a business capable of executing government contracts. Rough compensatory justice would be better served if we distributed lump-sum cash reparations to every member of the disadvantaged group, or concentrated compensation on the least well-off within the group.

Finally, the compensatory model offers an inadequate conception of the role of beneficiaries in the institutions practicing affirmative action. They are represented as passive victims of injustice, rather than as active contributors whose participation contributes to the mission of these institutions. This representation feeds stigmatizing thoughts that affirmative action's beneficiaries are not pulling their own weight in these institutions, that they do not deserve to be there, and that they lack real merit.

An adequate, nonstigmatizing conception of the beneficiaries of affirmative action would represent them as meritorious, as contributing to the missions of participating institutions through the roles they occupy. It would explain why, within the targeted classes, affirmative action often prefers the relatively more advantaged—those *least* injured by past discrimination. It would not locate the rationale for affirmative action in fast-receding events of the past, but in present- and future-oriented concerns. The diversity model of affirmative action meets these criteria.

THE DIVERSITY MODEL

The diversity model represents affirmative action as promoting a "robust exchange of ideas." In this model, (1) the institutions eligible to practice affirmative action are those whose mission would profit from a greater diversity of ideas brought by participants. (2) The targeted beneficiaries should be members of any group that would contribute to the epistemic diversity of the institution. (3) The weight given to preferences for including members from any group should be proportional to the diversity of ideas they bring, and inversely proportional to the degree to which they are already represented. (4) Those who should bear the costs of affirmative action are those whose perspectives and ideas are already well represented in the institution. (5) Race is presumed relevant to diversity because it is viewed as a proxy for possession of ideas distinct from well-represented groups. Finally, (6) individuals are targeted by affirmative action not to remedy injustice, but to advance the missions of the institutions that practice it.

The diversity model answers the surviving objections against the compensatory model. It is future-oriented, locating the point of affirmative action in continuing institutional needs for epistemic diversity rather than in receding events that, over time, lose their claim on how current institutions should be structured. It explains why affirmative action favors the more advantaged members of targeted groups. To effectively contribute to epistemic diversity, the beneficiaries must be otherwise qualified to perform up to the institution's standards. The more advantaged within the targeted groups possess those qualifications to a greater degree. The diversity model offers a nonstigmatizing account of why members of targeted racial groups are preferred: they bring valuable features to the institution—epistemic diversity—that advance the institution's mission. This is a meritocratic rationale, which represents the targets of affirmative action as contributing, deserving agents rather than as pitiful subjects of an institution's beneficence. It gives other participants positive reasons to value the presence of affirmative action's beneficiaries.

Yet the diversity model, when divorced from the aims of social justice, suffers from several flaws. First, its rationale does not fit the *scope* of the practice. It best suits educational institutions and the award of broadcast licenses. It can be extended to certain jobs that deal with producing new ideas and marketing products and services to diverse populations. It is harder to justify diversity-based affirmative action in employment for routinized blue- and pink-collar jobs that do not ask their occupants to contribute ideas, or for enterprises that produce undifferentiated commodities such as oil and coal, or undifferentiated services such as driving a bus or delivering mail. The diversity model seems inapplicable to much government contracting: it is hard to see how having a diverse set of subcontractors improves a road-building project. It even has a hard time explaining the scope of racial preferences by educational institutions. While it is plausible that the racial diversity of a classroom would enhance discussion of social, political, and cultural subjects by enriching the variety of perspectives, it is hard to see the cognitive relevance of racial diversity to investigations in mathematics, engineering, or the physical sciences. Yet schools extend racial preferences in admission to graduate programs in the latter fields.

Second, the diversity model, when separated from considerations of justice, cannot account for the special *weight* institutions give to race compared to other dimensions of diversity. In principle, race should figure no more than other background factors that affect a person's perspective, such as practicing an unusual religion, having lived abroad, or having grown up on a farm. In practice, schools give race enough weight to produce a "critical mass" of students from disadvantaged racial groups but are satisfied with mere token representation of people with other unusual backgrounds. The special weight given to admitting U.S. citizens from disadvantaged racial groups is even stranger. Blacks in the United States are as American as apple pie: they bring less cultural diversity to American schools than blacks, Asians, and Latinos from abroad and are already more heavily represented than the latter in most schools. Yet schools still place greater weight on admitting American blacks than the latter groups.

Third, the diversity model, when separated from justice concerns, promotes racial myths that may be stigmatizing. In stressing how different African Americans are from other Americans, it potentially primes stereotypes of blacks as alien and blocks recognition of common perspectives and identities. To the extent that it avoids issues of social justice, treats racial groups on a par with cultural groups, and refuses to specify precisely what kind of diversity race brings to the table, the diversity model invites the inference that the diversity represented by race is a matter of racially distinct cultures. Yet "race" denotes an identity group, a social category that has been made the basis of social inequality by means of in-group closure and out-group stigmatization. This is not the same as a cultural group. To suppose otherwise invites several potentially injurious ideas. In searching for the supposedly cultural content of black difference, people are liable to fix on stigmatizing representations of blacks in the folk anthropological account of black disadvantage, attributing such "underclass" behavior as gang membership, criminal conduct, welfare dependence, disdain for "acting white," and single teenage childbearing as cultural values of the black community. Blacks who do not conform to these stereotypes may thereby appear to be not "diverse" enough to satisfy the diversity model, while those who behave in ways that trigger these stereotypes (say, in listening to gangsta rap or wearing dreadlocks) may appear to lack the values needed to succeed in mainstream institutions and hence seem unqualified to participate. The multiculturalist account of diversity also suggests that all "cultural" differences ought to be celebrated and preserved. This thought undermines the quest for racial equality insofar as it insists on self-segregation within mainstream institutions for the sake of cultural preservation, and on the preservation of distinct forms of cultural capital, when black advancement requires social integration and the construction of common forms of cultural capital. Finally, the representation of the difference blacks make to institutions as "cultural" invites the misleading thought that "all blacks think alike."

The last thought misunderstands how the logic of diversity works. ⁎ ⁎ ⁎ The diversity defense says not that all blacks think alike, but that blacks have a range of diverse experiences and perspectives not well represented by the range of experiences and perspectives of members in other groups. This claim is hard to square with a cultural representation of the relevance of race. Cultures are understood, at least within folk anthropology, as shared, and hence as bases of in-group homogeneity. What is needed is an account of the difference race makes that is not cultural in this sense.

A fourth objection to the diversity model is that, in treating race as a proxy for relevant features—diversity of ideas and perspectives—it has a hard time explaining why institutions should not select directly for diverse ideas. If all that matters is that the whole range of ideas worth considering should be heard, why care about the racial identities of those who voice them? Schools should simply select students for ideological diversity, rather than using race as a crude proxy for this. Furthermore, if diversity of ideas is all that matters, why do we need the actual presence of racially diverse persons in schools? Why can't instructors and reading assignments represent all the diversity of information and opinion students need? * * *

An adequate model of affirmative action would explain the full scope and weight given to race in the institutions that practice it. * * *

THE DISCRIMINATION-BLOCKING MODEL

The discrimination-blocking model of affirmative action focuses on the practical difficulties of stopping current discrimination in a world saturated with stigmatizing stereotypes of disadvantaged groups and structured by entrenched habits that favor advantaged groups. To remedy this problem, merely passing antidiscrimination laws is insufficient to stop discrimination. Affirmative action is needed. In this model (1) the agents eligible to practice affirmative action are any institutions that are still discriminating. (2) The targets of affirmative action are qualified members of disadvantaged groups who would not gain access to opportunities in the absence of affirmative action. (3) Discrimination-blocking programs generally allow only "tie-breaking" preferences for members of disadvantaged groups. (4) The costs to innocents are very small since racial preferences that override meritocratic criteria are generally not involved. (5) Race, in the discrimination-blocking model, helps identify those who, but for affirmative action, would be victims of ongoing discrimination. (6) The discrimination-blocking model represents *current* discrimination as the fundamental cause of unjust race-based disadvantage.

The discrimination-blocking model arose from the experience of administrative agencies charged with enforcing antidiscrimination laws. They found that after the passage of antidiscrimination laws, nothing changed. Employers continued to discriminate, and members of groups suffering from discrimination made virtually no inroads into occupations and businesses that had been excluding them. * * *

Why does discrimination persist, despite antidiscrimination laws? Whenever the law has attempted to dismantle antiblack segregation and discrimination, it has met with massive resistance from recalcitrant whites. This was true for abolition, voting rights, school desegregation, and housing desegregation. It is true for equal employment opportunity as well. When recalcitrant actors repeatedly refuse to stop discriminating, antidiscrimination law must force outcomes on them that mirror what nondiscriminatory processes would produce. * * *

Discriminatory habits and unconscious evaluative biases can be somewhat offset by group-blind policies that reduce the scope for such biases to operate. Employers can advertise jobs formally, in places excluded groups regularly consult, abolish interviews, and "blind" job applications. They can formalize objective criteria for hiring, firing, and promotion, and reject subjective criteria that leave room for evaluative bias and aversive discrimination. They can create formal promotion ladders linking jobs. Affirmative action policies typically incorporate such group-blind measures.

Yet such measures are not sufficient to eliminate discrimination, especially if it is unconscious. Race can be inferred from many factors, such as applicants' addresses, association memberships, letters of recommendation, schools attended, and vocal signs recognized over the phone. Internal promotion decisions usually cannot be blinded and often rely on softer criteria that cannot be fully shielded from evaluation biases. Because biases can insinuate themselves at many points, formalized group-conscious measurement of outcomes is needed to ensure that discrimination has really ended. Hence, affirmative action programs typically include regular monitoring of employment practices to check for unexplained group disparities. * * *

Critics of discrimination-blocking race-conscious affirmative action goals also complain that they lead to reverse discrimination. Although there are some highly publicized cases—for instance, female firefighters—in which qualifying criteria have been substantially relaxed for traditionally excluded groups—the vast majority of employer-based affirmative action plans apply the same hiring and promotion criteria for members of all groups. Neither the purpose nor the result of affirmative action pressure in most employment contexts has been to override meritocratic criteria. Individuals hired or promoted under affirmative action programs perform as well as other employees. Private, for-profit establishments that employ more blacks do not suffer lower productivity than establishments with fewer black employees. Only a handful of reverse discrimination claims have been found credible in the courts. * * *

The discrimination-blocking model is indispensable to understanding how affirmative action operates in employment contexts. It introduces no novel or controversial moral principles. It simply requires recognition of the difficulty of avoiding discrimination in contexts organized around discriminatory habits and pervaded by group stigmatization. In the absence of concerned pressure to produce results, discrimination continues to undermine opportunities for stigmatized groups. Discrimination-blocking affirmative action is simply an application of Aristotle's point that to do the right thing in the face of a contrary inclination, we must drag ourselves in the opposite direction. * * *

Although indispensable, the discrimination-blocking model offers an incomplete rationale for affirmative action. * * * A more future-oriented rationale is needed—one that represents affirmative action as dismantling the continuing causes of discrimination, rather than simply opposing it with a countervailing force. The discrimination-blocking model also offers an incomplete account of current obstacles to equal opportunity: it focuses only on current discrimination, not on segregation and the lingering effects of past discrimination. This defect is particularly significant for affirmative action in higher education. Human capital deficits are among the stubborn legacies of historic discrimination, perpetuated by continuing segregation. To correct for these deficits, selective educational institutions that practice affirmative action give a weight to race that exceeds what can be justified on a discrimination-blocking model. To justify this weight, we need to resort to compensatory or integrative models of affirmative action.

THE INTEGRATIVE MODEL

The integrative model of affirmative action begins with the observation that Americans live in a profoundly racially segregated society. De facto racial segregation unjustly impedes socioeconomic opportunities for disadvantaged racial groups, causes racial stigmatization and discrimination, and is inconsistent with a fully democratic society. To remedy these problems, we need to practice racial integration. In this model, (1) the agents eligible to practice affirmative action are any institutions capable of promoting racial integration. (2) The targets of affirmative action are those individuals best placed to act as agents of racial integration. (3) The weight given to preferences for admitting these targets depends on how much integration is needed for its positive effects to be realized. I shall argue below that this justifies seeking a critical mass of any segregated and stigmatized racial group. (4) Since all citizens have a duty to promote the justice of social arrangements, and integration is instrumental to justice, it is just to expect all citizens to bear their fair share of the costs of integration. (5) Race, in the integrative model, is not a proxy for some other relevant characteristics but directly relevant to the integrative mission of affirmative action. (6) The integrative model represents racial segregation and stigmatization as the fundamental causes of unjust race-based disadvantage, treating discrimination as but one consequence of stigmatization. Affirmative action is a tool for dismantling the continuing causes of unjust race-based disadvantage. It offers a comprehensive defense of affirmative action that fits the practice and meets or avoids the objections against the other three models. ∗ ∗ ∗

Integration ∗ ∗ ∗ has distinct roles to play in particular domains. For professional schools, affirmative action helps remedy the severe deficit residents of segregated neighborhoods suffer in access to professional services. Black physicians are far more likely than white physicians to locate in underserved minority neighborhoods and serve far more black, Latino, and Medicaid patients, even after controlling for their location. For routinized, unskilled jobs, affirmative action ensures that blacks are not always in the back of the employment queue for lack of social connections. For government contracting, affirmative action promotes the acquisition of social, cultural, and human capital on the part of business owners from disadvantaged segregated groups, increases employment for racial groups suffering from high rates of unemployment, and provides its beneficiaries with experience working for racially diverse clients. In the case of black-owned businesses, the latter functions are particularly important because of the strong relation between the race of owners and the race of their employees. ∗ ∗ ∗ Such programs also promote integration, by connecting black-owned businesses to a wider, racially diverse customer base.

The integrative model offers a nonstigmatizing representation of affirmative action's targets. It identifies the proper targets of affirmative action as those who can function as agents of integration and destigmatization. They are not passive recipients of compensation delivered to them as victims, but partners with the practitioners of affirmative action in breaking down the barriers that block segregated groups' access to mainstream opportunities. Justice is part of the mission of all institutions of civil society, and the targets of affirmative action play an active, indispensable role in advancing this mission. They therefore win their places on the merits, by virtue of their capacity to contribute to institutional goals through their performance in their role. The beneficiaries of affirmative action play this role in multiple ways, corresponding to the ways integration breaks down segregation and stigmatization and promotes democracy. The targets of affirmative action remain linked to social networks of family, neighborhood, and friendship that are largely black and typically poorer than they are. They serve as sources of social capital to less advantaged black relatives, acquaintances, and neighbors. They transmit human and cultural capital (including knowledge of how to operate successfully in integrated settings). Through demonstrably successful functioning in their roles, the targets of affirmative action help break down racial stereotypes that underlie stigmatization and discrimination. This effect is not simply a matter of bringing counterstereotypical individuals to the attention of other participants in institutions practicing affirmative action. On a larger scale, affirmative action aims to break the public association of blacks with poverty and associated dysfunctional behaviors by moving blacks to secure middle-class positions, reproduced across generations. This reduces statistical discrimination against blacks and destigmatizes by reducing the usefulness of race as a basis for making inferences about an individual's position in society and conduct correlated with that position. Finally, the targets of affirmative action advance the democratic project of integrating civil society in central sites—schools and workplaces—making information about the asymmetric impacts of policies and other social phenomena on segregated communities more salient to others, and holding decision makers accountable for responding to this information.

The integrative model's representation of beneficiaries of affirmative action as agents of justice explains why affirmative action programs tend to select from within the disadvantaged racial groups those who are likely to be better skilled and more highly educated, who have suffered less from the racial caste system than their peers. These individuals are usually better able to perform their integrative roles since successful integration requires successful functioning in the position to which affirmative action opens access. The integrative model is based on a recognition of the fact that sometimes an effective way to help the disadvantaged is to give opportunities to their more privileged peers, who will then be better situated to help them.

The integrative model explains why affirmative action should give enough weight to race to yield a critical mass of representatives from disadvantaged racial groups, beyond tokenism. Integration of a critical mass of workers from underrepresented groups reduces the salience of social-group membership, enables others to view them as individuals, facilitates meritocratic evaluation, and undermines the stereotype incumbency effect. A critical mass is also needed to raise the probability that whites will have contact with blacks in large institutions, and thereby learn to interact more competently and comfortably with them.

Race, in the integrative model, does not function fundamentally as a proxy for some other morally relevant property. It is the direct object of moral and instrumental concern. It refers not to a biological classification, but to an identify that has been constituted as a ground of categorical inequality through segregation and stigmatization. The causal power of a person's race to break down race-based barriers to opportunity through integration is directly linked to these features. If the problem is racial segregation, then the most direct way to remedy this problem is to practice racial integration. Integration directly opens up hoarded opportunities to the targets of affirmative action and their in-group associates. As the contact hypothesis holds, institutionally supported cooperative interaction with members of stigmatized groups on terms of equality reduces stigmatization of and discrimination against them. As the accountability effect holds, the presence of members of stigmatized or excluded groups as equals in decision-making bodies reduces discrimination and increases responsible deliberation by decision makers. * * *

The compensatory, discrimination-blocking, and integrative models identify justice as the goal of affirmative action. They differ in their conceptions of the injustices that require correction, and their accounts of how affirmative action corrects it. For the compensatory model, the core injustice that affirmative action aims to remedy is past racial discrimination. Its remedy is post hoc: it waits for discrimination to happen and compensates for its effects after the fact. This stance raises questions about how long claims to compensation for long-past acts of discrimination should last. The discrimination-blocking model avoids this challenge by focusing on current discrimination. But it still offers a limited discrimination-based account of the causes of unjust racial disadvantage and only blocks discrimination without attacking its underlying causes. For the integrative model, the core injustices that affirmative action aims to remedy are segregation and stigmatization. Segregation has unjust effects that are not mediated by discrimination. So does stigmatization: it constitutes an expressive harm, depresses performance through stereotype threat, and promotes public policies that have harsh differential impacts on the stigmatized. The integrative model takes a proactive stance toward these injustices: its aim is to *dismantle* the continuing causes of racial injustice.

STUDY QUESTIONS

1. Why does Anderson think that the compensation and diversity models are inadequate to justify the full range of potential policies of affirmative action?
2. How strong does Anderson find the discrimination-blocking model to be?
3. Explain Anderson's reasons for endorsing the integrative model.

SHELBY STEELE
Affirmative Action: The Price of Preference

Shelby Steele (b. 1946) is an American writer and documentary filmmaker who considers himself a "black conservative."

In a few short years, when my two children will be applying to college, the affirmative action policies by which most universities offer black students some form of preferential treatment will present me with a dilemma. I am a middle-class black, a college professor, far from wealthy, but also well-removed from the kind of deprivation that would qualify my children for the label "disadvantaged." Both of them have endured racial insensitivity from whites. They have been called names, have suffered slights, and have experienced firsthand the peculiar malevolence that racism brings out in people. Yet they have never experienced racial discrimination, have never been stopped by their race on any path that they have chosen to follow. Still, their society now tells them that if they will only designate themselves as black on their college applications, they will likely do better in the college lottery than if they conceal this fact. I think there is something of a Faustian bargain in this.

Of course, many blacks and a considerable number of whites would say that I was sanctimoniously making affirmative action into a test of character. They would say that this small preference is the meagerest recompense for centuries of unrelieved oppression. And to these arguments other very obvious facts must be added. In America, many marginally competent or flatly incompetent whites are hired every day—some because their white skin suits the conscious or unconscious racial preference of their employers. The white children of alumni are often grandfathered into elite universities in what can only be seen as a residual benefit of historic white privilege. Worse, white incompetence is always an individual matter, but for blacks it is often confirmation of ugly stereotypes. Given that unfairness cuts both ways, doesn't it only balance the scales of history, doesn't this repay, in a small way, the systematic denial under which my children's grandfather lived out his days?

In theory, affirmative action certainly has all the moral symmetry that fairness requires—the injustice of historical and even contemporary white advantage is offset with black advantage; preference replaces prejudice, inclusion answers exclusion. It is reformist and corrective, even repentant and redemptive. And I would never sneer at these good intentions. Born in the late forties in Chicago, I started my education (a charitable term in this case) in a segregated school and suffered all the indignities that come to blacks in a segregated society. My father, born in the South, made it only to the third grade before the white man's fields took permanent priority over his formal education. And though he educated himself into an advanced reader with an almost professorial authority, he could only drive a truck for a living, and never earned more than $90 a week in his entire life. So yes, it is crucial to my sense of citizenship, to my ability to identify with the spirit and the interests of America, to know that this country, however imperfectly, recognizes its past sins and wishes to correct them.

Yet good intentions can blind us to the effects they generate when implemented. In our society affirmative action is, among other things, a testament to white goodwill and to black power, and in the midst of these heavy investments its effects can be hard to see. But after twenty years of implementation I think that affirmative action has shown itself to be more bad than good and that blacks—whom I will focus on in this essay—now stand to lose more from it than they gain.

In talking with affirmative action administrators and with blacks and whites in general, it is clear that supporters of affirmative action focus on its good intentions while detractors emphasize its negative effects. Proponents talk about "diversity" and "pluralism"; opponents speak of "reverse discrimination," the unfairness of quotas and set-asides. It was virtually impossible to find people outside either camp. The closest I came was a white male manager at a large computer company who said, "I think it amounts to reverse discrimination, but I'll put up with a little of that for a little more diversity." I'll live with a little of the effect to gain a little of the intention, he seemed to be saying. But this only makes him a halfhearted supporter of affirmative action. I think many people who don't really like affirmative action support it to one degree or another anyway.

I believe they do this because of what happened to white and black Americans in the crucible of the sixties, when whites were confronted with their racial guilt and blacks tasted their first real power. In that stormy time white absolution and black power coalesced into virtual mandates for society. Affirmative action became a meeting ground for those mandates in the law, and in the late sixties and early seventies it underwent a remarkable escalation of its mission from simple anti-discrimination enforcement to social engineering by means of quotas, goals, timetables, set-asides and other forms of preferential treatment.

Legally, this was achieved through a series of executive orders and Equal Employment Opportunity Commission guidelines that allowed racial imbalances in the workplace to stand as proof of racial discrimination. Once it could be assumed that discrimination explained racial imbalances, it became easy to justify group remedies to presumed discrimination rather than the normal case-by-case redress.

Even though blacks had made great advances during the sixties without quotas, these mandates, which came to a head in the very late sixties, could no longer be satisfied by anything less than racial preferences. I don't think the white mandate to achieve a new racial innocence and the black mandate to gain power in themselves were wrong, because whites clearly needed to do better by blacks and blacks needed more real power in society. But as they came together in affirmative action, their effect was to distort our understanding of racial discrimination. By making black the color of preference, these mandates have reburdened society with the very marriage of color and preference (in reverse) that we set out to eradicate.

When affirmative action grew into social engineering, diversity became a golden word. It grants whites an egalitarian fairness (innocence) and blacks an entitlement to proportionate representation (power). *Diversity* is a term that applies democratic principles to races and cultures rather than to citizens, despite the fact that there is nothing to indicate that real diversity is the same thing as proportionate representation. Too often the result of this, on campuses (for example) has been a democracy of colors rather than of people, an artificial diversity that gives the appearance of an educational parity between black and white students that has not yet been achieved in reality. Here again, racial preferences allow society to leapfrog over the difficult problem of developing blacks to parity with whites and into a cosmetic diversity that covers the blemish of disparity—a full six years after admission, only 26 percent of blacks graduate from college.

Racial representation is not the same thing as racial development, yet affirmative action fosters a confusion of these very different needs. Representation can be manufactured; development is always hard-earned. However, it is the music of innocence and power that we hear in affirmative action that causes us to cling to it and to its distracting emphasis on representation. The fact is that after twenty years of racial preferences the gap between white and black median income is greater than it was in the seventies. None of this is to say that blacks don't need policies that insure our right to equal opportunity, but what we need more of is the development that will let us take advantage of society's efforts to include us.

I think one of the most troubling effects of racial preferences for blacks is a kind of demoralization. Under affirmative action, the quality that earns us preferential treatment is an implied inferiority. However this inferiority is explained—and it is easily enough explained by the myriad deprivations that grew out of our oppression—it is still inferiority. There are explanations, and then there is the fact. And the fact must be borne by the individual as a condition apart from the explanation, apart even from the fact that others like himself also bear this condition. In integrated situations in which blacks must compete with whites who may be better prepared, these explanations may quickly wear thin and expose the individual to racial as well as personal self-doubt. (Of course whites also feel doubt, but only personally, not racially.) What this means in practical terms is that when blacks deliver themselves into integrated situations, they encounter a nasty little reflex in whites, a mindless, atavistic reflex that responds to the color black with alarm. Attributions may follow negative stereotypes, such as intellectual ineptness. I think this reflex and the attributions that may follow it embarrass most whites today, and thus it is usually quickly repressed. On an equally atavistic level, the black will be aware of the reflex his color triggers and will feel a stab of horror at seeing himself reflected in this way. He, too, will do a quick repression, but a lifetime of such stabbings is what constitutes his inner realm of racial doubt.

Even when the black sees no implication of inferiority in racial preferences, he knows that whites do, so that—consciously or unconsciously—the result is virtually the same. The effect of preferential treatment—the lowering of normal standards to increase black representation—puts blacks at war with an expanded realm of debilitating doubt, so that the doubt itself becomes an unrecognized preoccupation that undermines their ability to perform, especially in integrated situations.

I believe another liability of affirmative action comes from the fact that it indirectly encourages blacks to exploit their own past victimization as a source of power and privilege. Victimization, like implied inferiority, is what justifies preference, so that to receive the benefits of preferential treatment one must, to some extent, become invested in the view of one's self as a victim. In this way, affirmative action nurtures a victim-focused identity in blacks. The obvious irony here is that we have become inadvertently invested in the very condition we are trying to overcome. Racial preferences send us the message that there is more power in our past suffering than in our present achievements.

When power itself grows out of suffering, blacks are encouraged to expand the boundaries of what qualifies as racial oppression, a situation that can lead us to paint our victimization in vivid colors, even as we receive the benefits of preference. The same corporations and institutions that give us preference are also seen as our oppressors. At Stanford University, minority students—who receive at least the same financial aid as whites with the same need—recently took over the president's office demanding, among other things, more financial aid.

But, I think, one of the worst prices that blacks pay for preference has to do with an illusion. I saw this illusion at work recently in the mother of a middle-class black student who was going off to his first semester of college. "They owe us this, so don't think for a minute that you don't belong there." This is the logic by which many blacks, and some whites, justify affirmative action—it is something "owed," a form of reparation. But this logic overlooks a much harder and less digestible reality, that it is impossible to repay blacks living today for the historic suffering of the race. If all blacks were given a million dollars tomorrow it would not amount to a dime on the dollar for three centuries of oppression, nor would it dissolve the residues of that oppression that we still carry today. The concept of historic reparation grows out of man's need to impose on the world a degree of justice that simply does not exist. Suffering can be endured and overcome, it cannot be repaid. To think otherwise is to prolong the suffering.

Several blacks I spoke with said they were still in favor of affirmative action because of the "subtle" discrimination blacks were subject to once on the job. One photojournalist said, "They have ways of ignoring you." A black female television producer said, "You can't file a lawsuit when your boss doesn't invite you to the insider meetings without ruining your career. So we still need affirmative action." Others mentioned the infamous "glass ceiling" through which blacks can see the top positions of authority but never reach them. But I don't think racial preferences are a protection against this subtle discrimination; I think they contribute to it.

In any workplace, racial preferences will always create two-tiered populations composed of preferreds and unpreferreds. In the case of blacks and whites, for instance, racial preferences imply that whites are superior just as they imply that blacks are inferior. They not only reinforce America's oldest racial myth but, for blacks, they have the effect of stigmatizing the already stigmatized.

I think that much of the "subtle" discrimination that blacks talk about is often (not always) discrimination against the stigma of questionable competence that affirmative action marks blacks with. In this sense, preferences scapegoat the very people they seek to help. And it may be that at a certain level employers impose a glass ceiling, but this may not be against the race so much as against the race's reputation for having advanced by color as much as by competence. This ceiling is the point at which corporations shift the emphasis from color to competency and stop playing the affirmative action game. Here preference backfires for blacks and becomes a taint that holds them back. Of course one could argue that this taint, which is, after all, in the minds of whites, becomes nothing more than an excuse to discriminate against blacks. And certainly the result is the same in either case—blacks don't get past the glass ceiling. But this argument does not get around the fact that racial preferences now taint this color with a new theme of suspicion that makes blacks even more vulnerable to discrimination. In this crucial yet gray area of perceived competence, preferences make whites look better than they are and blacks worse, while doing nothing whatever to stop the very real discrimination that blacks may encounter. I don't wish to justify the glass ceiling here, but only suggest the very subtle ways that affirmative action revives rather than extinguishes the old rationalizations for racial discrimination.

I believe affirmative action is problematic in our society because we have demanded that it create parity between the races rather than ensure equal opportunity. Preferential treatment does not teach skills, or educate, or instill motivation. It only passes out entitlement by color, a situation that in my profession has created an unrealistically high demand for black professors. The social engineer's assumption is that this high demand will inspire more blacks to earn Ph.D.'s and join the profession. In fact, the number of blacks earning Ph.D.'s has declined in recent years. Ph.D.'s must be developed from preschool on. They require family and community support. They must acquire an entire system of values that enables them to work hard while delaying gratification. There are social programs, I believe, that can (and should) help blacks *develop* in all these areas, but entitlement by color is not a social program; it is a dubious reward for being black.

It now seems clear that the Supreme Court, in a series of recent decisions,[1] is moving away from racial preferences. It has disallowed preferences except in instances of "identified discrimination," eroded the precedent that

---

1 *Editor's note*: This article was published in 1990.

statistical racial imbalances are prima facie evidence of discrimination, and, in effect, granted white males the right to challenge consent decrees that use preference to achieve racial balances in the workplace. Referring to this and other Supreme Court decisions, one civil rights leader said, "Night has fallen . . . as far as civil rights are concerned." But I am not so sure. The effect of these decisions is to protect the constitutional rights of everyone, rather than to take rights away from blacks. Night has fallen on racial preferences, not on the fundamental rights of black Americans. The reason for this shift, I believe, is that the white mandate for absolution from past racial sins weakened considerably in the 80s. Whites are now less willing to endure unfairness to themselves in order to grant special entitlements to blacks, even when those entitlements are justified in the name of past suffering. Yet the black mandate for more power in society has remained unchanged. And I think part of the anxiety many blacks feel over these decisions has to do with the loss of black power that they may signal. * * *

But the power we've lost by these decisions is really only the power that grows out of our victimization—the power to claim special entitlements under the law because of past oppression. This is not a very substantial or reliable power, and it is important that we know this so we can focus more exclusively on the kind of development that will bring enduring power. * * *

The impulse to discriminate *is* subtle and cannot be ferretted out unless its many guises are made clear to people. I think we need social policies that are committed to two goals: the educational and economic development of disadvantaged people, regardless of race, and the eradication from our society—through close monitoring and severe sanctions—of racial, ethnic, or gender discrimination. Preferences will not get us to either of these goals, because they tend to benefit those who are not disadvantaged—middle-class white women and middle-class blacks—and attack one form of discrimination with another. Preferences are inexpensive and carry the glamour of good intentions—change the numbers and the good deed is done. To be against them is to be unkind. But I think the unkindest cut is to bestow on children like my own an undeserved advantage while neglecting the development of those disadvantaged children in the poorer sections of my city who will most likely never be in a position to benefit from a preference. Give my children fairness; give disadvantaged children a better shot at development—better elementary and secondary schools, job training, safer neighborhoods, better financial assistance for college, and so on. A smaller percentage of black high school graduates go to college today than 15 years ago; more black males are in prison, jail, or in some other way under the control of the criminal justice-system than in college. This despite racial preferences.

The mandates of black power and white absolution out of which preferences emerged were not wrong in themselves. What was wrong was that both races focused more on the goals of those mandates than on the means to the goals. Blacks can have no real power without taking responsibility for their own educational and economic development. Whites can have no racial innocence without earning it by eradicating discrimination and helping the disadvantaged to develop. Because we ignored the means, the goals have not been reached, and the real work remains to be done.

STUDY QUESTIONS

1. Explain the distinction between "racial representation" and "racial development."
2. Is it always true that those who benefit from affirmative action will experience feelings of self-doubt or inferiority?
3. Does affirmative action encourage a victim mentality?

GEORGE YANCY AND JUDITH BUTLER
Black Lives Matter

George Yancy (b. 1961) is an African American philosopher, noted for his work on the philosophy of race. Judith Butler (b. 1956) is a leading feminist philosopher and theorist of gender, best known for her book Gender Trouble *(1990).*

George Yancy: In your 2004 book, "Precarious Life: The Powers of Mourning and Violence," you wrote, "The question that preoccupies me in the light of recent global violence is, Who counts as human? Whose lives count as lives?" You wrote that about the post-9/11 world, but it appears to also apply to the racial situation here in the United States. In the wake of the recent killings of unarmed black men and women by police, and the failure to prosecute the killers, the message being sent to black communities is that they don't matter, that they are "disposable." Posters reading "Black Lives Matter," "Hands Up. Don't Shoot," "I Can't Breathe," communicate the reality of a specific kind of racial vulnerability that black people experience on a daily basis. How does all this communicate to black people that their lives don't matter?

Judith Butler: Perhaps we can think about the phrase "black lives matter." What is implied by this statement, a statement that should be obviously true, but apparently is not? If black lives do not matter, then they are not really regarded as lives, since a life is supposed to matter. So what we see is that some lives matter more than others, that some lives matter so much that they need to be protected at all costs, and that other lives matter less, or not at all. And when that becomes the situation, then the lives that do not matter so much, or do not matter at all, can be killed or lost, can be exposed to conditions of destitution, and there is no concern, or even worse, that is regarded as the way it is supposed to be. The callous killing of Tamir Rice and the abandonment of his body on the street is an astonishing example of the police murdering someone considered disposable and fundamentally ungrievable.

When we are taking about racism, and anti-black racism in the United States, we have to remember that under slavery black lives were considered only a fraction of a human life, so the prevailing way of valuing lives assumed that some lives mattered more, were more human, more worthy, more deserving of life and freedom, where freedom meant minimally the freedom to move and thrive without being subjected to coercive force. But when and where did black lives ever really get free of coercive force? One reason the chant "Black Lives Matter" is so important is that it states the obvious but the obvious has not yet been historically realized. So it is a statement of outrage and a demand for equality, for the right to live free of constraint, but also a chant that links the history of slavery, of debt peonage, segregation, and a prison system geared toward the containment, neutralization and degradation of black lives, but also a police system that more and more easily and often can take away a black life in a flash all because some officer perceives a threat.

So let us think about what this is: the perception of a threat. One man is leaving a store unarmed, but he is perceived as a threat. Another man is in a chokehold and states that he cannot breathe, and the chokehold is not relaxed, and the man dies because he is perceived as a threat. Mike Brown and Eric Garner. We can name them, but in the space of this interview, we cannot name all the black men and women whose lives are snuffed out all because a police officer perceives a threat, sees the threat in the person, sees the person as pure threat. Perceived as a threat even when unarmed or completely physically subdued, or lying on the ground, as Rodney King clearly was, or coming back home from a party on the train and having the audacity to say to a policeman that he was not doing anything wrong and should not be detained: Oscar Grant. We can see the videos and know what is obviously true, but it is also obviously true that police and the juries that support them obviously do not see what is obvious, or do not wish to see.

So the police see a threat when there is no gun to see, or someone is subdued and crying out for his life, when they are moving away or cannot move. These figures are perceived as threats even when they do not threaten, when they have no weapon, and the video footage that shows precisely this is taken to be a ratification of the police's perception. The perception is then ratified as a public perception at which point we not only must insist on the dignity of black lives, but name the racism that has become ratified as public perception.

In fact, the point is not just that black lives can be disposed of so easily: they are targeted and hunted by a police force that is becoming increasingly emboldened to wage its race war by every grand jury decision that ratifies the point of view of state violence. Justifying lethal violence in the name of self-defense is reserved for those who have a publicly recognized self to defend. But those whose lives are not considered to matter, whose lives are perceived as a threat to the life that embodies white privilege can be destroyed in the name of that life. That can only happen when a recurrent and institutionalized form of racism has become a way of seeing, entering into the presentation of visual evidence to justify hateful and unjustified and heartbreaking murder.

So it is not just that black lives matter, though that must be said again and again. It is also that stand-your-ground and racist killings are becoming increasingly normalized, which is why intelligent forms of collective outrage have become obligatory.

G.Y.: The chant "Black Lives Matter" is also a form of what you would call "a mode of address." You discuss questions of address in your essay, "Violence, Nonviolence: Sartre and Fanon," where Fanon, for example, raises significant questions about sociality in talking about his freedom in relationship to a "you." "Black Lives Matter" says something like: "*You*—white police officers—recognize my/our humanity!" But what if the "you," in this case, fails to be moved, refuses to be touched by that embodied chant? And given that "racism has become a way of seeing," is it not necessary that we—as you say in your essay "Endangered/Endangering: Schematic Racism and White Paranoia"—install "an antiracist hegemony over the visual field"?

J.B.: Sometimes a mode of address is quite simply a way of speaking to or about someone. But a mode of address may also describe a general way of approaching another such that one presumes who the other is, even the meaning and value of their existence. We address each other with gesture, signs and movement, but also through media and technology. We make such assumptions all the time about who that other is when we hail someone on the street (or we do not hail them). That is someone I greet; the other is someone I avoid. That other may well be someone whose very existence makes me cross to the other side of the road.

Indeed, in the case of schematic racism, anti-black racism figures black people through a certain lens and filter, one that can quite easily construe a black person, or another racial minority, who is walking toward us as someone who is potentially, or actually, threatening, or is considered, in his very being, a threat. In fact, as we can doubtless see from the videos that have swept across the global media, it may be that even when a black man is moving away from the police, that man is still considered to be a threat or worth killing, as if that person were actually moving toward the police brandishing a weapon. Or it could be that a black man or woman is reaching for his or her identification papers to show to the police, and the police see in that gesture of compliance—hand moving toward pocket—a reach for a gun. Is that because, in the perception of the police, to be black is already to be reaching for a gun? Or a black person is sleeping on the couch, standing, walking, or even running, clearly brandishing no gun, and there turns out to be evidence that there is no gun, still that life is snuffed out—why? Is the gun imagined into the scene, or retrospectively attributed to the standing or fleeing figure (and the grand jury nods, saying "this is plausible.")? And why when that person is down, already on the ground, and seeks to lift himself, or seated against a subway grate, and seeks to speak on his own behalf, or is utterly subdued and imperiled by the chokehold, he never stops looming as a threat to security, prompting a policeman to beat him or gun him down?

It may be important to see the twisted vision and the inverted assumptions that are made in the course of building a "case" that the police acted in self-defense or were sufficiently provoked to use lethal force. The fleeing figure is coming this way; the nearly strangled person is about to unleash force; the man on the ground will suddenly spring to life and threaten the life of the one who therefore takes his life.

These are war zones of the mind that play out on the street. At least in these cases that have galvanized the nation and the world in protest, we all see the twisted logic that results in the exoneration of the police who take away the lives of unarmed black men and women. And why is that the case? It is not because what the police and their lawyers present as their thinking in the midst of the situation is very reasonable. No, it is because that form of thinking is *becoming more "reasonable" all the time.* In other words, every time a grand jury or a police review board accepts this form of reasoning, they ratify the idea that blacks are a population against which society must be defended, and that the police defend themselves and (white) society, when they preemptively shoot unarmed black men in public space. At stake is a way that black people are figured as a threat even when they are simply living their lives, walking the street, leaving the convenience store, riding the subway, because in those instances this is only a threatening life, or a threat to the only kind of life, white life, that is recognized.

G.Y.: What has led us to this place?

J.B.: Racism has complex origins, and it is important that we learn the history of racism to know what has led us to this terrible place. But racism is also reproduced in the present, in the prison system, new forms of population control, increasing economic inequality that affects people of color disproportionately. These forms of institutionalized destitution and inequality are reproduced through these daily encounters—the disproportionate numbers of minorities stopped and detained by the police, and the rising number of those who fall victim to police violence. The figure of the black person as threat, as criminal, as someone who is, no matter where he is going, already-on-the-way-to-prison, conditions these pre-emptive strikes, attributing lethal aggression to the very figure who suffers it most. The lives taken in this way are not lives worth grieving; they belong to the increasing number of those who are understood as ungrievable, whose lives are thought not to be worth preserving.

But, of course, what we are also seeing in the recent and continuing assemblies, rallies and vigils is an open mourning for those whose lives were cut short and without cause, brutally extinguished. The practices of public mourning and political demonstration converge: when lives are considered ungrievable, to grieve them openly is protest. So when people assemble in the street, arrive at rallies or vigils, demonstrate with the aim of opposing this form of racist violence, they are "speaking back" to this mode of address, insisting on what should be obvious but is not, namely, that these lost lives are unacceptable losses.

On the one hand, there is a message, "Black Lives Matter," which always risks being misheard ("What? Only *black* lives matter?") or not heard at all ("these are just people who will protest anything"). On the other hand, the assembly, even without words, enacts the message in its own way. For it is often in public spaces where such violence takes place, so reclaiming public space to oppose both racism and violence is an act that reverberates throughout the public sphere through various media.

G.Y.: I've heard that some white people have held signs that read "All Lives Matter."

J.B.: When some people rejoin with "All Lives Matter" they misunderstand the problem, but not because their message is untrue. It is true that all lives matter, but it is equally true that not all lives are understood to matter which is precisely why it is most important to name the lives that have not mattered, and are struggling to matter in the way they deserve.

Claiming that "all lives matter" does not immediately mark or enable black lives only because they have not been fully recognized as having lives that matter. I do not mean this as an obscure riddle. I mean only to say that we cannot have a race-blind approach to the questions: which lives matter? Or, which lives are worth valuing? If we jump too quickly to the universal formulation, "all lives matter," then we miss the fact that black people have not yet been included in the idea of "all lives." That said, it is true that all lives matter (we can then debate about when life begins or ends). But to make that universal formulation concrete, to make that into a living formulation, one that truly extends to all people, we have to foreground those lives that are not mattering now, to mark that exclusion, and militate against it. Achieving that universal, "all lives matter," is a struggle, and that is part of what we are seeing on the streets. For on the streets we see a complex set of solidarities across color lines that seek to show what a concrete and living sense of bodies that matter can be.

G.Y: When you talk about lives that matter, are you talking about how whiteness and white bodies are valorized? In "Gender Trouble: Feminism and the Subversion of Identity," you discuss gender as "a stylized repetition of acts." Do you also see whiteness as "a stylized repetition of acts" that solidifies and privileges white bodies, or even leads to naïve, "post-racial" universal formulations like "all lives matter"?

J.B.: Yes, we can certainly talk about "doing whiteness" as a way of putting racial categories into action, since whiteness is part of what we call "race," and is often implicitly or explicitly part of a race project that seeks to achieve and maintain dominance for white people. One way this happens is by establishing whiteness as the norm for the human, and blackness as a deviation from the human or even as a threat to the human, or as something not quite human. Under such perceptual conditions built up through the history of racism, it becomes increasingly easy for white people to accept the destruction of black lives as status quo, since those lives do not fit the norm of "human life" they defend. It is true that Frantz Fanon sometimes understood whiteness in gendered terms: a black man is not a man, according to the white norms that define manhood, and yet other times the black man is figured as the threat of rape, hyper-masculinized, threatening the "virgin sanctity" of whiteness.

In that last formulation whiteness is figured as a young virgin whose future husband is white—this characterization ratifies the sentiments that oppose miscegenation and defend norms of racial purity. But whose sexuality is imperiled in this scene? After all, black women and girls were the ones who were raped, humiliated and disposed of under conditions of slavery, and it was black families who were forcibly destroyed: black kinship was not recognized as kinship that matters. Women of color, and black feminists in particular, have struggled for years against being the sexual property of either white male power or black masculinity, against poverty, and against the prison industry, so there are many reasons it is necessary to define racism in ways that acknowledge the specific forms it takes against men, women, and transgendered people of color.

Let us remember, of course, that many black women's lives are taken by police and by prisons. We can name a few: Yvette Smith, 48, in Texas, unarmed, and killed by police; or Aiyana Stanley-Jones, age 7, killed while sleeping on her father's couch in Detroit. After all, all of those are among the people on the street, outraged and demonstrating, opposing a lethal power that is becoming more and more normalized and, to that degree, more and more outrageous.

Whiteness is less a property of skin than a social power reproducing its dominance in both explicit and implicit ways. When whiteness is a practice of superiority over minorities, it monopolizes the power of destroying or demeaning bodies of color. The legal system is engaged in reproducing whiteness when it decides that the black person can and will be punished more severely than the white person who commits the same infraction, when that same differential is at work in the question, who can and will be detained? And who can and will be sent to prison with a life sentence or the death penalty? Angela Davis has shown the disproportionate number of Americans of color (black and Latino) detained, imprisoned and on death row. This has become a "norm" that effectively says "black lives do not matter," one that is built up over time, through daily practices, modes of address, through the organization of schools, work, prison, law and media. Those are all ways that the conceit of white superiority is constructed.

G.Y.: Yes. Whiteness, as a set of historical practices, extends beyond the skin. And yet, when a person with white skin walks into a store, it is assumed that she is not a threat. So, there is an entire visual technology that is complicit here, where the skin itself, as it were, is the marker of innocence. It is a visual technology that reinforces not only her sense of innocence, but that organizes the ways in which she gets to walk through space without being profiled or stopped. Hence, she contributes to the perpetuation of racial injustice even if she is unaware of doing so.

J.B.: Well, of course, class is also there as a marker of how anyone is perceived entering the door to the public building, the office, the post office, the convenience store. Class is in play when white people fail to look "moneyed" or are considered as working class, poor or homeless, so we have to be clear that the "white" person we may be talking about can be struggling with inequality of another kind: whiteness has its own internal hierarchies, to be sure. Of course there are white people who may be very convinced that they are not racist, but that does not necessarily mean that they have examined, or worked though, how whiteness organizes their lives, values, the institutions they support, how they are implicated in ways of talking, seeing, and doing that constantly and tacitly discriminate. Undoing whiteness has to be difficult work, but it starts, I think, with humility, with learning history, with white people learning how the history of racism persists in the everyday vicissitudes of the present, even as some of us may think we are "beyond" such a history, or even convinced that we have magically become "post-racial." It is difficult and ongoing work, calling on an ethical disposition and political solidarity that risks error in the practice of solidarity.

Whiteness is not an abstraction; its claim to dominance is fortified through daily acts which may not seem racist at all precisely because they are considered "normal." But just as certain kinds of violence and inequality get established as "normal" through the proceedings that exonerate police of the lethal use of force against unarmed black people, so whiteness, or rather its claim to privilege, can be disestablished over time. This is why there must be a collective reflection on, and opposition to, the way whiteness takes hold of our ideas about whose lives matter. The norm of whiteness that supports both violence and inequality insinuates itself into the normal and the obvious. Understood as the sometimes tacit and sometimes explicit power to define the boundaries of kinship, community and nation, whiteness inflects all those frameworks within which certain lives are made to matter less than others.

It is always possible to do whiteness otherwise, to engage in a sustained and collective practice to question how racial differentiation enters into our daily evaluations of which lives deserve to be supported, to flourish, and which do not. But it is probably an error, in my view, for white people to become paralyzed with guilt and self-scrutiny. The point is rather to consider those ways of valuing and devaluing life that govern our own thinking and acting, understanding the social and historical reach of those ways of valuing. It is probably important and satisfying as well to let one's whiteness recede by joining in acts of solidarity with all those who oppose racism. There are ways of fading out whiteness, withdrawing its implicit and explicit claim to racial privilege.

Demonstrations have the potential to embody forms of equality that we want to see realized in the world more broadly. Working against those practices and institutions that refuse to recognize and mark the powers of state racism in particular, assemblies gather to mourn and resist the deadly consequences of such powers. When people engage in concerted actions across racial lines to build communities based on equality, to defend the rights of those who are disproportionately imperiled to have a chance to live without the fear of dying quite suddenly at the hands of the police. There are many ways to do this, in the street, the office, the home, and in the media. Only through such an ever-growing cross-racial struggle against racism can we begin to achieve a sense of all the lives that really do matter.

STUDY QUESTIONS

1. What would be wrong with replacing the slogan "Black Lives Matter" with "All Lives Matter"?
2. How, according to Butler, have unconscious racist attitudes led to the killing of black people by police officers?
3. How can whiteness be understood as a form as social power?

■ Compare and Contrast Questions

1. Can Du Bois's notion of "double-consciousness" be applied to Steele's analysis of the effects of affirmative action?
2. Does Steele show that Anderson is wrong to advocate affirmative action?
3. Is the "Black Lives Matter" campaign evidence that the emancipation of people of color has failed to make significant progress since the time of Du Bois?

ECONOMIC JUSTICE

This section contains three important writings on questions of economic justice. In the first extract, from John Rawls's enormously influential book *A Theory of Justice*, Rawls outlines the theory of justice that, he claims, would be chosen by people in the "original position" which we encountered in an earlier extract. Rawls's theory calls for radical redistribution of wealth in society, and hence he is regarded as on the political left.

Rawls argues that the first priority of rational people in the original position would be what elsewhere in the book he calls "the liberty principle," which assures equal and extensive basic liberties to all. The second principle splits into two: the fair opportunity principle and the so-called difference principle, which is Rawls's most distinctive contribution. It requires income and wealth to be distributed in such a way that the worst-off group in society is as well-off as possible. Inequalities are permissible, but only if they are to the advantage of the worst-off. The principles are in "serial," or what Rawls later in the book calls "lexical," order, so that in case of clashes the liberty principle comes first, and then the opportunity principle over the difference principle. The only exception occurs if society is in very grave need, in which case it can be permissible to suspend the liberty principle until the crisis is overcome.

Rawls contrasts his theory, which he calls "democratic equality," with "natural liberty" and "liberal equality." Natural liberty guarantees rights but allows incomes to vary according to the free market, thereby allowing income to be influenced by family background and natural talents, which Rawls regards as "arbitrary from a moral point of view." Liberal equality insists on a principle of equality of opportunity that tries to mitigate the effects of differential family background, but still leaves distribution affected by natural talents. The difference principle, by contrast, uses any one individual's natural talents for the benefit of society as a whole, by allowing individuals to benefit from their talents, but only if they do so in a way that will help raise the position of the worst-off.

Robert Nozick's *Anarchy, State, and Utopia* appeared in 1974, shortly after *A Theory of Justice*, while Rawls and Nozick were colleagues at Harvard University. Nozick presents a form of libertarian political philosophy, reviving something close to the system of natural liberty criticized by Rawls. Nozick argues that a theory of justice needs three principles. First it needs a theory of justice in initial acquisition, which explains how property, especially land, can be acquired from its natural state of nonownership. Second, it needs a theory of justice in transfer, which explains how legitimately owned property can change hands from one person to another. And finally it needs a principle of justice in rectification, to correct for any injustices.

Nozick gives most of his attention to his own principle of justice in transfer, which, roughly, is that a transfer is justified if and only if it is voluntary. This idea is at the center of his "entitlement theory" of justice. While it may seem obvious, it is, in fact, a very radical principle. Taxation is a form of compulsory transfer, so Nozick's theory renders nonvoluntary taxation illegitimate. This amounts to the denial that the government has the right to tax and redistribute income and wealth, and, indeed, deliberately restricts the government's legitimate role to enforcing personal and property rights. For this reason, Nozick's theory is known as one of the "minimal state."

The entitlement theory is contrasted with a number of other approaches to justice, including "patterned" theories, which distribute resources according to the formula "each according to his X." Using the example of basketball player Wilt Chamberlain, in which one person amasses a fortune through voluntary exchange, Nozick argues that every patterned theory must restrict free trade and thereby illegitimately violates individual liberty.

In a very different approach, Iris Marion Young turns her attention to ways in which it can seem that a system conspires against an individual. Young takes the example of Sandy, a single mother who is compelled to move from her home because her new landlord wishes to redevelop the property. But she is unable to find accommodation she can afford and she and her children face homelessness. Many people live one or two paychecks away from disaster, but when, despite their best efforts, things fall apart, it can be very hard to attribute the cause to any one individual or company. There may have been no malice or negligence, but we may feel that the world as a whole, or at least society, has created an injustice for the person. This, Young suggests, is a "structural injustice."

Young wants us to rethink the idea of responsibility so that we can make more sense of cases such as the example she has given. While no individual is responsible for the Sandy's plight, there is a sense in which we all are. Structures are created and reinforced by the decisions we make. Our normal view of responsibility suggests that people are morally responsible for an outcome only if they can be shown to be liable for it in the sense of bringing it about. Young argues that this "liability" model is not adequate to understand the example of Sandy. Instead, Young proposes the "political responsibility" model in which everyone who is causally connected to the outcome bears some responsibility. However, each person's responsibility is likely to be to join in collective action to bring about structural change, rather than to take on an individual duty to compensate. Different people will have different responsibilities, owing to their connection to the injustice, their power, their privilege, and their interest (in the sense of self-interest) in structural change.

JOHN RAWLS
A Theory of Justice

John Rawls (1921–2002) was an American philosopher regarded as the most important political philosopher writing in English in the twentieth century. He is best known for his book A Theory of Justice *(1971).*

11. TWO PRINCIPLES OF JUSTICE

I shall now state in a provisional form the two principles of justice that I believe would be agreed to in the original position. The first formulation of these principles is tentative. As we go on I shall consider several formulations and approximate step by step the final statement to be given much later. I believe that doing this allows the exposition to proceed in a natural way.

The first statement of the two principles reads as follows.

First: each person is to have an equal right to the most extensive scheme of equal basic liberties compatible with a similar scheme of liberties for others.

Second: social and economic inequalities are to be arranged so that they are both (a) reasonably expected to be to everyone's advantage, and (b) attached to positions and offices open to all.

There are two ambiguous phrases in the second principle, namely "everyone's advantage" and "open to all." Determining their sense more exactly will lead to a second formulation of the principle in §13. ∗ ∗ ∗

These principles primarily apply * * * to the basic structure of society and govern the assignment of rights and duties and regulate the distribution of social and economic advantages. * * * Now it is essential to observe that the basic liberties are given by a list of such liberties. Important among these are political liberty (the right to vote and to hold public office) and freedom of speech and assembly; liberty of conscience and freedom of thought; freedom of the person, which includes freedom from psychological oppression and physical assault and dismemberment (integrity of the person); the right to hold personal property and freedom from arbitrary arrest and seizure as defined by the concept of the rule of law. These liberties are to be equal by the first principle.

The second principle applies, in the first approximation, to the distribution of income and wealth and to the design of organizations that make use of differences in authority and responsibility. While the distribution of wealth and income need not be equal, it must be to everyone's advantage, and at the same time, positions of authority and responsibility must be accessible to all. * * *

These principles are to be arranged in a serial order with the first principle prior to the second. This ordering means that a departure from the institutions of equal liberty required by the first principle cannot be justified by, or compensated for, by greater social and economic advantages.

12. INTERPRETATIONS OF THE SECOND PRINCIPLE

I have already mentioned that since the phrases "everyone's advantage" and "equally open to all" are ambiguous, both parts of the second principle have two natural senses. Because these senses are independent of one another, the principle has four possible meanings. Assuming that the first principle of equal liberty has the same sense throughout, we then have four interpretations of the two principles. These are indicated in the table below.

| | "Everyone's advantage" | |
"Equally open"	Principle of efficiency	Difference principle
Equality as careers open to talents	System of Natural Liberty	Natural Aristocracy
Equality as equality of fair opportunity	Liberal Equality	Democratic Equality

* * * In working out justice as fairness, we must decide which interpretation is to be preferred. I shall adopt that of democratic equality. * * *

∗ ∗ ∗ The system of natural liberty selects an efficient distribution roughly as follows. Let us suppose that we know from economic theory that under the standard assumptions defining a competitive market economy, income and wealth will be distributed in an efficient way, and that the particular efficient distribution which results in any period of time is determined by the initial distribution of assets, that is, by the initial distribution of income and wealth, and of natural talents and abilities. With each initial distribution, a definite efficient outcome is arrived at. Thus it turns out that if we are to accept the outcome as just, and not merely as efficient, we must accept the basis upon which over time the initial distribution of assets is determined.

In the system of natural liberty the initial distribution is regulated by the arrangements implicit in the conception of careers open to talents. ∗ ∗ ∗ These arrangements presuppose a background of equal liberty (as specified by the first principle) and a free market economy. They require a formal equality of opportunity in that all have at least the same legal rights of access to all advantaged social positions. But since there is no effort to preserve an equality, or similarity, of social conditions, except insofar as this is necessary to preserve the requisite background institutions, the initial distribution of assets for any period of time is strongly influenced by natural and social contingencies. The existing distribution of income and wealth, say, is the cumulative effect of prior distributions of natural assets—that is, natural talents and abilities—as these have been developed or left unrealized, and their use favored or disfavored over time by social circumstances and such chance contingencies as accident and good fortune. Intuitively, the most obvious injustice of the system of natural liberty is that it permits distributive shares to be improperly influenced by these factors so arbitrary from a moral point of view.

The liberal interpretation, as I shall refer to it, tries to correct for this by adding to the requirement of careers open to talents the further condition of the principle of fair equality of opportunity. The thought here is that positions are to be not only open in a formal sense, but that all should have a fair chance to attain them. Offhand it is not clear what is meant, but we might say that those with similar abilities and skills should have similar life chances. More specifically, assuming that there is a distribution of natural assets, those who are at the same level of talent and ability, and have the same willingness to use them, should have the same prospects of success regardless of their initial place in the social system. In all sectors of society there should be roughly equal prospects of culture and achievement for everyone similarly motivated and endowed. The expectations of those with the same abilities and aspirations should not be affected by their social class.

The liberal interpretation of the two principles seeks, then, to mitigate the influence of social contingencies and natural fortune on distributive shares. To accomplish this end it is necessary to impose further basic structural conditions on the social system. Free market arrangements must be set within a framework of political and legal institutions which regulates the overall trends of economic events and preserves the social conditions necessary for fair equality of opportunity. The elements of this framework are familiar enough, though it may be worthwhile to recall the importance of preventing excessive accumulations of property and wealth and of maintaining equal opportunities of education for all. Chances to acquire cultural knowledge and skills should not depend upon one's class position, and so the school system, whether public or private, should be designed to even out class barriers.

While the liberal conception seems clearly preferable to the system of natural liberty, intuitively it still appears defective. For one thing, even if it works to perfection in eliminating the influence of social contingencies, it still permits the distribution of wealth and income to be determined by the natural distribution of abilities and talents. Within the limits allowed by the background arrangements, distributive shares are decided by the outcome of the natural lottery; and this outcome is arbitrary from a moral perspective. There is no more reason to permit the distribution of income and wealth to be settled by the distribution of natural assets than by historical and social fortune. Furthermore, the principle of fair opportunity can be only imperfectly carried out, at least as long as some form of the family exists. The extent to which natural capacities develop and reach fruition is affected by all kinds of social conditions and class attitudes. Even the willingness to make an effort, to try, and so to be deserving in the ordinary sense is itself dependent upon happy family and social circumstances. It is impossible in practice to secure equal chances of achievement and culture for those similarly endowed, and therefore we may want to adopt a principle which recognizes this fact and also mitigates the arbitrary effects of the natural lottery itself. That the liberal conception fails to do this encourages one to look for another interpretation of the two principles of justice. ***

13. DEMOCRATIC EQUALITY AND THE DIFFERENCE PRINCIPLE

The democratic interpretation, as the table suggests, is arrived at by combining the principle of fair equality of opportunity with the difference principle. * * * Assuming the framework of institutions required by equal liberty and fair equality of opportunity, the higher expectations of those better situated are just if and only if they work as part of a scheme which improves the expectations of the least advantaged members of society. The intuitive idea is that the social order is not to establish and secure the more attractive prospects of those better off unless doing so is to the advantage of those less fortunate. * * *

To illustrate the difference principle, consider the distribution of income among social classes. Let us suppose that the various income groups correlate with representative individuals by reference to whose expectations we can judge the distribution. Now those starting out as members of the entrepreneurial class in property-owning democracy, say, have a better prospect than those who begin in the class of unskilled laborers. It seems likely that this will be true even when the social injustices which now exist are removed. What, then, can possibly justify this kind of initial inequality in life prospects? According to the difference principle, it is justifiable only if the difference in expectation is to the advantage of the representative man who is worse off, in this case the representative unskilled worker. The inequality in expectation is permissible only if lowering it would make the working class even more worse off. Supposedly, given the rider in the second principle concerning open positions, and the principle of liberty generally, the greater expectations allowed to entrepreneurs encourages them to do things which raise the prospects of the laboring class. Their better prospects act as incentives so that the economic process is more efficient, innovation proceeds at a faster pace, and so on. I shall not consider how far these things are true. The point is that something of this kind must be argued if these inequalities are to satisfy by the difference principle. * * *

* * * The outcome of the last several sections is that the second principle reads as follows:

> Social and economic inequalities are to be arranged so that they are both (a) to the greatest expected benefit of the least advantaged and (b) attached to offices and positions open to all under conditions of fair equality of opportunity. * * *

17. THE TENDENCY TO EQUALITY

I wish to conclude this discussion of the two principles by explaining the sense in which they express an egalitarian conception of justice. * * *

First we may observe that the difference principle gives some weight to the considerations singled out by the principle of redress. This is the principle that undeserved inequalities call for redress; and since inequalities of birth and natural endowment are undeserved, these inequalities are to be somehow compensated for. Thus the principle holds that in order to treat all persons equally, to provide genuine equality of opportunity, society must give more attention to those with fewer native assets and to those born into the less favorable social positions. The idea is to redress the bias of contingencies in the direction of equality. In pursuit of this principle greater resources might be spent on the education of the less rather than the more intelligent, at least over a certain time of life, say the earlier years of school.

* * * Now the difference principle is not of course the principle of redress. It does not require society to try to even out handicaps as if all were expected to compete on a fair basis in the same race. But the difference principle would allocate resources in education, say, so as to improve the long-term expectation of the least favored. If this end is attained by giving more attention to the better endowed, it is permissible; otherwise not. And in making this decision, the value of education should not be assessed solely in terms of economic efficiency and social welfare. Equally if not more important is the role of education in enabling a person to enjoy the culture of his society and to take part in its affairs, and in this way to provide for each individual a secure sense of his own worth.

* * * The difference principle represents, in effect, an agreement to regard the distribution of natural talents as in some respects a common asset and to share in the greater social and economic benefits made possible by the complementarities of this distribution. Those who have been favored by nature, whoever they are, may gain from their good fortune only on terms that improve the situation of those who have lost out. The naturally advantaged are not to gain merely because they are more gifted, but only to cover the costs of training and education and for using their endowments in ways that help the less fortunate as well. No one deserves his greater natural capacity nor merits a more favorable starting place in society. But, of course, this is no reason to ignore, much less to eliminate these distinctions. Instead, the basic structure can be arranged so that these contingencies

work for the good of the least fortunate. Thus we are led to the difference principle if we wish to set up the social system so that no one gains or loses from his arbitrary place in the distribution of natural assets or his initial position in society without giving or receiving compensating advantages in return.

In view of these remarks we may reject the contention that the ordering of institutions is always defective because the distribution of natural talents and the contingencies of social circumstance are unjust, and this injustice must inevitably carry over to human arrangements. Occasionally this reflection is offered as an excuse for ignoring injustice, as if the refusal to acquiesce in injustice is on a par with being unable to accept death. The natural distribution is neither just nor unjust; nor is it unjust that persons are born into society at some particular position. These are simply natural facts. What is just and unjust is the way that institutions deal with these facts. Aristocratic and caste societies are unjust because they make these contingencies the ascriptive basis for belonging to more or less enclosed and privileged social classes. The basic structure of these societies incorporates the arbitrariness found in nature. But there is no necessity for men to resign themselves to these contingencies. The social system is not an unchangeable order beyond human control but a pattern of human action. In justice as fairness men agree to avail themselves of the accidents of nature and social circumstance only when doing so is for the common benefit. The two principles are a fair way of meeting the arbitrariness of fortune; and while no doubt imperfect in other ways, the institutions which satisfy these principles are just.

A further point is that the difference principle expresses a conception of reciprocity. It is a principle of mutual benefit. At first sight, however, it may appear unfairly biased towards the least favored. * * *

One may object that those better situated deserve the greater advantages they could acquire for themselves under other schemes of cooperation whether or not these advantages are gained in ways that benefit others. Now it is true that given a just system of cooperation as a framework of public rules, and the expectations set up by it, those who, with the prospect of improving their condition, have done what the system announces it will reward are entitled to have their expectations met. In this sense the more fortunate have title to their better situation; their claims are legitimate expectations established by social institutions and the community is obligated to fulfill them. But this sense of desert is that of entitlement. It presupposes the existence of an ongoing cooperative scheme and is irrelevant to the question whether this scheme itself is to be designed in accordance with the difference principle or some other criterion.

Thus it is incorrect that individuals with greater natural endowments and the superior character that has made their development possible have a right to a cooperative scheme that enables them to obtain even further benefits in ways that do not contribute to the advantages of others. We do not deserve our place in the distribution of native endowments, any more than we deserve our initial starting place in society. That we deserve the superior character that enables us to make the effort to cultivate our abilities is also problematic; for such character depends in good part upon fortunate family and social circumstances in early life for which we can claim no credit. The notion of desert does not apply here. To be sure, the more advantaged have a right to their natural assets, as does everyone else; this right is covered by the first principle under the basic liberty protecting the integrity of the person. And so the more advantaged are entitled to whatever they can acquire in accordance with the rules of a fair system of social cooperation. Our problem is how this scheme, the basic structure of society, is to be designed. From a suitably general standpoint, the difference principle appears acceptable to both the more advantaged and the less advantaged individual.

STUDY QUESTIONS

1. Explain what Rawls means by the "difference principle."
2. How would Rawls respond to the suggestion that the introduction of slavery would make the worst-off better off than they are now?
3. What are Rawls's objections to the systems of "natural liberty" and "liberal equality"?

ROBERT NOZICK
The Entitlement Theory of Justice

Robert Nozick (1938–2002) was an American philosopher who wrote on a wide range of topics and was especially noted for his defense of the political philosophy of libertarianism.

The term "distributive justice" is not a neutral one. Hearing the term "distribution," most people presume that some thing or mechanism uses some principle or criterion to give out a supply of things. Into this process of distributing shares some error may have crept. So it is an open question, at least, whether redistribution should take place; whether we should do again what has already been done once, though poorly. However, we are not in the position of children who have been given portions of pie by someone who now makes last minute adjustments to rectify careless cutting. There is no *central* distribution, no person or group entitled to control all the resources, jointly deciding how they are to be doled out. What each person gets, he gets from others who give to him in exchange for something, or as a gift. In a free society, diverse persons control different resources, and new holdings arise out of the voluntary exchanges and actions of persons. There is no more a distributing or distribution of shares than there is a distributing of mates in a society in which persons choose whom they shall marry. The total result is the product of many individual decisions which the different individuals involved are entitled to make. *** Nevertheless, despite the title of this chapter, it would be best to use a terminology that clearly is neutral. We shall speak of people's holdings; a principle of justice in holdings describes (part of) what justice tells us (requires) about holdings. I shall state first what I take to be the correct view about justice in holdings, and then turn to the discussion of alternate views.

THE ENTITLEMENT THEORY

The subject of justice in holdings consists of three major topics. The first is the *original acquisition of holdings,* the appropriation of unheld things. This includes the issues of how unheld things may come to be held, the process, or processes, by which unheld things may come to be held, the things that may come to be held by these processes, the extent of what comes to be held by a particular process, and so on. We shall refer to the complicated truth about this topic, which we shall not formulate here, as the principle of justice in acquisition. The second topic concerns the *transfer of holdings* from one person to another. By what processes may a person transfer holdings to another? How may a person acquire a holding from another who holds it? Under this topic come general descriptions of voluntary exchange, and gift and (on the other hand) fraud, as well as reference to particular conventional details fixed upon in a given society. The complicated truth about this subject (with placeholders for conventional details) we shall call the principle of justice in transfer. ***

If the world were wholly just, the following inductive definition would exhaustively cover the subject of justice in holdings.

1. A person who acquires a holding in accordance with the principle of justice in acquisition is entitled to that holding.
2. A person who acquires a holding in accordance with the principle of justice in transfer, from someone else entitled to the holding, is entitled to the holding.
3. No one is entitled to a holding except by (repeated) applications of 1 and 2.

The complete principle of distributive justice would say simply that a distribution is just if everyone is entitled to the holdings they possess under the distribution.

A distribution is just if it arises from another just distribution by legitimate means. The legitimate means of moving from one distribution to another are specified by the principle of justice in transfer. The legitimate first "moves" are specified by the principle of justice in acquisition. Whatever arises from a just situation by just steps is itself just. ✳✳✳

Not all actual situations are generated in accordance with the two principles of justice in holdings: the principle of justice in acquisition and the principle of justice in transfer. Some people steal from others, or defraud them, or enslave them, seizing their product and preventing them from living as they choose, or forcibly exclude others from competing in exchanges. None of these are permissible modes of transition from one situation to another. And some persons acquire holdings by means not sanctioned by the principle of justice in acquisition. The existence of past injustice (previous violations of the first two principles of justice in holdings) raises the third major topic under justice in holdings: the rectification of injustice in holdings. If past injustice has shaped present holdings in various ways, some identifiable and some not, what now, if anything, ought to be done to rectify these injustices? ✳✳✳ How far back must one go in wiping clean the historical slate of injustices? What may victims of injustice permissibly do in order to rectify the injustices being done to them, including the many injustices done by persons acting through their government? ✳✳✳

The general outlines of the theory of justice in holdings are that the holdings of a person are just if he is entitled to them by the principle of justice in acquisition and transfer, or by the principle of rectification of injustice (as specified by the first two principles). If each person's holdings are just, then the total set (distribution) of holdings is just. ✳✳✳

HISTORICAL PRINCIPLES AND END-RESULT PRINCIPLES

The general outlines of the entitlement theory illuminate the nature and defects of other conceptions of distributive justice. The entitlement theory of justice in distribution is *historical;* whether a distribution is just depends upon how it came about. In contrast, *current time-slice principles* of justice hold that the justice of a distribution is determined by how things are distributed (who has what) as judged by some *structural* principle(s) of just distribution. A utilitarian who judges between any two distributions by seeing which has the greater sum of utility and, if the sums tie, applies some fixed equality criterion to choose the more equal distribution, would hold a current time-slice principle of justice. As would someone who had a fixed schedule of trade-offs between the sum of happiness and equality. According to a current time-slice principle, all that needs to be looked at, in judging the justice of a distribution, is who ends up with what; in comparing any two distributions one need look only at the matrix presenting the distributions. No further information need be fed into a principle of justice. * * *

Most persons do not accept current time-slice principles as constituting the whole story about distributive shares. They think it relevant in assessing the justice of a situation to consider not only the distribution it embodies, but also how that distribution came about. If some persons are in prison for murder or war crimes, we do not say that to assess the justice of the distribution in the society we must look only at what this person has, and that person has, and that person has, . . . at the current time. We think it relevant to ask whether someone did something so that he *deserved* to be punished, deserved to have a lower share. * * *

* * * Henceforth, we shall refer to such unhistorical principles of distributive justice, including the current time-slice principles, as *end-result principles* or *end-state principles*.

In contrast to end-result principles of justice, *historical principles* of justice hold that past circumstances or actions of people can create differential entitlements or differential deserts to things. An injustice can be worked by moving from one distribution to another structurally identical one, for the second, in profile the same, may violate people's entitlements or deserts; it may not fit the actual history.

PATTERNING

The entitlement principles of justice in holdings that we have sketched are historical principles of justice. To better understand their precise character, we shall distinguish them from another subclass of the historical principles. Consider, as an example, the principle of distribution according to moral merit. This principle requires that total distributive shares vary directly with moral merit; no person should have a greater share than anyone whose moral merit is greater. * * * Or consider the principle that results by substituting "usefulness to society" for "moral merit" in the previous principle. * * * Let us call a principle of distribution *patterned* if it specifies that a distribution is to vary along with some natural dimension, weighted sum of natural dimensions, or lexicographic ordering of natural dimensions. And let us say a distribution is patterned if it accords with some patterned principle. (I speak of natural dimensions, admittedly without a general criterion for them, because for any set of holdings some artificial dimensions can be gimmicked up to vary along with the distribution of the set.) The principle of distribution in accordance with moral merit is a patterned historical principle, which specifies a patterned distribution. "Distribute according to I.Q." is a patterned principle that looks to information not contained in distributional matrices. It is not historical, however, in that it does not look to any past actions creating differential entitlements to evaluate a distribution; it requires only distributional matrices whose columns are labeled by I.Q. scores. The distribution in a society, however, may be composed of such simple patterned distributions, without itself being simply patterned. Different sectors may operate different patterns, or some combination of patterns may operate in different proportions across a society. A distribution composed in this manner, from a small number of patterned distributions, we also shall term "patterned." And we extend the use of "pattern" to include the overall designs put forth by combinations of end-state principles.

Almost every suggested principle of distributive justice is patterned: to each according to his moral merit, or needs, or marginal product, or how hard he tries, or the weighted sum of the foregoing, and so on. The principle of entitlement we have sketched is *not* patterned. There is no one natural dimension or weighted sum or combination of a small number of natural dimensions that yields the distributions generated in accordance with the principle of entitlement. The set of holdings that results when some persons receive their marginal products, other win at gambling, others receive a share of their mate's income, others receive gifts from foundations, others receive interest on loans, others receive gifts from admirers, others receive returns on investment, others make for themselves much of what they have, others find things, and so on, will not be patterned. ✳ ✳ ✳

To think that the task of a theory of distributive justice is to fill in the blank in "to each according to his _____" is to be predisposed to search for a pattern; and the separate treatment of "from each according to his _____" treats production and distribution as two separate and independent issues. On an entitlement view these are *not* two separate questions. Whoever makes something, having bought or contracted for all other held resources used in the process (transferring some of his holdings for these cooperating factors), is entitled to it. The situation is *not* one of something's getting made, and there being an open question of who is to get it. Things come into the world already attached to people having entitlements over them. From the point of view of the historical entitlement conception of justice in holdings, those who start afresh to complete "to each according to his _____" treat objects as if they appeared from nowhere, out of nothing. ✳ ✳ ✳

So entrenched are maxims of the usual form that perhaps we should present the entitlement conception as a competitor. Ignoring acquisition and rectification, we might say:

> From each according to what he chooses to do, to each according to what he makes for himself (perhaps with the contracted aid of others) and what others choose to do for him and choose to give him of what they've been given previously (under this maxim) and haven't yet expended or transferred.

This, the discerning reader will have noticed, has its defects as a slogan. So as a summary and great simplification (and not as a maxim with any independent meaning) we have:

> *From each as they choose, to each as they are chosen.*

HOW LIBERTY UPSETS PATTERNS

It is not clear how those holding alternative conceptions of distributive justice can reject the entitlement conception of justice in holdings. For suppose a distribution favored by one of these non-entitlement conceptions is realized. Let us suppose it is your favorite one and let us call this distribution *D1*; perhaps everyone has an equal share, perhaps shares vary in accordance with some dimension you treasure. Now suppose that Wilt Chamberlain is greatly in demand by basketball teams, being a great gate attraction. (Also suppose contracts run only for a year, with players being free agents.) He signs the following sort of contract with a team: In each home game, twenty-five cents from the price of each ticket of admission goes to him. (We ignore the question of whether he is "gouging" the owners, letting them look out for themselves.) The season starts, and people cheerfully attend his team's games; they buy their tickets, each time dropping a separate twenty-five cents of their admission price into a special box with Chamberlain's name on it. They are excited about seeing him play; it is worth the total admission price to them. Let us suppose that in one season one million persons attend his home games, and Wilt Chamberlain winds up with $250,000, a much larger sum than the average income and larger even than anyone else has. Is he entitled to this income? Is this new distribution $D2$, unjust? If so, why? There is *no* question about whether each of the people was entitled to the control over the resources they held in $D1$; because that was the distribution (your favorite) that (for the purposes of argument) we assumed was acceptable. Each of these persons *chose* to give twenty-five cents of their money to Chamberlain. They could have spent it on going to the movies, or on candy bars, or on copies of *Dissent* magazine, or of *Monthly Review*. But they all, at least one million of them, converged on giving it to Wilt Chamberlain in exchange for watching him play basketball. If $D1$ was a just distribution, and people voluntarily moved from it to $D2$, transferring parts of their shares they were given under $D1$ (what was it for if not to do something with?), isn't $D2$ also just? If the people were entitled to dispose of the resources to which they were entitled (under $D1$), didn't this include their being entitled to give it to, or exchange it with, Wilt Chamberlain? Can anyone else complain on grounds of justice? Each other person already has his legitimate share under $D1$. Under $D1$, there is nothing that anyone has that anyone else has a claim of justice against. After someone transfers something to Wilt Chamberlain, third parties *still* have their legitimate shares; *their* shares are not changed. By what process could such a transfer among two persons give rise to a legitimate claim of distributive justice on a portion of what was transferred, by a third party who had no claim of justice on any holding of the others *before* the transfer? To cut off objections irrelevant here, we might imagine the exchanges occurring in a socialist society, after hours. After playing whatever basketball he does in his daily work, or doing whatever other daily work he does, Wilt Chamberlain decides to put in *overtime* to earn additional money. (First his work quota is set; he works time over that.) Or imagine it is a skilled juggler people like to see, who puts on shows after hours.

* * * The socialist society would have to forbid capitalist acts between consenting adults. The general point illustrated by the Wilt Chamberlain example * * * is that no end-state principle or distributional patterned principle of justice can be continuously realized without continuous interference with people's lives. * * * To maintain a pattern one must either continually interfere to stop people from transferring resources as they wish to, or continually (or periodically) interfere to take from some persons resources that others for some reason chose to transfer to them. * * *

REDISTRIBUTION AND PROPERTY RIGHTS

Taxation of earnings from labor is on a par with forced labor. Some persons find this claim obviously true: taking the earning of *n* hours labor is like taking *n* hours from the person; it is like forcing the person to work *n* hours for another's purpose. Others find the claim absurd. But even these, *if* they object to forced labor, would oppose forcing unemployed hippies to work for the benefit of the needy. And they would also object to forcing each person to work five extra hours each week for the benefit of the needy. But a system that takes five hours' wages in taxes does not seem to them like one that forces someone to work five hours, since it offers the person forced a wider range of choice in activities than does taxation in kind with the particular labor specified. * * *

The man who chooses to work longer to gain an income more than sufficient for his basic needs prefers some extra goods or services to the leisure and activities he could perform during the possible nonworking hours; whereas the man who chooses not to work the extra time prefers the leisure activities to the extra goods or services he could acquire by working more. Given this, if it would be illegitimate for a tax system to seize some of a man's leisure (forced labor) for the purpose of serving the needy, how can it be legitimate for a tax system to seize some of a man's goods for that purpose? Why should we treat the man whose happiness requires certain material goods or services differently from the man whose preferences and desires make such goods unnecessary for his happiness? Why should the man who prefers seeing a movie (and who has to earn money for a ticket) be open to the required call to aid the needy, while the person who prefers looking at a sunset (and hence need earn no extra money) is not? * * *

Whether it is done through taxation on wages or on wages over a certain amount, or through seizure of profits, or through there being a big *social pot* so that it's not clear what's coming from where and what's going where, patterned principles of distributive justice involve appropriating the actions of other persons. Seizing the results of someone's labor is equivalent to seizing hours from him and directing him to carry on various activities. If people force you to do certain work, or unrewarded work, for a certain period of time, they decide what you are to do and what purposes your work is to serve apart from your decisions. This process whereby they take this decision from you makes them a *part-owner* of you; it gives them a property right in you. Just as having such partial control and power of decision, by right, over an animal or inanimate object would be to have a property right in it.

End-state and most patterned principles of distributive justice institute (partial) ownership by others of people and their actions and labor. These principles involve a shift from the classical liberals' notion of self-ownership to a notion of (partial) property rights in *other* people.

STUDY QUESTIONS

1. What are the elements of Nozick's entitlement theory of justice?
2. What is the consequence of Nozick's theory for the legitimacy of government redistribution of income?
3. What use does Nozick make of the Wilt Chamberlain example?

IRIS MARION YOUNG
Political Responsibility and Structural Injustice

Iris Marion Young (1949–2006) was a feminist political philosopher who produced a wide range of influential works, including Justice and the Politics of Difference *(1990).*

The central city apartment building where Sandy, a white single mother, has been living with her two children, has been bought by a developer who plans to convert it into condominiums. The building was falling apart and poorly maintained, and she thought the rent was too high anyway, so she seizes the opportunity to locate a better place. She works as a sales clerk in a suburban mall, to which she has had to take two buses from her current residence, for a total of more than three hours commuting time each day. So she decides to look for an apartment closer to where she works, but she still needs to be on a bus line.

She begins looking in the newspaper and on line for apartment rental advertisements, and she is shocked at the rents for one and two bedroom apartments. One of the agents at an apartment finding service listens to her situation and preferences, diligently looks through listings, and goes out of his way to arrange meetings with Sandy.

Sandy learns that there are few rental apartments close to her workplace—most of the residential properties near the mall are single family houses. The few apartments nearby are very expensive. Most suburban apartments in her price range are located on the other side of the city from her job; there are also some in the city but few which she judges decent that she can afford and in a neighborhood where she feels her children will be safe. In either case, the bus transportation to work is long and arduous, so she decides that she must devote some of the money she hoped would pay the rent to make car payments. She applies for a housing subsidy program, and is told that the waiting time is about two years.

With the deadline for eviction looming, Sandy searches for two months. Finally she settles for a one-bedroom apartment forty-five minutes drive from her job—except when traffic is heavy. The apartment is smaller than she hoped she would have to settle for; the two children will sleep together in the bedroom and she will sleep on a foldout bed in the living room. There are no amenities such as a washer and dryer in the building or an outdoor play area for the children. Sandy sees no other option but to take the apartment, and then faces one final hurdle: she needs to deposit three months' rent to secure the apartment. She has used all her savings as down payment on the car, however. So she cannot rent the apartment, and having learned that this is a typical landlord policy, she now faces the prospect of homelessness.

This mundane story can be repeated with minor variations for hundreds of thousands of people across the United States. * * *

Presumably most of us would agree that Sandy and her children lack a basic element of minimal well being. Many will agree with me, further, that Sandy suffers an *injustice* in the fact that access to decent affordable housing is so difficult for her. What are the grounds of that judgment? Sandy's misfortune is not due to any personal or moral failing on her part. She plays by the socially accepted rules. She has a steady job and is a dutiful employee, swallowing a good deal of pettiness and complaint about her working conditions and interactions with people in the company. She does her best as a parent, spending most of her non-job time with her children, helping them with their homework, participating in school events, and taking them to doctor appointments.

Nor is Sandy's situation a matter of sheer bad luck, like being struck by lightning. On the contrary, it is predictable that there will be an insufficient supply of decent affordable housing in an urban area with a generally healthy capitalist economy and where large scale non-profit housing investment is absent. The major causes of Sandy's misfortune lie in the normal operations of markets and institutions of planning, building, land use regulation, investment, finance and exchange in the American city where she lives. The grounds for claiming that Sandy and those in a similar situation suffer injustice, that is, lie in the fact that her difficulties are socially caused.

✳ ✳ ✳ While socially caused, moreover, a scarcity of decent affordable housing does not result from the actions of one or a few specifiable perpetrators. Instead, this circumstance which affects many people is the outcome of the normal actions of a large number of agents—renters, home buyers, mortgage lenders, real estate brokers, developers, land use regulators, transport planners, and so on. The injustice Sandy and others suffer is *structural* or systemic.

How should moral agents, both individual and collective, think about their responsibilities in relation to such structural social injustices? ✳ ✳ ✳

STRUCTURAL INJUSTICE

In *A Theory of Justice*, John Rawls famously says that the subject of justice is the basic structure of society, which concerns "the way in which the major social institutions distribute fundamental rights and duties and determine the division of advantages from social cooperation."[1] Major institutions include, he says, the legal system's definition of basic rights and duties, market relations, the system of property in the means of production, and family organization. To these I would add the basic kinds of positions in the social division of labor.

✳ ✳ ✳ As I understand the concept, structure denotes a confluence of institutional rules and interactive routines, mobilization of resources, and physical structures; these constitute the historical givens in relation to which individuals act, and which are relatively stable over time. The term structure also refers to wider social outcomes that result from the confluence of many individual actions within given institutional relations, whose collective

---

1 *A Theory of Justice* (Cambridge, MA: Harvard University Press, 1971), p. 7.

consequences often do not bear the mark of any person or group's intention. For the purposes of using concepts of structure for thinking about justice and responsibility, I am particularly concerned with large scale or "macro" structures. If we wish to understand and criticize the way that many individuals and groups face too limited and unsavory sets of options, then we need an account of large-scale systemic outcomes of the operations of many institutions and practices that constrain some people at the same time that they enable others.

＊＊＊ Peter Blau offers the following definition: "A social structure can be defined as a multidimensional space of differentiated social positions among which a population is distributed. The social associations of people provide both the criterion for distinguishing social positions and the connections among them that make them elements of a single social structure."[2] ＊＊＊ The social structure consists in the connections among the positions and their relationships, and the way the attributes of positions internally constitute one another through those relationships. In my example, the apartment hunter stands in a particular position in relation to other positions in the structural processes that produce, set prices for, and market housing units. She mostly experiences effects of those processes as constraints on her options. Her position is very different from that of the owner of apartment complexes or the head of a municipal zoning board, though persons in these more powerful positions also experience structural constraints.

＊＊＊ Social structures exist only in the action and interaction of persons; they exist not as states, but as processes. Thus Anthony Giddens defines social structures in terms of "rules and resources, recursively implicated in the reproduction of social systems."[3] In the idea of the duality of structure, Giddens theorizes how people act on the basis of their knowledge of pre-existing structures and in so acting reproduce those structures. ＊＊＊ Our apartment hunter Sandy, for example, has decided she wishes to live in the suburbs not only because her job is there, but also because widespread social norms and behavior identify a suburban space and lifestyle as more comfortable in many ways than that of city centers. That people act on this assumption in fact helps produce more amenities in suburbs, such

---

2   Peter Blau, *Inequality and Heterogeneity* (New York: Free Press, 1977), p. 4.

3   Anthony Giddens, *The Constitution of Society* (Berkeley: University of California Press, 1984), p. 25.

as better schools and shopping centers. At the same time, action based on these assumptions helps depopulate some city neighborhoods and reduce their resource base, thus fulfilling the prophecy that they are less safe and comfortable. These judgments mediated through market processes then contribute to the situation in which Sandy finds herself, namely that she cannot afford the apartments in the neighborhoods she follows others in defining as desirable.

✳✳✳ The concept of social structure must also include conditions under which actors act, which are often a collective outcome of action impressed onto the physical environment. Jean-Paul Sartre calls this aspect of social structuration the *practico-inert*.[4] Most of the conditions under which people act are socio-historical: they are the products of previous actions, usually products of many coordinated and uncoordinated but mutually influenced actions over them. Those collective actions have produced determinate effects on the physical and cultural environment which condition future actions in specific ways. Housing options certainly are constrained by the practico-inert in this way. Past planning decisions have put highways and rapid transit rail lines in particular places, for example, and these are now part of the physical environment with significant influence on the housing market as well as home to work quality of life issues.

✳✳✳ The actions and interactions among persons differently situated in social structures using rules and resources ✳✳✳ often have future effects beyond the immediate purposes and intentions of the actors. Structured social actions and interactions often have collective results that no one intends and which may even be counter to the best intentions of the actors. Sartre calls such effects counter-finalities.[5] Even though no one intends them, they become given circumstances that help structure future actions. Presumably no one intends that a significant number of people in a metropolitan area will be forced to scrimp on food and dental care to pay the rent, or to live in substandard apartments, or seek shelter in a community center. ✳✳✳

✳✳✳ Justice and injustice concern primarily an evaluation of how the institutions of a society work together to produce outcomes that support or minimize the threat of domination, and support or minimize everyone's

---

4   Jean-Paul Sartre, *Critique of Dialectical Reason*, trans. Alan Sheeridan-Smith (London: New Left Books, 1976), Bk. I, ch. 3.

5   Ibid, pp. 277–92.

opportunities to develop and exercise capacities for living a good life as they define it. Social justice concerns the actions of particular individuals on the policies of particular institutions only secondarily, as these contribute to constituting structures that enable and constrain persons.

Structural injustices are harms that come to people as a result of structural processes in which many people participate. These participants may well be aware that their actions contribute to the processes that produce the outcomes, but for many it is not possible to trace the specific causal relation between their particular actions and some particular part of the outcome. Some upper income urban dwellers, for example, may be aware that their decisions to buy condominiums in renovated center city buildings contributes to processes that displace lower income renters like Sandy. No one can say, however, that their decisions and actions have directly caused Sandy's landlord to sell the building to a condo developer, thus necessitating Sandy's apartment search.

POLITICAL RESPONSIBILITY

* * * How should moral agents—both individual and organizational—think about their responsibilities in relation to structural social injustice? This question presents a puzzle for two reasons. * * * First, although structures are produced by actions, in most cases it is not possible to trace which specific actions of which specific agents cause which specific parts of the structural processes or their outcomes. The effects of particular actions often influence one another in ways beyond the control and intention of any of the actors. Second, because it is therefore difficult for individuals to see a relationship between their own actions and structural outcomes, we have a tendency to distance ourselves from any responsibility for them. The dominant concept of responsibility, I suggest, operates on a liability model that seeks causally to connect an agent to a harm in order to assign the agent responsibility for it. Because the relation of any actions to structural outcomes cannot be assigned in that direct way, we have a tendency to conclude that those structural processes and outcomes are misfortunes rather than injustices, circumstances we must live with rather than try to change.

* * * Many of the problems we collectively face are large scale structural problems, some of which cross national boundaries—global warming, volatility of financial systems, unemployment, and countless other issues. Yet the concepts of responsibility we operate with derive from and are most suited to issues of smaller scale interaction. We continue to rely on a phenomenology of agency that gives primacy to near effects over remote effects, to individual effects over group effects, and to people's positive actions more than what they have failed to do. This traditional notion of agency and the concept of responsibility derived from it, however, is not well suited to understanding and taking responsibility for the large scale social structural processes that are sources of many social and natural problems. * * *

* * * We need a plausible way of conceiving responsibility that connects individual agency to structural processes. I aim to offer some elements of such a conception, which I call political responsibility.

I find it helpful to contrast the model of political responsibility with a more common model of assigning responsibility which derives from legal and moral reasoning to find guilt or fault for a harm. Under this liability model, we assign responsibility to particular agents when we show that their actions are causally connected to the outcome for which we seek to assign responsibility. This agent can be a collective entity, such as a corporation or a government, but when it is, that entity can be treated as a single agent for the purposes of assigning responsibility. The actions found causally connected to the circumstances are shown to be voluntary and performed with adequate knowledge of the situation. If a candidate for responsibility in this sense can successfully show that their action was not voluntary or that they were excusably ignorant, then their responsibility is usually mitigated if not dissolved. When these conditions do exist, however, it is appropriate to blame the agents for the harmful outcomes. * * *

The liability model is primarily backward looking in its purpose; it reviews the history of events in order to assign responsibility, often for the sake of exacting punishment or compensation. Assigning responsibility to some agents, on this model, finally usually also has the function of absolving other agents who might have been candidates for fault. To find this person or group of persons guilty of a crime usually implies that others who were suspect are not guilty.

* * * By proposing a model of political responsibility, I do not aim to replace or reject the liability model of responsibility. My claim is, rather, that this model of responsibility is either insufficient or inappropriate for assigning responsibility in relation to structural injustice.

Let me illustrate how by referring again to the example of insufficient availability of affordable housing. Does it make sense to blame anyone * * * for Sandy's situation? One might argue that the landlord who has sold the building to a condominium developer is to blame. He didn't have to sell the building, or he might have done something to ensure that Sandy would nevertheless have a decent apartment that she could afford in reasonable proximity to her job. Current legal and social norms expect nothing of the sort from landlords such as this; indeed, expecting such action would itself involve structural changes that give building owners more influence over processes of housing allocation than they currently have. More generally, even though it may be appropriate to blame or hold liable particular agents at least for an aspect of the housing problems of particular persons—when they have discriminated against them, for example—there is no one in particular to blame for the general structural injustice of inadequate access to decent affordable housing for all. Vast numbers of actors contribute to the processes that produce this outcome, many of them with little awareness of how their actions contribute. The desire of young affluent professionals to move back to center cities from outlying suburbs, for example, gives incentives to investors to finance developers to convert old buildings into luxury condominiums. Each agent moves on their own interests within the existing legal and social norms, and their actions together contribute to the outcome that some people are displaced and have difficulty finding decent affordable housing. None ought to be *blamed* for that outcome, I am suggesting, because the specific actions of each cannot be causally disentangled from the structural processes to trace a specific aspect of the outcome.

The assignment of responsibility as liability is an indispensable aspect of moral judgment. ✳ ✳ ✳ The liability model of responsibility, however, is inadequate for understanding and evaluating much about the relationship of individual actors to large scale social processes and structural injustices. It needs to be supplemented with a notion of responsibility that implicates persons in the effects of structural processes because they participate in the production and reproduction of those structures. Thousands of actors in a metropolitan area and outside it contribute to the market, policy, and symbolic processes that produce the predictable outcome of a shortage of decent affordable housing in easy commuting distance from jobs. Most of these actors feel constrained by structures in their own decisions and outcomes. While together they produce the outcomes, they do not intend the consequence that denies some people a decent apartment, and many in fact condemn or regret such outcomes. A concept of political responsibility says that we who are part of these processes should be held responsible for the structural injustice, as members of the collective that produces it, even though we cannot trace the outcome we regret to our own particular actions in a direct causal chain. A concept of political responsibility fills this role without attributing blame.

When I designate this concept "political responsibility," the term "political" refers to something wider than what state institutions do. I use the term more in a sense like Hannah Arendt.[6] For her, the political refers to phenomena and movements of collective action, where people work together to form public works and institutions. The making of state institutions, and using them to enact collective goals, is often an important means of enacting political responsibility, but do not exhaust the concept or its organizational possibilities.

I have five features that distinguish the concept of political responsibility from a liability model. * * *

(1) Unlike a blame model, political responsibility does not seek to mark out and isolate those to be held responsible, thereby distinguishing them from others, who by implication then are not responsible. * * *

When harms or injustices have no isolatable perpetrator, but rather result from the participation of thousands or millions of people in institutions and practices that result in harms, such an isolating concept of responsibility is inadequate. Where there are structural injustices, finding that some people are guilty of perpetrating specific wrongful actions does not absolve others whose actions contribute to the outcomes from bearing responsibility.

(2) In a liability concept of responsibility, what counts as a wrong for which a perpetrator is sought and for which he or she might be required to compensate, is generally conceived as a deviation from a baseline norm. Implicitly we assume a normal background situation that is morally acceptable, if not ideal. A crime or an actionable harm consists in a morally and often legally unacceptable deviation from this background structure. The process that brought about the harm is conceived as a discrete, bounded event that breaks away from the ongoing normal flow. Punishment, redress, or compensation aims to restore normality or to "make whole" in relation to the baseline circumstance.

A concept of political responsibility in relation to structural injustices, on the other hand, evaluates not a harm that deviates from the normal and acceptable, but rather often brings into question precisely the background conditions that ascriptions of blame or fault assume as normal. When we

---

6 *Editor's note*: Hannah Arendt, 1906–1975, was a German-born political philosopher, especially known for her writings on totalitarianism.

judge that structural injustice exists, we are saying precisely that at least some of the normal and accepted background conditions of action are not morally acceptable. Most of us contribute to a greater or lesser degree to the production and reproduction of structural injustice precisely because we follow the accepted and expected rules and conventions of the communities and institution in which we act. Often we enact these conventions and practices in a habitual way, without explicit reflection and deliberation on what we are doing, having in the foreground of our consciousness and intention immediate goals we want to achieve and the particular people we need to interact with to achieve them.

(3) Political responsibility differs from a liability model of responsibility in being more forward looking. Blame and praise are primarily backward looking judgments. They refer back to an action or event assumed to have reached its terminus. Most often the purpose of assigning responsibility as fault or liability is to sanction, punish or exact compensation from those liable. To be sure, such backward looking condemnation and sanction may have a forward looking purpose; we may wish to deter others from similar action in the future, or to identify weak points in an institutional system that allows or encourages such blameworthy actions, in order to reform the institutions. Once we take this latter step, however, we have left a liability model and are moving toward a conception of political responsibility. The reform project likely involves responsibility of many people to take actions directed at those reforms, even though they are not to blame for past problems.

Political responsibility seeks less to reckon debts than to bring about results, and thus depends on the actions of everyone who is in a position to contribute to the results. Taking political responsibility in respect to social structures emphasizes the future more than the past. Because the particular causal relationship of the actions of particular individuals or even organizations to the structural outcomes is often not possible to trace, there is no point in seeking to exact compensation or redress only from those who have contributed to that outcome. The injustices produced through structures have not reached a terminus, but rather are ongoing. * * *

There is an important sense, then, however, in which political responsibility must be backward looking. An understanding of how structural processes produce and reproduce injustice requires understanding the history of those processes, often looking far into the past. The purpose of this analysis of past events is not to find perpetrators, however, but rather to understand how actions and policies have long term effects and how the effects can solidify into structures that condition new actions.

(4) Political responsibility is relatively open with regard to the actions that count as taking up the responsibility. It is distinct from duty in this sense. Like duties, responsibilities carry a burden and an obligation; carrying out responsibilities is not a matter of mere beneficence. Unlike duties, however, responsibility carries considerable discretion; one *must* carry out one's responsibilities, but *how* one does so is a matter for judgment according to what the responsibilities are for, the capabilities of agents, and the content of action. ＊＊＊ A duty specifies a rule that an agent should follow. One has fulfilled the duty if one has performed the required actions. Carrying out a responsibility, on the other hand, consists in seeking to bring about a specified outcome. It is possible to act in accord with rules of morality and yet not have discharged one's responsibilities, because one has not achieved the required outcomes even though it is feasible to do so.

(5) Political responsibility, finally, is responsibility shared in specific ways. As Larry May theorizes, the concept of shared responsibility is distinct from the concept of collective responsibility in that the former is a distributed responsibility whereas the latter is not. A collective of persons, such as a corporation, might be said to be responsible for a state of affairs without any of its constituent individuals being responsible as such. Shared responsibility, on the other hand, is a personal responsibility for outcomes or the risks of harmful outcomes, produced by a group of persons. As May sees it each is personally responsible for the outcome in a partial way, since he or she alone does not produce the outcomes; the specific part that each plays in producing the outcome cannot be isolated and identified, however, and thus the responsibility is essentially shared.[7]

May's treatment of shared responsibility is largely backward looking. He reflects on how persons who have not themselves been directly guilty of a harm such as a hate crime, may nevertheless contribute by their attitudes and actions to fostering a social environment in which such harms appear more acceptable than they might otherwise. If we follow my claim that political responsibility is more forward looking than backward looking, then the shared nature of the political responsibility refers primarily to the relationships with others that the responsibility involves. Taking political responsibility means acknowledging that one participates in social processes that have some unjust outcomes, and one participates with many others. Discharging the responsibility entails enjoining collective action with at least

---

7 Larry May, *Sharing Responsibility* (Chicago: University of Chicago Press, 1993), Chapter 2.

some of these others. We share responsibility to organize means of changing how the processes work so they will issue in less injustice. State institutions are often a most effective means of taking collective action to change structural processes, but government policy usually requires the active support of communities to be effective in its aims. The form of responsibility, then, is political in these senses that acting on my responsibilities involves joining with others in a public discourse in which we try to persuade one another about courses of collective action that will contribute to ameliorating the problem.

An important corollary of this feature of political responsibility is that many of those properly thought to be victims of harm or injustice may nevertheless have political responsibility in relation to it. In a fault model of responsibility, blaming those who claim to be victims of injustice functions to absolve others of responsibility for their plight. In a conception of political responsibility, however, those who can properly be argued to be victims of structural injustice can be called to a responsibility that they share with others in the structures to engage in actions directed at transforming the structures. Indeed, on many issues those who might be argued to be in less advantaged positions in the structures ought to take the lead in organizing and proposing remedies for injustice, because their interests might be argued as the most acutely at stake and their social position offers them a unique understanding of the likely effects of policies and actions proposed by others situated in more powerful and privileged positions. ＊＊＊

Conceptualizing political responsibility as distinct from blame is important not only philosophically, but also for the sake of motivating political action. Frequently the reaction of people being blamed for a wrong is defensive—to look for other agents who should be blamed instead of them, or to find excuses that mitigate their liability in those cases where they must agree that their actions do causally contribute to the harm. Such practices of accusation and defense have an important place in morality and law. In many contexts where the issue is how to mobilize collective action for the sake of social change and greater justice, however, such rhetorics of blame and finger-pointing displacement lead more to resentment and refusal to take responsibility than to useful basis of action. Banks that engage in redlining practices or landlords that fail to maintain the buildings they own should certainly be blamed for the effects their actions have on housing markets or living conditions, and should be punished in some way. Efforts to level blame for a generally tight market in affordable housing in a given metropolitan area, however, are more likely to create divisions among the agents that must work together toward remedies. Public discourse in our society is altogether too full of accusations of fault and the defensiveness and resentment such accusations usually produce.

KINDS AND DEGREES OF RESPONSIBILITY

Some people might object to the conception of political responsibility I have outlined on the grounds that it seems to make nearly everyone responsible for nearly everything. Most of us participate in a number of structural processes that arguably have disadvantaging, harmful or unjust consequences for some people in virtue of our jobs, the market choices we make, or other activities. Surely it is asking too much, the objection runs, for each of us to worry about all these modes of participating in structures and how we might adjust our lives and relation to others so as to reduce their unjust effects. Our relation to many of these structural processes is so diffuse, and the possibility that our own action can effect a change in outcomes is often so remote, that it is more reasonable to limit our moral concern to matters where we stand in direct relation to others and can see clearly the effect of our action on them.

One parameter of thinking here refers to the degree of injustice. Where basic rights are violated in a widespread fashion over a long term, moral agents have greater responsibility to take action directed at redress than for lesser injustices.

Approaching such structural injustice, we can appeal not to preassigned tasks that people have, but rather to their institutional or social *position*. What might be required from one's position is doing something different from or additional to the tasks normally assigned to that position, but different persons nevertheless stand in differing positions in structures that produce unjust outcomes, which afford them different opportunities and capacities for influencing those outcomes. I suggest that persons can reason about their action in relation to structural injustice along parameters of *connection, power, privilege,* and *interest.*

Connection—The theory of political responsibility argues that agents have forward looking responsibilities to take action to help undermine structural injustices not on the general grounds that right thinking people should be concerned about harm and suffering wherever it occurs, but on the more specific grounds that we are connected by our own actions to the processes that cause injustice for others. It is not obvious to the individual home buyer or renter that his or her location preferences and income allocation decisions may contribute to limiting the housing options of others, but in aggregate they often do, and home buyers and renters can become and often are aware of this. Faced with such an understanding of the outcomes of housing market processes, some people claim that these are matters of fate, or that the market will produce the best outcome for housing consumers in the long run. Certainly there is room for disagreement about just what are the structural causes of a lack of access to affordable, decent housing for significant numbers of people, and about what kinds of actions would best remedy such injustice. Political responsibility at this reflective moment of recognizing the connection of actions to outcomes, however, requires at least that the collective discuss these issues with an eye to collective action to improve the situation.

Power—A person's position in structural processes usually carries different degrees of potential or actual power or influence over the processes that produce the outcomes. Organizations and institutions, moreover, vary in their power and ability to influence structural processes. In structural processes producing and reproducing housing options, for example, certain government officials, corporate executives, property owners, all holding positions in particular types of institutions, have more power to influence these processes and influence their transformation than others. The power and influence parameter for reasoning suggests that where individuals and organizations do not have sufficient energy and resources to respond to all structural injustices to which they are connected, they should focus on those where they have more capacity to influence structural processes. * * *

Privilege—Where there are structural injustices, these usually produce not only victims of injustice, but persons who acquire relative privileges by virtue of the structures. Most who occupy positions of power with respect to the structures also derive privileges from this power. In most situations of structural injustice, however, there are relatively privileged persons who have relatively little power as individuals or in their institutional positions. Affluent home buyers or renters, for example, stand in a relatively privileged position in housing markets, especially compared with persons unable to locate decent affordable housing in reasonable distance from their workplaces. As housing consumers, however, they have less power than government officials, or financial officers, or heads of major real estate broker firms to influence and thus contribute to the transformation of structures. Persons who benefit relatively from structural inequalities have special moral responsibilities to contribute to organized efforts to correct them, not because they are to blame, but because they are able to adapt to changed circumstances without suffering serious deprivation.

Interest—People and organizations usually have different interests in the maintenance or transformation of structural injustices. Ironically, often those with the greatest interest in reproducing the structures are also those with greatest power to influence their transformation. Those who are victims of structural injustice have a great interest in structural transformation. Earlier I said that one of the distinctive things about a concept of political responsibility is that victims of injustice may nevertheless have political responsibility in relation to it. Those who suffer injustice have the greatest interest in its elimination, and often have unique insights into its social sources and the probable effects of proposals for change. To the extent that those with significant interests in transformation and those who are harmed through structural injustices have more insight and determination in such transformative projects, their voices should have particular influence in organizations and movements that aim to change the structures.

∗∗∗ Transformation in structures that produce or perpetuate injustice can occur only when many individuals take responsibility for making such transformation.

STUDY QUESTIONS

1. What does Young mean by structural injustice?
2. How does Young distinguish the liability model from the political responsibility model?
3. What is morally required from us, according to the political responsibility model?

■ Compare and Contrast Questions

1. Is Rawls's difference principle vulnerable to Nozick's objections to patterned theories of justice? If so, how strong is this objection?
2. How would Nozick respond to Young's example of Sandy?
3. How compatible are Rawls's and Young's accounts of justice?

WORLD HUNGER AND FOREIGN AID

This section contains three contrasting perspectives on what moral obligations people in wealthy countries have to people in grave need in distant lands and how we should fulfill those obligations. We begin with a much discussed paper by Australian philosopher Peter Singer. Suppose you are walking past a pond and notice a young child drowning. You could easily wade in and save the child, but it would be at some cost, as your clothes would get muddy. Most of us would think that we had a very strong moral duty to save the child. Peter Singer points out that we are in a position to save the life of a child on the other side of the planet simply by making a small charitable donation to famine relief. What is the difference between the cases? Singer thinks there is no morally significant difference, and therefore, just as we have a duty to save the life of the drowning child, we have a duty to make significant charitable donations to save many lives abroad.

The moral principle that underlies this intuition, according to Singer, is that "if it is in our power to prevent something bad from happening, without thereby sacrificing anything of comparable moral importance, we ought, morally, to do it."[1] One difference between the cases, of course, is distance. While distance can affect what we can know, Singer thinks that distance makes no other moral difference. And in the case of famines we have all the information we need. He also argues that the fact that others are in a position to help, in the case of famine, again is irrelevant. If there are others standing by the pond who do not act, this in itself does not reduce your duty. Indeed, Singer thinks his argument applies even if the intuition is weakened to remove the word *comparable* in the statement quoted above. Most of us are able to save lives without sacrificing anything of any moral importance. Doing so is a moral duty, not an act of charity. And while it's true that governments have a duty to act on our behalf, this does not excuse us from acting too.

Singer's piece is followed by a short extract from Zambian economist Dambisa Moyo. Moyo argues that international aid has done much more to harm developing economies than to help them. Moyo claims that more than a trillion dollars of aid has been sent to Africa in the last 50 years, but the results have been disastrous: Aid has made poor people poorer and slowed development.

It is important to note that Moyo's target is what she calls "development-related aid" and not humanitarian aid, which is typically aimed at famine relief or medical emergencies. Development aid is generally supplied by the governments of rich countries and is often in the form of loans rather than grants. These forms of development aid, she argues, are often siphoned off by corrupt governments, leaving the recipient country saddled with debt but without the benefits of the intended development. Moreover, independently of the crippling effect of debt, aid redirects energies and ingenuity within

---

1 *Editor's note*: See selections from Peter Singer's "Famine, Affluence, and Morality" on pp. 614–622 of this reader.

the recipient country to those activities where there is the greatest opportunity for extortion. This means, for example, that public contracts are often given to those who pay the biggest bribe, rather than those who will do the best work. Welfare and education services are often ignored. With lower growth and increased poverty, countries become ever more dependent on aid, yet the receipt of aid adds to their problems. This, for Moyo, is the "vicious cycle of aid."

In the final extract, in contrast to Peter Singer's more utilitarian arguments, Onora O'Neill approaches issues of world hunger from a Kantian perspective. While, of course, humanitarian aid is sometimes vital to save lives, Kantian moral theory requires a focus on the agency of individuals and not just their happiness or welfare. Accordingly, O'Neill emphasizes how important it is to seek solutions in which people in need are able to take control of their own lives and fates, come up with their own solutions, and, ultimately, achieve a sustainable state of affairs in which they will not need to rely on outside assistance.

O'Neill notes that utilitarian arguments have been used both for and against famine relief (and we can see the contrasting perspectives of Singer and Moyo in this light). Because utilitarianism is very much focused on outcomes, utilitarian theory means that the nature of our moral duties will depend on our calculation of consequences, which will very often be uncertain. The Kantian alternative proposes that morality requires us to treat people as ends in themselves and not merely as means to the ends of others. This requires us to rely on maxims of action to which famine relief recipients could consent, thereby ruling out deception, coercion, and violence. We can, though, fail to treat people as ends without treating them as means, as we might do by failing to treat them as rational, autonomous individuals. Some forms of humanitarian aid could be criticized on this basis. Against this, the Kantian insists on efforts to create the right type of background conditions so that people can act as the autonomous agents that they are.

PETER SINGER
Famine, Affluence, and Morality

Peter Singer (b. 1946) is a contemporary Australian utilitarian philosopher, known for his uncompromising views on many issues of contemporary morality, such as animal liberation and the moral necessity to address global poverty.

As I write this, in November 1971, people are dying in East Bengal from lack of food, shelter, and medical care. The suffering and death that are occurring there now are not inevitable, not unavoidable in any fatalistic sense of the term. Constant poverty, a cyclone, and a civil war have turned at least nine million people into destitute refugees; nevertheless, it is not beyond the capacity of the richer nations to give enough assistance to reduce any further suffering to very small proportions. The decisions and actions of human beings can prevent this kind of suffering. Unfortunately, human beings have not made the necessary decisions. At the individual level, people have, with very few exceptions, not responded to the situation in any significant way. Generally speaking, people have not given large sums to relief funds; they have not written to their parliamentary representatives demanding increased government assistance; they have not demonstrated in the streets, held symbolic fasts, or done anything else directed toward providing the refugees with the means to satisfy their essential needs. At the government level, no government has given the sort of massive aid that would enable the refugees to survive for more than a few days. ∗ ∗ ∗

∗ ∗ ∗ The Bengal emergency is just the latest and most acute of a series of major emergencies in various parts of the world, arising both from natural and from man-made causes. There are also many parts of the world in which people die from malnutrition and lack of food independent of any special emergency. ∗ ∗ ∗

What are the moral implications of a situation like this? In what follows, I shall argue that the way people in relatively affluent countries react to a situation like that in Bengal cannot be justified; indeed, the whole way we look at moral issues—our moral conceptual scheme—needs to be altered, and with it, the way of life that has come to be taken for granted in our society. ∗ ∗ ∗

I begin with the assumption that suffering and death from lack of food, shelter, and medical care are bad. I think most people will agree about this. ∗ ∗ ∗

My next point is this: if it is in our power to prevent something bad from happening, without thereby sacrificing anything of comparable moral importance, we ought, morally, to do it. By "without sacrificing anything of comparable moral importance" I mean without causing anything else comparably bad to happen, or doing something that is wrong in itself, or failing to promote some moral good, comparable in significance to the bad thing that we can prevent. This principle seems almost as uncontroversial as the last one. It requires us only to prevent what is bad, and not to promote what is good, and it requires this of us only when we can do it without sacrificing anything that is, from the moral point of view, comparably important. I could even, as far as the application of my argument to the Bengal emergency is concerned, qualify the point so as to make it: if it is in our power to prevent something very bad from happening, without thereby sacrificing anything morally significant, we ought, morally, to do it. An application of this principle would be as follows: if I am walking past a shallow pond and see a child drowning in it, I ought to wade in and pull the child out. This will mean getting my clothes muddy, but this is insignificant, while the death of the child would presumably be a very bad thing.

The uncontroversial appearance of the principle just stated is deceptive. If it were acted upon, even in its qualified form, our lives, our society, and our world would be fundamentally changed. For the principle takes, firstly, no account of proximity or distance. It makes no moral difference whether the person I can help is a neighbor's child ten yards from me or a Bengali whose name I shall never know, ten thousand miles away. Secondly, the principle makes no distinction between cases in which I am the only person who could possibly do anything and cases in which I am just one among millions in the same position.

I do not think I need to say much in defense of the refusal to take proximity and distance into account. The fact that a person is physically near to us, so that we have personal contact with him, may make it more likely that we *shall* assist him, but this does not show that we *ought* to help him rather than another who happens to be further away. If we accept any principle of impartiality, universalizability, equality, or whatever, we cannot discriminate against someone merely because he is far away from us (or we are far away from him). Admittedly, it is possible that we are in a better position to judge what needs to be done to help a person near to us than one far away, and perhaps also to provide the assistance we judge to be necessary. If this were the case, it would be a reason for helping those near to us first. This may once have been a justification for being more concerned with the poor in one's own town than with famine victims in India. Unfortunately for those who like to keep their moral responsibilities limited, instant communication and swift transportation have changed the situation. From the moral point of view, the development of the world into a "global village" has made an important, though still unrecognized, difference to our moral situation. Expert observers and supervisors, sent out by famine relief organizations or permanently stationed in famine-prone areas, can direct our aid to a refugee in Bengal almost as effectively as we could get it to someone in our own block. There would seem, therefore, to be no possible justification for discriminating on geographical grounds.

There may be a greater need to defend the second implication of my principle—that the fact that there are millions of other people in the same position, in respect to the Bengali refugees, as I am, does not make the situation significantly different from a situation in which I am the only person who can prevent something very bad from occurring. Again, of course, I admit that there is a psychological difference between the cases; one feels less guilty about doing nothing if one can point to others, similarly placed, who have also done nothing. Yet this can make no real difference to our moral obligations. Should I consider that I am less obliged to pull the drowning child out of the pond if on looking around I see other people, no further away than I am, who have also noticed the child but are doing nothing? One has only to ask this question to see the absurdity of the view that numbers lessen obligation. It is a view that is an ideal excuse for inactivity; unfortunately most of the major evils—poverty, overpopulation, pollution—are problems in which everyone is almost equally involved.

The view that numbers do make a difference can be made plausible if stated in this way: if everyone in circumstances like mine gave £5 to the Bengal Relief Fund, there would be enough to provide food, shelter, and medical care for the refugees; there is no reason why I should give more than anyone else in the same circumstances as I am; therefore I have no obligation to give more than £5. Each premise in this argument is true, and the argument looks sound. It may convince us, unless we notice that it is based on a hypothetical premise, although the conclusion is not stated hypothetically. The argument would be sound if the conclusion were: if everyone in circumstances like mine were to give £5, I would have no obligation to give more than £5. If the conclusion were so stated, however, it would be obvious that the argument has no bearing on a situation in which it is not the case that everyone else gives £5. This, of course, is the actual situation. It is more or less certain that not everyone in circumstances like mine will give £5. So there will not be enough to provide the needed food, shelter, and medical care. Therefore by giving more than £5 I will prevent more suffering than I would if I gave just £5. * * *

If my argument so far has been sound, neither our distance from a preventable evil nor the number of other people who, in respect to that evil, are in the same situation as we are, lessens our obligation to mitigate or prevent that evil. I shall therefore take as established the principle I asserted earlier. As I have already said, I need to assert it only in its qualified form: if it is in our power to prevent something very bad from happening, without thereby sacrificing anything else morally significant, we ought, morally, to do it.

The outcome of this argument is that our traditional moral categories are upset. The traditional distinction between duty and charity cannot be drawn, or at least, not in the place we normally draw it. Giving money to the Bengal Relief Fund is regarded as an act of charity in our society. The bodies which collect money are known as "charities." These organizations see themselves in this way—if you send them a check, you will be thanked for your "generosity." Because giving money is regarded as an act of charity, it is not thought that there is anything wrong with not giving. The charitable man may be praised, but the man who is not charitable is not condemned. People do not feel in any way ashamed or guilty about spending money on new clothes or a new car instead of giving it to famine relief. (Indeed, the alternative does not occur to them.) This way of looking at the matter cannot be justified. When we buy new clothes not to keep ourselves warm but to look "well-dressed" we are not providing for any important need. We would not be sacrificing anything significant if we were to continue to wear our old clothes, and give the money to famine relief. By doing so, we would be preventing another person from starving. It follows from what I have said earlier that we ought to give money away, rather than spend it on clothes which we do not need to keep us warm. To do so is not charitable, or generous. Nor is it the kind of act which philosophers and theologians have called "supererogatory"—an act which it would be good to do, but not wrong not to do. On the contrary, we ought to give the money away, and it is wrong not to do so.

I am not maintaining that there are no acts which are charitable, or that there are no acts which it would be good to do but not wrong not to do. It may be possible to redraw the distinction between duty and charity in some other place. All I am arguing here is that the present way of drawing the distinction, which makes it an act of charity for a man living at the level of affluence which most people in the "developed nations" enjoy to give money to save someone else from starvation, cannot be supported. ∗ ∗ ∗

One objection to the position I have taken might be simply that it is too drastic a revision of our moral scheme. People do not ordinarily judge in the way I have suggested they should. Most people reserve their moral condemnation for those who violate some moral norm, such as the norm against taking another person's property. They do not condemn those who indulge in luxury instead of giving to famine relief. But given that I did not set out to present a morally neutral description of the way people make moral judgments, the way people do in fact judge has nothing to do with the validity of my conclusion. My conclusion follows from the principle which I advanced earlier, and unless that principle is rejected, or the arguments shown to be unsound, I think the conclusion must stand, however strange it appears. ✳ ✳ ✳

The second objection to my attack on the present distinction between duty and charity is one which has from time to time been made against utilitarianism. It follows from some forms of utilitarian theory that we all ought, morally, to be working full time to increase the balance of happiness over misery. The position I have taken here would not lead to this conclusion in all circumstances, for if there were no bad occurrences that we could prevent without sacrificing something of comparable moral importance, my argument would have no application. Given the present conditions in many parts of the world, however, it does follow from my argument that we ought, morally, to be working full time to relieve great suffering of the sort that occurs as a result of famine or other disasters. Of course, mitigating circumstances can be adduced—for instance, that if we wear ourselves out through overwork, we shall be less effective than we would otherwise have been. Nevertheless, when all considerations of this sort have been taken into account, the conclusion remains: we ought to be preventing as much suffering as we can without sacrificing something else of comparable moral importance. This conclusion is one which we may be reluctant to face. I cannot see, though, why it should be regarded as a criticism of the position for which I have argued, rather than a criticism of our ordinary standards of behavior. Since most people are self-interested to some degree, very few of us are likely to do everything that we ought to do. It would, however, hardly be honest to take this as evidence that it is not the case that we ought to do it. ✳ ✳ ✳

It is sometimes said that overseas aid should be a government responsibility, and that therefore one ought not to give to privately run charities. Giving privately, it is said, allows the government and the noncontributing members of society to escape their responsibilities.

This argument seems to assume that the more people there are who give to privately organized famine relief funds, the less likely it is that the government will take over full responsibility for such aid. This assumption is unsupported, and does not strike me as at all plausible. ✳ ✳ ✳

I do not, of course, want to dispute the contention that governments of affluent nations should be giving many times the amount of genuine, no-strings-attached aid that they are giving now. I agree, too, that giving privately is not enough, and that we ought to be campaigning actively for entirely new standards for both public and private contributions to famine relief. Indeed, I would sympathize with someone who thought that campaigning was more important than giving oneself, although I doubt whether preaching what one does not practice would be very effective. Unfortunately, for many people the idea that "it's the government's responsibility" is a reason for not giving which does not appear to entail any political action either.

Another, more serious reason for not giving to famine relief funds is that until there is effective population control, relieving famine merely postpones starvation. If we save the Bengal refugees now, others, perhaps the children of these refugees, will face starvation in a few years' time. In support of this, one may cite the now well-known facts about the population explosion and the relatively limited scope for expanded production.

* * * I accept that the earth cannot support indefinitely a population rising at the present rate. This certainly poses a problem for anyone who thinks it important to prevent famine. Again, however, one could accept the argument without drawing the conclusion that it absolves one from any obligation to do anything to prevent famine. The conclusion that should be drawn is that the best means of preventing famine, in the long run, is population control. It would then follow from the position reached earlier that one ought to be doing all one can to promote population control (unless one held that all forms of population control were wrong in themselves, or would have significantly bad consequences). Since there are organizations working specifically for population control, one would then support them rather than more orthodox methods of preventing famine.

A third point raised by the conclusion reached earlier relates to the question of just how much we all ought to be giving away. One possibility, which has already been mentioned, is that we ought to give until we reach the level of marginal utility—that is, the level at which, by giving more, I would cause as much suffering to myself or my dependents as I would relieve by my gift. This would mean, of course, that one would reduce oneself to very near the material circumstances of a Bengali refugee. It will be recalled that earlier I put forward both a strong and a moderate version of the principle of preventing bad occurrences. The strong version, which required us to prevent bad things from happening unless in doing so we would be sacrificing something of comparable moral significance, does seem to require reducing ourselves to the level of marginal utility. I should also say that the strong version seems to me to be the correct one. I proposed the more moderate version—that we should prevent bad occurrences unless, to do so, we had to sacrifice something morally significant—only in order to show that even on this surely undeniable principle a great change in our way of life is required. On the more moderate principle, it may not follow that we ought to reduce ourselves to the level of marginal utility, for one might hold that to reduce oneself and one's family to this level is to cause something significantly bad to happen. Whether this is so I shall not discuss, since, as I have said, I can see no good reason for holding the moderate version of the principle rather than the strong version. Even if we accepted the principle only in its moderate form, however, it should be clear that we would have to give away enough to ensure that the consumer society, dependent as it is on people spending on trivia rather than giving to famine relief, would slow down and perhaps disappear entirely. There are several reasons why this would be desirable in itself. The value and necessity of economic growth are now being questioned not only by conservationists, but by economists as well. There is no doubt, too, that the consumer society has had a distorting effect on the goals and purposes of its members. Yet looking at the matter purely from the point of view of overseas aid, there must be a limit to the extent to which we should deliberately slow down our economy; for it might be the case that if we gave away, say, forty percent of our Gross National Product, we would slow down the economy so much that in absolute terms we would be giving less than if we gave twenty-five percent of the much larger GNP that we would have if we limited our contribution to this smaller percentage. * * *

* * * The issue is one which faces everyone who has more money than he needs to support himself and his dependents, or who is in a position to take some sort of political action. These categories must include practically every teacher and student of philosophy in the universities of the Western world. If philosophy is to deal with matters that are relevant to both teachers and students, this is an issue that philosophers should discuss.

Discussion, though, is not enough. What is the point of relating philosophy to public (and personal) affairs if we do not take our conclusions seriously? In this instance, taking our conclusion seriously means acting upon it. The philosopher will not find it any easier than anyone else to alter his attitudes and way of life to the extent that, if I am right, is involved in doing everything that we ought to be doing. At the very least, though, one can make a start. The philosopher who does so will have to sacrifice some of the benefits of the consumer society, but he can find compensation in the satisfaction of a way of life in which theory and practice, if not yet in harmony, are at least coming together.

STUDY QUESTIONS

1. Why doesn't Singer think that questions of distance and the number of people who can help make a morally significant difference between saving the drowning child and famine relief?
2. Is it true that "if it is in our power to prevent something bad from happening, without thereby sacrificing anything of comparable moral importance, we ought, morally, to do it"?
3. How should we draw the distinction between duty and charity?

DAMBISA MOYO
Dead Aid

Dambisa Moyo (b. 1969) is a Zambian economist specializing in development and international business.

We live in a culture of aid.

We live in a culture in which those who are better off subscribe—both mentally and financially—to the notion that giving alms to the poor is the right thing to do. In the past fifty years, over US$1 trillion in development-related aid has been transferred from rich countries to Africa. In the past decade alone, on the back of Live 8, Make Poverty History, the Millennium Development Goals, the Millennium Challenge Account, the Africa Commission, and the 2005 G7 meeting (to name a few), millions of dollars each year have been raised in richer countries to support charities working for Africa.

We are made to believe that this is what we ought to be doing. We are accosted on the streets and goaded with pleas on aeroplane journeys; letters flow through our mail boxes and countless television appeals remind us that we have a moral imperative to give more to those who have less. At the 2001 Labour conference, the UK's Prime Minister of the time, Tony Blair, remarked that "The State of Africa is a scar on the conscience of the world," and that the West should "provide more aid" as, thus far, amidst the multiple problems facing Africa, the continent had received inadequate amounts of aid.

Deep in every liberal sensibility is a profound sense that in a world of moral uncertainty one idea is sacred, one belief cannot be compromised: the rich should help the poor, and the form of this help should be aid.

The pop culture of aid has bolstered these misconceptions. Aid has become part of the entertainment industry. Media figures, film stars, rock legends eagerly embrace aid, proselytize the need for it, upbraid us for not giving enough, scold governments for not doing enough—and governments respond in kind, fearful of losing popularity and desperate to win favour. Bono attends world summits on aid. Bob Geldof is, to use Tony Blair's own words, "one of the people that I admire most." Aid has become a cultural commodity.

Millions march for it.

Governments are judged by it.

But has more than US$1 trillion in development assistance over the last several decades made African people better off? No. In fact, across the globe the recipients of this aid are worse off; much worse off. Aid has helped make the poor poorer, and growth slower. Yet aid remains a centrepiece of today's development policy and one of the biggest ideas of our time.

The notion that aid can alleviate systemic poverty, and has done so, is a myth. Millions in Africa are poorer today because of aid; misery and poverty have not ended but have increased. Aid has been, and continues to be, an unmitigated political, economic, and humanitarian disaster for most parts of the developing world. * * *

One of the most depressing aspects of the whole aid fiasco is that donors, policymakers, governments, academicians, economists and development specialists know, in their heart of hearts, that aid doesn't work, hasn't worked and won't work. Commenting on at least one aid donor, the Chief Economist at the British Department of Trade and Industry remarked that "they know its crap, but it sells the T-shirts."

Study, after study, after study (many of them, the donors' own) have shown that, after many decades and many millions of dollars, aid has had no appreciable impact on development. * * *

Even the *most* cursory look at data suggests that as aid has increased over time, Africa's growth has decreased with an accompanying higher incidence of poverty. Over the past thirty years, the most aid-dependent countries have exhibited growth rates averaging *minus* 0.2 per cent per annum.

For most countries, a direct consequence of the aid-driven interventions has been a dramatic descent into poverty. Whereas prior to the 1970s most economic indicators had been on an upward trajectory, a decade later Zambia lay in economic ruin. Bill Easterly, a New York University professor and former World Bank economist, notes that had Zambia converted all the aid it had received since 1960 into investment, and all of that investment to growth, it would have had a per capita GDP of about US$20,000 by the early 1990s. Instead, Zambia's per capita GDP was lower than in 1960, under US$500. In effect, Zambia's GDP should have been at least thirty times what it is today. And between 1970 and 1998, when aid flows to Africa were at their peak, poverty in Africa rose from 11 per cent to a staggering 66 per cent. That is roughly 600 million of Africa's billion people trapped in a quagmire of poverty—a truly shocking figure.

The evidence against aid is so strong and so compelling that even the IMF[1]—a leading provider of aid—has warned aid supporters about placing more hope in aid as an instrument of development than it is capable of delivering. The IMF has also cautioned governments, donors and campaigners to be more modest in their claims that increased aid will solve Africa's problems. If only these acknowledgements were a catalyst for real change.

What is perhaps most amazing is that there is no other sector, whether it be business or politics, where such proven failures are allowed to persist in the face of such stark and unassailable evidence.

So there we have it: sixty years, over US$1 trillion dollars of African aid, and not much good to show for it. Were aid simply innocuous—just not doing what it claimed it would do—this book would not have been written. The problem is that aid is not benign—it's malignant. No longer part of the potential solution, it's part of the problem—in fact aid *is* the problem. * * *

THE VICIOUS CYCLE OF AID

With aid's help, corruption fosters corruption, nations quickly descend into a vicious cycle of aid. Foreign aid props up corrupt governments—providing them with freely usable cash. These corrupt governments interfere with the rule of law, the establishment of transparent civil institutions and the protection of civil liberties, making both domestic and foreign investment in poor countries unattractive. Greater opacity and fewer investments reduce economic growth, which leads to fewer job opportunities and increasing poverty levels. In response to growing poverty, donors give more aid, which continues the downward spiral of poverty.

---

1 *Editor's note*: IMF—International Monetary Fund.

This is the vicious cycle of aid. The cycle that chokes off desperately needed investment, instils a culture of dependency, and facilitates rampant and systematic corruption, all with deleterious consequences for growth. The cycle that, in fact, perpetuates underdevelopment, and guarantees economic failure in the poorest aid-dependent countries.

CORRUPTION AND GROWTH

Ultimately, Africa's goal is long-term, sustainable economic growth, and the alleviation of poverty. This cannot occur in an environment where corruption is rife. There are, of course, any number of ways in which corruption retards growth.

In a context of high degrees of corruption and uncertainty, fewer entrepreneurs (domestic or foreign) will risk their money in business ventures where corrupt officials can lay claim to its proceeds, so investment stagnates, and falling investment kills off growth.

Development agencies would have us believe that aid helps build a lasting, credible and strong civil service. Indeed, the World Bank recommends that by providing more aid rich countries actually assist in the fight against corruption. Thanks to aid, poor governments can afford to support ethics training, increase the salaries of their public-sector employees (police, judges, medical staff, tax collectors), thereby limiting the need for corruption. Moreover, higher salaries will attract competent and higher-quality employees to the civil service.

Unfortunately, unfettered money (the prospect of sizeable ill-gotten gains) is exceptionally corrosive, and misallocates talent. In an aid-dependent environment, the talented—the better-educated and more-principled, who should be building the foundations of economic prosperity—become unprincipled and are drawn from productive work towards nefarious activities that undermine the country's growth prospects. Those who remain principled are driven away, either to the private sector or abroad, leaving the posts that remain to be filled by the relatively less-educated, and potentially more vulnerable to graft.

Endemic corruption also targets public contracts. In these environments, contracts which should be awarded to those who can deliver on the best terms, in the best time, are given to those whose principal aim is to divert as much as possible to their own pockets. What ensue are lower-quality infrastructure projects, and enfeebled public services, to the detriment of growth.

Similarly, the allocation of government spending suffers as corrupt officials are likely to choose projects less on the basis of public welfare and more on the opportunities for extorting bribes and diverting funds. The bigger the project, the greater the opportunity. Projects whose exact value is difficult to monitor present lucrative opportunities for corruption—it is easier to siphon money from large infrastructure projects than from textbooks or teachers' salaries. ✳ ✳ ✳

The net result of aid-dependency is that instead of having a functioning Africa, managed by Africans, for Africans, what is left is one where outsiders attempt to map its destiny and call the shots. Given the state of affairs, it is hardly surprising that, though ostensibly high on the global agenda, the Africa discourse has been usurped by pop stars and Western politicians. Rarely, if ever, are the Africans elected by their own people heard from on the global stage. And even though, as discussed earlier, the balance of power may have shifted supposedly in favour of the African policymakers, it is still the donors who are in the policymaking driving seat (which might help explain why, over the last five decades, independent African policymaking and national economic management have diminished considerably). So aid-dependency only further undermines the ability of Africans, whatever their station, to determine their own best economic and political policies. Such is the all-pervasive culture of aid-dependency that there is little or no real debate on an exit strategy from the aid quagmire.

STUDY QUESTIONS

1. In Moyo's view, what has been the effect of 50 years of development aid on Africa?
2. Why, according to Moyo, does development aid very often have detrimental effects for the recipient country?
3. If Moyo is right, should individuals stop giving to charity for famine relief and other forms of humanitarian aid?

ONORA O'NEILL
Ending World Hunger

Onora O'Neill, Baroness O'Neill of Bengarve (b. 1941), is a Northern Irish moral and political philosopher, who was made a life peer in the UK House of Lords in 1999. She specializes in the interpretation and development of Kantian moral philosophy and has taken on many roles in public life, such as chairing the UK Equality and Human Rights Commission.

ARE WORLD HUNGER AND FAMINE NEW MORAL PROBLEMS?

Through history millions have died of sheer starvation and of malnutrition or from illnesses that they might have survived with better food. Whenever there were such deaths, nearby survivors may have realized that they could help prevent some deaths and may have done so, or wondered whether to do so. But nobody sought to prevent faraway deaths. Distance made an important difference; with few exceptions there was nothing to be done for the victims of faraway famines.

In a global economy things are different. Food from areas with agricultural surplus (nowadays mainly North America, Australia, and western Europe) can be distributed to the starving in Bangladesh or Somalia. Longer-term policies that affect economic development, fertility levels, agricultural productivity, and the standard of living of the poorest may hasten or postpone far-off famines or make distant hunger more or less severe. Within the developed world, states can choose to have effective welfare systems, which eliminate hunger, or to leave the poorest to fend for themselves. Consequently we can now ask whether we ought to do some of these newly possible actions. Ought we to try to distribute food or aid, to control fertility, to further economic development, or to guarantee minimal entitlements to the means of life? Who should foot the bills and suffer the other costs? To whom (if anyone) should aid or welfare be given and to whom should it be denied? How much hardship or sacrifice, if any, is demanded of those who have the means to help? * * *

* * * I will try in this essay to show how certain moral theories *can* help us think about some questions about hunger and famine and also to use considerations about hunger and famine to show some of the strengths and limitations of these theories.

Some Utilitarian Controversies about Hunger

No disagreement over famine and world hunger could be more fundamental than one between (1) those who think that either individual citizens or social groups in the developed world are morally required to take an active part in trying to reduce and end the poverty of the Third World and (2) those who think that they are morally required not to do so. Yet utilitarian arguments have been offered for both conclusions. * * *

One well-known utilitarian dispute about famine has been between the basically Malthusian perspective of Garrett Hardin and the more optimistic, developmentalist perspectives of other utilitarian writers. For the latter position I shall draw particularly on Peter Singer's influential article, "Famine, Affluence and Morality."[1]

Hardin's argument may be summarized as follows: The citizens of developed countries are like the passengers of a lifeboat around which other, desperate people are swimming. Those in the lifeboats can rescue some of the drowning. But if the affluent rescue some of the starving, this will—unlike many lifeboat rescues—have bad consequences. It will mean that the affluent world will then have a smaller safety margin. In the short run this might be outweighed by the added happiness and benefit of those who have been rescued, but the longer-run effects are grim. The rescued will assume that they are secure; they will multiply, and next time that similar dangers arise they will be more numerous and rescue will not be possible. It is better, from a utilitarian point of view, to lose some lives now than to lose more lives later. So it would be morally wrong to rescue those who are desperate, and the starving must be left to starve.

Hardin's use of the lifeboat analogy has often been criticized. ✱ ✱ ✱ Those in the boats may be entitled to their seats, and they have no options except to stay put or to give up life itself. The affluent are in a different position. They may risk little in trying to help the hungry, they may lack clear title to all that they have (perhaps, for example, some of it has been acquired by unjust exploitation of parts of the Third World), and there are many ways in which they can give up something without sacrificing everything. Hardin does not take these points seriously because he thinks that the longer-term balancing of beneficial and harmful results of attempting to help the Third World points the other way. ✱ ✱ ✱ He writes:

> If poor countries received no food aid from outside, the rate of their population growth would be periodically checked by crop failures and famines. But if they can always draw on a world food bank in time of need, their population can continue to grow unchecked, and so will their "need" for aid. In the short run a world food bank may diminish that need, but in the long run it actually increases the need without limit.[2]

---

1   *Editor's note*: See selections from Peter Singer's "Famine, Affluence, and Morality" on pp. 614–622 of this reader.

2   Garrett Hardin, "Lifeboat Ethics: The Case Against Helping the Poor," in W. Aiken and H. La Folette, *World Hunger and Moral Obligations*, Prentice Hall, 1977, p. 17.

From this perspective it follows that the prosperous ought, if they are utilitarians, to leave the hungry to themselves to suffer, die, or survive as best they may.

Singer's utilitarianism, by contrast, leads to interventionist conclusions. He starts from the standard utilitarian assumption that "if it is in our power to prevent something bad from happening, without thereby sacrificing anything of comparable moral importance, we ought, morally, to do it." He then points out that contributions to famine relief, even if they amount to a large proportion of our income—say, 50 percent—do not sacrifice anything of moral importance comparable to that of the hunger they relieve. ✳✳✳ So he concludes that the prosperous, even the modestly prosperous, ought to help feed the hungry and to give up their affluence until they have so reduced their own standard of living that any further giving would sacrifice "something of comparable moral importance."

Singer's position ✳✳✳ has been challenged from within the famine-relief movement itself. Tony Jackson, an Oxfam food aid consultant, and many others have argued that giving food doesn't always benefit the hungriest.

Food aid commonly takes two forms. There is government-to-government food aid, which Third World governments obtain from food surplus countries and sell in their own countries. This food aid constitutes a form of budget and more general political support for Third World governments, and its harmful effects are often noted. It may do more to support a government that is failing to address needs than it does to meet those needs. The second form of food aid, so-called project food aid, is mostly channeled through the World Food Programme and various voluntary agencies. This food aid represents the very sort of action to relieve the greatest suffering that Peter Singer advocates on utilitarian grounds. ✳✳✳

✳✳✳ Jackson disagrees with Singer, not because he thinks the affluent should do nothing to meet the needs of the hungry, but because he thinks that providing food aid—even project food aid, which is intended to get the food where it is needed—has been shown to harm the needy. Project food aid competes with local food production, depriving vulnerable farmers of their living and driving them into the cities. Third World food production is then decreased rather than increased. Moreover, the food that is given often fails to reach those whose need is greatest and is diverted by others. ✳✳✳ In some cases food-aid dependence is institutionalized and development hindered rather than helped. Apart from genuine short-term emergencies, such as the plight of refugees or results of sudden natural catastrophes, project food aid often does more to benefit the prosperous farmers of the developed world, whose surplus is bought at subsidized prices, than it does to help the Third World. So the enormous international effort that goes into providing food aid preempts other and possibly more effective moves. * * *

It is not surprising that utilitarians disagree over famine and development policies. For utilitarians, it is *results* and not *principles* or *intentions* that count. The calculation of results must therefore be taken seriously and isn't adequate if it neglects remote and long-term consequences in global deliberations. * * *

* * * But our capacity to make accurate, if imprecise, judgments is on the whole restricted to matters that are relatively close at hand. We lack the sort of social science that provides an exhaustive list of available options or gives a generally accurate account of the long-term and overall likely results of each. Yet problems of world hunger, possible famine, and future population and resource growth cannot be considered without attending to the longer-term global results of available courses of action. If utilitarians lack a precise science of society and have only a limited ability to foresee results, they may have no general way to decide whether a proposed action or policy is morally required, forbidden, or neither. * * *

KANTIAN APPROACHES TO SOME FAMINE PROBLEMS

The second moral theory whose scope and determinacy in dealing with famine problems I shall consider was developed by the German philosopher Immanuel Kant (1724–1804). * * *

* * * Kant does not * * * try to generate a set of precise rules defining human obligations in all possible circumstances; instead, he attempts to provide a set of *principles of obligation* that can be used as the starting points for moral reasoning in actual contexts of action. The primary focus of Kantian ethics is, then, on *action* rather than * * * *results,* as in utilitarian thinking. * * * To know *what* sort of action is required (or forbidden) in which circumstances, we should not look just at the expected results of action * * * but, in the first instance, at the nature of the proposed actions themselves. * * *

* * * The famous Categorical Imperative plays the same role in Kantian thinking that the Greatest Happiness Principle plays in utilitarian thought. * * *

* * * [One formulation] of the Categorical Imperative [is] * * * *The Formula of the End in Itself.* * * *

Act in such a way that you always treat humanity, whether in your own person or in the person of any other, never simply as a means but always at the same time as an end.[3]

To understand this principle we need in the first place to understand what Kant means by the term "maxim." The maxim of an act or policy or activity is the *underlying principle* of the act, policy, or activity, by which other, more superficial aspects of action are guided. * * *

It is helpful to think of some examples of maxims that might be used to guide action in contexts where poverty and the risk of famine are issues. Somebody who contributes to famine-relief work or advocates development might have an underlying principle such as, "Try to help reduce the risk or severity of world hunger." This commitment might be reflected in varied surface action in varied situations. In one context a gift of money might be relevant; in another some political activity such as lobbying for or against certain types of aid and trade might express the same underlying commitment. Sometimes superficial aspects of action may seem at variance with the underlying maxim they in fact express. For example, if there is reason to think that indiscriminate food aid damages the agricultural economy of the area to which food is given, then the maxim of seeking to relieve hunger might be expressed in action aimed at *limiting* the extent of food aid. More lavish use of food aid might *seem* to treat the needy more generously, but if in fact it will damage their medium- or long-term economic prospects, then it is not (contrary to superficial appearances) aimed at improving and securing their access to subsistence. On a Kantian theory, the basis for judging action should be its *fundamental* principle or policy, and superficially similar acts may be judged morally very different. Regulating food aid in order to drive up prices and profit from them is one matter; regulating food aid in order to enable local farmers to sell their crops and to stay in the business of growing food is quite another.

When we want to work out whether a proposed act or policy is morally required we should not, on Kant's view, try to find out whether it would produce more happiness than other available acts. Rather we should see whether the act or policy is required if we are to avoid acting on maxims that

---

3 *Editor's note*: See selections from Immanual Kant, "The Categorical Imperative" on pp. 152–160 of this reader.

use others as *mere means* and act on maxims that treat others as ends in themselves. These two aspects of Kantian duty can each be spelled out and shown to have determinate implications for acts and policies that may affect the persistence of hunger and the risk and course of famines.

Using Others as Mere Means

We use others as *mere means* if what we do reflects some maxim *to which they could not in principle consent.* Kant does not suggest that there is anything wrong about using someone as a means. Evidently every cooperative scheme of action does this. A government that agrees to provide free or subsidized food in famine-relief agencies both uses and is used by the agencies; a peasant who sells food in a local market both uses and is used by those who buy the food. In such examples each party to the transaction can and does consent to take part in that transaction. Kant would say that the parties to such transactions use one another but do not use one another as *mere means.* Each party assumes that the other has its own maxims of action and is not just a thing or prop to be used or manipulated.

But there are other cases where one party to an arrangement or transaction not only uses the other but does so in ways that could only be done on the basis of a fundamental principle or maxim to which the other could not in principle consent. If, for example, a false promise is given, the party that accepts the promise is not just used but used as a mere means, because it is *impossible* for consent to be given to the fundamental principle or project of deception that must guide every false promise, whatever its surface character. ✳✳✳ In false promising, the deceived party becomes, as it were, a prop or tool—a *mere means*—in the false promisor's scheme. ✳✳✳

Other standard ways of using others as mere means are by violence or coercion. Here too victims have no possibility of refusing what is done to them. If a rich or powerful landowner or nation destroys a poorer or more vulnerable person, group, or nation or threatens some intolerable difficulty unless a concession is made, the more vulnerable party is denied a genuine choice between consent and dissent. ✳✳✳ Maxims of violence destroy or damage agents or their capabilities. Maxims of coercion may threaten physical force, seizure of possessions, destruction of opportunities, or any other harm that the coerced party is thought to be unable to absorb without grave injury or danger. For example, a grain dealer in a Third World village who threatens not to make or renew an indispensable loan without which survival until the next harvest would be impossible, unless he is sold the current crop at pitifully low prices, uses the peasant as mere means. The peasant does not have the possibility of genuinely consenting to the "offer he can't refuse." ✳ ✳ ✳

✳ ✳ ✳ To avoid unjust action it is not enough to observe the outward forms of free agreement, cooperation, and market disciplines; it is also essential to see that the weaker party to any arrangement has a genuine option to refuse the fundamental character of the proposal.

Treating Others as Ends in Themselves

For Kant, ✳ ✳ ✳ justice is only one part of duty. We may fail in our duty, even when we don't use anyone as mere means, if we fail to treat others as "ends in themselves." To treat others as ends in themselves we must not only avoid using them as mere means but also treat them as rational and autonomous beings with their own maxims. In doing so we must also remember that (as Kant repeatedly stressed, but later Kantians have often forgotten) human beings are *finite* rational beings in several ways. First, human beings are not ideal rational calculators. We *standardly* have neither a complete list of the actions possible in a given situation nor more than a partial view of their likely consequences. In a given situation nor more than a partial view of their likely consequences. In addition, abilities to assess and to use available information are usually quite limited. Second, these cognitive limitations are *standardly* complemented by limited autonomy. Human action is limited not only by various sorts of physical barrier and inability but by further sorts of (mutual or asymmetrical) *dependence*. To treat one another as ends in themselves such beings have to base their action on principles that do not undermine but rather sustain and extend one another's capacities for autonomous action. A central requirement for doing so is to share and support one another's ends and activities to some extent. Since finite rational beings cannot generally achieve their aims without some help and support from others, a general refusal of help and support amounts to failure to treat others as rational and autonomous beings, that is, as ends in themselves. Hence Kantian principles require us not only to act justly, that is, in accordance with maxims that don't injure, coerce, or deceive others, but also to avoid manipulation and to lend some support to others' plans and activities. Since hunger, great poverty, and powerlessness all undercut the possibility of autonomous action, and the requirement of treating others as ends in themselves demands that Kantians standardly act to support the possibility of autonomous action where it is most vulnerable,

Kantians are required to do what they can to avert, reduce, and remedy hunger. They cannot of course do everything to avert hunger: but they may not do nothing.

Justice to the Vulnerable in Kantian Thinking

For Kantians, justice requires action that conforms (at least outwardly) to what could be done in a given situation while acting on maxims that use nobody. Since anyone hungry or destitute is more than usually vulnerable to deception, violence, and coercion, the possibilities and temptations to injustice are then especially strong. ✳ ✳ ✳

✳ ✳ ✳ Where shortage of food is being dealt with by a reasonably fair rationing scheme, any mode of cheating to get more than one's allocated share involves using some others and is unjust. Equally, taking advantage of others' desperation to profiteer—for example, selling food at colossal prices or making loans on the security of others' future livelihood, when these are "offers they can't refuse"—constitutes coercion, uses others as mere means, and so is unjust. Transactions that have the outward form of normal commercial dealings may be coercive when one party is desperate. Equally, forms of corruption that work by deception—such as bribing officials to gain special benefits from development schemes, or deceiving others about these entitlements—use others unjustly. ✳ ✳ ✳

✳ ✳ ✳ Once we remember the limitations of human rationality and autonomy, and the particular ways in which they are limited for those living close to the margins of subsistence, we can see that mere "noninterfering" conformity to ordinary standards of commercial honesty and political bargaining is not enough for justice toward the destitute. If the demands of the powerful constitute "offers that cannot be refused" by the government or by the citizens of a poor country, or if the concessions required for investment by a transnational corporation or a development project reflect the desperation of recipients rather than an appropriate contribution to the project, then (however benevolent the motives of some parties) the weaker party to such agreements is used by the stronger. ✳ ✳ ✳

Beneficence to the Vulnerable in Kantian Thinking

In Kantian moral reasoning, the basis for beneficent action is that without it we fail to treat others of limited rationality and autonomy as ends in themselves. This is not to say that Kantian beneficence won't make others happier, for it will do so whenever they would be happier if (more) capable of autonomous action but that happiness secured by purely paternalistic means, or at the cost (for example) of manipulating others' desires, will not count as beneficent in the Kantian picture. Clearly the vulnerable position of those who lack the very means of life, and their severely curtailed possibilities for autonomous action, offer many different ways in which it might be possible for others to act beneficently. Where the means of life are meager, almost any material or organizational advance may help extend possibilities for autonomy. Individual or institutional action that aims to advance economic or social development can proceed on many routes. The provision of clean water, of improved agricultural techniques, of better grain storage systems, or of adequate means of local transport may all help transform material prospects. Equally, help in the development of new forms of social organization—whether peasant self-help groups, urban cooperatives, medical and contraceptive services, or improvements in education or in the position of women—may help to extend possibilities for autonomous action. * * * Where some activity helps secure possibilities for autonomous action for more people, or is likely to achieve a permanent improvement in the position of the most vulnerable, or is one that can be done with more reliable success, this provides reason for furthering that way of treating others as ends.

Clearly the alleviation of need must rank far ahead of the furthering of happiness in other ways in the Kantian picture. I might make my friends very happy by throwing extravagant parties: but this would probably not increase anybody's possibility for autonomous action to any great extent. But the sorts of development-oriented changes that have just been mentioned may *transform* the possibilities for action of some. Since hunger and the risk of famine are always and evidently highly damaging to human autonomy, any action that helps avoid or reduce famine must have a strong claim on any Kantian who is thinking through what beneficence requires. * * * Wherever we find ourselves, our duties are not, on the Kantian picture, limited to those close at hand. Duties of justice arise whenever there is some involvement between parties—and in the modern world this is never wholly lacking. Duties of beneficence arise whenever destitution puts the possibility of autonomous action in question for the more vulnerable. When famines were not only far away, but nothing could be done to relieve them, beneficence or charity legitimately began—and stayed—near home. In an interconnected world, the moral significance of distance has shrunk, and we may be able to affect the capacities for autonomous action of those who are far away.

The Scope of Kantian Deliberations about Hunger and Famine

In many ways Kantian moral reasoning is less ambitious than utilitarian moral reasoning. It does not propose a process of moral reasoning that can (in principle) rank *all* possible actions or all possible institutional arrangements from the happiness-maximizing "right" action or institution downward. It aims rather to offer a pattern of reasoning by which we can identify whether *proposed action or institutional arrangements* would be just or unjust, beneficent or lacking in beneficence. While *some* knowledge of causal connections is needed for Kantian reasoning, it is far less sensitive than is utilitarian reasoning to gaps in our causal knowledge. It may therefore help us reach conclusions that are broadly accurate even if they are imprecise. ✳✳✳

✳✳✳ The Kantian picture of beneficence is less mathematically structured than the utilitarian one. It judges beneficence by its overall contribution to the prospects for human autonomy and not by the quantity of happiness expected to result. ✳✳✳

✳✳✳ For utilitarians, paternalistic imposition of, for example, certain forms of aid and development assistance need not be wrong and may even be required. But for Kantians, who think that beneficence should secure others' possibilities for autonomous action, the case for paternalistic imposition of aid or development projects without the recipients' involvement must always be questionable.

In terms of some categories in which development projects are discussed, utilitarian reasoning may well endorse "top-down" aid and development projects that override whatever capacities for autonomous choice and action the poor of a certain area now have in the hopes of securing a happier future. If the calculation work out in a certain way, utilitarians may even think a "generation of sacrifice"—or of forced labor or of imposed population-control policies—not only permissible but mandated. In their darkest Malthusian moments some utilitarians have thought that average happiness might best be maximized not by improving the lot of the poor but by minimizing their numbers, and so have advocated policies of harsh neglect of the poorest and most desperate. Kantian patterns of reasoning are likely to endorse less global and less autonomy overriding aid and development projects; they are not likely to endorse neglect or abandonment of those who are most vulnerable and lacking in autonomy. If the aim of beneficence is to keep or put others in a position to act for themselves, then emphasis must be placed on "bottom-up" projects, which from the start draw on, foster, and establish indigenous capacities and practices for self-help and local action.

UTILITARIANS, KANTIANS, AND RESPECT FOR LIFE

In the contrasting utilitarian and Kantian pictures of moral reasoning and of their implications for hunger, we can also discern two sharply contrasting pictures of the value of human life.

Utilitarians, since they value happiness above all, aim to achieve the happiest possible world. If ✳✳✳ happiness is the supreme value, then anything may and ought to be sacrificed for the sake of a greater happiness. ✳✳✳

✳✳✳ We can see that on a utilitarian view lives must be sacrificed to build a happier world if this is the most efficient way to do so, whether or not those who lose their lives are willing. There is nothing wrong with using another as mere means, provided that the end in view is a happier result than could have been achieved any other way, taking account of the misery the means may have caused. In utilitarian thinking, persons are not ends in themselves. Their special moral status, such as it is, derives from their being means to the production of happiness. ✳✳✳

✳✳✳ Kantians reach different conclusions about human life. They see it as valuable because humans have considerable (but still quite incomplete) capacities for autonomous action. ✳✳✳

The fundamental idea behind the Categorical Imperative is that the actions of a plurality of rational beings can be mutually consistent. A minimal condition for their mutual consistency is that each, in acting autonomously, not preclude others' autonomous action. This requirement can be spelled out, as in the formula of the end in itself, by insisting that each avoid action that the other could not freely join in (hence avoid violence, deception, and coercion) and that each seek to foster and secure others' capacities for autonomous action. What this actually takes will, as we have seen, vary with circumstances. But it is clear enough that the partial autonomy of human beings is undermined by life-threatening and destroying circumstances, such as hunger and destitution. Hence a fundamental Kantian commitment must be to preserve life in two senses. First, others must not be deprived of life. ✳✳✳ Second, others' lives must be preserved in forms that offer them sufficient physical energy, psychological space, and social security for action. Partial autonomy is vulnerable autonomy, and in human life psychological and social as well as material needs must be met if any but the most meager possibility of autonomous action is to be preserved. Kantians are therefore committed to the preservation not only of biological but of biographical life. To act in the typical ways humans are capable of we must not only be alive, but have a life to lead.

On a Kantian view, we may justifiably—even nobly—risk or sacrifice our lives for others. When we do so, we act autonomously, and nobody uses us as a mere means. But we cannot justly use others (nor they us) as mere means in a scheme that could only be based on violence, deception, or coercion. Nor may we always refuse others the help they need to sustain the very possibility of autonomous action. ***

Where others' possibilities for autonomous action are eroded by poverty and malnutrition, the necessary action must clearly include moves to change the picture. But these moves will not meet Kantian requirements if they provide merely calories and basic medicine; they must also seek to enable those who began to be adequately fed to act autonomously. They must foster the capabilities that human beings need to function effectively. They must therefore aim at least at minimal security and subsistence. Hence the changes that Kantians argue or work for must always be oriented to development plans that create enough economic self-sufficiency and social security for independence in action to be feasible and sustainable. There is no royal road to this result and no set of actions that is likely to be either universally or totally effective. Too many changes are needed, and we have too little understanding of the precise causal connections that limit some possibilities and guarantee others. But some broadly accurate, if imprecise indication of ranges of required action, or ranges of action from which at least some are required, is possible.

STUDY QUESTIONS

1. How can utilitarian arguments be used both for and against famine relief?
2. In what ways could humanitarian aid fail to treat recipients of aid as ends in themselves?
3. Explain how a concern for the autonomous agency of individuals will influence how a Kantian will approach questions of world hunger.

■ Compare and Contrast Questions

1. How should Singer respond to Moyo's arguments?
2. Do Moyo's arguments apply to O'Neill as well as Singer?
3. How should Singer respond to O'Neill?

credits

index